THE DISPENSERS' FORMULARY

THE
DISPENSER'S FORMULARY

A Handbook of Over 2,500 Tested Recipes
with a
Catalog of Apparatus, Sundries and Supplies

COMPILED BY

THE TRADE MAGAZINE

Books for Business
New York-Hong Kong

The Dispenser's Formulary:
A Handbook of Over 2,500 Tested Recipes with
a Catalog of Apparatus, Sundries and Supplies

Compiled by
The Editors of the Soda Fountain Magazine

ISBN: 0-89499-093-4

Copyright © 2001 by Books for Business

Reprinted from the 1925 edition

Books for Business
New York - Hong Kong
http://www.BusinessBooksInternational.com

In order to make original editions of historical works
available to scholars at an economical price, this
facsimile of the original edition of 1925 is
reproduced from the best available copy and has
been digitally enhanced to improve legibility, but the
text remains unaltered to retain historical
authenticity.

DEDICATED TO THE

SODA FOUNTAIN INDUSTRY

OF THE UNITED STATES

TABLE OF CONTENTS

THE DISPENSERS' FORMULARY

INTRODUCTION

This new edition, the fourth, of the standard formulary book of the soda fountain and luncheonette trade is the direct descendant of the first collection of fountain recipes—a modest, paper-covered work of 116 pages, published just twenty years ago. The first edition contained 918 formulas—not one of them for a sundae or a sandwich; many of them calling for dashes of sherry wine or an ounce of creme de menthe. Assuredly times have changed, and we feel a certain fair and just pride in the marks of fountain progress that the successive editions of the "The Dispenser's Formulary" have recorded.

But this is not an historical work: it is a practical handbook of recipes for fountain use all of which have been not only devised by actual dispensers, but have also stood the test of sales to the public. Our thanks are due both to the authors of these formulas, many of them prize winners in the monthly formula contests in "The Soda Fountain," and to the hundreds of soda men all over the country who have co-operated in the preparation of this book by testing out these formulas.

Aside from the direct usefulness of this book to thousands of fountain owners in helping them to build up their business with successful specialties that earn extra profits, it has done a wider service to the entire fountain trade in assisting to standardize fountain practice and to promote uniformity in the naming of fountain drinks. Since the standard definitions of the various classes of fountain drinks and delicacies was first published in the last edition, it has been conclusively proved that the rage for trick and fancy names was not a sound selling policy. The public wants to know just what it is going to get when it orders a banana split or a frosted coffee. They will not gamble far with their own taste, and except in the case of the fancy sundaes, a fancy name is poor merchandizing. Even when, in this case, a catchy or timely name is used to push a specialty, it is money-making wisdom to indicate on menu or wall strip just what the principal ingredients and flavors are. The dispenser who studies the chapters in this book on standards and nomenclature and who then uses the given names of the formulas may be assured that he follows the well beaten path to fountain profits. He will be stepping right in the footsteps of thousands of successful fountain men who use this book continuously. This policy is certainly the line of least resistance to the patronage of the public.

It may be well to call attention to the arrangement of this book, designed particularly to increase the ease and quickness of its use. Formulas are collected into groups, and so far as has been possible are arranged so that those with the same principal flavors are together. Once this arrangement is understood it is an easy matter, for example, to locate a sundae whose dominating flavor shall be peach. The complete Index, in the back, makes instantly available any formula whose name is known.

The prices printed represent the average price at an average fountain in a small town—where, of course, the great bulk of the volume of business is done—but in the large cities or at the more pretentious fountain larger prices will naturally be charged.   —*The Publishers.*

FOUNTAIN SERVICE

Soda sales in the United States have grown to the astonishing total of $497,500,000.00, and when we add to this the luncheonette business of $176,650,000.00 and candy sales of $800,000,000.00 we reach a gross total for all three branches of the fountain trade's sales of nearly a billion and a half dollars. Competition for this business is keen for there are 91,241 real soda fountains in the country, giving an average daily sales of $46.10 per fountain.

Over forty thousand fountains—nearly half of the total—are in confectionery and soda shops; 38,503 in the drug trade; over 7,000 in department, general and five and ten cent stores; the balance, 4,561 fountains are in railway stations, theatres, barbers and cigar shops, and other miscellaneous places of business and amusement. All these fountains are distributed throughout the entire country pretty much in proportion to the population, although they are higher than the average in the various New England states and somewhat below the general ratio to population in the southern sections.

These are interesting and significant figures, and it is a wise thing for a fountain man once in a while to sit down and study his market so as to judge more wisely his opportunities. It is an encouraging feeling for the man of energy and ambition to learn that of all the fountains in the country there are a "best third"—33,510 to be exact—which do nearly three-quarters of the business and have an average daily sale of $91.40. It is a very tangible and attainable ambition to put your fountain into the class of the elite fountains, and here is a practical and convenient yardstick for measuring your trade accomplishments. If your fountain is doing a daily gross business of over ninety dollars a day, then, you are in that selected group of the top third of the trade where the leaders are always classed and where the real profits in the trade are being made.

You may not have set up before yourself any such definite measure of results as this figure; but presumably you have purchased this book with the intention of increasing your business and it is perfectly reasonable for you to expect to find it helpful to this end. It is therefore, incumbent upon us to furnish you with such practical material as will help most in this direction, and it is therefore fitting that you should find here something on the subject of using this book most profitably. Competition is keen in the fountain trade—it is keen in every profitable trade—but the bitterly bought experience of many successful dispensers and owners has proved that just as there are three branches to the modern fountain trade—soda, lunch, and candy,—so there are three factors in the success of a fountain store—quality, sanitation, and service.

Fountain sales are made up in the appeal to the taste of the public. That is fundamental, for it is the basis of the trade axiom, which has been proved and re-proved times without number, that no great success has ever been scored in the fountain trade unless built upon a foundation of quality.

The public is sensitive in the matter of its beverages and is becoming more and more discriminating in its tastes. The pure-food campaigns, the wide-spread propaganda for sanitation and hygiene, and the growing enlightenment of the people all are reflected in the demand at the soda fountain.

It is becoming increasingly difficult to deal in adulterants and substitutes, and the soda fountain which acquires and maintains a reputation for quality and purity automatically enjoys a profitable popularity.

FOUNTAIN EQUIPMENT

In addition to the fountain furniture and other essentials, fountain owners should be supplied with certain equipment with which to mix and prepare soda. This includes now the all-important matter of adequate refrigeration. Your customers, as a rule, expect truly ice-cold sodas and firm and compact ice cream and sundaes.

This subject of refrigeration merits rather broad discussion. Just at present, the science of mechanical refrigeration has approached a state of practical and economical application. Whether your fountain is supplied with a regulation ice-box or with regular mechanical appliances, your status is the same—your stock must be kept cold. This means "ice," and plenty of it, however it is secured.

For preparing and serving iced drinks, it is necessary to keep a good ice-shaver, a needle pointed ice-chipper and a sliding pick of iron. The first should be long, hard wood-handled, tempered and nickel plated to prevent rust. The ice-chipper is invaluable because it works rapidly and can be used in breaking up caked sugar or salt. A sliding iron pick, especially those made with adjustable points, permits cracking ice to any shape or size without noise or laborious effort.

Ice-shredders also are quick-action implements in the serving of iced drinks and foods.

In addition to the ice tools, such requisities as a machine for making simple syrup, syrup percolators, work board, lemon, lime and orange squeezers or reamers, wire strainers, ice cream dishers of various sizes, transfer ladles, ice scoops, and corkscrews are essential. Good tools stand for efficiency. Efficiency is an indispensable factor of success.

The fountain owner often can meet an emergency and save time and money by making small repairs himself. For this purpose, he should have a hammer, nails and screws, wrenches, pliers, brass, a brace and assortment of bits, a soldering outfit, and paint brushes. As in the case of everything else, it pays only to have the best of tools.

Perfect Cleanliness Indispensable

The term quality in relation to soda fountain products cannot be expressed without involving the element of cleanliness. It is impossible to conceive the former without the latter and it is reasonable to state that cleanliness is the most important factor in considering quality. No sense detects lack of care in sanitation more quickly than that of taste. How few of us who do not recollect with disgust a flavor—all too familiar in the past—of ice-cream cans refilled without scalding on a busy hot summer day; or who has not at some time or other been brought to the point of nausea by the odor of stale rinsing water or wiping cloths.

Happily the requirements of an increasingly fastidious public sharpened by the justifiable insistence of uplift societies, conscientious physicians and legislators have accomplished a great deal toward eliminating the old conditions. The mere consideration of pride should complete the transformation.

Undoubtedly, there are many fountain owners who consciously endeavor to keep their equipment scrupulously clean but who do not know how. A bulletin of the Illinois State Food Commission on this subject written by the commissioner, Douglas Scott Matthews, is so peculiarly apropos that we feel justified in reprinting it herewith.

Decomposition

Decomposition or spoilage is, in most cases, due to some one of three causes, molds, yeasts or bacteria.

Molds develop on substances containing sugars, starches or fruit acids. They injuriously affect the quality, flavor and food value of the substances which they attack and generally impart thereto a musty taste and odor. Moisture is necessary for their development.

Yeasts decompose the sugars present in fruit juices, syrups, etc., produce alcohol and give off a carbonic acid gas. Syrups which have been attacked by yeasts have a frothy appearance due to the rising of small bubbles of carbonic acid gas; they generally have a sour odor and are said to be fermenting

Bacteria attack the nitrogenous materials at the fountain such as nuts, milk and cream, and ice cream. They are the cause of putrefaction.

Most of the diseases of man are caused by bacteria. These bacteria multiply at an enormous rate during the progress of the disease. The disease-producing bacteria are carried to other persons by means of their food and drink.

Molds, yeasts and bacteria are everywhere present: in the air, in the water and on foodstuffs. They are generally present in an inactive "seed" (known as spore) condition.

These spores (germ seeds) develop only where they find suitable conditions.

In general, the conditions under which yeasts, molds and bacteria grow most readily (and consequently spoilage takes place most rapidly) are presence of moisture (water), a warm temperature and absence of sunlight.

While the spores of molds, yeasts and bacteria are everywhere present about the fountain, the numbers in which they are present are in proportion to the amount of dust and dirt present.

Clean fountains are comparatively free from molds and bacteria. Dirty fountains harbor large numbers.

From the standpoint of healthfulness, the kind of bacteria is of greater importance than the number.

Many bacteria are harmless to man when taken into his system. Others are the cause of tuberculosis, typhoid fever, diphtheria, Summer complaint and other disease. Harmful bacteria are carried to the fountain in the milk, cream and ice cream supply from diseased employees; in the glasses and spoons used by diseased patrons; or are carried from filthy places by flies, cockroaches, rats, mice, dogs or cats.

It is evident that cleanliness and sanitation are held in high regard by the health authorities and in view of the scope of their activities and the wide-spread publicity given their efforts, it is immensely important that the soda fountain be a model in this respect. When we consider that the mortality rate of the large cities has been reduced to an amazing degree and the average lifetime of the citizens lengthened correspondingly since sanitation became an important item in city administration, we are not surprised at the fastidiousness of the public.

Preventing and combatting bacteria should not be confined to the fountain itself. Every precaution should be taken to keep glasses, spoons, china and straws free from contamination. Careful washing, of course, takes care of the silver, glass, etc. but the straws frequently are unduly exposed. This can easily and economically be prevented by the use of containers which dispense only one straw at a time.

Hot water is an effective specific for germ. Neither bacteria and the tiny fungi known as mold nor ordinary dirt can be treated to a thorough saturation with boiling water and survive. Add a liberal proportion of sal soda' and you have a combination which not only will sterilize your equipment but will dissolve and remove grease as well. Wooden accessories—tables, chairs and floors—are going out of favor in the soda fountain. These pieces should be made of materials in tune with the modern spirit of sanitation, especially the floor which should be of tile in front of the fountain and plain cement with adequate drainage facilities in back; cooler boxes, cabinets, etc. should be made of metal enamelled or galvanized and raised from the floor so that they are accessible for cleaning.

We are stressing the sanitary side of the fountain because we believe it to be of dominant importance and because of the fact that in spite of constant effort of the authorities and the untiring activities of public-spirited organizations and individuals, many fountains exhibit a regrettable negligence in this matter.

The spread of such diseases as tuberculosis, diphtheria, pneumonia, influenza and the ordinary cold, not to mention certain more occult but none the less deadly diseases, by the common use of drinking glasses is so established that many states, including New York, have enacted laws prohibiting their use in public schools, factories and offices.

That the soda fountains are still permitted to dispense their beverages in glasses used repeatedly instead of paper or fibre, or some other material which naturally prohibits more than one service simply means that the authorities trust to the consciences of the fountain owners to make sure their glasses, spoons, etc. are not germ-carriers. It is up to the fountain proprietors to make good this trust, 100% strong.

The Process of Cleaning Equipment

Three processes are necessary to the real cleansing of glasses: first, the removal of material left by the last user by means of a thorough rinsing in water; second, washing both inside and outside with a glass brush using a warm solution of bicarbonate of soda or washing soda, 12 ounces to the gallon, and three rinsings in clear running water. Dry on the drain board.

Ice used in iced drinks and the tools with which it is handled all should be kept thoroughly clean. Of course, flies should not be tolerated. When they do succeed in getting through the screen doors as they inevitably do, they must be eliminated with the ordinary swatter which is the best agency for taking care of trespassing flies.

The following excerpt from the sanitary food laws of Illinois might well apply to fountains in other states:

1. The floors, walls and ceilings of every room, building or establishment occupied or used for the preparation, manufacture, packing, storage, sale or distribution of food, must at all times be kept in a clean and sanitary condition.

2. All utensils, implements, machinery and equipment used in moving, handling, cutting, chopping, mixing, canning and preparing food must be thoroughly cleansed daily.

3. All food in the process of manufacture, packing, storage, sale or distribution must be securely protected from flies, dust and dirt.

4. All refuse and dirt, and all waste products subject to decomposition and fermentation, must be removed daily.

5. The clothing of all operatives, employees and clerks, who handle or come in contact with the food, must be clean at all times.

6. Toilets and washrooms shall be supplied with soap, running water and towels, and shall be cleaned daily.

7. All employees who handle food or the materials from which it is prepared, shall wash their hands thoroughly in clean water before beginning work and after visiting the toilet.

8. Cuspidors shall be emptied and washed out daily. and when in use shall contain at least five ounces of water or disinfectant solution.

9. Employees shall not spit on the food or raw materials, nor on the utensils, floors or walls.

10. No person who is affected with any contagious or venereal disease, is allowed to work in any such establishment, nor is any person allowed to sleep therein.

Whoever violates or fails to observe any of the above provisions, is guilty of a misdeameanor, and may be punished by fine or imprisonment, or both, in the discretion of the court.

The familiar axiom "an ounce of prevention is worth a pound of cure" is peculiarly appropriate to sanitation in connection with the soda fountain. Naturally, occasional spilling of soda, syrups and ice creams, etc. is unavoidable but freshly spilled material of this kind is not filth. It becomes filth when it is allowed to remain on the floor, the back bar or the counter or elsewhere and decompose. It is a simple matter to keep a damp cloth handy to clean up the incidental but inevitable drippings as soon as they occur and before they have a chance to harden and require real effort to remove them.

Your customers appreciate a clean dry counter. What is more exasperating than to drag one's sleeve through a slop of syrupy water or melted ice cream? It would seem as though this was so elemental as to render unnecessary mentioning here but in this regard carelessness is encountered frequently. The dispenser should receive most emphatic instructions regarding this prevention of unclean and unsanitary top slab.

Personality of Dispensers

Too often the fountain education of a new dispenser is taken for granted. He may come with excellent references and perhaps long experience in other establishments but it does not necessarily follow that he is trained anent the idea of service. A wise plan is to give each new employee a course of instructions in your methods, as though he were a novice.

Eichelman's Rules

Peter Eichelman is manager of one of the largest and most successful fountains in the country and he has established a set of rules which are followed by himself and his dispensers. They possess sufficient merit to warrant reprinting them here.

"1. When serving customers, always serve crackers first, and then take their order. After a few moments, ask the customer whether the drink is sweet enough, or, if it is a sundae, how he likes the fresh fruit we serve. Let them know that we do serve fresh fruit. Give ice water with each sundae.

"2. Never use nicked or dirty glasses at the fountain, as they leave a bad impression about the fountain, which can easily be avoided. If you hear a customer speak about the cleanliness of our glasses, tell him that we employ three men who do nothing but wash glasses and dishes, first using hot water with soap, then clean rinsing water, then drying on clean towels.

"3. Be clean about your own person. Act like gentlemen with some intelligence. Don't stand around and talk about the good time you had the night before. Customers as a rule can hear this, and it certainly leaves a bad impression at a first-class fountain. We have everything here to make a successful fountain.—good, clean, sanitary conditions, crackers put up in waxed envelopes, fresh fruits, fresh syrups, good fresh eggs, pasteurized milk, best buttermilk, etc. All this shows nothing but quality. But you also must help. Quality alone, without good, clean dispensers and service is a failure. To bring success and a large increase in your earnings you must all work together. Try to have the honor of getting this fountain known as the best in town. You can do this if you will only try.

"4. If you break a glass or spill something, don't get excited or nervous about it. We know that it was not done on purpose, and fellow dispensers should never laugh at it. Try to be careful, but when unfortunate enough to spill a drink, get a clean towel at once, tell the customer you are sorry it happened, and assure him that our Prescription Department will take out all stains.

"5. Always be polite to a customer, no matter whether he is grouchy or polite himself.

"6. Keep drinks from overflowing. No matter how good a dispenser you are, if you let this happen it makes you look like a beginner. This may sound as if all theory to you, but put it into practice and you will soon notice the change. Remember that nine out of ten customers are the kind who, if treated right, will boost your reputation by telling what a good and courteous dispenser you are. Follow this advice; keep it always in mind, and you won't have to worry about the future. Any business is what a man makes it."

The right kind of service on the part of the dispenser is every bit as important as the quality of products. Bright, cheerful human dispensers mean personal following. After all, personality is essential in the fountain business as in any other, more than in most others because of the intimate touch associated with the serving of elements so close to the human heart as food and drink. Therefore, this question of service and the character and personality of those who do the serving is worthy of much careful thought.

One of the best means of getting your customers' angle on this question is to go out and shop among your competitors. Get the reaction on yourself of the various kinds of service you encounter in other shops. Note the impression made on you by the personalities of different dispensers who wait on you, in other words, get out in front of the counter and look at your fountain through your customers' eyes. Your success depends largely on your skill on securing this slant on your business.

Soda Fountain Publicity

Men and women are creatures of habit. Following an established path is one of the primitive instincts which we have retained. It is the natural thing for a man to shop until he finds a satisfactory place to eat or drink and then settle down there until something, poor service or poor quality, drives him elsewhere. Once away, he establishes new associations and remains loyal to them as long as they satisfy him. While women are inclined to be more restless and seek an occasional change for change's sake, they naturally will give the greater share of their allegiance to the place where they are served in the most satisfactory way. Moreover, the women patrons of luncheonettes and soda fountains are in the majority and fastidiousness as to service is an ever-increasing necessity to attract and hold this desirable class of trade. To satisfy, the customers are the best form of publicity. This is true in this field probably more than in any other due to the great American custom of treating.

The question of publicity is one always worthy of careful study. It must be remembered that publicity is a form of selling and in its way as important as the actual contact between yourself and your customers.

Roughly speaking, there are four kinds of publicity—window displays, local newspapers, circulars and bill boards. In the case of the soda fountain, the most powerful selling agent of all these undoubtedly is the window. This very likely is true of nearly every class of merchant and is so considered generally, but it is especially true in the case of the soda fountain. Yet, it unfortunately is a fact that no class of stores more generally fail to make the most of the opportunities in their windows than do the merchants in this field. Of course, there is a disadvantage in the fact that most soda fountain products are of a perishable character and, therefore, require very frequent if not daily changing. This entails a great deal of work and planning, but the effectiveness of a good window has such important results in attracting customers to the inside of the shop that it is worth the additional effort. Moreover, a good idea can be used for some time merely changing the items which make up the display.

Action in a window always attracts attention, and the man who invented the perpetually flowing bottle of wine must have reaped a bountiful reward because it is still used to advertise grape juice and one kind of liquid and another. Although it must be twenty-five or thirty years old, it always draws crowds. Action, of course, is not always practical, but "live" displays are always available and as a matter of fact are actually an essential of a worth-while display. By "live" we mean such items as a bowl of fruit punch in an attractive setting, fresh fruit sliced open and other edibles and drinkables actually ready for the customer to eat or drink.

Naturally, when these exhibits lose their freshness their utility as window-display items is gone. It admittedly is not easy to keep up a really attractive "live" window display with the kind of products at the hand of the soda fountain operator, but it is quite within the possibilities and is of inestimable value in attracting customers to the interior of the shop.

In your newspaper advertising it is well to present something of unusual or exceptional interest to the public—perhaps a "sale" for the day of some popular beverage at a reduced price or an announcement of a new drink.

The use of circulars should be exercised in a way somewhat similar to the newspaper advertising—some special appeal to the people you are addressing.

Bill boards are used for general publicity as a rule because of the longer periods of time during which the advertisements appear. It is not practical to change bill-board advertising frequently. It is too expensive and the results are probably not commensurate.

The best form of publicity any merchant can use is service in his shop. When you have succeeded in acquiring a reputation among your customers for the excellence of your products and service, you have not much to worry about concerning the volume of your business.

FOUNTAIN NOMENCLATURE
With Definitions and Classifications

A—BASIC MATERIALS

The basic materials from which are made the thousand and one drinks and delicacies served at the modern soda fountain have been defined by the Department of Agriculture and various State Boards of Health. The technical descriptions serve at once as an official definition and a standard of purity. As such they are doubly valuable to dispensers.

(a) Sugars and Syrups.

1. Sugar—is the product chemically known as sucrose (saccharose), chiefly obtained from sugar cane, sugar beets, sorghum, maple and palm.

2. Granulated, loaf, cut, milled and powdered sugars.—Simply different forms of sugar which contain at least 99.5% of sucrose.

3. Simple (Sugar) Syrup.—The product made by dissolving sugar to the consistency of a syrup and containing not more than 35% of water.

4. Rock Candy Syrup.—A heavy, concentrated sugar syrup just below the crystallization point, and having a specific gravity of about 1.320 at 15°C. As commercially obtained it is a heavy syrup from which candy is crystallized, or it may be prepared by dissolving sugar in the form of rock candy in water to produce a syrup of the proper density. It should be free from insoluble salts, coloring matter (ultramarine, etc.), and glucose, and not contain more than a slight amount of inverted sugar.

5. Concentrated Fruit Syrup.—Heavy syrup made by dissolving about 3½ pounds of granulated sugar in one quart of pure fruit juice of the required flavors; heating to the boiling point, straining and bottling. When wanted for fountain use this concentrated or "stock" syrup is diluted to the proper strength with simple syrup. Citric or fruit acid is frequently added to increase the acidity of these syrups.

6. Fountain Syrup.—The product of mixing the expressed juices of pure, ripe fruits or extracts of coffee, ginger or aromatics with simple syrup; or of cooking with sugar or syrup, as in the manufacture of chocolate syrups.

7. Maple Sugar.—The solid product resulting from the evaporation of maple sap and contains, in the water-free substance not less than 0 65% of maple sugar ash.

8. Maple Syrup.—The product of the evaporation of maple sap or solution of maple concrete and contains not more than 32% of water and not less than 0.45% of maple syrup ash.

9. Honey.—The nectar and saccharine exudations of plants gathered, modified and stored in the comb by honey bees; it contains not more than 25% of water, not more than 0 25% of ash, and not more than 8% of sucrose.

a. Comb Honey.—Honey contained in the cells of the comb.

b. Extracted Honey.—Honey which has been separated from the un-crushed comb by centrifugal force or gravity.

c. Strained Honey.—Honey which has been removed from the comb by straining or other means.

10. Caramel.—Literally burnt sugar, is prepared by heating sugar with occasional stirring at about 180° to 200°C., until a black viscid mass is formed, and adding to this while cooling one and a quarter times its weight of hot water. The resulting solution, after straining, is used for coloring purposes.

(b) Milk and Its Products.

1. Milk.—The fresh, clean, lacteal secretion obtained by the complete milking of one or more healthy cows, properly fed and kept, and contains not less than 8.5% of solids not fat, and not less than 3.25% of milk fat.

a. Blended Milk.—Milk modified so as to have a definite and stated percentage of one or more of its constituents.

b. Skim Milk.—Milk of which a part or all of its cream has been removed and which contains not less than 9.25% of milk solids.

c. Pasteurized Milk.—Milk that has been heated to a point below boiling but sufficiently to kill most of the active organisms present, and immediately cooled to 50°F. or lower.

d. Sterilized Milk.—Milk that has been heated to the temperature of boiling water, or higher, for a length of time sufficient to kill all the organisms present.

e. Condensed Milk (Evaporated Milk).—Milk from which a considerable portion of water has been evaporated and which contains not less than 28% of milk solids, of which not less than 27.5% is milk fat.

f. Sweetened Condensed Milk.—Milk from which a considerable portion of water has been evaporated and to which sugar (sucrose) has been added, and which contains not less than 28% of milk solids, of which not less than 27.5% is milk fat.

g. Condensed Skim Milk.—Skim milk from which a considerable portion of water has been evaporated.

2. Buttermilk.—The product that remains when butter is removed from milk or cream in the process of churning.

3. Whey.—The product remaining after the removal of fat and casein from milk in the process of cheese-making.

4. Kumyss.—The product made by the alcoholic fermentation of mare's milk or cow's milk.

5. Cream.—Cream is that portion of milk, rich in milk fat, which rises to the surface of milk on standing, or is separated from it by centrifugal force, fresh and clean, and contains not less than 18% milk fat.

a. Evaporated Cream (Clotted Cream).—Cream from which a considerable portion of water has been evaporated.

b. Whipped Cream.—Cream whipped or beaten to a stiff, spongy consistency and sweetened to taste.

(c) Fruits, Berries, and Their Products.

1. Fruits.—The clean, sound, edible, fleshy fructifications of plants, distinguished by their sweet, acid and ethereal flavors.

2. Berry.—In its restricted sense, the product of certain small shrubs or vines, such as gooseberries, blackberries, raspberries, etc.

3. Dried Fruit.—The clean, sound product made by drying mature, properly prepared, fresh fruit in such a way as to take up no harmful substance, and which conforms in name to the fruit used in its preparation.

  a. Sun-dried Fruit.—Made by drying without artificial means.

  b. Evaporated Fruit.—Made by drying with artificial means.

4. Crushed Fruit.—Clean, sound fruit, prepared with sugar, and heated to a point sufficient to destroy the greater part of the organisms, thus preventing fermentation, without heating to a point sufficient to cook and thus destroy the flavor and characteristics of fresh fruit.

5. Canned Fruit.—The sound product made by sterilizing clean, sound, properly matured and prepared fresh fruit by heating, with or without sugar, and spices, and keeping in suitable, clean, hermetically sealed containers, and which conforms in name to the fruit used in its preparation.

6. Preserve.—The sound product made from clean, sound, properly matured and prepared fresh fruit and sugar syrup, with or without spices or vinegar, and which conforms in name to that of the fruit used. In its preparation not less than 45 pounds of fruit are used to each 55 pounds of sugar.

7. Glace Fruits.—Fruits treated with sugar syrup which is subsequently allowed to crystallize, also known as candied or crystallized fruit.

8. Jellies.—The product produced by cooking the pure juice of fruits or berries, expressed from the pulp, with approximately equal portions of pure cane sugar.

9. Fruit Juices.—The expressed juices from the pulp of fruits and berries, ordinarily prepared by pasteurization to prevent fermentation, and not so sterilized by heat as to cook and change the character and taste of the product.

  a. Grape Juice.—The pure, undiluted and unfermented juice of grapes produced by crushing and sterilized by heat at a temperature of from 165°F. to 176°F., above which point the product is cooked and loses its distinctive flavor. When so prepared no artificial preservative is required. Normal grape juice contains no alcohol, glycerin, etc., has from 20-24% grape sugar, and some acids, mainly tartaric acid, mineral substances and protein. They are all substances of nutritive or therapeutic value.

10. Fruit Concentrates or Concretes.—(See Flavorings.)

(d) Flavors and Extracts.

1. Flavoring Extracts.—Solutions in ethyl alcohol of the flavoring and odorous principles derived from an aromatic plant or parts of a plant, with or without its coloring matter, and which conform in name to the plant used in their preparation.

2. Terpeneless Extract.—The flavoring extract derived by shaking an essential oil with dilute alcohol, or by dissolving a terpeneless oil (from which the constituents related to the turpentine group have been removed) in dilute alcohol.

3. Fruit Concentrates or Concretes.—The product resulting from the treatment of fresh fruit pulp, properly prepared and matured, so as to preserve its full odor and taste by the removal of its watery constituents without loss of flavor and with natural concentration of all its useful constituents into small bulk.

(e) Tea, Coffee and Cocoa Products.

1. Tea.—The leaves and leaf buds of different species of *Thea*, prepared by fermenting, drying and firing.

2. Coffee.—The seed of *Coffea arabica,* or *Coffea liberica,* freed from all but a small portion of its husk or outer skin.

Roasted Coffee.—Coffee, which by the action of heat, has become brown and developed its characteristic aroma.

3. Cocoa Beans.—The seeds of the cacao tree.

Cocoa Nibs, Cracked Cocoa.—The roasted, broken cocoa bean freed from its shell or husk.

4. Chocolate, Plain Chocolate, Bitter Chocolate, Chocolate Liquor, Bitter Chocolate Coatings.—The solid or plastic mass obtained by grinding cocoa nibs without the removal of fat or other constituents except the germ.

Sweet Chocolate, Sweet Chocolate Coatings.—A chocolate mixed with sugar, with or without the addition of cocoa butter, spices, or other flavoring materials.

5. Cocoa, Powdered Cocoa.—Cocoa nibs, with or without the germ, deprived of a portion of their fat and finely pulverized.

Sweet Cocoa, Sweetened Cocoa.—Cocoa mixed with not more than 60% of sugar.

_____

(f) Special Beverage Materials and Mineral Water.

1. Citric Acid.—A tri-basic acid prepared from the juice of limes, lemons and other fruits produced by species of *Citrus.* It should contain not less than 99 5% of pure citric acid, and otherwise conform to the standard prescribed by the United States Pharmacopoeia.

Fruit Acid.—A name employed by fountain operators to indicate a solution of citric acid, usually made by dissolving 2 ounces of citric acid in sufficient water to make a solution measuring 4 fl. ounces. This solution is extremely liable to spoil, and only small quantities should be made at one time. When part of the water is replaced with alcohol the solution is said to be more permanent Tartaric or mineral acids are inadmissible under the name of "fruit acid," and it is in violation of law to use them as substitutes.

2. Solution of Acid Phosphates (Acid Phosphates)—Made by adding sulphuric acid and water to bone ash and expressing as directed in the National Formulary. Under the Pure Food and Drugs Act the preparation so made is the only solution which, without other qualification, is legally entitled to the use of the name.

3. Foams.—A mucilaginous or saponaceous mixture added to carbonated beverages to increase their gas-retaining or foam-holding properties Among the substances used for the purpose are gum arabic, gelatin, white of egg, and quillaja (soap bark). Quillaja contains saponin, an acrid, irritating glucoside which renders the beverage to which it is added open to criticism; its use as a foam in some States is forbidden. Fruit syrups properly made from natural fruit juices, particularly where cream is used, need nothing to hold the foam, especially if the water is cold and highly carbonated. In most cases an ounce of gum arabic foam to the gallon of syrup is sufficient.

4. Mineral Water.—Non-contaminated natural water recommended as a beverage on account of its special therapeutic or hygienic properties. A manufactured mineral water, made in imitation of a natural water, may be named after such natural water in case the words "imitation" or "artificial" are used, but such manufactured waters must clearly resemble in chemical composition the natural waters after which they are named.

_____

(g) Carbonic Acid Gas.

1. Carbonic Acid Gas.—(Carbon dioxide CO_2.) At ordinary temperatures it is a colorless, transparent, tasteless (by some thought to be sweetish) gas. By a pressure of 38 atmospheres, at a temperature of 0°C. (32°F.), carbon dioxide is converted into a colorless liquid (*liquid carbon dioxide*). All carbonates liberate carbon dioxide when brought in contact with dilute acids. Carbon dioxide is also evolved in the process of fermentation as carried on in the brewing industries, and this source is extensively utilized for the commercial production of the gas at the present time. (For materials used in manufacture, see below.)

2. **Carbonated Water.**—("Plain soda.") Water saturated with carbonic acid gas, with resulting sparkle and pungency, to a pressure of from 150 to 200 pounds. The appellation "soda water" is a misnomer, as the liquid contains no soda in any form, but it continues to "stick."

3. **Sodium Carbonate.**—("Soda," neutral carbonate of soda, sal soda, washing soda, etc.) One of the most important of the sodium compounds for industrial purposes, and is employed as a source of carbonic acid gas which is evolved when the sodium carbonate is treated with sulphuric acid.

4. **Sodium Bicarbonate.**—(Baking soda and also acid sodium carbonate.) Occurs in small, rectangular prisms, which to the naked eye appear as a white, opaque powder. The salt is odorless, has a cooling, mildly alkaline taste, and is permanent in dry, but slowly decomposed in moist air. Also a source of carbonic acid gas when treated with sulphuric acid.

5. **Calcium Carbonate.**—Found in enormous deposits as limestone, marble, chalk, calcite, Iceland spar, and as the mineral basis of the corals, shells of the crustacea, etc. Prepared chalk is a native chalk, one of the common forms of calcium carbonate purified by grinding the chalk in water, allowing the mixture to partially subside, decanting the upper portion, allowing it to settle, and collecting and drying the fine powder. "Whiting," essentially the same as prepared chalk, is used in the production of carbonic acid gas.

6. **Sulphuric Acid.**—A colorless liquid, of oily consistence, inodorous, and very caustic and corrosive. As defined by the U. S. Pharmacopoeia, it should contain not less than 92 5% of absolute sulphuric acid, and about 7.5% of water. It should be andled with great care.

B—FROZEN PRODUCTS

The Standard Definitions adopted by the Association of Official Agricultural Chemists of the United States, and the Interstate Food Commission, and published in Circular No. 19, U. S. Department of Agriculture follow:

1. **Ice Cream.**—A frozen product made from cream and sugar, with or without a natural flavoring, and containing not less than fourteen (14) per cent. of milk fat.

2. **Fruit Ice Cream.**—A frozen product made from cream, sugar and sound, clean, mature fruits, and contains not less than twelve (12) per cent. of milk fat.

3. **Nut Ice Cream.**—A frozen product made from cream, sugar and sound, non-rancid nuts, and contains not less than twelve (12) per cent. of milk fat.

Trade Definitions Perfected by Usage.

All ice creams are classified by the ice-cream trade according to both ingredients and methods of preparation. *Philadelphia ice cream* is made without eggs. *Neapolitan, Delmonico* and *French* ice cream call for eggs, and include cream with a cooked body. But cooked body creams, made with eggs, flour or cornstarch, and cream or milk, are more properly designated *Frozen Custards*.

1. Plain Ice Cream.—Made from cream, sugar and flavoring, the latter either extract or such natural flavoring as coffee or chocolate, or the juice (not the pulp) of lemons, oranges or pineapples. (An ice cream made with grape *juice* would be a *plain* cream; one made with *pulp* would be a *fruit* cream.)

2. Fruit Ice Cream.—Made from sugar, cream and the pulp of clean, ripe fruit —strawberries, peach, pineapple, etc.—with or without additional flavoring.

3. Nut Ice Cream.—Made from cream, sugar and sound, non-rancid nuts. The nut meats must be incorporated, whether chopped, crushed or whole, for if the cream is flavored with peanut or almond oil it is a plain cream, as there are no nuts in it.

4. Bisque Ice Cream.—Made from cream, crumbled bread or cake, macaroons, nabiscos, grape nuts, etc., or such confections as marshmallows.

5. Sherbet.—(Water ice.) Made from water, sugar, egg whites and natural fruit flavoring (See also Fountain Sherbet.)

6. Parfait.—Made from sugar, cream and egg yolks, and may contain fruit, nuts or natural flavoring.

7. Souffle.—Made exactly the same as a sherbet except that the whole egg is used instead of the whites.

8. Milk Sherbet.—Made from milk, egg whites and flavoring. All the sherbets, no matter what the designation, must be frozen as smoothly as ice cream, for there are other titles for other sherbet formulas when frozen differently. For instance:

9. Frappe.—A half-frozen product containing water, sugar and fruit juice or natural flavoring, which when made according to formula is about the consistency of moist snow. They are simply half-frozen sherbets with the white of eggs omitted.

10. Frozen Punch.—Sherbet with an alcoholic flavoring; at the fountain frozen punches are sherbets with high flavor or with a mixture of several fruit juices.

11. Frozen Pudding.—Cream or rich milk, eggs, a filler of either flour or corn-starch, usually nuts, glacé fruits or crystallized cherries, citron, etc., and highly flavored before freezing. Caterers' frozen pudding or that served by hotel chefs is ordinarily flavored with Santa Cruz rum. Fountain frozen pudding cannot, of course, contain liquor, but is always highly flavored.

12. Mousse.—A frozen whipped cream to which has been added sugar and natural flavoring; if fruit flavors are used only the juice is employed. It must be light and spongy in texture or it belies its name.

13. Lacto.—A frozen product made of buttermilk, skimmed milk or whole sour milk, the product being indicated as "Buttermilk Lacto," etc. With the milk sugar, and flavoring are employed as in ordinary ice cream.

14. Plombiere.—A neapolitan ice cream mixture, to which has been added be-fore freezing, citron, greengages and pineapple, all chopped fine.

15. Aufait.—A brick or moulded ice cream packed in layers with one or more layers of frozen fruit (preserved or candied figs, etc.)

16. Baked Alaska.—A solidly frozen brick of ice cream which has been wrapped in a thick meringue of powdered sugar and egg whites whipped thoroughly and then placed in a very hot oven until the meringue browns. The cream will not melt if the oven is hot enough. A typical hotel dainty, which cannot be served economically at either luncheonette or soda fountain.

17. Glace.—Glace' in the trade means coated or glossed over, and bombe', mould-ed, hence a bombe' glace' is a moulded cream served with a colored meringue. Raspberry Bombe' Glace', for instance is made by lining a mould with raspberry sherbet, filling it with vanilla ice cream or moussé, and then topping with either mousse' or meringue and freezing.

C—FOUNTAIN DRINKS

(a) Sodas

1. Straight Soda.—(Solid soda. Plain soda.) A mixture of carbonated water and syrup, such syrups as do not harmonize with or contain milk or cream, as ginger, orange, lemon, ambrosia, grape fruit, nectar, raspberry, mint and cherry.

2. Cream Soda.—A mixture of carbonated water, cream or milk and such syrups as chocolate, vanilla, coffee, maple, etc.

3. Creme.—A syrupy liqueur, the principal flavor being usually specified, as creme de menthe, creme de rose, creme yvette, etc. As a fountain beverage the creme is related to the cream sodas, being very sweet and made with syrups of distinctive flavor, cream or milk, and topped with whipped cream.

4. Ice Cream Soda.—A measured quantity of ice cream added to the mixture of syrup and carbonated water. The best fountains use chocolate, vanilla and strawberry ice cream with syrups of the same flavor. In some fountains milk or cream is also added to the beverage, which is served with a spoon.

(b) Mixed Fruit Drinks

1. Punch.—At the soda fountain must be non-alcoholic, the place of the liquor being taken by a combination of crushed and sliced fruits, fruit juices and syrups, and usually the grated rinds of oranges and lemons. Mixed in quantity it is served from a glass bowl containing a cube of ice, some of the fruit being placed in each glass. If mixed, individually shaved ice, carbonated water, fruit syrups and sliced fruit or glacé cherries are added, and sometimes a sprig of mint.

2. Ades.—The juice of citrus fruit, lemon, orange or lime, with sufficient powdered sugar or simple syrup to sweeten, to which is added plain, mineral or carbonated water. It is customary, however, to designate the drink by prefixing the name of the water employed, as "seltzer lemonade." In fruit ades, slices of fruit, glace', cherries, etc. are added ingredients. All ades should be served very cold with straws.

  a. **Golden Ade.**—Made by adding the yolk of an egg before shaking.

3. Float.—An ade upon the top of which is floated a layer of grape juice, ginger ale, or in some cases, a disher of fruit sherbet or ice cream. In the latter case it would be known as a "sherbet float" or an "ice-cream float."

4. Freeze.—An ade or punch in which the shaved ice is allowed to remain when serving (to produce a very low temperature, hence the name), and ordinarily served with fruit, a sprig of mint, and straws.

5. Smash.—Similar to a freeze, and generally made with syrups of a rich, fruity flavor, shaved ice and carbonated water, the beverage being served in thin glasses with straws. Sometimes two or three dashes of solution of acid phosphate are added, and occasionally a sprig of mint.

6. Fizz.—Made from acid syrups, lemon, pineapple, etc., usually with lime juice or a dash of bitters, and served while effervescing. The fizz effect is gained after shaking by using the fine stream in quick dashes, or by the addition of a little sodium bicarbonate.

  a. **Silver Fizz.**—If the white of an egg is added and the drink shaken it becomes a silver fizz.

  b. **Golden Fizz.**—If an egg yolk is used the drink is a golden fizz.

7. Cup.—Fruit juice added to shaved ice and flavored with lemon and lime juice, the addition of carbonated water produces the cup, as grape cup or claret cup.

(c) Phosphates and Bitters

1. Phosphates.—A straight soda, with one or more flavors, to which dashes of solution of acid phosphate (see above, Basic Materials (f) 2) have been added. Usually served in a small, thin glass.

     a. Egg Phosphate.—An egg is added to a phosphate and the beverage well shaken before serving.

2. Rickey.—Nearly related to the phosphate is the rickey, the juice of a lime, a fruit syrup and carbonated water combined, but not shaken, lime juice always being a component.

3. Bitters Shake, or Cocktail.—A straight soda to which is added a dash or two of bitters as Angostura, wild cherry, elixir calisaya, etc.

(d) Mixed Fancy Drinks

1. Shake.—Any syrup or combination of syrups may be used, sometimes with the addition of solution of acid phosphate. Shaved ice is added with a little plain water. It is then shaken and strained and the glass filled with carbonated water. The shaking can be done by hand with a shaker or by machine.

     a. Milk Shake.—The milk shake is made without carbonated water by the shaking together of syrup and rich milk, either with or without crushed ice, and then serving after straining.

     b. Ice Cream Shake.—An ice cream shake is made in a similar manner, the ice cream being added before shaking.

     c. Egg Shake.—When an egg is added to a milk shake prior to the shaking it becomes an egg shake. Acid flavors should never be used in any of these as they curdle the milk.

2. Nogg.—Either hot or cold, is a combination of egg, milk or cream, sugar, an aromatic flavor (not an acid), over which grated cinnamon or nutmeg is usually sprinkled before serving. It differs from a milk shake or milk and egg shake in that the egg, milk and sugar are *beaten together* into almost emulsion form, before the flavor, etc., is added, and before the final shaking.

3. Puff.—A combination beverage containing one or more kinds of syrup, whipped cream or ice cream, white of egg, shaken well together. Into this carbonated water, fine stream, is injected in quick dashes, and a maraschino cherry is added before serving. Serve with a spoon.

(e) Hot Drinks

1. Hot Chocolate.—Chocolate powder, paste, or syrup, sweetened, with hot milk or water, usually topped with whipped cream and served in a cup with crackers, nabiscos, etc.

     a. Cocoa.—Made in the same way, cocoa powder being substituted for the chocolate.

2. Tea.—The leaves of tea steeped in boiling water, served in a cup with lump sugar and cream or sliced lemon.

3. Coffee.—An infusion or decoction of ground coffee, made by percolation (not boiled) with hot water and served with lump sugar and cream or whipped cream in cups.

4. Soup.—Meat, fish, or vegetables boiled with seasoning in water.

5. Bouillon.—A clear soup that has been strained

6. Chowder.—Usually made with fish and served with various vegetables and potatoes cut in small dice in it.

(f) Specialty Beverages

1. Root Beer.—A non-alcoholic drink made from extracts of various roots, and prepared for the fountain by the addition of syrup and carbonated water. This class includes Ottawa beer, sarsaparilla, and similar beverages which do not require the addition of cream and are mixed from the syrup and carbonated water. It is the common practice to carbonate such beverages in tanks and draw them from the draught arm of the fountain, or from a special dispenser.

2. Pop.—A non-alcoholic beverage made with sugar, flavoring (ginger, lemon, etc.), and carbonated water, and marketed in bottles. It is so named because the cork is expelled with a pop from the bottle on opening.

3. Ginger Ale.—A non-alcoholic beverage prepared from sugar, water and a soluble extract of ginger flavored with various aromatic substances or essential oils, frequently combined with capsicum or the pungent principle of capsicum, and charged with carbonic acid gas.

4. True Mead.—A product caused by the fermentation (with yeast or malt) of honey with two or three times its weight of hot water. It is alcoholic and cannot be served at the fountain.

a. Mead Syrup.—A product of aromatics and spices (such as mace, cloves, cinnamon, ginger, wintergreen and sassafras) and honey and water, heated together until the resulting syrup is impregnated with the flavor of the aromatics, or mead extract may be used.

b. Mead Extract.—In this preparation the honey flavor is simulated by the employment of sassafras, wintergreen, etc., from which drugs in crude form the extract is derived by percolation with alcohol; or by mixing certain syrups and extracts to simulate the honey and spice flavor.

D—FOUNTAIN DELICACIES

1. College Ice.—A service of a measured quantity of shaved or crushed ice, or, in some cases, a plain ice cream or sherbet of one flavor, with one kind of syrup or crushed fruit.

2. Sundae.—A service of a measured quantity of ice cream with one or more syrups, crushed fruits, nuts, or whipped cream, with or without a dressing or topping. It is in reality an elaborated college ice.

3. Dessert.—The dessert is an elaborate sundae, with one or more flavors of ice cream, sherbet, crushed or glacé fruits, nuts, whipped cream, cake or nabiscos, and usually served with a fancy dressing. Under this designation such a dish as a banana split would naturally fall. In reality, the college ice and sundae are less elaborate desserts.

SODA FOUNTAIN FORMULAS

(1) SYRUPS, EXTRACTS, AND FOAMS

The very basis of quality sodas and sundaes—the kind that bring patrons back to your fountain again for more—is good syrups, and the syrups are essentially sugar, water, and flavoring. Pure water is therefore the first necessity in making good sodas and good sundaes. If the city or town water is not clear and free from all bacteria, it should be distilled. This can be done at a cost of about *half a cent* a gallon, and is worth it! The sugar from which syrups are made should be free from the blue coloring matter which is sometimes added to give table sugar the whiteness housewives demand. The use of good grade granulated sugar in syrup making is true economy.

Fountain syrups even though made with pure water and good, clean sugar must be properly flavored. In making fruit syrups, none but ripe, sound, clean fruits should be employed. When extracts are used, only the highest grade will give satisfactory results.

In making chocolate and coffee syrups, the secret depends not so much upon the brand or blend employed or upon the special process used as upon a combination of just the best process for the particular chocolate and coffee employed. These two very popular flavors are often regarded by the public as a criterion by which they judge a fountain, and in making these syrups the greatest care should be exercised. A little experimenting will often prove to be very useful in obtaining the best possible results.

All syrups spoil—fruit syrups, chocolate, and coffee syrups easily deteriorate owing to the fact that they are readily attacked by spores and bacteria. It is economy therefore, especially during the warm months, to make up but little syrup at a time. In this connection it is well to note that heavy simple syrup keeps much longer than the fountain syrups, and it pays both in keeping qualities and also in storage facilities to have simple syrup in concentrated form.

The following general rules will be found to be invaluable in the syrup room:

1. Use only the best and purest materials.
2. Have all utensils scrupulously clean.
3. Do not cut acid fruits with a steel knife.
4. Fruit syrups should be cooked in agate or glass vessels, and if they are boiled too hard will lose much of their natural aroma and flavor.
5. Extracts should never be added to hot syrups—they are thereby lost through evaporation.
6. Syrups should be kept in sterile bottles, closely stoppered, and in a cool place, preferably upon ice.
7. Use coloring matter sparingly and eschew the old fashioned "foams." Brilliant, frothy sodas are suspiciously unpopular these days.
8. Throw out any syrup that has "turned"—it is false economy to try and sell such stuff—and profit by the experience to make up smaller quantities and keep them better.
9. Remember that syrup making is not a boy's job—it is a fine art.

SYRUPS

HINTS ON SYRUPS

Keep your extracts in a cool, dark place.
Never add flavoring extracts to hot syrup. It will cause them to evaporate and weaken the flavor.

Keep all your mixing utensils scrupulously clean.

Never mix your fruit syrups nor let them stand in the same vessels in which you mix or keep sarsaparilla, ginger, and similar extract flavors.

If possible always use distilled water in making syrups.

Make up your simple syrup often so that it will always be fresh.

Never allow a syrup containing acid to come in contact with any metal except pure block-tin.

Clean syrup jars each time before refilling.

Keep all packages of concentrated syrups and crushed fruits tightly corked.

Only mix a small quantity of crushed fruit in the bowl at a time so as to have it always fresh.

Use nothing but the best ingredients in making your syrups

ALMOND

Put 6 ounces of pulverized sweet almonds and 2 ounces of bruised bitter almonds into a saucepan with 1 quart of water, and let them simmer for a quarter of an hour; then add 1 pound of sifted sugar. When dissolved, strain through a hair sieve or jelly-bag, and add a teaspoonful of orange flower water. When cold, a wineglassful of the mixture should be put into a tumbler, which should be filled up with soda or seltzer water.

AMBROSIA

One-half gallon of raspberry syrup, 2 ounces of soda foam, ½ gallon of vanilla syrup.

AMBROSIA SYRUP

Orange syrup .... 1 quart
Vanilla syrup .... 1 pint
Strawberry syrup .... 1 quart
Port wine .... 3 ounces
Color red.

AMBROSIA

Raspberry juice, 1 quart bottle; hock wine, ½ pint; extract of vanilla, 2 ounces; granulated sugar, 6 pounds; water, 2 pints. Dissolve the sugar in the raspberry juice and water at a boiling point, strain, and when cool add the extract and wine.

AMBROSIA RICKEY

Syrup of raspberry ..... 2 parts
Syrup of orange .... 1 part
Syrup of pineapple .... 1 part
Into a glass squeeze the juice of half a lime, add 1 ounce of the foregoing syrup and then half fill with shaved ice; shake vigorously and add sufficient carbonated water to fill the glass. Serve with straws.

APRICOT

Three quarts of simple syrup, 1 quart of apricot juice, 2 ounces of soda foam, ½ ounce of citric acid solution. Color orange.

APRICOT

Apricot pulp (French)   1 pint
Solution of citric acid .   1 ounce
Rock candy syrup .....   3 pints
Orange flower water ...   1 pint
Two ounces to 14-ounce glass; crushed ice and straws. If this syrup is to be used with milk or cream it might be well to eliminate the citric acid solution from the formula.

BANANA

Peel any number of bananas, cut them in thin slices, and put in a wide-mouthed bottle of sufficient capacity; first a layer of banana slices, then a layer of sugar, until the bottle is filled, having as much sugar as banana. Place the bottle in a vessel of cold water, set it on the fire, and when the water boils remove the bottle containing the bananas Stir the contents thoroughly for several minutes, and when cool' press through a fine sieve or coarse linen cloth. Use as much of this as may be necessary to give a good, strong flavor.

BANANA

Peel and slice two bananas and beat them in a mortar until all lumps are reduced Then gradually add about two pints of syrup, mixing the whole thoroughly after each addition Lastly, add sufficient soda foam. This syrup should be made fresh each day, the quantity left at the close of each day being thrown away. The flavor may be strengthened by the addition of a small amount of banana essence. Instead of adding syrup to the bananas, the latter may be made into a smooth paste with hot water, then heated gently, 24 ounces of sugar being added for every pint of water used. Dissolve the sugar and add sufficient soda foam.

BANANA

Banana juice, 1 quart bottle; granulated sugar, 3 pounds. Mix, dissolve by heat, strain, and when cool add· Liquid foam, 1 ounce; fruit acid, 1 ounce; simple syrup, 4 pints.

BELFAST GINGER ALE

Dissolve 1 pound solid ginger ale extract in 1½ gallons of water at a temperature of 150° F., and filter through filter paper.

Dissolve 40 pounds of best granulated sugar in 6½ gallons warm water, and add 2½ ounces sugar color. Mix thoroughly with the dissolved and filtered extract and filter the whole through heavy flannel or a felt filter bag. Before using add to each gallon of syrup 1 ounce fruit acid.

BLOOD ORANGE

Fresh orange juice, 2 pints; water, 2 pints; sugar, 6 pounds; cherry juice (to color), ½ pint; solution of citric acid (1 in 2), 1 fluidounce.

BLOOD ORANGE

Tincture of orange .	2 fl. ounces
Solution of citric acid (50 per cent.) ...	2 fl. ounces
Raspberry juice ...	8 fl. ounces
Simple syrup, sufficient to make	1 gallon

Mix and strain through flannel. Tincture of orange for the above is made as follows: Oil of orange, 1 fl. ounce; peel of 2 oranges; alcohol, q s. to make 1 pint. Mix and filter. Blood orange syrup may also be made by adding 1 fl. ounce of compound tincture of cochineal to every gallon of ordinary orange syrup.

BLOOD ORANGE SYRUP

Fresh orange syrup ... 1 gallon
Juice of 12 raspberries ...
Color a light red.

CAPILLAIRE

Maidenhair	8 ounces
Boiling water	5 pints
Orange flower water ..	4 ounces
Sugar	sufficient

Infuse the maidenhair in boiling water. When nearly cold press out the liquid and filter. Add the orange flower water and dissolve in the solution about 7 ounces of sugar to each 4 fl. ounces of liquid.

CARAMEL

Extract of coffee	3 drams
Extract of vanilla	1 dram
Caramel	2 drams
Chocolate syrup	2 pints
Syrup to make	1 gallon

This syrup may be used to flavor a milk shake or egg drink, or as a sundae sauce.

CATAWBA

Three and one-half quarts of heavy simple syrup, 1 pint of catawba wine, 2 ounces of soda foam, ½ ounce of citric acid solution. Color red.

CELERY SYRUP

Lemon syrup	1 ounce
Celery extract	2 dashes

CHAMPAGNE

Crabapple extract	1 ounce
Pineapple juice	3 ounces
Citric acid	4 ounces
Simple syrup	1 gallon

CHAMPAGNE

Florida orange wine, 3 pints; water 1 pint; granulated sugar, 6 pounds. Dissolve by agitation or percolation, and add 1 ounce liquid phosphate.

CHERRY

Cherry juice, 1 quart bottle; granulated sugar 3 pounds. Mix, dissolve by heat, strain, and when cool add cochineal coloring, 1 ounce. Mix well, and then add: Liquid foam, 1 ounce; fruit acid, 1 ounce; simple syrup, 4 pints.

CHERRY

As the varieties of good cherries are not as abundant as in some other countries, it is best to use, as far as possible, the black varieties, which are of fine flavor and good color. Stone the cherries, pound about one-tenth of the kernels to a paste, mash and mix well together, let stand for a short time, stirring occasionally, and strain.

CHERRY COOLER

Cherry juice	10 ounces
Ess. of bitter almonds	1 dram
Sweet cider	2 quarts
Fruit acid	2 ounces
Foam extract	1 ounce
Sugar	5 pounds

Dissolve the sugar in the cider (pure apple juice) by stirring; do not heat; when dissolved add the other ingredients, mix well and strain.

CINNAMON

Oil of cinnamon, ½ fluidram; magnesium carbonate, 1 dram; water, 2 pints; sugar, 56 ounces. Rub the oil of cinnamon with magnesium carbonate, then gradually add the water, continuing the trituration; filter through paper, and in the filtrate dissolve the sugar.

CINNAMON (ARTIFICIAL)

One gallon of simple syrup, 10 drops oil of cassia, 2 ounces of soda foam. Color pink.

CHECKERBERRY SYRUP

Checkerberry essence or extract	1½ ounces
Simple syrup, enough to make	1 gallon

Color pink.

CLARET

Three quarts of simple syrup, 1 quart of claret wine, 1 ounce of citric acid solution, 2 ounces of soda foam. This syrup will be very thin unless sugar is added—14 pounds might be an advisable quantity. Bring to a boil.

CLOVE

One gallon of simple syrup, ½ ounce of essence of clove, 2 ounces of soda foam. Color pink.

CLUB COLA

Make a syrup of 2 drams of fluid extract kola, 6 drams tincture cinchona, enough fruit syrup to make 32 ounces. Make the

OR SODA WATER GUIDE

fruit syrup by mixing 16 ounces wild cherry phosphate syrup, 4 ounces vanilla syrup, 4 ounces orange syrup, 4 ounces lemon syrup, and 4 ounces strawberry syrup. Serve solid.

COCOA MENTHE

Chocolate syrup ..... ½ gallon
Mint syrup .... ½ gallon

Mix and strain and serve with cream. May be served as a milk shake or egg drink. For two ounces syrup and balance (to 10 ounces) milk, charge five cents; all milk and egg (12 ounces), 15 cents.

CONCENTRATED ORANGE

Grate 4 large oranges in a mortar, add 1 pound of sugar and rub it thoroughly with the grated oranges; squeeze in the orange juice and mix well; strain through cheese-cloth and add simple syrup enough to make a gallon, then add 2 ounces citric acid. Lemon syrup may be made in the same way, using however, 8 to 10 lemons.

CLARADE SYRUP

Equal parts claret syrup and orangeade syrup; 2 ounces fruit acid to gallon. Color red.

CREAM SYRUP

Condensed milk .... 1 pint
Water .... 1 pint
Sugar .... 1½ pounds

Heat to boiling point. Strain.

CREAM NECTAR SYRUP (SPECIAL)

Sweet cream, 32% ... 2 quarts
Pulverized sugar ..... 2 pounds
Orange syrup, from fruit,
   no acid .... 1 quart
Pineapple syrup ..... 1 quart
Vanilla extract ...... 7 drops

Color pink.

CREME DE MENTHE

Peppermint water, U. S. P. (freshly made), 4 pints; granulated sugar, 6 pounds; vegetable green, sufficient to color. Prepare by agitation or percolation. To dispense, place 1 ounce of the syrup in a glass, add 3 ounces of plain carbonated water, mix carefully with a twist bar spoon, and pour into a small goblet filled with finely cracked ice.

CRIMSON ORANGE

Red orange juice .... 1 quart
Fruit acid .... 1 ounce
Granulated sugar .... 3 pounds

Mix, dissolve by heat, strain, and add when cool:

Red fruit coloring .... ½ ounce
Liquid foam .... 1 ounce
Simple syrup .... 4 pints

CURRANT TART

Currant jelly .... 1 pint
Apple vinegar .... 1 pint
Sugar .... 3 pounds

Heat, stirring well, and use 2 ounces to 8-ounce glass.

FAVORITA

Strawberry juice ..... 4 ounces
Juice of 6 lemons
Maple syrup .... 1 pint
Soda foam .... 1 ounce
Syrup, enough to make ½ gallon

FELLOW FEELING

Strawberry syrup .... 10 ounces
Orange syrup .... 10 ounces
Pineapple syrup ..... 10 ounces
Lemon juice .... 2 ounces

Mix. Use 2 ounces of this syrup in a large glass which has been partially filled with shaved ice; fill the glass with carbonated water, top off with a slice of pineapple or other suitable fruit and serve with straws.

FLORIDA FRUITS

One dram vanilla extract, 1 dram orange essence, 1 dram lemon essence, 1 ounce pineapple juice, 1 ounce strawberry juice, sufficient soda foam, and syrup enough to make 32 ounces. Color with tincture of cudbear. Use 2 ounces in a 12-ounce glass. May be served as a phosphate in an 8-ounce glass for five cents.

FRESH STRAWBERRY

Pick two boxes of strawberries. Wash and clean them well. Add some sugar, about two 12-ounce glassfuls, and chop up the berries with a meat chopper. Add about two quarts of simple syrup. Care must be taken that the berries are not chopped too fine, just enough to bring out a good flavor.

FRUIT

Strawberry, raspberry, pineapple, blackberry, cherry, currant, etc. Fruit juice (desired flavor), 1 quart, plain syrup, 3 quarts; fruit acid, 1 ounce. A good plan is to mix the fruit juice and syrup, bring to boiling point and when cool add fruit acid and soda foam. This improves keeping qualities of syrup and develops taste of fruit more strongly.

FRUIT SYRUP ADVICE

The important thing that makes or mars the soda water trade is the quality of fruit syrups that form the flavors.

Only the real fruit syrups give the true fruit flavor.

The real essence of fruit is the best to give patrons to guarantee satisfaction and success

Crushed fruits should be made only from the fresh, ripe article.

To make and serve the best soda you must have the purest of syrups, the freshest crushed fruits and the truest flavorings.

In former years it was the general custom to use nothing but essences and extracts for soda beverages, but during the last ten years a change has taken place and nearly all first-class dispensers are using pure fruit syrups and so-called crushed or liquid fruits; which are made from selected fruits and sugar only. The fruit syrups are made from pure fruit and put up with sugar, either in gallon jugs, kegs or barrels. The crushed or whole fruits are made from selected fruits, either of domestic or foreign origin, and pure cane sugar, and put up generally in half-gallon air-tight jars after being duly pasteurized. The natural flavor of the respective fruits is preserved without the addition of any chemicals whatever. Some few flavors, such as ginger, orange and lemon, cannot very well be produced from the fruits by crushing the fruit and pressing it, but must be made by distillation.

FRUIT CHOCOLATE

Strawberry syrup, 10 ounces; vanilla syrup, 10 ounces, raspberry syrup, 8 ounces; chocolate syrup, 4 ounces. To dispense, draw 2 fl. ounces of this syrup into a 12-ounce glass, add 1 or 2 fl. ounces of cream, nearly fill the glass with carbonated water, coarse stream, then top off with the fine stream.

CHOCOLATE SYRUPS

BARNABY'S PRIZE CHOCOLATE

Cocoa powder (good quality) ..1 lb.
Granulated sugar ....2 lbs.
Mix thoroughly, then add just enough water to make a thick paste—taking care to rub out all the lumps—thin again with boiling water to the consistency of molasses; place receptacle in a water bath and cook 15 minutes with the water boiling. To serve, place small ladleful of mixture in seven-ounce hot soda cup, add one ounce of standard cream, and top off with whipped cream. Serve with wafers.

CHOCOLATE

One pound of cocoa, six pounds of sugar and one gallon of water. This will make about 1½ gallons of syrup at a cost of 53 cents a gallon, figuring cocoa at 35 cents and sugar at six cents a pound. If you use two ounces of this to a soda, it will cost about one cent, and you have a very good syrup for reasonable money. Some dispensers also add a little vanilla extract which will make it more expensive, and rather spoil the wholesome chocolate flavor.

CHOCOLATE

Take 24 pounds of sugar, 3½ pounds cocoa, 12 quarts water, make a paste with hot water, take out the lumps and slowly add the remaining water. Let the mixture come to a boil. (John Moore)

CHOCOLATE

Powdered chocolate, 8 ounces; sugar, 7½ pounds; water, 2½ quarts, extract of vanilla, 1 ounce. Make chocolate into a thick paste by addition of hot water and gradually add rest of water; add sugar; place on fire and boil one or two minutes, stirring constantly; strain while hot, and when cool add extract of vanilla. In serving add about 2 ounces of plain cream to each glass. Chocolate syrup is best made in small quantities, as it is liable to fermentation. Keep in cool place.

CHOCOLATE

Confectioners' chocolate, half pound; hot water, 2 quarts; condensed milk, 1 can; granulated sugar, 5 pounds; whites of 2 eggs; extract of vanilla, 1 ounce Cut the chocolate finely into a porcelain-lined evaporating dish, and with the aid of heat and a pestle reduce it to a smooth paste. Add the water (boiling hot), stirring constantly, then stir in the condensed milk and sugar. Allow to cool, skim off the cacao butter, particles of chocolate, etc., add the white of egg, previously beaten to a froth, and the vanilla, and strain through muslin.

CHOCOLATE

One pound chocolate, 1 gallon water, 20 pounds sugar; rub the chocolate in a mortar with 1 quart of hot water, add 1 gallon of water with the sugar and bring it to the boiling point; let it cool, add 1 ounce vanilla extract and strain into a pitcher or kettle, cover when cool and keep ready to serve.

CHOCOLATE COFFEE

Take one pound good chocolate powder and run it through a medium fine sieve. Mix this with 3 pounds granulated sugar, and sufficient salt. Now put about ½ ounce of this mixture into a cup or hot soda mug, and fill with hot coffee, adding cream to taste and topping off with whipped cream. Serve with wafers. (F. A. Ferguson.)

CHOCOLATE CORDIAL

Powdered cocoa	5	ounces
Powdered tea leaves	45	ounces
Deodorized alcohol .	20	ounces
Water	15	ounces
Diluted alcohol	1½	ounces
Simple syrup	1	pint

Macerate the cocoa and tea with the alcohol and water for eight days, shaking once in a while, then filter. Through the filter add the diluted alcohol. Flavor the liquid with equal parts of cinnamon and vanilla extracts, add the syrup and color with caramel. Used as a flavoring.

CHOCOLATE PASTE (HOT)

Soluble choc. powder .	8 ounces
Sugar, powdered	26 ounces
Glycerin	1 ounce
Rose water	1 ounce
Vanilla syrup	8 ounces
Water	8 ounces

Mix thoroughly. If too thick to mix well, add more water. Keep the paste in a shallow dish. To dispense take off:

Chocolate paste	1 ounce
Sweet cream	½ ounce

Turn on hot water stream and stir with spoon while filling; top off with whipped cream. Serve with a few crackers on a dish.

CHOCOLATE RATAFIA

Powdered cocoa .	2½ ounces
Cassia bark	1 ounce
Mace	30 grains
Vanilla	30 grains
Cloves	30 grains
Sugar	2 pounds
Deodor'd alcohol	56 fl. ounces
Water, distilled, enough to make	1 gallon

Reduce the cassia, mace, vanilla and cloves to coarse powder; mix these and the cocoa with the alcohol; macerate for seven days, agitating occasionally; strain, add the sugar, dissolved in the water and filter

CHOCOLATE VOTAN

Extract of malt, 8 ounces; extract of vanilla, 1 dram; chocolate syrup, enough to make two pints. Place 2 ounces in glass and fill with carbonated water, or serve as cocoa malt phosphate by adding a few dashes of acid phosphates to a glass.

COCOA

Cocoa, best grade ..	8 ounces
Sugar	5 pounds
Hot water	3½ pints

Mix cocoa and sugar thoroughly in a large mortar, add the hot water and boil the mixture for three minutes in a double boiler or granite kettle, stirring constantly with a wooden spoon. By adding a small piece of vanilla bean and allowing it to remain during the heating process the vanilla flavor desired is attained without the alcoholic taste, as when the extract is used. Strain through wire cloth or filter

COCOA

Cocoa, 4 ounces; sugar, 2 pounds; boiling water, 1 quart; extract of vanilla, 1 ounce. Dissolve the cocoa in the hot water by stirring, then add the sugar and dissolve. Strain and when cold add vanilla. Take two ounces of this syrup, 1 ounce of cream, turn on hot water stream, stir while filling and top off with whipped cream.

COSTELLO'S CHOCOLATE

Cocoa	5 ounces
Chocolate	12 ounces
Sugar	2 pounds
Water	1 gallon

Use two quarts of this syrup with two quarts of milk; boil for 15 minutes.

COFFEE SYRUPS

COFFEE

Take three ounces of prepared coffee, which dissolves instantly in either cold or hot water, three quarts of water and from 3½ to 4½ pounds of sugar. Mix the coffee first with one quart of cold water, then add two quarts more of water and sugar and stir until the sugar is dissolved.

COFFEE

Place one pound coffee, mixed with bird gravel and glycerin in long tin percolator, and percolate two quarts of boiling water through it several times. Add simple syrup to make one gallon. Glycerin will preserve the syrup and help retain the flavor. ("Happy" Ward.)

COFFEE

One pound of good coffee, place in a percolator and add a pint of cold water. Let stand for about five hours, then add 2½ gallons of boiling water and again let stand for from six to 12 hours. Drain off the percolate and add from 2½ to 3½ pounds of sugar, warming a little in order to dissolve the sugar. Strain and allow to cool before using. This process will make about three quarts of syrup at a cost of 44 cents or 60 cents a gallon.

COFFEE A LA POUGHKEEPSIE

Mocha coffee, 3 ounces; Java coffee, 5 ounces; boiling water, sufficient (about 40 ounces) to make 28 ounces of infusion; sugar, 3½ pounds. Pour the boiling water on the freshly ground coffee contained in a closed vessel and draw out after a half hour 28 ounces of infusion, which should be filtered. Pour the filtrate upon the sugar, previously placed in a percolator, and make the syrup by percolation. To the finished syrup add two or three drams of soda foam (tincture quillaja of the N. F.), as desired.

FRUIT SYRUPS, FANCY

ALHAMBRA

Seven ounces cream, 2 ounces peach syrup, 6 ounces orange syrup, 9 ounces vanilla syrup.

Use ounce of this mixture when dispensing. Fill the glass half full. Then add carbonated water, coarse and fine streams, in quick dashes until filled.

It might be well to put the cream in the syrups on serving. The acids in the peach and orange are liable to curdle the cream on standing.

AUGUST COOLER

Cherryallen syrup	2 pints
Orangeade	2 pints
Simple syrup	2 pints

Serve in 10-ounce glass as a phosphate. Charge 5 cents.

BALTIMORE CREAM

Peach syrup	3 ounces
Orange syrup	8 ounces
Vanilla syrup	8 ounces
Strawberry syrup	4 ounces
Cream to make	32 ounces

Use one ounce to the glass, filling with alternate coarse and fine streams of carbonated water. A better way to serve this feature might be to add the cream at time of dispensing. Syrup makes a good milk shake or ice cream soda.

BRAZILIAN BRACER

Raspberry juice	2 ounces
Orange juice	8 ounces
Rose water	8 ounces
Orange flower water	1 ounce
Ess. bitter almonds	20 drops
Fruit acid	½ ounce
Simple syrup	20 ounces
Water	20 ounces

Mix well and serve as fruit lemonade made with coarse stream.

BURBANK SPECIAL

Plum extract	2 drams
Quince extract	2 drams
Fruit acid	4 drams
Pineapple juice	10 ounces
Simple syrup	1 gallon

Mix well. Serve as a phosphate.

CHAMPAGNE SMASH

Champagne syrup	1 pint
Sweet mint syrup	1 pint
Essence of peppermint	5 drops
Solution of phosphates	1 ounce
Simple syrup	5 pints

Mix thoroughly. To serve place about 2 ounces in a 10-ounce glass and fill with carbonated water. Charge 5 cents.

CHERRO LIMETTO

Cherry juice	8 ounces
Lime juice	8 ounces
Angostura bitters	2 drams
Foam extract	4 drams
Cochineal coloring	½ dram
Simple syrup	3 quarts

Mix thoroughly. This is one of the best popular tart flavored specials.

CHERRY BLOSSOM

Prepare a syrup of ½ dram cherry essence, ½ dram strawberry essence, 2 drams vanilla extract, 1 dram solution of citric acid, 32 ounces syrup, sufficient cochineal color.

Use 1½ ounces of the syrup to a 12-ounce glass, fill with finely shaved ice and then with carbonated water, stirring well and serving with straws. In the above formula concentrated fruit syrups may be used instead of the essences.

COLUMBIA SPRAY

Pineapple syrup	8 ounces
Extract vanilla	¾ ounce
Strawberry syrup	8 ounces
Port wine	4 ounces
Syrup, enough to make	32 ounces

Draw 1½ ounces in a mineral water glass and fill with carbonated water. Serve with straws. Price—8 ounces, 5 cents.

• CONNER'S FRUIT PUNCH

Strawberry syrup	10 ounces
Orange syrup	10 ounces
Pineapple syrup	10 ounces
Lemon juice	2 ounces

Use 1½ ounces to a large glass one-third full of shaved ice, then fill glass with carbonated water, add a few strawberries, a slice each of pineapple and orange, and serve with straws and a spoon. For 13 ounces charge 10 or 15 cents.

CUBANA DELIGHT

Prepare a syrup of 3 lemons, 3 oranges, 1 pound granulated sugar, 4 ounces strawberry juice, 1 ounce solution citric acid, sufficient carmine solution and water, and enough syrup to make 1 gallon. Grate the yellow portion of the peel from the lemons and oranges, triturate with sugar, add the juice and enough water to make a solution; strain, and add the coloring and the syrup. Makes a good syrup for phosphates —8 ounces, 5 cents.

DON'T CARE

Blackberry juice, 1 quart bottle; grape juice, 1 quart bottle; lemon syrup No. 2, 1 pint; granulated sugar, 4½ pounds. Dissolve the sugar in the fruit juices at the boiling point, strain, and when cool, add the lemon syrup. Especially good for use in phosphates—8 ounces, 5 cents.

DON'T CARE SYRUP

California brandy	10 ounces
Pineapple syrup	½ gallon
Vanilla syrup	½ gallon

Color red and dispense in any kind of soda drink except a phosphate.

EGYPTIAN

Orgeat syrup	1 pint
Strawberry syrup	2 pints
Catawba syrup	2 pints
Cherry syrup	2 pints
Cranberry syrup	1 pint

Mix and strain.

This syrup is recommended for use in milk shakes or egg drinks.

ENGLISH PEACH, 'ONEY AND CREAM

Peach juice	1½	pints
Strained honey	1	quart
Simple syrup	1	quart
Rose water	4	ounces
Foam extract	1	ounce

Mix well. To dispense: Mix in a 12-ounce glass, fancy drink style, 2 ounces of the syrup with 2 ounces of sweet dairy cream; fill up with almond cream from the draught arm if you have it, and stir rapidly with the mixing spoon. If you have no almond cream on draught fill the glass with carbonated water instead.

FAIRIES' WISH

Cream		1 pint
Syrup		2 pints
Extract of vanilla		2 fl. drams
Strawberry syrup		1 fl. dram

Serve by drawing 2 ounces in a 12-ounce glass, fill the latter about one-half with the coarse stream of carbonated water, completing the operation with the fine stream. Price—10 cents; with egg, 15 cents.

FLORIDA FRUIT

Vanilla extract	1 dram
Orange extract	1 dram
Lemon extract	1 dram
Pineapple juice	1 ounce
Strawberry juice	1 ounce
Syrup, enough to make	32 ounces

Mix well and serve in 8-ounce glass. Charge 5 cents.

FOREST FLOWER

Anise water, freshly made, 1 pint; water, 2 pints; granulated sugar, 4½ pounds. Dissolve by agitation or percolation, and add: Syrup of tolu, U. S. P., 2 pints; extract of vanilla, 1 ounce; red fruit coloring, 1 ounce; liquid foam, 1 ounce. Mix and strain.

FRENCH PUNCH

Vanilla syrup, 2¼ pints; pineapple syrup, 2½ pints; sherry wine, ½ pint; grape juice, ¼ pint. Mix and strain. Price—10 ounces, 5 cents.

FRUIT PUNCH

Strawberry syrup, 10 ounces; 10 ounces orange syrup, 10 ounces pineapple syrup, 2 ounces lemon syrup; ½ ounce solution acid phosphate.

Use 1½ ounces of this to a large glass one-third full of shaved ice, then fill glass with carbonated water and a small amount of crushed strawberry, pineapple and orange, and serve with straws. Serve a 10-ounce glass, plain for 5 cents; with the fruit, 10 cents.

FRUIT SAUER

Strawberry syrup, pineapple syrup, cherry syrup and pear syrup, of each 8 fluid ounces, acid phosphate, 1 ounce.

Mix. To serve, draw 2 ounces in a mineral glass and fill with carbonated water. Drop a piece of twisted lemon peel on top of this beverage. For 8 ounces charge 5 cents.

FRUIT SPRAY

Four ounces pineapple syrup, 4 ounces strawberry syrup, 4 drams vanilla extract, 2 ounces port wine.

Mix and serve solid like phosphate. Price—8 ounces, 5 cents.

GINGER MINT

Prepare a syrup from ½ ounce peppermint essence, 2 ounces ginger essence, ½ ounce magnesium carbonate, water, and enough syrup to make 32 ounces. Mix the essence of peppermint intimately with the magnesium carbonate, add 2 ounces water, shake thoroughly, filter, adding through the filter enough water to make 2 ounces of filtrate. Add the remaining ingredients and serve like ginger ale syrup.

GINGER MINT

Con'trated mint syrup	1 pint
Rock candy syrup	2 quarts
Ginger ale extract	2½ ounces

Mix well by pouring. Serve solid at 5 cents for 8 ounces.

This formula is recommended as being the better of the two Ginger Mint formulas presented.

HOBSON'S JAP ROSE

Strawberry juice	8 ounces
Maple syrup	20 ounces
Lemon juice	10 ounces
Lime juice	5 ounces
Cherry syrup	10 ounces
Soda foam	1 ounce
Simple syrup	2 gallons
Caramel to color a reddish-amber.	

Use 2 ounces of syrup to a 10-ounce glass. Serve with shaved ice and fill with fine stream. Charge 10 cents.

HONEY BOY

Pineapple syrup	1 pint
Vanilla syrup	1 pint
Lemon syrup	1 pint
Strained honey	3 drams
Fruit acid	2 fl. drams
Soda foam	4 fl. drams

Serve 2 fluid ounces in glass and fill with carbonated water. Price—10 ounces, 5 cents.

HONEY MINT

Mint leaves	1 ounce
Sugar (gran.)	1 ounce
Strained honey	1 pint
Vanilla extract	2 drams
Simple syrup	2 quarts

Bruise mint leaves and sugar thoroughly in a mortar. Add ½ pint water and stir till sugar is dissolved; then strain and add other ingredients, mixing well. This makes a good milk shake or egg drink. For latter charge 5 cents; all milk, 12 ounces, 15 cents.

IDLEWILD FRUIT PUNCH

Strawberry syrup .... 10 ounces
Orange syrup .... 10 ounces
Pineapple syrup ...... 10 ounces
Lemon juice .... 2 ounces

Draw 1¼ ounces into a 12-ounce glass one-third filled with shaved ice; then fill the glass with the coarse stream of carbonated water; add a few strawberries, a slice of pineapple and a slice of orange and serve with straws and a spoon. Charge 15 cents.

IMPERIAL GRENADINE

Extract grenadine .... 2 ounces
Liquid foam .... 1 ounce
Red fruit coloring .... 1 dram
Simple syrup .... 1 gallon

Mix thoroughly, then add:

Fruit acid .... 2 ounces
Strain. Serve solid; 8 ounces, 5 cents.

JOHNNIE JONES

Peach syrup .... 2 ounces
Orange syrup .... 6 ounces
Vanilla syrup .... 9 ounces
Cream to make .... 24 ounces

Draw one ounce of this syrup into a 12-ounce glass and fill the glass with carbonated water, beginning with the coarse stream and finishing with the fine stream. Makes a delicious egg drink or milk shake.

JULIET

Crushed ice .... ½ glass
Ginger ale syrup ..... 1 pint
Pineapple juice ...... 8 ounces
Grape juice .... 8 ounces
Water .... 1 quart
Simple syrup .... 5 ounces

Serve solid; 10 ounces, 10 cents.

JUNE PUNCH

Strawberry syrup ...... 1 pint
Orange syrup .... 1 pint
Pineapple syrup .... 1 pint

Draw 2 ounces in a 12-ounce glass and fill with carbonated water, coarse stream. Dress with a strawberry, slice of orange and pineapple. Charge 10 cents. May be used for a phosphate, milk shake, egg drink or ice cream soda.

KENTUCKY BELLE

One pint prepared strawberry; 1 pint vanilla syrup. To 1½ ounces of this mixture add ½ ounce rich cream and a teaspoonful of pulverized sugar.

Draw carbonated water, fine stream, first to mix cream and syrup, then coarse stream to nearly fill the glass, and finish with fine stream. Price—12-ounce glass, 5 cents.

GINGER

Essence Jamaica ginger, 4 ounces; plain syrup, 1 gallon; caramel, 1 ounce.

GINGER ALE

To make 12 gallons of syrup take 1½ ounces ginger ale extract, place it in a No. 10 Wedgewood mortar, add 2 ounces of calcined magnesia, and mix thoroughly. Add 8 gallons hot water, and filter through filter paper. Then add 50 pounds granulated sugar, 2 quarts lime juice, 8 ounces fruit acid, 1½ ounces acetic acid, and 3 ounces sarsaparilla color.

For dispensing, use 1½ ounces to a thin 9-ounce tumbler.

For bottling, use 1½ ounces to a half-pint bottle, 2 ounces to an imported ginger ale bottle, and 4 ounces to a quart apollinaris bottle.

The directions given are for 12 gallons of syrup, which is a convenient quantity for a bottler to make. The dispenser can make a smaller quantity by using the ingredients in smaller quantities, but same proportions.

GINGER ALE

Jamaica ginger, 8 pounds; capsicum, 6 ounces; alcohol, a sufficient quantity. Mix the powders intimately, moisten them with a sufficient quantity of alcohol and set aside for four hours Pack in a cylindrical percolator and percolate with alcohol until 10 pints of percolate have been obtained. Place the percolate in a bottle of the capacity of 16 pints, and add to it 2 fl. drams of oleoresin of ginger. Shake, add 2½ pounds of powdered pumice stone, and agitate thoroughly at intervals of one-half hour for 12 hours. Then add 14 pints of water in quantities of 1 pint at each addition, shaking briskly meanwhile. This part of the operation is most important. Set the mixture aside for 24 hours, agitating it strongly every hour or so during that period. Then take: oil of lemon, 1½ fl. ounces; oil of rose or geranium, 3 fl. drams; oil of bergamot, 2 fl. drams; oil of cinnamon, 3 fl. drams; magnesium carbonate, 3 ounces. Rub the oils with the magnesia in a large mortar and add 9 ounces of the clear portion of the ginger mixture, to which has previously been added 2 ounces of alcohol, and continue the trituration, rinsing out the mortar with the ginger mixture. Pass the ginger mixture through a double filter, and add, through the filter, the mixture of oils and magnesia. Finally pass enough water through the filter to make the resulting product measure 24 pints, or 3 gallons. An extract of more or less pungency may be obtained by increasing or decreasing the quantity of powdered capsicum in the formula. Four ounces of the extract are to be used with each gallon of syrup.

GINGER ALE

Jamaica ginger, ground, 12 ounces; ounces; lemon peel, fresh, cut fine, 2 ounces; capsicum, powdered, 1 ounce; calcined magnesia, 1 ounce; alcohol, water, of each, sufficient.

Extract the mixed ginger and capsicum by percolation so as to obtain 16 fluid ounces of liquid, set the mixture aside for 24 hours, shaking vigorously from time to time, then filter, and pass through the filter enough of a mixture of 2 volumes of alcohol and 1 of water to make the filtrate measure 32 fluid ounces. In the latter macerate the lemon peel for seven days, and again filter.

GINGER FRUI-TANA

To make the ginger frui-tana syrup take 6 ounces soluble essence of ginger, 8 ounces pineapple juice, 2 drams fruit acid, 1 gallon simple syrup. Mix well. To serve take one ounce ginger frui-tana syrup and 3 dashes essence ginger. Add hot water and a slice of lemon. This feature syrup would make up well as a ginger fruit phosphate.

GINGER SNAP

Take ¼ ounce of American Dublin ginger ale syrup, ½ ounce grape syrup, ¼ ounce orangeade in a soda glass. Fill glass with carbonated water and mix thoroughly. May also be served with shaved ice.

Ginger cordial syrup, 1½ ounces; carbonated water, 6 ounces.

Concentrated ginger syrup, 1 quart; plain syrup, 3 quarts. Mix well.

GINGERADE

Make syrup of 2 ounces ginger essence, 2 drams lemon essence, 2 drams solution citric acid, syrup to make 32 ounces. Serve solid and add small spoonful powdered sugar to each glass.

GRAPE

Boil together one pound of sugar with ½ pint water until it threads. Take from the fire and when cool add the juice of six lemons and a quart of grape juice. Let stand over night. Serve with soda water, apollinaris or plain water, ice cold. This is an excellent formula but the beverage thus prepared will not keep well and should be dispensed soon after making. (U. S. Dept. of Agriculture.)

GREEN MOUNTAIN FAVORITE

Strawberry juice ..... 4 ounces
Juice of lemons ..... ½ dozen
Maple syrup .... 2 pints
Simple syrup .... 2 pints

Mix well. To serve, place 2 ounces in a 12-ounce glass and fill with carbonated water.

GOODNER'S SARSAPARILLA

Two drams essence sarsaparilla root; 2 drams essence wintergreen; 1 gallon plain syrup. Color with caramel.

HONEY BOY

Mix thoroughly 1 pint of pineapple syrup, 1 pint of vanilla syrup, 1 pint of lemon syrup, and ½ pint of strained honey. Serve with sweet or ice cream.

HONEY DEW

One pint pineapple syrup, 1 pint vanilla syrup, 1 pint lemon syrup, 3 drams strained honey and 2 drams solution citric acid. Serve like ordinary lemon syrup. Price, 8-ounce glass, 5 cents.

ICED CHOCOLATE

Put into a porcelain-lined or granite kettle ¼ pound grated, unsweetened chocolate; add 6 ounces of sugar and half a cup of water, and cook until shiny and smooth. Add 3 cups more hot water and boil until the chocolate is of the consistency of thick cream; remove from the fire and beat while cooling; flavor with vanilla, and, if desired, a little cinnamon; then set on the ice until chilled. Serve in tall glasses with a little chopped ice and a spoonful of whipped cream on top; this chocolate syrup may be made in quantity and kept in glass jars in the refrigerator ready for an emergency. It would make a good "special" at the fountain and on that account is deserving of attention.

INDIAN BIRCH

Birch essence .... 2 ounces
Oil of sassafras ...... 2 drops
Syrup, enough to make 64 ounces
Soda foam ...., sufficient

To make the essence of birch dissolve 5 ounces oil of sweet birch, 2 drams oil of lemon, and ½ dram oil of cloves in 12 ounces of alcohol, and then add 4 ounces extract of vanilla.

KOLA CHAMPAGNE

Stock champagne syrup, 7 pints; kola wine, 1 pint; fruit acid, 3 ounces; sarsaparilla color, ½ ounce; extract vanilla, 1½ ounces. Serve 2 ounces to each 12-ounce glass.

KOLA PUNCH

Prepare syrup of 2 drams fluid extract kola; 8 ounces grape juice; 6 ounces pineapple syrup; 1½ ounces solution citric acid; 14½ ounces syrup. Serve solid.

LADY DAINTY

Raspberry juice ...... 1 ounce
Lemon juice .... 2 ounces
Orange juice .... 4 ounces
Angostura bitters .... 2 drams
Fruit acid .... 4 drams
Simple syrup .... ½ gallon

This syrup makes a very fine egg phosphate as well as a plain one. Price—10 ounces, 5 cents.

LEMON

Lemons with smooth, thin skin are preferable to the rough, thick ones which are spongy and dry. Choose only sound fruit, wash them lightly in cold water and wipe them dry with a soft cloth, after which wrap in soft paper again and store away in a dry and cool box, well covered with a lid. By doing this the fruit will keep a good sound flavor, and all the odor of the box or the bad smell from the decayed fruit, so often noticed with lemons or oranges, will be removed, and an ice cream or water ice of superior quality will be the reward for the little trouble. To prepare the lemon for cream or other ices, the rind may be rubbed on a large lump of sugar. The fruit is then cut in half. After having removed all the white rind, pick out the seeds, squeeze out the juice, add the sugar, strain it and it is ready for use or it may then be bottled. By removing the seeds the juice will have a finer taste, as the seeds, especially when some are mashed in the squeezer, will impart a bitter flavor to the juice. Many ice cream makers neglect these little things.

LEMONA MINT
Spirit of peppermint, 4 fl. drams; lemon juice, 4 fl. drams; solution of citric acid, 1 fl. dram; syrup, enough to make 32 fl. ounces. Dispense either solid or foamed. In the latter case gum must be added.

LORD BELPER
Extract of Jamaica ginger, ½ ounce; solution of citric acid, 2 drams; raspberry juice, 1 ounce; tincture of spearmint, ½ dram; syrup, enough to make 16 fl. ounces. In dispensing use two ounces of this syrup and draw solid. Add a couple of sprigs of mint.

MAGIC MINT
Lemon juice .... 1 pint
Essence peppermint .. ½ dram
Fruit acid .... ½ ounce
Simple syrup .... 1 gallon
Mix.

MALTESE ORANGE SYRUP
This syrup is made from the maltese orange fruit. It is very sweet and fragrant, but is more expensive than any other orange flavor. Take one quart of maltese orange juice, three quarts of rock candy syrup and two ounces citric acid solution. Serve phosphate style.

MANDARIN
Syrup mandarin orange, 1 gallon; soluble essence of mandarin, 3 ounces; solution of citric acid, 2 ounces; liquid saffron, ¼ ounce; liquid cochineal, ¼ ounce. Liquid saffron is made by macerating 1½ ounces of saffron in 1 pint hot distilled water for 24 hours and then filtering the solution through paper pulp.

MAPLE
Five pounds of maple sugar, 1 quart of water, 1 pound of glucose. Bring to a boil, color with burnt sugar and pour in a jug.

MAPLE
Maple sugar .... 3 pounds
Water .... 2 pints
Solution of citric acid   4 drams

Dissolve the sugar in the water by the aid of heat, strain and add the solution of citric acid. Extract of vanilla may be added if desired.

MARSHMALLOW
Seven pints rock candy syrup, 1¼ ounces powdered gum arabic, 4 ounces orange flower water, 2 ounces fruit acid and water enough to make 1 gallon.

MAY QUEEN FIZZETTE
Blood orange syrup ... 3 pints
Raspberry fruit syrup   2 pints
Fine sweet catawba ... 2 pints
Rose syrup .... 8 ounces
Pineapple syrup ...... 7 ounces
Fruit acid .... 1 ounce

Mix well together and filter. For dispensing, place 2 ounces of the syrup in a tumbler, add shaved ice, fill up with plain carbonated water, and top off with two raspberries and a piece of lemon.

MEAD
Cloves .... ½ ounce
Nutmegs .... 2 drams
Coriander .... 2 ounces
Jamaica ginger ...... 2 ounces
Allspice .... ½ ounce
Cinnamon water ..... 4 ounces
Alcohol .... 4 ounces

Pulverize the spices coarsely and macerate them for 24 hours in the alcohol and cinnamon water; then transfer the whole to a percolator, and pour on dilute alcohol till 16 ounces of fluid are obtained; percolate slowly, and add to the mixture ½ ounce of genuine orange flower water. For making a mead syrup take 1 ounce of the above extract and enough rock candy to make 2 pints.

MEAD A LA CHAUCER
Pineapple syrup, 2 ounces; soluble essence of ginger, 4 drams; essence of sarsaparilla, 15 drops; spirit of nutmeg, 1 dram; honey or malt extract, 2 ounces; syrup, enough to make ½ gallon; caramel, sufficient to color. Mix.

METROPOLITAN SOUR
Strawberry syrup, 3 pints; lemon syrup, 8 ounces; infusion of wild cherry, fresh, 8 ounces; tartaric acid, 1¼ drams.
Dissolve the tartaric acid in the infusion and mix with the syrups. Serve without foam in a thin mineral water glass. Price —8-ounce glass, 5 cents.

MINT CORDIAL

Raspberry vinegar, 4 ounces; fruit acid, 1½ ounces; extract ginger ale, 1½ ounces; brandy, 1 ounce; simple syrup, 1 gallon. Mix, strain.

Serve as follows: Shaved ice, 1 tumblerful; mint cordial syrup, as above, 2 ounces; fresh mint (pressed to side of glass with spoon), 4 sprigs; carbonated water, 1 tumblerful. Stir and serve with straws.

MINT CORDIAL

Make a syrup of ½ ounce ginger essence, ½ dram tincture capsicum, 1 ounce grape juice, 3 drams solution of citric acid, 1 ounce raspberry vinegar, enough syrup to make 32 ounces. Use 2 ounces of this syrup in 12-ounce glass, add fresh mint sprigs, press latter against side of glass to get flavor, fill glass two-thirds full of shaved ice, fill with coarse stream, top with mint, serve straws.

MINT NECTAR

Make a syrup of 1½ ounces peppermint essence, 4 drams vanilla extract, 1 ounce solution citric acid, ½ gallon syrup, sufficient water and soda foam, and enough tincture of grass to impart a green tint. Mix the essence with 2 ounces of water and filter through powdered magnesium carbonate, passing enough water through to make 3 ounces of filtrate. Add the remaining ingredients. Serve solid in 8-ounce glass.

MINTOLA

Make a syrup of 4 ounces lemon juice; 4 drams peppermint essence, 1 dram solution of citric acid, enough syrup to make 32 fl. ounces, and sufficient gum foam. Dispense solid.

MINTORANGE

Orange stock syrup, 1 pint; green mint stock syrup, 1 pint; simple syrup, 2 quarts; juice of 6 lemons. Serve from punch bowl in 8-ounce glasses.

MORNING DEW

Make a syrup of 4 drams brandy, 1 dram sweet catawba wine, 1 dram clove essence, 1 dram blood orange extract, 2 drams rose essence, 1 ounce strawberry juice, 1 ounce pineapple juice, simple syrup enough to make one-half gallon. Price—8-ounce glass, 5 cents.

MOUNTAIN PINK

Vanilla extract	½ ounce
Lemon essence	½ ounce
Pineapple juice	2 ounces
Sugar	2½ pounds
Sodium bicarbonate	60 grains

Mix well and then add

Sweet cream	2 pints
Vegetable coloring (red)	sufficient

The sodium bicarbonate to neutralize fruit acid. Serve as an ice cream soda.

NECTAR

Make a syrup from 3 ounces pineapple syrup, 3 ounces strawberry syrup, 2 ounces raspberry syrup, 2½ ounces orange flower water, ½ ounce citric acid, 8 ounces sherry, 3 pints syrup. By this formula may be prepared a syrup which will make a delicious egg drink.

NECTAR

Pineapple syrup, 1-3 gallon; strawberry syrup, 1-3 gallon; lemon syrup. 1-3 gallon; oil bitter almond, 6 drops; color deep red and add 1 ounce soda foam.

NECTAR

One-half gallon of simple syrup, 1 quart of strawberry syrup, 1 quart of vanilla syrup, ¼ pint of port wine, 2 ounces soda foam, 1 ounce of burnt sugar.

NECTAR PUNCH

Lemon syrup	1 pint
Strawberry syrup	1 pint
Orange syrup	1 pint
Solution phosphates ....½ ounce
Orange, sliced	1

Put into a punch bowl, ladle 1½ ounces into a mineral water glass, add shaved ice, fill the glass with carbonated water, coarse stream, top off with maraschino cherries, and serve with a straw.

NEW ORLEANS MEAD

This beverage, an old stand-by of a quarter of a century ago, is still a favorite in many localities. It may be made as follows:

Tonka beans	2 ounces
Cloves	7 ounces
Cinnamon	7 ounces
Ginger	7 ounces
Nutmeg	7 ounces
Mace	2 ounces
Simple syrup	20 gallons

Bruise the spices in a mortar, placing those containing the most oil in a bag by themselves and the others in another bag. Immerse all in the syrup, and boil for 12 hours, no longer. Then take 2 pounds of sassafras bark, add 3 gallons of water. and boil slowly until reduced to 2 gallons; 8 ounces of allspice may be added to advantage. After the spices are sufficiently boiled, add the decoction of sassafras and 2 gallons of honey. Put 5 quarts of the syrup thus made into a suitable fountain, add enough water to make 10 gallons, and charge to 100 pounds pressure.

NIPPONESE

Cherry juice (fresh) ..	1 pint
Essence bitter almonds	1 dram
Citric acid	1 dram
Simple syrup	2 quarts

Served either solid or with ice cream.

OPERA BOUQUET

Rose water	3 fl. ounces
Strawberry juice or	
concentrated syrup	8 fl ounces
Syrup enough to make	32 fl ounces
Solution of carmine ..	q. s.

ORANGE

Eight large thick-skin oranges, 2 ounces fruit acid. Take oranges unpeeled and chop with meat chopper into pieces about one-quarter inch thick. Add 10 pounds of sugar and allow to sit overnight if possible so as to give the sugar a chance to draw. Add 1 gallon of water and strain through cheese-cloth. Rub together thoroughly while straining until you can see a thick yellow juice coming from the skins. This last point is very important. This is a much quicker process than the old way of grating the oranges and produces better results.

ORANGE

Grate six orange skins, then mix with a little sugar, in order to break up the oil cells. Squeeze the oranges into the gratings and add enough simple syrup to make one gallon. Put the mixture in the ice box until the next day, then strain well through a cheese cloth. Only good oranges should be used, the rough skinned variety are the best, purchased at a cost of, say, five cents apiece.

ORANGE BLOSSOM

Blood orange syrup....	3 quarts
Orange flower water ..	4 ounces

Mix well.

ORANGE CHOCOLATE

Extract of vanilla, 1 ounce; orange flower water, 2 ounces; chocolate syrup, 1 gallon.

Serve with cream in a soda glass. If all milk and egg are used in dispensing charge 15 cents, otherwise five cents for a 12-ounce glass.

ORANGE (CRUSHED FRESH FRUIT)

Oranges	8
Sugar (gran.)	5 pounds
Citric acid	1 ounce
Simple syrup	5 pints
Water	2 pints

Peel oranges carefully and cut into small cubes, removing seeds and putting in cheese cloth bag. Squeeze out juice and add pulp, sugar and water. Heat gently to help melting of sugar, and when cool add syrup and acid, mixing well.

ORGEAT

Almond extract	½ dram
Orange peel essence ...	4 drams
Sugar (granulated) ..	8 ounces
Sweet cream	6 ounces
Simple syrup	3 quarts

Dissolve sugar in cream by heating, then add other ingredients, mix well, strain, and cool. This syrup should be used at once as it does not keep well.

ORGEAT

One gallon simple syrup, 1 ounce of bitter almond extract, 2 ounces of soda foam, 1 ounce of caramel. This formula for orgeat syrup is commended, but the dispenser may prefer green to caramel color.

ORGEAT

Almond paste	2 pounds
Blanched bitter almonds	2 ounces
Water	1 quart
Orange flower water ..	1 gill
Vanilla extract	1 ounce
Sugar (powdered) ...	4 pounds

Mix and pound into a paste with the water, then pressing the mixture in a towel to extract milk. Add other ingredients and bottle securely after sugar has dissolved. Must be kept cold to prevent fermentation.

ORGEAT

Take 2 pounds of almond paste; add 2 ounces of blanched almonds, pounded fine, and mix and pound the whole with 1 quart of water, 4 ounces of orange flower water, 1 ounce of vanilla extract; then press the mixture through a towel or napkin so as to get the milk of almonds all out of it; add 4 pounds of powdered sugar to the mixture dissolved in the milk, and put in a large bottle placing it on ice to keep the syrup from fermenting. This is a good formula but the syrup must be used quickly.

OUR NEW MEAD

Tincture of Jamaica ginger, 4 fluiddrams; lemon essence, 4 fluiddrams; oil of cloves, 3 drops; honey, 4 fluidounces; simple syrup, enough to make 32 fluidounces. Color with caramel. Charge 5 cents for an 8-ounce glass.

PEACH SHRUB

Peel 10 pounds of peaches and mash them, and simmer gently in two quarts of the best cider vinegar, to which have been added two quarts of water, and a muslin bag containing three sticks of cinnamon and two ounces of whole cloves. Strain through coarse muslin. Add five pounds of sugar and boil 20 minutes. Bottle while still hot, first sterilizing the bottles by boiling in water for 20 minutes. Serve with carbonated water. The remaining peach pulp may be sweetened and used as a marmalade, adding a little citric acid solution, if needed to bring up the flavor. Use pint snap top bottle. Peach shrub makes a nice sundae flavor or dressing.

PEAR

One gallon of simple syrup, 2 ounces of soda foam, 3 ounces of pear extract, ½ ounce of citric acid solution. Color yellow.

PHANTOM

Vanilla syrup	8 ounces
Pineapple syrup	1 pint
Orange syrup	24 ounces
Orange flower water ..	2 ounces

Mix well. To serve add milk or sweet cream to 13-ounce glass. This syrup makes a good egg drink flavor using all milk and charging 15 cents.

PHOSPHATE SYRUPS

BITTER ORANGE

Ess. of orange peel ..	½ ounce
Angostura bitters ....⁻	½ ounce
Phosphate sol.	½ ounce
Orange syrup	2 quarts

Price—8-ounce glass, 5 cents.

BLOOD ORANGE

Extract of orange (fresh), 2 ounces; raspberry juice, 2 ounces, solution of citric acid (1 : 2), 2 ounces; simple syrup, 1¼ gallons; tincture of cudbear, N. F., q. s. to color. Place 1 ounce in a mineral water glass, add a dash of solution of phosphate and fill with carbonated water.

BOWLER'S PUNCH

Three ounces wild grape juice (ordinary juice will do), 16 ounces strawberry syrup; ½ ounce fluid extract of kola; ½ ounce solution of acid phosphate; enough syrup to make a gallon and sufficient soda foam. Use 2 ounces to a glass, and fill with carbonated water.   Charge 5 cents for 8 ounces

CELERY PHOSPHATE

Celery Extract	2 ounces
Syrup	1 gallon

Acid phosphate—A few shakes per tumbler.

CHERRY-COLA

Coca Cola syrup	1 pint
Cherry syrup	2 pints

Serve as phosphate. Price—8 ounces, 5 cents.

CHERRY SPECIAL

Cherry phosphate syrup	1 quart
Plain syrup	3 quarts

Draw 1½ ounces in a mineral glass, add a dash of phosphate, draw soda into another glass, and pour into glass containing the syrup. Stick a Maraschino cherry on a wooden toothpick and drop into the glass. The customer enjoys the drink, and finishes by eating the cherry off the end of the toothpick, and goes away pleased. Price—8 ounces, 5 cents.

CHOCOLATE LACTART

Lactart	12	ounces
Chocolate syrup ...	6	pints
Vanilla syrup	1	pint
Cinnamon syrup ...	¼	pint

For stock syrup. Dispense 1½ ounces with 1 ounce of cream and 8 or 10 ounces of carbonated water.

DELHI PUNCH

Grape juice	6	ounces
Orange juice	4	ounces
Phos. sol.	2	ounces
Cochineal color	½	dram
Simple syrup	2	quarts

Serve as a phosphate.

EGG MINT

Two fresh eggs; orange juice, 3 ounces; raspberry syrup, 12 ounces; phosphoric acid, syrupy, 30 minims; spirit of peppermint (1 :15), 30 minims. Mix. Trim with sliced orange and sprigs of fresh mint.

Shake well for some time, strain and use 2 ounces to a 12-ounce glass. Serve with fine ice on which crush the mint. Stir up with fine stream. When 2/3 full with the coarse stream, finish with the fine. Price—10 cents; extra egg to each glass, 15 cents.

EGYPTIAN

Grape juice	6	ounces
Orange juice	2	ounces
Raspberry juice	2	ounces
Phosphate solution .	3	ounces
Foam extract	1	ounce
Cochineal coloring .	½	dram
Simple syrup	2	quarts

Mix thoroughly. This syrup is a good one to use in phosphates and egg drinks.

GINGER BOUQUET

Sol. ess. of ginger...	2½	ounces
Citric acid	½	ounce
Extract of vanilla ..	1	ounce
Ess. of sarsaparilla	1	ounce
Syrup, to make	4	pints
Burnt sugar	1	dram

Serve solid. Price—8 ounces, 5 cents.

GOODNER'S MINT PHOSPHATE

Fresh mint leaves, 1 handful Scald in hot water; add ½ pound granulated sugar and rub in mortar; when cool strain through cheese cloth into 1 gallon plain syrup; add 4 drops oil lemon; 1 ounce fruit acid; color green. Price—8 ounces, 5 cents.

GRAPE CUP

One pint grape juice, 1 ounce English breakfast tea (concentrated), 4 ounces prepared lime juice, ½ ounce solution acid phosphate, 1 pint water. Add a lump of ice and let stand until cold. Fill glass ¾ full and fill with carbonated water as it is served.

HARVEST HOME

Tea syrup	1	pint
Maple syrup	½	pint
Acid phosphate sol. .	½	ounce
Foam extract	½	ounce
Simple syrup	3	pints

Mix and color green with a solution made from spinach leaves or any vegetable green color.

INDIAN PHOSPHATE

Make a syrup of ½ ounce ginger essence, ½ dram wine flavor, 1 ounce glycerin, 2 ounces solution acid phosphate, enough syrup to make ½ gallon and sufficient foam. Draw 1½ ounces in an 8-ounce glass, filling with shaved ice and carbonated water. Add cherry, and serve solid with straws.

LACTART

Orange syrup, 10 ounces; pineapple syrup, 10 ounces; vanilla syrup, 10 ounces; lactart, 6 ounces. Mix.

LEMON LACTIC

Lemon syrup	1	quart
Lactic acid	½	ounce
Fruit acid	¼	ounce
Curcuma coloring ...	30	drops
Simple syrup	1	quart

Price—8 ounces, 5 cents   Serve solid.

L...... PHOSPHATE

Solution of acid phosphate, 2 fluid ounces; lemon syrup, sufficient to make 1 gallon. Mix.

N. A. R. D. FAVORITE

Red orange syrup	5½	pints
Orange wine	1	pint
Pineapple syrup	1	pint
Sol. of acid phos.	½	pint

Put two ounces in thin 8-ounce glass and fill with carbonated water coarse stream. Charge 5 cents.

ORANGE PHOSPHATE

Solution of acid phosphate, 2 fluid ounces; orange syrup sufficient to make 1 gallon; mix. Blood orange phosphate syrup may be prepared in the same manner by using blood orange syrup. Price—8 ounces, 5 cents.

PALM BEACH QUEEN

Blood orange syrup...	6	ounces
Raspberry syrup	4	ounces
Grape juice	4	ounces
Rose syrup	1	ounce
Pineapple syrup	1	ounce
Acid solution	1	dram

Mix. Place 2 ounces in a glass partly filled with ice, fill up with carbonated water and dress with two raspberries and a piece of pineapple. Price—10 ounces, 10 cents.

PARISIAN BLEND

Compound tincture cardamom, 2 ounces; simple syrup, 1 gallon. Mix well, then add lactart, 1 ounce, and strain.

PINEAPPLE PHOSPHATE

Solution acid phosphate, 2 fluid ounces; orange syrup, 16 fluid ounces; vanilla syrup, 8 fluid ounces; pineapple syrup, sufficient to make 1 gallon; mix.

The elimination of the orange and vanilla syrups in this formula might give the pineapple syrup more of a chance to be brought out.

PRESIDENT'S PHOSPHATE

Blood orange juice, 8 ounces; red raspberry juice, 4 ounces; vanilla extract, 2 drams; claret, 4 ounces; juice of 3 oranges; solution of acid phosphate, 3 ounces; simple syrup, enough to make 1 gallon. To serve, place 2 ounces in an 8-ounce glass, and fill with carbonated water, coarse stream.

RAPID TRANSIT

Tea syrup, 1 pint; vanilla syrup, 8 ounces; solution acid phosphate, ½ ounce; foam extract, ½ ounce; simple syrup, 3 pints. Color with caramel.

RASPBERRY PHOSPHATE

Solution of acid phosphate, 2 fluid ounces; raspberry syrup, sufficient to make 1 gallon, mix. A bit of certified color might be added to this syrup to advantage.

SENIOR

Strawberry syrup ..	6	fl. ounces
Pineapple syrup ...	6	fl. ounces
Cherry syrup	6	fl. ounces
Sol. acid phosphate	1	fl. ounce

Serve 1½ fluid ounces in an 8-ounce glass and fill with carbonated water.

SPRING FRUIT

This phosphate may be announced by the following "ad.":

....

    SPRING FRUIT PHOSPHATE:

       5 Cents and 10 Cents

    DRAWN FROM THE ICE

....

Pineapple fruit	1	pint
Strawberry fruit	1	pint
Oranges, in slice	6	
Lemons, in slice	6	
Simple syrup	1	gallon
Phosphate	6	ounces

Mix well and place in a large bowl on the counter in plain view of your customers. Keep the bowl covered with glass. To serve, fill one-quarter of the glass with cracked ice and to within an inch of the top with soda. Completely fill glass with one or two dippers of the above mixture. Mix well with a spoon, top with a cherry and serve with straws

THE ALLIES (PHOSPHATE)

Strawberry syrup
Pineapple syrup
Cherry syrup
Pear syrup

Take of each of the above ingredients 8 fluid ounces and of dilute phosphoric acid 1 fluid ounce.

TUTTI 'FRUTTI EGG PHOSPHATE

First make a syrup according to the following: Lemon syrup, 1 pint; orange syrup, ½ pint; vanilla syrup, ½ pint, grape juice, 4 ounces; solution of acid phosphate, 2 ounces. Mix in the syrup 16 fresh eggs, using an egg beater. For dispensing, place 1½ ounces of the syrup in a 12-ounce glass, add some ice shavings, fill with carbonated water and stir vigorously with a spoon. It might be well to eliminate the eggs from the above formula and to add an egg with each service. Customers paying for eggs nowadays want to see the real egg.

WILD CHERRY COOLER

Make syrup of 9 ounces wild cherry syrup, 4 ounces sherbet syrup, 2 drams elixir calisaya, 2 drams solution acid phosphate, 1½ ounces port wine, 2 ounces water. Price—8 ounces, 5 cents.

WILD CHERRY PHOSPHATE

Solution of acid phosphate, 2 ounces; German black cherry juice, 8 fluid ounces; syrup of wild cherry, U. S. P., 16 fluid ounces; oil of bitter almond, 10 drops; syrup, sufficient to make 1 gallon; mix. Price—8 ounces, 5 cents.

WILD CHERRY PHOSPHATE

Oil of bitter almond, 8 drops; water, 4 ounces; mix thoroughly and add fluid extract of wild cherry, soluble, 1 ounce; extract of vanilla, 1 ounce; dilute solution of acid phosphate, 1½ ounces; syrup of red raspberry, concentrated, 8 ounces; certified red color, ½ ounce; syrup, enough to make 1 gallon. Price—8 ounces, 5 cents.

WILD CHERRY PHOSPHATE

Cherry juice, 4 fluid ounces; syrup of wild cherry, U. S. P., 3 fluid ounces; dilute phosphoric acid, 1 fluid ounce; oil of bitter almond, 2 minims; simple syrup, 8 fluid ounces, and ½ ounce pure food color.

WILD STRAWBERRY PHOSPHATE

Strawberry syrup ...	6	pints
Lemon syrup	1	pint
Wild cherry syrup ..	1	pint
Tartaric acid	2½	drams

Dissolve acid in wild cherry and add in order lemon and strawberry syrups.
Serve solid.—H. B. Dunham in *American Druggist.*
A first class drink. Advertise it in season.

PINEAPPLE

The best pineapples for ices are the dark, orange-colored variety; indeed, much better than the Sugar Loaf, which is better adapted for preserving whole, while the Bird's Eye and others are more juicy and of better flavor. Pare and cut them into slices, cut out the core, which is hard and of very little flavor, grind or pound the pulp in a stone mortar and after straining use it right away, as most of the fruit will darken or change color. One quart of the juice thus made should be mixed with 3 quarts of water and made into a syrup with sugar, using 12 to 14 pounds of sugar. Heat to boiling, cool and cover.

PINEAPALE

Pineapple juice	4 ounces
Essence ginger sol. ...	4 ounces
Citric acid	½ ounce
Simple syrup	3 pints

A good phosphate syrup. Charge 5 cents for an 8-ounce glass.

PINK PUNCH

Pineapple syrup ...	1	pint
Strawberry syrup ...	½	pint
Raspberry syrup	½	pint
Sherry wine	2	ounces
Citric acid	20	grains
Red vegetable coloring	sufficient.	

PLUM

Three quarts of simple syrup, 1 quart of plum juice, 1 ounce of citric acid solution.

POMEGRANATE

First make grenadine essence, as follows:

Oil of sweet orange ...	3 parts
Oil of clove	1 part
Tincture of vanilla ...	15 parts
Tincture of ginger	10 parts
Maraschino liqueur ...	150 parts
Tincture of cochineal .	165 parts
Distilled water	150 parts
Dilute phosphoric acid	46 parts
Alcohol, 95 per cent. ..	810 parts

Mix and dissolve
To make the syrup, add 1 part of the essence to 50 parts of simple syrup, and dissolve in the mixture 1 part of citric acid. The dispenser may find it more satisfactory to buy his essence.

PRESERVATION OF SYRUPS

The preservation of syrups is purely a pharmaceutical operation. They must be made right, in order to keep right. Syrups, particularly fruit syrups, must be kept aseptic, especially when made without heat

The containers should be of glass, porcelain, or of pure block tin, so that sterilization may be effected with promptness and facility. No syrup should ever be filled into a container without the container being first sterilized with scalding water. The fruit acids in the presence of sugar serve as media for the growth and development of germ life upon exposure to the air, hence the employment of pasteurization and sterilization in the preserving of fruits, etc.

A pure fruit syrup filled into a glass bottle, porcelain jar or block-tin can which has been rendered sterile with boiling water and kept at a cool temperature, will keep for any reasonable length of time. Care should be taken not to break the bottle by pouring boiling water into it.

PRESERVING FRUIT JUICES

A practical method is to fill the freshly prepared cold juice into bottles until it reaches the necks, and on top of this fruit juice a little glycerin is placed. Juices thus preserved will keep in unchanged condition in any season. Probably one of the best methods of preserving fruit juices is to add 15 per cent. of 95 per cent. alcohol. On such an addition, albumen and mucilaginous matter will be deposited The juices may then be stored in large bottles, jars or barrels, if securely closed, and when so clear that further clarification is unnecessary, they may be decanted or siphoned off. An efficient way of clarifying fruit juices is to heat them with a small quantity of albumen (white of egg) in an enameled vessel provided with a close-fitting lid, without stirring, to near the boiling point of water The impurities under this treatment coagulate, and either rise to the surface of the juices or fall to the bottom; the juices should then be filtered through felt or flannel. This heating process most effectively destroys the germs of fermentation and the subsequent filtration clarifies the juices, which should be kept in a cool place; so stored they will remain unchanged for an indefinite period if they have been properly and carefully prepared. Corks should be coated with wax, and, if possible, the bottle necks dipped. Great care should be observed in heating the juices, no more being applied than is absolutely necessary, or the delicate aroma will suffer.

PUGILISTS' PANACEA

Champagne syrup, pineapple syrup, grape juice, of each 1 pint; lime juice, 4 ounces; soda foam, ½ ounce; syrup, 1 quart.

Mix and color red with tincture of cudbear, N. F. This syrup is a good one for use in phosphates.

QUEEN NECTAR SYRUP

Milk or light cream .. 32 ounces
Granulated sugar .... 48 ounces
Extract vanilla .... 6 ounces
Extract lemon .... 1 ounce

Dissolve sugar in milk, add vanilla extract, then the lemon. Color dark red.

RASPBERRY

One quart concentrated raspberry, 3 quarts simple syrup, 1 ounce citric acid and coloring. For use with milk or cream soda, omit the acid.

RASPBERRY AND HONEY

Equal parts of maple syrup, honey and raspberry juice.

Serve solid in 8-ounce glass, using 2 ounces of above syrup for the flavor, and fill glass with carbonated water.

RASPBERRY AND HONEY

Equal parts of maple syrup, honey and raspberry juice.

Serve solid in 8-ounce glass, using 2 ounces of above syrup for the flavor, and fill glass with carbonated water.

RASPBERRY SHARP

Fill a two-quart glass or jar with fresh red raspberries, pour over them cider vinegar until the jar is full. Screw on the cover and allow the mixture to stand for a week, then scald, pour in a jelly bag and drain off the juice. To every pint of juice add one pound of sugar. Boil fast 20 minutes and skim off any scum that arises. While hot put in bottles. One spoonful in a glass of cold carbonated water makes a drink of delicious flavor.

RED CURRANT

Extract of red currant, 1 ounce; red fruit coloring, 1 ounce; simple syrup, 1 gallon. Mix thoroughly, then add solution of fruit acid, 2 ounces, and strain. Serve solid; no milk.

RHUBARB

Carefully clean and scrape a dozen stalks of rhubarb, then boil them in 2 quarts of water for 15 minutes. Strain through cloth, add sufficient extract of lemon to flavor and 2 fluid drams of fruit acid. Let stand for a few hours to clarify and decant into a vessel containing 4 ounces of sugar. Serve in sherbet glasses with shaved ice. Said to be a delicious drink for the spring and early summer months.

ROOT BEER

Root beer extract, 5 ounces; simple syrup, 1 gallon; fruit acid, 2 ounces; soda foam, ½ ounce. Put 2 ounces in a 12-ounce stone mug and draw in the usual way.

To charge for fountain use· Place in a suitable fountain 1½ gallons of above syrup, omitting the soda foam, and water enough to make 10 gallons, and charge with gas to a pressure of 100 pounds. To be drawn from the apparatus in the manner of soda water, but without syrup. The beverage can be dispensed more readily by use of a beer pitcher (made to draw from the bottom), from which the tumbler is partially filled with the solid beverage, and the remainder drawn directly into the tumbler. This pitcher should always be kept on ice.

ROOT BEER

One gallon of simple syrup, 3 ounces of

root beer extract, 2 ounces of soda foam, 1 ounce of burnt sugar. This formula might be improved by eliminating the soda foam and by using more of the root beer extract.

ROSE

Extract of rose, 1 dram; extract of orris; ½ ounce; extract of vanilla, ¼ ounce; red fruit coloring, ¼ ounce; simple syrup, 1 quart. Mix and strain.

ROSEBUD

Four ounces strawberry juice, 1 ounce rose water, 29 ounces syrup, certified color to make reddish tint To serve, put 2 ounces syrup in soda glass with 2 ounces sweet milk and fill with carbonated water. Price—5 cents for a 10-ounce glass.

ROYAL FRUITED CHAMPAGNE

Champagne syrup, 27 ounces; raspberry juice, 3 ounces; black cherry juice, 2 ounces; citric acid, ½ ounce; soluble essence of red orange, 1 fl. dram. Place 1½ ounces in a 10-ounce glass and fill with carbonated water.

ROYAL MUSCADINE

Raspberry syrup ..... 1 pint
Grape juice syrup .... 1 pint
Raspberry vinegar .... 2 ounces
Mix. Pour two ounces into a mineral water glass, fill with carbonated water and serve. This syrup is a good one for use in a phosphate.

SARSAPARILLA

Boil down sassafras bark with water to an extract of considerable degree of concentration. To a gallon of simple syrup add sufficient of this extract to make the mixture taste slightly bitter; add 4 drops of oil of wintergreen and color to a light brown with caramel. This makes a good sarsaparilla syrup, and may be dispensed either plain or with ice cream. With the addition of a few dashes of compound tincture of gentian it makes a good tonic.

SARSAPARILLA

Oil of wintergreen, 10 drops; oil of sassafras, 10 drops; alcohol, ½ ounce; fluid extract of licorice, ½ ounce; caramel, ½ ounce; syrup, 5 pints. Dissolve the oils in the alcohol, add to the extract of licorice and syrup, then add caramel and shake well.

SARSAPARILLA

Compound syrup of sarsaparilla, 4 fl. ounces; simple syrup, not too heavy, ½ gallon; caramel, 1 fl. ounce; essence of wintergreen, 1 fl. dram; essence of sassafras, 1 fl. dram.

SARSAPARILLA

One and one-half ounces sarsaparilla extract in one-gallon bottle, sugar coloring, then add simple syrup enough to make 1 gallon.

SARSAPARILLA

Extract sarsaparilla, 1½ ounces; plain syrup, 1 gallon; soda foam, 1 ounce; caramel, 1½ ounces.

SARSAPARILLA (ARTIFICIAL)

"Sarsaparilla flavoring," so-called, for preparing the syrup which usually goes under the name of "sarsaparilla": Oil of wintergreen, ¾ fl. ounce; oil of sassafras, ¼ fl. ounce; oil of cassia, 1½ fl. drams, oil of cloves, 1½ fl. drams, oil of anise, 1½ fl. drams; alcohol, enough to make 8 fl. ounces.

To prepare a syrup from this add 2 fl. drams to 1 quart of simple syrup and color with caramel (about ¾ fl. ounce). To serve in a 10-ounce glass use 1½ ounces syrup.

SHAMROCK

Essence of bitter almond, 10 minims; grape juice, 4 ounces; extract of vanilla, 2 drams; compound tincture of cardamom, 2 drams; sweet cider, 10 ounces; white sugar, 14 ounces; soda foam, 3 drams.

Mix. Place 2 ounces in 10-ounce glass and fill with carbonated water.

SHERBET

Pineapple syrup ...... 1 pint
Orange syrup .... 1 pint
Vanilla syrup .... 1 pint
Sherry wine .... 4 ounces
Color red or pink.

SHERBET

One quart claret wine, 1 quart strawberry, 1 quart raspberry, 1 quart pineapple, 1 ounce foam, 1 ounce solution of citric acid to make 1 gallon sherbet. This beverage is said to be very popular in Rhode Island.

SILURIAN

Rose water .... 10 ounces
Pineapple juice ...... 1 pint
Fruit acid .... ½ ounce
Simple syrup .... 4 pints
Mix.

SIMPLE SYRUP

If possible use sugar free from ultramarine color, such as druggists' granulated sugar—all refiners make it.

SIMPLE SYRUP

Thirty pounds of sugar, 2½ gallons of water. Bring to a boil, and pour out at once into a crock; strain before using.

SIMPLE SYRUP (COLD PROCESS)

Granulated sugar .... 12 pounds
Water .... 1 gallon
This will produce almost two gallons simple syrup.

Put the sugar in a stone crock, pour on the water, and agitate with a wooden paddle until the sugar is entirely dissolved.

SIRUP DES QUATRE FRUITS

Sirup des Quatre Fruits or "Four Fruits," is the name given by the French to equal parts of the syrups of cherry, strawberry, raspberry, and currant.

SLOAN'S NECTAR

Extract of vanilla, 2 drams; orange flower water, 2 ounces; rock candy syrup, 1 gallon. Mix, using sufficient carmine solution to color. This is an old time formula and makes a delicious syrup for an egg drink.

SPICE OF LIFE

Red currant syrup	...	3 quarts
Lemon syrup	....	1 quart
Raspberry syrup	......	1 quart

Mix well and serve in 8-ounce glasses with cracked ice.

This formula provides for an excellent beverage to be featured as the dispenser's own "Thirst Quencher."

SPICED CHOCOLATE

Powdered cocoa	...	6 ounces
Powdered cinnamon		½ ounce
Vanilla bean, cut fine	1	dram
Water	....	30 ounces
Alcohol	....	2½ pints
Simple syrup	....	4 pints

Place the first three ingredients in a suitable vessel, add the water and alcohol and macerate eight days with an occasional agitation, then express, adding the simple syrup to the product thus obtained. Used as a flavoring.

SPRING CUP

Con'd. orange syrup	.	1 dram
Con'd. lemon syrup	..	1 dram
Extract of vanilla	....	1 dram
Pineapple juice	......	2 drams
Grape juice	....	2 ounces
Strawberry juice	.....	2 ounces
Sol. of citric acid	....	2 ounces
Syrup	....	4 pints

STRAWBERRY AND RASPBERRY

In selecting strawberries the opinions differ a great deal as to which berry to use. While some prefer a large berry, others again say that the small berries contain more juice and flavor. From our own experience, dark red, medium sized, pointed-on-the-top berries gave the most satisfaction for color as well as for flavor and juice, while the extra large berries are more for the eye and well adapted for dessert or fruit stand. Mash the berries with a wooden masher; never use iron or copper, as these metals will discolor the fruit; then mix with the sugar, and bottle or use immediately. As the strawberry has not much acid it is best to add a little lemon juice, which will heighten the flavor and color as well. For raspberries follow the same rules. Use the dark berries, pick and mash them, and finish as quickly as possible; never let any juice stand overnight unless you have some sugar mixed with it, and then keep in a porcelain-lined bowl in the refrigerator.

STRAWBERRY PUFF

Sugar	....	2 pounds
Cream	....	1 pint
Water	....	1 pint
Strawberry juice	....	4 ounces

Mix, bring to a boil, cool, then add a few drops of vanilla extract. Pour into a punch bowl and cover partly with very stiff whipped cream. Drop a few strawberries on the cream. Serve 2 ounces of the syrup in a soda glass, using the fine stream. Top off with whipped cream and a strawberry. Price—10-ounce glass, 10 cents.

SWEETS FOR THE SWEET

Strawberry syrup, 10 ounces; vanilla syrup, 10 ounces; raspberry syrup, 8 ounces; pineapple syrup, 8 ounces

Mix thoroughly and serve 2 ounces in a 12-ounce glass, add 1 or 2 ounces of sweet cream and nearly fill the glass with carbonated water, topping off with fine stream. This is a good all-around syrup for a fancy milk shake.

TANSY ROOT BEER

Extract of root beer, 6 ounces; essence of tansy (1 in 10), 1 dram; tincture of quillaja, 1 ounce; syrup enough to make 1 gallon. Color with caramel. The tansy imparts a delicious musky flavor that has a peculiar charm for many people. Use about 1½ ounces of this syrup to each glass and fill with carbonated water.

TEA

Green tea	....	4 ounces
Black tea	....	4 ounces
Liquid foam	....	1 ounce
Granulated sugar	....	6 pounds
Boiling water, a sufficient quantity		

Place the tea in a suitable vessel, pour upon it 3 pints of boiling water, cover up tightly, macerate until cool, express and set aside. Repeat the operation twice, using the same tea and quantity of boiling water each time. Then mix the three expressed liquids and evaporate to 4 pints. In this solution dissolve sugar at boiling point, strain, and when cool add the liquid foam.

TEA

Orange Pekoe tea (true) 4 ounces

Bring to a fast boil 2 pints of water, pour over tea, let stand 8 minutes, using a porcelain or aluminum kettle—never a tinned- or agate-iron one. Strain through several folds of cheese cloth, and add 4 pints heavy rock candy syrup and ½ ounce fruit acid. Will keep when well cooked. Tea syrup is recommended for iced tea, but should not be used for hot tea.

THREE-IN-ONE
Raspberry syrup .... 1 pint
Wild cherry syrup ...... 1 pint
Nectar syrup .... 1 pint
Simple syrup .... 1 pint
Equal parts of each well mixed. Three-in-One makes a good milk shake flavor.

TONIC SYRUPS

A. B. C.
Syrupy ext. of malt. ...- 2 ounces
Syrup of vanilla ..... 4 ounces
Syrup of almond ..... 4 ounces
Simple syrup, heavy .. 6 ounces
Mix. To one ounce of this syrup in an 8-ounce glass add a teaspoonful of solution of acid phosphates, nearly fill the glass with carbonated water, coarse stream, stir with a spoon and serve solid. Charge 5 cents. (John Gilpin.)

ASPEPSIN
Pepsin (pure crystals), 1 dram; liquid phosphate, 2 drams; vanilla syrup, 2 pints; raspberry syrup, 6 pints. Mix and strain; serve in mineral water tumbler. Charge 5 cents.

BEEF, WINE AND IRON
Beef, wine and iron.... 8 ounces
Vanilla syrup .... 24 ounces
Mix well.

BLAIR'S NERVE TONIC
Comp. syrup sar'p'illa 1 pint
Syrup of ginger .... 8 ounces
Comp. tinct. of gentian 8 ounces
Rock candy syrup .. 1½ pints
Sol. of acid phos. .. ½ pint
Caramel .... q. s.
Dispense 1½ ounces to an 8-ounce glass. Mix well with carbonated water and serve quickly

BRACER PHOSPHATE
Glycerite of pepsin, N.F. 8 ounces
Syrup of wild cherry . 8 ounces
Syrup of vanilla ..... 8 ounces
Grape juice .... 3 pints
Sol. acid phosphates .. 8 ounces
Simple syrup .... 4 pints
This formula is especially recommended. Charge 5 cents for an 8-ounce glass.

CELERTONE
Celery extract .... 2 ounces
Fruit acid .... 3 ounces
Syrup .... 1 gallon

CELERY MALT TONIC
Malt extract, 8 ounces; tincture of celery seed, 2 drams; orange syrup, 4 ounces; comp. tincture of gentian, 1 dram; lemon syrup, to make 2 pints. Mix and serve 1 ounce in an 8-ounce mineral glass, with or without solution of acid phosphate.

CRABAPPLE TONIC
Sweet cider ..... 1 gallon
Granulated sugar 7 pounds
Malt extract .... 4 fl. ounces
Sol. citric acid .. 1½ fl. ounces
Evaporate the cider to ½ gallon and in it dissolve the sugar, strain, and add the extract of malt and solution of citric acid This beverage may be served "solid" with carbonated water in an 8-ounce glass.

FRIGIDINE
Make a syrup of 1 ounce citric acid; 4 drams lemon essence; 4 drams compound tincture gentian; ½ gallon syrup Color with ½ ounce caramel. Do not serve with ice cream, or make the drink too sweet.

HERCULINE
Extract orange, 2 ounces; extract vanilla, 2 ounces; solution of phosphate, 2 ounces; tasteless tincture of iron, 4 ounces; simple syrup, 7½ pints; sugar coloring, 30 drops. Mix and strain.

HOT SCOTCH
Prepare a syrup as follows · Soluble extract of ginger, 4 ounces; soluble extract of capsicum, ¼ ounce; fluid extract of gentian, 1 dram; compound spirit of orange, 4 fl. drams; syrup of lemon, 20 ounces; caramel, sufficient. Mix thoroughly. To dispense, take 1 ounce of this syrup, place in cup, and fill with hot water.

ORANGE CORDIAL
Scale pepsin, 20 grains; curacoa cordial, 3 fl. ounces; syrupy phosphoric acid, 4 fl. drams; orange syrup, 13 fl. ounces. Trim with grated nutmeg. Charge 5 cents per service.

ORANGE FERRONE
Orange syrup (from fruit), 2 pints; raspberry syrup, 1 pint; vanilla syrup, ¼ pint; elixir of iron phosphate, 6 ounces; elixir of gentian, N. F, 8 ounces. Mix. Serve plain. Dispense 2 ounces in a mineral water glass and fill with carbonated water.

OXFORD CORDIAL
Sixteen ounces calisaya syrup, 1 quart claret phosphate, 3 quarts rock candy syrup. Mix and serve in mineral glass with crushed ice. A splendid tonic for the fount. Price—eight ounces, 5 cents.

PEPSIN PHOSPHATE
Solution of pepsin, N. F., 8 ounces; raspberry syrup, 16 ounces; solution of acid phosphates, 4 ounces; syrup, enough to make 4 pints. Lime juice, orange, grape and other phosphates are made in the same manner.

REX
Orange syrup, 8 ounces; pineapple syrup, 4 ounces; strawberry syrup, 4 ounces; solution of acid phosphate, ½ ounce; fruit

acid, 1 ounce; alcohol, to preserve, 3 ounces Mix and add to 1 gallon of simple syrup.

SPARTACUS

Essence of pepsin ...	15 minims
Phosphoric acid syrupy..	30 minims
Fresh eggs	½ dozen
Essence peppermint .	1 dram
Raspberry syrup	12 ounces

Place 2 ounces in a glass, fill with carbonated water and top off with grated nutmeg. Charge 10 cents.

TEXAS TONIC

Calisaya	
Angostura bitters, of each	1 ounce
Maple syrup	
Simple syrup, of each...	1 quart
Caramel color	1 dram

WONDER WORKER

Lemon syrup		
Orange syrup		
Moxie syrup, of each..	½	pint
Spirits of juniper ..	1	ounce
Simple syrup	2	quarts

VANILLA

Vanilla syrup is prepared by adding vanilla extract to syrup, the proportions depending upon the strength of the extract, which in turn depends upon the quality of the vanilla used, the method of extraction and care in manipulation. Enough of the extract should be added to the syrup to insure the requisite degree of flavor to the resulting product. Generally, 1½ to two ounces of extract to a 12-pound syrup is sufficient. The addition of two ounces of good sherry wine will give a vanilla syrup which will be a "winner."

VERMONT MAPLE SPECIAL

Dissolve 5 cakes of maple syrup in 1 gallon of water, cool and strain. To the syrup thus made add an equal quantity of simple syrup and, if desired, flavor with extract of vanilla. Dispense two ounces in glass with cream and a little nutmeg, and sufficient carbonated water to fill.

WALNUT OR HICKORY

Take 1 pound of hickory nut or walnut kernels and remove the skin by blanching, which, if left on, would give an unpleasant, bitter taste; then powder in a Wedgewood or porcelain mortar, adding a few drops of lemon juice to prevent the separation of oil in the kernel and sufficient water, gradually added, to make a thick emulsion. As fast as the kernels are reduced put them in a linen cloth, which should be gathered around them so that they may be squeezed through the cloth. Whatever is left in the cloth should be returned to the mortar and pulverized further, the lemon juice and water being added as needed. All should eventually pass through the strainer. The result of this process (about 2 pints) is to be added to 2 quarts of cream syrup. This formula may be varied, and perhaps improved, by a slight addition of extract of lemon or vanilla, or any other flavor to suit the taste; likewise a little coloring to suit the fancy.

WILD PLUM

Plum juice	8 ounces
Plum jelly	8 ounces
Sugar	3 pounds
Water	3 pints

Dissolve the jelly and sugar in the juice and water mixture by heating and add when cool

Ess. bitter almonds	½ dram
Citric acid	4 ounces
Sol. tartaric acid ...	6 drams
Grape juice	8 ounces

Color deep purple and serve very cold.

WILD ROSE

Triple rosewater	2 ounces
Strawberry juice	8 ounces
Soda foam	2 ounces
Tincture of cochineal..	q. s.

Syrup to make 1 pint.

WILD STRAWBERRY

Strawberry syrup, 16 ounces; almond essence, 2 drams; cherry juice, 8 ounces; diluted phosphoric acid, 1 ounce; syrup, enough to make 32 ounces.

YUM YUM

Vanilla syrup	4 ounces
Orgeat syrup	4 ounces
Pineapple syrup	4 ounces
Orange flower water .	1 ounce
Syrup to make	1 quart

EXTRACTS

CHOCOLATE

Curacao cocoa	400 parts
Vanilla beans, cut	1 part

Macerate for 14 days with alcohol, 55 per cent., 2,000 parts. After straining and pressing, the alcoholic extract is set aside and the residue percolated with hot water so as to obtain 575 parts of percolate, which are then mixed with the alcoholic liquid. If a sweetened preparation is required, sugar, 1,000 parts, is dissolved with heat in the aqueous liquid before mixing it with the reserved portion.

COFFEE

Ground coffee	½ pound
Boiling water	1 quart

Percolate three or four times. The lower end of the percolator should be carefully introduced into the receiver and protected to preserve the aroma.

HOP ALE

Fresh hops .... 4 ounces
Quassia (coarse pow.) 2 ounces
Alcohol .... 6 ounces
Water .... sufficient

Mix the hops and quassia, pour on 12 fluid ounces of boiling water, set aside for several hours, agitating occasionally; then add the alcohol, macerate for several days, stirring from time to time, and filter, adding through the filter enough water to make the filtrate measure 16 fluid ounces.

HYACINTHA

American saffron ... ½ ounce
Juniper berries...... ¼ ounce
Dates .... ¼ ounce
Raisins .... ¼ ounce
Aniseed ....15 grains
Cinnamon .... 8 grains
Coriander .... 8 grains
Mace .... 8 grains
Cloves .... 8 grains
Diluted alcohol ....19 ounces

Reduce the solids, add the diluted alcohol, macerate for six days, agitating occasionally, and filter. Use the resultant tincture for flavoring syrup, which is then to be served solid like the phosphates.

LEMON

Fresh lemon peel......10 pounds
Rectified spirit (60%). 1 gallon

Macerate for 28 days, with occasional stirring, press, and add:

Terpeneless oil of lemon 2 drams

Shake well, allow to stand seven days, draw off the clear tincture, and filter the rest. The author parenthetically states that "more or less terpeneless oil of lemon may be added according to the desired cost," and also, that "a full year's supply of this preparation should be made each year in January when the fruit arrives in its best condition."

MEAD EXTRACT

Cloves .... ½ ounce
Nutmeg .... 2 drams
Coriander .... 2 ounces
Jamaica ginger .... 2 ounces
Allspice .... ½ ounce
Cinnamon water ... 4 ounces
Alcohol .... 4 ounces

Pulverize the spices coarsely and macerate them for 24 hours in the alcohol and cinnamon water, then transfer to a percolator and pour diluted alcohol until 16 ounces of the fluid are obtained. Percolate slowly and to the mixture add half ounce of orange flower water. For dispensing at the fountain take 1 ounce of the above compound and 2 pints of plain syrup.

TANGO EXTRACT

Tincture avena sativa.... 3½ ounces
Tincture cinchona comp. 2½ ounces
Tincture nux vomica.... 1 ounce
Fluid ext. of cocoa...... 1 ounce
Angostura bitters .... 5 ounces
Oil of wintergreen...... 1 dram
Oil of sassafras .... 1 dram
Caramel coloring ....24 ounces

This is the old Moxocolo extract closely similar to the well known Moxie.

SODA FOAMS

SODA FOAM

Ground quillaja bark 8 ounces
Boiling water....... ½ gallon

SODA FOAM

Let stand for 24 hours and filter.
Sarsaparilla bark, finely ground 8 ounces
Quillaja bark............... 8 ounces
Diluted alcohol to obtain..... 4 pints

Prepare by percolation. Of this 1 to 2 ounces is sufficient to a gallon of syrup and will produce an excellent foam Tincture of quillaja, N.F., or fluid extract of quillaja may be used for the same purpose, the former in the proportion of 1 ounce in 2 gallons of syrup, or 1 ounce of the fluid extract in 8 or 10 gallons of syrup. It is not likely that either of these preparations could be employed as "gum foam," although we believe there can be no objection to lawful use under their proper names.

SODA FOAM

Take of gum arabic 8 ounces, and water 1 pint; wash the gum with water, to free it from impurities, and add the water, stirring occasionally until dissolved. It should be used in the proportion of 3 or 4 ounces to the gallon of syrup.

SODA FOAM

Wash an ounce of Irish moss to free it from impurities, add 1 pint of water and boil for 5 minutes; or heat in a water bath for 15 minutes; or macerate in cold water for 24 hours, with occasional stirring; filter through purified cotton on a muslin strainer, in a hot water funnel. It can be used with soda syrup, in the proportion of from 2 to 4 ounces to 1 gallon of syrup.

(2) Fruit Mixed Drinks

Within this classification come a host of ades, punches, and similar fruit drinks that are widely popular, especially during the summer time.

Many of the drinks in this class antedate the soda fountain for centuries —lemonade, so the story goes, was brought back to Europe from the East by the Crusaders—while others are more modern concoctions.

The tart drinks, those with the vinous flavor of grapes, and the citrous flavor of lemons, oranges, limes, and grape fruit, are all famous as quenchers of thirst. In the following pages will be found any number of drinks that will prove to be capital sellers on the piping hot days. Many people cherish the belief that nothing "touches the spot" during the dog days quite so well as plain, cold lemonade, but the clever dispenser will find that he has in the class of the mixed fruit drinks scores that are more palatable and just as effective for the thirst as that "old reliable."

A most effective way of pushing these hot weather drinks is to select an attractive formula and then make up a big bowl of the mixture and set on the counter. If the bowl be of cut glass—or pressed glass— so much the better, but it must contain a big chunk of ice and as the ice melts it must be kept up to standard strength by the judicious addition of more of the concentrated flavoring materials. Fresh fruits, berries in season, slices of orange and pineapple, add very much to the attractiveness of such a display. The punch should be served in small punch glasses at five or ten cents according to the formula and the trade catered to, or at double the price in tall, thin glasses with straws.

Generally speaking the dispensers of the country north of the Mason and Dixon Line have neglected the mixed fruit beverages. In the South, as one would naturally expect, such drinks are well appreciated and form an important percentage of the fountain business. Almost without exception these beverages yield a handsome profit, and a fountain that wins such a trade will build up a reputation for service, besides having added a very profitable feature to its menu.

When made up as stock syrups or served from a punch bowl fruit mixed drinks offer the added attraction of being very easily and quickly served. This is much in their favor especially during the rush of the hot days when they are always most in demand. In making these stock syrups, punches, etc., it should be remembered that all such mixes are very liable to decomposition. Do not mix up more than one day's supply at a time in the summer, nor more than a couple of days' stock during the cooler months.

MIXED FRUIT DRINKS

Ades, Punches, Shrubs, etc.
APPLE JULEP

Squeeze half a lemon into a 12-ounce glass, add a little cracked ice, and two ounces of simple syrup. Arrange green mint leaves in the glass, in the good old Southern style, and then fill the glass with cider. Sprinkle a little grated nutmeg on the surface, and collect 10 or 15 cents, according to the price of cider. Fresh made cider is preferable as an ingredient in this feature. A good fall special at 10c.

FROSTED APPLE JACK

Take 6 sour green apples, stick into them 36 cloves and then half bake. In a glass or porcelain dish put 36 allspice, one lemon sliced thin, and the apples while hot and cover all with sugar. Let the mixture stand twelve hours, add 1 quart of syrup and stew until the apples, except the cores, fall to pieces. Take off the fire before the mixture separates, let cool, add thin slices of lemon and over all put two bananas. Add 1/4 teaspoonful of powdered cinnamon, 2 teaspoonfuls of extract of Jamaica ginger, 4 teaspoonfuls of extract of vanilla and enough syrup to make a half gallon. Serve 2 tablespoonfuls to each glass with a similar quantity of cream or ice cream, and fill the glass with carbonated water, small stream. See that each glass has a slice of lemon and banana in it. Price—10 ounces, 15 cents. (Thurman Wilcox.)

CHERRY COCKTAIL

Pineapple syrup ...... ½ ounce
Cherry syrup .... ½ ounce
Lemon syrup .... ½ ounce
Angostura bitters ...... 2 ounces
Carbonated water ...... 2 ounces

Strain into cocktail glass and serve with cherry. Charge 10 cents.

CHERRY FIZZ

Cherry syrup .... 1½ ounces
Lemon .... ½ ounce

Squeeze juice of ½ lemon in cherry syrup in mixing glass half full of carbonated water. Strain into 12-ounce glass, add little sodium bicarbonate from end of spoon and fill glass with fine stream. Price—10 ounces, 10 cents.

CHERRY JULEP

Half fill 12-ounce glass with shaved ice, 1½ ounces red cherry syrup, 1 dash sherry wine and a sprig of fresh mint crushed with the ice. Add carbonated water to fill glass. Serve with straws and decorate with creme de menthe cherries Charge 10 cents.

CHERRY PUNCH

Into a tall glass put some shaved ice, add 2 ounces of cherry syrup, a little lime juice, a spoonful of crushed pineapple, and shake; then fill up the glass with carbonated water and top with a slice of orange and slices of strawberries. Serve with straws. Price—10 ounces, 10 cents.

FASCINATION

Cherry syrup .... 2 ounces
Cracked ice .... ½ glass
Juice of ¼ lemon
Plain water .... enough

Mix well and top with orange and cherry. Price—10 ounces, 10 cents.

CRACKER JACK

Cherry syrup, 1 ounce, cracked ice to fill glass and then pour in grape juice to fill glass. Price—8 ounce glass, 10 cents.

RESOLUTION FIZZ

Cherry syrup ...... 1½ ounces
Lemon juice .... ½ ounce

Pour into a mixing glass half full of cracked ice, stir well, strain into a fancy glass which has previously been filled about one-third full of fine ice, add a little sodium bicarbonate on the end of a spoon, stir well, add a slice of lemon and orange, or a cherry, and a slice of orange. Price—10 ounces, 10 cents.

WILSON PUNCH

Cherry syrup .... ½ ounce
Lemon syrup .... ½ ounce
Sarsaparilla syrup .... 1 ounce

Draw syrups in large glass, add cracked ice. Fill with carbonated water, using

fine stream. Finish with a cherry and a cube of pineapple. The punch is a good special and should be priced at 10 cents for 10 ounces.

CHERRY-MINT COOLER

Wild cherry syrup ... 2 ounces
Creme de menthe syr. ½ ounce

Serve with fine ice in 8-ounce glass and charge five cents. The juice of a quarter lemon might be added to the cooler to advantage.

CLARET RINGUE

Claret syrup .... 1 ounce
Lemon syrup .... 1 ounce
Port wine .... ½ ounce
Sweet cream .... ½ ounce

Mix and serve 2 ounces in an 8-ounce glass. Charge five cents.

OLD ENGLISH PUNCH

Claret syrup .... 1 ounce
Pineapple syrup .... 1 ounce
Juice of ½ lemon.
Plain water ice.........½ glassful

Mix in 10-ounce glass, fill with coarse stream, mix well and serve with spoon. Charge 10 cents.

KLARET KLONDIKE

Fill sherbet glass with fine shaved ice, pour over the ice 1 ounce claret syrup and garnish with a slice of lemon. Serve with spoon. Charge 10 cents.

COLD CLAM BROTH

Place 1½ ounces of good clam bouillon in an 8-ounce glass, add a little shaved ice and fill up with cold soda water, a dash of salt, a dash of phosphate, and a slice of lemon. A quick money getter. Price, 10 cents.

CROWN PRINCE FIZZ

Into a 12-ounce glass put:
Strawberry syrup .... 2 ounces
Orange syrup .... 1 ounce
Juice of half a lemon
Shaved ice .... ¼ glassful

Shake, strain and fill with carbonated water. Price 10 cents for 10 ounces, and sells well in summer. (Martin S. Meyer.)

DORIAN CREAM

Orange syrup .... ¾ ounce
Maple syrup .... ¾ ounce
Plain cream .... 1 ounce
Shaved ice .... ⅓ glassful

Place in a suitable glass, fill with carbonated water, sprinkle powdered nutmeg on top and serve with straws and crackers. Makes a delicious drink. Charge 10 cents for a 12-ounce glass. (F. Mintzer.)

EASTERTIDE SPECIAL

Claret syrup .... 1 ounce
Peachblow syrup .... 1 ounce
Orange cider .... 4 ounces
Shaved ice .... ¼ glass

Place in glass and fill with carbonated water, fine stream, and mix with spoon. Price 15 cents for 12-ounce glass.

FEDORA

Shaved ice as usual, usual quantity of orgeat syrup, a small timball glass of kirschwasser; shake well and fill the glass with vichy and throw in one or two white French cherries for decoration. Price— 10 ounces, 10 cents.

FIRE EXTINGUISHER

Blood orange syr.... 1   ounce
Lemon juice 1   fluid dram
Raspberry syrup.. ½ ounce
Shaved ice ...... ½ glass

Add several ounces of carbonated water, stir well, strain into an 8-ounce glass, and fill the latter with plain soda water, coarse stream. Serve with two straws.

FRUIT FRAZZLE

Fruit syrup .... 2 ounces
Powdered sugar ... 1 teaspoonful
Cracked   ice ...... 2 ounces
Carbonated water, sufficient.

Mix syrup, sugar and ice with about 9 ounces of the water, stir, strain into glass containing slice of pineapple, peach, orange or lemon, and a few selected berries or small fruit. Price—10 ounces, 10 cents.

FRUIT PUNCH

Make a syrup of equal parts of strawberry, pineapple and orange syrup. Use 1½ ounces of this syrup to glass third full of ice. Fill with carbonated water, coarse stream, and add a few strawberries, a slice of pineapple, a slice of orange, and serve with straws. The juice of half a lemon will bring out the fruit flavor in the punch. Price—12 ounces, 10 or 15 cents.

FRUIT-ADE

Juice of ½ orange
Juice of ⅓ lemon
Pineapple juice.. 2 tablespoonfuls
Powdered sugar. 2 tablespoonfuls
Crushed   ice ....½ glass

Fill glass with water; shake well and serve with straws. Price—12 ounces, 15 cents.

FRUITED FREEZE

Crushed fruits served in the following manner are delicious and refreshing:

Crushed fruit ...... 1½ ounces
Juice of half a lemon
Shaved ice, q. s.

Put the shaved ice in a small glass, add the fruit and lemon juice, stir well, and serve with a spoon and straws. Price— 8 ounces, 10 cents.

GINGER ALE BOUNCE

Into a 6-ounce phosphate glass put 1 ounce of grape juice; add a little cracked ice and fill the glass with ginger ale; serve with two straws. "A splendid hot weather drink, easily and quickly made " Charge 10 cents for domestic ginger ale and 15 for the imported. The Bounce does not pay at 5 cents. (Alonzo Draine)

GINGER ALE COBBLER

Dissolve a teaspoonful of powdered sugar in a small quantity of carbonated water, add a large slice of pineapple, nearly fill the glass with shaved ice, and then add enough ginger ale to fill the glass. Decorate with fruit and serve with straws. Some dispensers use ginger ale syrup instead of ginger ale, then adding a little carbonated water to fill the glass. Price 10 cents for 10 ounces.

GINGER ALE SOUR

Lemon syrup .... 4 drams
Lemon juice .... 2 drams
Ginger ale to fill an 8-ounce glass.
Charge 10 cents for eight ounces.

GINGER COLD SNAP

Ginger ale .... 1½ ounces
Orange syrup .... ½ ounce
Shaved ice .... ½ glass
Pineapple slice.

Fill glass with carbonated water and stir with spoon. Charge 10 cents for 10 ounces.

GINGER FIZZ

Carbonated water .. 4½ ounces
Ginger syrup .... 1½ ounces

Mix carefully with twist bar spoon then add small spoonful powdered sugar Serve 8 ounces for 5 cents.

GINGER FIZZ

About 6½ ounces carbonated water, 1½ ounces ginger syrup. Mix and add a small spoonful powdered sugar.

GINGER-GINGER

Ginger syrup 1   ounce
Lemon syrup .... ½ ounce
Cream syrup .... ½ ounce
Whipped cream ...... 1 spoonful

Place in a 12-ounce glass half filled with carbonated water, using coarse and fine streams, and then fill with ginger ale on draught.

GINGERADE

Into an eight-ounce glass pour one-half ounce of ginger syrup, of the imported variety. Add one-half ounce of simple syrup, the juice of one lemon and fill the glass with shaved ice. Top off with a slice of orange and sell for 10 cents. Can be varied by using orange juice. (Wade T. Surratt.)

GOLDEN MINT ORANGEADE

Squeeze the juice of one-half an orange into a 12-ounce glass, then add one-half ounce of mint syrup and one-half ounce of plain syrup. Fill a wine glass three-fourths full of shaved ice, then fill the remainder of the glass with distilled water (ice cold). Put the mixture into a shaker and shake a minute to make it real cold, then pour back into the glass. Place two straws in the glass and top off with a sprig of mint and a Maraschino cherry. Price—12 ounces, 15 cents. Crushed fresh mint makes a good addition to this formula. (P. W. McCole.)

GOOD CHEER

Blood orange syrup... ½ ounce
Catawba syrup ...... ½ ounce
Pineapple syrup ..... ½ ounce
Lemon juice .... 1 ounce
Place in a 12-ounce glass and serve "solid" with carbonated water. Price—10 ounces, 10 cents.

GORDON COOLER

Orange syrup .... 1 ounce
Cherry syrup .... 1 ounce
Juice of ½ lemon
Some shaved ice
Fill glass with carbonated water, top with slice of pineapple and a cherry; serve with straws and spoon.

GRAPE ALE

Take 1 ounce of any good brand grape juice, a little shaved ice, place in an 8-ounce glass and fill with ginger ale. This is a 10 cent drink.

GRAPE COOLER

Grape juice .... 1 ounce
Orange syrup .... 1½ ounces
Lemon syrup .... ½ ounce
Sol. acid phosphate.. ¼ teaspoonful
Cracked ice .... ¼ glass
Mix in 14-ounce lemonade glass. Decorate with pineapple. Price—10 ounces, 10 cents.

ROYAL RUBY

Grape juice .... 2 ounces
Strawberry syrup ..... 1 ounce
Rose leaves 6; mint leaves, 6; crushed well against side of glass with ice
Cracked ice .... ½ glassful
Stir thoroughly, then add carbonated water, coarse stream, and serve in tall lemonade glass. Decorate with creme de menthe cherries and a slice of lemon. Price—12 ounces, 15 cents.

GRAPE FLOAT

Fill a 12-ounce glass to within an inch of the top with plain lemonade, then carefully float on the top a sufficient quantity of grape juice to fill the glass, being careful not to disturb the lemonade. A good, long drink, and a thirst quencher. Price—10 ounces, 10 cents.

GRAPE FLOAT LEMONADE

Make a plain lemonade, fill a glass within 1 inch of top, then hold a teaspoon in center of glass and pour in slowly grape juice until the glass is full. Price—12 ounces, 15 cents.

QUAKER FREEZE

Pure grape juice .... 1 ounce
Raspberry syrup ... ½ ounce
Orange syrup ...... ½ ounce
Juice of ½ orange
Fine ice shavings.... ½ glassful
Fill glass with carbonated water; mix with a spoon. Decorate with fresh mint and seasonable fruits; serve with straws. Price—12 ounces, 15 cents.

GRAPE-LEMO

One ounce lemon syrup, 1 ounce grape juice in mineral glass, fill up with carbonated water, stir well and serve.

GRAPE GURGLE

Into a suitable glass place one No. 10 ladleful of ice cream, 1 ounce of grape syrup and enough chipped ice; mix thoroughly, strain into a 12-ounce glass and fill with carbonated water (fine stream). Sprinkle with powdered nutmeg or cinnamon.

GRAPE ORANGE COOLER

Lemon syrup .... 1 ounce
Grape juice .... 1 ounce
Orange water ice.... 1 scoopful
Dispense in 12 ounce glass. Shake and fill the glass with carbonated water. Decorate with a slice of lemon and orange and serve. Price—10 ounces, 10 cents.

PRESIDENTIAL FAVORITE

Grape juice .... 1 ounce
Lemon juice .... ¼ ounce
Orange juice .... ¼ ounce
Powdered sugar ...... 2 drams
Place all in a glass, half filled with cracked ice, adding enough ice-cold plain water to finish. Shake, serve in a 12-ounce lemonade glass and trim with a slice of orange and a cherry. Charge 10 cents.

GRAPE SYLLABUB

Grape juice .... 2 ounces
Simple syrup .... 1 ounce
Lukewarm cream ..... 2 ounces
Mix the grape juice and syrup, adding the cream slowly so as to froth. Ten ounces, ten cents.

ORIENTAL MAGI

Draw into a 12-ounce glass 1 ounce of strawberry syrup and 2 ounces of unfermented grape juice and fill the glass two-thirds full of shaved ice; break into the mixture a few sprigs of mint, shake thoroughly, fill with carbonated water, mix with a spoon, and decorate with fruit, etc. Rose syrup may be substituted for strawberry syrup or the syrups may be used in equal quantities. Price—10 ounces, 10 cents.

GRAPE TRICKLE

Place in a 12-ounce glass partly filled with cracked, not shaved, ice, ½ ounce of lemon syrup, ½ ounce of pineapple syrup, ½ ounce of orange syrup, and a little more than ½ ounce of grape juice. Fill the glass with carbonated water and stir until all is thoroughly mixed. Can also be dispensed as a float, adding the grape juice last. The author states that this formula makes a very refreshing drink and can be readily sold for 10 cents at a good profit. To advertise the beverage he has used with good results a placard bearing the phrase: "Grape Trickle for that Thirsty Spot." (J. M. Bingaman.)

GUNTHER'S EXCELSIOR

German cherry juice . 1 ounce
Rhine wine .... 1 ounce
Lemon juice .... 1 dash
Simple syrup .... 1 ounce

Draw into 12-ounce glass, fill with carbonated water, garnish with cherries and pineapple and serve with straws. Can be made acceptably with American cherry juice. Price—10 ounces, 10 cents.

HAPPY PUNCH

Raspberry vinegar syrup. 1 ounce
Orange cider .... 2 ounces
Bitters .... 3 dashes

Half fill glass with ice Complete with coarse stream.

HELENA FREEZER

Vanilla syrup . 1½ ounces
Orange pulp .. 1 tablespoonful
Shaved ice .... ¼ glassful

Place all in a 12-ounce soda glass, fill with carbonated water, fine stream, and top off with whipped cream.

HOKIE POKIE COOLER

Simple syrup .... 1 ounce
Pure cream .... ½ ounce
Extract nectar .... 1 dash
Carbonated water, fine ¾ glass
Shaved ice to fill glass

Serve with whipped cream and spoon. Price—8 ounces, 10 cents.

IRISH ICEBERG

Fill a champagne glass half full of finely shaved ice, then pour in creme de menthe syrup and decorate with creme de menthe cherries on toothpicks. Cut straw in two, put the pieces in the glass and serve. The Iceberg makes a good St. Patrick's Day special. Charge 10 cents.

JOVE'S OWN DRINK

Into a 12-ounce glass draw ½ ounce of pistachio syrup, ½ ounce Catawba syrup and nearly fill with shaved ice. Fill glass with carbonated water, fine stream, and top off with a creme de menthe cherry. Price—12 ounces, 10 cents.

KOLA COOLER

Kola punch .... ½ ounce
Red cherry syrup .... ½ ounce
Pineapple syrup ..... ½ ounce

Serve in 12-ounce glass two-thirds full cracked ice, and carbonated water. Straws.

LADIES PUNCH

Into a glass partly filled with shaved ice draw three-fourths ounce of pineapple syrup, 1 teaspoonful of lemon juice, and a teaspoonful of raspberry vinegar. Place a mixing spoon in the glass and almost fill the glass with carbonated water, coarse stream. Add a little more shaved ice, on the top of which place crushed strawberries. Between the glass and the ice insert a slice of orange. Serve with spoon and straws. Price—10 cents for 10 ounces.

LEMONADE (WHOLESALE)

Water .... 3 gallons
Lemons (juice) ..... 4 dozen
Citric acid .... 3½ ounces
Granulated sugar ...20 pounds

Mix and stir adding the paste made from 4 ounces of granulated sugar and the grated rind of 4 lemons. This formula is recommended.

PLAIN LEMONADE

With many individuals the old-fashioned lemonade is still a great favorite. To make it at the fountain counter place 2 tablespoonfuls of powdered sugar in a 12-ounce glass one-half full of crushed ice. Now cut a lemon in two, slice each section in two or three pieces, add the juice of the lemon and fill the glass with plain ice-cold water. Shake thoroughly, pour from shaker into glass, and serve with straws. It should be observed that some patrons object to a too great abundance of ice.

FANCY LEMONADE

Make a lemonade in the regular manner and pour in a teaspoonful of raspberry or strawberry syrup, which will go to the bottom of the glass. Now carefully pour on the top the same amount of grape juice without stirring. A piece of pineapple, orange or other fruit may be added to decorate the drink. The drink may also be made with the glass half full of shaved ice and the fruit on top. Serve with straws. Charge 15 or 20 cents for a 12-ounce glass.

SELTZER LEMONADE

Juice of 1 lemon
Powdered sugar.. 1 tablespoonful
Seltzer water ... 4 ounces
Shaved ice ...... 2 ounces

Stir vigorously in a shaker with a spoon, strain into a 12-ounce glass, fill the glass with seltzer water and stir with a spoon.

LEMON-RASPBERRY-ADE

Put into a large soda tumbler 1 tablespoonful of raspberry syrup, 1 tablespoonful of lemon squash and a lump of ice; nearly fill the glass with carbonated water and ornament with a thin slice of lemon and a few red and white raspberries. Drink through straws.

AMERICAN CITIZEN LEMONADE

Orange syrup .... 1 ounce
Lemon syrup .... 1 ounce
Powdered sugar ...... 1 teaspoonful
Solution acid phosphate 1 dash
Shaved ice ....1-3 glass

Add slice of orange and run two straws through it. A better flavor and more "life" may be brought to this 'ade by using the fruit juices.

TROPICAL LEMONADE

Juice of 1 lemon.
Pineapple syrup .... 1½ ounces

Place in a 12-ounce glass, fill glass with carbonated water, coarse stream, add a slice of pineapple and a ladleful of crushed pineapple, and serve with spoon and straws. Price—10 or 12 ounces, 15 cents.

BROADWAY LEMONADE

Juice of 1 lemon
Powdered sugar ..... 2 tablespoons
Grape juice .... ½ ounce
Claret wine .... ½ ounce
Small scoop shaved ice

Fill glass with plain water, shake, put in 12-ounce lemonade glass, finish with a slice of orange and a cherry, serve with spoon and straws.

GRAPE LEMONADE

Make a soda lemonade, filling the glass to within about an inch of the top. Mix and decorate with lemon and orange slices pour on top enough to fill the glass with the desired grape juice, and serve without mixing, with straws. Price—12 ounces, 15 or 20 cents.

VINO-LEMO

Into a 10-ounce glass put 2 ounces shaved ice, the juice of 1 lemon, and 2 ounces claret syrup. Shake well, nearly fill the glass with carbonated water, stir, strain, add one slice of lemon and enough carbonated water to fill the glass; serve with two straws. Charge 10 cents.

GRAPE LEMONADE

Grape syrup .... ½ ounce
Lemon syrup .... ½ ounce
Carbonated water, large stream 7 ounces
Solution acid phosphate........ a dash
Stir gently with spoon.

SARATOGA COOLER

Juice of ½ lemon
Sugar .... 1 teaspoonful
Water .... 1 ounce
Shaved ice .... ½ glass
Fill 12-ounce glass with ginger ale. Price—10 ounces, 10 cents.

INDIAN LEMONADE

Wash well 2 dozen lemons, dry, pare thinly and squeeze the juice over the shaved rinds. Let stand for 12 hours, then add 2 glasses of grape jelly; dissolve 4 cupfuls of sugar in 3 quarts of scalded milk and add it to the fruit juice. When cold strain through double cheesecloth without squeezing and serve with chopped ice. Better results may be obtained with this formula by grating the lemonpeels.

KITRO LEMONADE

Kitro syrup ...... ½ ounce
Juice of 1 lemon
Powdered sugar.... 1 tablespoonful
Shaved ice.

Fill up with plain water and serve in 12-ounce lemonade glass. Decorate with cherries.

QUEEN LEMONADE

Juice of ½ lemon
Orange syrup ...... 1½ ounces
Grape juice .... 2 ounces
Cracked ice, enough.
Carbonated water to fill glass.

Shake and serve in a tall glass, without straining. Top off with a slice each of orange and pineapple.

SOUTHERN LEMONADE

Take a good size watermelon, hollow out the inside, first cutting a small slice from the narrow end to act as a lid or cover, place on the counter and surround with shaved or cracked ice; then fill with lemonade, adding enough extract of Jamaica ginger to suit the taste. When serving to the customer, fill a glass one-fourth full of shaved ice, add one or two pieces of the melon taken from the inside, then fill the glass with lemonade and serve with straws and napkins. Price—12 ounces, 10 or 15 cents. A big "hit" on "Fair Day" or "Old Home Week." (F. Mintzer.)

RUBY SMASH

Cracked ice .... ½ glass
Juice of ½ lemon
Cherry malt phosphate syrup 2 ounces
Lactart .... 2 dashes
Shake well, then fill with carbonated

water and serve with two straws. Price—8 ounces, 5 cents.

OLD FASHIONED LIMEADE

Squeeze the juice of 1 lime into a 12-ounce glass, put in one-half the rind, add 1 ounce of lemon syrup and 2 tablespoonfuls of powdered sugar, fill glass two-thirds full of crushed ice and draw on carbonated water, coarse stream, until the glass is nearly full. Mix by pouring from glass to strainer several times; finally strain into the glass and serve with straws. Price —12 ounces, 10 cents.

WILD LIMEADE

Lime juice .... ½ ounce
Or juice of half lime
Strawberry juice ... ½ ounce
Powdered sugar.... 2 spoonfuls
Wintergreen essence.. 2 dashes

Shake with cracked ice, strain and add carbonated water. Price—10 ounces, 5 cents.

LIME AND GINGER

Ginger syrup ...... 1 ounce
Lime juice syrup... 1 ounce

Use mineral water glass and draw full of carbonated water, coarse stream, and stir with spoon. The juice of half fresh lime may be used in this formula. Price —8 ounces, 5 cents.

LIME COOLER

Express the juice of the large ripe lime into a 12-ounce glass and add one ounce of plain syrup and one-half ounce of pineapple syrup. Fill the glass one-half full of snow ice and add carbonated water, coarse stream; top off with pineapple aces and Maraschino cherries, at the same time adding a teaspoonful of cherry juice. Then float on a round slice of orange of the same diameter as the top of the glass and insert two straws.

This drink is a trade winner, more especially with men and boys. It can be served at ten cents, but 15 cents is a better price. Only good fresh limes should be used in its preparation. (J. E. Bradley.)

MAID MARION

Into a 12-ounce glass two-thirds full of shaved ice draw half ounce of pineapple juice, and 1 dram each of lemon juice and raspberry vinegar. Fill glass nearly full with carbonated water (coarse stream) and garnish with a strawberry and a slice of fresh orange. Serve with spoon and straws. Price—10 ounces, 10 cents.

MAN FRIDAY

One measure of ice cream (16 to-the-quart); two-thirds glass of carbonated water; 1½ ounces coca-cola syrup; ¼ ounce wild cherry syrup. Put ice cream and carbonated water in a 10-ounce glass, stir with spoon until the cream is melted and has a nice foam; then add the syrups and fill with fine stream, which will give a dark drink with a white foam. Charge 10 cents.

MARATHON REFRESHER

Into a 12-ounce glass place three-fourths ounce each of strawberry, raspberry and orange syrups, juice of one-half lemon, and one-half glass shaved ice. Fill glass with carbonated water, coarse stream, mix with spoon, decorate with fruit in season, and serve with straws. Charge 10 cents.

MAY BIRD

Blood orange syrup.. ½ fluid ounce
Catawba syrup ..... ½ fluid ounce
Pineapple syrup .... ½ fluid ounce
Lemon juice .... 1 fluid dram

Serve solid in an 8-ounce glass with carbonated water. Charge 5 cents.

MENTHE-ADE

Powdered sugar....... 2 teaspoonfuls
Creme de menthe syrup ¼ ounce
Roman punch syrup.. 1 ounce

Dispense above ingredients in a mineral water glass one-fourth full of crushed ice. Draw full of carbonated water, coarse stream, and serve with straws. Price—10 ounces, 10 cents.

MINT COOLER

Crush or mash some fresh green mint leaves with a little coarse or granulated sugar; add some shaved ice, a small quantity of milk or almond syrup or sweet cream, flavored with almond; shake well and fill up the glass with Apollinaris. Price, when served in an 8-ounce glass with plain soda, 5 cents; with Apollinaris, 10 cents.

MINT FREEZE

Chop fine several sprigs of mint and put them in a mixing glass; add 2 ounces crushed ice, ½ ounce of black raspberry syrup; ½ ounce of claret syrup; ½ ounce of ginger syrup; the juice of half a lemon, and 1 ounce of grape juice. Fill the glass with carbonated water and stir; strain into a 12-ounce glass one-half full of crushed ice and trim with a slice of pineapple, one cherry and a sprig of mint. Charge 10 or 15 cents.—(E. V. Kayner.)

FROZEN MINT

Pour into a small sundae glass nearly filled with shaved ice 1 ounce of creme de menthe syrup; top off with creme de menthe cherries and a sprig of mint. Or, serve in 8-ounce glass with plain carbonated water. Charge 5 cents.

TRIO GRANDE

Creme de menthe syrup 1 ounce
Orange syrup .... ½ ounce
Tame cherry syrup.... ½ ounce

Dispense in a tall 12-ounce glass, filled one-quarter with shaved ice, and fill with carbonated water, coarse stream. Top off with orange, mint leaves and a Maraschino cherry. Serve with two straws. Price, 15 cents.—(Henry O. Peters.)

MENTHE FRESHER

Crush fresh mint leaves with small amount of granulated sugar, add 4 ounces shaved ice, 2 ounces almond cream syrup and 4 ounces plain water. Shake, strain and fill with Apollinaris. Price—10 ounces, 10 cents

MEXICAN MINT GLACE

Into a fancy 8-ounce glass put a heaping ladleful of shaved ice, and ½ ounce cherry syrup; then add a No. 16-to-the-quart dipperful of vanilla ice cream, and another ladleful of shaved ice; now add ½ ounce of mint syrup, and top off with a cherry. Can be sold profitably at 10 cents per glass. The name is suggested by the fact that the beverage duplicates the colors of the Mexican flag. It is recommended for use as a special.

KENTUCKY COOLER

Fill a 10 ounce glass with crushed ice and four sprigs of fresh mint; then with a mallet bruise the mint until the pungent juice mingles with the ice Next add blood orange syrup and fill with soda. Then put on the finishing touches—sprig of mint, slice of pineapple and Maraschino cherry. Price—10 ounces, 10 cents.—(Willis Wood)

LOUISVILLE COOLER

Fill glass half-full with shaved ice, add a teaspoonful of sugar, a dash of lemon juice and two or three sprigs of fresh mint. Crush the mint against the sides of the glass to get the flavor; then add ½ ounce of claret syrup, 1½ ounces of raspberry syrup and nearly fill the glass with carbonated water. Insert a bunch of mint and fill the glass with carbonated water. Serve with straws and decorate with fruits of the season.

MONT BLANC

Strawberry syrup ... 1   ounce
Orange syrup ...... ½   ounce
Vanilla syrup ...... ½   ounce
Grape juice .... ½   ounce
Shaved ice .... ¼   glassful

Mix the first three ingredients in a 12-ounce glass, fill glass with carbonated water, add the ice, top with the grape juice and float the whipped cream over all. Charge 15 cents.

NECTAR PLUSH

A very pretty feature; beat up 2 ounces of nectar syrup with 2 ounces of ice cream, add 2 dashes of Maraschino and sherry wine, and enough carbonated water (fine stream) to fill 12-ounce glass. Top off with whipped cream and nutmeg Serve with straws and spoon.

ORANGE-ADE (FROM FRESH FRUIT)

Juice of 1 orange.
Powdered sugar ... 1   tablespoonful
Lemon juice 3   dashes
Fine ice .... ½ glass

Fill glass with plain water and shake well. Dress with fruits. Price—10 ounces, 10 cents. Use Florida orange.

ORANGEADE (FANCY)

Juice of 1 orange
Juice of ½ a lime
Orange syrup ..... ½ ounce
Powdered sugar.... 1   tablespoonful

Mix; shake all well with plain water and quite a bit of shaved ice. Garnish with a creme de menthe cherry (a Maraschino cherry will do) and a slice of orange. Price—12 ounces, 15 cents. Use Florida orange, size 150.

SPANISH BLOOD ORANGE-ADE

Juice of 1 orange
Raspberry syrup .. ½ ounce
Lemon juice 1   dram
Sugar 1   tablespoonful
Shaved ice .... ½ glassful

About half fill the glass with the coarse stream, stir, strain into a mineral water glass and fill with carbonated water. Price —10 ounces, 10 cents

TRIO-ADE

Juice of 1 orange
Grape juice .... ½ ounce
Raspberry syrup .... ½ ounce
Lemon juice 1   teaspoonful

Mix; add a tablespoonful of sugar and ¼ glassful shaved ice. Half fill the glass with carbonated water, coarse stream, stir, strain into a mineral water glass and fill with fine stream.

ORANGE CRESS

In a 12-ounce lemonade glass squeeze the juice of half a lemon and half an orange, add a dash of cherry juice and 1½ ounces of simple syrup. Fill the glass about two-thirds full of cracked or shaved ice and fill with plain water. Turn all over in a shaker and mix well. Put in two straws and decorate with a red cherry and a couple of sprigs of water-cress.

This is a long, cooling drink, and customers once trying it come back for more. As the season advances it will be found among the best sellers and thirst quenchers. Cress being an edible plant makes a perfect decoration for lemonades and other fancy drinks, such as freezes, etc. Price— 10 or 15 cents, the latter being the fairer price —(H. R. Rowe.)

PUNCHINE

Cracked ice .... 2 ounces
Juice of ½ orange
Lemon juice .... 1 dash
Curacoa cordial .... 1 dash
Claret syrup .... 1 ounce
Catawba syrup ..... 1 ounce

Fill glass with carbonated water, stir, strain and serve. Price—10 cents for 10 ounces.

ELKS' DELIGHT

Juice of half an orange
Juice of half a lemon
Pure grape juice..... 1 ounce
Powdered sugar .... 2 teaspoonfuls

Cracked ice to half fill glass, carbonated water to finish; shake, serve in 12-ounce lemonade glass. Garnish with a slice of orange and a cherry. Charge 15 cents.

PERSONAL REGARDS

Orange syrup ...... 2 ounces
Raspberry juice ... 1 ounce
Orange juice ...... ½ ounce

Place in a 12-ounce glass one-fourth full of shaved ice. Shake well, fill with carbonated water, coarse stream, mix with a spoon, add a slice of orange or a small quantity of crushed pineapple and serve with two straws. Price—12 ounces, 10 cents.

CREAMED ORANGE

Vanilla syrup..... 1½ ounces
Shaved ice ...... 1 tablespoonful
Orange pulp ...... 1½ tablespoonfuls
Pure cream ..... 1 ounce

Fill with carbonated water, fine stream. Price—12 ounces, 10 cents. This feature has also been recommended as a flavor for ice cream soda.

ORIENTAL NECTAR

Sherbet syrup ..... 1 ounce
Red orange syrup... ½ ounce

Fill a mineral glass half full of crushed ice, finish with carbonated water and serve with straws. Price—8-ounce glass, 5 cents.

PINEAPPLE FREEZE

Pineapple syrup .... 1 ounce
Powdered sugar .... 1 teaspoonful
Shaved ice .... ½ glassful

Add some carbonated water, stir vigorously in a shaker, strain into an 8-ounce glass, fill the latter with the coarse stream of carbonated water, stir again, and add a piece of pineapple or some crushed pineapple.

TOMMY ATKINS

Crushed pineapple .. 2 spoonfuls
Pineapple syrup .... ½ ounce
Shaved ice.

Serve in punch glasses. For an 8-ounce bell top with whipped cream, or two ice cream soda spoonfuls of vanilla in cream, and charge 10 cents.

SHERBET FLOAT

Two ounces pineapple syrup, one ounce sweet cream. Fill glass two-thirds full of carbonated water and float a ball of sherbet on top. Use pineapple or orange sherbet. Price—10 ounces, 10 cents. (Harry G. Frame.)

PINEAPPLE CREAM PUNCH

Grated pineapple syrup.. ½ ounce
Crushed strawberry syrup ½ ounce
Nectar syrup .... 1 ounce
Ice cream .... 1 spoonful

Add a little shaved ice, fill with orange cider and stir. Price—10 ounces, 10 cents.

PINEAPPLE FREEZE

One ounce pineapple syrup, half glass shaved ice. Draw into 12-ounce glass, fill with carbonated water, stir, add spoonful crushed strawberry; top with slice of orange; serve with straws; or, draw ounce of syrup into 8-ounce glass; add large spoonful of either canned or fresh grated pineapple; fill with shaved ice, stir, serve with spoon.

PINEAPPLE PUNCH

Pineapple syrup .... 2 ounces
Blood orange syrup. 1 ounce
Shaved ice .... sufficient

Serve solid in 12-ounce glass garnished with slice of fresh fruit. Charge 10 cents.

PINEAPPLE PUNCH

Pineapple syrup .... 2 ounces
Claret syrup .... ½ ounce
Finely shaved ice.. 1-3 glass
Crushed pineapple.... 3 teaspoonfuls

Fill in 12-ounce glass with coarse stream of carbonated water and serve with a spoon and straws. Price—10 ounces, 5 cents.

PINEAPPLE SMASH

Pineapple syrup ... 1 ounce
Powdered sugar ... 1 teaspoonful
Shaved ice .... ½ glass

Add carbonated water, shake, strain into 8-ounce glass and fill with coarse stream; stir again and add a piece of pineapple or some crushed pineapple. Add a small amount of lemon juice. Price—10 ounces, 10 cents.

RASPBERRY PUNCH

Raspberry syrup ... ¾ ounce
Orange syrup ...... ¾ ounce
Juice of one lime
Grape juice .... 1 ounce

Draw the syrup into a 12-ounce glass, then add the lime juice and grape juice. Fill the glass one-third full of shaved ice and complete the filling with carbonated water. Mix and decorate with two cherries and two pineapple cubes on toothpicks. Price—10 ounces, 10 cents.

RASPBERRY ROYAL

Shaved ice .... ½ glass
Raspberry vinegar .. ½ ounce
Raspberry juice .... ½ ounce
Crushed raspberry
  fruit syrup ...... 1 ounce

Draw solid, using sufficient carbonated water to fill; stir gently. Price—8 ounces, 5 cents.

RAZZLE-DAZZLE

Pineapple syrup .... ½ ounce
Lemon juice .... ½ dram
Raspberry vinegar .. 1 dram
Powdered sugar .... 1 teaspoonful

Fill soda glass two-thirds full of fine cracked ice, put mixing spoon in glass and turn on coarse stream of carbonated water. Fill nearly to the top of the glass and stir with spoon, adding more cracked ice. Over all place a teaspoonful of crushed raspberry and insert a small piece of orange between the ice and glass. Serve in ordinary thin soda glasses with straws.

RUSSIAN FRAPPE

Make an infusion of tea, as for iced tea, using one level teaspoonful of tea to each pint of water. Strain and cool. In a glass place a small scoop of lemon sherbet, an ounce of lemon syrup, and a dash of phosphate solution. Add a little cracked ice, and fill with the cold tea to within one-third of the top. Finish with carbonated water. This furnishes a pleasing variation of the ordinary iced tea with lemon, and brings a better price. (H. M. Houpt.)

SPRING PUNCH

Strawberry syrup... ½ ounce
Orange syrup ...... ½ ounce
Pineapple syrup .... ½ ounce
Lemon juice .... 2 dashes
Shaved ice .... 1-3 glassful

Place ice in glass, draw on the syrups and fill with carbonated water. Trim with slice of pineapple and two strawberries. Serve with straws. Charge 10 cents for 10 ounces.

STRAWBERRY A LA WASHINGTON

Shaved ice .... 1-3 glass
Strawberry juice ... 1 dash
Strawberry syrup ... 2 ounces
Crushed strawberries 2 teaspoonfuls

Fill with carbonated water. Stir with spoon and add four halves of strawberries. Serve with spoon and straws. Two ounces of sweet cream added to this formula might enhance its delectability. Add cream to syrup, then add juice and fruit.

PINK PLUSH

Shaved ice .... 1-3 glass
Strawberry syrup ... 2 ounces
Orange cider .... 2 ounces
Sweet cream .... ½ ounce

Fill up with carbonated water and stir gently. Serve with straws.

STRAWBERRY LIME CORDIAL

Shaved ice .... 2-3 glass
Lime juice .... 1 ounce
Strawberry syrup ... 2 ounces

Fill with carbonated water, drawing solid; stir gently. Straws. Use fresh limes when possible.

STRAWBERRY-ADE

Juice of one lemon
Strawberry juice ... 1 ounce
Powdered sugar ... 1 spoonful

Add shaved ice, shake, strain and fill solid with plain soda. Stir and serve with straws. Charge 10 cents for 12 ounces. The formula may be improved by adding more sugar.

(3) Phosphates, Bitters, and Rickeys

It has been well said that "drinks may come and drinks may go but the orange phosphate goes on forever," and although the great popularity that all these phosphate drinks enjoyed a few years ago has waned somewhat of late, still even in the face of severe competition from all sorts of beverage novelties, there are hundreds of fountains where the phosphates have kept in the lead.

The most popular members of the phosphate family are, of course, the lemon, the orange, and the egg. This last is an especially good drink to push during the hot weather when the patrons who want egg drinks do not want so heavy and heating a drink as the egg and milk shakes that have the call during the winter.

Dispensers make a mistake in always having their specials in the sundae class. The phosphates have many friends, and a reputation for the right kind of a phosphate is, especially in the business section of large cities, a great asset. The more unusual and the more elaborate phosphates make capital specialties to push and feature on certain days.

The drinks of the bitters division are practically "temperance cocktails." They can be confidently recommended as stomach tonics and appetizers. As a class they offer a too-little appreciated special for fountains that cater to men's trade.

Rickeys, containing as they all do, the juice of limes, are classed among thirst quenching beverages. What applies to the advantages of pushing the mixed fruit drinks in hot weather applies to the rickey, with the exception that the latter must be mixed as served, a proceeding which requires more time at the fountain. For this reason care should be exercised in pricing the rickeys, in order to cover both time and service, as well as the cost of the materials.

PHOSPHATES, BITTERS AND RICKEYS

ANGOSTURA

A popular drink in New York is made by adding 1 teaspoonful of angostura bitters to a regular lemon phosphate, in which a little more than the regular quantity of lemon syrup is used. Price—8 ounces, 10 cents.

ARCTIC PHOSPHATE

Strawberry syrup ... ½ ounce
Pineapple syrup .... ½ ounce
Vanilla syrup ...... ½ ounce
Orange syrup ...... ½ ounce
Acid phosphate ..... 3 dashes
Cracked ice .... ½ glass
Carbonated water sufficient to fill 12-ounce glass.

Stir thoroughly with a spoon. Serve with spoon and straws. Charge 5 cents for 8 ounces.

BERRY

Half an ounce each of strawberry, raspberry, checkerberry and lemon syrups. Add a dash of phosphate and fill 10-ounce glass with cold, well carbonated water.

BOSPHO

Raspberry syrup ..... ¾ ounce
Orange syrup .... ¾ ounce
Lemon syrup .... 1 ounce
Lime syrup .... ¼ ounce
Solution of acid phos-
   phates .... 1 dash
Cracked ice .... ½ glass

Mix in a 10-ounce glass and decorate with slices of orange and pineapple, and a Maraschino cherry. Serve with spoon and straws. It might be better for the soda man to keep the syrups called for blended together as a stock syrup Use 1½ ounces of this to a 10-ounce glass. Add other ingredients and charge 10 cents.

CELERY WHITE CAP

Celery syrup .... ½ ounce
Orange syrup ...... ½ ounce
Lemon syrup ...... ½ ounce
White of 1 egg
Acid phosphate .... 1 dash
Cracked ice .... ¼ glass
Shake, strain, toss and serve.

CENTRAL PARK

Pineapple syrup ..... 1 ounce
Red orange syrup.... 1 ounce
Solution acid phosphate.6 dashes

Put into an 8-ounce soda glass in the order named and fill with carbonated water. Serve "solid." Charge 5 cents for 8 ounces.

CHERRY

One ounce of wild cherry syrup, 4 dashes of phosphate. Fill glass with carbonated water, using coarse stream; stir well with spoon.

CHERRY ROOT

Cherry syrup .... 1 ounce
Root beer .... 4 ounces
Phosphate .... 2 dashes

Draw syrup in 10-ounce glass and fill half full with carbonated water, fine stream, then draw in charged root beer and dash of phosphate.

CHERRY SOUR

1 lime
Cherry syrup ...... 1 ounce
Simple syrup ...... ½ ounce
Acid phosphate..... dash
Shaved ice .... ½ glass
Carbonated water ... sufficient

Mix well and top with Maraschino cherry. Charge 10 cents.

CLARINE

Claret syrup .... ½ ounce
Catawba syrup ..... ½ ounce
Solution acid phos.. 1 dram

Serve like other phosphate drinks. For 8-ounce glass charge 5 cents.

FRATERNITY

Champagne phosphate 1½ ounces
Lime syrup 1   ounce
Lemon syrup ...... ½ ounce
Shaved ice .... ¼ glass

Mix in a 14-ounce lemonade glass and decorate with pineapple or cherries.

FROST BITE

Fill an 8- or 9-ounce glass with finely shaved ice, add three dashes of solution of acid phosphate, and then cover the ice with orange syrup or syrup of any desired flavor; serve with spoon. Sells quickly in hot weather for 10 cents.

FROZEN PHOSPHATE

Make a delicious orange or other fruit phosphate, nearly filling an eight or 10-ounce glass. Float on top of liquid one ball unflavored ice. Serve with long spoon. Charge 10 cents. This drink is very cold.

FROZEN

This name is applied to a combination of unflavored water ice, solution of acid phosphate and any specified flavor. To prepare it, have the ice cream manufacturer make a batch of unflavored water ice; of this take a No. 10 dipperful and place it in a mixing glass; add 2 or 3 dashes of solution of acid phosphate and a ladleful of any specified fruit syrup (2 or 3 ounces). After stirring the mixture thoroughly, transfer it to a sundae cup, and top with a Maraschino cherry. Price 10 cents. (L. W. Garnett.)

FRUIT

Fill glass half full of fine ice; then add in the following order:

Powdered sugar.... 1   tablespoonful
Orange syrup ..... ½ ounce
Lemon syrup 2   dashes
Raspberry syrup ... 1   dash
Solution of acid phos-
phates .... ¼ ounce

Fill the glass with soda water, stir well, strain into a mineral water glass and serve. Price—10 ounces, 5 cents.

GINGER

Fill a glass containing 2 ounces of shaved ice with ginger ale, adding a dash of Maraschino flavor and a squeeze of a lemon. Garnish with slices of orange and lemon, and serve. If bottled ginger ale is used, charge 10 cents.

HAPPY HOOLIGAN

Malaga wine .... ½ ounce
Raspberry syrup ... 1½ ounces
Solution acid phos-
phate 2   dashes

Draw into phosphate glass and fill with solid stream of carbonated water. This delicious phosphate can be made into a fancy 10-cent beverage by drawing into a 10-ounce glass and garnishing with slice each of orange, pineapple and cherry.

HIAWATHA

Cherry syrup .... ½ ounce
Orange syrup ...... ½ ounce
Pineapple syrup 1   ounce
Phosphate 6   dashes
Cracked ice and soda.

Fountain operators may find it advantageous to keep the above fruit syrups blended as a stock syrup.

JACK FROST

Grape syrup .... ½ ounce
Orange syrup ...... ½ ounce
Carbonated water,
large stream 7   ounces
Solution acid phos-
phate .... a dash
Stir with a spoon.

JAPANESE THIRST KILLER

Orgeat syrup 1   ounce
Cracked ice 1   ounce
Solution of phosphate 2   dashes
Angostura bitters ... 2   dashes

Fill up with grape juice, and add a slice of pineapple. Charge 10 or 15 cents.

LIQUID AIR

Use 10-ounce phosphate glass. Fill one-third full of pineapple or lemon ice, using 1 ounce of flavor, preferably vril, wild cherry or lemon. Add a dash of phosphate, draw glass full of ice water, stir well and serve with straws. (Geo. P. Stockton.)

MANHATTAN

Lime syrup .... ½ ounce
Acid phosphate 1   dash
Angostura bitters .. 2   dashes
Grape juice 2   ounces
Sherry wine 1   dash
Powdered sugar ... 2   teaspoonfuls
Cracked ice .... ¼ glass

Add carbonated water in a coarse stream to fill 10-ounce glass. Decorate with orange and pineapple fruit. Charge 10 cents.

MARYLAND MINT

Creme de menthe syrup ½ ounce
Ginger syrup .... 1½ ounces
Solution acid phosphate 1   dash

Serve in 8-ounce mineral water glass, 2-3 full of cracked ice. Add sprig of fresh mint. Price—5 or 10 cents.

MEXICAN REBEL

Strawberry syrup 1   ounce
Orange syrup 1   ounce

A dash each of phosphate and tincture of capsicum. Quarter fill glass with shaved ice and fill with coarse stream. Serve with straw. Price—8 ounces, 5 cents.

MIXED MINT

Orange syrup	½	ounce
Ginger ale	½	ounce
Grape syrup	½	ounce
Pineapple syrup	½	ounce
Solution acid phosphate	2	dashes
Fresh mint leaves...	4	
Shaved ice	½	glass

Press the mint to the sides of the glass, then add coarse stream to fill the glass. Stir and serve with straws. Decorate with fresh mint. Price—10 ounces, 10 cents.

NECTARINE

Fill 8-ounce glass seven-eighths full carbonated water, in coarse stream, add an ounce of nectar syrup and a dram of solution acid phosphates, and stir, serving solid.

NIPPONESE PHOSPHATE

Orange syrup	½	ounce
Ginger syrup	½	ounce
Grape syrup	½	ounce
Pineapple syrup	½	ounce
Acid phosphate	2	dashes
Shaved ice	½	tumblerful
Four fresh mint leaves.		

Press leaves against the sides of the glass to flavor, fill glass with carbonated water (coarse stream), and serve with two straws. Price—5 cents.

ORANGE

This drink is so universally dispensed that a formula for it is hardly necessary here, but it might be mentioned that a little orange syrup in a mineral-water glass, a little acid phosphate squirted into it, carbonated water from the coarse stream enough to nearly fill the glass, and cracked ice or not, as the occasion or the drinker may require, the whole well stirred with a spoon, constitutes this most popular, perhaps, of all orange drinks.

RED ORANGE

Red orange syrup.....	1 ounce
Solution of acid phosphates	1 teaspoonful
Plain soda	7 ounces

Mix the syrup and solution of acid phosphates and draw coarse soda stream till glass is full; stir with spoon. Serve in 8-ounce mineral water glass.

PHOSPHATE FRAPPE

Fill 8- or 9-ounce glass with finely shaved ice, add 3 dashes of solution of acid phosphate and nearly cover the ice with the desired syrup; serve with a spoon.

PINEAPPLE

Pineapple syrup	2 ounces
Solution of acid phosphate	3 dashes

Half fill a soda glass with crushed ice, pour over it the syrup and phosphate, fill with carbonated water, stir and drain into a mineral glass. Price—5 cents.

ROSE CELERY

Straight raspberry phosphate with a dash of celery.

SCORCHERS' DELIGHT

Shaved ice	½	glass
Solution acid phosphate	5	dashes
Compound tincture of cardamom	3	dashes
Vanilla syrup	1½	ounces

Add carbonated water, stir, strain and serve with straws.

SUNLIGHT

Fine ice	½	glassful
Powdered sugar ...	1	tablespoonful
Orange syrup	½	ounce
Lemon syrup	2	dashes
Prepared raspberry.		dash
Solution of acid phosphate	¼	ounce

Fill with carbonated water and stir well, strain into a mineral glass and serve.

SUNSHINE

Pineapple syrup.....	1	ounce
Raspberry syrup ...	¼	ounce
Lemon juice	1	dash
Solution of acid phosphate	2	dashes

Place in an 8-ounce glass and fill with carbonated water. Price—5 cents.

THIRST QUENCHER

Raspberry syrup	2 fluid ounces
Sol. acid phosphate....	1 fluid dram
Juice of one-half lemon	
Shaved ice	2 ounces
Water	8 fluid ounces

Mix well by agitating in a shaker; strain and add enough water to fill a 12-ounce glass. Charge 10 cents.

US FELLERS

Place in a 10-ounce glass:

Orange syrup	2 ounces
Grape juice	1 ounce
Sol. acid phosphates..	3 dashes
A little fine ice	

Shake, fill with carbonated water, and strain. Price—10 cents.

EGG PHOSPHATES

BOARD OF TRADE TONIC

One egg.

Creme de menthe syrup	1	ounce
Lemon syrup	½	ounce
Pineapple syrup	1	ounce
Sol. acid phosphate...	2	dashes

Add the syrups first. Shake, strain, toss and serve. Price—12 ounces, 10 cents.

BROADWAY EGG

Half fill mixing glass with shaved ice, crush 2 large sprays of mint on the ice, and add 1½ ounces blood orange syrup, 2 dashes of solution of acid phosphate, 1 egg, and shake well and strain. Add carbonated water, fine stream, toss several times, grate nutmeg on top and serve with straws. Charge 10 cents.

CENTRAL PARK EGG

Into a 12-ounce glass draw 1 ounce of blood orange syrup and 1 ounce of pineapple syrup. Into this break an egg, add a few dashes of acid phosphate and a little finely shaved ice. Shake thoroughly and fill with carbonated water, as is done in preparing all egg phosphates. Strain into a clean glass and serve. Charge 10 cents.

CHERRY EGG

Cherry syrup ...... 1½ fluid ounces
Sol. acid phosphates. 1 fluid dram
Shaved ice .... 2 ounces
1 egg

Shake well, draw on coarse stream of carbonated water, strain into a 12-ounce glass, nearly fill the glass with the coarse stream of soda, finishing the operation with fine stream; sprinkle on a small amount of powdered nutmeg.

EGG

Into mixing glass add 1½ ounces orange syrup and 1½ ounces lemon syrup, break one egg, and add acid phosphate to customer's taste. Add shaved ice, shake well, fill with fine stream and serve in bell glass. This formula is recommended for the preparation of egg phosphate. Add one ounce plain water before shaking. Price—12 ounces, 10 cents.

EGG

Small quantity cracked ice
Lemon syrup .... 1½ ounces
Egg 1
Sol. acid phosphate..30 drops

Shake together with hand shaker and add enough plain carbonated water to fill the glass. Mix well by pouring from glass to shaker, and serve, after adding a little grated nutmeg.

FAMOSA

Raspberry syrup ...... 1 ounce
Sweet cream .... 1 ounce
Essence Jamaica ginger 1 dash
Crushed ice .... 2 teaspoonfuls
Egg 1

Place the egg in a glass, add syrup, cream, shaved ice and a few dashes of solution acid phosphate. Shake well and strain into glass. Draw enough carbonated water through coarse stream to fill glass. Pour from one glass to another a few times. Price—12 ounces, 10 cents.

FIZZY EGG

One egg
Lemon syrup .... ½ ounce
Sol. acid phosphate.... 1 dash
Angostura bitters .... 1 dash
Shaved ice .... sufficient

Shake well, pour into a mineral water glass, fill with fine stream soda water.

FLIPPED EGG

One whole egg
Lemon syrup .... 1 ounce
Catawba syrup ..... 1 ounce
Sol. acid phosphate.. ½ teaspoonful

Shake and fill glass with carbonated water. Mix by pouring from glass to shaker, strain into glass, add grated nutmeg and serve.

FROZEN EGG

Lemon syrup ...... 1½ ounces
Orange syrup ...... 1½ ounces
Phosphate .... 5 or 6 dashes
One egg
Two pieces ice.
Orange or lemon water
  ice .... 1 dipperful

Shake until very cold, use fine stream serve in 12-ounce glass with a dash of nutmeg. Price should be 15 cents. The water ice makes it very cold. (Irvin K. Scott.)

GOLD MINE

Put the yolk of two eggs in a 14-ounce glass, add two ounces of orangeade syrup, two dashes of port wine and two of acid phosphate. Then add one 16-to-the-quart dipper of vanilla ice cream and fill with cracked ice. Carbonate with the fine stream. Charge 15 cents. (E. J. Howard.)

GOODNER'S EGG

Lemon syrup ...... 1 ounce
Orange syrup ...... 1 ounce
Several dashes solution
  acid phosphate (50
  per cent.)
Port wine .... 2 dashes
Plain sweet cream... ½ ounce
1 egg

Dispense in a mixing glass half filled with cracked ice, shake thoroughly, add carbonated water from fine stream, pour 3 times and top with nutmeg By too much pouring the gas will be lost and as a result the drink will be flat and heavy. Charge 10 cents.

HERCULES EGG PHOSPHATE

Wine syrup .... ½ ounce
Pineapple syrup .... 1 ounce
Juice of 1 lemon
1 egg
Acid phosphate ..... 3 dashes
Shaved ice, enough

Place all in a suitable glass, fill with carbonated water, and serve. Price—12 or 14 ounces, 15 cents.

IMPERIAL EGG
White and yolk of 1 egg
Lemon syrup ...... ½ ounce
Catawba syrup ..... 1 ounce
Sol. acid phosphate.. ½ teaspoonful
Shake well, then add carbonated water, enough to fill glass. Mix well by pouring from tumbler to shaker, strain through julep strainer into tumbler, then add a little grated nutmeg and serve. Price—12 ounces, 10 cents.

KITRO EGG
Kitro syrup .... 1½ ounces
Lemon syrup .... 1 ounce
Acid phosphate to suit
1 egg
Shake above with shaved ice. Strain into mixing glass, return to shaker and add carbonated water with fine stream. Serve in 12-ounce thin glass. Add nutmeg if desired.

KNIGHT'S EGG
One egg, one ounce lemon syrup, one-half ounce red raspberry syrup, four dashes of acid phosphates, shaved ice. Shake thoroughly, then fill the mixing glass nearly full with coarse stream, then fizz. This makes a very light, foamy acid drink that should be poured back and forth two or three times in order not to have it all foam.

By leaving out the phosphate and adding four ounces of milk and two ounces ice cream, you have another delicious egg drink but *not* egg phosphate. Price—First formula, 10 cents; second formula, 15 cents. (A. G. Knights.)

MALTESE EGG
Into a 10-ounce glass put 2 ounces blood orange syrup, add one egg, a few dashes of solution of acid phosphate, and some shaved ice. Shake well, fill the shaker with carbonated water, large stream only, and strain into a thin glass.

MOONBEAM EGG PHOSPHATE
Egg (white) 1
Lemon syrup .... 1 ounce
Pineapple syrup ...... 1 ounce
Phosphate .... 3 dashes
Price—12 ounces, 10 cents. (F. X. Sullivan.)

PARISIAN FLIP
Formulas differ somewhat for this drink. As good as any, perhaps, is this one:
Orange syrup .... 1 ounce
Pineapple syrup ..... 1 ounce
1 egg
Sol. phosphates ...... 1 dash
Angostura bitters ..... 2 dashes
Shaved ice ....¼ glass
Mix thoroughly by pouring from shaker to glass. Fill glass with carbonated water and strain. May be served with straws. Price—12 ounces, 10 cents.

PHROSO
Ginger syrup .... 1 ounce
Lemon syrup .... 1 ounce
Angostura bitters ..... 1 dash
1 egg
Sol. of acid phosphate to suit.
Cracked ice
Shake well together, strain, add carbonated water, fine stream, and serve with nutmeg and straw.

PISTACHE A LA CREME
1 egg
Pistache syrup .... 2 ounces
Phosphate .... 3 dashes
Shake, strain, fill with fine stream and serve with straws. By eliminating the phosphate and making this beverage all milk (12-ounce glass) a real pistache a la creme may be obtained.

REGULATION EGG
Lemon syrup .... 1½ ounces
Orange syrup ...... 1½ ounces
Phosphate .... 6 dashes
Egg 1
Two pieces of ice. Shake it well. Strain and serve with nutmeg.

ROYAL EGG PHOSPHATE
Sherry syrup .... 1½ fluid ounces
Sol. acid phosphates. 2 fluid drams
Shaved or cracked ice 2 ounces
Egg 1
Shake well, draw on the coarse stream of carbonated water, strain into a 12-ounce glass, again nearly fill the glass with the coarse stream of carbonated water, completing the operation with fine stream, sprinkle on a small amount of powdered nutmeg.

ROYAL GOLF
Into a suitable glass put 1 ounce syrup of raspberry, then break one egg. Next add 2 ounces of sweet cream, ¼ glassful shaved ice, and a few dashes of solution of acid phosphate. Fill the glass with carbonated water, coarse stream, and then pour all into another glass, repeating the operation, until a foaming drink is produced. Sells for 10 cents. (Bert Taylor.)

ROYAL ROYSTERER
Egg (yolk) 1
Orange syrup ...... 1½ ounces
Gentian bitters .... 1 dash
Serve as egg phosphate. Price—12 ounces, 10 cents.

SPRAGUE'S SPECIAL
Egg 1
Pineapple syrup
Strawberry syrup
Sol. acid phosphate.. 1 dash
Angostura bitters.... 1 dash
Sweet cream .... ½ ounce
Fill glass with ice, shake, strain and add

carbonated water, fine stream, then pour from glass to shaker, top with nutmeg and serve with straws. Price—12 ounces, 10 cents.

THREE-IN-ONE

One whole egg		
Malted milk	1	teaspoonful
Clam bouillon	½	ounce
Hock syrup	1	ounce
Cracked ice	¼	tumblerful

Shake well, strain and add 1 dash solution of acid phosphate, filling with carbonated water. Pour from shaker to tumbler and serve with nutmeg and straw. Charge 15 cents.

TRUE NEW YORKER

One egg		
Lemon syrup	1	ounce
Catawba syrup	1	ounce
Sol. acid phosphate....	2	dashes

Shake and fill glass with carbonated water. Mix by pouring from shaker to glass and vice versa. Strain into 10-ounce glass, add nutmeg and serve. Price—12 ounces, 10 cents.

ZIZZ EGG MINT PHOSPHATE

One egg		
Syrup of orange	1	ounce
Syrup of lemon	1	ounce
Creme de menthe.....	1	dram
Acid phosphate	2	dashes
Milk	2	ounces
Cracked ice		sufficient

Shake, strain and add soda to fill 12-ounce glass. Dispense with straws. This concoction might be improved by shaking a little before adding the phosphate. (Robt. B. Batcheller.)

BITTERS

AROMATIC BITTERS

Angostura bitters ..	4	drams
Chamomile flowers ..	1½	drams
Cinnamon bark	½	dram
Cardamom seeds	1	dram
Bitter orange peel...	1	dram
Proof spirit	1	quart

Macerate 15 days, press out and filter.

PIQUANT BITTERS

Extract of cardamom..	1	ounce
Extract of vanilla	½	ounce
Extract of licorice	¼	ounce
Extract of coriander...20		minims
Oil of bitter orange....	4	minims
Essence of ginger, soluble	½	ounce
Rectified spirits	1	pint
Maple syrup	1	pint
Water	1	quart

Mix oil of orange and the extracts thoroughly with spirits, add other ingredients and mix again.

WORMWOOD BITTERS

Oil of lemon........	2	drops
Oil of absinthe......	1	drop
Oil of caraway......	1	drop
Extract of licorice ..	½	ounce
Extract of chamomile	¼	ounce
Rectified spirits	1	pint
Simple syrup	1	pint
Water	1	quart

Mix well.

AULD LANG SYNE

Shaved ice	½	glass
Angostura bitters ...	4	dashes
Elixir of calisaya....	2	dashes
Curacoa cordial	4	dashes
Compound tincture of gentian	2	dashes
Cherry malt phosphate syrup	1	ounce

Shake well and add enough carbonated water to fill 8-ounce glass. Serve in mineral water glass. This appetizer might be made up as a stock syrup and dispensed 1½ ounces to an 8-ounce glass; 10 cents.

BLAZE DU BARRY

Lemon syrup	½	ounce
Lemon juice	1	dram
Angostura bitters ...	1	dram

Carbonated water, coarse stream, enough to fill three-fourths of a 12-ounce glass. Stir in a teaspoonful of powdered sugar and drink during effervescence.

CAPITOL

Blood orange syrup..	1	ounce
Grape juice	½	ounce
Sherry syrup	½	ounce
Angostura bitters ...	1	dash

Mix in a 12-ounce glass, shake vigorously, fill with carbonated water, coarse stream, and serve with straws. This formula makes a fine bitters at 5 cents for 8 ounces; also a delicious egg drink with soda, at 10 cents, or all milk at 15 cents for 12 ounces.

CHERRY COCKTAIL

Cherry juice	1	ounce
Lemon juice	2	ounces
Angostura bitters ...	1	dram
Sugar	1	teaspoonful
Shaved ice	¼	glass
Carbonated water ...	2	ounces

Strain with a long thin stream into a cocktail glass with a cherry in it; twist a piece of lemon rind over the drink and serve. The lemon juice, cherry and lemon rind are frequently omitted. Price—10 ounces, 10 cents.

DELMONICO

Orange syrup	1	ounce
Sherry syrup	1	ounce
Angostura bitters ...	1	dash

Serve as a phosphate. Price—8 ounces, 5 cents.

FAKIR FREEZER

Claret syrup	1	ounce
Catawba syrup	1	ounce
Lemon juice	1	dash
Orange juice	3	dashes
Sol. acid phosphate.	1	dash
Cracked ice	½	glassful

Mix in 8-ounce glass, fill with carbonated water, and serve. Charge 5 cents.

FESTIVAL FIZZ

Rose syrup	½	ounce
Lemon juice	⅛	ounce
Pineapple syrup	1	ounce
Angostura bitters ...	1	dash
Shaved ice	enough	

Place in glass, fill with carbonated water, top off with slice of orange and cherry and serve with spoon and straws. Price—10 ounces, 10 cents.

KNICKERBOCKER BRACER

Cracked ice	¼	tumblerful
Cognac syrup	1	ounce
Cherry malt phosphate syrup	¼	ounce
Extract of anise.....	1	dash
Catawba cordial	2	dashes
Carbonated water ..	4	ounces

Stir with a spoon and strain into a wine glass in which has been previously placed a seedless cherry, then immediately over the glass express the oil from a small piece of fresh lemon peel by twisting it between the thumb and forefinger.

LEMON SOUR

To 7½ ounces of well-charged water in an 8-ounce glass add the juice of one-half lemon. Serve at once. Charge 5 cents.

NEWPORT BITTERS

Into a 10-ounce glass draw ½ ounce cherry syrup, ½ ounce orange syrup and ½ ounce of lemon syrup. Add a dash of orange bitters and fill the glass one-third full of finely shaved ice. Fill the glass with carbonated water, mix thoroughly and decorate with a slice of orange and a cherry. Serve with straws. Charge 10 cents.

SAFETY FIRST

Lemon syrup	4	drams
Lemon juice	1	dram
Angostura bitters ...	1	dram

Fill with carbonated water, coarse stream, and add teaspoonful powdered sugar.

SEA BREEZE THIRST QUENCHER

Mint syrup	1	ounce
Orange syrup	½	ounce
Angostura bitters ...	2	dashes
Shaved ice	½	glass

Garnish with a thin slice of pineapple, creme de menthe cherry and sprig of mint.

Serve with straws and spoon. Charge 10 cents.

SUNSET EGG SIZZLE

Sarsaparilla syrup ...	2	ounces
Angostura bitters	1	dram
Yolk of one egg		
Shaved ice	2	ounces

Prepare and dispense like other egg drinks. Price—12 ounces, 10 cents.

THIRD DEGREE

Shaved ice	¼	glassful
Sweet cherry juice..	1	fluid ounce
Lemon juice	1	teaspoonful
Angostura bitters ...	1	dash
Powdered sugar	1	teaspoonful

Add 2 ounces of carbonated water, mix and strain into a cocktail glass, add a cherry and small slice of lemon peel and serve. Charge 10 cents.

TONIQUE FIZZ

Fill glass half full shaved ice, add white of 1 egg, 3 spoonfuls powdered sugar, 3 dashes angostura bitters, 4 dashes lime juice, 8 dashes solution of acid phosphate. Shake well, pour into 12-ounce bell top glass and fill with vichy in short dashes to make fizz.

WALL STREET PEPSIN CORDIAL

Sol. of pepsin, N.F.	1	dram
Lime syrup	1	ounce
Curacoa cordial	½	dram
Shaved ice	½	glassful
Carbonated water ...	6	ounces

Place in a glass, stir, strain and serve in mineral water glass. Price—10 cents.

WORLD'S FAIR

Shaved ice	¾	glass
Lemon juice	½	ounce
Checkerberry syrup..	1½	ounces
Angostura bitters ...	3	dashes

Shake and fill glass with ginger ale. Serve with straws. Price—10 ounces, 10 cents.

RICKEYS

AMBROSIA

Juice of half lime		
Ambrosia syrup	1	ounce
Shaved ice	½	glass

Mix in a 10-ounce glass, shake vigorously, fill with coarse stream and serve with straws. Charge 10 cents.

AUGUST SPECIAL

Into a 10-ounce glass draw ½-ounce each of vanilla and pineapple syrups and 1 ounce of grape juice; squeeze the juice of half a lime into the glass, add two-thirds glassful of shaved ice and fill with carbonated water. Mix by tossing. "A delightful thirst-quencher." Charge 10 cents.

BOSTON

Into a tall, slender 12-ounce glass pour 1½ ounces of grape juice and add the juice of 1 lime freshly expressed (bottled lime juice may be used when necessary); three dashes of angostura bitters, a couple of dashes of solution of acid phosphate, a dash of sherry and sweeten with simple syrup to taste. Fill the glass one-third full of fine shaved ice and the remainder with carbonated water. Mix with a spoon and serve with straws. Price—10 or 15 cents.

CHICAGO

Raspberry syrup ... ½ ounce
Pineapple syrup .... 1 ounce
Lime juice .... 1 dram
Grape juice .... 1 ounce
Lemon juice ...... 2 drams

Place all in a 12-ounce glass which has previously been half filled with shaved ice, then fill nearly to the top with carbonated water and mix thoroughly. Decorate with a maraschino cherry. Before serving the "Chicago" crush fresh mint on the ice. Price—10 ounces, 10 cents.

GOLDEN GATE

Blood orange syrup.... 1 ounce
Lime juice .... 1 fluid dram
Fill an 8-ounce glass seven-eighths full of carbonated water, coarse stream, add the above syrup, stir, and serve solid. Price—8 ounces, 5 cents.

GRAPE RICKEY

Into an 8-ounce mineral glass put 1 ounce pineapple syrup and 2 ounces grape juice; then add carbonated water, coarse stream, to nearly fill the glass and mix by pouring from one glass to another two or three times; lastly, add a dash of carbonated water, fine stream, and pass the glass to the customer in a "fizzing" condition.

The author found that "grape rickey is the most popular new drink we ever started at our fountain. We now sell it fast enough to open half-gallon containers of grape juice and put in regular syrup tank. The formula is very easy to dispense and the only sign which does the work that we have so far used is the following: Try a Grape Rickey, 5c. It is Sodalicious." Fountain operators may find this special price too low. (Jas. L. Tuohy.)

LIME A LA MEMPHIS

Mint syrup .... ½ ounce
Lemon syrup ...... ½ ounce
Pineapple syrup .... ½ ounce
Fill tall 6-ounce stem glass one-fourth with shaved ice, squeeze on lime juice and stir. Use carbonated water, fine stream, and serve with Maraschino cherry placed on slice of lime. Charge 10 cents.

LIMETTA

Four dashes bottled lime juice or juice of one-half lime, two-thirds glass shaved ice, 2 spoonfuls powdered sugar, dash angostura bitters; fill with carbonated water, mix, add a slice of lime or lemon or sprig of fresh mint. Serve with straws. Lemon or plain syrup might be used to advantage in this formula in place of the powdered sugar. Charge 5 cents for 8 ounces.

LLOYD'S

Lime juice .... 6 dashes
A little cracked ice
Essence of orange
flower .... 3 dashes
Lemon syrup ...... 1 ounce
Fill glass nearly full with carbonated water, stir and cloud with grape juice. Price—10 ounces, 10 cents.

RASPBERRY

Raspberry syrup ... 1 ounce
Lime juice .... ½ ounce
Sol. acid phosphate.. 1 dash
Mint .... 1 dash
Serve in an 8-ounce glass; place a slice of lemon and cherries on top and serve with straws.

SANTIAGO

Pineapple syrup .... 1 ounce
Roman punch syrup. 1½ ounces
Lime juice .... 2 dashes
Shaved ice .... 1-3 glassful
Place in glass, draw nearly full of carbonated water, coarse stream, stir well with spoon and serve with straws, using large glass. Price—10 ounces, 10 cents.

SUMMER COOLER

Into a parfait glass half filled with chipped ice draw half ounce of claret syrup, half ounce of lemon syrup and half ounce of pineapple syrup. Squeeze into the mixture the flavor of half a lime rind and fill the glass with plain water, toss, top with a Maraschino cherry and a sprig of mint and serve with two straws. Charge 10 cents. (Wm. Chalk.)

(4) Shakes and Egg Drinks

Within the past few years no drinks have so increased in popularity as the various nutritious and palatable beverages that are included under this heading. The consumption of eggs at the larger fountains in the business sections of the cities has reached tremendous proportions, and is paralleled by the increasing use of malted milk.

The shakes fall naturally into three general classes, dependent upon their principal basic material. The milk shakes are essentially sweet milk and a flavoring to which can be added an egg (egg milk shake), malted milk (malted milk shake) or both (egg malted milk shake). The cream shakes are enriched by the use of sweet cream, and the ice cream shakes by the use of ice cream. All of the shake drinks are in the nature of liquid lunches—in fact the food value of such a drink as egg chocolate malted milk shake is high enough to serve as a substantial meal.

In the preparation of all these shakes the mechanical mixers, usually of the electric type, effect a great saving in time and labor. In fact, in the making of ice cream shakes and malted milk shakes it is not possible to get the smooth, creamy consistency demanded unless a mixer is used.

Except for the simple milk shakes, these drinks should always be served with a couple of crisp, salty crackers. All shakes should be served with straws. Milk and cream used in the preparation of shakes should be cold—a little lump of ice cream in a pinch will remedy any trouble in this respect—for these beverages should always be served very cold to be at their best.

Many fountains have proved that a reputation for shakes and egg drinks makes the best foundation for successful business. This is, of course, more particularly true in the business office neighborhoods, though in the theatre districts there is always a big demand for these lunch beverages.

Fresh eggs are probably the one most important item in the building up of such a trade, and if a dispenser can make arrangements with some farmer or producer of poultry to supply him regularly with day-old eggs, using the announcement of the fact as an advertising feature, he has gone a long way towards capturing this trade. Photographs of the hens and poultry yards from which the eggs come, and signs that tell "All Eggs Used at This Fountain are Delivered *each morning* fresh from the Hazelhurst Farms" or "We use only White Leghorn Eggs, Delivered Daily from the F. H. Smith Farms, Pleasantville" can be used to advantage. Such little wrinkles, (and the enterprising dispenser will find many along this line that he can employ) will afford wonderfully effective publicity for the egg drinks.

SHAKES—PLAIN, CREAM, EGG, ICE CREAM, MILK, ETC.

OLD-FASHIONED MILK SHAKE

Put 4 ounces, or less, of shaved ice into a thick 12-ounce tumbler, add 1 ounce vanilla syrup, fill the glass with milk and agitate the whole thoroughly. The shaking may be done in the special machine known as a "milk shaker," or by means of a small hand shaker like that used for making egg drinks. After shaking, strain into another glass and serve. Sprinkle on some powdered nutmeg, if desired. Chocolate or any other non-acidulous syrup may be used if desired (acid syrups tend to curdle the milk). Price—12 ounces, 10 cents.

MILK CHOCOLATE SHAKE

Chocolate syrup ..... 1 ounce
Sweet milk .... enough

Fill a glass full of shaved ice, put in the syrup, and add the milk until the glass is almost full. Shake well, but do not strain. Top off with whipped cream and serve with straws. Price—10 ounces, 10 cents.

CHOCOLATE BOUCHE

Chocolate syrup ... 2 fluid ounces
Shaved or cracked ice ½ glassful
Milk, enough to make 12 ounces.

Mix, shake well, strain and top off with whipped cream.

SAFETY FIRST (MILK SHAKE)

Into a shaker put a ladleful of whipped

cream, 1 ounce of chocolate syrup, and one banana, previously mashed. Mix thoroughly, add one dipperful of ice cream, and enough milk to nearly fill a 12-ounce glass; mix thoroughly, and strain into another 12-ounce glass. On top of the mixture float a ladleful of whipped cream and a cherry. Serve with two straws, into the end of one of which a small American flag has been inserted. The author used the following sign to call attention to his "special":

```
.. .. .. .. .. .. .. .. .. .. ..
:                               :
:       Safety First 15 Cents   :
:                               :
: Safe,   Sane and Refreshing   :
:                               :
.. .. .. .. .. .. .. .. .. .. ..
```

(J. T. Clapsattle.)

CREME DE COCOA

One-third glass of shaved ice, 1½ ounces chocolate syrup, 2 ounces sweet cream, ¾ tumbler pure milk. Shake and strain into another tumbler into which has been placed 1 tablespoonful whipped cream. Grate chocolate on top and serve.

The above formula makes up a genuine creme de cocoa milk shake.

DARK HORSE SPECIAL

Into a 10 or 12-ounce glass pour 1½ ounces of good chocolate syrup; add a 16-to-the-quart ladleful of chocolate ice cream and fill the glass with sweet milk to within a half-inch of the top; stir, allowing the spoon to remain in the glass; put in two straws and fill the glass with whipped cream, colored dark brown with caramel, smoothing the top into a conical shape.

In advertising this special the author used placards on which were printed the words, "Try the Dark Horse Special." The placards were placed at various prominent points in the store so as to catch the eye of prospective customers. He states that he wrote the name of this special in black ink on his menu cards, the other special being written in red ink. Price—12 ounces, 15 cents. (Paul J. Grafe.)

COFFEE MILK SHAKE

Coffee syrup .... 1½ ounces
Powdered sugar .... 1 tablespoonful
Shaved or cracked ice ½ glassful
Milk enough to fill glass.
Shake well, strain, and top off with whipped cream.

COFFEE SHAKE

Serve in a 12-ounce glass. One-half fluid ounce of coffee, fill glass half full of shaved ice, then add sugar or simple syrup to sweeten to taste, fill glass with milk and shake thoroughly, top off with nutmeg or cinnamon and serve with straws.

MALTED SHAKE AU CAFE

Two ounces malted milk coffee syrup, two-thirds glass shaved ice, 4 ounces milk. Fill with milk, stir rapidly, serve spices to please.

COFFEE SHAKE (PHILADELPHIA STYLE)

Serve in a 12-ounce glass. Fill glass half full of fine shaved ice, half ounce of pure sweet cream, 1 ounce of coffee syrup, half ounce vanilla syrup, 3 ounces of milk, shake and strain, add sufficient milk to fill glass and pour from shaker to glass.

COFFEE SHAKE A LA RIO

Fresh cream .... ½ ounce
Coffee syrup .... 1½ ounces
Extract vanilla ..... 1 dash
Plain milk .... ¾ tumblerful
Shake well in glass half filled with shaved ice, strain and add plain soda in a fine stream. Price—10 ounces, 5 cents.

GOLFER'S DELIGHT

Plain cream .... 4 ounces
Malted milk .... 1 ounce
Coffee syrup .... ¾ ounce
Grape juice .... 6 dashes
Shake in glass quarter filled with ice, strain, toss and serve. Price—All milk, 10 cents.

COFFEE CABARET

Into a 10-ounce glass put 1 ounce of coffee syrup, 7 ounces of milk and shake well. Add a No. 16-to-the-quart dipperful of coffee ice cream, and top off with a spoonful of chopped English walnuts. Price, 15 cents.

OLD BROADWAY

Equal proportions vanilla, coffee and cream, with whipped cream, served with cracked ice, milk and straws.

PEACH MILK SHAKE

Peach syrup .... 1 ounce
Grape juice .... ½ ounce
Pineapple syrup .... ½ ounce
Shaved ice .... ½ glass
Fill the glass with milk, shake well and serve with two straws. Price—10 ounces, 5 cents. The amount of syrup in this formula may be reduced.

PINEAPPLE SHAKE

Shaved or cracked ice ½ glassful
Vanilla syrup ...... 1 ounce
Pineapple syrup .... 1 ounce
Milk, enough to fill the glass.
Mix and shake as in the preceding. Price—10 ounces, 5 cents.

MILK ORANGE

Orange syrup ...... ¼ ounce
Milk .... 4 ounces
Shaved ice .... sufficient
One or 2 eggs
Horlicks Malted Milk 1 tablespoonful
Put all in a shaker, shake thoroughly,

strain and fill the glass with plain or carbonated water. Price, when using all milk and one egg, 15 to 20 cents.

PERSIAN

Shaved ice	½	glass
Ice cream	1	tablespoonful
Milk	1	ounce
Vanilla extract	1	dash
Crushed strawberry	1	teaspoonful
Crushed raspberry	1	teaspoonful
Crushed pineapple	1	teaspoonful
Catawba syrup	1½	ounces

Shake well, then fill glass with carbonated water, in a fine stream. Serve with spoon. Price—12-ounce glass, all milk, 10 or 15 cents.

FINDLAY'S FRUIT MILK SHAKE

Claret syrup	1	ounce
Sweet cream	2	ounces
Mixed fruits	3	ounces
Cracked ice		sufficient

Fill the glass with milk and shake well. Pour into serving glass Sells for 20 cents.

COMMANDER IN CHIEF

Shaved ice	½	glass
Strawberry syrup	½	ounce
Pineapple syrup	½	ounce
Vanilla syrup	½	ounce

Milk to nearly fill glass.
Shake well, add soda water, fine stream, and pour from tumbler to shaker several times. Serve in a 12-ounce glass, with straws. Charge 10 cents.

JAPANESE MILK SHAKE

Almond syrup	2	ounces
Cream	2	ounces
Strawberry syrup	2	ounces

Fill glass nearly full of milk and shake. Add small portion of pistachio ice cream.

KEY WEST SHAKE

Vanilla syrup	½	ounce
Strawberry syrup	½	ounce
Orgeat syrup	¼	ounce

Place in 10-ounce glass, fill with milk, and top off with whipped cream. Charge 10 cents.

SNOWDRIFT SHAKE

Catawba syrup	1	ounce
White of an egg		
Shaved ice	½	glass

Milk, enough to fill glass.
Shake well, strain into a 12-ounce glass and serve with whipped cream and a spoon. Price—12 ounces, 15 cents.

SPORTSMAN'S SHAKE

One fresh egg.

Raspberry syrup	1	dash
Sugar	1	teaspoonful

Place in a glass in the order named and fill with milk; shake well and strain in fizz glass. Top off with grated nutmeg. Charge 15 cents.

MINT AND MILK

Mint syrup	1½	ounces
Angostura bitters	½	dram
Milk	3	ounces

Carbonated water, coarse stream, to make 8 ounces. Serve solid.

CLAM MILK SHAKE

Clam juice	1½	fluid ounces
Milk	2	fluid ounces
Soda water	5	fluid ounces

Add a pinch of salt and a little white pepper to each glass; shake well. Price— 8 ounces, 5 cents.

COCOA-COFFEE

Chocolate syrup	1½	ounces
Coffee syrup	½	ounce
Cream	2	ounces

Mix well and add carbonated water.

CREME DE CHOCOLATE

Two fluid ounces chocolate syrup, 1 ounce shaved ice, fill with charged whipped cream. Half fill another glass with cream, and mix by pouring. Price—12 ounce glass, 15 cents

FRUIT CHOCOLATE SHAKE

Chocolate syrup	2	ounces
Sweet cream	3	ounces
Cracked ice	¼	glass

Shake, strain, then add fine stream carbonated water to fill 12-ounce glass three-quarters full, and ice cream one ladle, dressing the mixture with sliced pears and whole cherries.

COFFEE ARCTIC

Serve in a 12-ounce glass. Use 1½ ounces of syrup, fill one-third full of shaved ice, 1 ounce of pure rich cream, shake thoroughly, withdraw the glass from the shaker, allowing the syrup, etc, to remain in the shaker. Now fill with carbonated water, using the fine stream only, until the shaker contains sufficient to more than fill glass. Pour into glass and back once, then strain into clean glass. Much is added to the appearance of this drink if it is topped off with whipped cream. A spoon of ice cream may be used instead.

CREME DU CAFE

Serve in a 12-ounce glass Coffee syrup, 1½ ounces, ice to fill half full; sweet cream 1 ounce; shake thoroughly, fill with soda water, strain and top off with whipped cream.

CREAM SHAKE A LA ORLEANS

Cream	2	ounces
Chocolate syrup	1	ounce
Orange syrup	½	ounce

Fill one-fourth of the glass with ice and add cream and syrups and milk enough to fill. Shake well and strain into bell-shaped glass. Serve with straws. This formula makes up as a real cream shake. Add a 16-to-the-quart scoop of ice cream and charge 10 cents.

ZEPHER SHAKE

Draw 1 ounce of any desired syrup into a 12-ounce glass and half fill the glass with carbonated water. Draw into another glass 3 ounces of whipped cream and pour the contents of the two glasses together until well mixed. Or, draw about 1 ounce of cream into a 12-ounce glass, add from another glass 4 or 5 ounces of carbonated water and about an ounce of syrup, any desired flavor, then fill the glass with the cream, using a slow stream, stirring constantly meanwhile with a spoon. (Ralph Sprague.)

MOUNTAIN NECTAR

Pure cream	....	½ ounce
Orange syrup	......	½ ounce
Vanilla syrup	......	½ ounce
Shaved ice	....	1 glassful

Shake well and add enough carbonated water to fill the glass, and serve with nutmeg. Price—10 ounces, all milk, 10 cents.

CREAMED PINEAPPLE

Crushed pineapple	..	1½ ounces
Cream	....	2 ounces
Shaved ice	....	¼ ounce

Fill 12-ounce glass with rich milk. Shake, toss and serve. Charge 15 cents.

SENATORIAL CREAM SHAKE

Pineapple syrup	....	1 ounce
Vanilla syrup	......	½ ounce
Strawberry syrup	...	½ ounce
Sweet cream	....	2 ounces
Ice cream	....	1 teaspoonful

Place in a mixing glass, shake well and nearly fill glass with carbonated water; transfer to thin glass, fill with carbonated water, fine stream, and top off with a slice of orange or pineapple. Serve with spoon and straws. Price—With the fruit topping, 15 cents.

LADIES' DAY SPECIAL

Mix in regulation glass:

Vanilla syrup	......	1 ounce
Strawberry syrup	...	½ ounce
Shaved ice	....	½ ounce
Cream	....	1½ ounces

Shake and fill the glass with milk, finishing with just a dash of fine stream.

GEYSER

Strawberry syrup	...	1 ounce
Orange syrup	......	1 ounce
Sweet cream	....	4 ounces
Grape juice	....	1½ ounces
Cracked ice	....	¼ glass

Mix, shake, strain, toss and serve with straws.

FRUITS AND FLOWERS

Rose syrup	....	½ ounce
Pineapple syrup	....	½ ounce
Vanilla syrup	......	½ ounce
Orange syrup	......	½ ounce
Plain cream	....	1 ounce
Shaved ice	....	¼ glass

Shake, strain, toss and serve.

DAISY CREAM SHAKE

Place a small portion of vanilla ice cream, ½ ounce of orange flower syrup, 1 ounce of raspberry syrup and 2 ounces of sweet cream in a shaker with some cracked ice; shake vigorously, transfer to a tall glass, fill up with milk and top off with whipped cream and chopped citron.

COLONIAL

Rose syrup	....	¾ ounce
Pineapple syrup	....	½ ounce
Orange syrup	......	½ ounce
Sweet cream	....	4 ounces
Cracked ice	....	½ glass

Shake, strain, toss and serve. Dress with whipped cream. Price—All milk, 12 ounces, 10 cents; whipped cream, 15 cents.

ATLANTIC CITY SHAKE

Orange syrup	......	1 ounce
Pineapple syrup	....	1 ounce
Sherry wine	....	2 dashes
Aromatic bitters	....	2 dashes
Plain cream	....	4 ounces

Shake, add seltzer and strain. An egg may be added if desired.

IRISH LACE CREAM SHAKE

Strawberry syrup	...	¾ ounce
Pineapple syrup	....	¾ ounce
Sweet cream	....	1 ounce
Angostura bitters	...	1 dash

Add a small quantity of ice cream (one No. 16 scoopful), shake well, put in a 12-ounce glass, add carbonated water, fine stream, and enough ice cream to fill the glass. Garnish with a slice of pineapple and a cherry. Charge 15 cents.

TROPICAL CREAM SHAKE

Strawberry syrup	...	¾ ounce
Pineapple syrup	....	¾ ounce
Sweet cream	....	1 ounce
Angostura bitters	...	1 dash

Put in a shaker with a small quantity of ice cream, shake well, transfer to a 12-ounce glass, add a little carbonated water, small, fine stream, and ice cream to fill the glass. Garnish with pineapple and cherry. Charge 10 cents per service.

HASTY PUDDING

1 egg

Pineapple syrup	......	1 ounce
Lemon juice	....	2 dashes
Sweet cream	....	1 ounce
Shaved ice		

Shake well. Add carbonated water, fine

stream. Strain into a fancy glass. Top off with nutmeg if so desired. Price—12 ounces, 10 cents.

BANANA CREAM

Shaved ice .... ½ tumblerful
Banana syrup ...... 2 ounces
Cream of milk ...... 8 ounces

Shake well, add a few pieces of banana, and fill with soda water, using the fine stream, and serve in a 12-ounce tumbler with spoon and straws. This special may also be served with all milk.

MADAGASCAR SHAKE

Shaved ice .... ½ glass
Claret syrup .... ¾ ounce
Catawba syrup ..... ¾ ounce
Whipped cream .... 1 tablespoonful

Shake, strain and fill with carbonated water. Charge 10 cents.

FLOATING ISLAND

Catawba syrup .... 1 ounce
Cherry syrup .... 1 ounce
White of 1 egg
Sweet cream .... 1 ounce

Shake well and strain, using shaved ice in shaking. Fill with milk. Top off with whipped cream and serve with straws.

GINGER MINT

Crush a small amount of fresh mint with some granulated sugar, then add a small quantity of ginger syrup, about 2 dashes of soluble ginger and an ounce of sweet cream. Fill the glass half full of shaved ice and shake thoroughly. While the drink is still in the shaker, add carbonated water to nearly fill the glass, and then mix well with the fine stream. Pour into a glass, add a couple of cherries and serve with straws.

The ginger mint must be mixed very carefully. It is liable to curdle.

VIENNA

A small quantity of shaved ice, some delicately colored pistachio syrup (green) and a small quantity of sweet cream; shake the whole well and fill up the glass with vichy water. Price—10 ounces, 10 cents.

GARDEN SHAKE

Rose syrup .... ½ ounce
Pineapple syrup .... ½ ounce
Vanilla syrup ...... ½ ounce
Orange syrup ...... ½ ounce
Plain cream .... 1 ounce
Shaved ice .... ¼ glassful

Shake, strain, toss and serve. Price—10 ounces, all milk, 10 cents. The syrup in this formula might be cut down. The Garden Shake is a very sweet affair with the 2 ounces of syrup called for above.

CREAM ROOT BEER

Root beer .... 1½ ounces
Sweet cream .... 3 ounces
Cracked ice .... ¼ glass

Shake, fill glass with carbonated water. Strain and serve.

CREAM PUFF

Draw 1 ounce of the syrup of the flavor desired into a 12-ounce glass and half fill the glass with carbonated water. Draw another glass of the same size half full of charged whipped cream, and pour the contents of both glasses together until mixed.

CHOCOLATE ICE CREAM SHAKE

Into a 12-ounce glass place 1 ounce of chocolate syrup, add 8 ounces of milk and a scoopful of vanilla ice cream (20-to-the-quart); stir and serve. Price 10 cents. The author of this formula states that if chocolate is not desired the best flavors to use are pineapple, vanilla, coffee and strawberry. The cost of the materials employed will not be more than 5 cents, he says.

CHOCOLATE A LA ARCTIC

Shake well together 1 ounce of chocolate syrup, 2 ounces of plain cream, 2 ounces of ice cream and sufficient shaved ice. Serve in a 10-ounce bell glass, filling with carbonated water, fine stream. Price —10 cents.

WIGGLE-WAGGLE

Into a mixing glass put 1½ ounces of chocolate syrup and a No. 12 disherful of vanilla ice cream. Mix thoroughly together with a bar spoon and "fluff" up with carbonated water, fine stream; pour the mixture into an 8-ounce stem glass until the contents reach within half an inch of the top. Then put in a layer of nuts and top off with whipped cream. Price—15 cents. (Harper Huntley.)

BUFFALO SHAKE

Chocolate syrup .... ½ ounce
Maple syrup .... ½ ounce
Vanilla ice cream ... ½ tablespoonful
Plain cream .... 1 ounce

Ice and shake. Pour into a frappe glass, garnish with whipped cream and a cherry and serve with a spoon and straws. Price —10 cents.

COFFEE CREAM SHAKE

Coffee syrup .... 2 ounces
Plain cream .... 3 ounces
Ice cream .... 1 teaspoonful

Shake well with ice; use only fine stream and serve in bell glass.

COFFEE CORDIAL

Yolk of 1 egg
Coffee syrup .... ½ ounce
Bitters .... 3 dashes
Cream or rich milk.. 2 ounces

Shake with cracked ice, strain and fill

with carbonated water. Price—10 cents with carbonated water; 15 cents for all milk.

CZAR OF RUSSIANS SHAKE
Vanilla syrup ...... 1 ounce
Red orange syrup ... 1 ounce
Ice cream .... 2 ounces
Shaved ice .... ½ glassful
Shake, strain, toss and serve. Price—12 ounces, 10 cents.

MAPLE SHAKE
Maple syrup .... 2 ounces
Plain cream .... 3 ounces
Ice cream ....large teaspoonful
Shake well with ice, use only fine stream and serve in bell glass. Charge 10 cents.

MAPLE CREAM SHAKE
Maple syrup ...... 2 ounces
Plain cream .... 3 ounces
Ice cream .... large spoonful
Shake well with shaved ice; fill glass with carbonated water, fine stream, and serve.

MAPLE PINE
Maple syrup .... 1 ounce
Pineapple syrup .... 1 ounce
Shaved ice .... ½ glassful
Ice cream .... 1 spoonful
Mix in 10-ounce glass with spoon, fill glass with carbonated water, mix again, and top off with grated pineapple. Price, all milk, 10 cents.

CREME DE MAPLE
Maple syrup .... 2 ounces
Ice cream .... 2 ounces
Plain cream .... 1 ounce
Mix, thoroughly shake, then fill with milk and add a spray of mint. A slice of orange goes well here, but such addition is at the option of the dispenser.

CREAMED NUT SHAKE
Nut fruit syrup...... 2 ounces
Sweet cream .... 1 ounce
Ice cream .... 1 ladleful
Shake thoroughly; finish with fine stream and serve with spoon and straws.

CREAM FREEZE
Shaved ice .... ½ glass
Ice cream .... 3 spoonfuls
Orgeat or pistache
syrup .... 2 ounces
Shake, fill with carbonated water and mix with spoon. Price—12 ounces, all milk, 10 cents.

SPICY SHAKE
Mint syrup .... 1 ounce
Wintergreen syrup .... 1 ounce
Sweet cream .... 1 ounce
Soft ice cream .... ladleful
Shake well, use fine stream carbonated water, serve in regular frappe style, top

with whipped cream. Price—12 ounce glass, 15 cents.

PINEAPPLE CREAM
Pineapple syrup .... ½ ounce
Ice cream .... 1 ounce
White of two eggs
Place in a shaker with shaved ice, shake, strain, fill with all milk, and serve, topped with nutmeg, if desired. Price, 15 or 20 cents.

ORGEAT CREAM
Orgeat syrup .... 2 ounces
Sweet cream .... 4 ounces
Ice cream .... dash
Maraschino cherry
This makes a 10-ounce drink, adding four ounces of milk.

ORANGE BLEND
Vanilla syrup ...... 1 ounce
Red orange syrup ... 1 ounce
Ice cream .... 2 ounces
Ice .... ¼ glass
Shake, strain, toss and serve. Price—12 ounces, all milk, 10 cents.

OCEAN GROVE SHAKE
Put into a glass:
Vanilla syrup ...... 2 ounces
Orange syrup .... ½ ounce
Ice cream .... 1 ladleful
Shake thoroughly; fill the glass with carbonated water, strain into a clean glass, and top off with whipped cream. In this formula the amount of syrup called for might be cut down. Price—12 ounce glass, 10 cents.

MONARCH SHAKE
Place a small portion of vanilla ice cream, half ounce of orange flower syrup, 1 ounce of raspberry syrup and 2 ounces of sweet cream in a shaker with some cracked ice; shake vigorously, transfer to a tall glass, fill up with carbonated water, using coarse and fine streams alternately, and top off with whipped cream and chopped citron. Price—12 ounce glass, 10 cents.

"CO-ED" SHAKE
Vanilla syrup ...... 1 ounce
Orange syrup ...... 1 ounce
Ice cream .... 1 spoonful
Shaved ice .... ¼ glass
Shake, strain, toss and serve. Charge 10 cents for 12-ounce glass.

BLIZZARDINE
Shaved ice .... ½ glass
Ice cream .... 1 tablespoonful
Orgeat syrup .... 1 ounce
Catawba syrup ..... ½ ounce
Shake well and fill glass with carbonated water. Price—12 ounce glass, 10 cents.

ANGEL FOOD

Vanilla syrup	1	ounce
Red orange syrup	1	ounce
Ice cream	2	ounces
Ice	¼	glass

Shake, strain, toss and serve. Price—12 ounces, all milk, 10 cents.

BANANA A LA MANHATTAN

Draw 1 ounce of sweet cream in a 12-ounce glass, add 1 ounce of vanilla syrup and into the mixture slice half of a banana. Now add a portion of ice cream, shake thoroughly and fill glass with the milk. Pour without straining into a clean glass and top off with whipped cream and serve with spoon. Price—all milk, 15 cents.

DIPLOMATIC SHAKE

Grape juice	2	ounces
Sweet cream	2	ounces
Ice cream	1	spoonful
Bitters	3	dashes

Shake thoroughly, strain, pour back into shaker and add carbonated water to fill glass; throw as in mixing egg drinks. Serve with paper napkin and place nutmeg handy. Price—12 ounces, 10 cents.

FRUIT MIX

Two ounces punch syrup and a small lump of ice cream. Shake until smooth and add 1 large spoonful cut candied fruits. Add carbonated water, then another lump of the cream and serve. Price—12 ounces, 15 cents.

FROSTED FRUIT

Shaved ice	½	tumblerful
Ice cream	1	tablespoonful
Pure milk	1	ounce
Extract of vanilla	1	dash
Crushed strawberry	1	teaspoonful
Crushed pineapple	1	teaspoonful
Crushed raspberry	1	teaspoonful
Catawba syrup	1½	ounces

Shake well, then add carbonated water. Serve with spoon.

TROPICAL SHAKE

Crushed orange	½	ounce
Crushed cherry	½	ounce
Crushed pineapple	½	ounce
Sweet cream	1	ounce
Ice cream	1	spoonful

Shake well, using both streams, fine and coarse. Serve in a frappe glass. Top off with sliced pineapple and cherry, and serve with straws. (Ralph Sprague.) Charge 15 cents.

SUPERLATIVE SHAKE

Shaved ice	½	tumblerful
Ice cream	1	tablespoonful
Pure milk	1	ounce
Vanilla syrup	½	ounce
Crushed fruits	3	teaspoonfuls
Catawba syrup	1½	ounces

Shake well, then add enough carbonated water, fine stream, to fill glass. Serve with spoon.

GLAD WE'RE HERE

Into a mixing glass put:

Strawberry syrup	¾	ounce
Pineapple syrup	¾	ounce
Sweet cream	1	ounce
Angostura bitters	1	dash

Add a small quantity of ice cream. shake well, put into a 12-ounce glass, add a little carbonated water, fine cream, and enough ice cream to fill glass. Garnish with sliced pineapple and a cherry. Price—12 ounces, 15 cents.

BEAUX AND BELLES

Draw ¾ ounce each of pineapple and orange syrups into a 12-ounce glass, add 2 or 3 dashes of acid phosphate, shaved ice, and 1 tablespoonful of ice cream. Shake well, add enough carbonated water to fill glass, pour from glass to shaker and serve.

GARDEN OF EDEN

Shaved ice	½	glass
Ice cream	1	tablespoonful
Sweet milk	1	ounce
Extract of vanilla	1	dash
Crushed strawberry	1	teaspoonful
Crushed raspberry	1	teaspoonful
Crushed pineapple	1	teaspoonful
Catawba syrup	1½	ounces

Shake well, fill glass with carbonated water, and serve with spoon.

CARDINAL SHAKE

Raspberry syrup	1	ounce
Pineapple syrup	1	ounce
Sherry wine	3	dashes
Ice cream	ladleful	
Cracked ice		

Shake well, add carbonated water, fine stream, and strain into fancy glass.

EGG MILK SHAKE

Syrup, any desired flavor	1	ounce
Ice, finely shaved	¼	glassful
Milk, enough to make 12	ounces	

Shake and strain.

This formula makes a genuine milk shake. Use very little ice. Charge 15 cents.

EGG VICHY

One egg		
Shaved ice	½	glass
Pure water	1	ounce

Shake thoroughly; then add slowly, while constantly stirring enough vichy water to fill the glass. Price—12 ounces, 10 cents.

CHOCOLATE EGG SHAKE

Chocolate syrup	2	ounces
Cracked ice	1	ladleful
Egg	1	

Milk, enough to nearly fill glass.

Draw the syrup into the glass, add the egg and cracked ice, then fill the shaker about one-third full of milk and shake again. Finally add the balance of the milk to fill the shaker about two-thirds full Shake well and strain into a clean glass. Top off with a little powdered mace, nutmeg or cinnamon.

The above formula is recommended for making chocolate egg shake. Price—12 ounces, 15 cents.

EGG CHOCOLATE

Chocolate syrup .... 1 ounce
White and yolk of 1 egg
Crushed ice, small quantity

Shake well, then add plain carbonated water sufficient to fill tumbler. Stir with twist bar spoon, strain, then pour alternately from tumbler to shaker, and serve. This drink is rather thin and should not be priced at more than 10 cents.

MALTED MILK EGG CHOCOLATE

One ounce chocolate, plain cream, 2 spoonfuls, malted milk, small amount ice cream, 1 beaten egg. Shake well, strain and serve, all milk, with nutmeg, if desired. Charge 15 or 20 cents.

EGG MALTED MILK

Egg 1
Vanilla syrup ...... 1 or 2 ounces
Plain cream .... 3 ounces
Malted milk .... 2½ teaspoons

Put syrup in mixing glass, adding the malted milk last, just before shaking. Shake well with ice, use fine stream only, and serve in bell glass. This drink is much more satisfactory if all milk is used. Use very little ice—the shake is easily spoiled. Price—12 ounces, 15 or 20 cents.

THE IRON CROSS

Chocolate syrup .... 1½ ounces
Grape juice .... 2 ounces
Sweet cream .... 1 ounce
Malted milk .... 1 teaspoonful
Egg 1

Mix, shake, strain in 12-ounce glass and fill with fine stream. Price—15 or 20 cents. (J. M. Hahne.)

PIFF PAFF PUFF

Place in a glass the white of one egg, sweet cream, 2 ounces, and whip well. Then add chocolate syrup, 1½ ounces. Shake well, fill with carbonated water, pour into a 12-ounce glass and serve without straws.

HAWAIIAN CHOCOLATE SHAKE

Break and separate an egg; beat up the white with half an ounce of chocolate syrup, and the yolk with a similar quantity of pineapple crushed fruit syrup; beat the two mixtures well together and then shake up with an ounce of chocolate syrup

and a 16-to-the-quart disherful of vanilla ice cream. Pour into a 12-ounce glass and fill with carbonated water, fine stream. Serve with two straws. This formula may be much improved by dispensing all milk and charging 20 cents for 12 ounces. (Beverly F. Towne.)

CONGER'S EGG CHOCOLATE

Chocolate syrup .... 1 ounce
Vanilla syrup ...... ½ ounce
1 egg
Piece of ice, size of walnut

Shake well together, add plain soda and pour from shaker to glass three times; top off with nutmeg. Price—12 ounces, 10 cents.

EGG CHOCOLATE

Put 2 ounces chocolate syrup in a heavy glass, break and drop in one egg, add 3 ounces plain cream and shaved ice, shake well and use only fine stream of soda water.

EGG COFFEE

Serve in a 12-ounce glass. Use:
Coffee syrup .... 1 ounce
Egg 1
Sweet cream .... 1 ounce
Ice .... a little

Shake thoroughly and proceed as in preparing of other egg drinks. Charge 15 cents.

AFTER WORK

Coffee syrup .... 1½ ounces
Cream .... 1 ounce
Angostura bitters ... 3 dashes
Don't care syrup.... ½ ounce
One egg
Shaved ice .... ½ glassful

Shake, fill glass with carbonated water and strain. Price—12 ounces, 10 cents.

BOSTON EGG FLIP

Serve in a 12-ounce glass:
Egg 1
Coffee syrup .... 1½ ounces
Fresh, sweet cream. 1 ounce
Angostura bitters ... 3 dashes
Fine shaved ice..... a small quantity

Shake thoroughly, add carbonated water and strain as in preparing other egg drinks.

EGG MALTED MILK COFFEE

Prepare same as malted milk coffee with the exception of adding the egg before shaking, and top off with a little nutmeg if desired. This drink is sometimes called Coffee Light Lunch, sells readily at 15 cents a glass.

CREME DE LUXE

Cream syrup ...... 1 ounce
Extract of vanilla... 1 dash
Shaved ice .... ½ glassful
White of 1 egg

Shake well, strain, fill glass with milk, and serve with nutmeg. Price—15 cents.

ORANGE SPRAY

Egg	1	
Orange syrup	1	ounce
Orange bitters	2	dashes
Sweet cream	1	ounce

Dispense in glass half filled with shaved ice, shake and use fine stream carbonated water. Top off with nutmeg. Price—12 ounces, 10 or 15 cents.

AMERICAN GENTLEMAN

Juice of 1 orange		
Powdered sugar	3	teaspoons
Egg	1	
Grape juice	1	ounce
Port wine	¼	ounce
Shaved ice	small quantity	

Fill glass with plain water; shake, put in lemonade glass, finish with a slice of pineapple and a cherry. The "American Gentleman" may be livened up by the application of a little fine stream. Price—12 ounces, 20 cents.

EGG PUFF

Into a 12-ounce mixing glass, put one egg, 1 ounce orange syrup, 1 No. 16-to-the-quart dipperful vanilla ice cream, 2 ounces sweet milk; shake thoroughly, add carbonated water, fine stream first, and completing with coarse stream. Top with whipped cream. Price—12 ounces, 15 cents. (Paul Anderson.)

WHITE MOUNTAIN

Orange syrup	2	fluid ounces
Cream	3	fluid ounces
White of 1 egg		
Shaved or cracked ice	½	glassful

Shake well, strain into a 12-ounce glass and fill with milk. Price—15 cents.

CANARY PUFF

Into a shaker or mixing glass put 1½ ounces of blood orange syrup, the white of an egg, three or four teaspoonfuls of Maraschino cherry syrup, one ladleful of vanilla ice cream; shake well, add carbonated water, fine stream, and a Maraschino cherry. Serve with a spoon in a 12-ounce glass. Price—15 cents. (Otis Brown.)

NARANGA SHAKE

Shaved ice	½	tumblerful
1 egg		
Vanilla syrup	1	fluid ounce
Orange syrup	1	fluid ounce
Ice cream	1	tablespoonful

Add a few dashes of bitters and orange extract. Fill the glass nearly full of cream, grate a little nutmeg on top, add sufficient carbonated water, fine stream, and serve with spoon and straw. Charge 15 cents.

BIG GUN EGG

Juice of 1 lemon		
Egg	1	
Powdered sugar	1	tablespoonful
Shaved or cracked ice	2	ounces

Shake thoroughly, strain into a 12-ounce glass, and fill with ginger ale. Charge 15 cents. The Big Gun Egg is a good thirst quencher.

MALTED MILK LEMONADE

Break a fresh egg into a mixing glass and add the juice of one lemon, 1½ ounces rock candy syrup, shaved ice, a sufficient quantity, 1½ teaspoonfuls of malted milk, and a dipperful of ice cream. Shake well, transfer to a bell glass and fill with carbonated water, fine stream, and serve. (John S. Flemming.)

LIME SOUR EGG SHAKE

Take a 12- or 14-ounce glass and place in it one ounce of lime freeze, one egg, one small dipperful of ice cream and about 8 drops solution of acid phosphate. Shake well and fill the glass with carbonated water; stir with a spoon. Price—12 ounces, 10 cents.

PINEAPPLE PUFF

Into a mixing glass containing 2 ounces plain, sweet cream, add 1 egg white, beat with spoon until well whipped, add 1½ ounces pineapple syrup, transfer into shaker and add carbonated water from both streams; then pour from shaker to 12-ounce glass and serve without straws. Charge 10 cents.

EGG FLIP

Vanilla syrup	1	ounce
Pineapple syrup	1	ounce
Plain cream	3	ounces
Shaved ice		
Egg	1	

Shake, strain and toss and serve with straws. Price—All milk, 15 cents.

SNOW FLURRIES

Pineapple syrup	¾	ounce
Vanilla syrup	¾	ounce
Ice cream	2	ounces
Shaved ice	¼	glassful
Egg	1	

Break the egg into the glass, add the other ingredients, shake, strain and toss, adding the carbonated water last. (S. M. Sanborn.)

CUPID'S DELIGHT

Use a lemonade shaker. Put in a No. 16 dipperful of soft vanilla ice cream, 2 teaspoonfuls pulverized sugar, one dipperful of pineapple ice and one egg; beat the mixture well with a spoon and draw on fine stream of carbonated water to make a 12-ounce drink; top off with whipped cream and serve with two straws. No syrup is required in this drink. Price—12 ounces, 10 cents. (Howard E. Rollison.)

NIAGARA

Pineapple syrup .... 2 fluid ounces
Plain water ice..... 2 ounces

Beat the white of an egg and add to the above mixture in a 12-ounce glass, mix with a spoon, and fill the glass with carbonated water, fine stream. Charge 10 cents.

CHERRYBLOSSOM EGG SHAKE

Cherry syrup .... 1½ ounces
Ginger .... ½ ounce
Ice cream .... 2 ounces
White of one egg

Mix and shake with cracked ice. Serve in 12-ounce glass and top with nutmeg. (B. K. Keeler.)

GRAPE

Break into a suitable glass one egg and add 4 ounces of sweet cream, about 2 ounces of grape juice, and 1½ ounces of shaved ice. Add sufficient sugar to sweeten, shake thoroughly, toss and serve with straws. A 15-cent drink. Might charge 10 cents and make a present of it.

CHAUTAUQUA SHAKE

Into a mixing glass break one egg and upon it draw 1 ounce of vanilla syrup, 1 ounce of grape juice and 1 ounce of sweet cream. Add sufficient cracked ice, mix well, fill glass with carbonated water or milk, and top off with nutmeg. Serve with two straws.

CIDER EGG

Vanilla syrup .... 2 ounces
Sweet cider .... 6 ounces
One egg
Shaved ice .... 3 ounces

Shake well, put into a 12-ounce glass and serve with straws. A little of the fine stream might make this a snappier drink.

EGYPTIAN EGG SHAKE

Orgeat syrup .... 2 ounces
Egg 1
Sweet cream .... 2 ounces

Shake with ice and fill 12-ounce glass with milk, touching up at end with fine stream. Charge 15 cents. (Henry Lee.)

LITTLE RED HEN

Raspberry vinegar .. ½ ounce
Raspberry syrup .... 2 ounces
Egg 1
Shaved ice .... ¼ glassful

Mix and transfer to a 12-ounce glass, fill with carbonated water, strain and serve with straws. Charge 10 cents.

STRAWBERRY EGG SHAKE

To 1 egg in mixing glass, add 2 ounces of strawberry syrup, 2 ounces plain cream, shake well with ice; use fine stream and serve in bell glass. Charge 10 cents.

CALIFORNIA EGG MILK SHAKE

White and yolk of 1 egg
Cracked ice .... ¼ tumblerful
Nectar syrup ...... 1¾ ounces

Shake, strain, finish with milk, and serve in a thin soda glass with grated nutmeg. Price—12 ounces, 15 cents.

GOOD SAMARITAN

White and yolk of 1 egg
Cracked ice .... ¼ glassful
Nectar syrup ...... 1¼ ounces
Milk .... ¼ glassful

Shake, strain, and serve in thin soda glass with grated nutmeg. Price—15 cents.

CHARLOTTE SHAKE

To small quantity of shaved ice in a tumbler, add 1 whole egg, a little sweet cream and highly flavored Maraschino syrup; shake the whole well and fill up the glass with milk. Price—12 ounces, 15 cents.

PALL MALL SHAKE

Queen nectar syrup.. ½ ounce
Clarade syrup ...... 1 ounce
White and yolk of 1 egg
Fresh cream .... 1 ounce
Cracked ice .... ¼ glass

Shake well together, strain and add 1 dash curacoa cordial and carbonated water sufficient to fill tumbler.

ARION

Apricot syrup ...... ½ ounce
Peach syrup .... ½ ounce
Rose syrup .... ½ ounce
Plain cream .... 2 ounces
Egg 1
Ice .... ¼ glass

Shake, strain, toss and serve. Price—12 ounces, all milk, 15 cents.

REPUBLIC EGG SHAKE

Raspberry syrup ... 1 ounce
Angostura bitters ... 1 dash
Egg 1
Malted milk .... 1 teaspoon
Sweet milk .... 2 ounces
Cracked ice........ a few pieces

Shake well, strain, add fine stream carbonated water to fill 12-ounce glass; finish with whipped cream; serve with straws. (Maud Irma.)

PATRIOTIC

Into a mixing glass break 1 egg; then add ½ ounce cherry syrup, ½ ounce strawberry syrup; ½ ounce claret syrup and 1 ounce vanilla ice cream, as follows: First break the egg into the glass, put in the ice cream, syrup, and two dashes of solution of acid phosphate. Add two small pieces of ice. Shake, strain, toss and serve with nutmeg on top. Should bring 15 cents. (J. D. Hamble.)

ALAN DALE

Lemon syrup ...... ½ ounce
Raspberry syrup ...•. ½ ounce
Orange syrup 1   ounce
Sweet cream 2   ounces
Egg 1
Cracked ice

Shake, strain, add carbonated water, toss and serve.

OLYMPIC EGG SHAKE

Shaved ice, a small
   quantity
Juice of 1 lemon
Grape juice 1   ounce
Egg 1
Powdered sugar ..... 2 tablespoonfuls

Dispense in a 12-ounce glass and fill with carbonated water, fine and coarse streams. Serve straight in a 12-ounce lemonade glass and garnish with orange and cherry. Charge 15 cents.

NADJA

Shaved ice, a little heavy raspberry syrup, the white of one egg and a little cream; shake well and fill the tumbler with vichy water. Price—10 ounces, 10 cents.

ROYAL MIST

Orange syrup .... 1 ounce
Catawba syrup ..,.... 1 ounce
Cream .... 2 ounces
One egg

Mix according to art and finish with soda. Serve with straws. Price—12 ounces, 10 cents.

KING OF HEARTS

Pineapple syrup ...... 1 ounce
Raspberry syrup ...... 1 ounce
Egg 1
Rich milk .... 2 ounces

Add dash of bitters and shake with spoonful of ice cream, strain and serve as other egg shakes. Finish with coarse and fine streams. Charge 10 cents for 12-ounce glass.

MIDGET EGG

Into a mixing glass draw half ounce of pineapple and half ounce of orange syrup, and into this break one egg and add a little sweet cream and shaved ice. Shake thoroughly and add a small amount of carbonated water, fine stream, and strain into an 8-ounce bell-shaped glass. Charge 10 cents.

QUEEN'S FAVORITE

Strawberry syrup .... 1 ounce
Pineapple syrup ...... 1 ounce
Vanilla syrup .... 1 ounce
Sweet cream .... 4 ounces
Egg 1
Ice and carbonated wa-
   ter .... sufficient
Charge 15 cents.

LUNAR BLEND

Take two mixing glasses, break an egg, putting the yolk in one glass, the white into the other, into the glass with the yolk add one ounce cherry syrup and some cracked ice, shake, add small quantity carbonated water and strain into a 12-ounce glass. Into the other mixing glass add one ounce plain sweet cream and beat with bar spoon until well whipped, add one-half ounce lemon syrup, then transfer it into shaker and add carbonated water from fine stream only and float on top of the yolk and cherry syrup. Serve with two straws.

MARINGO SHAKE

Mix in glass one egg, equal parts of vanilla and pineapple syrups to make 1½ ounces, dash of ice cream, a little cracked ice. Shake well. Have ready a large bell glass with half ounce of crushed strawberry. Now turn the fine stream into the shaker, pour into the mixing glass, which empty by pouring from a height into a bell glass, so as to mix the strawberry with the rest of the syrup. Price—12 ounces, 15 cents.

MANHATTAN EGG CREAM SHAKE

Pineapple syrup .... ¾ ounce
Vanilla syrup ...... ¾ ounce
Ice cream 2   ounces
Cracked ice .... ¼ glass
Egg 1

Shake, strain, toss and serve. Price—12 ounces, 15 cents.

CASHIER'S EGG SHAKE

Strawberry syrup ... ¾ ounce
Pineapple syrup .... ¾ ounce
Sweet cream 2   ounces
Angostura bitters ... 1   dash
Shaved ice 1   ounce
One egg

Shake, strain, using carbonated water, coarse stream. Pour from glass to shaker and vice versa. Grate nutmeg on top. May be served as a hot drink by using hot water instead of carbonated water, but served cold this shake is much more tasty. Should attract the "junketers." Price—12 ounces, 10 cents.

OLD KENTUCKY

One egg
Don't care syrup.... 1   ounce
Champagne phosphate
   syrup 1   ounce
Sweet cream 1   ounce
Shaved ice .... ¼ glassful

Shake thoroughly, fill glass with carbonated water and strain. Price—12 ounces, 10 cents.

LUNARETTE

Grape syrup .... 1 ounce
Vanilla syrup ...... ½ ounce
Ice cream .... 2 tablespoonfuls
Egg 1
Shaved ice .... ¼ glass

Shake, strain, finish with milk, and serve. Price—12 ounces, 15 cents.

AMERICAN BEAUTY

Rose syrup .... ½ ounce
Pineapple syrup ... 1 ounce
Port wine .... 4 dashes
Egg 1
Plain cream .... 2 · ounces
Ice .... ¼ glass

Shake, strain, toss and serve. Price—12 ounces, all milk, 15 cents.

CANADENSIS SHAKE

Almond syrup ...... ½ ounce
Raspberry syrup .... 1 ounce
Egg 1
Milk to fill glass
Ice .... ¼ glass

Shake, strain, toss and serve. Charge 15 cents.

WASHINGTONIAN EGG SHAKE

Grape juice .... 2 ounces
Juice of half a lemon
Powdered sugar .... 2 teaspoonfuls
Egg 1
Cracked ice
Plain water .... 2 ounces

Shake together well. Prepare a large goblet in the following manner: In bottom of glass put pieces of ice, one tablespoonful of pineapple sherbet. Over this pour a ladleful of grated pineapple, then strain the contents of shaker over all, garnish with fruit and serve with a spoon and straws. Charge 20 cents.

AMERICAN DERBY

One egg
Sherry syrup .... 2 ounces
Ice cream .... 2 tablespoonfuls
Shaved or cracked ice ¼ glassful

Shake, strain, toss and serve. Price—12 ounces, all milk, 15 cents.

BRAZILIAN SHAKE

Raspberry syrup ... 2 ounces
Pineapple syrup ... ½ ounce
Sweet cream .... 3 ounces
One egg
Cracked ice .... ¼ glass

Shake, strain, toss and serve. Price—12 ounces, all milk, 15 cents.

ROYAL GOLF

Into a suitable glass break the egg and add the syrup of raspberry, cream, shaved ice, a few dashes of solution of acid phos-

phate. Fill glass with carbonated water, coarse stream, and then pour all into another glass, repeating the operation until a foaming drink is produced. Charge 10 cents.

SEA-SIDE SHAKE

Vanilla syrup ...... 1 ounce
Orange syrup ...... ½ ounce
Grape juice .... ½ ounce

Draw into a 12-ounce glass; into this mixture break an egg and add a dash or two of angostura bitters, 1 ounce of sweet cream and a little ice; shake thoroughly, fill the glass with carbonated water, and strain into a clean glass; top with spice, if desired.

KANSAS HIGH BALL

Juice of 1 lemon
Grape juice .... 3 ounces
Egg 1
Simple syrup to sweeten
Cracked ice .... half a scoop
Water

Mix in a glass, shake well, jerk up with carbonated water, fine stream, strain and serve in 8 or 10-ounce stem glass. Price, 15 cents. (Vance R. Thralls.)

HUMDINGER

Cherry syrup .... 1½ ounces
1 egg
Ginger extract ..... dash
Sol. of acid phosphate dash

Shake well, strain and fill 12-ounce glass with fine and coarse streams. Charge 10 cents. (H. C. Baldwin.)

ALASKA SNOWBALL

Pineapple syrup .... ½ ounce
Lemon syrup ...... ½ ounce
Orange syrup ..... ½ ounce
Egg 1
Plain cream .... 2 ounces
Shaved ice .... ¼ glass

Shake, strain, toss and serve. Drop in a ball of pineapple ice or ice cream to float on the surface and the Alaska Snowball is a winner. Price—15 cents; all milk, 20 cents.

SEA BREEZE

Shaved ice .... ½ tumblerful
Egg 1
Vanilla syrup ...... 1 fluid ounce
Orange syrup ...... 1 fluid ounce
Grape juice .... ½ ounce
Bitters .... 2 dashes

Fill the glass nearly full of milk, shake well, grate a little nutmeg on the top, add a little soda water (fine stream), and serve with spoon and straws.

HINDOO

White of 1 egg
Pure cream	½ ounce
Shaved ice	¼ glass
Catawba syrup	½ ounce
Lemon syrup	½ ounce
Pineapple syrup	½ ounce

Shake well and add carbonated water, both streams. Serve with nutmeg.

GLASGOW EGG SHAKE

Cherry syrup	½ ounce
Orange syrup	½ ounce
Sherbet syrup	½ ounce
Plain cream	1½ ounces
Egg	1
Ice	¼ glass

Shake, strain, toss and serve. Price—12 ounces, 10 cents.

FRUIT BLEND

Pineapple syrup	½ ounce
Vanilla syrup	½ ounce
Orange syrup	½ ounce
Egg	1
Plain cream	2 ounces
Sherry wine	2 dashes
Ice	¼ glassful

Shake, strain, toss and serve. Price—12 ounces, all milk, 15 cents.

POCAHONTAS SHAKE

Raspberry syrup	½ ounce
Orange syrup	½ ounce
Pineapple syrup	½ ounce
Lime juice	½ dram

One egg

Break the egg into a soda glass containing some fine ice, add the other ingredients, shake thoroughly, fill glass with carbonated water and strain. Price—12 ounces, 10 cents.

EGG SHAKE A LA NEW ORLEANS

Break 1 egg in mixing glass, add 1 ounce catawba syrup, 1½ ounces brandy syrup, 2 ounces plain cream, shake well with ice and use carbonated water, fine stream, to fill; serve in bell glass.

CAMPUS SHAKE

Raspberry syrup	2 fluid ounces
Orange syrup	½ fluid ounce

One egg
Ice shavings	2 ounces

Milk enough to fill a 12-ounce glass

Shake well, strain, fill the glass with the fine stream of carbonated water and sprinkle over the foam a small quantity of grated nutmeg. Charge 15 cents.

EGG SHAKE A LA KALAMAZOO

Celery syrup	2 ounces
Cream	2 ounces
Egg	1

Shake, strain and toss. Price—12 ounces, all milk, 15 cents.

NEW ENGLAND EGG SHAKE

Lemon syrup	½ ounce
Pineapple syrup	1 ounce
Egg	1
Cracked ice	¼ glass

Shake, strain, toss and serve with nutmeg or cinnamon. Price—12 ounces, 10 cents.

SCIENTIFIC EGG SHAKE

Pineapple syrup	½ ounce
Lemon syrup	½ ounce
Orange syrup	½ ounce
One egg	
Plain cream	2 ounces
Shaved ice	¼ glass

Shake, strain, toss and serve in a 12-ounce glass, filling with fine and coarse streams.

EGG SHAKE A LA FRANCAIS

Champagne syrup	1 ounce
Egg	1
Cracked ice	small quantity

Shake together with hand shaker; then add enough carbonated water to fill the glass. Mix well by pouring from tumbler to shaker; strain through julep strainer into tumbler. Add a little grated nutmeg and serve.

EGG NUTRINE

Egg	1
Raspberry syrup	½ ounce
Claret syrup	½ ounce
Angostura bitters	2 dashes
Sweet cream	2 ounces
Shaved ice	

Shake well, strain, transfer to a 10-ounce glass, fill with carbonated water, and serve. Charge 10 cents. (James N. Morris.)

DON'T CARE EGG SHAKE

"Don't Care" syrup	1 ounce
Sherry	4 dashes
Egg	1
Cream, a little	
Cracked ice	

Shake well, fill glass with carbonated water, fine stream, strain into a clean glass and sprinkle ground nutmeg on top. This beverage is improved by serving all milk.

WHITE VELVET

Pineapple syrup	1 ounce
Orange syrup	½ ounce
Colonial punch syrup	½ ounce
White of egg	
Cracked ice	1-3 glass

Shake, strain, toss and serve. Price—All milk, 15 cents.

VARSITY EGG SHAKE

Into a 12-ounce glass draw one ounce of orange syrup, one ounce of pineapple syrup. Into this break an egg and add one ounce of port wine and a little finely shaved ice. Shake thoroughly and proceed to fill the glass with milk. Strain into a soda glass and serve. Price—12 ounces, 15 cents.

DELIGHT

Strawberry syrup ...	½ ounce
Raspberry syrup ...	½ ounce
Grape syrup	½ ounce
Egg	1
Plain cream	1½ ounces
Ice	¼ glass

Shake, strain, toss and serve.

CHICAGO EGG SHAKE

Into a 12-ounce glass draw one ounce of strawberry syrup and half ounce each of raspberry and pineapple syrups; then add 1½ ounces of sweet cream. Into the mixture break a fresh egg and add a little ice. Shake thoroughly, fill glass with carbonated water, dispensing as you would other egg drinks.

PRINCETON TIGER

Orgeat syrup	2 ounces
Fresh cream	½ ounce
Yolk of one egg	
Shaved ice	¼ glass
Milk 12	ounces

Price—15 cents.

SOROSIS EGG SHAKE

Draw one ounce of strawberry syrup and one-half ounce of pineapple syrup into a 12-ounce glass and add one and one-half ounces of sweet cream. Into this break an egg, add sufficient shaved ice, shake thoroughly, fill with carbonated water and serve with a spoon. If desired a whole strawberry or two may be added. Charge 10 or 15 cents.

CATCH OF THE SEASON

Into a suitable glass containing half ounce each of strawberry and pineapple syrups, break an egg, adding two teaspoonfuls of sweet cream and two ounces of shaved ice. Shake thoroughly, add a little carbonated water and strain into a ten-ounce glass. Fill with fine stream.

SANS SOUCI SHAKE

Pineapple syrup	½ ounce
Orange syrup	½ ounce
Vanilla syrup	½ ounce
Egg	1
Ice cream	1 ounce
Cracked ice	¼ glass

Shake, strain, fill with carbonated water, toss and serve. Price—12 ounces, 15 cents.

BOSTON SPECIAL SHAKE

Into a 12-ounce mixing glass break a fresh egg, add half ounce vanilla syrup, half strawberry syrup, two or three dashes of solution of acid phosphate, half teaspoonful of malted milk, and fill the glass to

within two inches of the top with sweet milk. Shake well, strain and toss, then add carbonated water to fill the glass and finally sprinkle with ground nutmeg. Price, 15 cents.

NORTH POLE SHAKE

White and yolk of 1 egg	
Lemon syrup	½ ounce
Orange syrup	½ ounce
Raspberry syrup	½ ounce
Fresh cream	½ ounce
Shaved ice	1 tumblerful

Shake well in milk shaker, then add carbonated water to fill glass. Stir and serve with straws.

MERRY WIDOW

Grape syrup	1 ounce
Orgeat syrup	1 ounce
Sweet cream	1 ounce
One egg	

Place in glass, add a little ice, shake, fill with milk and strain. Price—12 ounces, 15 cents.

BONNIE BELLE

Pineapple	¾ ounce
Vanilla syrup	¾ ounce
Ice cream	2 ounces
Cracked ice	¼ glassful
Egg	1

Shake, strain, toss and serve. Charge 15 cents.

ROYAL SHAKE WITH EGG

Break one egg in mixing glass and add:

Catawba syrup	1 ounce
Vanilla syrup	1 ounce
Strawberry syrup ...	½ ounce
Plain cream	2 ounces

Shake well with ice; use milk and serve in bell glass. Charge 15 cents.

NAVY EGG SHAKE

Into a 14-ounce glass draw two to two and a half ounces of strawberry syrup. Into this break two eggs and add a few dashes of Jamaica ginger, one to two ounces of sweet cream, and a little fine shaved ice. Shake thoroughly and fill with carbonated water, using fine stream mostly. Strain into a clean glass and serve. May be topped with spice, if desired. The carbonated water should be added to the syrup and eggs in the shaker and from the shaker strained into the serving glass. Price—12-ounce glass, 20 cents.

EGG BIRCH

Birch syrup	1½ fluid ounces
Egg	1

Place in shaker, fill with milk, shake, and strain into a 12-ounce glass. Charge 15 cents.

MAY TONIC

Yolk of egg......... 1
Sarsaparilla syrup ... 2   ounces
Milk .... ½ glass

Shake and strain. Fill with broad stream. (S. S. Jones.)

SIZZLER SHAKE

Sarsaparilla syrup .... 2 ounces
Angostura bitters ..... 1 dram
Egg 1
Shaved ice .... 2 ounces

Prepare and serve as other egg shakes, using fine and coarse streams. Price—12 ounces, 10 cents.

FLORAL CREAM

Syrup of fragrant
  flower .... 1½ ounces
Cream 4   ounces
White of one egg

Mix. Violet syrup and rose syrup are best adapted for this composition, the cream being named accordingly.

MARSHMALLOW EGG SHAKE

Marshmallow syrup.... 1 ounce
Ice cream .... 1 ounce
Egg 1

Shake together in a shaker, or glass, and strain into a 12-ounce glass, nearly filling the latter with carbonated water, coarse stream, and "finish" with the fine stream. The use of milk improves this shake.

BEST BRACER

Mint syrup 1   ounce
Lemon syrup ...... ½ ounce
Pineapple syrup 1   ounce
Egg 1

Add carbonated water, shake and strain into a 12-ounce glass, then add two dashes of acid phosphate.

TEMPTRESS EGG SHAKE

Catawba .... 2 ounces
White of 1 egg
Shaved ice

Fill with milk and shake thoroughly. Top off with whipped cream and serve with a spoon. Charge 15 cents.

CUPID'S DREAM

Egg 1
Champagne syrup ... 1   ounce
Catawba syrup ..... ½ ounce
Lactart 1   dash
Cracked ice .... ½ tumblerful

Shake well and fill with carbonated water, both fine and coarse streams. Pour from tumbler to shaker and strain and serve with grated nutmeg.

HEAP OF COMFORT

Into a 12-ounce glass one-fourth full of cracked ice, break one egg and add one teaspoonful of malted milk, half ounce of clam bouillon, and 1 ounce of hock syrup. Shake well, strain, add a dash of solution of acid phosphate, and fill with soda water. Pour from shaker to tumbler, top off with nutmeg and serve with straws.

YAMA

Shaved ice as usual, a small quantity of ginger syrup, a few drops of cognac and one whole egg; shake well and fill up with apollinaris.

EGG CALISAYA

White and yolk of 1
  egg
Cracked or shaved ice ½ tumblerful
Elixir calisaya 3   dashes
Lemon syrup ...... 1¼ ounces

Shake well, strain, and add carbonated water, first coarse, then fine, stream. Pour from tumbler to shaker alternately several times, and grate nutmeg on top and serve. Price—12-ounce glass, 10 cents.

---

(5) Specialty Beverages

Here are included those drinks of a standard proprietary nature and medicinal value.

Many progressive dispensers have come out as flatly against the serving of medicines at the fountains. Others in charge of large and successful establishments have been equally positive in their defence of the sale of certain preparations of this nature.

There is room for argument on both sides and the individual fountain owner or manager must, in each case, decide what he had best do.

Those who do not consider that medicinal drinks have any place on the fountain menu point out that taking medicine is never a pleasant thing and that the sight of a person taking medicine may take the keen edge off one's appetite. The contortions of a man struggling with a dose of castor oil, for example, would not tend to increase the gustatory delight of a young lady eating a sundae. But notwithstanding these possible objections, there are many fountains which do no inconsiderable business in "bracers," "headache cures," "salts," etc.

Mineral waters and specialty beverages like kumyss are standard fountain products throughout the trade and no objections can be advanced against their sale.

SPECIALTY BEVERAGES

GINGER ALE

The ale is more brilliant if the syrup is used on the day it is made.

To make a temporary filter, take a large tub, perfectly clean and sweet, having a faucet at the bottom, over the top of the tub stretch a clean, wet, cotton cloth, firmly secured in position by a cord around the outside of the tub, press the cloth down in the center firmly with the hand, and lay on it a large No. 80 size filter paper. With a long-handled dipper or ladle pour the mixture on the center of the filter until it is full. Draw from the tub the first run, and if not clear, return it to the mixture, and again pass through the filter.

The filter when set can be used for several lots.

The filter tub should be scalded after use to keep it sweet.

Tin-lined copper tanks are preferable to tubs for mixing and filtering.

Acid and color must not be added until after filtering.

The best way to use color is to mix a pint of color and a pint of hot water, and filter. Use one-fourth ounce to the gallon.

Fruit acid is made as follows:

Citric acid .... 4 ounces
Boiling water .... 8 ounces

Dissolve thoroughly, and strain through a flannel cloth. Keep the acid solution in a glass or stone bottle or jug, well corked. Prepare in small quantities, as the solution will deteriorate if kept too long.

The same ginger ale does not suit all localities. To make the beverage stronger use more extract; if sweeter, use more sugar; if dryer, use more acid. Stick to the method of manipulation. The quality depends to a great degree on the method.

GINGER ALE (TO CHARGE IN FOUNTAIN)

Place in a suitable fountain 1½ gallons of any ginger ale syrup and water enough to make 10 gallons, and charge with gas to a pressure of 100 pounds. To be drawn from the apparatus in the manner of soda water, but without syrup.

The beverage can be dispensed more readily from a beer pitcher (made to draw from the bottom) by use of which the tumbler is partially filled with solid beverage, and the remainder drawn directly into the tumbler.

HOP BEER

Hops 6   ounces
Ginger, bruised 1   ounce
Molasses .. .. ½ gallon
Water .... sufficient

Pour 1 gallon water on the mixed hops and ginger, heat to boiling and boil for half an hour, strain and add water through the strainer to make the liquid measure one gallon. To the latter add the molasses, about half pound of bread which has previously been well browned, dried and reduced to a coarse powder, and a pint of brewer's yeast or a cake of compressed yeast. Put the whole in a warm place until fermentation ceases, then draw off the clear liquid, put into bottles or a jug or a keg, and keep in a cool place.

HOP BEER

Burdock root, bruised 8   ounces
Essence of sassafras.. 2   fluid drams
Hops .... 1½ ounces
Corn meal, roasted
   brown 4   ounces
Molasses and water,
   of each .... sufficient

Boil the hops, corn and burdock (if latter is used) with 1½ gallons of water for half an hour, strain and add enough water through strainer to make 1½ gallons, add the molasses (and essence), using enough of the latter to make the mixture palatable but not too sweet, add the yeast, and ferment like the preceding.

OLD FASHIONED GINGER POP

Boil 2 ounces of best white Jamaica ginger, bruised, in 6 quarts of soft water; strain and add 1 ounce of cream tartar and 1 pound of sugar. Put on the fire and stir until the sugar is dissolved, then pour into an earthen jar and add 2 drams of tartaric acid and the grated rind of one lemon. Let cool down to the surrounding temperature, add 1 ounce of fresh yeast, stir well and bottle at once, tying the corks down firmly. The "pop" will be ready for use in two or three days if the weather is warm, or if kept in a warm place.

OLD FASHIONED GINGER BEER

Boiling water	2 gallons
Sugar	2 pounds
Cream of tartar	2 ounces
Ginger root	2 ounces
Lemon (sliced)	1 ounce

Let the ingredients stand until lukewarm, then put into a stone jar, add a large slice of stale bread and two cakes of compressed yeast. Allow to remain over-night in a warm place. Strain and bottle, filling bottles only two-thirds full and fasten corks. Bottles with patent corks are best. In from three to four days the ginger pop will be ready for use.

KUMYSS

"Kumyss" is a liquor originally prepared by the Tartars from the milk of mares, but recently imitated with cow's milk to a great extent. It is said to be prepared in Tartary by putting the mare's milk in a tall vessel, while warm adding kumyss, 1 part for every 10 of milk, stirring thoroughly every few minutes, and in three or four hours taking out and bottling in champagne bottles. The National Formulary contains a formula for kumyss which may be recommended.

Another formula contributed to *The Pharmaceutical Era* some years ago is as follows:

Fresh milk	12	ounces
Water	4	ounces
Brown sugar	2½	drams
Compressed yeast	24	grains
Milk sugar	3	drams

Dissolve the milk sugar in the water, add to the milk, rub the yeast and brown sugar down in a mortar with a little of the mixture, then strain into the other portion.

In the manufacture of kumyss strong bottles should be used, champagne bottles being the best. The corks should fit very tightly; in fact, it is almost necessary that a bottling machine should be employed for the purpose, and once the cork is properly fixed it should be wired down. Many failures have been reported because the corks did not fit properly, the result being that the carbonic gas escaped as formed, leaving a worthless preparation. It is further necessary to keep the preparation at a moderate temperature, and to insure the article being properly finished. The bottles are to be gently shaken each day for about 10 minutes to prevent the clotting of the casein. It is well to take the precaution of rolling a cloth around the bottle during the shaking process, as the amount of gas generated is great, and should the bottle be of thin glass or contain a flaw it

may give way. Some few days elapse before the fermentation passes into the acid stage, and when this has taken place the preparation is much thicker. When this stage is reached the kumyss is ready to be used.

KUMYSS (RUSSIAN)

Sweet milk	7	fluid ounces
Yeast (see below)	1	fluid ounce
Water	4	fluid ounces
Sugar	½	ounce

Take 1 cake of yeast and dissolve in 1 pint of water. Take 1 ounce of the solution, place in a bottle with the other ingredients, cork tight and tie with string, sealing top of bottle with wax. Keep in temperature of 75 to 80 degrees until it separates, which takes 4 to 8 hours. Then shake bottle well and put in ice box for 48 hours, when it is ready for use. It may be sold at 10 or 15 cents and can be called Russian or Turkish Kumyss.

ANTI-BRAIN STORM

Wine of pepsin, N.F.	8 fluid ounces
Comp. elixir celery, N.F.	6 fluid ounces
Syrup of orange, fresh	32 fluid ounces
Syrup of raspberry	16 fluid ounces
Syrup of pineapple	8 fluid ounces

Mix, place 2 ounces in a glass one-third full of shaved ice and fill with carbonated water. Charge 5 cents.

ROYAL GRAPE

One ounce grape syrup, 2 ounces grape juice, sufficient carbonated water to fill glass. Price, 5 cents for 8-ounce glass.

PINEAPPLE TONIC

Pineapple syrup	6 ounces
Elixir of Lactated Pepsin	4 ounces
Syrup, to make	1 quart

Good, healthful stomach drink. Dispense 1½ ounces in an 8-ounce glass, fill with soda, and charge 5 cents.

PEP-PHO

Make a syrup of 60 grains pure pepsin, 1 dram of solution acid phosphates, 2 ounces water, 1 pint vanilla syrup, and raspberry syrup enough to make 2 pints. Dissolve the pepsin in the acid solution mixed with the water and add the remaining ingredients. Serve 1½ ounces in an 8-ounce glass and charge 5 cents.

LIME JUICE AND PEPSIN

To half gallon of lime syrup add 8 ounces of essence of pepsin and mix thoroughly. This may also be served by adding a few dashes of lime juice to any pepsin syrup. It is a fine after-dinner drink and thought by some to be much preferable to plain pepsin as a digestant. Serve 1½ ounces in an 8-ounce glass. Charge 5 cents.

CHERRY PEP

Tame cherry syrup....21 ounces
Concentrated syrup ...11 ounces
Essence pepsin ......40 drops
Simple syrup, to make.. 1 gallon
Dispense 1½ ounces in an 8-ounce glass, fill with soda and charge 5 cents.

MILK AND SELTZER

In serving this drink, which is strictly "temperance," half fill the glass with seltzer water, and the rest with milk. This order of procedure is necessary to avoid the excessive formation of foam, which would cause delay in serving. Use a medium-sized glass (10-ounce). Charge 5 cents.

MINERAL MILK

Draw 6 ounces plain carbonated water into 8-ounce tumbler; fill with plain sweet cream; stir and serve.

ARTIFICIAL KISSENGEN

Potassium chloride ... 160 grains
Sodium chloride ....3390 grains
Magnesium sulphate
(anhydrous) ..... 560 grains
Sodium bicarbonate ..1015 grains
Mix intimately by trituration, and dissolve in—

Pure water, gradually
added .... 10 gallons
Filter and charge to 100 pounds pressure.

The above is a standard formula, but the soda man may find it better to buy his salts already prepared by a reliable drug house; not so expensive and better results obtained. Carbonation at 150 pounds pressure may give a more satisfactory product than at 100 pounds.

BROMO-FRUIT

Bromo seltzer .... a dose
Fruit (any flavor) syrup ½ ounce
Use 2 glasses to mix.

CASTOR OIL—TO SERVE

One small ounce concentrated sarsaparilla syrup, 1 ounce castor oil. Fill glass with carbonated water and serve.

Use fine stream on inside of glass first, then add the sarsaparilla syrup and next the oil. Fill glass two-thirds full with fine stream, directed to center of contents. Drink at once.

Orangeade is another good flavor to disguise the taste of castor oil.

---

(6) Mixed Fancy Drinks

The formulas following cover a lot of miscellaneous drinks, the number of which is not large enough to warrant a division into sections of their own.

A number of the formulas in this department are in the nature of a "glorified soda"—that is, they are of the ice cream soda types in method of mixing and serving, but by the combination of various flavors, fruits, and unusual syrup combinations employed, they graduate out of the staple into the fancy class.

Others in this section are specialty drinks pure and simple, and some of these are deserving of special attention.

The extra fancy ice cream soda possesses certain advertising advantages that one must not overlook. Everyone knows what an ice cream soda is, and the combination of cream, flavor, and charged water is so widely popular that with this fact known the appeal is already made. A fancy soda, therefore, starts with a certain handicap over a drink or delicacy whose composition cannot be guessed by the name.

In this connection it is interesting to note that many expert specialists print on their menus information showing the nature of the ingredients of their offerings. This gives the patron the clue, and avoids the disappointment that may arise in attempting to select a drink or dish by name only and then to discover it contains a flavor or fruit that is distasteful.

FANCY MIXED DRINKS

CHOCOLATE NOIR
Chocolate syrup 2   ounces
Plain milk .... ½ glass
Ice cream 3   spoonfuls
Mix in 12-ounce glass, fill with coarse stream and serve with spoon. Price—10 cents.

CHOCOLATE MINT
Chocolate syrup, 2 ounces, sprig of mint. Crush the mint against side of glass. Add ice cream and fill glass with coarse and fine stream. Price 10 cents.

FROSTED CHOCOLATE
Place 2 ounces of chocolate syrup and 2 ounces of cream in a glass, and half fill with carbonated water. Add 1 ounce of vanilla ice cream, then fill the glass with carbonated water. Top off with whipped cream. Sells for 15 cents.

FROZEN CHOCOLATE
This is an easily made and a satisfactory chocolate beverage. Shake together 1½ ounces of chocolate syrup and 2 ounces light, sweet cream, or rich milk, with 2 ounces of shaved ice, then add carbonated water to fill a 12-ounce glass. Charge 10 cents.

KOKO CREME
For each glass of soda water mix equal parts of chocolate and vanilla syrups and add one tablespoonful of cream. The syrups should be made as follows:
Vanilla—Plain syrup, 1 gallon; extract of vanilla, 4 ounces   Mix.
Chocolate—Powdered chocolate, 8 ounces; granulated sugar, 8 pounds; water, 5 pints. Heat the water to the boiling point, then add 7 pounds of sugar and dissolve. To this solution add the powdered chocolate, previously triturated with the remainder of the sugar. Boil for 10 minutes, stirring constantly with a wooden spoon or paddle, then pass through a wire milk strainer. Chocolate syrup prepared in this manner meets all the requirements for soda fountain use. The flavor is well developed. The syrup is smooth and of proper density, and in warm weather will keep for one week. It should be kept in quart bottles, tightly corked, and shaken when dispensed. (Chas. R. Rhodes.)

PING PONG
Make an emulsion of 1 ounce of cocoanut oil in 3 ounces of mucilage of acacia; add gradually 3 pints of heavy foam syrup and 1 pint of chocolate syrup. Heavy foam syrup is made as follows: Dissolve 1 gallon of water and 1 ounce of gelatin and 12 pounds of sugar. This drink should be very cold and should contain a generous quantity of ice cream.

MIXED FRUITS
Vanilla syrup 1   ounce
Cream .... ½ ounce
Carbonated   water,
fine stream .... ½ glass
Add 2 tablespoonfuls of the mixed fruit, finely cut and thoroughly saturated with simple syrup. Serve with spoon and straws.

TUTTI-FRUTTI
Take small amount of each fruit in season, cut very fine into a dish, adding enough syrup to cover, and let stand for several hours. In serving put 2 tablespoonfuls of the mixture into a 12-ounce glass, add ice cream and carbonated water as in other crushed fruit drinks. Price, 10 cents.

FROU-FROU
Fruit nectar syrup.. 1   ounce
Peach ice cream.... 2   ounces
Fill glass two-thirds with carbonated water, add a small amount of shredded pineapple, and top with whipped cream. Price, 10 or 15 cents.

PANAMA
Strawberry syrup ... 1 fluid ounce
Vanilla syrup ...... 1 fluid ounce
Ice cream .... 1 spoonful
Place the ice cream in a 12-ounce glass, add the syrup and fill with carbonated water.

NEW YORK BEAUTY
Strawberry syrup ... 1   ounce
Plain syrup 1   ounce
Ice cream .... 1½ ounces
Mix in 12-ounce glass and fill with carbonated water, fine stream.

ALLEE SAMEE
Strawberry syrup ... ¾ ounce
Vanilla syrup .... ¾ ounce
Rich cream .... ½ ounce
Powdered sugar ... 1   teaspoonful
Place in a glass and mix with fine stream carbonated water, filling the glass with coarse stream.

STRAWBERRY SODA DE LUXE
Mix 2 ounces of fresh strawberries with an equal weight of powdered sugar and allow to stand all night; in the morning crush the fruit, and use with a No. 12 disherful of ice cream in a large soda glass. Now take an egg, and whip it in a machine to a foamy froth, which add to the fruit and cream mixture, and fill the glass with carbonated water. Top with whipped cream. Sells for 20 cents. The author classes this beverage with the "sodas." Made up in larger quantities than called for in this formula a better flavor may be produced.

LADIES' CHOICE

Raspberry syrup ..... 2 ounces
Sweet cream .... 2 ounces
Peach ice cream..... 2 spoonfuls
Serve with 12-ounce glass like any soda drink with coarse and fine streams of carbonated water. Charge 10 cents.

ALMOND SPONGE

One large spoonful plain ice cream, 1 ounce orgeat syrup. Draw into 12-ounce glass, fill with carbonated water, coarse stream, top with whipped cream and serve with a spoon. This may also be prepared by drawing the same amount of the syrup into a mixing glass, adding a little strawberry syrup, half filling the glass with ice, then filling with milk, shaking thoroughly, straining into a 12-ounce glass, holding the shaker high so as to have a nice foam on the drink, and sprinkling on powdered nutmeg. Price—10 cents.

MAPLE FROSTBITE

Maple syrup ...... 1 ounce
Vanilla syrup ..... ½ ounce
Shaved ice .... ½ glassful
Rub the rim of a tall frappe glass with a piece of orange and dip the rim of the glass into powdered sugar, which will adhere to it. Shake the syrup and ice, using a heavy glass and a shaker, pour carefully into the frappe glass so as not to wash off the crusting sugar, and fill to about half an inch of the top with plain soda. Add a slice of orange. Serve with paper napkin and straws. Price—10 cents.

ROOT BEER CREAM FLOAT

Fill 12-ounce glass within an inch of the top with root beer, then float on top with spoon about 2 ounces plain, sweet, rich cream. The Cream Float serves well as a novelty and should be priced at 10 cents.

SOUTHERN SARSAPARILLA

Essence sarsaparilla ... 4 drams
Burnt sugar .... 2 drams
Soda foam .... 2 drams
Syrup enough to make..64 ounces
The essence is made as follows·
Oil of wintergreen.... 1 ounce
Oil of sassafras....... 1 ounce
Alcohol enough to make 16 ounces
To serve, dispense 1½ ounces in a 10-ounce glass and fill with soda.

CREAM PUFF

One-half ounce of ice cream beat up with 1 ounce of orange syrup; then fill the glass with carbonated water, fine stream. An ounce of ice cream is then put in around the top of the glass by using a silver tablespoon. This piles the thick creamy soda up in center. Price—10 cents.

---

(7) Hot Drinks

Hot drinks, originally introduced to increase the financial returns during the slacker trade of the winter months, particularly before the egg drinks and the shakes became so popular, were undoubtedly the forerunner of the modern luncheonette department. In a way, they may be considered the stepping stone to this more recent development, but because one serves hot drinks it does not of necessity mean that he will turn his attention later to the more elaborate lunch service. It is an axiom that any fountain which is open the year round should serve hot drinks during the cold months. Such drinks are trade winners and they are money makers.

THE SODA FOUNTAIN has summed up the gist of hot soda success in the following rules that dispensers will find a thoroughly dependable guide:

1.—Have all drinks piping hot.

2.—Serve hot beverages in perfectly clean, unchipped cups or mugs. A woman prefers a cup and saucer any day. The saucer protects her gloves and clothes, affords a rest for the spoon, and is generally more attractive

3.—Keep spoons in a covered glass dish on the fountain. Have this dish bear the words, "These spoons have been sterilized since being used," and see to it that they are. Keep on hand a sufficient spoon supply to permit this precaution.

4.—Do not allow any hot beverage to be served which is a watery, flavorless, insipid decoction. It will kill your trade. Hold each dispenser up to a certain standard in the serving of every hot drink.

5—Insist on counters and tables being kept clean—that means so clean that a damp, spotless linen cloth will find no dirt to remove.

6.—See that salt, pepper, and spice shakers are filled and sift freely.

7.—Use the decorated hot soda sets, which are the cup and china tray, where crackers or simple sandwiches are to be served.

8.—Maintain a varied menu so that all tastes may be pleased.

9.—Sweeten hot beverages moderately. Too sweet ones cloy, while more sugar is easily added.

10.—In using malted milk powder, bouillon cubes, beef extract, or other ingredients necessary to dissolve in hot water, see to it that every particle is dissolved. Gummy particles floating on the top or sticking to the china cup, are disgusting. Very hot water is necessary and sufficient manipulation. Neither should be stinted.

11.—Serve napkins with hot soda. Attractive paper ones may be purchased in quantities at negligible cost.

12.—Milk and cream must be absolutely fresh or the heat will cause curdling.

13.—Advertising strips, displays, or newspaper items should be changed almost daily so that the public eye may not become weary and indifferent.

14.—Menus become soiled more readily in winter than in summer. Never use a soiled menu.

15.—Hot chocolate should be cooked thoroughly. Too often it is insufficiently prepared and so has a grainy appearance.

16.—All meat extracts and bouillons should be tested each morning by the head dispenser lest some one of them is off flavor. This is fatal to the trade.

17.—Onion and celery salts are inexpensive and add much to make drinks distinctive in flavor.

18.—Never serve scorched syrups.

19.—Do not over-do the flavoring of any drink.

20.—Be exact in the preparation of syrups, flavor blends, and finished drinks. Only in this way can uniformity be gained.

21.—Never serve a syrup which has begun to ferment. It is a mistaken idea to think this is an economy.

22.—A cold cup or mug will cool a hot drink. Have dishes clean and warm.

23.—If a customer finds fault with a drink, rectify the trouble or give him another without dispute.

24.—Keep wafers, sandwiches, etc., in covered glass jars.

25.—Never permit soiled dishes to remain on a counter or table an instant after the customer has left.

26.—Obtain the catalogues of the leading houses manufacturing hot soda supplies, and do not neglect the advertisements in your favorite trade journal. These are the printed market-places which will travel willingly to your side. What they have to offer is worth finding out. The other man is going to do it and you canot afford to be left behind.

27.—There is no time when hot top dressings are more popular for sundaes or for finishing a hot drink, than in the winter.

28.—A fudge warmer with three compartments will keep the top dressings at just the right temperature to serve.

29.—Purchase only the best of materials, prepare them properly, and serve them right.

30.—Introduce something new from time to time. Variety is the spice of business.

31.—Chili-con-carne bowls, sanitary paper cups served upon request, a new broth, an electric toaster or grill, are inexpensive additions which will attract attention.

32.—Plan early, keep your eye on all the details, balance outgo and income, serve the best, serve it in the most approved way, advertise your service persistently and honestly, and there is no reason why you should not make good money in the hot soda business.

HOT SODA

HOT BRACER

Shaved ice .... ½ glass
Angostura bitters ... 5 dashes
Elixir calisaya ..... 2 dashes
Curacoa cordial .... 4 dashes
Compound tincture
gentian .... 2 dashes
Cherry malt ...... 1 ounce
Phosphate syrup

Shake well and add soda to fill mug. Salt to season. Serve with wafers and celery. The Hot Bracer may be made up as a stock syrup, using 1½ ounces per service. (Geo. A. Zahn.)

HOT BEEF TEA

First make an extract by taking 6 ounces extract of beef, 16 ounces hot water, 5 drams tincture of black pepper. Dissolve the beef extract in the hot water and add the tincture of black pepper. To make the tincture of black pepper, take 2 ounces of whole black pepper, crush it, add 10 ounces alcohol. Steep and filter. To dispense, take 1 ounce of the beef tea extract, dash of cream, dash of salt, and dash of celery salt, and place in mug. Fill up with hot water, stirring with a spoon while filling. Place the salt, pepper and celery salt convenient to the customer, should he wish more of the seasoning.

HOT BEEF TEA

Put half a teaspoonful of beef extract into a cup, fill the cup with hot water, stir well, and add salt and pepper to suit.

HOT BOVILINE

One ounce extract of beef and 2 ounces cream. Add hot water and serve with pepper and salt.

JERSEY CITY BOUILLON

Take 10 hot soda serving cups and fill them to the brim with water. The ensuing shrinkage will make just 10 ordinary services of bouillon. Pour the water over one pound of chopped beef, the best you can get. Add two spoonfuls of salt, stir and let stand over night. Do not heat during this period. In the morning place over a slow fire, but do not bring to a boil. Boiling keeps the meat juices in by coagulating the tissues. Slow heating permits the water to pass through.

CHICKEN BOUILLON

Two ounces concentrated chicken and half ounce sweet cream. Stir while adding hot water, after seasoning with a little spice. Price, 10 cents.

RICE CHICKEN BOUILLON

First make a good chicken soup as follows: Take one average sized chicken (not a young or spring chicken), cut into small pieces and add two gallons of cold water, put on a slow fire and cook until the chicken is tender. Strain the liquid and after seasoning to suit the taste, put into the urn and keep piping hot. Now take the chicken meat, cut it into cubes and set aside in a handy place on fountain. This will keep well if placed between damp cloths. Boil or steam a small quantity of rice, which also keep in a handy place on the fountain. In serving place a tablespoonful of rice in a bouillon cup, add a few dice of chicken meat, a very small piece of butter, and then draw on this the chicken bouillon which, if kept inside the urn, will be good and hot. With each cup serve a few nice crisp crackers.

The author states that "it is no trouble to get 15 cents for this bouillon, which should not be served in anything but a good china cup. Throw out the old broken cups and saucers and buy some good china. (H. R. Rowe.)

HOT MOCK TURTLE BOUILLON

Make an extract of mock turtle by taking:

Extract of beef....... 2 ounces
Concentrated chicken.. 2 ounces
Clam juice .... 8 ounces
Hot water .... 3 pints
Tincture black pepper. 1 ounce
Essence of celery..... 3 drams
Essence of orange peel 1 dram

Mix and dissolve thoroughly. To dispense, take 2 ounces of the mock turtle extract and half ounce sweet cream. Stir while adding the hot water. Serve with spices.

MOCK TURTLE BROTH

Liebig's beef extract. 1 ounce
Armour's vigoral ... 1 ounce
Barley, oatmeal or
starch .... ½ ounce
Gelatin .... ¼ ounce
Tincture bitter orange
peel .... 3 drams
Tincture of capsi-
cum ....18 drops
Lime juice .... 3 drams
Worcestershire sauce 3 drams
Salt .... ¾ ounce
Hot water to make..16 ounces

Make a thin paste from the starch or other material; swell the gelatin in cold water; dissolve the beef extract in hot water with the salt; add to the hot mixture the starch paste and softened gelatin and bring all to a boil; strain through a wire strainer; add the flavoring and hot water to finish. Use 1½ ounces of the mixture to a mug.

CLAM BOUILLON

Be sure the clams are absolutely fresh; pick them over carefully and throw out all which are not plainly alive. Then wash thoroughly in cold water and scrub the shells with a clean brush until they are absolutely clean. Put a peck of clams in a kettle with two quarts of cold water, and steam until the shells open wide. Strain the liquor, allow it to cool and then clear as usual. The clam meats can be used in any manner desired.

CLAM BOUILLON

As many people are unable to obtain clams in the shell the following recipe is given for bulk clams:

Take two quarts of solid clam meat. With a sharp knife cut off the tough black head, and separate the soft parts from the remainder of the tough portion. Chop both fine but keep separate. To the tough portions—not the black tips—add two quarts of water, a tablespoonful of salt, two stalks of celery cut fine and a dash of cayenne pepper. Simmer slowly for one hour. Then add the soft parts of the clams, previously chopped, and simmer another hour to extract all the juices. Bring to the boiling point and boil briskly for a few minutes. Then cover and place on the back part of the stove and allow it to stand for a while. Strain through clean cheesecloth doubled. Return the contents of the strainer to the kettle and add two quarts of white stock, two quarts of cold water, and the clam liquor strained previously from the clams. Bring to the boiling point again and then strain. It is now ready to serve.

CLAMCEL

Clam juice, 1½ fluid ounces; add about half a teaspoonful of celery extract and a small quantity of mixed spices, seasoning to taste; fill mug with hot water and serve.

HOT CLAM CREAM

Concentrated clam
 juice, any good
 brand .... 1½ ounces
Hot milk 2   ounces
Hot water 4   ounces
Serve in a fine china cup and add a pinch of salt and a little white pepper.

Clam juice should be transferred to a glass or porcelain container immediately on opening the can.

HOT CLAM JUICE

Clam juice may be served in the proportion of two ounces to an eight-ounce mug, filling the latter with hot water and serving with a spoon; also giving the patron celery salt, salt and pepper cellars and soda crackers. The clam juice is served more acceptably by adding an ounce of milk, better yet by using half water and half milk, and still better by using all hot milk. A small amount of butter causes a marked improvement. Clam juice, like beef tea, must always be served hot. It spoils very readily and must be kept on ice. If a distinction is desired between clam bouillon and clam broth, the latter may be served with a spoonful of butter and the former without it. A fine way to make a distinction is to apply the name "clam juice" to a mixture of clam juice with hot water, "clam bouillon" to a similar mixture with a dash of lemon juice added, and "clam broth" to clam juice mixed with cream or milk. Clam juice with hot water and seasoned well may be known as "clam night cap." "Clam juice cocktail" is made with two ounces of clam juice, two drams of lemon juice and hot water.

SELECT OYSTER BOUILLON

In an 8-ounce bouillon cup put 1 select oyster of medium size and add 1½ ounces of hot water. Then with an oyster fork crush the oyster into small bits until nothing but the skin and hard parts remain. Remove the largest pieces and add 1 ounce of concentrated clam juice, 1 small ladleful of unsweetened whipped cream. Fill the cup with hot water and season with salt, pepper and celery salt. In this formula concentrated oyster juice is not used. Price, 10 cents. (H. Wendell.)

HOT OYSTER JUICE

Fresh juice or liquid
 taken from the top
 of a quantity of
 oysters 1   ounce
Sweet cream 1   tablespoonful
Fill the mug with hot water and add a small piece of fresh butter and season with salt and pepper. (Geo. A. Zahn.)

OYSTER SPICED

Six oysters
Clam juice 1   ounce
Fill mug with hot water and flavor with salt, pepper or other spices.

CREME TOMATO BOUILLON

First obtain regular tomato bouillon of your choice, there are a number of good ones on the market, or make one like the following:

Tomatoes .... 1 can
Maggi beef .... 1 teaspoonful
Cayenne pepper .... ¼ ounce
Cloves .... 1 ounce
Bay leaves .... 1 ounce
Extract of celery... a few drops
Worcestershire sauce. season to suit

Strain the above through a fine sieve, bring to a boil, and strain through cheesecloth. Add to this 1½ quarts of water, and the mixture is ready to use. A little sodium bicarbonate will prevent curdling.

Use 1 to 2 ounces to the regular bouillon cup; to this add a teaspoonful of whipped cream, 1 teaspoonful powdered cracker dust, season to suit and serve with long thin crisp crackers. If you have an urn with a top, keep your crackers in it and you will be able to serve hot crisp crackers at all times.

The author says that "broken crackers should never be served at the fountain, and as they are too good to throw away just run them through the fine plate of the food chopper and you will have the very best cracker dust to use for cream tomato bouillon. This drink sells for 10 cents and is very quickly and easily made. Try it and see how soon the trade will take notice." (H. R. Rowe.)

HOT CREAM TOMATO BOUILLON

Into a small cooker put one can of any good brand of tomato soup, one bottle of catsup, one-fourth ounce of cayenne pepper, a piece of butter the size of an egg, and season with salt and pepper. Lastly, put in one-fourth of an ounce of fluid extract of celery seed and bring the mixture to a boil. The addition of the celery gives the cocktail a delicious and characteristic flavor. Strain the mixture and it is ready to serve.

HOT TOMATO BISQUE

Usual amount of tomato extract, spoonful malted milk, little cream, hot water.

RICE TOMATO BOUILLON

First boil a small quantity of rice and keep it in a convenient place on the fountain. Put the regular amount of prepared tomato in a bouillon cup, add a teaspoonful of the rice, fill the cup with hot water, season to suit, and serve with an olive, a small piece of celery and a couple of saltine wafers. Price, 10 or 15 cents.

TOMATO BOUILLON

Use 1 ounce tomato bouillon (any good brand) in a 7-ounce cup of hot water, season with celery salt and serve. By adding a small amount of rich, sweet cream you have "tomato puree."

TOMATO BOUILLON

Tomatoes .... 1 quart
Arrowroot .... 2 ounces
Extract of beef..... 1 ounce
Bay leaves .... ½ ounce
Cloves .... ½ ounce
Red pepper .... ¼ ounce
Worcestershire sauce, to flavor

Remove the seeds from the tomatoes by rubbing through a strainer; add the other ingredients and half gallon of hot water; bring to a boil and strain.

PUREE OF TOMATO

Pour 2 ounces of tomato soup into a cup, add half ounce of sweet cream, fill with boiling water, and season with salt, pepper and celery salt.

HOT CELERY BOUILLON

Clam juice .... ¼ ounce
Beef extract ...... ¼ ounce
Cream .... 1 ounce
Essence of celery... 4 dashes

Stir while adding hot water. Serve with spices.

HOT CELERY WITH CREAM

To one teaspoonful of beef extract add one ounce of sweet cream and season with extract of celery. Celery salt may be used if desired. Serve in an eight-ounce mug, filling same with hot water. Serve with salted wafers. (George A. Zahn.)

DELMONICO NOGG

Extract of beef ..... 1 ounce or less
Cream .... 1 ounce
Extract of celery... 1 dram
Egg 1

Beat egg up with the cream. Mix thoroughly with mixing spoon and stir while adding the hot water. Top off with grated cinnamon. Price—Eight or 10-ounce mug, 10 cents.

HOT LACTATED BEEF

Aromatic extract of
beef .... 1 teaspoonful
Fresh cream .... 1 teaspoonful
Extract of celery..... 1 dash
Hot water .... 1 cupful

Season with pepper and salt.

HOT STUFF

Beef extract .... ½ teaspoonful
Clam bouillon ..... 1 teaspoonful
Sweet cream .... 1 tablespoonful
Port wine .... 1 teaspoonful

Place in mug which fill with boiling water. Serve with salt, pepper and celery salt.

ROASTER

Use 1 ounce beef bouillon in cup of hot water; season with salt, pepper and celery salt; add 1 dash sherry wine; top with whipped cream.

WALL STREET'S HOT FAVORITE

Liquid beef extract..	1	ounce
Egg	1	
Essence of celery ...	1	dash
Cream	1	ounce

Beat or stir the egg well with the cream; add the extract of beef and celery and fill the cup with hot water; serve with powdered nutmeg and cinnamon on the side. Charge 10 or 15 cents. (H. T. Schultz.)

DOUBLE B BOUILLON

Extract of beef....	½	ounce
Extract tomato bouillon	1	ounce

Place in cup, fill with hot milk and serve with graham wafers, salt and pepper. A bit of sodium bicarbonate will prevent curdling.

CURRIED BOUILLON

Extract of beef (any good kind)	4	drams
Salt	1	dram
Water	1	pint

Dissolve and mix; bottle the product and keep on ice. To dispense, pour 1 ounce into mug, add a pinch of curry, stir, and fill with hot water, again stirring before serving.

AROMATIC BEEF BOUILLON

Aromatic extract of beef, 1 teaspoonful; extract of celery and pepper, 10 drops; place in mug and fill with hot water.

BLIZZARD BREAKER

Extract of beef.....	1	teaspoonful
Tomato catsup	½	fluid ounce
Hot water	6	ounces

Season to taste.

HOT KLONDIKE

Clam juice	2	drams
Liquid beef	2	drams
Cream	1	ounce
Essence of celery.....	4	dashes
Extract of spices......	1	dash

Place all in cup and fill with hot water.

HOT PRIZE

Clam juice	2	ounces
Lemon juice	2	dashes
Celery salt		sufficient
Hot water	6	ounces

PICKLED CLAM BROTH

Ginger syrup	1	ounce
Cream	1	ounce
Clam bouillon	1	ounce

Fill mug with hot water and add a dash of celery salt.

TOMATO CLAM BROTH

Clam juice	1	ounce
Tomato catsup	¼	ounce
Butter	¼	ounce
Cream		dash

Add hot water, stirring well, and serve with spices.

HOT CHOCOLATE

Take one heaping teaspoonful of rich chocolate powder, dissolve it in a little hot water, then fill the cup with hot milk and top off with whipped cream. Serve with saltines or flake wafers.

FINISHED HOT CHOCOLATE

To be served from a hot apparatus having large cans. Two quarts water, 2 pounds sugar, 1 quart milk, 1 pound powdered chocolate, or 1 quart cream chocolate. Put the water into a can over a slow fire, let it come almost to a boil, add the chocolate, milk and sugar, and simmer for five minutes; pour into the urn and keep it·hot. To serve, draw this chocolate into cup, add more sugar if desired, and top with whipped cream. Charge 10 cents.

HASTY HOT CHOCOLATE

This syrup is quickly and easily prepared. Take 16 ounces of powdered cocoa (any good brand), five pints of water, six pounds of granulated sugar and one-half ounce of vanilla extract. Reduce the cocoa to a smooth paste with a little warm water. Place the water over the fire in a suitable container and when it reaches the boiling point add the cocoa paste. Allow to boil for five minutes, stirring carefully meanwhile to prevent burning. Then strain and add the vanilla extract. This is a practical formula and has been used with success

HOT CHOCOLATE

Sugar	4	pounds
Cocoa	2	pounds
Water	2	gallons
Milk	3	gallons

This formula makes about 6½ gallons of hot chocolate.

HOT CHOCOLATE

This formula makes "a good hot chocolate":

Cocoa	3	pounds
Sugar	10	pounds
Water	8	quarts
Vanilla	1	ounce

To the above chocolate stock add 25 quarts of milk. The formula may be cut and the milk added in proportion—approximately 10 quarts of milk to a gallon of stock. The formula as given makes close to two gallons of stock. Ten cents per cup is the proper price.

A "cheaper" formula, based upon the above, is as follows:

Cut the quantity of milk used in half and substitute in place thereof one-half condensed milk and one-half water. Cut the cocoa to 12 ounces. Add the remaining ingredients in the same proportion as above.

Hot Chocolate

Sugar	5	pounds
Cocoa	3½	pounds
Water	2	gallons
Milk	6	gallons

This formula was used for three and a half years with great success. It costs about 22 cents per gallon and makes up approximately 10 gallons.

Hot Chocolate

Cocoa (French)	1 pound
Sugar	3 pounds
Heavy cream	1 quart
Milk	11 quarts

This formula makes up nearly 3½ gallons and costs about 3 1/3 cents per cup. With the whipped cream, cakes, etc., the cost per cup is about 4½ cents. This is, of course, a 10-cent product. (F. V. Edmonds.)

Hot Chocolate

Cocoa	2½	pounds
Water	1	gallon
Condensed milk	4	quarts
Granulated sugar	4	pounds
Salt		sufficient

This hot chocolate should be served "straight" and not diluted. It may prove advantageous in this formula to reduce the amount of cocoa to two pounds.

Hot Chocolate

Cocoa	1 pound
Sugar	2 pounds

Mix thoroughly and keep in covered container. At time of serving put two teaspoonfuls of mixture in cup, fill with boiling water, stir thoroughly and serve with whipped cream. Evaporated milk or standard cream may be added. Ten cents should be the price for this hot chocolate.

Hot Chocolate

Boiling water	5	gallons
Cocoa	5	pounds
Salt	½	ounce
Milk	5	gallons
Sugar	20	pounds

This syrup may be served by adding hot milk or hot water, preferably the former—two ounces of the syrup to the cup. Charge 10 cents per service.

Hot Chocolate

Take of a good soluble cocoa, 3½ ounces; 2 pints water, 40 ounces granulated sugar, 4 drams vanilla extract. Heat the water to boiling, stir in the cocoa, gradually added; add the sugar, when latter is dissolved, strain and add the extract.

Hot Chocolate

Eight ounces chocolate, 4 ounces granulated sugar, 28 ounces boiling water, chocolate syrup enough to make a gallon. Select a rich brand of chocolate. Grate or scrape fine and triturate with the sugar; then in a large warm mortar form a paste by trituration, gradually adding 18 ounces of boiling water; transfer to a porcelain vessel, heat slowly, stirring well, gradually add the remainder of the water, bring to a boil and ·boil for five or six minutes, stirring constantly; stir for some time after removing from the fire, then bring to a boil again and boil for one minute. By this means separation of cacao butter is prevented, and the mixture does not require straining, but simply skimming. Add the syrup and flavor with vanilla extract or other flavoring. Care must be exercised to make a smooth paste in the beginning, and to avoid scorching at the last. A quantity of the chocolate may be kept on hand, in grated or scraped form, mixed with the proper amount of sugar. In serving use 1½ ounces of the syrup, add an ounce of cream, fill the mug with hot water, top with whipped cream, and serve with crackers and a spoon.

Hot Chocolate

Four ounces powdered chocolate, 2½ pints water, 2½ pounds sugar, 2 drams vanilla extract. Mix the chocolate and starch by trituration with part of the water, pour on the remainder of the water in a boiling condition, stir well and heat to boiling until the starch is cooked, stirring constantly; add the sugar, stir until dissolved, add the vanilla extract. Serve like the preceding.

Hot Chocolate

Cocoa	2	pounds
Lukewarm water	1½	gallons
Milk	5	gallons
Sugar	3	pounds

Stir cocoa into water until latter boils; boil five minutes; then add sugar and milk; bring again to boiling point, and keep ready for service at temperature of about 140° F.

Hot Chocolate

Bitter choc. (ground)	12	ounces
Warm water	1	pint
Granulated sugar	24	ounces
Sweet milk	2	gallons
Extract vanilla	1	ounce
Salt		pinch

Add the chocolate to the warm water, and heat to boiling point, stirring to produce a smooth paste. Dissolve the sugar in the milk, then add to the paste. Then add vanilla flavoring and the salt. (Raymond Wells.)

Hot Chocolate

Cocoa	18	ounces
Sugar	4	pounds
Milk	2	quarts
Vanilla extract	1½	ounces
Glycerin	1½	ounces
Cocoa butter	1	ounce

Warm the milk, add the sugar and cocoa previously mixed. Bring to a boil, add the cocoa butter and stir. Take from the fire, add the glycerin and stir again. When cool add the vanilla. Add four ounces of condensed milk to 28 ounces of the syrup Serve 1½ ounces to an eight-ounce mug, which fill with hot water. Top with whipped cream and serve with crackers.

HOT CHOCOLATE

Good cocoa .... 1½ pounds
Water .... 7 quarts
Sugar .... 2½ pounds
Extract of vanilla .. ½ ounce
Pure cream .... 3 pints

Have the water *boiling,* and then with one quart of the water make a paste of the chocolate. Then smooth the paste with two or more quarts of water and let it come to a boil. Then add the sugar, the vanilla and the ice cream and let it come to a boil again. Strain it before putting in your dispensing urn. (Sam. Schusterman)

HOT CHOCOLATE

Three pounds powdered Dutch cocoa, ½ gallon water, 2 pints cream, 5 ounces tincture of vanilla, 1 teaspoonful salt, and enough simple syrup to make 1 gallon This syrup must be used in a day or it will sour It may prove advantageous to reduce the quantity of cocoa.

HOT CHOCOLATE

Powdered cocoa, 1 pound; boiling water, 1 pint; syrup (12 pounds of sugar to gallon of water), 7 pints. Put the cocoa in a double boiler, add 1 pint of syrup, rub into a smooth paste, add the pint of boiling water, place over fire and bring to a boil. Remove from fire, add the balance of the syrup and strain. When cold add I ounce of vanilla extract, if desired

HOT CHOCOLATE

Cocoa, 5 ounces, sugar 7 ounces; water, 1 quart, milk, 2 quarts; put into a suitable vessel over the fire, bring to a boil, then place in the urn. This formula may be improved by the addition of more cocoa.

HOT CHOCOLATE PASTE

Cocoa .... ¼ pound
Fine granulated sugar ½ pound
Evaporated milk ... ½ cupful
Water .... ½ cupful

Mix the cocoa and the milk smoothly, rubbing out all lumps Add the water and bring slowly to the boiling point, stirring all the time. Boil steadily for four or five minutes. Keep in covered container. In serving place small dipperful in cup of boiling water. Add cream to taste.

HOT CHOCOLATE PASTE

Cocoa .... ¼ pound
Fine granulated sugar ½ pound
Lukewarm water.... 1 cupful

Mix as above, and proceed exactly as outlined in the preceding formula. Serve about an ounce to a cup and fill cup with hot milk and water.

HOT COCOA

Cocoa, 8 ounces; corn starch, 1 ounce; sugar, 5 pounds; water, 5 pints. Dissolve the corn starch in water brought to a boil and add the cocoa previously mixed with sugar. Place 1 ounce of the mixture in a cup, fill with hot water and top off with whipped cream.

HOT COCOA

Place in a double boiler three pounds of powdered sugar, one pound of best cocoa and after mixing well add two quarts of water. Cook for one hour. When ready, take off fire and add three pints of unsweetened condensed milk, stir and mix well and keep in cold place until used. To dispense, take one ounce of this syrup in a seven-ounce mug and fill with hot water, top off with whipped cream and serve. Price 10 cents (Theodore Louvis)

IMPROVED HOT CHOCOLATE

Powdered cocoa, best, 8 ounces; water, 4 pints; sugar, 2½ pounds; place the cocoa in double boiler, adding the water slowly. Strain the syrup through a cheesecloth to remove all lumps.

INWRIGHT'S CHOCOLATE (HOT)

Milk .... 3½ gallons
Water .... 3 gallons
Powdered chocolate 1 pound
Sugar .... sufficient

Flavor with vanilla.

LOUVIS HOT CHOCOLATE

Best cocoa .... 1 pound
Powdered sugar ..... 3 pounds
Water .... 2 quarts
Unsweetened cond milk 3 pints

Mix the cocoa and sugar, add the water, cook for one hour in a double boiler. Take off the fire and add condensed milk, stir well and set aside for use. Dispense one ounce of this syrup in a seven-ounce mug, fill with boiling water, top with whipped cream and serve

MOORE'S CHOCOLATE MILK

Chocolate .... 1 pound
Water .... 6 quarts
Milk .... 4 quarts
Vanilla .... 1 dram
Sugar .... q. s

"REAL" CHOCOLATE (HOT)

Cocoa (any good brand)1 pound
Sugar .... 2½ pounds
Milk .... 10 quarts

Boil the milk in a double boiler; add the cocoa and the sugar which have been mixed together. Let the mixture come to a *good* boil. Serve with saltines, 20 cups to the gallon. Charge 10 cents per cup.

Hot Cocoa Royale

Chocolate paste ..... 1 ounce
Grated cocoanut .... ½ ounce
White of egg 1

Mix thoroughly with a spoon, then add boiling water, stir well, and top off with whipped cream and a dash of grated cinnamon if desired.

Benedict's Hot Persian Chocolate

Two spoonfuls of cocoa, a shake of cinnamon, hot milk; top off with whipped cream; serve with wafers.

Aviation Hot Chocolate

Chocolate syrup .... 1½ ounces
Egg 1
Sweet cream .... ¼ ounce

Mix the syrup, cream and egg together in an egg shaker as in dispensing cold egg drinks, add hot water, and mix by pouring back and forth several times from shaker to mug, or break the egg into the shaker, beat with a spoon, add the syrup, cream and sufficient hot water, stirring constantly all the while. Strain into a mug and serve with whipped cream.

Hot Swiss Chocolate

Malted milk .... 1 spoonful
Sweet cream ...... 1 ounce
Chocolate paste (see
formula below)... ½ ounce

Add hot water to fill the cup and top off with whipped cream.

Paste for Hot Chocolate

Pure chocolate .... ½ pound
Plain syrup, enough
to make a paste
Evaporated milk ... ½ pint
Vanilla extract ..... ½ ounce
(Smoot Drug Co.)

Hot Swiss Chocolate

Malted milk .... 1 spoonful
Sweet cream ...... 1 ounce
Chocolate paste .... ½ ounce

Add hot water to fill the cup and top off with whipped cream. Chocolate paste is made as follows:

Pure chocolate .... ½ pound
Water, enough to
make a paste
Evaporated milk ... ½ ounce
Extract of vanilla... ½ ounce

Hot Ice Cream Chocolate

Hot chocolate, very hot, with a spoonful of ice cream to top it off. Charge 10 cents.

Celery Cocoa

Chocolate paste .... 1 ounce
Cream .... 1 ounce
Essence of celery ... 4 dashes

Stir while filling up with hot water.

Top off with whipped cream and serve with celery salt.

Hot Coffee Punch

Egg 1
Extract of mocha
coffee .... 1 dessertspoonful
Lime juice .... 1 teaspoonful

Dispense in an 8-ounce glass. Prepare like hot egg checkerberry.

Coffee Bouquet

Strawberry syrup .. ¾ ounce
Vanilla syrup ...... ¾ ounce
Egg 1
Sweet cream .... 1 ounce

Shake well and fill mug with hot coffee; top off with whipped cream.

Hot Vanilla Creme

Vanilla syrup ..... 1 ounce
White of 1 egg
Cream .... 1 ounce

Shake well; add whipped cream and fill cup with hot water. Cream in hot drinks is often replaced by ice cream where ice cream soda is served all winter.

Oloroso

Pistache or almond
syrup .... 1 ounce
Egg cream syrup... 1 ounce
Cream .... ½ ounce
Aromatic tincture,
N.F. ....15 minims

Mix in soda mug and fill with hot water, stirring well. Top off with cinnamon.

Hot Caramel

Cream .... 1 ounce
Chocolate paste .... ½ ounce
Vanilla syrup ..... ½ ounce
Hot coffee .... 2 drams
Egg 1

Beat up egg in cream, add paste, then syrup and coffee, filling with hot water, fine stream, stirring meanwhile. Serve with grated nutmeg or cinnamon. Price—10-ounce glass, 15 cents.

Hot Mint

Milk .... 2 ounces
Essence of mint....10 drops
Sugar .... 2 teaspoonfuls

Fill mug with hot water, top with whipped cream and serve with nutmeg.

Birch Tea (hot)

Birch beer syrup.... 1 ounce
Hot water to fill mug

Birch beer syrup for the above may be made as follows:

Extract of birch... 6 ounces
Caramel .... sufficient
Soda foam .... 1 ounce
Syrup, enough to
make .... 1 gallon

HOT MALTED MILK

Add to several teaspoonfuls cream in a mug two tablespoonfuls malted milk and make a paste. Then add hot water or milk to fill, gradually stirring while doing this. Season with salt and pepper, or with celery salt and serve with soda crackers.

HOT MALTED SPECIAL

Malted milk may be added to a mixture of hot coffee and chocolate and makes a very fine beverage.

MALTED MILK COFFEE

Coffee syrup 1   ounce
Malted milk powd.. ½ ounce

Mix the powder thoroughly with the syrup to reduce the lumps, fill up with hot water and stir again. Top off with whipped cream. Serve with salt and celery salt.

HOT MALTED COFFEE

Malted milk 1   ounce
Coffee extract 1   dram
Cream 1   ounce

Reduce the lumps with a spoon. Stir briskly while adding hot water.

HOT MALTED MILK COFFEE

Malted milk 1   teaspoonful
Coffee, ground 1   teaspoonful
Hot water to fill cup
Sugar, to sweeten as desired.

Mix the malted milk, coffee and water with vigorous stirring, and boil for three minutes. Add the sugar and serve hot, using a fine strainer. Or, 1 to 4 teaspoonfuls of malted milk are placed in a cup and ordinary hot coffee poured directly upon it with constant stirring.

MALTED OYSTERETTE

Mix a teaspoonful of malted milk with a little milk, add 1½ ounces oyster juice and season with a little salt. Fill with hot milk, being careful to mash all lumps of the malted milk. Charge 10 cents.

MALTED TOMATO-BEEF

Into a well-heated hot-soda mug put a teaspoonful of malted milk. Mix to a smooth paste with a little milk. Add one ounce of beef bouillon and one ounce of plain tomato bouillon. Fill mug with hot water. Stir and serve. Charge 10 cents

HOT MALTED MILK BRACER

Place in an electric mixer:

Orange syrup ...... ½ ounce
Sweet cream 1   ounce
Malted milk .... 2 soda spoonfuls
Hot milk 8   ounces

Mix for about five seconds and pour into a 12-ounce glass; then top with whipped cream and nutmeg. Can be sold for 10

cents. The author states that the sale of this beverage has increased his malted milk trade 50 per cent. Price—12-ounce glass, 10 cents. (E. J. Harshman)

HOT MALTED GINGER

One level tablespoonful malted milk mixed to a paste with cream. One ounce ginger syrup. Hot water to fill cup.

HOT EGG DRINKS

The hot egg drink is delicious if it be nicely prepared, but it certainly requires skill. An egg may be served as a phosphate, as an egg chocolate or coffee. Prepare same as for cold, after shaking strain and draw off 1 glass of hot water to be sure the water is very hot, then add the water slowly, stirring constantly so that the egg will not separate and lump up.

HOT EGG BOUILLON

Egg 1
Beef tea extract.... 1   ounce or less
Dairy butter ...... ½ spoonful

Beat up the egg, add several ounces hot water and stir until the butter is dissolved. Fill up with hot water. Serve in an 8- or 10-ounce mug.

HOT EGG BOUILLON

Shake the egg and extract in a shaker, add the water, and mix by pouring back and forth several times from shaker to mug.

PARISIAN CONSOMME

Extract of beef..... 1   ounce
Egg 1
Butter, a small quantity

Mix in mug with several ounces of hot water, stirring until the butter has dissolved. Then fill up with hot water and serve with celery salt.

IMPERATRICE BOUILLON

Tomato bouillon .... ½ ounce
Liquid extract of
    beef .... ½ ounce
Egg 1
Extract of celery... 1   dash
Mixed spices, to season

Stir the extracts, egg and seasoning together, add the hot water, strain and serve. Or, shake together in a mixer and strain. Charge 10 cents.

HOT BEEF EGG

Break fresh egg into mixing glass with a little water and shake well. Draw hot water to fill, then take a bouillon cup and add half ounce of beef tea extract or a cube of the same   Serve with graham wafers and salt. Price—Eight or 10-ounces, 10 cents. (Geo. A. Zahn.)

EPICUREAN LUNCH

Sweet cream .... 1 ounce
Beef extract .... 1 ounce
Extract of celery...... 3 dashes
Egg 1

Break the egg by shaking and mix thoroughly while pouring in hot water enough to fill an 8-ounce mug. Float a teaspoonful of whipped cream on top, and sprinkle with nutmeg.

SKY SCRAPER

Break 1 fresh egg into a mixing glass without ice, but containing a very little hot water, and shake well. Pour into a hot soda mug, add half ounce beef tea extract, and fill cup with hot water; serve with two graham wafers, pepper and salt.

HOT MALTED MILK WITH EGG

One ounce of malted milk. Put into a mug and add a little hot water to dissolve the powder. Then break an egg and beat it with a spoon, stir into malted milk, add hot milk or hot water, and flavor with either chocolate or vanilla. Charge 15 cents (Geo. A. Zahn.)

HOT EGG CHOCOLATE

Egg 1
Chocolate syrup ... 1¼ ounces
Sweet cream ...... 1 teaspoonful

Shake well, strain and add one cupful hot water and one tablespoon whipped cream. Serve in a 10-ounce glass.

HOT EGG CHOCOLATE

Chocolate syrup .... 1 ounce
Egg 1
Cream .... ½ ounce
Hot water enough to fill a 10-ounce mug

HOT EGG COFFEE

Extract of Mocha
coffee .... 1 dessertspoonful
Sweet cream ...... 2 teaspoonfuls
Sugar .... sufficient

Beat egg, cream and sugar together; add coffee extract and then the hot water. Shake well, strain and add one cupful hot water and one teaspoonful whipped cream. Price —10 ounces, 10 cents.

EGG COFFEE

Beat the yolk of one egg, add sugar to sweeten, two ounces of hot cream. Nearly fill cup with hot coffee and fold in the beaten white. Serve at once.

HOT EGG NOGG

Break fresh egg into shaker. Shake well and pour into 5-ounce bouillon cup. Flavor with sherry and one teaspoonful of sugar. Sprinkle a little cinnamon before drawing hot milk. Serve in a 10-ounce glass with two 5 o'clock tea cakes.

HOT EGG CREAM

One egg, one ounce each of cream and vanilla syrup; shake and add hot milk. Price, 15 cents.

HOT EGG MILK

Two teaspoonfuls sugar, 1 ounce cream, 1 egg, a "touch" of vanilla syrup to improve flavor, hot milk to fill an 8-ounce mug. Prepare like hot egg checkerberry, top with whipped cream and sprinkle with nutmeg. If hot milk is not available, use about 2 ounces of cream, and fill the mug with hot water.

HOT EGG CARAMEL

Cream .... 1 ounce
Chocolate paste .... ½ ounce
Vanilla syrup ...... ½ ounce
Coffee .... 2 drams
Egg 1

Mix thoroughly and stir while adding hot water. Serve with grated nutmeg or cinnamon.

HOT EGG CLARET

Prepare like the hot egg checkerberry, using claret syrup.

HOT EGG CHERRY BLAZE

Prepare like hot egg checkerberry, only use cherry syrup and lemon juice in proportions of 1 ounce and 1 dram respectively, instead of the wintergreen or orange syrups. Sprinkling on the beverage a few drops of alcohol and igniting the latter will make it a real blaze.

HOT EGG CHECKERBERRY

Take 1 ounce wintergreen syrup or the same quantity of wintergreen and orange syrups, half and half; 1 egg, half ounce cream, and hot water enough to fill an 8-ounce glass. Mix the syrup, egg and cream together in an egg shaker, add the hot water, and mix all by pouring back and forth several times from shaker to mug. Or, prepare by beating the egg with a spoon, add the syrup and cream, mix all quickly with the spoon and add hot water, stirring constantly, and strain.

CHECKERBERRY EGG

Syrup checkerberry.. 1 ounce
Egg 1
Sol. acid phosphates ½ dram

Mix thoroughly and fill mug with hot water. Top off with nutmeg and cinnamon.

HOT EGG PINEAPPLE

Prepare like hot egg checkerberry, using pineapple syrup.

HOT EGG LEMONADE

Prepare like hot egg checkerberry, substituting lemon syrup for the other syrup, adding a small amount of lemon or lime juice and omitting the cream and whipped cream. Charge 15 cents.

HOT LEMON AND EGG

Egg 1
Juice of half lemon
Sugar 2   teaspoonfuls
Hot water, enough to
   make 8   ounces

Charge 15 cents.

HOT LIME-EGG-ADE

Egg 1
Lime juice 1   ounce
Powdered sugar ... 1   spoonful

Mix the egg thoroughly, strain if necessary. Add hot water, stirring while filling. Serve nutmeg and cinnamon.

HOT EGG LIME FIZZ

Lime juice 1   ounce
White of 1 egg
Powdered sugar ... 2   teaspoonfuls

Add hot water and top off with a small spoonful of whipped cream.

HOT EGG ORANGE

Orange syrup .... 1½ ounces
Egg 1
Cream 1   ounce
Hot water, enough to
   make 8   ounces

Mix the syrup, egg and cream together in an egg shaker, shaking as in making cold egg drinks. Add a little hot water before serving. This drink may be prepared by breaking the egg with a spoon, adding the syrup and cream and mixing quickly with the spoon. Then add the hot water, stirring constantly meanwhile, and strain. (George Zahn.)

HOT EGG ORANGE

Orange syrup ...... 1 to 1½ ounces
Egg 1
Cream .... ½ ounce
Hot water enough to
   make 10   ounces

Mix the syrup, egg and cream together in an egg shaker as in making cold egg drinks, add the hot water, and mix all by pouring back and forth several times from shaker to mug. Charge 15 cents.

HOT EGG ORANGEADE

Egg 1
Juice of half orange
Powdered sugar 2   teaspoonfuls

Shake well, strain into mug and fill with hot water. Stir and serve with nutmeg.

HOT EGG ORANGEADE

Egg 1
Juice of half orange
Powdered sugar ... 2   teaspoonfuls

Shake well (use electric mixer), strain and add one cup of hot water. Stir and serve with nutmeg. Price—10-ounce glass or mug, 10 cents. (George A. Zahn.)

HOT EGG GINGER

Prepare same as hot egg checkerberry, using ginger syrup.

HOT GOLDEN FIZZ

Ko-kola syrup 1   ounce
Yolk of egg........ 1
Bitters 2   dashes

Mix the egg thoroughly with a whirling spoon. Add hot water, stirring while filling. Serve with grated nutmeg and cinnamon.

HOT EGG PUNCH

Serve in a long, thick soda glass. Take 2 ounces of cream, 2 ounces of hot milk, 1 ounce of plain syrup—or vanilla, one whole egg. Shake the egg with the above ingredients and then add a teaspoonful of Jamaica rum (or enough for the flavor required). Pour from shaker to glass four or five times. After putting glass in holder add hot water, stir; top with whipped cream and nutmeg.

This makes a fine drink when a person is feeble or has been exposed to cold (Geo. A. Zahn.)

HOT EGG PHOSPHATE

Break fresh egg into shaker and add half ounce pineapple syrup, half ounce orange syrup, 1 dash solution of acid phosphate. Shake, without ice, and pour into bouillon cup. Draw cup full of hot water sprinkle a touch of cinnamon and serve with Long Branch wafers. Serve in a 10-ounce glass.

HOT EGG PHOSPHATE

Lemon syrup ..... 1 to 1½ ounces
Sol. acid phosphate 1   dash
Egg 1
Hot water to make 8   ounces
Lemon syrup 2   ounces

Hot egg phosphate may also be made as follows·

Egg 1
Sol. acid phosphate. ⅛ ounce

Mix in a glass and shake together thoroughly; pour into another glass, heated previously, and slowly draw full of hot water; season with nutmeg. Serve in a 10- or 12-ounce glass (heavy) and charge 10 cents.

HOT EGG PHOSPHATE

Break a fresh egg into a shaker; add a small piece of ice to break the yolk of the egg in shaking; then add one ounce of strong lemon syrup and one ounce of strong orange syrup. Shake thoroughly, then pour into hot-soda mug and add hot water. Top with grated nutmeg and a dash of phosphate. Serve in a 10-ounce mug or glass and charge 10 cents. (Geo. A. Zahn.)

HOT EGG PHOSPHATE

Lemon juice, sugar to sweeten, 1 fresh egg, 1 dram solution of acid phosphate, 1 ounce cold water; put into a combination shaker and shake thoroughly; strain into a cup, then fill with hot water; top with nutmeg. Price—10- or 12-ounce glass, 15 cents.

HOT EGG PHOSPHATE

Egg 1
Lemon juice .... 3 teaspoonfuls
Soluble extract lemon 10 drops
Confectioners' sugar 3 large teaspoonfuls
Sol. acid phosphate.. 1 dash
Prepared spice ...... small quantity

Place all in a combination shaker and thoroughly shake; then strain through julep strainer into hot soda cup; to this add two large tablespoonfuls of whipped cream. Draw hot water into side of cup, and stir bottom only. Charge 15 cents.

HOT LEMON

Lemon essence ...... 4 drams
Solution citric acid.. 1 ounce
Syrup to make..... 32 ounces

Draw 2½ ounces to a mug and serve with a spoon. The formula may be improved by using lemon juice instead of the essence.

HOT LEMONADE

Lemons 3
Solution citric acid.. 4 drams
Granulated sugar ... sufficient
Syrup enough to make .... 32 ounces

Grate peel from the lemons and triturate with half its weight of granulated sugar; express the lemons, add the syrup to the mixed juice and peel, let stand for several hours in a covered glass or porcelain vessel, strain and add the acid solution.

HOT LEMONADE

Juice of half a lemon, 1 teaspoonful powdered sugar, twist a small portion of lemon peel over the cup so as to impart a flavor of the lemon, then fill up with hot water and stir.

HOT LEMONADE

Squeeze half a lemon into cup and add one or two teaspoonfuls of sugar; fill with hot water. This is the proper way to make hot lemonade.

HOT ROYAL LEMONADE WITH EGG

White of one egg, juice of one lemon, three spoonsfuls powdered sugar. Mix with spoons and stir while adding hot water. Serve with nutmeg and cinnamon. Charge 15 cents. (Geo. A. Zahn.)

HOT SODA TODDY

Lemon juice .... 2 drams
Lemon syrup .... 1 ounce
Aromatic bitters ... 1 dram
Hot water enough to make .... 8 ounces

Sprinkle with nutmeg or cinnamon.

HOT LEMON SOUR

Lemon syrup ...... 1 ounce
Lemon juice .... 2 ounces
Hot water to fill

Instead of lemon juice 1 dram of lime juice and a dash of solution of acid phosphate may be used.

HOT CREAM LEMON

Lemon 1
Alcohol .... 1 ounce
Solution citric acid.. 2 drams
Sugar .... 20 ounces
Water .... 20 ounces
White of egg....... 1

Grate the peel of the lemon and macerate with alcohol for a day, express, also express the lemon, mix the juice and extract, add the sugar and water, dissolve by agitation and add the solution of citric acid and the egg white, the latter being first beaten to a froth.

FROSTED HOT LEMONADE

For this use two ounces of lemon syrup made from fresh fruit. Fill the mug with hot water. Mix and finish with a spoonful of marshmallow dressing. Serve with cheese wafers.

HOT CITRIC PHOSPHATE

Lemon syrup .... 1½ ounces
One fresh egg
Citric phosphate .... 1 dram

Mix well in a shaker, transfer to a mug and fill with hot water. Have the water a few degrees below the boiling point to prevent the egg from becoming stringy.

HOT SILVER FIZZ

White of 1 egg, juice of 1 lemon, 3 spoonfuls powdered sugar. Mix with spoon and stir while adding hot water. Serve with nutmeg and cinnamon. Charge 10 cents.

HOT LEMON PUNCH

This can be made from cold lemon syrup prepared from the fruit, but a special syrup may be made with the gratings of 6 and juice of 18 lemons to the gallon. The latter is the better method.

HOT LEMODINE

Lemon essence ..... 1 ounce
Orange essence or compound spirit of orange .... 2 drams
Nutmeg essence ....15 drops
Lime juice .... 4 drams
Solution citric acid.. 4 drams
Syrup enough to make .... 32 ounces

STATESMAN'S BRACER

Lemon juice 2   drams
Lemon syrup 1   ounce
Aromatic bitters 1   dram

Mix and add enough hot water to fill an 8-ounce glass. Top off with mixed spices. Price, 10 cents.

ORANGE GOLD MINE

Orange syrup 1   ounce
Sol. acid phosphate.. 1   dram
Hot water to fill an
    8-ounce mug
Price, 5 cents.

HOT LIMETTA

Lime juice 1   ounce
Strawberry juice ... ½ ounce
Sugar 1   spoonful

Fill up with hot water, stirring well.

HOT LIMEADE

Lime juice .... ½ ounce
Orange syrup 1   ounce
Ginger syrup ...... ½ ounce
Hot water.

HOT LIME JUICE

Lime juice .... ½ ounce
Lemon   or   ginger
    syrup 1   ounce
Hot water to fill

Lime juice with lemon or plain syrup or with sugar and hot water may be dispensed as "hot limeade."

HOT GRAPEADE

Grape juice .... 1 ounce
Lemon syrup .... 1 ounce
Hot water to fill mug.

HOT RASPBERRY

Raspberry vinegar syrup ½ ounce
Raspberry juice .... ½ ounce
Lime juice .... ½ ounce

Place in mug and fill with hot water.

LAMBRAKIS HOT LUNCH

Into a mixing glass put:
    Coca-cola .... ½ ounce
    Chocolate syrup .... ½ ounce
    Plain cream 2   ounces
    Malted milk 3   teaspoonfuls

Shake well, transfer into a 12-ounce bell glass and fill with hot water This drink can be made with an egg or it may be served cold. Price—10 cents, with egg, 15 cents.

HOT ROYAL NECTAR

Nectar syrup 1   ounce
Lime juice .... ½ ounce
Grape juice .... ½ ounce

Fill with hot water, add a slice each of orange and lemon.

HOT CHECKERBERRY

Draw half ounce of wintergreen syrup and 1 ounce of red orange syrup into a mug and fill with hot water. Top with whipped cream. It may also be served by using 1 ounce wintergreen syrup and omitting the orange.

HOT APPLE FLOAT

Place in a shell glass one ounce each of pineapple juice or syrup and one ounce of crabapple syrup. Fill with hot water and stir well, then float a spoonful of whipped cream on the liquid.

HOT CRAB APPLE

Pour 1 ounce of crab apple syrup into a mug and fill with hot water, stir well and serve.

BONNE BOUCHE

Egg 1
Cherry juice or syr-
    up 2   ounces
Powdered sugar 1   spoonful

Mix thoroughly, continuing the stirring while adding the hot water. Then add two cherries and a slice of orange, and top off with nutmeg.

CHERRY KICKER

Cherry juice 1   pound
Sugar .... 1¾ pounds
Water .... ½ pint

Make a syrup. To dispense, pour 1½ ounces in an 8-ounce soda mug, add 1 dram of solution of acid phosphates and fill with hot water. The juice of a quarter lemon is often preferable to acid phosphate in a hot drink.

HOT PUFF

One ounce of vanilla syrup, white of 1 egg, 1 ounce of cream. Shake well; add whipped cream and fill cup with hot water.

CHIN CHIN

Loaf sugar .... cubes
Extract of mint julep 10 drops
Warm milk 2   ounces
Hot water .... sufficient

Top off with whipped cream and powdered nutmeg.

CHRISTMAS HOT PUNCH

Place the juice of 1 lemon and ½ ounce sherbet syrup in an 8-ounce mug; draw 6 ounces of hot water into another mug and mix with the liquid in the other mug by pouring back and forth from one mug to the other a few times. Price, 10 cents

HOT DON'T CARE

Don't care syrup.... ½ ounce
Egg 1
Bitters 3   dashes
Cream 1   ounce

Mix thoroughly and stir while adding hot water. Top off with grated nutmeg or cinnamon.

HOT FRUTESCENS

Strawberry juice ...	½	ounce
Raspberry juice	½	ounce
Vanilla syrup	1	ounce
Hot water	1	cupful

Top off with whipped cream.

HOT PARISIAN BLAZE

Champagne syrup ...	1	ounce
Sweet mint syrup ...	½	ounce
Sol. acid phosphate..	3	dashes

Fill with hot water and add a slice of lemon, and, if obtainable, a sprig of mint. Fresh mint leaves can usually be obtained from any first-class butcher shop.

HOT PINEAPPLE FIZZ

Pineapple syrup	1	ounce
Lemon syrup	1	ounce
Saturated sol. bicarbonate soda	½	ounce

Hot water and a dash of phosphate.

JONES' SPECIAL HOT PUNCH

Take the yolk of one egg, one ounce of grape juice, one-half ounce lemon juice, two spoonfuls powdered sugar and mix thoroughly. Continue to mix while filling up mug with hot soda. Top off with whipped cream and sprinkle a little nutmeg on top. This preparation is said to be a "winner" and affords a good profit when sold at 15 cents. (George A. Zahn.)

TANT MIEUX

Strawberry juice	½	ounce
Pineapple juice	½	ounce
Vanilla syrup	1	ounce

Place in cup, fill with hot water, and top off with whipped cream.

GINGER SNAP (HOT)

Break an egg into a suitable glass, add 1 ounce each of ginger syrup and grape juice and 3 or 4 dashes of lemon juice Shake thoroughly, add about 4 ounces of hot water to the mixture in the shaker, strain carefully into a mug, top off with whipped cream and a sprinkle of nutmeg or cinnamon, and serve.

GINGER HOT

Loaf sugar	4	cubes
Soluble extract ginger ale 10		drops
Soluble extract lemon 10		drops
Fruit acid 10		drops
Hot water	1	cupful

HOT GINGER

Ginger syrup	1	ounce
Sweet cream	2	ounces

Fill with hot water and top with whipped cream.

GINGER TODDY

Ginger syrup	½	ounce
Tea syrup	1	ounce
Currant juice	½	ounce

Add hot soda and serve with grated cinnamon.

HOT GINGERADE

Fluid extract of ginger 10		fluid drams
Precipitated calcium phosphate	4	drams
Sugar 20		ounces
Water 20		ounces

Triturate the fluid extract with the precipitated calcium phosphate, expose in a warm place until the alcohol has evaporated, triturate with the water, macerate for several hours, stirring occasionally, filter, and in the filtrate dissolve the sugar by agitation. To dispense, pour 1½ ounces in an 8-ounce soda mug and fill with hot water. Cream (about 1 ounce) may be added if desired. The "soluble essence of ginger" of the National Formulary may be used in place of the solution of ginger here directed.

HOT SCOTCH

One ounce hot Scotch syrup; add hot water, stirring constantly. Top off with cream.

To make the hot Scotch syrup, take:

Soluble essence of ginger	4	ounces
Soluble extract of capsicum	¼	ounce
Solution extract of gentian	1	dram
Essence of orange peel	3	drams
Lemon syrup 20		ounces
Caramel coloring ...	½	ounce

Mix thoroughly and keep in a syrup bottle.

RED HOT

Vigoral	1	ounce
Worcestershire sauce	10	drops
Tabasco sauce	2	drops
Lemon juice	1	dram
Hot water to fill mug		

Season with salt and pepper or celery salt.

HOT CATAWBA PUNCH

Catawba syrup	1	ounce
Sweet cream	2	ounces
Angostura bitters ...		dash

Stir while filling with hot water. Serve with grated cinnamon.

QUIP RIDOTTO

This drink possesses a vinous flavor; take of:

Lemon juice	3	drams
Sugar	3	drams
Port wine	½	dram
Fresh essence of lemon 10		drops
Whipped cream		sufficient

Place the first four ingredients in the mug, then draw half full of hot water, stir.

add the whipped cream, and finally fill the cup with hot water. Stir from the bottom.

HOT PEPSIN PHOSPHATE

Liquid pepsin	1	teaspoonful
Sol. acid phosphate .	2	dashes
Lemon syrup	1	ounce
Hot water	1	cupful

HOT PEPTO-BEEF

Crystal pepsin	5	grains
Warm water	½	ounce

Dissolve, then add 1 teaspoonful beef bouillon, 1 cupful hot water. Serve with pepper and salt.

HOT PEPTO-LIME

Lime juice	½	ounce
Lemon syrup	½	ounce
Essence of pepsin..	1	dram

Stir while adding hot water. Price—Eight-ounce mug or glass, 5 cents.

PEPSO-LEMO

Lime juice	½	ounce
Lemon juice	½	ounce
Essence of pepsin...	1	dram

Add two teaspoonfuls sugar, a bit of peel, spice, and serve in a hot mug.

PREPARED MILK

The prepared milk prescribed for the dispensing of many of the hot drinks is made by taking 1 pint of pure milk, 4 ounces evaporated milk or 16% cream, ⅛-ounce extract vanilla, 5 grains of bicarbonate of soda and mixing all together.

CELERY SALT

Powdered celery seed	3	ounces
Salt	12	ounces
Pulverized mace, pulverized allspice, of each 180 grains.		

HOT TEA

Loaf sugar	4	cubes
Extract Oolong tea..	1	dessertspoonful
Prepared milk	1	dessertspoonful
Hot water sufficient to fill cup		
Whipped cream ...	1	tablespoonful

ORIENTAL TEA

Tea syrup	1	ounce
Red orange syrup ...	½	ounce
Aromatic bitters	½	dram

Place in hot soda mug and fill with hot water. Sprinkle with cinnamon.

TEA A LA RUSSE

Peel a juicy lemon, slice thin, taking out the seeds; put one slice in each teacup, sprinkle the lemon with sugar and pour hot tea over it. Should be served with hot cream on the side.

TURKISH TEA

Tea syrup	1	ounce
Blood orange syrup.	½	ounce
Cream		dash

Fill up with hot water, stirring well.

---

(8) Sundaes and College Ices

Probably the average dispenser will consult the pages in this section more than any other. Syrup and ice cream formulas constitute an important part of his stock in trade and business equipment, but in the profitable pushing of specialties he will avail himself of the experience and genius of his fellow workers in the field of good soda. Since most dispensers prefer to push specials of the sundae class, the following pages are sure to be of peculiar value.

The two hundred and seventy-five formulas presented in this section are the most complete collection of sundaes published and, with the following divisions on desserts (which are highly elaborated sundaes) and special sundae toppings, total five hundred and sixty-two different formulas.

In serving sundaes it is important that an appeal should be made to the eye as well as to the palate. It is poor policy to slap together a messy concoction. Never let the syrups run over the edge of the sundae glass. See that the handle of the spoon is not sticky with syrup. Place nuts, cherries, or knobs of whipped cream carefully on the sundae so that the effect may be pleasing.

It is customary to serve a glass of iced water with all sundaes. This should not be omitted, and do not wait for the customer to ask for it. Many dispensers serve a cracker with the sundae. This is desirable, especially in many neighborhoods, but such service is not absolutely necessary. A reasonable amount of judgment must be exercised as to the kind of cracker served. With chocolate, coffee, maple, and similar flavors a salty cracker is very acceptable, but with the fruity flavors and with fresh or crushed fruits a sweet cracker is correct.

Words of warning can advantageously be sounded in the matter of naming sundaes. The names in the following pages are standard in many cases. A great number of the following formulas are prize winners in the SODA FOUNTAIN's monthly contests and as such, have a wide reputation. There is always a danger in carrying the fancy name idea too far—for a fine name does not of necessity mean a fine sundae, while the too fancy names are apt to be fantastic and even funny to one who possesses a sense of humor. Stick to original names of the sundaes and help to make them more and more standard and uniform. The Formulary contains typical formulas for sundaes for every special occasion. A decidedly local event or an intimate personal touch is the only reasonable excuse that can be advanced for the use of a specially coined name.

Sundaes offer the widest possible range in advertising. Window strips and slips in or on the menu are the favorite means of bringing a special to the attention of the public. A little skill in lettering and a little ingenuity in cutting out magazine covers and pasting them on white cardboard is often all that is necessary to make a most attractive advertising sign. Unless well done, however, it is better not to attempt such signs. A poorly made amateurish sign does not create a favorable impression on the prospective patron.

SUNDAES AND COLLEGE ICES

CHOCOLATE (PLAIN)

Make a thick, smooth paste with powdered cocoa and hot water and add simple syrup until the correct consistency is obtained. Pour over vanilla ice cream.

Vanilla syrup may be added in this formula for flavor.

CHOCOLATE NUT FREEZE

Into a sundae glass place ½ ounce of chocolate syrup, ½ ounce of sweet cream, one teaspoonful of vanilla ice cream, and two teaspoonfuls of nut meats mixed well. Add one 20-to-the-quart scoopful of vanilla ice cream, cover with whipped cream, and place a whole Maraschino cherry on top. Sells for 15 cents. The author says the name is "very catchy." (Theo. Louvis.)

CHOCOLATE NUT

Chocolate syrup, 2 quarts; cover thickly over chopped English walnuts. Serve a ladle of this dressing over a ladleful of ice cream and top off with whipped cream and 1 whole cherry. Price, 10 cents.

MALTED CHOCOLATE

Chocolate syrup, 1 ounce; malted milk, 1 tablespoonful. Mix thoroughly and pour over one measure of ice cream.

GRAPE NUT

On a suitable footed sundae dish put one 12-to-the-quart disherful of any special ice cream; over this pour a small portion of chocolate syrup, top with about four spoonfuls of grape nuts and two red cherries. The "grape nuts" are the kind used as a breakfast food. Sells for 10 cents. (Warren Thomas.)

ARABIAN

Take a dish full of chocolate ice cream (or a dish of vanilla ice cream with a layer of chocolate syrup over it). Over this place a spoonful of crushed figs and a large spoonful of whipped cream, putting on each side a Nabisco wafer. Serve in a sherbet glass with a spoon, topping off with a maraschino cherry.

LADY DEVONSHIRE

Chocolate ice cream, orange ice, whipped cream, nuts, fruits. (Geo. Dauernheim)

BILTMORE

In a high-ball glass place a scoopful of vanilla ice cream and cover with strawberry syrup. Add two spoonfuls of chopped nuts and fill glass with chocolate frappe. Cap it off with whipped cream and a Maraschino cherry, selling for 15 cents. (Wade T. Surratt.)

EUCHRE SPECIAL

On a china ice cream plate place half of a banana, which cover with chocolate whipped cream. On this lay a slice of a pint brick of vanilla ice cream one-half inch thick. In two diagonal corners and in the center of the slice of ice cream put red Maraschino pineapple aces, to represent the different aces of the cards. On the side of the dish beside the frappe lay two nabiscos and serve. Sells for 15 or 20 cents.

The author explains that the so-called pint bricks of ice cream are used because, when sliced, the slices are near to size of the playing card they are supposed to represent. To make the chocolate whipped cream, use 3 ounces of cocoa and mix thoroughly with a little simple syrup; then pour the mixture into a quart of heavy cream when it is almost whipped. (Sterling Miller.)

MT. WASHINGTON

On a sundae dish place a No. 10 disherful of chocolate ice cream. Cover with whipped cream, add three Maraschino cherries and sprinkle over all a spoonful of walnut meats.

PIKE'S PEAK

Dish chocolate ice cream topped off with whipped cream and a blanched almond on top.

CHOCOLATE FRAPPE

Frozen whipped cream, sufficient; shaved ice, sufficient; chocolate syrup, 2 ounces Fill a glass half-full with frozen whipped cream, fill with shaved ice nearly to the top, and pour in the chocolate syrup Charge 15 cents.

PRIDE OF THE ROCKIES

Into a glass sundae dish, place a large ball of chocolate ice cream. Then with a knife cut it into four quarters. Separate the parts so that they will nearly touch the sides of the dish. Into the opening thus formed, put a ladle of crushed cherries, being careful to drain off the syrup first. Then fill in the openings on the sides with a teaspoonful of whipped cream beaten very stiff. Lastly sprinkle over all some shredded cocoanut. Price 15 cents. (Hector Johnson.)

BLACK HILLS

In a banana-split dish place a No. 10 disherful each of vanilla and chocolate ice cream side by side. Over these pour chocolate syrup and nut meats, and top each cone with a cherry. At the side of each cone place a nabisco wafer. The two cones covered with chocolate are supposed to represent the Black Hills in which the city of Lead, S. D., is located. (C. H. Bigalow.)

BULL MOOSE

Place a No. 10 scoopful of ice cream in a sundae glass; pour over the cream a ladleful of chocolate marshmallow dressing, add a spoonful of chopped nuts and top with a chocolate bud. Stand two froufrou wafers, one on each side of the cream, to represent the horns of a moose. Prepare the marshmallow cream as follows: Make a smooth paste with chocolate and hot water, and add to the marshmallow cream. About one ounce of chocolate to the quart of cream will give the desired flavor. This sundae sells readily for 15 cents.

The author enclosed with his formula a photograph to show how he advertises this specialty by means of a picture of a moose head painted on a mirror inside and also on the window outside. He wrote that a picture of this kind will attract the attention of the public much quicker than the ordinary lettered sign, and it is not at all difficult to make. Unfortunately, this picture was not adapted for reproduction. An ordinary newspaper cartoon is enlarged on a large piece of wrapping paper, the enlargement being outlined with a tracing wheel. This serves as a pattern, which is then held against the glass and patted with a powder bag, the powder dusting through leaving a clear outline of the moose head on the glass, the figure being then filled in with a brush. (Harry P. Ayers.)

CONEY ISLAND

A rounded helping of chocolate ice cream, dressed with a thickened orange dressing and topped with a marshmallow. Serve with a macaroon or a nabisco.

HIGH SCHOOL

Take three portions of chocolate ice cream (No. 16 disher) and place them in triangular form on a flat ice cream saucer; then place some whipped cream in the center and dust over with finely chopped walnuts, or, if preferred, a Maraschino cherry may be used. Price 15 cents.

SORORITY

Into a tall goblet put one No. 12 dipperful of chocolate ice cream, then add a small quantity of chopped nuts and a small ladleful of maple syrup. Put a No. 16 dipperful of vanilla ice cream on top of this and over it put a spoonful of thick bitter-sweet chocolate. Top off with whipped cream and a chocolate-dipped maraschino cherry. Charge 15 cents. (A. E. Perkins.)

TANGO

In an 8-ounce phosphate glass put a No. 20-to-the-quart disherful of chocolate ice cream. Over this pour ½ ounce butterscotch dressing and a soda spoonful of finely ground nuts. On this put a No. 20-to-the-quart disherful of vanilla ice cream, ½ ounce marshmallow dressing, and a dash of ground nuts. Over this pour a very little heavy chocolate dressing, and top with a cherry or slice of fresh peach, and one cloverleaf wafer. Charge 20 cents. (Philip W. Traker.)

THE MIDNIGHT SUN

Into a fancy sundae dish place a ladleful of vanilla ice cream and over it pour a suitable quantity of "sauce princessia." Over the latter pour a spoonful of chocolate syrup and surround all with a ring of whipped cream; on this place bits of cherries. "Sauce princessia" is made as follows: Stir well together 6 yolks of eggs and 4 pounds of sugar; add ½ gallon of pure cream, stirring all the while and then boil the mixture for five minutes. Add a sufficient quantity of orange coloring to produce the desired tint. This makes a very delicious sauce. (Shirley B. Ware.)

PALMER HOUSE

Place a dipperful of vanilla ice cream (eight-to-the-quart) on a large sundae dish. Place four clover leaf wafers on each side of the cream, and over the whole place the peeled half of a peach. On the peach place a Maraschino cherry. In one end of the dish put a few ground nuts over a small sprig of mint. Over all pour some chocolate syrup. Sells for 15 or 20 cents. (Charles T. Dakes)

PARISIAN BON BON

Serve in an 8-ounce glass as follows· Place in the glass a small scoopful of chocolate ice cream, then cover the cream with a few crushed macaroons, a little chocolate syrup, and a pinch of shredded cocoanut. Fill the glass even to the brim with vanilla ice cream and top with a cherry. Sells for 10 or 15 cents. The author states that it has proved "a great seller." (Carl F. Mock.)

THE KNICKERBOCKER

Ice cream, 4 ounces, chocolate syrup, ½ ounce; raspberry crushed fruit, ½ ounce; whipped cream, 3 ounces, 2 brandied cherries. Place the ice cream in a glass and add chocolate syrup, some of the whipped cream and 2 dashes of essence of rose. Add raspberry fruit and then balance of whipped cream and the rose essence; top with cherries. Each of the separate portions will appear as a separate layer in glass. This sundae should be served in a tall, narrow, 10-ounce, thin glass, and the dispenser in serving should insert long spoon to the bottom of glass just once and draw slowly towards top, so as to slightly mix the ingredients. This is done for appearance only. Fifteen cents should be secured for this sundae and all materials should be of the very best.

VICTORY

On a long dish place a small dipperful each of vanilla ice cream and orange ice. Over these pour a small ladleful of chocolate syrup and top off with whipped cream and cherries beaten together. Serve with two nabisco wafers. Sells for 15 cents.

COUNTRY CLUB

Cone of ice cream in sundae cup. Pour on top 1 ladleful of chocolate, 1 ladleful of chopped nuts, and put 1 green and 2 red cherries on each side. Sprinkle over all 1 teaspoonful of malted milk Price, 15 cents.

DESSERT FRANCAIS

Ice cream in sundae glass, chocolate flavor; slice one fresh banana around edge, sprinkle with chopped nuts, top with whipped cream and maraschino cherry. Price, 15 cents.

GOLD DUST TWINS

Take a suitable dish or plate and place on it two No. 20 disherfuls of chocolate ice cream and cover each with chocolate syrup. Over each sprinkle powdered nabisco wafers and top with a red cherry, one on each cone of cream. Sells for 10 cents

CHOCOLATE PECAN PUFF

Put into a suitable glass one No. 10-to-the-quart ladleful of vanilla ice cream, and cover it with a mixture of ½ ounce chocolate syrup, 1 spoonful of whipped cream, and ½ ounce of pecans. The dressing should be prepared fresh as called for. Yields a good profit at 15 cents. The author writes that this is a favorite with the "sorority girls" of his city. (Wallis H. Brown)

YAMA YAMA

Place one (No. 12) scoopful of chocolate ice cream into a sundae dish and over it pour one ladleful of crushed pineapple. Top off with whipped cream, a few pecans and a cherry. Charge 15 cents. (Joseph Casiragh.)

BACHELOR'S SPECIAL

Into a stem frappe glass place one disherful of chocolate ice cream and over the cream sprinkle a few chopped nuts. Pour over the ice cream and nuts a small quantity of vanilla syrup, then well cover with "bitter sweet" chocolate syrup. Cut three marshmallows into cubes, making four cubes to each marshmallow. Place these around the edge of the sundae, an equal distance apart. Top off with whipped cream and decorate with one red cherry and one cube of marshmallow. Price 15 cents. (Walter J. Taber.)

BUSTER BROWN

Fill a punch glass with half chocolate ice cream and half pineapple sherbet, and pour over the mixture a ladleful of caramel nut sauce or catawba syrup.

WALNUT CHOCOLATE

Take the usual quantity of ice cream and pour over it a heavy chocolate syrup. Garnish with walnut halves, or a ladle of walnut russe. Price, 10 cents.

STARTLER

Into a 6-ounce glass put a No. 16-to-the-quart dipperful of chocolate ice cream;

take a spoon and push it down into the cream on one side of the glass so as to leave a hollow in the middle of the glass; in the hollow or cavity thus made, pour a ladleful of crushed Hawaiian pineapple and a Maraschino cherry; then put a No. 16-to-the-quart dipperful of vanilla ice cream on top and over it a ladleful of marshmallow dressing; cover it with some dry chopped nuts and top off with a red or green cherry. Sells at 15 cents. (W. Sidney Stevens)

RUBAIYAT

Place a ladleful of ice cream in a sundae dish and over it pour 1½ ounces of chocolate syrup. Top off with whipped cream and two thin slices of pineapple. Price, 15 cents. (Epworth Reilly.)

PEG O' MY HEART

Into a footed sundae cup put a small dipperful of vanilla ice cream; cover with marshmallow whip and then add ½ ounce chocolate syrup Insert slices of banana around the inside of the glass, and top with whipped cream and chopped nuts. Decorate with red and green cherries. Sells for 15 cents. (Bruno Schubet.)

HYDROX

In a regular sundae dish place a 20-to-the quart dipperful of chocolate ice cream, and over it pour a dipperful of "chocolate nut fudge"; on top of the mixture put a ladleful of marshmallow whip. On the dish and beside the sundae stand a chocolate hydrox biscuit and serve. To make the "chocolate nut fudge" mix and boil to 120°, 1 quart of milk, 1 teaspoonful of butter, and 3 ounces of cocoa; when cold, add chopped walnuts. This recipe makes a most delicious fudge and one which can be served at any fountain.

A window sign to advertise the sundae can be made of heavy paper, the lettering being done with a dark brown ink to simulate the color of chocolate, as follows:

```
..........................
:        Special To-day.        :
:     HYDROX  SUNDAE     :
:        At the Fountain        :
:            10 Cents.            :
..........................
```

This sundae is worth 15 cents. (Sterling Miller.)

LONE STAR

Over a ladleful of ice cream in a sundae glass pour some chocolate syrup and cover with Texas pecans, almonds and dates chopped together. Price, 15 cents.

IMPERIAL CHOCOLATE

Stand two bars of sweet chocolate in a sundae cup in such a manner that a cone of vanilla ice cream can be dropped between them; put chocolate syrup and whipped cream over the cone; in an indentation made in the top of cream with a spoon, place a scoopful of ground nuts; on one side of the dish place a green cherry and on the opposite side put a red cherry. Price, 15 cents.

CHOCOLATE SHOP TEMPTATION

In a sundae glass place a scoopful of chocolate ice cream and pour on some rich chocolate syrup; over the latter dash a spoonful of whipped cream and sprinkle on some ground roasted almonds. Top off with a blanched almond. Price, 10 cents. (Miss Ida Eleanore Johnson.)

CHOCOLATE NOUGATINE

Over a ladleful of vanilla ice cream put a large spoonful of chopped nuts and over the nuts pour marshmallow whip syrup; over this pour a mixture of ½ ounce of chocolate syrup with 2 ounces of stiff whipped cream and top off with ½ of a walnut. Price, 15 cents (Emil J. Bastion.)

CHOCOLATE MARSHMALLOW

In a sundae glass put a disherful of chocolate ice cream (French) and over it pour a marshmallow sauce made by diluting marshmallow whip with simple syrup and adding a few dashes of vanilla to flavor. Top off with nuts and a red cherry.

COFFEE (PLAIN)

Make a rich syrup of coffee and pour over vanilla ice cream. Top with whipped cream and charge 10 cents.

AUSTRALIAN

Vanilla cream and New York cream in a regular sundae cup; pour over the ice cream port wine syrup, then add grated nuts and top off with whipped cream and maraschino cherries.

CLARET TRICKLE

In a six-ounce flare phosphate glass place a small dipperful of vanilla ice cream; over the cream pour a small ladleful of chopped pecan nuts in maple syrup, then a small dipperful of pineapple sherbet; on top place three large Maraschino cherries in a little of the Maraschino liquor and then pour over them one-half ounce of rich claret syrup mixed with one dash of phosphate; top with whipped cream. Place glass in a soda holder and serve with spoon by the side and a glass of clear ice water. Price, 15 cents. (Alonzo Draine.)

AULD IRELAND

Take a ball-shaped portion of pistachio ice cream filled with ground pistachio nuts. Color the cream a light green. Over the cream pour about 2 ounces of orange flower flavored syrup, which should be very heavy and also colored green. Now drop in 6 or 8 roasted filberts (to represent the stones). Then take a tooth pick and with it place around the ice cream round strips of crystallized ginger, previously colored green (to represent the snakes); on top of the cream drop some well whipped cream, colored light pink, and sweetened and flavored with rose (for the rose of Old Ireland), dropping a green cherry with a roasted filbert inside of it in the center of the cream. Place the above in a stem sundae glass on a 5-inch plate on which has been laid a St. Patrick napkin and a dainty spoon. Serve with a glass of Vichy, well charged, giving with each order a white carnation having green colored edges. Price 15 to 25 cents. (C. L. Hadley.)

MAPLE NUT

Vanilla ice cream, 1 dipperful; maple syrup (the real thing), 2 ounces; place in a sundae glass, sprinkle with chopped English walnuts, and top with whipped cream. Price—10 or 15 cents.

MAPLE CARAMEL

In an ordinary sundae cup place one (16 to the quart) dipperful of vanilla ice cream. Over the ice cream pour 1 ounce of maple caramel syrup and 1 large spoonful of ground English walnuts. Top off with whipped cream and one Maraschino cherry. Price, 15 cents

"Maple Caramel" for the above is made as follows: Beat up 9 eggs very lightly, add 1 quart xx sweet cream, 1 quart of pure maple syrup and 4 ounces solution of caramel; strain and cook in a double boiler until the mixture comes to a boil; allow to cool and place on ice; the maple caramel is then ready for use. (Low W. Garnett.)

MAPLE HONEY

Prepare a syrup of 16 ounces of maple syrup, 4 ounces of strained honey and 4 ounces vanilla syrup. Into a mineral water glass (7-ounce is best size) put 4 or 5 ounces of vanilla ice cream, add 1 ounce of of the above syrup, mix well with spoon. Care should be used in mixing, as the beverage must not be made mushy. Then sprinkle over this a heaping spoon of ground English walnuts, add some whipped cream over the nuts and over it sprinkle a very little powdered sugar, dress with a slice of orange and a cherry, set the glass into a small plate and serve. Charge 15 cents.

MAPLE LEAF

Take a saucer, such as are commonly used for sundaes and around its edge place five macaroons. Place a cone of vanilla ice cream (measured out with a 12 to the quart ice cream disher) in the center of the saucer. Over the ice cream pour one-half ladleful of pineapple fruit and one ounce of maple syrup. Top off with a small measure of maple sugar. This formula is especially recommended.

The author writes: "We used fifty gallons of maple syrup last season, supplying customers with 'maple leaf sundae' Guess that's going some for Canada, 'the land of the maple leaf.'" (Harry G. Frame.)

WHIPPED MAPLE CREAM

Place a cone of vanilla ice cream on a dish. Put three whipped cream chocolates around evenly on the bottom; pour maple syrup over the ice cream. Sprinkle over a few nuts and top off with whipped cream and a cherry. Price, 15 cents.

PEANUT SUNDAE

Place 2 ounces of Spanish peanuts, freshly roasted, shelled and blanched, in a mortar, and mash with a pestle. Add 4 ounces of peanut butter and rub together. Then add a little salt, 2 drams of powdered acacia, and rub again, gradually adding an ounce of water. Reduce to a smooth paste, and gradually add ½ gallon of simple syrup. To serve, pour over a portion of ice cream.

PEANUT

On a suitable sundae dish place one scoopful of ice cream and over it pour peanut butter syrup; top off with whipped cream and a cherry. Sells for 10 cents. (Logan Taylor.)

VIRGINIA SUNDAE

Fill a No. 12-to-the-quart dipper with plain vanilla ice cream, and before releasing the cream from the dipper, make a hollow or cavity in the center of the cream with a sundae spoon. In the cavity place a spoonful of good peanut butter. Now turn the ice cream into a sundae dish, and cover over the top with a ladleful of marshmallow dressing and some ground nutmeg. Sells for 15 cents and is easily and quickly dispensed. To use the author's recommendation· "It's a humdinger for taste." (Max H. Karlsruher.)

CREAMED PEANUT

On a small flat dish place a dipperful of vanilla ice cream, over which pour a ladleful of peanut butter, which has been mixed with simple syrup, and kept in a crushed fruit bowl. Add a ladleful of chocolate syrup, which should be made rather heavy. Top with whipped cream and half an English walnut.

COCOANUT SPECIAL

Four ounces and a half of vanilla ice cream, 1 ounce of orgeat syrup, 1 ounce grated cocoanut. To serve glace, cream glace and ices use a broad, short glass. Place ice cream in 7-ounce glass, add on top the orgeat syrup, then the cocoanut. Serve a glass of plain ice water and a paper napkin. Charge 10 cents.

COCOANUT CREAM

Take a 6-ounce sundae dish and in it place a 10-to-the-quart scoopful of vanilla ice cream; over the ice cream pour a ladleful of whipped cream and on it a teaspoonful of chopped nuts; over all, sprinkle some good, well-toasted cocoanut and top with one chocolate cream. Sells for 15 cents. (Paul Hurwity.)

MACARONI COCOANUT

Use a long plain "banana split" dish and place upon it, in the order named, beginning at one end, three small cones of caramel ice cream, nesselrode pudding and chocolate ice cream, the pudding being in the center of the dish. Around the pudding and between the cones of cream, pour a small ladleful of stiff whipped marshmallow cream. Have previously prepared in an air-tight bowl crisply toasted shredded cocoanut and crumbed macaroni mixed, sprinkle this freely over the whipped cream. On the cones of caramel and chocolate ice cream place a small cube of maraschino pineapple and on the nesselrode pudding put a chocolate cherry. Serve with a glass of ice water and two lady fingers or sweet wafers.

The author says this sundae has proved very popular with his trade and can be served for 25 cents at a good profit if the dispenser is careful and uses a small disher; it can also be as easily made and as quickly turned out in a rush as a banana split and a hundred other similar dishes. (Chas. Greenberg.)

FROZEN COCOANUT BALL

Vanilla ice cream, 1 small ladleful; clover leaf wafer, 1; marshmallow sundae, 1 ladleful; freshly grated cocoanut, a sufficient quantity. Place the small ladleful of vanilla ice cream on a square of oiled paper and with another square of oiled paper form the ice cream into a round ball. (It is advisable to have these balls made up ahead. Keep them in cold cabinets.) Roll this ball into a plate of freshly grated cocoanut until it is well coated, then place the ball on a square clover leaf wafer on a fancy plate and over all pour a ladleful or 1½ ladlefuls of marshmallow sundae. Use a No. 10 disher for the ice cream, which must be firm. The cocoanut may be ground with a food chopper, using a very fine knife. Sells readily for 15 cents and is a winner. (C. E. Denton.)

TASTY TOASTY

Into a suitable dish put a dipperful of vanilla ice cream; cover it with maple syrup and then sprinkle over the syrup a spoonful of toasted corn flakes.

The author states that he realizes the fact that but few 5-cent dishes are offered at the soda fountain counter for the public, and he therefore submits the above formula for a 5-cent specialty which has proved a big winner with him. (D. J. Fitz-Gerald '

CREME DE MENTHE

Serve a ladleful of creme de menthe syrup over strawberry ice cream, adding a sprig of mint.

DEW DROP

Fill a stem glass two-thirds full of vanilla ice cream; then nearly fill the glass with mint and cherry syrup, drop a cherry in the syrup and finish with a lump of whipped cream on top.

SPRINGTIME

Serve ice cream in the shape of an egg on a dish. Pour over the cream creme de menthe syrup. Around the ice cream lay ½ dozen creme de menthe cherries and a spray of menthe.

SUNDAE A LA VENICE

Cocktail glass two-thirds full New York ice cream; fill glass with mint and sherry syrup and top off with whipped cream and creme de menthe cherry. Price—10 cents.

DE MENTHE PINEAPPLE

Pour creme de menthe pineapple over ice cream in a sundae dish.

STRAWBERRY

Strawberry ice cream, 4½ ounces; strawberry crushed fruit syrup, 2 ounces; add a couple of fresh ripe berries on top if in season.

STRAWBERRY SNOW AND CREAM

In a seven-ounce glass put one ounce of vanilla syrup and two spoonfuls of crushed strawberries; add a sufficient quantity of shaved ice and enough whipped cream to fill the glass. Mix well. Price, 10 cents.

Strawberries for the above may be prepared by adding one pound of sugar to each pint of crushed berries. (E. J. Sivley.)

CANTERBERRY

One dipper strawberry ice cream, one spoonful crushed strawberries, one dipper vanilla cream; top with crushed pineapple and sliced bananas, and decorate with two English walnut meats. (E. D Howe.)

BROKEN HEARTS

Put a slice of brick vanilla ice cream on a 6-inch plate. Cover the ice cream with fresh, sweetened, and slightly mashed strawberries, and over these put sweetened whipped cream; top off with two whole strawberries and serve with two nabisco wafers. Sells for 20 cents. (C. F. Wagner.)

MILITANT

Into a suitable dish place a cone of strawberry ice cream, cover with a ladleful of fresh strawberries, and place a large red cherry on top. The "militant" feature is represented by a small hatchet stuck in one side. Sells for 20 cents. (F. Varney.)

STRAWBERRY PUFF

Put into a 6-ounce fancy glass one 20-to-the-quart disherful of vanilla ice cream, pour over it one ladleful of fresh crushed strawberries, and sprinkle on a few chopped nuts; fill the glass nearly full with whipped cream, making the latter stand high in the glass. Top off by sprinkling with chopped nuts and a whole cherry or a strawberry. Any other crushed fruit can be used in place of strawberries, if desired. Can be served at 10 or 15 cents with a good profit. (E. C. Edwards, Jr.)

NEW YORK

Champagne syrup, crushed strawberry. Pour over New York ice cream, serve in fancy sundae cup, top off with whipped cream.

OWL

Put into a tall flaring stem glass a No. 16 dipperful of vanilla ice cream and over it pour a small ladleful of strawberry fruit. Add a No. 8 dipperful of orange ice and top off with a ladleful of whipped cream and a Maraschino cherry. Sells for 15 cents. (H. M. Norris.)

STRAWBERRY CREME

Place a disherful of fresh strawberry ice cream in a sundae dish, pour over it marshmallow sauce, put on a spoonful of nuts, and top off with whipped cream and a nice ripe strawberry. Price, 15 cents. The whipped cream may be left out.

STRAWBERRY DELIGHT

Into a neat saucer place a No. 12 to-the-quart disherful of strawberry ice cream; over the cream put a small ladleful of strawberry crushed fruit, pour on a small quantity of mallo-creme, then sprinkle on a few nuts and top off with a cherry. Around the edges of the cream place a few slices of banana fruit. Sells readily for 15 cents, or it can be served with wafers and sold for 20 cents. (Paul Hurwitz.)

THE HOUN' DOG

Into a bell-shaped phosphate glass place one 12-to-the-quart dipperful of vanilla ice cream. Pour over it crushed raspberries, add ½ ounce of chopped and fresh roasted Spanish (blanched) peanuts, finally placing on top a small piece of cinnamon (the bark!). Sells for 10 cents. (Roy V. Proffitt.)

TRIO

Use a 5-ounce tall stem glass and in it put a small scoopful of vanilla ice cream, a spoonful of ground walnuts and a small scoopful of orange ice. Then pour some raspberry crushed fruit over the mixture. Smooth down, top off with whipped cream and place a cherry on top. Sells for ?0 cents. (G. R. Siegwald.)

MALTED GRAPE

In a sundae dish place a No. 8-to-the-quart disherful of vanilla ice cream; over this sprinkle a light quantity of malted milk, cover with 1½ ounces of grape juice;

top off with whipped cream, and decorate with ripe, purple Concord grapes. The author remarks that "there is just enough absence of sweetness to make this dish a popular favorite with those who do not wish for anything too sweet." Charge 15 cents. (G. W. Lehmann.)

SUNSET

A ladleful of vanilla ice cream in sundae cup. Pour over it a thin grape syrup; top with whipped cream and a fresh strawberry.

CHAUCEREAN

Fill a sundae cup two-thirds full of ice cream; fill the cup with iced grape juice, top off with whipped cream and red Maraschino cherries. Charge 15 cents.

DAMON AND PYTHIAS

Serve on an ice cream dish or in a sundae glass by placing on one side vanilla ice cream, and on the other side pineapple sherbet, filling the center along the "median line" with grape juice. Charge 15 cents.

METROPOLITAN

In any deep sundae glass place vanilla ice cream molded out in a 12-size ice cream disher; pour over the cream 2 ounces of grape juice; then put one large Maraschino cherry on top of the cream and a spoonful of crushed walnuts on the side of the dish. Price, 10 cents.

IMPERIAL GRAPE

Dish of half vanilla ice cream and half grape water ice topped off with whipped cream. (G. L. Loeffler.)

PEACH ROYAL

In a sherbet glass place a large spoonful of whipped cream and over it place a ladleful of sliced peaches. Then add a scoopful of vanilla ice cream (16 to the quart); on one side of the ice cream place a ladleful of crushed pecan nuts, and on the other put a Nabisco wafer. On top and in the center place a ladleful of whipped cream. Decorate with a few whole pecan meats and top off with a Maraschino cherry. The whipped cream should be properly sweetened with pulverized sugar and flavored with a little vanilla extract. Price, 15 cents. (P. A. McCole.)

PEACH BASKET

Place one disherful (No. 12 size) of peach or vanilla ice cream on a comport glass, surround with crushed peaches; over the ice cream put one wafershell, one ladleful of whipped cream and top with Maraschino cherries. Sells for 15 cents. The author of this formula states that "it is named after the 'peach basket hat'; it is a great novelty and takes with everybody." (Erna Hertzberg.)

LADY MARY

Into a cocktail glass put a small portion of sliced peaches, add a small ladleful of plain or fancy ice cream, as desired, and over it place whipped cream. In the center of the top of the cream place a cherry and over all pour some cherry juice, allowing the latter to run down over the sides of the mixture. The juice imparts a nice pinkish tint to the sundae. Put the glass on a fancy plate with two wafers. Price 15 cents. (C. H. Wilkinson.)

ALBERTA

Peel and slice one large Alberta peach, dropping the slices into a deep Colonial sundae cup; cover the slices with a layer of ground nuts, and on them place a cone of strawberry ice cream, decorate the cone with a sliced banana, pineapple cubes and maraschino cherries, artistically arranged. Top off with a ladleful of whipped cream. As an advertising medium the author uses the photograph of an attractive young lady with the name "Alberta" printed below the picture. Price high enough to at least cover costs. (Fay W. Fraker.)

DATE-WITH-A-PEACH

Take a "pin special" sundae dish and place in the bottom one-half ladleful of vanilla ice cream, then add half a scoopful of vanilla marshmallow cream, one 16-to-the-quart scoopful ice cream, one ladleful of crushed fresh peaches, and top with a seeded date on a toothpick. "Is a winner and can be profitably sold for 10 cents." This special was advertised by means of a window display and by "liners" in a local newspaper, which read as follows: "Get a 'Date-with-a-Peach' at ———'s soda fountain for 10 (or 15) cents." (Henry P. Ayers.)

SWEETHEART

Split one lady finger, place the pieces in the bottom of a sundae dish and over them put one small scoop of ice cream, placing on it another lady finger and covering the whole with one fruit ladle of crushed peaches; top off with whipped cream. Price, 15 cents.

PEACHERINE

Two ounces raspberry syrup; one No. 10 disherful peach ice cream. Serve.

LADY MARY SOMERSET

Use fancy custard or dessert cup. Put in one small ladle of strawberry ice cream, add 4 slices of sliced peaches, fill glass with whipped cream, and top off with cherry and nutmeg. Price, 15 cents.

DREAMLAND SUNDAE

Into a banana special dish lay two good sized slices of a peach. In the center place a medium-sized scoopful of vanilla ice cream. Put a spoonful of whipped cream at each side of the ice cream and cover with walnuts and a cherry. Over the vanilla ice cream put a spoonful of crushed pineapple and top with a red and green

cherry. Serve with two nabisco wafers. "A simple dish to prepare and sells readily for 15 cents." (Miss Florence E. Cavanaugh.)

MIDNIGHT SONS

In an oval dish place one 16-to-the-quart measure each of vanilla and strawberry ice cream, putting in the center of the dish a similar measure of pineapple sherbet Over these pour some fresh sliced peaches, then sprinkle on a few pignolia nuts and top off with whipped cream and one each of red, white, and green Maraschino cherries. Sells for 15 or 20 cents.

The author states that this sundae has never failed to delight the ladies who are connoisseurs of choice delicacies. (Thos. Keriakedes.)

PEACH OF A SUNDAE

Over a ladle of peach ice cream pour a sauce made of the following: One pound of mixed nuts chopped fine, mixed with 1 pint of rich maple syrup.

CHERRY

On a measure of ice cream in a saucer champagne glass, place several maraschino cherries and pour over them 1 ounce of cherry phosphate syrup. Top off with whipped cream and serve with a spoon.

MARASCHINO CHERRY

Into an ordinary sundae glass place a No. 16 disherful of Maraschino cherry ice, top off with whipped cream and cherry. To make the Maraschino cherry ice, use the following formula: juice of one lemon, 8 ounces sugar, 2½ pints water, one pint Maraschino cherries (chopped fine) and the beaten whites of three eggs Mix well and put the mixture, which should measure ½ gallon, into a freezer and freeze. Sells for 10 cents. (John H. Gassman.)

CHERRY ROYAL

Take a 5-inch saucer, such as are used for serving ice cream. In the center place a No. 12-to-the-quart scoopful of vanilla ice cream. Around the base of the cream arrange a ring of large, fresh black cherries, with the stems removed; pour over the ice cream a ladleful of cherry royal sauce; top off with a spoonful of whipped cream and a red and green cherry.

The author writes that black cherries can be bought at any fruit store for 20 cents per pound. Open them on the bottom end with a sharp knife, and remove the pits. Prepare "cherry royal sauce" as follows. Put one pound of fresh fruit red cherries in one quart of water on the stove and cook until the cherries are thoroughly done; strain through cheesecloth, squeezing the pulp up well. Return the juice to the cooking vessel, add 3 pounds of granulated sugar, and boil until the mixture reaches the consistency of molasses; when cool, flavor with 2 ounces of port wine; keep the mixture cool. "This sundae will make a hit with your male patrons, as it is not too rich, and most men like cherries. Advertise the sundae by signs in the window or at the fountain, and charge 20 or 25 cents." (Harry G. Frame.)

DIXIELAND

Take a cone of ice cream in sundae cup, dash a little red cherry syrup over it. (Keep cherry syrup in phosphate bottle, dilute the concentrated cherry syrup with water, so it will come out of bottle) Top off with a little whipped cream, another dash cherry syrup or orange syrup over the whipped cream and top off with a maraschino cherry. If you haven't whipped cream, serve without.

Creme de menthe cherries may be served same way with mint syrup.

BLOSSOM

Maraschino cherry ice cream, shaped into flower, whipped cream. (Geo. Dauernheim.)

CHERRY TEMPTATION

On a banana-split dish place two scoopfuls (No. 10) vanilla ice cream, cover with crushed cherries, top with marshmallow cream and decorate with one red and one green cherry. Charge 15 cents.

FROZEN CHERRY BON BON

Spoonful ice cream in 8-ounce stem glass. Almost fill with shaved ice. Add 2 ounces cherry syrup, top with layer of ice cream, and add a maraschino cherry. Price, 10 cents.

HOT CHERRY SUNDAE

In a sundae glass containing pineapple cream pour a ladleful of hot cherry syrup.

CHERRY SANDWICH

Layer of whipped cream in a cocktail glass followed by vanilla ice cream and an ounce of cherry syrup. Top off with pineapple sherbet and whipped cream and sell for 15 cents. (G. A. Kinney.)

NABISCO

One 16-to-the-quart dipper vanilla ice cream; four nabisco wafers; half a dozen whole cherries. Sells for 15 cents. (John C. Muse, Jr.)

CHERRY NEWPORT

Cherries, whipped cream, grated cocoanut. Price, 10 cents. (Geo. Dauernheim)

SPRING SONG

On a banana split dish place two small scoopfuls of vanilla ice cream, and over the cream and on the dish between the two portions of cream put two teaspoonfuls of whipped cream, topping off with two maraschino cherries and cherry syrup. Then put on one of the scoopfuls of cream, some cocoanut, and on the other some strawber-

ries and nuts Finally, place a chocolate marshmallow at each end of the dish. Sells for 15 to 25 cents. (Harry Slantchek.)

CHERRY CREAM AND EGG

Place in the bottom of an 8-ounce fancy or good flint glass tumbler with stem bottom, one small ladleful of crushed cherries and over the cherries place a ladleful of ice cream (16 to the quart). Into a shaker glass (about 14-ounce capacity) put one whole egg, 1 ounce cherry syrup, 1 tablespoonful of sweet cream (ice cream), and cracked ice. Shake well and strain on to the contents of the tumbler. Place a medium sized spoon across the top of the tumbler after the ice cream has risen to the top of the mixture. By using strawberry syrup and crushed strawberries or different flavors, any customer may be served to taste. Charge 15 or 20 cents. (R. K. Snow.)

BUNKER HILL

Into a fancy sundae glass put a scoopful of vanilla ice cream and over it pour a little cherry syrup; sprinkle over the syrup some ground nuts and cover with a little whipped cream. Then with a spoon make a notch through the whipped cream into the ice cream and in the notch insert a cherry pierced by the pole of a small souvenir flag. The flag measures $1\frac{1}{4}$x2 in., and can be procured at any kindergarten supply house for about 50 cents per gross The author explains: "As we employed them the flags were desirable souvenirs and pinned on the coats and hats of our customers, they proved a moving advertisement for us the rest of the day." He writes that he served this special on Feb 22 with most satisfactory results, although it can be served on any national holiday. On St. Patrick's Day he served the sundae as "Pat's Shamrock," substituting creme de menthe for the cherry syrup directed in the above formula, and a shamrock pin piercing a creme de menthe cherry instead of the U.S. flag and the red cherry. Charge 15 cents. (Henry Mertens.)

CHERRY DIP

On a measure of ice cream arrange in a circle 6 red Maraschino cherries, with one green cherry in the center, using a pair of tongs, and pouring over the "dip" a ladle of the Maraschino liquid. Charge 15 cents.

CHERRY BLOSSOM

Take ordinary whipping cream, flavor with cherry syrup, adding enough syrup to make the cream a dark pinkish, almost red color, and whip thoroughly. Keep on ice. To serve, put a small dipperful over a cone of ice cream (any flavor except strawberry or other cream of a reddish color), and top with a red cherry. Place two nabisco wafers at the side and serve. Sells for 10 cents, and according to the author, "it is a hummer with transient trade, which is our specialty, being close to the Union Station and the different street-car lines of our city." May also be dispensed under the name of "Cherry Puff." (V. C. Studney.)

FLEUR D'ORANGE

Sundae proportion ice cream, orange syrup, whipped cream and orange cut in cubes Strawberry Flower is prepared in the same manner, only strawberries are used instead of orange.

BOSTONIAN

Place a measure of ice cream in a sundae glass, and over it artistically arrange sliced orange cut in diamond shaped pieces, sliced pineapple, maraschino cherries and English walnut halves. Charge 15 cents.

CUBANOLA

Peel and slice an orange. Cut a slice in half and place a half one each side of the plate. Set a cone of ice cream in the center, filbert nuts on one side, walnuts on the other, a green cherry on one-half of the orange, a red cherry on the other half. Sells for 15 cents.

DOVE OF PEACE

Into a stem sundae glass place a No. 10-to-the-quart dipperful of vanilla ice cream, and cover the cream with orgeat syrup. Around the cream stand three half slices of orange, round side up; between each slice place a small spoonful of whipped cream; garnish each slice of orange with the half of a cherry, and the ice cream with ground pistachio nuts. On top of the sundae put an "icing dove," about 1½ inches in length (these "doves" can be procured at any baker's supply house). Sells for 20 or 25 cents. (H. T. Pierson.)

E. B.

Put a No. 8 dipper of orange ice on a fancy sundae dish, and pour over it a ladle of fresh crushed orange.

GOLDEN SUNSET

Into a suitable sundae dish place a No 16-to-the-quart dipperful of vanilla ice cream; add a ladleful of crushed orange, sprinkle with finely chopped cherries, and top off with a whole cherry. Charge 10 or 15 cents.

KANSAS CITY SUNFLOWER

Take a nice, sweet, smooth-skinned orange, and beginning at the top of the fruit, cut the rind in about eight or ten places, following the natural divisions of the juicy pulp, and then peel the several sections of the rind thus cut outward and downward for about half the height of the fruit, so as to simulate the structure of a sunflower. Separate and spread out the divisions of the juicy pulp of the orange in the same way, and place on a dainty 6-inch sundae plate. In the center of the orange put ice cream of two different colors (or if preferred, vanilla ice cream alone) to represent the heart of the sunflower, and then decorate with pieces of oranges, cherries and nabisco wafers. Sells for 25 cents. (Robt. R. Russell.)

MEXICAN TIP TOP

On a sundae dish place a No. 16 to-the-quart cone-shaped disherful of peach ice cream. Diagonally up and down the cone of ice cream place the sections of an orange, top with a cherry and sprinkle with Mexican pecans. Serve with Mexican pecan wafers and a small spoon. Price, 15 cents.

PELL MELL

Take a navel orange, remove the peel and cut the orange into small cubes; cover the cubes with powdered white sugar and freshly grated cocoanut; let the mixture stand for two hours when it will be ready for use. In the center of a salad dish place a dipperful of vanilla ice cream and orange ice, half-and-half, placing at either end of the dish a small dipperful of sweet, whipped cream and cover with the orange and cocoanut mixture. Top off the center cone with a Maraschino cherry and each of the whipped cream cones with the half of an English walnut. Sells readily for 20 cents. (Ralph Hilligass.)

TANGO ICE

Into a fancy saucer place a slice of orange. Over this place one five-cent disherful of orange ice. Top with a maraschino cherry. Place nuts around the outer edge of the glass. The color-scheme of this dish is about as near as one can come, while working with soda-fountain products, to the now popular "tango" shade, and for this reason it makes a special appeal to customers of the fair sex. The price is 15 cents. (Harry Crum.)

DAISY

From the center to the edge of a dainty wafer dish, about six inches in diameter, place thin slices of banana so as to represent the petals of a flower; over the center of this place a large dipperful of vanilla ice cream and over the cream pour a dipperful of strawberry syrup and sprinkle on a few crushed nuts, and the sundae will closely resemble a daisy. Price, 15 cents. (J. Harold Searls.)

BRYN MAWR (COLORS GOLD AND WHITE)

Split a banana lengthwise, place in a suitable dish and cover it with vanilla ice cream. Around the edges of the dish place slices of orange and top off with grated cocoanut. Price, 20 cents.

OMAR SUNDAE

Fill an 8-to-the-quart cone rounded full of ice cream, place it in a champagne glass and pour over it a small ladle of the crushed fruit. Take half a banana and peel it, cut into thin slices and place arou..d the sides of the cone.

RUNABOUT

Put large measure of ice cream in a tall sundae glass, cover with fresh crushed banana fruit and fill the glass with whipped cream. Place on one side maraschino cherries. Other fruit may be used if desired

TALLYHO

Put a large dipperful of vanilla ice cream into a tall sundae dish, cover with freshly crushed banana fruit and fill the glass with whipped cream. Cover the top of the mixture on one side with chopped pecans, and on the other side sprinkle powdered mace. Top with maraschino cherries or other fruit, as may be desired. Charge 15 cents.

PINEAPPLE FREEZE

Fill sundae cup two-thirds full pineapple ice, then fill up with pineapple crushed fruit. Top off with sliced pineapple and orange and chopped brandied cherries.

MARASCHINO PINEAPPLE

Over ice cream in sundae dish pour maraschino pineapple.

WALNUT PINEAPPLE

Make a regular sundae with crushed pineapple and top with a spoonful of whole or chopped walnut meats. Price, 10 cents.

HAVANA

Over half a slice of pineapple in a fancy saucer place a cone of ice cream. Top off with two or three cherries, whipped cream and nuts. Charge 15 cents.

MOUNT VESUVIUS

Take a scoopful of strawberry ice cream and a scoopful of vanilla ice cream and over them put some fresh pineapple juice. Decorate with one or two marshmallows and then pour on a ladleful of marshmallow cream; top off with several Maraschino cherries. Price 15 cents.

The author is of the opinion that if more druggists and confectioners would encourage the sale of fancy sundaes they would find a greater profit and 5-cent sundaes would be seldom called for. (Gilbert Crawford.)

PINEAPPLE SNOW

Pineapple snow is a mixture of shaved or cracked ice, cream and pineapple syrup with or without carbonated water, the whole being topped off with shaved ice and dispensed in a glass with a spoon.

PINK LADY

Place in a fancy sundae dish ½ ounce of pineapple syrup, then add a No. 16-to-the-quart dipperful of vanilla ice cream. Over this pour a small ladleful of whipped cream previously colored a pink tint by the incor-

poration of a small quantity of strawberry syrup. Top with a maraschino cherry or some chocolate-dipped peanuts. Sells for 10 cents. (P. H. Kutz.)

SUNSHINE

Put into a sundae glass or dish one ladleful of pineapple sherbet. Place on top and down four sides of the sherbet whipped cream, putting grated pineapple over the whipped cream and topping off with a Maraschino cherry.

Pineapple sherbet is made as follows: Water, 3 quarts; sugar, xxxx, 6 pounds; 6 pineapples cut very fine; solution of citric acid, 1 ounce. Dissolve the sugar in the water, add the other ingredients and the white of one egg, pass through a fine hair sieve, strain into a freezer and freeze Canned pineapple may be used in place of the fresh fruit, one can of pineapple being taken in place of two pineapples. (Walter Luick.)

HAWAIIAN BEAUTY

Into a glass sundae dish place one 12-to-the-quart disherful of pineapple sherbet and cover with a ladleful of fresh strawberries. Top off with a spoonful of whipped cream and a cherry.

PINEAPPLE PRINCE

Put pineapple fruit in ice cream dish, place cone of ice cream on the fruit, pour a small quantity of Roman punch syrup over it, and top off with violettas or rose petals. Charge 15 cents.

"CO-ED"

Serve in a fancy sherbet glass Place one measure of lemon nut sherbet in the glass; pour over it one ladleful of crushed pineapple, and top off with a whole red cherry.

AUTOMOBILE

On a 6-inch plate put a nabisco wafer over which place a No. 20 disherful each of orange ice and vanilla ice cream; then pour over them an ounce of crushed pineapple. Decorate with four candy cream wafers used as wheels, two maraschino cherries to represent lights, using a toothpick to hold them in place, and top off with whipped cream and a few ground or powdered nuts. Place a candy figure on the finished sundae to represent the driver. Should sell for 25 cents. (Ed. Mockler.)

PINEAPPLE PIE

Place a large slice of pineapple on a small china plate and upon this put an 8-to-the-quart dipper of vanilla ice cream. Imbed three pineapple red aces or hearts in the cream and top with vanilla marshmallow upon the crest of which is placed another pineapple ace or heart.

This makes a handsome, appetizing sundae and is a winner. Charge 15 cents. (E. J. Howard.)

BLUEBERRY DREAM

Buy one quart of blueberries, wash them thoroughly, then pour over them 1½ pounds of sugar Let the mixture stand for three hours, then add to it six bananas sliced, and two quarts of simple syrup. Mix well in a glass bowl and proceed as follows In a sundae cup put one disherful (20-to-the-quart) of strawberry ice cream and one of pineapple water ice; over these put a ladleful of the blueberry mixture and a few chopped nuts. Then cover with some marshmallow cream, surmounting all with a lady finger placed between a green and red cherry.

The author states that he has no trouble in selling this mixture for 15 cents, and it is a new use for blueberries. (Clinton W. Waldorf.)

NUT APRICOT

Into a sundae glass turn a cone of ice cream. Over the top of the cream stick a few hickory or walnut meats broken into small pieces. Over all pour an ounce of strong apricot syrup and serve with a spoon.

MERRY COUNTESS

One No. 20 ladle each of vanilla and strawberry ice cream in a sundae dish. A ladle each of crushed pineapple and strawberry. A small quantity of sliced bananas. Top with whipped cream and a red and green cherry. Sells for 15 cents. (Don C. Vann.)

NOUGAT FRAPPE SUNDAE

Into a 7-ounce high-ball glass put a No. 16 disherful of strawberry ice cream; over the strawberry cream put one ladleful of nougat frappe dressing; then add a No. 16 disherful of orange frappe, and then top off with a liberal supply of nougat frappe dressing, a few pecan halves and a maraschino cherry. Sells for 15 cents. (C. Lawson Hughes.)

ROOF GARDEN FAVORITE

In a stemmed sundae glass put a spoonful of crushed peaches, then a small ladleful of ice cream, and over all sprinkle some ground nuts. Nearly fill the glass with whipped cream and finish with hot claret syrup.

SEPTEMBER MORN

Into an 8-ounce goblet place 3 ounces of white grape juice; float on the juice a ladleful of whipped cream and on top of the whipped cream put a No. 12 disherful of strawberry ice cream. Now insert two veronique wafers opposite each other in the ice cream next to the glass. Decorate with maraschino pineapple and cherries, and pecan halves arranged artistically. Price—15 or 20 cents. (Fay W. Fraker.)

SEA FOAM

Shake up separately the yolk of an egg with 1 ounce of orgeat syrup, and beat the white with some powdered sugar. Put a cone of peach ice cream in a sundae cup, pour around it the beaten egg white, putting in the center the syrup and yolk, and serve. Charge 15 cents.

SALAMANDER

Ginger cordial syrup, mix with ginger fruit, pour over vanilla ice cream and sprinkle cinnamon on top. Serve in sundae cup and top off with maraschino cherries. Vanilla syrup may be used in this formula and crystallized ginger cut up in it.

FRUITS AND FLOWERS

A glass basket is filled with peach ice cream covered with slivers of fresh fruits. A wreath of crystallized violets is placed around the edge of the peach cream. On top, place a rosette of vanilla whipped cream in the center of which put a preserved or candied strawberry. At this season of the year, the author states, preserved fruits may be used. The glass basket is served on an ice-cream plate, regular size, on which a fancy paper doily mat has been placed. The glass baskets can be bought for 10 cents apiece. The combination, the author says, can be sold for 20 cents. (Edward Pennock)

"ROOSEVELT" SPECIAL

At one end of a split banana dish place a No. 12 ladleful of strawberry ice cream, and at the other, a No. 12 ladleful of vanilla ice cream, which is to represent an iceberg, the strawberry cream representing a ship. Decorate the vanilla cream with crushed pineapple fruit, and the strawberry with red raspberries and chopped nut meats. Place two nabisco wafers on edge, one on either side of the strawberry ice cream, and pointing toward the vanilla cream. Also put two nabiscos in a vertical position on the strawberry cream to represent sails. Serve with a spoon and glass of water.

To advertise this delicacy the author used short window strips which read:

```
: Try Delicious                    :
: "ROOSEVELT" SPECIAL, 15c. :
```

The "Roosevelt" was the ship used by Admiral Peary on his voyage toward the North Pole. (Kenneth E. Paul.)

PERFECTO

Into a fancy ice cream dish place a disherful of vanilla-strawberry-chocolate ice cream, and over it pour a small ladleful of strawberry, pineapple, and peach fruits; then add a small quantity of claret and champagne syrups, a ladleful of chopped walnuts, a teaspoonful of whipped cream, and put a red cherry on top. Serve with a napkin and a glass of ice water. Sells for 10 cents and "costs only five if made right." It might well be priced at 15 cents.

The author states that "this is a big seller and every patron likes to tell his friends about it." (Edwin H. Shortiss.)

ORIENTAL FRUIT SUNDAE

Into a sundae dish put a small spoonful of lychu nuts and cover them with a No. 10 to-the-quart disherful of vanilla ice cream, add ½ ounce of vanilla syrup; place half way round the base of the ice cream a sprinkling of ground figs, completing the circle with a sprinkling of ground dates. Top with a sprinkling of ground nuts and a cherry Sells for 15 or 20 cents.

FLUFFY RUFFLES

Take two cones of ice cream, 20 to the quart, and put one ladleful of marshmallow sauce, chopped walnuts and a red cherry on one cone, and one ladleful of raspberry fruit, chopped pistachio nuts and a green cherry on the other cone. Serve on a pickle dish. The walnuts and pistachio nuts should be chopped in a meat chopper and not cut too fine. Where green cherries with vegetable color cannot be procured, use two red cherries or one red and one white cherry.

The author states that "'Fluffy Ruffles' is a pretty dish. Its appearance will cause people to try it who never saw or heard of it before. It is a big favorite at our fountain." It is worth 15 cents. (D. Charles O'Conner.)

OLD GREY BONNET

Place in a colonial sundae cup one cone (No. 3 disher) of caramel ice cream; around the base of the cream arrange at regular intervals cubes of pineapple, orange and Maraschino cherries. Take a whole slice of pineapple with a hole in the center and fit it down over the top of the cone. This will represent the bonnet. On the pineapple put a ladleful of whipped cream, vanilla flavored, and top off with a green cherry

The song "Put on your old grey bonnet" was very popular in Lincoln, Nebr., the author's city, when he originated this sundae, and he advertised it by taking the picture off the music and pasting the word "sundae" after "grey bonnet" in the title. It sells for 20 cents. (Fay W. Fraker.)

HOBBLE

Into a fancy sundae glass put a scoopful of caramel ice cream and over it sprinkle some ground nuts; cover with a little whipped cream, putting on the latter a little pink marshmallow. Now around the cream and in such a position that the ends will come to a point stand four lady fingers, topping off with whipped cream and surmounting the whole with a cherry, the lat-

ter being flanked on each side with two pieces of pecan meats.

The author states that "this sundae made according to the above formula is not only artistic but very delicious when correctly made." Sells for 20 cents. (Justin Loubere)

GOO GOO

Ice cream, 1 large ladleful; nut frappe, 2 ounces; stir together thoroughly, cover with whipped cream and trim with Maraschino cherry and cut pineapple.

CREAMED FIG

Take a dish full of chocolate ice cream (or a dish of vanilla ice cream with a layer of chocolate syrup over it). Over this place a spoonful of crushed figs and a large spoonful of whipped cream, putting on each side a Nabisco wafer. Serve in a sherbet glass with a spoon, topping off with a Maraschino cherry.

Regarding this formula, the author says· "On account of the popularity of figs and the great number of people who eat figs for so many different purposes, this formula is a trade winner." Charge 15 cents. (Patrick McCole.)

BALTIMORE BELLE

Make a syrup of 1 orange, 1 peach, 1 banana, ½ pineapple, 1 ounce strawberries, and enough simple syrup to make one-half gallon. Leave the peel on the oranges and cut into cubes, peel the banana and peach and cut into cubes, grate the pineapple and crush the strawberries. Add the syrup and color the mixture pink. To serve put ice cream in the bottom of the glass. Add one ounce of the above topping

CABARET

Place in a suitable dish one ball of pistachio nut ice cream (green), and one ball of frozen pudding (pink). Pour over the ice cream cabaret dressing, and then stick a toothpick in each ball of the cream, placing on one of the toothpicks an olive and on the other a red cherry. Drop six roasted and blanched almonds around the base of the cream, and shake over all one tablespoonful toasted cocoanut

The "cabaret dressing" is made as follows: Take 1 quart pure maple syrup, ¼ pound cut seeded raisins, ¼ pound cut figs, mix, and bring to a boil; cool, add ½ pound cut Malaga grapes, mix well, and use as a dressing. Charge 15 cents. (C. I. Hadley.)

ORIENTAL DELIGHT

Take a fancy stem glass, holding about 4 ounces, and in it place a No. 20 dipperful of vanilla ice cream, add a ladleful of chopped figs which have been previously soaked in maple syrup, then a sprinkling of ground nut meats, and a dipperful of equal parts of pistachio ice cream and orange ice.

On top place a spoonful of whipped cream, then a chocolate Maraschino cherry; on each side put a red cherry, and serve with the glass on a fancy plate. The fact that chopped figs are used in the preparation of this beverage makes the name "Oriental Delight" particularly appropriate. Charge not less than 15 cents. (Geo. W. Eldon.)

FIG SPECIAL

Take three small preserved figs, cut them in half, and lay the halves on a small plate; add one No. 12 dipperful of vanilla ice cream and sprinkle with chopped nuts; top with whipped cream and cherry. Sells for 20 cents. The author, a dispenser in the Hawaiian Islands, states that the figs can be bought in 2-pound packages or in 1-gallon cans. (Hazel P. Wilson.)

OLD VIRGINIA

Into a tall flaring stem glass place a No. 16 dipperful of strawberry ice cream and add in the order named, a small ladleful of red raspberry fruit, a No. 8 dipperful of pineapple ice, and top off with whipped cream and a chocolate-covered Maraschino cherry. Sells for 15 or 20 cents. (Robt Landis.)

BULGARIAN

Into a high sundae glass of cylindrical shape place a teaspoonful of vanilla ice cream; over this pour creme de menthe syrup (which is green); then add a teaspoonful of chocolate ice cream, on top of which place a little crushed strawberry fruit; now add a teaspoonful of maple nut ice cream, and top the whole with two slices of peaches and one cherry, thus reproducing the colors—white, green, brown, red-tan orange, and red. The author writes that this sundae is named after the popular Bulgarian colors, and "would seem to be a big sundae to sell for 10 cents. But the capacity of this kind of sundae dish isn't much, and by using a spoon instead of a ladle for measuring out the various ingredients the sundae may be sold at a good profit." (Miss Louise Heinze.)

FRUITED SUNDAE

Mix together ¼ pound ground roasted almonds; ½ pound candied cherries cut in halves, and 1 pint fresh crushed strawberries. Mix with 1 gallon of vanilla ice cream, pack in ice and salt, and allow to stand 3 hours. To serve, place one No 10-to-the-quart scoopful of the fruited ice cream in a sundae cup and pour over it a ladleful of cherry juice. Sells for 15 cents. (T. Louvis.)

TURKISH DELIGHT

Into a sundae cup place one-half scoopful each of pistachio ice cream and orange water ice. Over these pour a ladleful of Turkish Delight mixture and a few ground walnuts; top off with whipped cream and a whole green fig, sprinkling a little ground nutmeg on top of the cream. Place the sundae cup on a saucer and serve.

The Turkish Delight mixture is made by taking candied citron, 1 pound; preserved ginger, 1½ pounds; water, 3 pints; simple syrup, 3 pints; and strawberry crushed fruit, ½ gallon. Run the citron and ginger through a food chopper equipped with the fine knife cutter, place the mixture in a suitable vessel and add the water and syrup. Cook the mixture slowly over a fire for about half an hour, stirring occasionally to keep from burning; then add the strawberries; a few drops of red vegetable color may also be added if the mixture is not dark enough. Whole figs can be bought from any grocery store.

The author states that when he first thought of asking 25 cents for this sundae he was afraid the price would scare everybody, but he took a chance and on the Saturday previous to submitting the formula he sold forty-one of the sundaes, which made quite an addition to his receipts for that day. (Clinton W. Waldorf.)

FROU FROU

In the bottom of a four-inch glass saucer having a handle, lay three "frou frou" wafers, their ends touching so as to form the outline of a triangle. In the center of the triangle put a No. 8 cone of vanilla ice cream, which will hold the wafers in place. Pour over all one ladleful of crushed raspberry, filling in the three corners left by the wafers with chopped Brazil nuts. Then add a ladleful of whipped cream, three walnut halves and a Maraschino cherry on a toothpick. Now lay a fern leaf on a six-inch fancy plate and on it place the saucer containing the sundae. Serve with a glass of water and a paper napkin.

"A good seller at 15 cents the year round." (Raymond J. Williams.)

BROOKLYN BRIDGE

On an oblong dish place two (No. 16) scoopfuls of chocolate ice cream, one at each end of the dish. Over each cone of ice cream scatter a few chopped pecans and top with a little whipped cream, being careful to leave the space between the ice cream cones vacant. Then fill this space with mint syrup; connect the two cones of ice cream with a half slice of orange. The chocolate ice cream cones represent the banks of the river, the mint syrup the water, and the orange, the bridge. Charge 15 cents. (Pendel Poledor.)

VERMONT

Take a saucer, such as are commonly used for sundaes, and around its edge place 5 macaroons. Place a cone of vanilla ice cream (measured out with a 12-to-the-quart ice cream disher) in the center of the saucer. Over the ice cream pour ½ ladleful of pineapple fruit and 1 ounce of maple syrup. Top off with a small measure of maple sugar. Charge 20 cents or more.

RIKER-HEGEMAN'S PARISIAN

Made of vanilla ice cream served with chocolate sauce, with a layer of sliced bananas, a dash of chopped walnuts and a toothsome, red cherry on top.

"Nothing more delicious and nourishing could be served even though you bought it as a fancy ice cream in a great restaurant and paid 30 or 40 cents for it. Try our Parisian Sundae this week." Price, 15 cents.

U-WANA

In a six-inch dish place a scoop of vanilla ice cream, one of strawberry and one of chocolate (20 to quart), round-bowl shape. In the center place half a Bartlett pear. Top off with a teaspoonful of whipped cream, sprinkle a few crushed pecans. Top each mold with a cherry pierced with a toothpick. Price 20 cents.

To advertise the "U-Wana Sundae" place a card to read:

```
: ........................... :
:      SPECIAL TODAY       :
:     "U-WANA SUNDAE"      :
:         20 Cents.        :
: ........................... :
```

This feature might well be priced at 25 cents. (Theo. Louvis.)

BISQUE BLUSH

At the bottom of a cocktail glass place a scoop of bisque ice cream. Cover with a spoonful of crushed pineapple and chopped nuts, followed by a layer of orange sherbet. Top off with a spoonful of claret syrup, so placed that it will trickle down the glass and produce a pretty effect, whipped cream and Maraschino cherries, selling for 15 cents. (Clarence Bess)

BRIDAL PATH

Take six bananas, crush and mix them with 1 quart jar of cherries, and 1 pound of walnut meats. To serve, take a banana split dish and into it put a No. 16-to-the-quart dipperful of vanilla, peach and banana ice cream. On top of the cream and close together lay lengthwise two Cameo wafers. Cover with the mixture of bananas, cherries and walnut meats, and place at each end a cherry. With each sundae when served give a spray of lily of the valley (artificial). Sells for 20 or 25 cents. (Peter Eichelman.)

MILITARY

One dipper of ice cream, sliced orange cut in diamond shaped pieces, sliced pineapple cut in triangular shape, whole English walnuts, maraschino cherries, the nuts and fruits to be arranged artistically. No syrups are used. Charge 15 cents.

DUNCE CAP

In a regular sundae glass place a ladleful of fresh raspberries, cover with raspberry whipped cream, over the whipped cream lay a few walnut halves and a sphere of vanilla ice cream. Then fill a small ice cream cone with raspberry whipped cream and place on the sphere of cream so as to form a cap.

To make raspberry whipped cream, take one quart of heavy cream and whip until almost stiff, pour in one-half teacupful of crushed raspberries and whip until the mixture becomes stiff. Price, 20 cents. (Sterling Miller.)

DUNCE CAP SUNDAE

On a sundae saucer or dish put one spoonful of whipped cream, pressing it into a circular shape. Upon it place one large-sized *cone-shaped* disher of vanilla cream. Press the ice cream down so as to form a roll or ridge of whipped cream all around the base of the cone. Stud the ice cream with choice currants, top with a fresh cherry, and sprinkle over with a spoonful of chopped roasted almonds. Sells for 15 cents. (C. Bassman.)

SPECIAL MATINEE

Take a tall-footed sundae glass, place in it a 16-to-the-quart dipperful each of chocolate and vanilla ice cream, and pour over the top of each a ladleful of the following dressing· Marshmallow, 1 quart, plain syrup, 1 pint, and enough concentrated blackberry and old rose to color and flavor. Then mix in ¼ pound each of chopped walnuts and pecans. Sells for 10 cents.

To advertise the sundae, the author makes use of the following ad, which he has found of direct value as a trade promoter, in that it excites interest as relating to something new, without going too deeply into details as to what the Matinee Sundae really is:

```
: ............................. :
:   On Saturday we will serve a  :
:  Special MATINEE Sundae that   :
:  will be a pleasure to take in. :
:    Something smooth and so deli- :
:  cious that you will enjoy it from :
:  beginning to end              :
:         (Three Acts)           :
:     Be Sure to Attend.         :
:     Tell Your Friends.         :
: ............................. :
```
(C. E. Wilber.)

SOUVENIR

Serve in a tall stem frappe' glass a No. 16-to-the-quart dipperful of vanilla ice cream, putting over the ice cream a ladleful of a mixture consisting of chopped figs, fresh sliced peaches, crushed pineapples, whole strawberries and fresh orange fruits, top with whipped cream and a wafer. Serve with the sundae a small silver spoon, which may be bought in gross lots for four cents apiece. The customer may keep the spoon as a souvenir. Price of this feature would necessarily vary considerably. It might be 20 or 25 cents. (Sterling Miller.)

RIGOLETTO

Over a ladle of peach ice cream pour a sauce made of the following: One pound of mixed nuts chopped fine, mixed with 1 pint of rich maple syrup.

EPICURIAN

Place a tall cone of strawberry ice cream in a flat dish, pour a little grape syrup and a little "champagne syrup" around the bottom; add two slices of peach, and on top of the cone balance a thin slice of pineapple topped off with an arabesque dab of whipped cream and a red cherry. Charge 15 cents.

FLIRTING PRINCESS

In a highball glass place a scoopful of vanilla ice cream, covered by half an ounce of grape juice. Add several teaspoonfuls of chopped bananas and cover with a layer of strawberry ice cream. Top off with whipped cream and cherries and serve for 15 cents. (R. J. Reynolds.)

CLUB HOUSE

Peel six bananas and one pineapple, slice and cut the pineapple into small cubes, cut the bananas in thin slices and put both fruits into a fruit bowl. Sprinkle with as much sugar as the fruit will take up and place on the ice until the sugar is dissolved. Then add about three dozen Maraschino cherries and mixture is ready for use. This should be prepared, small quantity at a time, so as to keep fresh.

Take one-half cone each of strawberry and vanilla ice cream, place in a six-ounce sundae cup, and pour on a ladleful of the above mixture. Be sure to get about three cherries neatly placed on the top and finish with whipped cream. Can be served without the whipped cream. If served with whipped cream it should bring 20 cents (James L. Humble.)

MYSTERY MIX

Put one ladleful of vanilla, chocolate and strawberry ice cream, mixed, into a sundae glass, over which pour rainbow sauce, topping off with whipped cream. Rainbow sauce is made as follows: Chop fine one pound of candied cherries, one pound of pineapple, one-half pound each of candied citron, apricots and pears, and a few pistachio nuts; mix all well together and boil in enough simple syrup to make a nice dish. Pour one ladleful of this mixture over the mixed ice cream. Price, 15 cents (W. Luick.)

FLORIDA MIXTURE

The Florida Mixture consists of one ball of orange ice, one-half dipperful of crushed strawberries and one-half dipperful of crushed pineapple. Top off with a cherry on a toothpick. Charge 10 cents.

FREE LUNCH

Take a deep sundae dish, one that will hold two disherfuls of cream, and put in one disherful of vanilla ice cream. Over this put some chocolate syrup, a few pieces of sliced bananas and a half teaspoonful of malted milk. Now put in another disherful of vanilla cream and cover with chocolate syrup. Place sliced bananas all around the top with a spoonful of chopped pecans over all. At the top, in the center, place a Maraschino cherry with a toothpick through it.

"This delicacy sells readily for 15 cents and is a trade winner. Of course, you must use your judgment in the making and not be too liberal, because if you are careful you can make a good per cent of profit on each sundae. This one has been especially popular with the students in our neighborhood." (W. Arthur Golding)

SKYSCRAPER

Place two small scoopfuls of vanilla ice cream on a china platter; over the ice cream pour cherry syrup with cherries and place a Nabisco wafer over the cream; then add a scoopful of strawberry ice cream, placing it on the middle of the Nabisco wafer; place another Nabisco wafer on top of the strawberry ice cream so that it will balance evenly and top off with whipped cream and a whole cherry. Charge 20 cents. (Sydney Trau.)

COMMODORE PERRY

Into a large sundae dish place a large dipperful each of strawberry, vanilla and French vanilla ice cream, putting crushed strawberries over the strawberry ice cream, crushed pineapple over the vanilla ice cream, and grape juice over the French vanilla ice cream. Top off with whipped cream and red cherries. Sells for 15 to 20 cents (H. Bayless.)

QUEEN

Pour over ice cream mixed blackberries and grated black walnuts and top off with two whole strawberries. Or, pour over ice cream the same mixture as in the preceding, adding a little powdered cinnamon and syrup of raspberry vinegar.

This sundae may also be topped with marshmallow.

MILITANT HOPE SUNDAE

Use a small neat china or cut glass plate. Upon it in triangular shape arrange three cones of ice cream—strawberry, chocolate and vanilla flavors respectively. Upon the strawberry ice cream place a white cherry;

upon the chocolate ice cream put a pine-apple cube, and upon the vanilla ice cream put a whole English walnut. Fill the center with shredded cocoanut and on it place a thin slice of orange Decorate the edge of the plate with whipped cream and half pecans Charge 15 cents. (Clinton B. Ellis.)

CUBIST

Cut into cubes equal parts of oranges, pineapples and bananas; mix with fresh strawberry syrup, and add one pint of chopped nuts to each two quarts of the mixture. To serve, use a No. 1½ cube-shaped sundae mould. Fill the mould with alternate layers of chocolate and vanilla ice cream, then empty out on a small hexagonal plate. Pour over the cream a ladle-ful of the "cubist art" mixture, and top with whipped cream and a cube-shaped piece of orange or pineapple. This is a good seller at 20 cents.

The author writes that he uses "cubist art" drawings to advertise this specialty. (Philip W. Fraker)

SILVER SUNDAE

Make a thin paste of marshmallow whip, which pour over a cone of ice cream (No. 12-to-the-quart dipper); sprinkle over with cocoanut, and top off with marshmallow. Sells for 15 cents.

The author of this formula asserted that "this sundae made a great hit with our trade and we gave a silver spoon with each dish."

MEXICANA

Put a dipperful of vanilla ice cream on a sundae dish, and cover with a dressing made by mixing equal parts of pecans, pignolia nuts and pistachio nuts, chopped together, and a sufficient quantity of heavy caramel syrup.

DING-A-LING

Take a 6-inch fancy flat glass dish and place on it a large (10-to-the-quart) cone-shaped dipperful of vanilla ice cream. Then pour a small ladleful of crushed orange around the edge of the ice cream and over it put a small ladleful of crushed strawberries. Cover with whipped cream, dashing a little of it extra heavy on one side to imitate a feather.

The author says the name was suggested to him from the fact that in his city the ladies were all wearing the style of covering for the head known as "ding-a-ling" hats. Charge 10 cents. (Ed. C. Swain.)

DUTCH TREAT

To dispense a "Dutch Treat" sundae make a frozen fruit cream consisting of three bananas freshly cut, 1¼ pounds of sugar, 7 ounces of chopped walnut meats, 1 ounce of vanilla extract and 7 ounces cut cherries for each gallon of cream desired.

As a base in dispensing, use four frou frou wafers, over which sprinkle chopped Brazil nuts, add one ladleful (size No. 8) of fruit cream, circle the top with pecan halves, add a dash of caramel whipped cream and one creme de menthe and one Maraschino cherry. The frou frou wafers used in this sundae are imported from Holland, hence the name "Dutch Treat" Charge 15 cents. (Raymond J. Williams)

TRIPLE-FRUIT

Into a sundae glass put a No. 16 disher-ful of ice cream, pour over it a ladleful of crushed pineapples, then hollow out a No. 6 cone of ice cream and place it on top of the ice cream first put on the dish. Cover this with crushed strawberry and decorate with Maraschino cherries.

The author says this makes a desirable and showy sundae and can be made from the material or supplies on hand at any fountain, large or small. (Chester Schlabach.)

MEXICAN SPECIAL

On a large sundae dish place a No. 16-to-the-quart disherful of Mexican pecan ice cream; cover with penoche sauce and then with whipped cream, adding some jelly beans to represent Mexican beans.

Mexican pecan ice cream is a maple cream with which pecan nut meats have been incorporated. Penoche sauce is made as follows· Mix together 4 pounds brown sugar; 1½ quarts of sweet cream and ½ pound glucose and boil for three minutes, being careful not to scorch the mixture. Let cool, and when cold, stir in chopped pecan nut meats. Sells for 20 cents. According to the author, this special has been a trade-winner in Los Angeles. (W. G. Turner.)

FESTINO ALMOND NUT

Into a tall Buffalo glass put one 16-to-the-quart ladleful of ice cream; over the cream put a ladleful of crushed cherries and caramel nut fudge. Then place a ladle-ful of ice cream on top and arrange 6 festino almonds around the cream. Top with whipped cream and a red or green cherry. Sells for 15 to 20 cents. (W. H. Marsh.)

FRUIT COCKTAILS

Chopped and iced fruits, commonly known as "fruit cocktails," always find favor with children, and may be substituted for the richer frozen creams. Shredded pineapple and ripe bananas, sliced and mixed together with pulverized sugar, may have poured over them a little lemon or orange juice and then be set in a refrigerator to ripen, time being given for the various fruit flavors to combine. When ready to serve fill sherbet glasses with chopped ice and add a couple of spoonfuls of the shredded fruit with the juice formed around it. Charge 10 cents.

UNCLE JAKE

Place a cone of ice cream on a dish around the edge of which lay three vanilla wafers flat, the wafers marking the points of a triangle; now put a slice of banana at each point where the cakes join together, placing crushed peaches on one side of the dish and crushed strawberries on the other. Sprinkle a little chopped nuts over the ice cream, and top off with whipped cream and a cherry. Price, 15 cents.

MAHOMET

Take of fresh figs, 1 pound; dates, 1 pound; English walnuts, 1½ pounds; pistachio nuts, 1½ pounds; raisins, 1 pound. Put all through a meat grinder and when well ground and mixed add ½ gallon maple syrup. Boil in a porcelain kettle until the mixture is reduced in volume to a heavy, thick liquid. When it has become cool add ½ ounce vanilla extract and color a dark brown with sugar coloring.

To serve, place a No. 10 dipperful of ice cream in an oblong dish, over the cream put some of the Oriental mixture and top with burnt almonds, whipped cream, colored a light green and flavored with pistachio, and a Maraschino cherry. The burnt almonds can be run through a grinder and put on a tin lid held over a gas range until roasted a light brown, the almonds being kept from burning by a movement similar to that employed in making popcorn; 15 cents. (Ellis N. Rowe.)

FRUIT PUDDING

One-half ounce crushed strawberries, ½ ounce crushed peaches, ice cream to fill small glass. Serve with spoon. Charge 15 cents.

HIPPODROME

In a sundae dish place a scoopful of chocolate ice cream, one of orange sherbet and one of cherry nougat. Cover this foundation with a layer of chopped bananas and top off with whipped cream and cherries, selling for 15 cents. This combination may be advertised by the phrase, "See all the colors of the Hippodrome in our Hippodrome Sundae." (R. J. Reynolds.)

HONOLULU FRUIT

Take one scoop of vanilla ice cream, one scoop strawberry cream, one dipper of strawberry fruit, one round slice of pineapple and top off with whipped cream and a cherry.

: HONOLULU FRUIT FRAPPE :
: 15 Cents :
: ONE CALLS FOR TWO :

JOY

Into a silver sundae cup place a cone of vanilla ice cream and raspberry ice, a ladleful of joy fruit, and decorate with whipped cream and one cherry. To prepare the "joy fruit," take two bananas, two oranges, a cupful of fresh strawberries, and a cupful of raspberries and cut and chop up very fine. Put into a suitable dish, cover them with a half pint of whipped cream and stir all well together. Sells for 10 cents.

ROYAL SALAD OF FRUITS

Take 1 gallon of rock-candy syrup and flavor with a little N. E. rum, then add the following ingredients: Strawberries, 1 quart; maraschino pineapple aces, 1 pint; ripe cherries, ½ pound; pecan halves, ¼ pound; oranges, 2; Spitzenberg apples, 2; and one fresh pineapple, each of the fruits being sliced in cubes. Add a pint of maraschino cherries, and mix all of the ingredients named in the syrup and let it stand for two hours. Serve in a parfait glass, using a No. 16-to-the-quart dipperful of ice cream, covering it with the salad and topping off with whipped cream. Price, 15 cents.

GLACED NUTS

In an ordinary sundae cup place one 12 to the quart disherful of vanilla ice cream. Pour over this 1 ounce of double chocolate and 1 large spoonful of ground glaced nuts. Top with a Maraschino cherry.

"Double chocolate" for the above is made as follows: To half a gallon of boiling water add 1 pound of any good fountain chocolate. Stir and boil for two minutes, then add 6 pounds of granulated sugar and 1 can of condensed milk. Boil the mixture a minute longer, remove from the fire and strain; when cold, add 1 ounce of vanilla extract. The chocolate is then ready for use.

"Glaced nuts" are made by placing in a kettle 4 pounds of granulated sugar, 1 quart of water and 1 pound of glucose (or 1 level spoonful of cream of tartar). Bring to a good stiff boil and add 2 pounds of shelled almonds. Stir constantly until the nuts are brown. Remove from the fire and pour into a sieve or colander. When the syrup has drained off pour on a greased slab of marble or into a pan; when cold, pass through a food chopper and put into a glass jar for future use.

The author says: "This formula may seem a bit complicated, but after making the first batch it will be found to be very simple. Glaced nut sundae is original with me and is the biggest hit I have had in my ten years' experience back of the fountain counter. I would suggest that glucose be used, if convenient; if not, cream of tartar works nearly as well, but care should be taken to wash down the sides of the kettle with a wet cloth, as if this is not done the batch may 'grain.' I use small shelled almonds which can be bought of any supply house. The syrup drained from the batch should be saved, as it can be re-melted and to it added more stock for the next batch" (Lew. S. Snyder)

TOWER OF BABEL

A mold about 4 x 3 x 1½ inches is preferred, but any other size will answer. Put 2 red and 2 green whole Maraschino cherries in opposite corners of the mould and a thin round slice of an orange in the center; now fill the mold with two different kinds of cream. Place 2 Nabisco wafers on a china platter and empty the contents of the mold on the wafers. To take the cream out of mold, cut around the sides with a knife.

"This sundae is very appetizing and neat looking if made right and is a sure winner." (Sydney Trau.)

TOWN TALK

Place in a footed ice cream sundae cup 1 cone (No. 12 disher) of strawberry ice cream, and around the base pour 1 ladleful of "fruit mix," in the top of the cone place 1 Maraschino cherry and finish with a small ladleful of claret syrup, extra heavy Charge 10 cents.

To make "fruit mix" for the above · Take a small cupful of chopped oranges, a similar quantity of seeded raisins and 2 ounces each of coarsely ground walnuts and pecans, and a sufficient quantity of extra heavy maple syrup to make 1 quart. Put the fruits and nuts in the maple syrup and boil to a heavy syrup (G. W. Irwin)

SWEET HEART

Into a sherbet glass place a cone of vanilla ice cream; over this pour a spoonful of caramel syrup (made from best pure caramels and rich cream or heavy cream); on one side of the glass place a spoonful of crushed walnuts. Serve with a spoon and on the top in the center place a Maraschino cherry.

The author says: " 'To appeal to the taste it must be attractive to the eye' is a very true saying. There is no sundae that 'is more attractive to the eye than 'sweet heart sundae' when properly served. It is a very popular dish with the ladies and a sundae that brings the people to your store." (P. W. McCole)

SUNDAE A LA ESCOFFIER

Place a cone of lemon ice in a sundae cup, arrange fresh strawberries over it; pour over all some grape juice and sprinkle with vanilla sugar.

CUPID'S DELIGHT

Place on a 5-inch plate one slice of red pineapple, cut heart-shaped, one cone of cherry bisque ice cream well filled with broken red cherries(to represent the broken hearts) ; add a ladleful of crushed red cherries, one ladleful of marshmallow (pink in color), sprinkling over the latter a sundae spoonful of chocolate nibs. Top with a red pineapple heart cut out of the pieces left from the slice of pineapple used in preparing the foundation. Serve with a Valentine napkin. Sells for 15 cents.

The "stock" for making "Cupid's Delight" is prepared as follows: Procure 2-pound cans of sliced pineapples; then make a sherry wine syrup, using 1 quart of sherry wine and 3 quarts of very heavy rock candy syrup Color a deep red, and in this syrup place the sliced pineapples, and stand in the ice box over night, so that the pineapple will take up the flavor and color Then cut each slice of the fruit with a heart-shaped cookie cutter, and the remaining pieces or what is left of the slices with a vegetable cutter. Make the cherry fruit by mixing 1 pint crushed maraschino cherries, ½ pint concentrated cherry syrup and ½ pint simple syrup, colored red. The chocolate nibs are tiny rolls of sweet chocolate and make a good "finish" when sprinkled on the marshmallow. They can be purchased from dealers in fountain supplies.

The author writes that this is his "Valentine Day Special" To advertise it he uses a 14 x 28 white card on which at the top and center is the reproduction of the head and shoulders of a beautiful young lady (cut out), while around the sides and bottom of the card are pasted red figures of cupids with arrows aimed at "Cupid's Delight." In the center of the card are the words "A Dainty Morsel. A Cupid's Delight Sundae, 15 Cents." (C. L. Hadley.)

SUMMER BEAUTY

Take a rather large flat sherbet dish, preferably one with a large stem. Put on it one ladleful of red strawberry ice cream. Put in the center of the cream shredded cocoanut, and top this with a Maraschino cherry. Make a ring around the cream with sliced bananas. When made in this manner the sundae will resemble the form and coloring of a flower. Price, 15 cents. (Forest M. Walters.)

SUMMER TIME

Cut up one banana in slices and place them around the edge of an ice cream plate. Add one measure of ice cream in center of the plate; then put a row of fresh strawberry fruit (or cherries) around the cream, pour on ½ ounce vanilla syrup and ½ ounce strawberry syrup and sprinkle a few nuts on top. Price, 20 cents. (L. W. Marshall.)

SALADE DE LEUX

Into a champagne or tall fluted glass of some fancy kind, put on one side a small portion of lemon sherbet and on the other side put a small portion of vanilla ice cream; then place a ladleful of the salad between the two and top off with shredded whipped cream (whipped cream with shredded cocoanut beaten into it) and a red cherry. Serve with a glass of ice water and two "frou frou" wafers. Can be sold for 10 or 15 cents

The salad is made as follows Take 3 fresh eggs and beat thoroughly; then add 2 ounces of concentrated lemon and orange syrups, 1 dram extract of vanilla and 4 ounces sherry wine. Mix all thoroughly together, add ½ pound shredded cocoanut (unsweetened), ½ pound pecan nuts (ground, but not too fine), and enough simple syrup to make ½ gallon. If the ingredients are carefully put together the mixture will possess a fine flavor. Price, 15 or 20 cents. (Guy E. Cla Vell.)

PANAMA SURPRISE

Into a banana-split dish place two No 16-to-the-quart dipperfuls of vanilla ice cream, and add six pieces of cut orange and four dashes of grape juice. Over the whole slice the half of a banana and top off with whipped cream and a cherry Serve with a glassful of ice water, crackers and a napkin. Sells for 15 cents. (John Lentz)

FRESH FRUIT DELIGHT

In a sundae cup place a ladleful of fresh pineapple fruit, add half a ladleful of oranges cut into small slices, then nearly fill the cup with sliced bananas, placing two maraschino cherries, one directly opposite the other and across the top of the contents of the cup. Put a quarter of a dipperful of whipped cream in the center Sells for 15 cents. To call attention to his delicacy, the author uses the following sign

```
:............................:
:                            :
:       Special Today        :
:   Fresh Fruit Delight—15c. :
:         Very fine.         :
:........ ...................:
```

(Paul E. Anderson.)

ASTOR

Vanilla ice cream, one small cone; ice or special cream, one small cone; Astor salad, one ladleful.

The "Astor salad" is made as follows Take three seedless oranges, cut in small cubes; two ounces walnut meats, chopped fine; two ounces Brazil or pecan meats; one-half pint crushed strawberries; one-half pint crushed pineapple. Place all in a half-gallon fruit bowl, add one quart of simple syrup, mix together and serve. Price, 15 cents. (Lew S. Snyder.)

COUPE JACQUE

Put in a sundae glass one mixed ice with chopped apple, orange, banana, green and red cherries, grapes, peaches, pears, apricots, pineapple and any candied fruits you like. This is best made up every morning in a glass dish. In serving one large

spoonful is poured over the mixed ice. Top off with whipped cream from a star-shaped piping bag. Make four small stars and one large star on top and set it off with one red cherry. Fresh fruit makes much the best combination. This dish is very popular at Fuller's Cafe, Ranelagh street, Liverpool. Price in U. S., at least 15 cents (Fred. S. Longley.)

CATHEDRAL CLUB

Take a frappe cup, place in it 1 scoopful of vanilla ice cream, flatten the cream and on it put about six slices of banana, then a scoopful of chocolate cream. Surround the last named with a small quantity of claret syrup. On each of the opposite sides of the dish place a slice of peach and on the chocolate cream place three walnut halves. Sells for 15 or 20 cents.

The author states that although he named the above sundae "Cathedral Club" it can be given a name suggestive of any club with quarters near one's place of business (E. Dean Mattison.)

FRUIT SALAD A LA MODE

On a small plate place a lettuce leaf, over it put a small portion of fruit salad, on the salad put a No. 16 disherful of vanilla ice cream and over the ice cream pour a small ladleful of sliced strawberries in syrup.

In making the fruit salad use the following formula: Four bananas, sliced thin, 2 oranges, cubed; ¼ pound walnuts, halved; 6 Maraschino cherries, chopped fine; 14 strawberries, sliced. Mix all and drain off the juice. This mixture will keep well in a cool place. After the "fruit salad a la mode" is ready to serve, top off with a spoonful of whipped cream and a fresh strawberry. Sells for 20 cents (H. R. Rowe.)

FRISCO FAVORITE

Place enough vanilla ice cream in a glass to reach a depth of one inch and cover it with crushed strawberries; add 1 ounce of raspberry syrup and 1 ounce of orange fruit and fill the glass with whipped cream. Serve in 14-ounce straight mineral glasses, and dress with whole cherries. Insert a long spoon on side of glass to bottom.

FANDANGO SANDWICH

Place a layer of whipped cream in the bottom of a cocktail glass. Surmount with succeeding layers of chocolate and vanilla cream, covered with an ounce of raspberry syrup. Top off with a layer of orange sherbet, whipped cream and cherries for 15 cents. (G. A. Kenney.)

BON BON

A bon bon as served in Norfolk, Va., and other Southern cities is a seven-ounce glass (bell) filled to the brim with shaved ice, the flavor poured on top so it may trickle down through the ice. Place a spoonful of ice cream on side of glass. Both five and ten-cent bon bons are served.

ALL TOGETHER

Take a banana split dish and place on it side by side three 16-to-the-quart scoopfuls of ice cream—chocolate, strawberry and vanilla, the strawberry ice cream in the middle. On top of the chocolate ice cream place a ladleful of crushed pineapple, on the strawberry ice cream a ladleful of crushed strawberries, and on the vanilla ice cream a couple of red cherries with a little of the juice. On the chocolate ice cream place a spoonful of whole walnuts, on the vanilla ice cream a spoonful of whole walnuts, on the vanilla ice cream a spoonful of ground walnuts, and in the center on the strawberry ice cream place a dipperful of whipped cream. Sells for 15 or 20 cents. (John Collins.)

ROSE BUD

In an ordinary college ice dish place ½ ounce of claret sauce and on it put a No. 10 scoopful of pistachio ice cream. Flatten down the mixture with the scoop, then cut into four pieces to represent four leaves; in the center of the mass place a ladleful of crushed Maraschino cherries to represent a rosebud, and around the border put maple syrup or dry walnut meats. Sells for 15 cents. (D. G. Bromley.)

CHRISTMAS DELIGHT

Take an eight inch plate and place holly leaves around the edges; in the center put a No. 10 dipperful of chocolate and vanilla ice cream. Cover the ice cream with a sauce made as follows: To a quart of cranberries add a quart of sugar and the juice of three lemons and boil all to a nice thick pulp. Top with whipped cream colored pink and flavored with cranberry juice; decorate with a Maraschino cherry and a small sprig of mistletoe. A few holly berries scattered around the margin of the plate add to the attractiveness, while the decorative effect is still further enhanced by using a sprig of mistletoe bearing a berry. Sells for 15 or 20 cents.

The author wrote that this delicacy may be also sold under the name of "Sleigh Bell Sundae" and "advertised with Christmas pictures and branches of holly with a hanging sign or a square sign fitted in a wreath. This sundae made a decided hit in St. Louis." (Ellis N. Rowe.)

COMBINATION

In a sundae dish (China preferred) place one 12-to-the-quart dipperful of vanilla ice cream; over this put a ladleful of butter-scotch dressing; cover this with ground black walnut meats, and top off with a spoonful of chocolate ice cream or chocolate whipped cream and cherries.

To prepare the butter-scotch dressing. Take 1 pound of brown sugar, ¼ pound of glucose or karo corn syrup, and ¼ pound of best butter. Add a little cream (water can be used) and cook to a thick syrup. In boiling, care must be taken to keep the mixture from burning.

The author states that the use of black walnuts and butter-scotch dressing has won great favor for this combination with his patrons. It can profitably be sold at 15 cents, and the name really suggests a happy combination to would-be customers. (R. W. Irwin.)

ROBIN HOOD

In a banana split dish put one disherful of pineapple ice; then place a banana, previously sliced in four pieces, down the sides of the glass. On top of the pineapple ice place a small disherful of strawberry ice cream and over it pour marshmallow paste; add ground nuts and a Maraschino cherry. Should be served with a few cakes. Sells for 15 or 20 cents. (O. L. Bunyan.)

X'MAS SUNDAE DINNER

On a banana split dish at one end place a No. 12 to-the-quart dipperful of cherry ice; at the other end, place a similar quantity of vanilla or walnut ice cream. On the cherry ice, place a ladleful of cranberry sauce, sweetened; on the ice cream, put a ladleful of pudding dressing. Put half a slice of sliced pineapple on each of the ends of the dish, covering each slice with a spoonful of whipped cream. Sprinkle with crushed pecans and top with a red and green cherry. Price, 15 cents. (Charles Held.)

NOUGATINE SUNDAE

Fill one cake cup (using a No. 12 to-the-quart dipper) with walnut or vanilla ice cream (walnut ice cream is preferable). Cover the ice cream with a ladleful of nougatine dressing and top off with a cherry. Serve a small piece of nougatine candy with each sundae.

Nougatine dressing is made as follows: To one gallon of marshmallow whip add three ounces of walnut extract, one-fourth pound each of walnut and pecan meats. Mix thoroughly together. If the marshmallow whip is too thick, as is often the case, thin with a little simple syrup. (W. S. Bachman.)

NIAGARA

Dissolve 4 pounds of sugar in 1 gallon of water add 1½ cupfuls of straight lemon juice, color the mixture with a suitable leaf green and freeze. To serve, put one ladleful of the mixture into a champagne glass, covering the surface of the frozen mixture with finely chopped nut meats. Also dot or fleck the surface of the mixture here and there with whipped cream to represent the white caps on Niagara river. Place the glass on a fancy plate with a paper doily to fit the plate and serve with a glass of ice water. (Walter Luick.)

NEW YEAR SPECIAL

In a fancy china plate put a large No. 12 cone of chocolate ice cream. Take a cone of vanilla ice cream of similar size, invert and place it on top of the chocolate ice cream. Around the cones place four Nabisco wafers upright. Cover with whipped cream and put the numerals of the new year on top with pistachio flavor. Garnish with parsley. The design is that of an hour glass, the chocolate ice cream representing the full side and the vanilla ice cream the empty side. (B. B. Farr.)

DOUBLE DOSE

On a sundae dish put one No. 12 to-the-quart disherful of vanilla ice cream and one disherful of strawberry ice cream. Over one disherful of the ice cream sprinkle powdered almonds, and over the other sprinkle powdered pistachio nuts. Top each with a little whipped cream and a maraschino cherry. Charge 15 cents.

TRUTH

Put a ladleful of ice cream in a 12-ounce glass, then add one ladle of cherries over the ice cream. Mix. In another glass mix 1 ounce of strawberry syrup, 1 ounce of sweet cream, 1 egg, and ¼ glass of cracked ice. Shake, strain, toss and pour over the ice cream and cherries

NEXT YEAR'S

To make, have handy a small tin of good cocoa, some granulated sugar, a teaspoon and a cup Then in the cup mix together one teaspoonful each of cocoa and sugar, and an ounce of rich sweet cream, stirring vigorously until a smooth mixture is made. Pour this over a No. 16 scoopful of vanilla ice cream, placing over all chopped pecan nuts. Serve in a regular sundae dish. Price 15 cents. (Leonard L. Whetmore)

NEAPOLITAN NUT

First purchase from an ice cream dealer several bricks of Neapolitan ice cream (which is strawberry, chocolate and vanilla ice cream in layers); lay the brick on the table and cut it into five equal slices; place one of these slices on a saucer-shaped dish and on it put a No. 20 disherful of vanilla ice cream; over the latter pour a ladleful of pineapple fruit and a ladleful of chopped nut meats. Top off with whipped cream and fruit

The author states that he has made a "special" of this sundae during the month of June and part of July, and he has good success with it. From the fact that it contains three flavors of ice cream and is sold at a reasonable price (15 or 20 cents) he says it has been a winner. (John H. Gassman.)

JAPANESE

The Japanese sundae is served in tall, thin sundae glasses and consists of any flavor of ice cream topped with a marsh-mallow-whipped cream dressing full of English walnuts. This brings ten cents and is so popular at Lord's, Portland, Me., that the fame of "Lord's Japanese" has been carried the country over by summer people who have been won by the delicious dish. ("Lord's".)

ITALIAN

Serve in a regular sundae cup, part strawberry and part chocolate ice cream. Pour over the ice cream a chop suey mixture. Top off with whipped cream and a few fresh strawberries. Charge 15 cents.

DARDANDO

Figs and dates, of each (cut very fine), 2 ounces; English walnut meats, 3 ounces; heavy chocolate syrup to make 2 quarts; pour a sufficient quantity of this mixture over the ice cream in a sundae glass and top off with whipped cream and a cherry. Price, 10 cents. (Elmer E. Pierce.)

CHOP SUEY MIX

Take an average-sized spoonful of hard vanilla ice cream and lay it in an ordinary sundae glass, cover with "Arabian Eats," prepared as given below, and top off with a spoonful of whipped cream, in the center of which place a big red maraschino cherry. To make the "Arabian Eats," take an equal amount of dates and figs, grind and mix them together with a little maple syrup, and finally add a few chopped pecans, or whole ones may be used if preferred. "A good seller at 10 cents " (Carl Buchanan.)

DECORATION

Place in a regular sundae glass equal quantities of strawberry and chocolate ice cream; over this put a ladleful of crushed walnuts and top off with whipped cream and a few fresh strawberries. Charge 15 cents when dispensed with fresh fruit. (Patrick McCole.)

BISMARCK

Sundae cup two-thirds full vanilla ice cream, fill up with chopped dates and figs and pour over some maple syrup. Top off with whipped cream.

BACHELOR

Take one ladleful of vanilla ice cream, put in sundae glass, and pour on the ice cream one ladleful of sauce No. 1. Take one ladleful of chocolate ice cream and pour on it sauce No. 2. Place both of the mixtures in a dish and top off with whipped cream and a stuffed raisin.

No. 1 Sauce—Take one pound of hickory nut meats and grind very fine; add one pint of sweet cream and one-half pound of sugar and boil the mixture until thick enough to serve. Put into a cool place until ready to serve.

No. 2 Sauce—Take one pound of raisins with which prepare a sauce similar to No. 1, using the raisins instead of hickory nut meats.

Stuffed Raisins—Remove the seeds from the raisins, which fill with finely chopped hickory nut meats.

Price—15 or 25 cents. Prepare sauce in small lots and keep cold. (Walter Luick.)

HOT MAPLE

Pour a ladleful of hot maple syrup over vanilla ice cream, and over the whole sprinkle ground hickory nuts. Serve with Nabiseo wafers.

HOT CHOCOLATE

Hot, rich chocolate syrup poured over a ladle of plain or nut ice cream. A few chopped nuts may be sprinkled over the top. Price, 10 cents.

HOT MAPLE

Over a ladle of vanilla ice cream pour a heavy hot cream. Sprinkle ground hickory nuts over the top and serve with Nabisco wafers. (Geo. A. Zahn.)

HOT MENTHE

Over a ladle of vanilla ice cream pour a heavy hot menthe syrup and place three creme de menthe cherries on top. (Geo. A. Zahn.)

HOT TEMPTATION

Take a banana split dish, and on one end place a cone of vanilla ice cream (16-to-the-quart); at the other end place a similar-sized cone of chocolate ice cream. Over the vanilla cream pour a ladleful of maple temptation sauce, and over the chocolate cream put a similar quantity of chocolate temptation sauce; top each cone of cream with whipped cream and a cherry, and place two water-ice wafers across the dish between the cones of ice cream. Charge 20 or 25 cents. (Harry G. Frame.)

ICE CREAM CROQUETTES

Shape vanilla ice cream into croquette forms and then roll them in macaroon crumbs that have been powdered fine.

ICE CREAM CROQUETTES WITH CREAM SAUCE

On a 5-inch fancy plate place a large ladleful of sweetened whipped cream; in the center of this put a cone-shaped dipperful of chocolate ice cream (10-to-the-quart) which has been coated with toasted cocoanut, and top with one green cherry. Sells for 15 cents. (L. W. Garnett.)

MOSS BRAE

Into a fancy ice cream dish, preferably one ornated with a foliage design, place a disherful of well congealed ice cream so ladled from the container that the cone of cream will have a hollow interior. Repeat this process, placing the second disherful athwart the first, pressing slightly on the ladle so as to join the two disherfuls of cream. Over these mounds, which are intended to represent hills, sprinkle some ground nut kernels; then apply some thick, well-made chocolate syrup, and on it place some white of egg, which has been colored with chlorophyl or some other kind of harmless green coloring, and beaten to a stiff froth. Lay a sprig of mint on the dish in juxtaposition to the finished product, and serve with a tiny spoon. Sells for 15 cents. (G. G. Rice.)

MOUNTAIN

Hard ice cream is necessary for this. Serve on a small china plate one 6-to-the-quart dipper of vanilla ice cream, then one 10-to-the-quart chocolate ice cream, pressing down firmly, then one 16-to-the-quart strawberry ice cream, pressing down hard enough to insure each of the latter to stand firmly on the lower one but not enough to spoil the mountain peak effect. On top place a spoonful of whipped cream and vanilla marshmallow and encircle the base with grated cocoanut. (E. G. Howard)

RED CROSS SPECIAL

Cover the bottom of a 12-ounce glass with sliced orange, then add, in the order named, 1 disherful of pistachio ice cream, a few sliced peaches, a disherful of New York ice cream, and a few strawberries or sliced apricots. Then fill the glass with whipped cream, placing red cherries on top to form the outlines of a cross. Charge 20 cents. (A. Frank.)

THE GREAT DIVIDE

On a flat plate place a No. 8 cone-shaped dipperful of vanilla ice cream. Divide the cone by splitting it deep enough from the top downward to allow a rich, ripe slice of orange to be placed in the cleft. Over the orange pour creme de menthe syrup; over one-half of the ice cream pour crushed raspberry, and over the other put a thick paste made of ground nuts and chocolate syrup. Around the base of the ice cream pour a thin ribbon of white marshmallow (made by mixing marshmallow cream with plain water and allowing the mixture to stand, using only the top). The author states that "this sundae is very simple and can be easily made Sells for 15 cents at a good profit." (J. M. Bingamon.)

STATE CAPITOL

On a fancy china plate place a large No 12 scoopful of chocolate ice cream. On top of it put a cone of vanilla ice cream, placing the cone in an inverted position, the apex downward. Around the ice cream place four Nabisco wafers (standing upright). On top of the vanilla ice cream put a spoonful of pink marshmallow and on the latter a Maraschino cherry. Around the ice cream, between the wafers, place two squares of peach fruit and two squares of pineapple fruit; the marshmallow and cherry are supposed to represent the tower of the Capitol. (Calvin Arnold.)

REGATTA PRIDE

On a boat-shaped dish place three nabisco wafers on edge so that they meet in the center. In one compartment put a small portion of vanilla ice cream; in the next, one of strawberry, and in the third another of chocolate.

Over the whole turn a ladleful of chopped fruit—pineapple, bananas, strawberries and cherries. Top with whipped cream and garnish with a chocolate almond. Price— 20 cents.

MISS NEW LONDON

One cone of peach ice cream (that's for the girl!). Pour over it one ounce pink pistachio sauce and one ladleful vanilla marshmallow (to represent her pretty cheeks). To the mixture add one ladleful of crushed walnuts, 4 slices of banana and one cherry. Serve with two Nabiscos and a 3-ounce glass of vichy water. Charge 15 cents.

To exploit this sundae make use of the phrase: "Looks good, smells good and tastes good " (C L. Hadley.)

MAXIXE SUNDAE

On a 5-inch ice cream plate lay a very thin slice of angel food cake. On this place a No. 12 to-the-quart disherful of mixed strawberry, chocolate and vanilla ice cream. On the cream place a small portion of five kinds of crushed fruits, preferably pineapple, raspberries, strawberries, cherries and peaches, or a good fruit salad dressing and chopped walnuts will answer. Top off with whipped cream and a green cherry. Charge 15 cents. (W. C. Herget.)

"500"

In a suitable sundae dish put an 8-to-the-quart disherful of vanilla ice cream; smooth it out flat and over it pour a ladleful of pineapple aces, or pineapple cut into the shape of hearts, diamonds, clubs or spades, with maraschino flavor, may be used. In the center on top place some whipped cream.

A sign which helped to make this sundae "take" read as follows:

```
...............................
·        500 SUNDAE         :
ı     As Good as the Game   :
:         15 Cents          :
...............................
```

(Carl D. Shults.)

NORTH POLE SUNDAE

On the edge of a six-inch plate lay a half slice of thin orange to represent the sun on the horizon. Now take one lady finger and split lengthwise in two pieces and place in a standing position in a six-ounce parfait glass, then fill the glass with vanilla ice cream, pressing the cream down firmly; holding the hand around the glass while filling will melt the cream enough to let it slip easily from the glass mold. This, when turned out upon the plate, forms a tall cone about the size of an empty ice cream cone. Put a pink gum drop on a toothpick and stick on one side of the cone near the top, then finish by putting a small paper United States flag on a stick on top. Charge 25 cents. (H. R. Rowe.)

NORTH POLE SUNDAE

Place a 5-cent cone of chocolate (vanilla, if preferred) ice cream in a fancy sundae glass and over it pour a small quantity of bitter sweet chocolate syrup, or ordinary chocolate syrup, if the former is not convenient; now take a large Maraschino cherry and place it on a toothpick so that the cherry rests in the center of the toothpick and the same distance from either end of the pick; place this cherry on top of the ice cream so that one end of the pick is inserted down into the cream, the other pointing upward (to represent a pole). Pour over the cone several spoonfuls of white marshmallow syrup, covering the pick, cherry and all; then trail over this covering a small teaspoonful of purple-colored marshmallow syrup, and finish by placing two English walnut halves on the side.

The author writes: "This makes a very pretty sundae, representing a field of ice and snow ('purple tinted,' as Dr. Cook says the snow at the pole is), with the pole standing in the center. I use chocolate cream and chocolate syrup because chocolate is the most popular flavor for the majority of people and that is what makes it sell so well." (W. Franklin Spayth.)

NORTH POLE SUNDAE

Split a banana and put the pieces on a long special plate to represent the runners of a sleigh. On these and to represent a "pack" put a No. 10 scoopful of vanilla ice cream, and to simulate the snow effect, cover the "pack" well with marshmallow syrup. On one end of the plate put a small candy polar bear; at the other end, put 6 small gum drops (jelly gum drops, if possible). On top of the ice cream place a small American flag. This special, the author informs us, made a very decided hit with the theater-goers in his home town, a thriving California city. Price, 20 cents. (Ray H. Chaffee.)

POLAR BEAR SUNDAE

Into a tall stem sundae glass put 1½ ounces of almond syrup, on the syrup place a No. 20 to-the-quart dipperful of vanilla ice cream, and top with a large ladleful of very stiff whipped cream. Serve. This makes a dainty white concoction.

To introduce this formula the author used a display extending from the fountain back bar over the fountain. He first built a canopy frame of 1-inch hemlock and covered it with muslin. On the frame canopy he pinned cotton, pulling it out at the ends so as to give it the appearance of a snow slide, the cotton being then dusted with four boxes of artificial snow to further heighten the snow effect. In the center of the mirror or back bar he made a large stand and covered it with cotton. On the stand he then placed a large white, pressed-paper polar bear he had borrowed from a hardware store. The shelving at the ends of the back bar were also decorated with cotton to give the "wintry" effect. The electric light globes at the top of the mirror were covered with paper shades of a red color, with the result that when the light was turned on the display showed up most attractively, and was much commented on by patrons. On the mirror was painted with white water color pigment a dotted snow storm, and over this was lettered in red "Polar Bear Sundae, 10c." (Sterling Miller.)

Lollie Popp

Put into a parfait glass 1 teaspoonful of crushed pineapple fruit and a cherry; then on top of the fruit put equal parts of vanilla, strawberry and chocolate ice cream so that the mixture will look like a "pousse cafe." Garnish with whipped cream and a cherry, shaping the cream into the form of a point. When correctly made the "lollie popp" looks very appetizing. Serve with a few Nabisco wafers. Sells for 15 cents. (Justin Laubere.)

Divinity

Into a stem sherbet glass place a No. 16-to-the-quart disherful of chocolate and vanilla ice cream, half and half; put on each side a piece of angel cake, also a piece of devil cake. Over all pour strawberry fruit and whipped cream, and top with a cherry. Sells for 15 cents, or 20 cents with two pieces of cake. (H F McCafferty.)

Cho-Van-Ca

Place a slice of cake in a shallow bowl or dish. On one end of the cake put a small cone of chocolate ice cream and on the other end put a small cone of vanilla ice cream. Sprinkle over this a few English walnuts and fresh strawberries. Put a dash of whipped cream and a cherry on each cone.

The name is derived from the words "chocolate," "vanilla" and "cake." Charge 15 cents. (Irwin K. Scott.)

Pousse Cafe

Chocolate ice cream, 1 ounce; grated co-coanut, 1 ounce; strawberry ice cream, 1 ounce; crushed orange, 1 ounce; vanilla ice cream, 1 ounce; crushed raspberries, 1 ounce. Use a 7-ounce glace glass, add the above ingredients in alternate layers, so as to show six distinct colors. Add the chocolate ice cream first, then a layer of cocoanut, and so on, until the six layers are filled in. Serve the same as you would serve maple glace. Two ounces of any suitable flavor may be added to 4 or 5 ounces of vanilla ice cream, or ice cream of the same flavor as the syrup or fruit used.

Progressive

Place 2 ounces of vanilla ice cream in the bottom of a 7-ounce parfait glass. Add a small ladleful of fresh crushed strawberries, pack down well, and put over them about 2 ounces more of vanilla ice cream. Then add a spoonful of sliced pineapple, two or three drops of creme de menthe syrup to give color, and fill the glass almost to the top with stiffly whipped cream. Over this sprinkle a few broken pecan nuts and top off with fresh cherries and one maraschino cherry.

The author writes that this formula will stand the test of practical dispensing and yield a good profit at 15 cents a glass. (Frank W. Hallock.)

Rainbow

Take an 8-ounce short-stem cocktail glass and pack it with vanilla ice cream up to within a quarter inch of the top. Now take a pointed soda spoon and from down the inside of the glass take out a spoonful of ice cream on three different sides. In the cavities thus made pour claret syrup in one, pineapple syrup in the second and mint syrup in the third. Then over all put a small ladleful of crushed cherry fruit and top off with a Maraschino cherry. Serve on a flat dish with spoon and two wafers. Charge 20 cents. (Harrison W. Wendell.)

Battleship Sundae

In the center and lengthwise of a banana split dish place a long scoopful of ice cream, giving to the ends of the ice cream a battleship appearance by means of nabisco wafers, by placing two of the wafers at either end on their sides in the form of the letter V turned on its side, the sharp point being turned forward to represent the prow of the boat; the rear of the ship is reproduced in the same way, except that the wafers forming the V are turned in the other direction. For masts, two Veronique wafers are stuck upright in the ice cream. Now put a whole cherry on each end and in the center, first running a toothpick through each cherry to represent cannon, and stick a small flag in the stern of the ship (small flags of each of the countries at war, as well as that of the U. S. are easily obtained). Along the sides of the "battleship" pour some good brand of puree to represent the ocean. Sells for 25 cents.

The author states that to advertise this specialty he has reproduced six "battleships" in his window, making them of cotton, each ship of which carries a small streamer indicating the country it is supposed to represent On the stern of each boat is placed the flag of the country named on the streamer. In the back of the window appears a large map of Europe The window display proved a big drawing card and helped him to sell many "battleship sundaes." (F. J. Arnoldy.)

EGG UP

Serve on a small sandwich platter. Place two leaves of fresh lettuce on the platter. Take two small disherfuls of vanilla ice cream and lay them side by side. Turn the disher over and smash a hole in the center of each portion of cream to represent a hollow; in each "hollow" put one-half an apricot to simulate "fried eggs up." To add to the flavor and realistic appearance of the dish (*i. e.*, pepper and salt effect), sprinkle with a little cinnamon and powdered sugar. (Jos. B. Clark.)

MUTT AND JEFF

On a long platter put an "animal" cracker representing a horse; on the cracker put a No. 10 dipperful of vanilla ice cream and a No. 20 dipperful of strawberry ice cream. The two portions of ice cream represent "Mutt and Jeff" and the cracker is used because the two characters represented like to bet on the "ponies." Over these pour a caramel sauce made of equal parts of glucost, sugar and cream, as follows:

Heat the glucose and sugar almost to the boiling point and add the cream, stirring until thoroughly mixed.

Then place a spoonful of whipped cream on each of the figures, a green cherry on "Jeff" and a red one on "Mutt." Sells for 20 cents. (Will McDonald.)

FLAG DAY SPECIAL

Place three small nabisco wafers flatwise across a boat-shaped dish so as to form a bridge; on the wafers place one No. 10-to-the-quart dipperful of fresh strawberry ice cream, and around the base put about 10 strawberries with a ladleful of whipped cream. Then put two nabisco wafers on two sides of the cone of cream so as to meet at the top. Crown with a large strawberry surmounted by an American flag, the staff of the latter being held in place by pushing it into the strawberry. Suitable flags can be bought for five cents per dozen. Price, 20 cents. (John Lentz.)

NATIONAL

Take two small dishes of marshmallow cream and color (with cake coloring), one red and the other blue. Then in a fancy sundae dish put a No. 10 ladleful of vanilla ice cream; on one side of the cream put a spoonful of red marshmallow cream, and on the other side a spoonful of blue marshmallow cream, allowing the ice cream to show in the center of the dish so as to represent the national colors. Sprinkle a spoonful of ground nut meats on top of the dish and serve.

To advertise this sundae the author uses a window strip like the following.

        Be Patriotic !
     Try National Sundae, 10c.

(R. E. Paul.)

LIVERPOOL

Put a small dipper of water ice in a stemmed glass; top with whipped cream from a fancy piping bag. Decorate with red and green cherries, and small pieces of angelica arranged in the form of green leaves. (Jas. M. Johnson.)

U. S. A.

Make strawberry, lemon and grape sherbet, as follows: Strawberry water, 3 quarts; sugar, 6 pounds; solution of citric acid, 1 ounce; white of one egg. In the same manner make lemon sherbet, using the juice of two lemons, and grape sherbet, using four quarts of ripe grapes. Press the berries through a fine sieve, add sugar, water, white of egg, and solution of citric acid. Place each sherbet mixture into separate freezers and freeze. To serve, take a ladleful of each of the sherbets and place them in a suitable glass in the order of their colors, emblematic of the flag—red, white and blue. After this has been done top off with whipped cream; now in the whipped cream make three grooves, filling one groove with lemon syrup, the second with strawberry syrup and the third, with grape syrup. Place in the center of the dish a small United States flag. Serve with a glass of water and paper napkin bearing the U. S. colors, red, white and blue. Price high enough to cover costs. The U. S. A. is a great holiday feature. (Walter Luick.)

EASTER

First have a mould made in the shape of a cross. This is not so difficult as any tinsmith can make one at a slight cost. This mould works on the same principle as that employed for the "club sundae" and with which nearly all dispensers are familiar; or one can take for his model the form used for the ice cream, push the moulded form out on a six-inch plain white hollow cross instead of a square or oblong shape. Having provided the mould, make a few wax paper linings by placing the mould upside down on a piece of wax paper and tear out the paper in the shape of the cross These paper linings keep the cream from sticking to the mould when the ice cream form comes out of the mould. Now place a wax paper in the bottom of the mould and fill it with plain vanilla ice cream, push the mould form out on a six-inch plain white plate and you have a perfect cross of white. Whip up some cream that has had added to it a little purple color and place it in a pastry tube or paper cornucopia. With the tube squeeze out the colored cream on the cross of ice cream in the form of letters to spell the word "Eastertide." This sundae is very simple to make and can be turned out as fast as any common sundae The mould should be made to hold about as much as the regular No. 12 disher. Price, 15 or 20 cents.

The author submitted with his formula a diagram of a sundae in the form of a cross, the first two syllables of the word "Eastertide" appearing on the upright section and the last syllable, reading from left to right, on the arms of the cross. (H. R. Rowe.)

ST. PATRICK'S DAY SPECIAL

On a 4-inch sundae plate place a No. 8 scoopful of vanilla ice cream and on it put a slice of creme de menthe pineapple. Place pecan halves around the cream and scatter a few chopped walnuts over the top. Then add whipped cream and a creme de menthe cherry with a toothpick through it.

ST. VALENTINE'S OWN

To dispense this sundae have a tinner make a heart-shaped mould, about 2½ inches in diameter and 1¼ inches in depth. This mould works similarly to the club house mold with which nearly all dispensers are familiar. In the mould place a layer of vanilla ice cream, a layer of strawberry ice cream and another layer of vanilla ice cream. Trim the moulded ice cream even with the top of the mould, then place the cream on a china plate of fancy design, measuring about 6 inches in diameter. Pour over the cream a ladleful of crushed strawberries, add a spoonful of mixed ground nuts and top off with a spoonful of whipped cream, a cherry, and a sprinkle of ground cinnamon.

The author states that this sundae is a good seller at 20 cents. He has advertised it in the daily papers of his town with much success. (Philip W. Fraker.)

(9) Fountain Desserts

In catering for the public taste for novelties in the sundae line dispensers have gradually elaborated the original idea of ice cream plus a syrup, till many of these concoctions have become so complicated that it is no longer possible to recognize them as the children of the simple sundae and college ice.

The first of these fancy fountain desserts to win favor—and it still maintains its popularity—was the banana split. This too has been elaborated and in the following pages will be found many very fancy and special splits. The use of other fruits, notably cantaloups, pineapples and oranges, was early introduced.

A more recently introduced feature of the development of the dessert is in the use of cakes. All the various staple cakes are now used as the basis upon which the delicacy is built. Angel cake is very popular, and serves admirably for this purpose. From the bakers, eclair and puff shells can be bought, and these when filled with ice creams and dressed with toppings, make easily prepared, yet very elaborate looking and tasty specialties.

Good service is essential in serving these "extra specials." The more elaborate the dessert, the greater care should be exercised to see that the result is not merely a "mess." Some dispensers show a tendency to put "everything but the kitchen stove" into their desserts. This is a mistake. Too many flavors mean the destruction of all good flavor. It is a safe rule to be sure that you have a good predominating flavor, and then to take care that the accessories blend with it. Strawberry and raspberry, both capital flavors, kill each other. This often happens, especially among the fruit flavors. Strawberry and currant, however, make a fine combination. If a dispenser will do a little experimenting himself, he will soon discover the best combinations to employ.

Like the sundaes, all desserts should have a glass of iced water served with them. It is not necessary, however, to serve a cracker or cake with those that have a cake basis. The fruit mixtures are often served with a sweet cooky or biscuit.

BANANA SPLITS

BANANA SPLIT WITH CHERRY

Slice a banana in two. Place a spoonful vanilla ice cream in the center, and top off with maraschino cherries, and pour cherry syrup over it. Price, 15 cents.

BANANA NUT SPLIT

In a suitable dish place a banana which has been split in two lengthwise. At each end put a small cone of ice cream, a portion of whipped cream being used to fill the center. On the whipped cream place a Maraschino cherry and around it a few slices of citron. Cover one of the cones of ice cream with chopped mixed nuts and the other with chopped mixed fruits. Price, 20 cents.

CULEBRA CUT

Use a boat-shaped dish. Peel and cut lengthwise one banana, place on the dish, spreading the slices of banana apart. Cut a small slice of pineapple in the center, place one cut on outside of banana in the center (to represent Culebra cut through which the boat is passing). Now pour pistachio-flavored syrup colored a pale green (representing the ocean) on the outside of the banana and on each side of the pineapple so as to trickle under the fruit. On top of this shake a tablespoonful of ground pistachio nuts and put a tablespoonful of malted milk on each side of the banana (the rock and sands of the cut). Near each end of the banana place a No. 20 to-the-quart cone of fruit ice cream. In the top of one place a tiny U. S. flag, and in the other stick a Union Jack. In the center put a ball of chocolate ice cream into the sides of which stick two chocolate cigarettes (the guns), and between the cones sprinkle a teaspoonful of chocolate tidbits (the people on board). A toothpick placed upright in each end of the banana, one carrying a red cherry, the other a green cherry, will reproduce the signal lights. Serve with a tiny glass of vichy water. The author states that this delicacy "costs 12c to make and easily sells for 20c. Can be made in a couple of minutes and is pleasing to the eye and taste. All the people talk about it." (C. L. Hadley.)

ELFIN DELIGHT

Cut a banana into four thin slices, which place to form a square with the ends overlapping. Fill the space within the square with a sundae portion of vanilla ice cream Now pour a syrup composed of 10 ounces each of crushed strawberries and cherries (Morello), and 6 ounces of grape juice. In the right angles formed by the overlapping ends of the banana slices place a point of whipped cream. Garnish with creme de menthe or maraschino cherry and a few whole pecan meats. With a little practice this specialty may be quickly and nearly prepared Price, 15 or 20 cents.

AVIATION GLIDE

Place in an oblong suey dish one split banana, flat side up. Use three scoopfuls (No 16 disher) of chocolate, vanilla and strawberry ice cream. On either side of the chocolate ice cream place a nabisco wafer for forward ends of the air ship, and in the strawberry ice cream stick a nabisco wafer to represent the tail piece of the machine. On the chocolate ice cream place a red cherry to represent a man riding in the air ship. Between the scoopfuls of ice cream sprinkle crushed cherries and pineapple, and top with chopped pecans and whipped cream. "Has sold well to students of the University at 20c," writes the author of the formula. (M. C. Thurber.)

BANANA BON TON

Slice a banana lengthwise and lay the pieces on a suitable dish; add 2 No. 10 ladlefuls of ice cream or 1 ladleful of ice cream and 1 ladleful of lemon, orange, or pineapple sherbet. Cover the ice cream with fresh strawberries, and the sherbet or other portion of ice cream with vanilla marshmallow. Top off with a red and green cherry. Price 20 cents.

MAID O' MY DREAMS

Slice one-half of a banana crosswise and place the slices on a small butter plate. Over the slices place a ladleful of good stiff ice cream and over the cream sprinkle finely ground nuts and top off with Maraschino cherry. Over all place a ladleful of whipped cream that has been sweetened. Price, 20 cents. (Mrs. E. L. Feagan.)

HINDOO

Split a banana and lay the pieces on a small plate; on one end of the banana put one dish of nut cream, and on the other put vanilla or strawberry cream, placing midway on the banana and between the ends a whole fig. On top of the nut cream put a creme de menthe cherry and on top of the vanilla or strawberry cream a Bigarreaux cherry. Whichever cream is used, pour crushed strawberries over it and then sprinkle chopped nuts over all. Price, 20 cents. (Mark C. Wilhoite.)

LAVENDER LADY

On a banana split dish place a sound, ripe banana which has been sliced lengthwise. Place on one end a disherful of vanilla and strawberry ice cream, and on the other a disherful of vanilla and chocolate ice cream. Over the whole pour sufficient lavender dressing, prepared as follows: Marshmallow paste, 1 pint; raspberry syrup, 4 ounces; grape juice, 1 dash; shredded cocoanut, 2 ounces, and sufficient simple syrup to bring the dressing to the proper consistency. Color the mixture the desired shade by means of red and blue coloring, both of which may be had in certified food colors. Red cherries may be used to top with, but the lavender marshmallow will carry out the color scheme to better advantage.

The author writes as follows concerning his formula: "The name came to me by reason of the fact that one of our patrons, a very popular Southern girl, 'blossomed out' in a very becoming attire of lavender. Her frequent appearance at the fountain in this garb helped to draw attention to the sign I had in mind. To advertise the specialty, I took a 22 x 28 gray card, on the right side of which I pasted a picture of a 'lavender lady' cut out of lavender colored paper. The headline to the wording was 'COMING,' and in smaller letters, 'to be a great favorite. She's brand new, sweet and attractive. You'll miss a treat if you do not meet her.'" Price, 20 cents. (B. C. Archibald.)

PETER PAN

Place in an oval dish one banana sliced lengthwise and at the sides place four frou frou wafers. After this has been done place one ladleful of vanilla ice cream on each end of the bananas; in the center of each put an ice cream cone filled with chocolate ice cream and around this pour vanilla syrup. Top off with whipped cream, placing over the cream sliced bananas. Place the dish on an extra plate, and serve with frou frou wafers and a glass of water on the side. (Walter Luick.)

THREE TWINS

Into a suitable dish place a No. 10-to-the-quart dipperful of rich vanilla ice at one end of the dish place a No 16 cone of vanilla ice cream; at the other end place a cone of maple ice cream with a cone of chocolate cream in the center of the dish Between the cones place a tablespoonful of whipped cream and top each cone with a red Maraschino cherry. Place a nabisco wafer on each end of the dish and serve.

The author states: "To advertise 'Three Twins' we hung up a sketch of three small boys with large straw hats and ragged trousers and it sold readily at 20 cents. It is a good scheme to give the customer three kinds of ice cream and there is a nice profit in the sale of this sundae at the price named." (Mrs. E. J. Beattie.)

GOODY GOODY

Into a suitable dish place a No. 10-to-the quart dipperful of rich vanilla ice cream; over this pour an ounce of maple syrup and sprinkle on 1 tablespoonful of fresh broken walnuts; cut a banana in half and use one of the halves sliced in about 4 pieces, standing the pieces one on each side of the dish. Also place a Maraschino cherry on each side and a tablespoonful of good whipped cream on top. Sprinkle over all powdered red sugar. Use a dainty dish, spoon, and napkin, and serve with a glassful of water. Price, 15 or 20 cents. (Edwin Horace Shortiss.)

FOOT BALL DESSERT

Take a banana, freed from its skin, place it in an oblong dish and cut lengthwise, then place two 16-to-the-quart ladlefuls of chocolate ice cream in the center, the cream being in the form of half globes; smooth off the cream and press the half globes together to represent a foot ball; then cut the ice cream lengthwise in the center, with a few cuts crosswise, and on this put a few walnut meats, some chocolate syrup and a ladleful of whipped cream; place a nabisco on each side and top off with red cherries. According to the author, this specialty can be served for 15 or 20 cents For advertising purposes he uses a window sign made of heavy paper with the lettering done in brown ink to represent the color of a football. A sample advertisement submitted carries the following lines:

```
: ..........................  :
:          Special          :
:   FOOT BALL DESSERT       :
·       at the Fountain      
:   Get in the game for 15 cents  :
  ..........................
```

(Gus Scholl.)

FAN'S SPECIAL

In an ordinary frappe dish slice half a banana, over it put a few fresh strawberries, and cover with a layer of whipped cream. On the cream place a dipperful of ice cream made in the form of a sphere to represent a ball. Serve with the dish a nabisco wafer, standing it on end and alongside of the cream. When fresh berries are out of season, use crushed strawberries. Sells for 15 cents.

FAIR HARBOR

Use a dome of ice cream for the foundation, half a banana cut crosswise for the tower, three toothpicks for the light supports, four cherries, one green, two red and one white, for the signal lights, a ladleful of pistachio flavored syrup, colored a light green, for the ocean, five pieces of banana cut in odd shapes for the shells that cling to the base, and a teaspoonful of broken nuts to represent rocks. To dispense, use a footed sundae dish. Place in it the vanilla ice cream, then take half of a banana (cut across the peel) into the lower or cut end of which, in the center, push a toothpick, and through the upper end or top of the banana insert two toothpicks so that they will cross each other and emerge from the sides On the ends of the toothpicks place the four cherries for the signals, one cherry for each light. The "tower" is now placed on the dome of cream and is held in position by the toothpick extending from the bottom of banana down into the cream. Pour pistachio syrup over all, add the odd pieces of bananas and broken nuts, and serve with crisp saltines. Sells for 20 cents. (C. L. Hadley.)

COMET

Peel one banana, slice in two lengthwise and lay the slices parallel on a plate; place a ball of vanilla ice cream on one end of the slices, place over the banana crushed fresh strawberries and over all pour a thick marshmallow cream, then put a Maraschino cherry on a toothpick on the ice cream. The ball of ice cream represents the head of the comet, while the two slices of banana represent the tail. This dish should bring 15 cents. (C. Ray Wait)

BASE BALL FRAPPE

In an ordinary frappe dish slice half a banana, over it put a few fresh strawberries and cover with a layer of whipped cream. On the cream place a dipperful of ice cream made in the form of a sphere to represent a ball. Serve with the dish a nabisco wafer, standing it on end and alongside of the ice cream. When fresh berries are out of season, use crushed strawberries. Sells for 10 or 15 cents. (Sterling Miller)

BANANA, NUT AND FRUIT

Slice a good ripe banana in halves and place the pieces flat side down on an oblong hand-painted china plate; between the slices put a 20-to-the-quart mold each of vanilla ice cream and chocolate ice cream; over one of these pour some chopped pecans and over the other, some pineapple fruit. Place a cherry on each side of the molds of ice cream and top off with whipped cream. On top of the cream put a few fresh pecan meats. Price, 20 cents. (Willie Burch.)

BAHAMA BANANA

Split a banana lengthwise and place the pieces on an oval plate. Over the pieces put a No. 12 dipperful of vanilla ice cream, cover with mayonnaise dressing and top off with a spoonful of ground nuts.

The author states that this dressing can be bought as prepared in the market, or it can be made as follows: Take 3 eggs, 1 tablespoonful each of butter and sugar; 2/3 cupful of vinegar, 2/3 cupful of milk or cream, a dash of salt, some mustard and a little pepper. Mix the dry ingredients together and stir them into the beaten eggs, then add the vinegar, boil for a couple of minutes and when cool add the milk The sundae sells for 15 cents. (Miss Beulah Lucas.)

DELMONICO SPECIAL

Use a long dish and put a small ladle of ice cream at each end. Then cut half of a banana into four thin slices lengthwise. Put two of the pieces on the dish in an outward V-shape between the two molds of ice cream, and then place a slice of sweet orange around the entire dish in each of the vacant places, or four all told. Pour over this an ounce of cherry wine syrup and a sprinkle of nuts; top off each mold with whipped cream and a cherry. Price, 20 cents.

BABY GRAND

Take a half of a banana, slice it in two, and lay the pieces in the center of a banana split dish. In the center place some ice cream. Cut the other half of the banana in round pieces and lay around the ice cream Top the ice cream with whipped cream and a cherry, and put ambrosia dressing at each end of the dish. Serve with a cereal tea wafer or a wafer of any other kind. Sells for 15 cents. (Harry Slavitchek.)

BRASS BAND

Into a saucer place a 5-cent dipperful of fruit ice cream. inserting into the cream a toothpick carrying a cherry. Along one side of the cream lay one-half of a frozen banana, decorating it with salted peanuts laid in a row. The fruit cream represents a drum, the cherry on the toothpick the drum stick, the banana any horn instrument, and the peanuts, the keys of the instrument

The frozen bananas are prepared as follows: Take nice, solid bananas, perfectly but not too ripe, skin and cut in two crosswise; run a soda straw into each banana half from end to end; bend the protruding end of the straw and reinsert it into the banana so as to form a hook or handle; take the banana halves by the straws and set them into a well-packed ice-cream freezer, using a sufficient number of the pieces of banana to cover the bottom of the freezer. Over the bananas pour some half-frozen sherbet, or orange ice will do. Let stand until well frozen. If the batch should freeze so hard as not to permit the bananas to be lifted from the packer by the straws, remove the packer from the tub and allow the mixture to soften, or loosen the banana halves from the bottom of the packer by means of two soda spoons. The cherries should be stuck on the toothpicks and placed into a cup or bowl in readiness to serve.

The author states that he sold this sundae for 10 cents, making thereby a profit of 6½ cents, the occasion being that of a Chautauqua celebration. (John Griffith.)

DIRECTOIRE

A modification of the banana split. Slice a banana lengthwise and spread open on a dish, the lower ends of the pieces being held together by the peel. Now fill the center with ice cream, over which pour vanilla syrup. Top off with whipped cream and a maraschino cherry. Price, 15 cents.

THAT MYSTERIOUS

Make a paste or thick syrup by boiling together a pint each of white cane syrup and lukewarm water with four pints of granulated sugar for four minutes. Beat the whites of four eggs to a stiff froth and to the mixture gradually add the syrup, stirring rapidly until free from lumps. To prepare the sundae, place a split banana upon an oblong dish and on it put a No. 10-to-the-quart dipperful of vanilla ice cream. Over all pour a ladleful of the syrup first described; on top of the ice cream put a few drops of chocolate syrup which will serve to "stripe" the sundae. (J. M. Bingaman.)

CHOCOLATE A LA HONDURAS

Serve in a rather shallow and broad dish Peel a fine ripe banana, slice it in two and between these sections pile up a liberal allowance of chocolat ice cream. Then over the ice cream pour some whipped cream, adding two or three strawberries and a little grated chocolate to give the proper color and taste.

UNCLE SAM

Put a whole banana on a platter; then take 2 ounces of white ice cream and ½ cunce of lemon syrup and make an emulsion, which pour around the banana. Put one cone-shaped scoop of white ice cream at the end of the banana, and top with a small U. S flag. Sells for 10 or 15 cents. (Sydney Trau.)

ROYAL BANANA SURPRISE

Take one dozen large, ripe bananas and split the skins carefully lengthwise on one side only, and remove from the fruit Next cut up six of the bananas in a mixing bowl, add one cupful of ground pecan nut meats, one-half cupful of shredded cocoanut, one pint of maple nut ice cream, and mix all well together; then take a spoon and refill the banana skins with the mixture, moulding it so that the cut edges of the skins will meet when filled; then place the sundaes thus made in a brick ice cream cabinet to freeze and keep hard To serve, place one of the stuffed banana skins on a plate, put a ladleful of whipped cream on the side, sprinkling over it lightly a little ground cinnamon; serve with a spoon, glass of water and a napkin. Sells for 25 cents. The author states that "the beauty of this sundae is that it has the customer guessing until he opens the banana skin and finds it loaded with a delicious dessert." (Harry G. Frame.)

BANANA NEAPOLITAN

Peel and split a banana and place the pieces on an oblong glass or china dish On the sliced banana place a No. 20 disherful each of chocolate, vanilla and strawberry ice cream. Over these sprinkle a few chopped nut meats and a little rich fresh strawberry dressing made by mashing the berries in granulated sugar. Top each cone of ice cream with a dash of whipped cream, and a large strawberry or cherry. A good seller at 20 cents.

BANANA MARTINIQUE

Peel and split a banana and lay the halves on a small oblong dish. On this put a No. 16-to-the-quart disherful of strawberry ice cream, and a similar quantity of coffee or vanilla ice cream. Over each cone of ice cream put a little whipped cream, sprinkle with macaroon crumbs and top with a cherry. Price, 20 cents.

FANCY FRUIT DESSERTS

CANTALOUPE SPLIT

Take a cantaloupe, remove the rind and then slice it lengthwise into ten parts; place two of the slices lengthwise in an oblong dish and a ladleful (eight-to-the-quart and cone-shaped) of vanilla ice cream in the center. Then pour on a ladleful of fresh pineapple fruit, adding a spoonful of walnut meats and whipped cream; place nabisco wafers, one on either side of the ice cream, and top off with a red cherry. Can be served for 10 or 15 cents.

The author used a window sign made of heavy paper to advertise this sundae, the lettering being done with red ink, as follows:

```
: . . . . . . . . . . . . . . . . . . . . . . . . . . . . . . . . .
:               Special!                :
:        CANTALOUPE SPLIT               :
:            at the Fountain.           :
:    It's Real.          15 Cents.      :
. . . . . . . . . . . . . . . . . . . . . . . . . . . . . . . . .
```

(Gus V. Schall.)

MELON A LA MODE

Small, ripe cantaloupe (or musk melon), cut lengthwise. Scoop out seeds and fill with ice cream (vanilla generally used); sprinkle with powdered sugar to taste. Price, 15 cents.

MELON MAID

In a round dish of about 4 inches in diameter, place half of one cantaloupe (small muskmelon) and in the center of the melon place a ball of ice cream. On one side of the ice cream put crushed peaches and on the other crushed strawberries. Top off with whipped cream and a cherry. Price, 15 cents. (Donald Strauss.)

CANTALOUPE A LA CLEVELAND

Select a ripe cantaloupe and cut in half; then cut a thin slice off of the end so as to make the half of the cantaloupe rest evenly on a china platter. Take out the seeds and add a small scoopful of vanilla ice cream (about 16 to the quart), unless other flavor is specified. Then take a spoon and make a concave opening on the top of the ice cream and fill it with fresh strawberries and grated English walnuts. Top off with a whole red cherry. "A splendid seller when cantaloupes are in season." Price, 20 cents. (Sydney Trau.)

THAT HEAVENLY DREAM

Take a ripe Osage cantaloupe (these cantaloupes are ripe to the rind and make good sundaes), cut it in two, take the seeds out, and slice off the bottom so that each half will stand upright on an oblong dish. The cantaloupe should stand on the ice at least six hours before it is wanted for use. Now place in the melon some pineapple fruit and on it put a disherful of rich maple cream. For a dressing, take four oranges which are not dry or spongy, four ripe bananas, and one pound of fresh ripe cherries; chop all up together and cover with powdered sugar; let stand for 12 hours. Use enough of the dressing, and top off with whipped cream and three cherries, placing the cherries lengthwise and about an inch apart. Should bring 25 cents. (Willie Burch.)

FROZEN CANTALOUPES

Select small, sweet, and very ripe cantaloupes. Press all the ripe portion after rejecting the seeds through a sieve. To each two quarts of pulp and juice add one pint of orange juice, one pint of grape juice, and one-half pint of lemon juice. Sweeten this with three pounds of sugar. Let stand until a thick syrup has formed. Color with a little green and amber coloring. When the mixture has begun to stiffen fold in the stiffly beaten whites of two eggs and one pint of whipped sweetened cream. Pack and let stand four hours. Price, 15 cents.

MAPLE MELON MIX

Cut an ordinary sized round nutmeg muskmelon or cantaloupe into halves; remove the seeds; cut off a small slice on the bottom of one of the halves so that it will set level, then place it on a china saucer. Fill the center of the half of the melon with one 10-to-the-quart scoopful of vanilla ice cream; over the cream pour a ladleful of "maple mix," top with whipped cream and a couple of red cherries. "Maple mix" is prepared as follows: Put one quart of milk in a double boiler and bring it to the boiling point; add 14 ounces of maple syrup, two well-beaten eggs and stir well. Now burn one cupful of brown sugar, until it becomes the color of maple sugar, add it to the mixture, and stir until dissolved. Then dissolve 2½ teaspoonfuls of corn starch in a little cold water, add this to the mixture and boil until just thick enough to pour; remove from the fire, and add ½ pound ground walnuts, stirring in well and cooling before using. Can be sold at a good profit for 20 cents. (Harry G. Frame.)

CANTALOUPE IMPERIAL

Take a cantaloupe, cut in half, take out the seed and put a scoopful of vanilla ice cream in the cavity, pour over the ice cream vanilla syrup and over this put a scoopful of peach ice cream, topping off with finely chopped nuts and whipped cream. On the whipped cream place a piece of cantaloupe. Put the sundae on a fancy dish and serve with Nabisco wafers. Sells for 25c.

A PEAR OF PEACHES

Procure a number of rather large nice ripe cantaloupes. Cut one of them in two, lengthwise. Then cut one of the halves into strips of about two and a half or three inches in diameter across the middle. Cut a slice off the bottom so that the pieces will lie flat. Place two of the pieces side by side on a fancy china plate, putting on each piece a small ball of peach ice cream (about half the side of a No. 16 mold). Over these pour a ladleful of fresh crushed pears, and between them put two red Maraschino cherries. Price 15 or 20 cents.

The author says that by having a number of cantaloupes cut up one can prepare this sundae in a very short time. (Victor Johnson.)

CANTALOUPE SURPRISE

On a six-inch plate place one No. 16 disherful of vanilla ice cream. Over this invert half a small ripe cantaloupe, which has been peeled, taking care to hide all of the ice cream. Now arrange four slices of banana at regular intervals around the cantaloupe, and top with whipped cream and a cherry. The author states that this is a sure winner at 20 cents, but that the price may be varied according to the cost of cantaloupes.

CANTALOUPE WITH A PEACH

Take half a cantaloupe, clean out the seeds and cut a small slice from the bottom so that the cut cantaloupe will stand on a small plate. In the cantaloupe place a ladleful of fresh sliced peaches, add a 16-to-the-quart scoopful of fresh peach ice cream, pour over a ladleful of whipped cream and top with a creme de menthe cherry; on the dish beside the cantaloupe lay two nabisco wafers and serve. Sells for 15 cents. (Sterling Miller)

ROCKY FORD SPECIAL

On a small breakfast plate place half of a medium size Rocky Ford cantaloupe Into this put a small ladleful of caramel nut, tutti-frutti or strawberry ice cream Over the cream pour a ladleful of pineapple fruit and top with whipped cream and a cherry Price, 20 cents.

WATERMELON ROYAL

Take a long glass dish and on it lay a neat slice of the heart of a ripe watermelon, avoiding the seeds. On one end of the dish put a small ladleful of pineapple water ice; at the other end place a similar quantity of orange water ice; pour over all a little strawberry syrup and put a maraschino cherry on the water ice at each end of the dish. Serve. Price, 20 cents.

WATERMELON A LA ATLANTA

Take a watermelon and cut it into one and a half inch cubes. Place one of the cubes in an oblong dish; on one side of the cube of melon put a ladleful of vanilla ice cream, and on the other side a ladleful of strawberry ice cream (16-to-the-quart) Then pour a ladleful of strawberry fruit over the vanilla ice cream, and a ladleful of pineapple fruit over the strawberry ice cream. Put a ladleful of walnut meats and some whipped cream over the melon, and top off with red and green cherries, placing a nabisco wafer on each side of the melon. Sells for 15 cents and up.

The author states that a window sign can be made of heavy paper, the lettering being done in red and green ink to represent the colors of a watermelon. (Gus V. Schall.)

PEACH MELBA

Use half a large preserved peach, free from stone. Place in a suitable glass or china dish of the saucer type. This dish should be about 4 inches in diameter and 1½ inches from base to rim. Over the peach place a suitable quantity of ice cream, either free from flavor or vanilla flavor, and over the ice cream and peach pour from 2 to 3 ounces of rich and strong strawberry syrup. This syrup should be at least twice the strength of ordinary syrup utilized in the regular manner. A number of strawberries in their whole form can be added, especially when the fruit is in season Price, 20 cents.

PEACH MELBA

Ice cream for the foundation, covered with imported fresh peaches sliced, covered with a syrup sauce of raspberry kirsch and maraschino. This is a variation of the original "peach Melba" in which the peach is served whole and covered with a raspberry puree. Price, 15 cents.

BABY MINE

Place one spoonful of vanilla ice cream in a sundae dish; cover the ice cream with half a peach, and base it with whipped cream, then sprinkle a few nuts around the base Charge 15 cents.

This above formula has been tried by the author's brother, who runs a store in an Indiana town, and the demand has been excellent. He says he sells on an average 25 cans of peaches each day in the Summer to supply the trade in this sundae   (Theo Louvis.)

PEACHES SUPREME

On a 5-inch fancy plate place a dipperful (16-to-the-quart) of vanilla ice cream, on either side of the ice-cream place the half of a peach (the peach having been previously pared, cut in two and the halves sprinkled with powdered sugar), over the whole pour one ladleful of sliced fresh peaches, and sprinkle with one spoonful of walnut meats broken into small pieces; top with whipped cream and one red cherry The author of this formula writes that he has been selling this dish for 15 or 20 cents and it has been a winner. (P. A. Ritto.)

PEACH CREME

Wipe and remove the skin from one peach Force the pulp through a sieve, and if there is much juice, drain. Beat the white of one egg, using a silver fork. Gradually incorporate the peach pulp while continuing the beating. Sweeten with powdered sugar, pile on a glass dish, and serve with steamed custard or cream.

PEACH A LA REINE

Place on a china plate one 6-to-the-quart dipper of vanilla ice cream, cover with vanilla marshmallow cream, encircle the base with quartered peaches, sprinkle cocoanut over all, and top with a Maraschino cherry. Charge 15 or 20 cents. (E. J. Howard.)

PINEAPPLE SUPREME

Pare and grate one pineapple, add as much sugar as you have pulp; place in a saucepan on a medium hot fire and boil like a jam Let cool, then beat the whites of five or six eggs to a very stiff froth; beat in the pineapple and pile on a glass dish. Serve with custard or with pineapple syrup. Price, 15 cents.

SNOWBALL

Into an ordinary mixing glass put 1 disherful each of pineapple ice and vanilla ice cream, and 1 fruit ladleful each of grated pineapple and whipped cream. With a mixing spoon frappe the whole well together. Put the frapped mixture into a 10-ounce fancy stem glass and top off with a little whipped cream and a Maraschino cherry. Serve with a teaspoon and nabisco wafers on a flat dish; also serve the customer with a glassful of water. It sells for 20 cents. (H. Wendell.)

PINEAPPLE A LA HONOLULU

In a long stem champagne cup glass place a No. 10 disherful of vanilla ice cream. Take a round slice of Hawaiian pineapple and cut from the center, making eight triangular pieces. Place these points upward around the ice cream. Over the cream sprinkle some chopped walnut meats and pour on a little grape syrup. Top with a tablespoonful of whipped cream and one red cherry. Serve on a 4-inch china plate on which are two nabisco wafers. Sells for 15 cents. (Sam Davis.)

ARCTIC ORANGES

Cut oranges in half and scoop out the pulp. Separate pulp from seeds and tough portions and to each quart of pulp take one tablespoonful of granulated gelatin and dissolve it in a little cold water, then add one pint of hot water. Combine gelatin mixture with orange pulp, fold in half a pint of whipped cream and sweeten to taste. Fill orange shells and set aside to harden. When mixture is stiff in shells heap with whipped cream and serve very cold. Twenty cents is suggested as a price for this feature.

ORANGE MELBA

Take one orange, cut away the rind so as not to remove any of the fleshy part of the fruit. Peel down the skin until the bottom of the orange is nearly reached. Then, with the skin still attached to the lower end of the orange, run your finger down into the center of the orange, spreading the sections and being careful not to break the orange or allow the juice to run out. Carefully separate the divisions or parts of the orange and while still holding the fruit in the hand, make a cup-shaped cavity in the orange and into it put a dipperful of ice cream; pour over the ice cream half an ounce of nectar syrup, add a spoonful of flaked cocoanut and top off with a red Maraschino cherry. Sells for 15 cents. (Alfred Miller.)

HARVEST MOON

In a banana special dish place a good clean corn husk; on one end of the husk put a good-sized ball of orange ice cream. It is quite necessary that the cream have a good orange or golden color so as not to defeat the object of the name. The author uses a specially prepared cream, although a cream made by any good formula will answer. On the other end of the corn husk place a copious supply of toasted corn flakes. All around and partially covering the flakes place well-sweetened whipped cream.

According to the author, this makes an edible and very nourishing dish. The name and dish are harmonious, as the orange cream is intended to represent the harvest moon, while the husk makes a good foundation and together with the flakes represents the corn harvest. The whipped cream is to represent the early frosts which arrive about the time of husking. He states that the dish may be sold profitably in most localities for 15 cents. It is a question whether this price would provide an adequate profit. (B. C. Archibald.)

SCHOOL MAID'S DELIGHT

On a 4-inch fancy plate place a thin slice of orange and over the orange put a No. 16 dipperful of vanilla ice cream; over the ice cream pour one ladleful of freshly crushed orange and one spoonful of chopped nuts; top with marshmallow whip and one Maraschino cherry; serve with two Coronado wafers. Price 10 cents; more fruit, 15 cents.

CATCH OF THE SEASON

Boil 4 pounds of sugar with 4 cupfuls of water, then add 8 cupfuls of orange juice; scald 4 cupfuls of light cream, add the yolks of 8 eggs and cook over hot water until the mixture thickens; when cool add to the mixture 4 cupfuls of heavy cream beaten stiff, mix well and put into the freezer and partly freeze; then add 1 cupful of shredded orange and citron peel (candied); cut two pieces from each orange so that the part remaining will represent a basket having a handle; remove the pulp and cut portions of the orange so as not to injure the "basket," which place in cold water until ready to serve. Now fill each basket with the above mixture, covering it with whipped cream sweetened and flavored with orange. Price, 20 cents. (Walter Luick.)

ORANGOLA

Place in a round, glass saucer one slice of a large orange; add one full size (10-to-the-quart) dipperful of vanilla ice cream, stand the two halves of an orange, each half on opposite sides of the cream and dress with orange syrup and whipped cream. Top off with a Maraschino cherry. Sells for 15 cents. (Morris B. Benjamin.)

KEY WEST

Peel a good-sized seedless orange, slice off three slices and lay on a round plate. Over each slice place a spoonful of ice cream, using chocolate, vanilla and strawberry. Shape up round, and over the cream pour Maraschino syrup, topping off with Maraschino cherries. Serve with glass of ice water. Price, 15 cents.

EL CAPITAIN

On a long, shallow dish place side by side two slices of orange. On one of the slices place a small 20-to-the-quart disherful of chocolate ice cream, and on the other a tall measureful of vanilla ice cream. The vanilla cream may be formed by filling a tall tapered 4- or 5-ounce glass with the cream, then dipping the glass into warm water and turning the contents out upon the orange slice. Around the cream, but not covering it, place a dressing which is made as follows:

(a) Make a gelatine dessert by cooking 5 cards of gelatine in a quart of water. Before the mixture has entirely cooled, add orange syrup to flavor and sufficient red coloring to tint. This does not make a very solid mixture. (Prepared gelatine may be used to advantage.)

(b) Take a quart of marshmallow (half paste and half syrup) and to this add a quart of the gelatine dessert and 4 ounces of shredded cocoanut. Beat this mixture until the gelatine dessert is broken up into small particles. The dressing is then ready for use.

Price, 20 cents (B. C. Archibald.)

ORANGERBET

In an ordinary mixing glass put one disherful of smooth orange ice and add one and a half disherfuls of vanilla ice cream and a fruit ladleful of whipping cream. Then with an ordinary soda spoon proceed to frappe the mixture, stirring the ingredients well together. Put the frapped mixture into a fancy 10-ounce stem glass, and top off with a little whipped cream and a cherry. This parfait should sell for 20 cents.

The author adds that in his opinion and that of his customers, orangerbet is, if prepared right, the most delicious parfait ever introduced and is always a repeater. The

blending of the flavors of the orange ice and the vanilla ice cream could not be finer, the whipped cream giving the desired smoothness. (Julius M. Kortlang.)

ORANGE DAINTY

Take a large orange cut into the shape of a basket and from which the meat has been removed; fill up with orange water ice, spread on a thin layer of strawberry ice cream, and top off with a Maraschino cherry. Serve the basket in a dish of shaved ice to keep it cold. A bow of red ribbon may be tied to the handle of the basket to add to the color effect. Price, 20 cents.

GRAPE FRUIT A LA PERU

Cut a grape fruit horizontally in two, remove the fleshy part, section by section, finally cutting out the remaining hard parts. Put the fleshy pulp of the grape fruit with a similar quantity of good ripe strawberries into a bowl, add powdered sugar and flavor with curacao, then set on ice cream to macerate for at least 30 minutes. When ready to serve, fill the grape fruit shell with the fruit mixture, and garnish with whipped cream, flavored with curacao. Price, 15 or 20 cents, according to size of fruit used. (Victor B. Miller.)

MALAY MIX

Into a long-stem sundae glass place a sufficient quantity each of strawberry, vanilla and chocolate ice cream; over these press a No 10 cone disher to form all into a cone, around which place thin slices of banana, standing the slices on end, pouring over all some pineapple fruit, and sprinkling on top some walnut meats, coarsely ground; finally top off with a cherry. Can be sold for 10 or 15 cents, according to the class of trade. (J. B. Lytell.)

SPECIAL FIG

Take an ordinary frappe dish and in it place a No. 16-to-the-quart ladleful of chocolate ice cream; over the ice cream pour a ladleful of crushed figs, then a ladleful of chopped walnut meats, a ladleful of whipped cream, and top off with a whole ripe cherry. Place a piece of fig cake on one side and serve for 15 cents. (Gus. Schall)

TWO-IN-ONE BEAUTY

Take a small side dish in platter shape and place in the bottom of the dish one lettuce leaf. Then take a No. 16 cup disher and with it put vanilla ice cream on one end of the dish and strawberry ice cream at the other end. On the vanilla ice cream put one-half ladleful of strawberry fruit; on the strawberry cream end put one-half ladleful of pineapple fruit. Then place one large Maraschino cherry on top of the strawberry ice cream and one creme de menthe cherry on top of the vanilla ice cream. Top off the "Whole Beauty" with a small portion of grated walnuts. Charge 15 cents. Be sure and place fruits in the manner directed so as to make a perfect blend of colors. (C. P. Finkle.)

THE GRISWOLD

Take 3 red plums, 3 blue plums, 3 yellow peaches, 2 ripe Bartlett pears, 3 ripe bananas, 1 8-ounce glassful crushed pineapple, 1 8-ounce glassful whole red raspberries, juice of 3 lemons, 1 8-ounce glassful sherry wine, and 1 pint of plain marshmallow. Cut up the fruit in a dish, over it pour the wine and then the marshmallow, adding enough heavy syrup to bring the mixture to the right consistency to serve. If necessary, add a bit of red coloring to brighten the mixture. To serve, take a ball disher, fill it with real fresh fruit peach ice cream and highly flavored coffee ice cream (half and half). Drop the ice cream on a serving dish, pour over it a ladleful of the Griswold blend given above, and "you will have something that will make 'em look wise." A dainty slice of sponge cake may be served with the dessert if desired. (C. L. Hadley.)

THE CASTLE WALK

On a banana-split dish put at one end a No. 16 disherful of vanilla ice cream, and at the other end place a similar quantity of orange ice. Cover the ice cream and orange ice with a dressing made by mixing together 1 pint of marshmallow, 3 ounces of raspberry syrup, 4 ounces of lemon syrup, 2 ounces of cocoanut and 8 or 10 whole cherries chopped fine, the mixture being thinned to the proper consistency with simple syrup. Use one or two ladlefuls of the dressing; sprinkle on some ground nuts and top with a red and green cherry.

The author states that this dessert has proved to be a phenomenal seller with him. He uses the following window sign:

```
:    They All Eat 'Em!    :
: THE CASTLE WALK—20c :
```

(Mason Laurie.)

QUEEN OF BOHEMIA

Take a small mold (about 3 x 2 x 1 inches), put into it two red and two green cherries in opposite corners and a thin round slice of an orange; in the center of the orange put a festino and then fill the mold with cream of any flavor desired. Place two nabisco wafers on a china platter and empty the contents of the mold on the wafers. Then top off with whipped cream and English walnut, the walnut on top of the whipped cream.

An easy way to keep the cream from sticking to the mold and also to assist in

the removal of the cream is first to wet the mold then cut the side with a knife when the cream will fall out. Price, 15 cents. (J. H. Makler.)

MY MAID'S FAVORITE

Into an 8-ounce bell glass put 1 No. 12 dipperful of ice cream; take a good ripe banana, slice it over the ice cream (½ inch slices), and over this pour 1 ounce of pineapple fruit; top with whipped cream and a Maraschino cherry, and serve with a long spoon in a glass holder.

The author says that he has tested this formula over his fountain for some time. Price, 15 cents. (Geo. E. Engle.)

MEXICAN SALUTE

Into an ice-cream saucer place a small ladleful each of vanilla, chocolate and strawberry ice cream; fill in the center of the plate and around the ice cream with chopped nuts, fruit salad, or any kind of fruit. Directly over the fruit, which should rest in the center of the plate, place a cone-shaped ladleful of water ice. Stick a small American flag in the top of the water ice. The author who is a Canadian, states that this dessert has made a big hit in his city, and believes that it should appeal to the American public at the present time. Sells for 20 cents. (J. Arthurs.)

SOUL KISS

On a small fancy platter place a quarter of a brick of nesselrode or tortoni ice cream; on top of this put some stiff whipped cream in which lay some slices of banana; put a cherry at either end and also in the center, and sprinkle with nuts, if desired. Price, 15 or 20 cents.

MEXICAN REMINDER

Take 1 pound of French candied fruits, 4 cupfuls of water, 2½ cupfuls of sugar, 3 lemons and 4 oranges. Chop the fruit fine; put the sugar and water into a suitable kettle with the rinds of 2 lemons and one orange, and boil for five minutes When cold, add the juice of 2 lemons and 3 oranges, stir well, strain, and freeze; then stir in the fruit, place in deep-fluted moulds and again freeze hard. To serve, place one of the frozen sections on a fancy plate, cover with pistachio sauce and marshmallow, and top with a cherry. May be served with a Mexican pecan wafer The following sign was used to advertise this dessert:

```
:    MEXICAN REMINDER    :
: Something New at the Right Time :
```

(J. T. Clapesattle.)

ROSE OF THE ORCHARD

Take a ripe, yellow Bartlett pear, cut off the top and bottom, take out the core, and remove the seeds with a small sundae spoon. Put the small ends of the pear one on top of the other on a plate, and place on them a small cone of peach fruit ice cream. Pour over all a ladleful each of chopped maraschino cherries and pistachio-flavored heavy marshmallow, and put a green mint cherry on top of the cone of cream Serve on a 5-inch heavy plate, if possible, with rose leaves for the decoration. Sells for 15 cents.

The author of the formula writes that he advertises the specialty by a picture of a large, yellow pear in a wreath of bright red roses on a card 10 x 20 inches, with the words, "Try a Dainty Treat; 'Tis Worth 15 Cents." (C. L. Hadley.)

ICE CUP

Pack a dozen flat champagne glasses or other small tumblers in a tub with pounded ice, and salt around them. Fill these glasses with any fruit syrup, such as raspberry, strawberry, or cherry. Cover the tub with a cloth and leave for 15 or 20 minutes, or until the syrup is frozen about an eighth of an inch in thickness all around the sides of the glass. Pour out the unfrozen syrup and replace the glasses in the ice for a few minutes longer in order to thoroughly set the inside of the syrup case. Turn these ice cups out carefully and fill them with Curacao ice cream, nut ice cream, or any ice of a different color from the cups, and serve

PRESIDENTIAL DELIGHT

Into an 8-ounce colonial stem glass put 1 ounce of chocolate syrup, one 10-to-the-quart disherful of vanilla ice cream, some sliced bananas, 1 ladleful of crushed strawberries, one 20-to-the-quart disherful of pineapple sherbet, all to come level with the top of the glass. Then put one 10-to-the-quart disherful of chocolate ice cream on top, and around the base of the cream in the form of a square put the four pieces of a marshmallow previously quartered. In the center and on top put a maraschino cherry with a small U. S. flag, the flag being raised by thrusting the flagstaff through the cherry. Price, 20 or 25 cents. (Ulysses Degman.)

NEED YOU

Put into a 6-ounce sundae glass one No. 8 scoopful of vanilla and strawberry ice cream mixed; then take a half of a banana and quarter in lengths like a finger; take two pineapple fingers and cut in half lengthwise, and place around the ice cream so that the ends of the pieces will project on the outside of the sundae dish, pour over the dish so prepared a ladleful of crushed pineapple with some sliced bananas, and top off with whipped cream and a couple of fresh strawberries. (J. Casiragh.)

HUG-ME-TIGHT

Take a large ripe pear, cut lengthwise, place one half on a small decorated china plate, preferably a heart-shaped plate. Over the pear put a ladleful of vanilla ice cream, then over the ice cream pour a ladleful of mallow cream. Around the cream place walnut halves and top off with a Maraschino cherry. Price, 15 cents. (Fay W. Fraker)

EMERALD ISLE

Over a dipperful of vanilla ice cream (colored green), pour a ladleful of custard, top with whipped cream into which embed a green cherry; sprinkle over all a little shredded cocoanut and a shaking of nutmeg. Serve with whole wheat Mansfield wafers. To color the ice cream, boil spinach for 3 or 4 minutes, drain, and mash, then strain through muslin.

The custard referred to above is made by using 8 eggs, a gallon of milk and 1 pound of sugar. Let the milk come to a boil on a gas stove or electric heater, stir in a mixture of the sugar and the yolks of the eggs beaten to creaminess, and let the whole come to a boil once more. The boiling point must be carefully watched, for if the mixture stays at that temperature for more than a couple of seconds after the eggs and sugar have been stirred in, the mixture will eventually curdle and settle into soured milk and lumps of eggs and sugar. The use of a double boiler simplifies this part of the work. The custard so made may be flavored in any manner. Price, 15 cents. (Arthur A. Capwell)

EASTER EGG

Cover the bottom of a small round china plate with several leaves of lettuce; upon these place a "bird's nest" prepared with finely spun candy. In the nest place a 12-to-the-quart mold of vanilla ice cream in the form of a setting hen. Around and partially under the hen put red, white, and green cherries to represent Easter eggs. Price, 25 cents. (Ralph S. Hay.)

DARKEST AFRICA

Into an oval dish about 6 inches long place ½ ball of chocolate ice cream, dark in color on one side, and ½ ball vanilla ice cream, placing the two halves side by side; over both balls of cream pour 2 ounces of heavy catawba wine syrup, colored pale green to represent the Congo River. On top of the chocolate cream which is for Africa, place a large white cherry (on a toothpick) to represent the white explorer in Africa; over the white ball pour a small ladleful of chopped green cherries and stick in a few pieces of bark cinnamon to represent the foliage and trees. Now take 8 tiny candy toys, or babies, to represent the natives (can be bought in

New York), placing four on each ball of cream. Over all pour a good ladleful of ground Brazil nuts (niggertoes). Can be sold for 15 cents, but ought to bring 20 cents. By having the ingredients in one place the dessert can be put up in two minutes. (C. L. Hadley.)

COUNTRY CLUB SPECIAL

Cover the bottom of a small round china plate with several leaves of lettuce. Upon these place a slice of brick ice cream (8-to-the-quart), vanilla and caramel flavor, and orange pudding. In the center on the brick of cream place two long slices of a fresh peach and cover them with stiffly whipped cream. Sprinkle finely ground walnut meats over the whipped cream and place a whole Maraschino cherry upon each corner of the ice cream. Orange pudding, used in making this sundae, consists of orange cream in which ground walnut meats and small pieces of cherries are frozen. Price, 20 cents. (Ralph S. Hay.)

BULGARIAN DESSERT

Use a 7-ounce glass; put into it ½ ounce of strawberry syrup, 1 small scoopful of strawberry crushed fruit, 1 small scoopful of vanilla ice cream, 1 small scoopful of chocolate ice cream, 1 spoonful of crushed pecans, cover with chocolate syrup and top with whipped cream, and one green and one Maraschino cherry. Sells for 15 or 20 cents.

ST. JACOB'S COAT

Fill a sundae glass with plain ice cream in the usual way. Around the rim place one layer of neat, thinly sliced bananas; on top of the bananas and around the cream arrange in the form of a circle whole cherries; then a circle of pineapple cubes, assorted nuts, etc., continuing the operation upward until the cone of ice cream is completely covered. On top place a thin slice of orange, glaze with whipped cream and a dash of grape juice. It takes time to make St. Jacob's Coat, which, with the cost, should not be forgotten in setting the price. (Clinton B. Ellis.)

WALNUT LANE BRIDGE

On a banana-split dish place a No. 12 cone or dipperful of vanilla ice cream and a cone of chocolate ice cream; make a bridge across the two cones of ice cream with two nabisco wafers, pouring over the wafers when placed in position, one ladleful of crushed peaches, top off with marshmallow whip, place a cherry on each end of the bridge and serve with a glass of water. Price, 15 cents. (Macy Wright.)

THE MONORAIL

A mold to form the cream in the shape of a gyroscope or monorail car is necessary. This can be very easily obtained at any hardware store where the tinner will make one for about 75 cents. The size of the mold will depend upon the size of the car one wishes to represent. A colonial style "happy-thought" dish is recommended for dispensing the sundae. The cream when molded should measure 3 x 1 x ¾ inches and have the shape of a car with a seating capacity of eight. The mold is so made that it leaves the inside of the car hollow. Into this cavity is poured a mixture of crushed pineapple and strawberry fruits and over it is sprinkled a few finely ground nuts. Then place small candy Teddy Bears around the car—three on either side and one at either end. Then put wto spoonfuls of whipped cream evenly along the center of the car and serve the sundae with three assorted wafers on a small china plate.

The author states that "This sundae sells readily for 25 cents and is a good advertiser. It can be put up very rapidly after a little practice." (Philip W. Fraker.)

PANAMA DELIGHT

Cut a brick of ice cream of three flavors into slices. Take one of the slices and cut into two pieces and place the pieces on the plate 1½ inches apart. At each end push a nabisco wafer down to the plate through the cream, also inserting a wafer in the cream midway between the wafers at the ends. If the cream is hard, start the insertions with a knife. This will represent two locks of the canal. Fill one with raspberry syrup and the other with pineapple fruit; place fresh strawberries or cherries on the four corners and some raspberry fruit around the plate. Sprinkle with crushed nuts, and stick two half toothpicks, each holding the half meat of a pecan nut, into the cream to represent boats. Sells for 15 cents.

The author says that he advertises this specialty by using pictures of the Panama Canal. (Ellis N. Rowe.)

OVUM UPP

Take an oblong pickle dish and place in it one ladleful of soft vanilla ice cream; smooth out the cream so as to make it look like the white of an egg; place on the cream two halves of an apricot (the Wedding Ring or Wishbone apricots are preferred on account of their size and golden color), one at each end or a short distance from the end to represent the yolk of an egg; on one side of the dish place a nice piece of lettuce. Sprinkle nutmeg on the white portion of the beverage to represent pepper and "you will have a very pretty dish and one that will talk for itself."

The author states that if just a little care is taken in putting up this formula it will be pretty hard to distinguish the mixture from the genuine dish indicated by the name he has selected. Price, 20 cents (P. S. Williams.)

MUTT AND JEFF

Take a tall, slender mold, fill it with chocolate ice cream, mold the cream and then let it slide out upon an oblong dish. At the bottom of this molded cream place two chocolate almonds representing Mutt's feet. Now pour chocolate over all this. Next take about one-third of a veronique wafer, stick one end of a toothpick into it, and then stick this in the cream. This is Mutt's neck. On top of the wafer place a white marshmallow. That's all of Mutt.

Now for Jeff. Take a small dipper of vanilla cream and place it beside Mutt. Stick a couple of chocolate peanuts at the base of the cream for Jeff's feet. Pour a smooth, thick marshmallow dressing over this, then proceed to finish just as Mutt, with the exception of having the neck a little shorter.

When properly made this is a comical dish, and one that "takes." This feature is worth 25 cents. (R. C. Sellers.)

LOBSTER DELIGHT

On either end of a fancy plate place lettuce leaves so that the half of each protrudes over the side. Take an ice cream cone, break it apart to simulate a "shell." Lay the shell in middle of the plate, and then with a No. 10-to-the-quart disher put in a mound of one-half strawberry and one-half vanilla ice cream, placing the cream partly on the shell and partly on one of the lettuce leaves. Cut a Maraschino cherry in two and lay the hemispheres on cream so as to make two "eyes." To represent the "mouth" employ a whole cherry. Take half a banana, slice down the center and use the two pieces thus formed to make the claws, laying them in the corners of the shell on the side of the ice cream. Then take two nabiscos and lay them crossed on a lettuce to constitute a side lunch for the salad. Sells for 20 cents.

The author says the Lobster Delight takes about two minutes to prepare if the cones are already made into shells and the lettuce is ready for use. (Morris Bialac.)

CLUB SANDWICH

Have an individual mold made by a tinsmith. He may use for a model a small ice cream sandwich mold, making it three inches wide and two and one-half inches long. Have the bottom plate made to fit very closely and perfectly flat on the inside so as not to retain any soft cream or water that may accumulate during the rush hours. Take two saucers, one smaller than the other, put a napkin between them, place a fresh, crisp lettuce leaf on the top saucer, then proceed with the sundae.

Cut a slice of orange, trim all the rind off carefully and put it on the bottom of the mold Place a creme de menthe cherry in each corner and fill mold half full of vanilla ice cream. Then cover with two nabisco wafers, several slices of pineapple (creme de rose pineapple adds to the color scheme), and fill balance of mold with orange sherbet or water ice. Press firmly, turn out and place before your customer. Always be careful to thoroughly drain your fruit before using and it works easier if chilled. Should the sandwiches be desired to fill outside orders use lady fingers instead of wafers.

CHESTNUT FRAPPE

Into a regular frappe dish put a ladleful of sliced peaches and cover with whipped cream. Then take a sphere of chocolate ice cream and push it down into the whipped cream so that it cannot move out of the center of the dish. With a small knife cut the chocolate ice cream into quarters, pulling each quarter open to represent the opening of a chestnut burr; then drop into the center or opening thus made a few shelled marrons. Place a nabisco wafer alongside of the ice cream and serve. Sells for 15 cents. (Sterling Miller.)

BILLIARD DESSERT

On a small china plate place two ladlefuls of chocolate whipped cream; on the cream lay a thin slice of a 2-quart brick of light green pistachio ice cream; then press the ice cream on the whipped cream so that some of the latter will be squeezed out under the sides of the ice cream. This represents the top of a billiard table. Place in different positions on top of the slice of pistachio cream three spheres of ice cream about the size of English walnuts, one sphere being made of strawberry ice cream, the other two of vanilla ice cream. These represent the billiard balls. On the cream near one of the spheres of cream lay a "sunshine veronique" sugar wafer stick to represent the billiard cue. Serve. Price, 15 cents or more.

The author uses a window sign of heavy paper lettered as follows to advertise the frappe:

```
: ............................. :
:        A CUE FOR YOU!       :
:     Try our Billiard Frappe  :
:            15 Cents          :
:        At the Fountain.      :
: ............................. :
```

(Sterling Miller.)

CHOCOLATE WHIP

Pour about one-third of a glassful of ice cold rich milk into a 12-ounce glass (straight glass preferred), place the button of the electric mixer on the surface of the milk, and hold it there until the milk becomes thick and creamy, and its volume increased to within an inch and a half from the rim. Flavor to suit with chocolate while mixing; add one dipperful of chocolate ice cream (24 to the quart).

The author calls this a product of the electric mixer, and writes that with a little practice this drink can be made quickly. Serve with a long spoon and a glass of water. Sells for 10 cents. The author also states that he dispensed the beverage for some time before he realized its value. He believes the formula deserves consideration for the reason that it took and that in spite of the fact that a cold special dispensed in the dead of Winter is usually a failure. He writes that it is not an uncommon occurrence for him to have eight or nine orders for this specialty out of every eleven or twelve orders he receives. The cost anywhere in the United States will not exceed 4 cents, and it will readily sell for 10 cents; the profit is larger than on ice-cream soda and the demand, the author states, is three times greater. (Alex McDonald.)

CHOCOLATE PUFFEE

In a tall parfait glass draw an ounce of heavy chocolate syrup, add a medium ladleful of whole pecans, then a spoonful of chocolate ice cream, leaving the spoon in the glass for mixing purposes. Fill the glass with good, heavy whipped cream, and well mix all with the spoon so as to thoroughly distribute the chocolate flavor, which can be done very quickly. Then top with a ladleful of whipped cream, smoothing over the top to give the dish a neat appearance. Sprinkle with ground nuts and place a cherry or a frou-frou almond on top. By using claret syrup, instead of chocolate syrup as given above, a "claret nut puffee" may be made. In fact, the customer can be given any flavor he may desire. Charge 15 or 20 cents. (W. B. Moreland.)

FIFTH AVENUE

Take a cake of Huyler's frozen chocolate or Buiscuie; with a small spoon place a small quantity of whipped cream on each corner of the cake. With the end of the spoon dig a small hole in the middle of the cake and fill with crushed strawberry. On top of the whipped cream put a cherry pierced with a toothpick. Serve the dish with two nabiscos cut in halves, a half on each side of the dish. Charge 20 cents. (F. J. Beaucoudray)

MARBLE BRICK

Cut lengthwise into two pieces a slice of marble brick ice cream (strawberry, chocolate and vanilla). Put one of these pieces on a banana-split dish, and cover with a thin coat of chopped English walnut meats, placing over the latter some marshmallow dressing. Then pour some thick chocolate syrup over the marshmallow dressing, allowing the syrup to run down through the dressing to give the dessert an artistic appearance. Top with a red and green cherry. Sells for 15 cents. (J. T. Clapesattle.)

THE WHITE HOPE

To dispense this sundae, use a mold which will give a brick of ice cream 2½ inches high and 2 x 2 inches on the top or base. Such a mold can easily be made by any tinsmith. Place a layer of vanilla ice cream one inch thick on the bottom of the mold, then a mixture of strawberry fruit and nuts, and finish filling the mold with an inch and one-fourth layer of rich, chocolate ice cream. Turn out the mold on a white china plate, top with whipped cream, and red, white and blue cherries. Lay a chocolate wafer on one side and a vanilla wafer on the other side of the dish and serve. (Philip W. Fraker.)

REAL TEMPTATION

(a) Take one quart of light cream, boil and add two pounds of sugar; then beat up the yolks and whites of five eggs separately, mix with the cream and sugar and boil the mixture for five minutes; let it stand over night in a cool place, and skim it off the next morning.

(b) Take six ounces of roasted peanuts and four ounces of peanut butter and rub into a paste in mortar, adding about three ounces of water. Gradually mix a and b together until a rich peanut custard is produced.

(c) Take 1 quart of milk, bring almost to a boil, add 3 pounds of sugar and remove from the fire; put one pound of cocoa in a mortar and gradually work into it the hot sugar and milk (about one pint) until a very smooth thick paste results; take one-half pound of butter, heat until dissolved and then work it into the chocolate paste; add the balance of the milk and sugar slowly while mixing When thoroughly mixed, boil for about 15 minutes. This makes a chocolate fudge which should be kept warm in a chafing dish or double boiler.

To serve, put a cone of vanilla ice cream in a sundae dish; cover half of it with peanut custard and the remainder with chocolate fudge (one side light, the other dark); top off with whipped cream, chopped pecan nuts and a cherry; place two small size nabisco wafers so as to meet on top. Price, 20 or 25 cents. (John Fox.)

SENSATION CHOCOLATE

Scrape or cut up four ounces of cocoa paste; put it in a bright stew pan with half a tumbler of water; reduce it to a very smooth consistency over a moderate fire, stirring continually with a spatula, and be very careful not to burn or scorch it; then add one quart of the richest cream and eight ounces of pulverized sugar; boil together for eight or ten minutes, stirring without ceasing; remove from the fire and add one ounce of strong vanilla sugar. When ready to serve, fill cups half full of whipped cream, staunch, well drained and highly flavored with vanilla sugar; pour the hot chocolate upon it; stir together and top off with more of the whipped cream and serve immediately with some zweiback biscuits, which are the proper accompaniments of all table chocolate. Price, 15 cents.

DESSERTS WITH CAKES, ETC.

PINEAPPLE BON BON
Into a plain white saucer place one slice of pineapple, cut round; on this put a No. 12 mold of vanilla ice cream, and surround it on three sides with three sponge lady fingers (small ones are best); over all pour a ladleful of crushed pineapple with the thick, sweet juice, and finish by placing a red cherry on top. Sells for 15 cents (Lamar B. Talley.)

HOBBLE BON BON
Into a glass about 4 inches deep place a small amount of chocolate, vanilla or strawberry ice cream; split two lady fingers and stand the four halves on end in a vertical position, so that the upper ends will reach the top of the glass. Add about ½ ounce of chocolate syrup, or syrup of any flavor desired, one disherful of vanilla ice cream, whipped cream, one teaspoonful of English walnuts and top off with a slice of fig or a Maraschino cherry. In pricing this feature be sure to at least cover the costs. (J. E. Stallings.)

BELL'S SPECIAL
Take one pint of marshmallow and syrup, q.s. to make the dressing. Then incorporate about 2 ounces of crushed cherries, 4 ounces of ground nuts, and 3 crushed bananas. To serve: Place in the center of a 6-inch plate one piece of plain cake (about 4 x 4 inches), and on top of it put one No. 12-to-the-quart dipperful of strawberry ice cream. On each corner of the cake put a lady-finger cracker and top off with the preceding dressing. Scatter a few strawberries around the top of the cake in suitable places. Can be sold for 20 cents and will yield a good profit. (A. Karl Beh.)

CHARLOTTE RUSSE WITH NUTS
Sweet cream, 40 per cent, 1 quart; powdered sugar, 6 ounces; extract of vanilla, 2 fl. drams, ice cream powder, 2 teaspoonfuls; chopped nuts (very fine), 6 ounces. Mix by whipping the cream until almost stiff with the sugar, ice cream powder and extract, then add the chopped nuts and

whip until the mixture will stand. Having previously ready 1 dozen ice cream saucers, take 24 lady fingers, slice them into halves and place four of the halves around on each saucer and fill the center with charlotte russe. Then take a small quantity of whipped cream, colored a light red or pink, and decorate the dish, topping off with a Maraschino cherry. Sells for 15 cents and yields a nice profit. (Jos. H. Wadsley.)

SQUARE MEAL
Take three lady fingers and halve them lengthwise. Lay two halves on a six-inch plate and lay the other halves across the first two at right angles to them, thus making a criss-cross pile. Over this place one dish of vanilla ice cream (about 6 to a quart); cover with "bitter sweet" chocolate and top off with a Maraschino cherry and two walnut halves. Price, 15 cents. (W. Arthur Goulding.)

LADY FINGER DESSERT
Stand four lady fingers upright around a paper case. Fill center with strawberry ice cream and top with a cherry. Price, 15 cents.

MASTERPIECE
Line a champagne sundae glass with four or five split lady fingers in upright position, and then put into the center a disherful of Neapolitan ice cream, made by filling the disher with equal parts of vanilla, strawberry and chocolate ice cream; over all pour a ladleful of vanilla marshmallow, or cover with whipped cream and close to the top insert peaches, the slices pointed toward a cherry placed in the center. Price, 15 or 20 cents. (Jos. B. Clark.)

MILADY
Place on one end of an oblong or "banana split" dish two lady fingers, side by side; cover each with another lady finger using four in all At the other end of the dish place a 12-to-the-quart disherful of rich vanilla ice cream. Over the lady fingers and ice cream pour two ladlefuls of fresh strawberries, and finish by pouring some whipped cream on the lady fingers. Can be sold at a profit for 15 cents. (C. E. Wilber.)

FRENCH GLACE FRUIT
On a platter 10 x 7 inches place three slices of angel food and on each of slices put a small disherful of vanilla ice cream On each of the two outer portions place pineapple and strawberry fruit, respectively. Over the center portion of ice cream put whipped cream and over all sprinkle chopped pecans. Top off with two Maraschino cherries. Then on one side of the platter place a fourth of a slice of pineapple fruit and mixed imported French glaced fruits. Price with due regard to costs and work involved.

The blending of the French fruits against the white background makes the sundae look very attractive. The French fruits are cut in small dices and preserved in simple syrup to keep them soft. (Miss Anna Finigan.)

MAUDE ADAMS

Chop and mix well together in a small bowl five bananas, four oranges, one apple, a small bunch of grapes, one ounce of cocoanut and 30 cherries Add one ounce of sherry wine for flavoring, one-half pound of sugar, 1 ounce of cherry syrup, and 6 ounces of simple syrup. Put the mixture into a fruit bowl and let stand an hour before serving. To serve, place on a plate one slice of angel cake and a 12-to-the-quart dipperful each of chocolate and vanilla ice cream; then over the ice cream and cake add a ladleful of the mixed fruit and top off with whipped cream, a few walnut meats and a cherry. Sells for 15 or more cents. (Wesley Smith)

ANGEL OF EDEN

Place a thin slice of angel food cake in a sundae dish and over the cake put a small scoop of vanilla ice cream and 1 ladle of finely chopped Maraschino figs, previously prepared in a fruit dish. Over all put another slice of angel cake and pour on ½ ounce of sherry syrup and 3 or 4 dashes of claret wine. Price with due consideration to costs.

NORTHERN LIGHTS

In dispensing the Northern Lights use a fine china plate, six inches in diameter, decorated with a winter design (ice and snow). First, place a piece of angel food on the plate. Around the angel food lay three slices of orange, on the first of which place a red cherry, on the second a white cherry and on the third a blue cherry. Now place a (large size) mold of ice cream on the cake and insert in the top of the ice cream a Veronique wafer, leaving about one inch to appear above the cream (this is to represent the pole). Stick a small American flag on the top of the pole.

Place three spoonfuls of pineapple ice around the bottom of the cream between the three slices of orange. Then spread whipped cream over the top of the mold of ice cream just below the pole, so that it looks like snow. Lastly, arrange four chocolate "Teddy Bears" around in the whipped cream so that they appear to be trying to reach the pole—one at the very top. Sells for 20 cents. (Philip B. Fraker.)

DESSERT A LA PLAZA

Take one slice of vanilla ice cream (10-to-the-quart), one slice of pound cake similar in size to the slice of cream, some crushed pineapple syrup, and whipped cream with a little sugar and a few drops of Maraschino liquor added to it. Now spread two teaspoonfuls of the pineapple syrup over the cake; over the syrup put the slice of ice cream, trim on the side and cut across from corner to corner. Put some of the whipped cream on a dessert plate and on it lay the sandwich, the cream on top, and add a little fine whipped cream in the center apple syrup. Place a little whipped cream in the center of each piece of the sandwich and top off with two cherries; 20 cents. The author says this has proved to be a most attractive and delicious special, and that some days he has sold as many as 250. He charged only 15 cents. (D. Negri.)

RENO CHOCOLATE DROP

In a fine china dish, saucer-shaped, place a slice of chocolate cake 2½ inches square and ⅛ inch thick. On the cake place a No. 10 mold of chocolate ice cream, around which arrange four chocolate drops. Top off with whipped cream and red cherry and put two dashes of blood orange syrup over all. "A good seller at 25 cents." (Philip W. Fraker.)

CHOCOLATE SOLDIER

Place a mold of chocolate brick ice cream on a fancy Melba plate and on it lay a slice of devil's food cake. Over all pour a float of chocolate syrup and top with a Maraschino cherry. "A very delicious and dainty dish when correctly served. Sells for 15c." (Everett Kelley)

FIFTH AVENUE SUPPER

Take a quart brick ice cream mold and cover the bottom with a layer of strawberry ice cream about an inch thick; on this place a layer of sponge cake about half an inch thick; covering it with a layer of chocolate ice cream; then add another layer of sponge cake and top off with vanilla ice cream. Pack away the mold in ice and salt for about an hour, when the delicacy will be ready to serve. Cut the mixture in four slices; serve in oblong dishes, pouring a ladleful of crushed strawberries over the slice and topping off with whipped cream and a cherry. Price, 25 cents a slice. (Clyde J. Klingelsmith.)

DAFFODIL

Take eight pieces of 5-cent sponge cake, cut off the brown crust and chop the cake to fine crumbs; take 6 eggs, beat them up well, and then mix all well with 3 ounces of shredded cocoanut, 6 ounces of bisque and 6 ounces of pineapple syrup. To serve, take a 4-ounce claret glass with a tall stem, and put into it on the bottom, a spoonful of the mixture, add a 16-to-the-quart dipperful of vanilla ice cream, pressing it down to conform to the shape of the glass and leaving a hollow or cavity in the center. In the hollow put 3 pieces of cake, and top with a little more of the mixture and a cherry so as to resemble a daffodil. When in season a daffodil can be given with each dish of the sundae served

The sponge cake is most economically prepared by taking the whole cake, cutting off the brown crust, and slicing the cake lengthwise so as to make eight pieces; then cut each of these pieces in the center, which will make 16 pieces in all. Price, 20 cents. (K. C. Bronson.)

CREAMED APPLE SPONGE

Peel six large apples; grate four of the apples (squeeze lemon juice over grated apple, so latter will hold color) and chop the other two; add to them 3 ounces of vanilla syrup, and enough whipped cream to make one-half gallon. To serve, take a five-cent piece of sponge cake, cut it in two and place the pieces in a glass saucer; on top of the cake put a No. 16-to-the-quart dipperful of vanilla ice cream and cover with the apple mixture; top off with a Maraschino cherry. Price, 15 cents. (Peter Eichelman.)

RECALL FRAPPE

In a china saucer place a piece of sponge cake, about 1½ inches square. Over it pour ½ ounce of claret sauce. Then place a twelve-to-the-quart scoopful of vanilla ice cream on the cake and over this a ladleful of fresh strawberries. Cover with whipped cream and top off with dry walnut meats Sells for 15 cents. For advertising this frappe Mr. Bromley uses a card lettered as follows:

```
.....................................
:          Up to the minute         :
:               the                  :
:          Recall Frappe             :
:               15c                  :
.....................................
```

(D. G. Bromley.)

STRAWBERRY DELIGHT

Take a sponge cake, cutting eight pieces or slices to the pound of cake. Put one piece of the cake cut in halves on a small plate (such as is used for a banana split), and on each half of cake place a dipperful of fresh strawberry ice cream (No. 20 to-the-quart). Over this pour fresh strawberry syrup, then add whipped cream, topping each cone of ice cream with a whole strawberry. Sells for 10 cents and costs, according to the author's figures, 6 cents to produce, as follows: Sponge cake, 2 cents; ice cream, 2 cents; fresh strawberries, 1 cent, and whipped cream, 1 cent. The author used this announcement:

```
.....................................
:   STRAWBERRY DELIGHT              :
:   Contains Fresh Strawberry Ice    :
:     Cream, Fresh Strawberries,     :
·    Sponge Cake & Whipped Cream     :
.....................................
```

STRAWBERRY WHIP

Fresh strawberries, 1 cupful; powdered sugar, ⅓ cupful; whites of 2 eggs. Wash and hull the strawberries and mash slightly. Beat the whites of the eggs until stiff, add sugar and berries; beat until very stiff, using a broad bowl and a wire egg beater, beating with a long and steady stroke. Pile lightly in a glass dish and serve with white or sponge cake. Price, 15 cents.

MOONBEAM

Place a No. 8 scoopful of fruit-cake ice cream in a sundae dish and on this put whipped cream to form a half-moon on one side; on the other side place a few walnuts and top off with a red cherry on a toothpick.

Here is the formula for the "fruit cake ice cream": Sugar, 3 pounds; ice-cream powder, any standard make, 4 ounces; sweet cream, 20 per cent., 2 gallons, sweet milk, 1 gallon; raisins, currants, figs, dates, citrons, of each 4 ounces; allspice, ½ teaspoonful; brandy, sufficient to flavor, caramel, to color brown. Cut the fruit fine and mix with the flavor. (J. H Wadsley.)

DESSERT A LA COPLEY SQUARE

Serve individuals of vanilla ice cream in this manner: Secure dainty white paper cases of a square shape, half fill a case with ice cream and then introduce a spoonful of guava jelly or a layer of chopped nut meats and figs. Fill the case even full of ice cream. Mound the top with whipped cream and garnish with four blanched almond meats arranged like the petals of a flower and with a bit of candied citron for a center. Lay on one side of the plate a spray of crystallized mint, also a square piece of delicate white cake frosted with white and decorated with a slight touch of pale green frosting. This feature is worth 25 cents.

MACAROON DELIGHT

Fill one-half of a macaroon shell with bisque ice cream and one-half with tutti frutti ice cream. Surround the macaroon with whipped cream in which has been placed a number of fresh strawberries, selling at 20 cents. (Clarence Bess.)

CREAM PUFF

Take 2 quarts of sweet milk, heat, then add four eggs previously beaten up, stirring the mixture constantly, then add 1½ pounds of sugar, and bring the whole to a boil; now add 4 tablespoonfuls of cornstarch (previously rubbed up with enough water to dissolve it,) stirring constantly all the while so as not to allow the mixture to scorch or burn, and when it thickens, remove from the fire, and add 10 teaspoonfuls of vanilla extract. Then stand in an ice box and let cool. An asbestos mat may be used to keep the mixture from burning when cooking on the stove, although the sundae mixture is best made in a farina boiler   To serve, take the half of a cream puff shell, lay it in a Colonial sundae cup, and cut crosswise into four pieces   This obviates the necessity of the customer attempting to cut the shell into smaller pieces with his spoon. Put a No 16-to-the-quart dipperful of strawberry ice cream on the pieces of cream puff shell and top with the above mixture and a cherry. Sells for 10 or 15 cents.

The author states that he also serves a chocolate eclair sundae with the same mixture and in the same manner, the only difference being that he uses vanilla ice cream instead of strawberry ice cream, and tops the whole sundae with chocolate syrup. (Peter Eichelman.)

PEACH CREAM PUFF

Take an empty cream puff shell, cut the bottom out and place it on a sundae plate. On the shell put a disherful (20-to-the-quart) of peach ice cream, add a small portion of whipped cream and about two quarter portions of a small peach; over all pour a little peach syrup and cover with the top of the shell, then put a little whipped cream over this shell and top off with a quarter of a peach and a Maraschino cherry. Sells readily for 15 cents.

The author states that the cream puff shells can be bought at any pastry shop. (Wm. H. Anders.)

ICE CREAM CHARLOTTE

Take an empty charlotte russe cup, and place in it two lady fingers cut in halves, standing the pieces on the narrow ends. Then fill up the cup as follows   One dipperful of vanilla or bisque ice cream, over which pour charlotte dressing until the cup is filled; then place one cherry on top. The dressing for the above is made by dissolving ¼ ounce of gelatin in hot water, and then heating the solution with whipped cream, 1 quart; yolk of one egg well beaten; pulverized sugar, 1 ounce, and sherry wine, 1 ounce.   Keep all in a cool place until wanted for use. Price 15 cents.

SURPRISE ECLAIR

On a five-inch plate place a lettuce leaf. Cut an empty eclair shell which can be purchased from any bakery, in half and lay the bottom half on the lettuce leaf on the plate. Then put one disherful (16 size) of ice cream on the shell and over the cream put the top part of the shell. Over this pour a little chocolate syrup and decorate with a slight sprinkling of cocoanut, whipped cream and cherry.

ECLAIR DELIGHT

Cut an eclair shell in two lengthwise, place on a banana split dish and fill with delight ice cream. Place top on the shell

and cover with a ladle of marshmallow whip. Dust over all a sweet powdered chocolate and top with a couple of red cherries. Sells for 25 cents

Delight ice cream, used in the above, is made as follows   Take one gallon of vanilla ice cream, slice into it 10 ripe bananas, then add 6 ounces of maple syrup, 1 pound of chopped pecan nuts (meats), add ½ pound of seeded Muscat grapes which have been previously soaked in simple syrup for three hours   Mix all well together, place in a storage can and keep hard.   (Harry G. Frame.)

CREME DE LA CREME

Rub the peel of a large lemon on 6 ounces of loaf sugar, pound the sugar with the juice of a lemon, add half a pint of double cream and whip until very stiff. Pour into punch cups with handles and set on ice for a few hours before the evening rush is on. Serve cup on plates with two nabisco wafers and two toasted marshmallows.

ICE CREAM SANDWICH

Take two nabisco wafers, chocolate, vanilla or strawberry, whichever the customer may prefer, and place a slice of ice cream between them. Serve on a small plate with an ice cream fork. It is necessary to have a regular ice cream sandwich mold to make a neat service.

HAYSTACK

In dispensing "Haystack" use a fine china plate of rose design decoration and measuring six inches in diameter. For the base of the stack use a piece of chocolate cake about 2½ inches square; on this place a mold (large size) of vanilla ice cream   On each of two sides of the plate place a slice of orange and on each of the other two sides lay a slice of banana. Pour over the cream a heavy caramel syrup, sifting over it shredded cocoanut which has been previously browned. On top of the stack put a Maraschino cherry and lean against the sides of the stack so that they will come to a "peak" four Veronique wafers, arranging them so that the cherry appears to rest on top of the wafers. Around the base of the stack arrange four Maraschino cherries, put a little whipped cream on the slices of orange and insert a spoon in the side of the stack. Price, 25 cents. (Philip W. Fraker.)

GOODNERS CEREAL CREAM

Fill mixing glass two-thirds full with soft ice cream; add quantity desired of maltavita or egg-o'see, and mix with bar spoon. Transfer into sundae glass or large sherbet cup and serve.

TEASER LUNCH

Take one whole shredded wheat biscuit, place in deep saucer. Vanilla syrup, 1 ounce; malted milk, 1 heaping teaspoonful;

1 egg and enough milk to fill glass, then shake together, strain and pour over the wheat biscuit, allowing plenty to stand in saucer, and sprinkle powdered sugar over. Price, 15 cents.

JELLO AND GELATINE DESSERTS

BERRY JELLY

Dissolve one package of strawberry flavored gelatin in a pint of boiling water and add half a cup of sugar. When it begins to set fold in a pint of whipped cream. In tall stemmed glasses place a spoonful of ripe berries, a spoonful of the hardened jelly and a topping of vanilla ice cream. Price, 10 cents.

ITALIAN TUTTI FRUTTI

Soften one teaspoonful Knox's sparkling gelatin in one-half cup of cold water. Dissolve in one quart of hot water and add two cups of sugar. Add strained juice of three lemons and four oranges. Stir in one pound of mixed candied fruit which has been soaked several hours in cherry juice. Set in individual cups to harden. Price, 10 cents.

MOUSSE AVEC PARFAIT D'AMOUR

Place into a bowl 12 ounces of pulverized sugar, 4 whole eggs; beat the mixture up well, then add 1 quart of double cream. 3 small glassfuls of parfait d'amour liquor and a few drops of red color. As soon as the sugar is well dissolved set the bowl on ice and beat and finish. Any kind of fancy liquor or flavor may be used with advantage, only great care should be taken that the sugar is entirely dissolved in the composition before it is set on ice to be beaten up.

NEAPOLITAN GLACE

Take a quart-brick mold; place a layer of strawberry ice cream in the bottom, then a layer of glace fruit, then a layer of pineapple sherbet. Fill the mold with stiff whipped cream, colored green and flavored with creme de menthe. To serve put a lettuce leaf on a small salad plate, cut off a slice from the brick and serve with wine jelly. Sells for 25 cents. (E. M. R. Brown.)

RUBY SALAD

Simmer until tender two pounds of juicy pitted cherries with one and a half cups of cold water and three cups of sugar. Remove from fire and add one ounce of powdered gelatin dissolved in a cupful of boiling water. Make a deep ruby color with a pure food red coloring. Add two ounces of rose extract. Mold in oblong brick. Serve in slices on lettuce leaves, dress with equal parts of whipped cream and mayonnaise and garnish with ripe cherries.

CREME NOYAU

Blanch about ¼ pound of Jordan almonds and 1 ounce of bitter almonds and threw into cold water. Rinse well and pound in a mortar with two ounces of powdered sugar and four ounces of cream. Mix well together and rub through a sieve into a basin, add one pint of cream, whipped, and flavored with noyau, and an ounce of dissolved gelatin. Pour into a mold, set on ice and serve at any time after the mixture has set.

CREME DE ROMA

One-third box of any good gelatin, 1 cupful of rich milk, 1½ cupfuls sugar, 8 eggs, flavor with vanilla. Soak the gelatin in the milk for an hour, then put a quart of milk on to boil, stir in the yolks of the eggs, well beaten, and then sugar and gelatin; when the mixture begins to thicken take it off and pour into a deep bowl in which the whites of the eggs have been beaten to a stiff froth. Mix well together and flavor to taste. Put in molds and allow four hours to cool. May be served with or without cream.

A AND A SPECIAL

One individual brick of Neapolitan ice cream, topped with a salad made from jello, sliced bananas, oranges and pineapple served with sugar wafers. (W. N. Maher.)

SOCIETY

Take a small one-ounce package of sparkling gelatin and place it in a pint of cold water, then add one pint of boiling water and stir until the gelatin is dissolved. Now add to the solution one pint of a mixture made of grape juice, figs, berries, pineapples cut in cubes, cherries, dates, nuts and thin slices of limes. Pour the mixture into 8-ounce parfait glasses and set in an ice box to cool. When the mixture has solidified or "set" it is ready for dispensing. To serve, place a No. 16 scoopful of vanilla ice cream on top of each sundae, cap with whipped cream, halves of pecans and a green creme de menthe cherry. Sells for 15 or 20 cents. (Ellis N. Rowe.)

STRAWBERRY MOLDS

Express two or three quarts of fresh strawberries through a fine sieve; add two ounces of dissolved gelatin and the juice of one lemon and stir the whole on ice until the mixture begins to thicken. Pour into a cylindrical mold previously thinly oiled with sweet almond oil, and set in a cool place or on ice to cool. Shortly before serving dip the mold in hot water and turn out on a shallow dish. The top may be garnished with sugar or whole strawberries on leaves. Raspberries may be treated in a similar manner, and any kind of almond wafer or fancy cake may be served with these molded fruits.

YE QUALITY SPECIAL

Into a cup put one tablespoonful of gelatin, and one red color tablet enclosed with the gelatin. Fill with boiling water, allow to cool, and after becoming thoroughly dissolved, strain into a large earthen mixing bowl. Add the unbeaten whites of two eggs, five heaping tablespoonfuls of powdered sugar, and one tablespoonful of vanilla extract. Beat from 20 to 30 minutes with a wire egg whip until very light. Cut up one can of Hawaiian pineapple into cubes, free from juice, and add to the gelatin and egg mixture, stirring well. Place the whole on ice, and allow to ripen till next day.

To serve at the fountain, place a small disherful of vanilla ice cream on a dessert dish, over this pour a small ladle of marshmallow dressing, and a ladleful of the above dressing; then pour on some crushed pineapple, a tablespoonful of whipped cream, with a little strawberry syrup. Top off with chopped walnuts and a creme de menthe cherry. This dessert should be sold for 25 cents. (Miss Anna C. Fuchs.)

GRAPE JUNKET

Heat slowly to blood heat a quart of fresh milk, sweeten to taste, flavor with a teaspoonful of strained orange juice and turn into a large mixing bowl. Crush and dissolve one junket tablet in two tablespoonfuls of lukewarm water, stir it quickly into the milk and set the mixture aside, being careful not to jar it, until it is firm. Have ready a pound of Concord grapes that have been freed from the skins and seeds, blend them with a large cupful of stiff meringue and when ready to serve, fill slender chilled glasses, using alternate spoonfuls of the fruit and junket. Garnish each glass with a tiny pyramid of sweetened whipped cream colored with a little unfermented grape juice. Price, 15 cents.

PEACHES AND CREAM

To one quart can of sliced peaches (cut fine) and syrup add one quart of boiling water, one pound and a half of sugar and juice of four lemons. Bring to a boil and simmer a few moments until peach bits are tender. Cool and add one-half pound very finely chopped English walnuts. When mixture has begun to freeze, fold in a pint of whipped cream. Serve in tall glasses and decorate with a cherry.

NORTH POLE BANANAS

Slit the skins of any desired number of bananas and take out the edible portion of the fruit without destroying its shape; mash to a pulp, and to each cupful add a pint of whipped cream and powdered sugar to taste; fill the skins to their original shape and pack in ice two or three hours before serving. Price, 20 cents each.

ORANGE JELLY

Peel the oranges and run them through a fruit press, if you have one; if not, cut the oranges in two crosswise and rub the juice and pulp through a sieve. A lemon squeezer or any device of that sort will not do, as the pulp must be taken with the juice. If you have 2 quarts of juice and pulp, cook it down to 3 pints, then add sugar and treat as any other jelly. Of course, the white of the orange makes it bitter.

NOMINATION

On a fancy 6-inch plate lay two slices of fruit dessert lengthwise. On this place a 16-to-the-quart dipperful of ice cream and put two more slices of the dessert on each side of the cream. Cover with a spoonful of good sweet chocolate and lay a Maraschino cherry on top. For making the fruit dessert, take a pint of boiling water and into it stir a box of jello, any desired flavor. When the mixture is nearly ready to set, stir in a few English walnuts and Maraschino cherries. Then pour the mixture into a square dish about the size of the slices desired and cool until ready to slice. This sells for 15 cents. (Logan Taylor.)

MARRON WHIP

One box of sparkling gelatin soaked in two cups of cold milk five minutes. Add beaten yolks of eight eggs to two cups of plain hot milk and bring to a boil. Combine softened gelatin and egg mixture. Whip two quarts (possibly 3 pints will permit product to set better) of cream and add four cups of sugar, two tablespoonfuls vanilla and gelatin mixture. Fold in beaten whites of eggs and four cups of prepared French chestnuts. Very pleasing and unusual. Price, 20 cents; more if you can get it. (Henry J. Burke.)

PINEAPPLE GLAZE

To one box of pineapple jello add a pint of boiling water, and set in a refrigerator until nearly hard; then add the beaten whites of two eggs and one pint of crushed pineapple fruit, and set the mixture back into the refrigerator until it becomes hard. To serve, place one ladleful of vanilla ice cream in a sundae dish and over it put a large spoonful of pineapple glaze, prepared as above. Cover the top with whipped cream and place on the summit a Maraschino cherry or a cube of pineapple. Charge 15 cents. (Miss Florence Rae.)

SNOW PYRAMIDS

Beat the white of 12 eggs to a stiff froth. Add a glassful of currant or lemon jelly and whip all together. Serve on individual ice cream dishes, first putting on each a large spoonful or layer of vanilla or strawberry ice cream. Top off in pyramid shape with the whipped egg and jelly preparation.

(10) Sundae Toppings

In no department of fountain work has greater progress been made during the past few years than that of sundae toppings, and this new section in this formulary attests to the advances in this direction.

The introduction of the chop suey topping was an epoch marking event. This was followed by the use of the marshmallow dressing. These two innovations had important results in the development of the sundae topping. From the chop suey dressing have come a host of attractive formulas of the fig and nut type, while from the marshmallow have come the popular maple and butterscotch dressings.

In making up special or standard sundae toppings the dispenser must remember that all are very liable to spoil. Time, trouble, and money will be saved if only one day's supply is made up at a time. It is the height of foolishness to serve a dressing that has begun to turn. Many of these dressings are of a character that calls for costly ingredients—nuts, French candied fruits, imported gingers, figs, and other delicacies—and it will soon wipe out a lot of profit if half a bowl of this must be thrown out at the end of every two or three days.

The more careful keeping of dressing would also reduce this waste. There is no excuse for keeping a dressing in any but covered bowls. Especially in hot weather, it would be wiser if the bowls were set in ice rather than on the top of the counter. Stopping the leaks of wasted material through spoilage has turned more than one fountain from a money loser into a money maker.

TOPPING

CHOCOLATE

Cut up one-half pound of cake chocolate in one pint and a half of milk. Place in water bath until smooth. Add half a pound of sugar into which a teaspoonful of powdered arrowroot has been mixed. Cook thoroughly. Flavor with five drops of extract of cinnamon. Good on plain creams.

COCO-MARSH-NUT

Mix one cupful of powdered chocolate with three cupfuls of simple syrup. Let the mixture come to a boil, then beat in sufficient marshmallow whip. When about cold add one cupful of walnuts chopped not too fine. To serve, put one scoopful of ice cream in an ordinary sundae dish and over it pour one ladleful of the above chocolate marshmallow nut mixture. If desired a Maraschino cherry may be placed on top of the mixture to give it a more attractive appearance. (William H. Sullivan.)

BITTER CHOCOLATE

Cocoa, 2 pounds; sugar, 5 pounds; water, 6 pints; cornstarch, ½ pound. Boil 5½ pints of the water, and add to it a paste of ½ pound of cornstarch and ½ pint of water. Heat until a thick paste is formed, stirring constantly to keep from lumping. To this add the cocoa, previously sifted, and the sugar, and beat all into a smooth paste. This may be thinned either with syrup or water to suit. The contributor of this formula states that this dressing has proved to be his best seller and "always makes a regular customer."

AMPHION SAUCE

Shave four 5c cakes of milk chocolate in hot water and dissolve. Then take 2 cupfuls or 1¼ pounds of good cocoa and 5 cupfuls or 2½ pounds of granulated sugar, and mix them well together. Convert the mixture of cocoa and sugar into a paste with the solution of milk chocolate, using just enough water to bring the paste to the right consistency. Into the paste put 5 ounces of maple syrup or 2 ounces of maple extract and 1 teaspoonful of cinnamon. Heat, but do not boil, 24 ounces of milk and mix with the paste. Place the mixture on the fire and boil for three minutes, stirring constantly. Remove from the fire and, while still hot, strain, adding a pinch of salt. Take 25 teaspoonfuls of malted milk and dissolve it in just enough hot water to make the resulting solution easy to pour. Heat, and mix with the cocoa mixture to make a sauce. When lukewarm, add 2 ounces of vanilla extract and 3 drams of rose water to flavor.

To serve, place a No. 8 cone of vanilla

ice cream on a suitable dish, cover with the "Amphion sauce" and sprinkle on some dry ground nut meats. "Costs about 6½c to make and sells easily for 15c." The author of the formula writes that he has worked up quite a large local trade for this sundae, the name for which was suggested by a well known organization in his city (Leo Birdsong.)

Choco-Nut

Make a thick paste of powdered cocoa and hot water, and add simple syrup until the correct consistency is obtained. Stir in pecans, walnuts and almonds, chopped together, until the syrup is sufficiently thickened. Serve over vanilla ice cream in a sundae glass.

Turkey Trot

To prepare, grind together in equal proportions to make 1 pound, four kinds of nuts, viz., walnuts, pecans, almonds and filberts; pour the ground nuts into a pint of thick chocolate and a pint of marshmallow whip, and mix so as to make a pudding.

To serve, take a silver sundae cup, into it put a No. 12-to-the-quart dipperful of vanilla ice cream, then add the pudding and over it put 2 spoonfuls of whipped cream; lastly, put a green cherry on one side of the dish and a red cherry on the opposite side.

League Winner

Boil together 5 ounces of cocoa, 3 pounds of sugar, and 1 quart of water; add one 10-cent can of evaporated milk, 1½ pounds of chopped dates, ½ pounds of pistachio nuts, and 15 drops of almond extract (This mixture is to represent a baseball field.) Mix well, and pour a ladleful over a round ball of ice cream (the baseball) in a suitable dish, and serve with 2 veronique wafers (long and round to represent bats) and a glass of water (the refreshment at the big game).

The author writes that this sundae was originally devised in honor of the local baseball club again joining the "league" of his section, and the delicacy has been a winner and steady seller from the start. (C. L. Hadley.)

Nancy Brown

Best cocoa, 8 ounces; granulated sugar, 6 pounds; water, ½ gallon. Heat the water to the boiling point, add the cocoa and sugar mixed and stir in. Cook the mixture until it boils good, take off from the fire and add the following while the syrup is still hot: Ground assorted nuts, 3 pounds; ground cloves, 1 ounce; ground cinnamon, 1 ounce; glycerin, 3 ounces; Eagle condensed milk, 2 cans, and coffee extract, 8 ounces   The latter must be obtained fresh every time the syrup is made up by letting two quarts of boiling water drip through one pound of very finely ground Mocha and Java coffee. The water should be returned and passed through the coffee twice. Mix well together and serve this way:

Take a tall stem glass, large enough to hold a ball of vanilla ice cream (size 16). On this place in a neat manner 2 teaspoonfuls of the mixture with heavy whipped cream and top off with a piece of glace fruit on a toothpick. Serve with two nabisco chocolate wafers and a glass of water. A glass of Nancy Brown can be sold for 10c and costs about 6c. (C. L. Hadley.)

Nugo Chocolate

Chocolate, 8 ounces; sugar, 10 pounds; oil of nutmeg, 10 drops; extract of vanilla, 2 drams; finely ground mixed nuts, ½ pound. Mix the chocolate, sugar and oil of nutmeg, make a paste with 2 pints of water, then add 3 pints more of water and boil for five minutes; add the vanilla extract and mixed nuts. Serve as ordinary chocolate syrup from a chocolate pot or decanter.

Milk Chocolate Morello Cherry

Take 5 pounds of milk chocolate (cake) and melt it in a double boiler. Mix together 2 quarts of milk and 1 quart of condensed milk, boil, and then add the mixture, little by little, to the melted milk chocolate, and beat to a smooth paste. Let the mixture come to a boil, then remove from the fire and cool. Add 2 ounces of vanilla extract. This formula is for the preparation of the milk chocolate.

To prepare the Morello cherries· Take a No. 10 can of the cherries and boil the contents for 10 to 15 minutes, adding, while boiling, a little red coloring. Remove from the fire and cool. Mix equal parts of the Morello cherries and the milk chocolate in a fruit bowl and serve as follows: Take a No. 10-to-the-quart dipperful· of either vanilla or chocolate ice cream, and cover with the cherry-milk chocolate mixture Add a teaspoonful of whipped cream and place a cherry on top. Sells for 10 cents.

The author states that "the beauty of this formula is that it provides for three sundaes. The dispenser, if desired, can serve 'milk chocolate Morello sundae,' 'milk chocolate sundae,' or 'plain Morello cherry sundae.' There is nothing like it on the market ,and it is easy to make and very popular. I sell from 200 to 250 a day. I have two jars of the materials on the bar even at this time of the year." To advertise it he uses the following sign:

.. .. ·· .. ··

Milk Chocolate Morello Cherry Sundae :
· Never Tasted Anything Like It Before :

.. ..

CHOCOLATE TEMPTATION

To a pint of rich chocolate syrup add 1 pound of granulated sugar; bring to a boil over a slow fire, remove and add one cupful each of ground walnuts and seeded raisins.

Keep sauce hot in chafing dishes or by placing it on steam tables. The hot sauces when poured over the cream become hard and make a dainty dish. These sauces can also be used for hot maple or chocolate fudge nut sundaes, which, according to the author, are very popular in his part of the country. (Harry G Frame.)

CHOCOLATE NOUGAT

Granulated sugar, ½ pound; chocolate, ½ pound; milk, 8 ounces; lemon juice, ¼ ounce; crushed pineapples, 1 can, nuts, 6 ounces. First mix the milk, chocolate and sugar together, cook over a slow fire for about five minutes, then slowly add the lemon juice and cook until the mixture comes to a boil; add the nuts and crushed pineapples, mix, and set aside to cool. To serve, place a No. 12 scoopful of chocolate ice cream on a suitable dish, cover with chocolate nougat, and top off with whipped cream and a cherry. Sells for 15 cents.

CHOCOLATE MARSHMALLOW NUT

Mix one cupful of powdered chocolate with 3 cupfuls of simple syrup. Let the mixture come to a boil, then beat in 2 dozen marshmallows. When about cold, add one cupful of walnuts chopped not too fine. To serve, put one scoopful of vanilla ice cream in an ordinary sundae dish and pour over the cream one ladleful of the chocolate marshmallow nut mixture. If desired, a maraschino cherry may be placed on top of the mixture to give it a more attractive appearance.

FLYING DUTCHMAN

Dutch chocolate ...... 1 pound
Water .... 1 pound
Corn starch .... 3 ounces
Granulated sugar ..... 7 pounds

Dissolve the chocolate in hot water, taking care not to burn it; mix the corn starch with cold water, add to the chocolate and heat over a slow fire, stirring constantly; strain through a sieve to remove coarser particles and dissolve the sugar in the strained liquid while it is still hot.

ENGLISH CHOCOLATE NUT SUNDAE

Rich cream, ½ gallon; granulated sugar, 4½ pounds; marshmallow whip, 4 heaping ladlefuls. Boil until this mixture has a smooth appearance; then add to it ½ pound Baker's bitter chocolate, previously grated and rubbed to a smooth paste with hot milk. Boil until the mixture reaches the desired consistency, remove from the fire, place on a cake of ice and whip until cool; then incorporate 1½ ounces of vanilla extract and enough blanched unsalted peanuts to make the mixture into a thick paste. This makes a fine sundae dressing.

To serve, place a ladleful of the paste over a No. 20-to-the-quart disherful of ice cream on a fancy dish, sprinkling over the dressing enough soluble malted milk to give a little added contrast in color. Sells for 10 cents. (W. E. Kefover.)

CHOCOLATE DAINTY

Sift together 1 cupful powdered cocoa and 1½ cupfuls of powdered sugar. Put a pint of cream over the fire and sugar and cocoa to make a paste, stirring to reduce all lumps while adding the cream; pour in the rest of the cream and cook in a double boiler for about 10 minutes. Remove from the fire and after the mixture has become cool add a few drops of vanilla extract. To serve place a No. 12 disherful of vanilla ice cream in a sundae dish and cover with the chocolate prepared as above. Top with whipped cream and a cherry. Sells for 15 cents. (Harper Huntley.)

CHOCOLATE FRUIT

Strawberry syrup, 10 ounces; vanilla syrup, 10 ounces; raspberry syrup, 8 ounces; chocolate syrup, 4 ounces. Pour a ladleful of this sauce over plain ice cream.

DIXIE

Into a silver sundae dish put two scoopfuls of vanilla ice cream and add a ladleful of "Dixie Dessert Syrup." Top with whipped cream and cherry. Dixie Dessert Syrup is made as follows: Mix into a paste 1 pound of peanut butter and ½ pound of cocoa by gradually adding 3 quarts of cold water. When the mixture is rubbed up smooth, add 2 ounces of butter, and slowly heat until it boils; dissolve in it 3 pounds of sugar and set away to cool; then stir in 2 ounces of vanilla extract and the mixture is ready for use.

The author writes that by using cold water and gradually bringing the mixture of peanut butter and cocoa to a boil, the combination will thicken like gravy, and will not separate when cold. To make an adequate margin of profit on this feature it should be dispensed at 15 cents per service. (E. Dean Matteson.)

CHOCOLATE BUFFALO SUNDAE

Nuts ground fine... ½ pound
Crushed orange (J.
  H. S. & Co.'s)... 2   pounds
Claret syrup, heavy... 1   quart
Chocolate syrup, heavy 1   quart

Mix all well together, let stand for some time, and then pour a ladleful over vanilla ice cream.

This sundae was much in demand and served for a long time at a large Boston fountain. (C. L. Hadley.)

BROWN STONE FRONT

Make a thick, smooth paste of powdered cocoa and hot water, and add simple syrup until the correct consistency is obtained. Stir in sufficient pecans, walnuts and almonds chopped together and serve over ice cream.

HOT CHOCOLATE

Melt 1 pound of bitter cake chocolate and add to the melted liquid 1 pint of light cream; keep the mixture hot. To dispense, pour a ladleful over a dish of chocolate ice cream. Price 15 cents.

HOT CHOCOLATE

Boil one cup each of sugar and water for five minutes. Melt half a pound of unsweetened chocolate and add to sugar. Season with one teaspoonful of extract of vanilla and half a teaspoonful of extract of cinnamon.

HOT MILK CHOCOLATE

In a suitable dish place a No. 10 disherful of vanilla ice cream, and cover it with a ladleful of hot milk chocolate sundae sauce. Decorate with a little whipped cream and red cherry (a little of the cherry liquor will not be amiss). The hot sundae is made by shaving 2 pounds of milk chocolate (which may be bought in 5- or 10-pound cakes at 30 cents per pound). Place the chocolate in a double boiler, heat till dissolved, stirring with a wooden paddle; add a pinch of salt and 1 quart of unsweetened condensed milk. This will somewhat chill the mix, but continue the heat and stirring until the mixture is thoroughly homogeneous, then add about a pint of sweet cream or milk, scalded but not boiled. Keep the saucer in a hot-water bath where the customer can see it. If it becomes too thick, the water in the bath is not hot enough; if gas be used under the bath it tends to make the sauce too dry; this is remedied by adding a little more milk and well stirring the mixture. The sauce so used may also be used with hot drinks. Served with whipped cream and wafers. Sells for 15 cents. (J. K. Taylor.)

HOT MILK CHOCOLATE

Sweet milk chocolate, 1 pound; milk, 1 pint; sugar, 4 ounces. Shave the chocolate and melt in a double boiler, then add the milk very gradually and with constant stirring; when thoroughly dissolved, stir in the sugar. Place a No. 12-to-the-quart disherful of chocolate ice cream (vanilla ice cream may be used) in a sundae cup, pouring over it a ladleful of the above syrup, and top with whipped cream. Sells for 15 cents. "Can be advertised on the windows and on the menu cards."

HOT FUDGE SUNDAE

Fountain chocolate, 1 pound; sweet milk, 8 ounces, granulated sugar, 8 ounces; butter, 4 ounces. Mix and let boil on a water bath till thick, then add 2 drams of extract of vanilla; keep warm on the water bath and serve in that condition on slices of brick ice cream cut from bricks One or two attempts at the "fudge" in small quantities may be necessary to get the right article for serving, but the finished product, if rightly made, is a winner.

HOT COCOA SAUCE

Water .... 7 cups
Sugar .... 2 cups
Arrowroot .... 2 tablespoonfuls
Cocoa .... 2 tablespoonfuls

Boil water and sugar and add arrowroot dissolved in cold water, stir and boil till clear. Dissolve cocoa in hot water and add with pinch salt and stir and boil 2 minutes. Remove from fire and add teaspoon vanilla. (Mrs. Cornelia G. Bedford.)

HOT COCOA

Boil together one and one-half cupfuls of water and one cupful of sugar for two minutes; add one tablespoonful of arrowroot dissolved in a little cold water, stir for a moment, then boil until clear. Add two tablespoonfuls of cocoa, which have dissolved in a little hot water, and a tiny pinch of salt, and boil for three minutes longer. Take from the fire and add one teaspoonful of vanilla extract.

HOT CHOCOLATE NOUGATINE SUNDAE

To prepare the nougatine take 6 pounds sugar, 2 pounds corn syrup, 2 quarts water, and 3 pounds honey. Mix and boil until the mixture becomes quite thick, then remove from the fire.

In a separate kettle take the whites of 1 dozen fresh eggs and beat them until quite stiff; then add of the beaten whites, a little at a time, to the above preparation, stirring all the while, until the mixture is thoroughly incorporated. Add ½ gallon marshmallow whip, 5 pounds of pistachio nuts, 2 pounds bitter chocolate and 4 ounces vanilla, mix thoroughly together and keep warm. In serving, take silver sundae cups and place on each a

No. 10-to-the-quart dipperful of vanilla ice cream, cover with chocolate nougatine, and dress with a spoonful of whipped cream. Sprinkle on a little nutmeg to suit the taste, if desired. "A delicious sundae and a good seller." Price, 15 or 20 cents.

COFFEE NUTTEE

Chop ½ pound of English walnuts, ½ pound hickory nuts, ¼ pound filberts and mix with the desired amount of coffee syrup. To serve pour a small quantity over a portion of ice cream and tip with whipped cream.

CREAM ALMOND

In a mortar mash 1 pound, bring to a scald; then pour enough of the cream over the blanched almonds until reduced to a fine paste; add ½ pound of sugar and 1 quart of water, and cook for half an hour; then add 1 quart of pure cream and again cook for five minutes. Remove from the fire and when cold, add 1 ounce of vanilla extract and 10 drops of orange flower water. Pour a ladleful of almond mixture over ice cream. (Theodore Louvis.)

BUTTER NUT

Bring to a boil 1 pint of cream and 2 pounds of pulverized sugar; then add 6 ounces of ground mixed nuts and 8 ounces of butter When cool, serve a ladleful of the mixture over a disherful of walnut ice cream The dressing can also be served to good advantage over ice cream of other mixture over ice cream. Edward C Swain)

WALNUT FUDGE

One quart chopped walnut meats, 2 pounds brown sugar, 1 ounce vanilla, 2 ounces caramel, 2 quarts cream, 8 eggs, 2 quarts milk, 4 ounces butter, 4 level tablespoonfuls flour.

Make a custard of the milk, flour, sugar, butter and whole slightly beaten eggs. Add to hot custard one quart cream. Cool. Mix with this vanilla and caramel. Add nuts when mixture stiffens.

PENOCHE SAUCE

Sugar .... 4 pounds
Cream .... 1½ quarts
Glucose .... ½ pound

Mix, boil 3 minutes, cure; hot, scorch, cool and stir in sufficient chopped pecans. (W. G. Turner.)

NUGGET SUNDAE

Take ½ gallon of vanilla marshmallow 1 quart of maple syrup, 1 quart of pineapple fruit, and ¾ pound chopped pecan nut meats. Mix the marshmallow and maple syrup and incorporate the pineapple. Then mix in the chopped pecans. Color a golden brown with caramel or burnt sugar coloring. To serve, place a sufficient quantity over vanilla ice cream, topping off the sundae with whipped cream and a maraschino cherry. Can be sold at a good profit for 15 cents.

To advertise this specialty the author used a sign on the window which read:

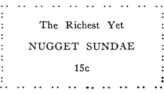

The Richest Yet

NUGGET SUNDAE

15c

(J. L. Miller.)

BUTTER-SCOTCH

Take the yolks of five eggs, place in a granite pan, add a cupful of granulated sugar, and stir well. Then add 3 cupfuls of granulated sugar, 1 cupful of brown sugar, 1 cupful of glucose, ½ cupful of good butter, ¼ teaspoonful ot salt, 1½ cupfuls of water, and 1 cupful of milk. Stir all well together, then place on the fire, continuing the heat and stirring with a small ladle until cooked.

BUTTER SCOTCH

Tablets—Cut up 1 pound of best butter, put it into a clean, bright, copper kettle and melt down, stirring constantly with a paddle, then add 6 pounds of good brown sugar. Continue to stir, and boil to "crack" degree; pour out on greased slab. When sufficiently cool, cut into tablet size. Vanilla or lemon flavoring may be added, if desired, or the candy may be left without additional flavoring.

BUTTER SCOTCH

With glucose—White sugar, 16 pounds; brown sugar, 1 pound; glucose, 5 pounds; butter, 1½ pounds; lemon flavor, enough. Put the sugar with a little water into a pan to melt, add the glucose and cook to 210°. Take off the fire, work in the flavor, and add the butter. Pour into a large pan, or on an oiled slab, to cool.

BUTTER SCOTCH DRESSING

Cook to a thick syrup in a copper pan 2 pounds of brown sugar, ½ pound of glucose, and ½ pound of good butter, adding a little cream to produce the required density.

BUTTER SCOTCH PECAN FUDGE

Cook over a slow fire until the mixture comes to a boil 2 pounds of sugar and 1½ pints of milk; then add ½ pound of butter, stirring until dissolved, a teaspoonful of table salt, and color a light shade with caramel; slowly pour in two teaspoonfuls of lemon juice and 3 handfuls of pecans.

When cool, serve a scoopful on a cone of vanilla ice cream, and "dress" with whipped cream and a cherry. Price, 15 cents. (T. J. Beaucoudray.)

BUTTER SCOTCH

Sugar, 4 pounds; water, 15 ounces; cream of tartar, ½ dram; butter, 2 ounces. Put the water, sugar and cream of tartar into a pan and stir until boiling, do not stir after the mixture begins to boil. Add the butter after removing from the fire, but do not stir in.

CARAMEL DRESSING

Extract of coffee... 1½ fluid drams
Extract of vanilla.. 1   fluid dram
Caramel 1   fluid dram
Chocolate syrup.... 8   fluid ounces
Simple syrup, enough
   to make 32   fluid ounces

To serve, put a sufficient quantity of the syrup in a 12-ounce glass, with or without ice cream, and fill the glass with carbonated water. The syrup can also be used for a dressing, etc. This formula is known under the title of "caramel syrup," although many variant formulas have been printed under the same name. A "caramel syrup" suitable for dressings, etc., can also be made by adding caramel directly to simple syrup, and using the product so made to flavor sauces, frosting, ice cream, etc, this being the plan followed by most operators.

CARAMEL

Take 1 pound of vanilla caramels, which may be obtained from any first class confectionery store, put them in a porcelain container, add 1 pint of hot water, and stir until dissolved, or put over a slow fire and heat until dissolved, being careful not to burn; remove from the fire, let stand for five minutes; then add 1 ounce of vanilla extract and 1 quart of pure cream, 20 per cent.; mix thoroughly, and keep in a glass bottle in a cool place. To serve, place a 10-to-the-quart scoopful of vanilla ice cream in a sundae dish and pour over it a ladleful of the caramel sundae mixture; sprinkle on a teaspoonful of ground pecans, and top with a Maraschino cherry. (Theodore Louvis.)

CARAMEL FRUIT

One quart of heavy caramel syrup, 1 pint of crushed pineapple, 1 pint broken Maraschino cherries, mix well and serve in fancy stem sundae glasses, garnishing with whipped cream and a whole cherry.

NUT CARAMEL

Mix equal parts of pecans, English and black walnuts, pignolia and pistachio nuts. Chop together and mix with an extra heavy caramel syrup.

CARAMEL NUT FUDGE

Take 3 pounds of granulated sugar and burn over a slow fire (do not scorch) until smooth and thoroughly dissolved; then stir in slowly 1 quart of pure rich milk, 1 pound grated English walnuts, and boil the mixture for three minutes so that the oil from the nuts will boil out and flavor the fudge, add ¼ ounce extract of vanilla and let the mixture cool. As thus prepared one has ½ gallon of rich nut fudge which is original and true to name To dispense, use a small round "Yokomay" dish or bowl and into it, in the center, place a dipperful of ice cream, pouring over the cream a ladleful of caramel nut fudge. Top off with whipped cream, placing on the cream three walnut halves and in the center a marshmallow. (Charles Greenberg.)

CARA-MALLOW

Make a good caramel syrup and mix with marshmallow paste, using 2 parts of the former to 1 part of the latter. Pour a sufficient quantity over vanilla ice cream and top off with nuts, whipped cream and a cherry. (P. H. McNulty)

MARSHMALLOW SALAD

Peel and slice one dozen bananas and mix with marshmallow sauce (see Marshmallow Creme), add a few chopped Maraschino cherries, ½ pint of diced strawberries (not crushed) fresh, and 4 ounces of crushed pineapple. Mix well, pour the mixture over vanilla ice cream and top with nuts and a cherry.

FRUITED MARSHMALLOW

Take 1 quart of fresh strawberries, ½ pound pecan meats and 2 quarts of fresh marshmallow syrup. Sort the strawberries and cut each berry in three or four pieces Chop up the pecan meats, mix with the cut strawberries and let stand for five minutes. Incorporate the marshmallow syrup and color red, using a sufficient quantity of fruit coloring. To serve, pour a ladleful of the fruited marshmallow dressing over a dish of strawberry or peach ice cream, and top with a small spoonful of whipped cream, one cherry, and a dash of cinnamon. The author says of his Fruited Marshmallow feature: "It is a dandy seller at 20 cents." The following sign was used to advertise the specialty:

```
.. ........ .. ... .. ........ ..
:    Wanted 100,000 Recruits    :
:            to try             :
:FRUITED  MARSHMALLOW:
:             at                :
:    BLANK'S SODA FOUNTAIN      :
.. .. .... .... .. .. .. .. .. ..
```

(Philip W. Fraker.)

MALLOWRAIPINE SUNDAE

Take 2 pounds of seedless raisins and cook in 1 quart of simple syrup until they swell; then cool. Take 1 quart of marshmallow whip, mix down to a smooth paste with 3 ounces of distilled water, then add 18 ounces of raisins and 12 ounces of crushed pineapple. In these proportions the mixture is not sickening and is liked by most customers. To serve, take a No. 16-to-the-quart ladleful of vanilla ice cream and place it in a fancy china cup large enough to hold ice cream; top the ice cream with the mallowraipine mixture and a Maraschino cherry. Place the cup in which the sundae is served on a fancy china saucer of the same design.

The author states that the reason he works the marshmallow down with distilled water is because the product thus made does not become so "sickening sweet" when the raisins are added. The name, he explains, was suggested by the names of the principal ingredients used in making the dressing. Sells for 10 cents. (Peter Eichelman.)

MARMALADE SAUCE

Add half a cup of orange marmalade to one cup of marshmallow dressing. Beat smooth.

SNOWBALL

Mix in a large bowl 1 quart marshmallow frappe, 1 quart maple syrup, 1/4 pound chopped walnuts, 1/4 pound chopped pecans, 3 bananas, sliced, 1 pt. grated pineapple. Marshmallow frappe can be bought ready for use at any first class soda fountain supply house, while maple syrup can be made according to the following formula: Maple sugar, 15 pounds; granulated sugar, 12 pounds; water, 2 gallons; mix and let boil for about 4 minutes. This concentrated syrup will stand dilution, using 1 gallon of the maple syrup to 2 gallons of simple syrup. The bowl in which the mixing is done should be used for displaying the mixture. To serve, put one 10-to-the-quart dipperful of ice cream on a suitable sundae dish and over it pour two ounces of the above Snowball mixture. Top with one cherry. Price, 15 cents. (James Whalen.)

YELLOWMALLOW SUNDAE

Prepare a dressing composed of marshmallow, 14 ounces; lemon syrup, 1 1/2 ounces; tincture of curcuma (turmeric), 1/2 ounce; chopped pecans, 2 ounces. Mix well.

Over a 10-to-the-quart disherful of ice cream pour two ladlefuls of the dressing. Insert a piece of soda straw about four inches long in the cream ,and on the tip of this stick a cherry. Sells for 10 cents.

In order to make the dish more attractive, states the author, the fountain should be trimmed in yellow. He has found that the sundae is a great repeater, and it has been a record breaker at his fountain this year. (Wm. J. Holley.)

ROSE BUD

Mix 'thoroughly one pound of fresh marshmallows (previously cut into small pieces) with one quart of strawberry fruit and syrup, one-half pint of Maraschino cherries and enough nuts to make it palatable, bringing the mixture to the desired viscosity through the addition of claret syrup. To make the Rose Bud Sundae: In a silver service place a scoop of vanilla ice cream and one of strawberry ice cream. Cover the creams with a liberal quantity of the Rose Bud syrup and bank with whipped cream, topping off with a fresh strawberry. This mixture has sold rapidly in Louisville at 15 cents per portion. (Clarence Bess.)

TANGO SUNDAE

Place in a sundae dish a No. 12-to-the-quart disherful of vanilla ice cream, over which pour a ladleful of "tango dressing." This dressing is made by taking one pint of marshmallow topping and one pint of simple syrup, and beating them well together until the mixture is light and smooth. Add to the mixture one pint of crushed pineapple, one-half pint of Bigarréaux cherries (Maraschino flavor), 4 ounces of chopped pecans, 2 ounces of citron, also chopped very fine, and one-half pound of marshmallows, cut in cubes. (Leslie Bauslin.)

MARSHMALLOW PUFF

Take one apple and cut it into small pieces about the size of a small finger nail; in a similar manner cut up one banana. Now make a thin paste of marshmallow whip and syrup and mix it well with the apple and banana.

MARSHMALLOW CREME

Place a disherful of vanilla ice cream in a sundae glass and over it pour a sauce made of marshmallow whip, 2 parts, simple syrup, 1 part, and sufficient extract of vanilla to flavor. Top off with a little whipped cream and a red cherry. Place a few pieces of pink marshmallows around the edge of the sundae dish and serve with nuts or not, as desired.

MAPLE

Beat the whites of four eggs stiff, add one cupful of boiling hot maple syrup, and beat vigorously with a spoon. Cool and add to the mixture one cupful of cream. Whip the mixture with an egg beater, adding, if desired, chopped nuts. Price, 15 cents.

HOT MAPLE DELIGHT

Run through a coarse food chopper 1 pound pecan nuts, ½ pound walnuts, ¼ pound preserved ginger and ½ pound citron, then add 1 quart strawberry fruit and 1 pint simple syrup and stir to form a heavy paste. Into a china saucer place one disherful (20-to-the-quart) vanilla ice cream and one of orange ice. Over these pour a ladleful of the paste, putting on top of the orange ice a red cherry, and on the vanilla ice cream a green cherry. Over all pour hot maple syrup, then place the saucer on a five-inch plate and serve immediately. The maple syrup can be kept hot in an urn or steam table. (Clinton Waldorf.)

MAPLE NUT

Chop up half pound or more of pecan meats, and mix with enough maple syrup to give the desired consistency. To serve, place a portion of ice cream in a sundae glass, pour over it a small quantity of the syrup, finishing with a sprinkling of cinnamon, whipped cream and cherry.

DOWN TOWN

Put in a double boiler half pint of pure maple syrup and bring to a boil. Add 1 box of clean, fresh strawberries and 1 chopped fresh pineapple. Stir all together and boil over slow fire for five minutes; when cool, put into a dispensing bowl. To serve, take a long parfait glass, place a No. 24-to-the-quart scoopful of strawberry ice cream in the bottom, on it pour a ladleful of the prepared mixture, then add a scoopful of pineapple sherbet, and over it another ladleful of the prepared mixture; top with whipped cream and a fresh strawberry. Sells for 20 cents. (Harry G. Frame.)

BROTHERHOOD

One-half pound marron glace chopped fine, half gallon maple syrup, half pound grated nuts. This will make nearly two-thirds of a gallon. Mix well and pour ladleful over ice cream. Top off with whipped cream.

SHERWOOD SPECIAL

On a sundae dish put a No 10-to-the-quart disherful of vanilla ice cream, and cover with a dipperful of a dressing made as follows· Marron glaces, chopped fine, half pound; grated nuts, half pound, maple syrup, half gallon. Mix well. After pouring the dressing over the ice cream, top off with whipped cream.

MAPLE TEMPTATION SAUCE

Crushed pineapple, very fine and heavy.....	1	quart
Maple syrup, genuine..	1	quart
Pecan nuts, cut fine..	½	pound
Marshmallow, undiluted	1	pint

Whip all together for 10 minutes. Pour ladleful over ice cream.

MAPLE TANTILIZER

Dissolve over a slow fire in 1½ cupfuls of water 2 pounds of brown sugar; bring to a boil, remove from the fire and add to the mixture one cupful each of grated cocoanut and ground roast almonds. (Harry G. Frame.)

MAPLE CHOP SUEY

Seeded raisins	½	pound
Shredded cocoanut...	2	ounces
Green cherries	4	ounces
Red cherries	4	ounces
Sliced pineapple	4	ounces
Dates	4	ounces

Chop and mix, adding enough maple syrup to thin to the right consistency to serve, then add 3 ounces of angelica or port wine.

MAPLE CRYSTAL

Maple syrup	2 pints
Honeycomb, cut in small pieces	1 ounce
Simple syrup	3 pints

HONEY WHIP

Strained honey	1 pound
Granulated sugar	1 pound

Cook to a boil and add the well-beaten whites of one dozen eggs. Beat for 15 minutes and add an ounce of vanilla extract. A very white, creamy whip and a great favorite.

HONEY BOY

Chop together with a chopping knife ¼ pound lemon peel, ¼ pound orange peel and ¼ pound citron peel, using in each case the dried peel. Add ¼ gallon strained honey and ½ gallon simple syrup. Heat to the steaming point, remove from the fire and let stand in a cool place for forty-eight hours. When cool, add chopped pecans. To dispense, pour one ladleful of the above mixture over vanilla ice cream placed on a suitable dish. Top with whipped cream and one cherry. Price, 15 cents. (James Whalen)

CHOP SUEY

Chop and mix thoroughly ½ pound of seeded raisins, ¼ pound of lychu nuts, ⅛ pound of shredded cocoanut, ⅛ pound of candied pineapple, 1 pound of mixed nuts, ⅛ pound of citron, ¼ pound of dates, and ¼ pound of figs To serve, place a portion of ice cream in a sundae glass and cover with the mixture, adding a sprinkle of cinnamon. Price, 15 cents.

CHOP SUEY

Seeded raisins, ½ pound; shredded cocoanut, 2 ounces; green cherries, 4 ounces; red cherries, 4 ounces; sliced pineapple, 4 ounces; dates, 4 ounces Chop and mix; add maple and cherry syrup, equal parts, to thin enough to serve; port and sherry wine, of each, enough to flavor. Price, 15 cents.

DEMOCRATIC

One-half pound grated walnuts, 2 pounds grated orange, claret syrup enough to make half gallon. Fill sundae glass two-thirds full of ice cream and pour 1 ladleful of the nut mixture.

DEVIL'S FOOD

Run through a food chopper 4 ounces (by measure) of roasted almonds, 4 ounces of crushed cherries, 4 ounces of crushed pineapple, 5 whole figs and 1 drop of oil of rose (or sufficient extract of rose) to impart a delicate flavor. Then mix thoroughly with one pint of cherry syrup. To serve, take one 10-to-the-quart disherful of chocolate ice cream, place it in a sundae dish and over it pour a ladleful of the "devil's food" mixture, place whipped cream around the edge of the dish and top with pecan nut meats or a maraschino cherry. Sells for 15 cents. (Guy C. Malone.)

FIG NUT

Put into a pan one quart of good marshmallow sundae syrup and color pink with a few drops of liquid cochineal. Add 6 or 8 ounces of ground nuts and mix well; then add 4 ounces of figs previously cut fine and again mix all well together.

HOT CHOP SUEY

Crush and thoroughly mix: Walnuts, ½ pound; pecan nuts, ½ pound; filberts, ½ pound; figs, ½ pound; dates, ½ pound. Add water, 1 quart and sugar, 2½ pounds, and marshmallow whip, ¼ pound. Keep the mixture warm and serve in the following way: Ice cream, 1 dipperful; chop suey, 1 ladleful; top off with whipped cream and a dash of nutmeg. To be served in a silver sundae cup on a fancy plate and napkin. Price, 15 or 20 cents.

SYRIAN

Figs .... 1½ pounds
Sugar .... 4 pounds
Water .... ½ gallon

Chop figs small, adding sugar and water, and boil briskly, stirring for 5 minutes.

PUDDING DRESSING

The pudding dressing is made as follows: Mold a pint of plain gelatin and after allowing it to become cool, crush and mix it with one-fourth crushed raisins, a similar quantity of seeded raisins, and one pint of marshmallow whip. Mix thoroughly, when the pudding should be ready to serve. A sundae can also be made by using the pudding dressing alone

with the ice cream, the delicacy being thus served as "Xmas Pudding Sundae." When dispensed in this way, the author of the formula gets 10 cents For the "Xmas Sundae Dinner" he gets 20 cents. (Chas. Held.)

IRISH STEW

Take one pound of raisin cake finely broken, ½ pound of English walnuts finely chopped, one pint of mallocreme caramel and one pint of simple syrup. Mix the mallocreme caramel with one quart of hot water (this quantity of water may be a little too much—add slowly, until a sufficient amount has been used), and while stirring add the cake and nuts. Bring to a boil, and add one pint of syrup. Remove from direct fire, but keep hot. This delicacy is served as follows: Into a silver sundae dish place one 12-to-the-quart dipperful of vanilla ice cream; pour over this the "Irish stew," add whipped cream, and top off with one green cherry. Sells for 10 cents.

The author states that as an advertising medium he uses a paper strip 18x8 inches on the front window of his store; on the strip is painted a green shamrock under which, excepting the word "hot," which is in red, appears in green letters the legend ·

```
: ... .. .. ... .. .. ... .. .. .. :
:                                    :
:  OUR LATEST HOT IRISH STEW    :
:                                    :
:  Served With Whipped Cream    :
:                                    :
:         10 Cents               :
:                                    :
: .. .. ... .. .. .. ... .. .. ..:
```

MAIDEN BLUSH

One cupful of golden brown sugar, 8 ounces of apple cider, 2 ounces of good vinegar, a couple of bay leaves, 15 or 20 whole cloves, ½ dozen whole allspice, 2 small sticks of cinnamon and a splinter or band of mace. Put into a saucepan and bring to a boil. Pare and core eight medium size maiden blush apples, quarter, add the pieces to the syrup and simmer gently until tender.

Serve on a small decorated china plate by placing a disherful of cream in the center and arranging around the cone quarters of an orange and cover with the same amount of dressing that you would use on any sundae. Top with whipped cream and two whole red cherries. (Fay W. Fraker.)

ORIENTAL

Equal parts of seedless raisins, currants and English walnuts.

NUT KRINKLE

Cut 2 pounds of assorted glace fruits into small pieces and put them into 2 quarts of simple syrup colored a bright red; boil till the pieces no longer stick to each other and then remove from the fire. To the mixture add half pound of shelled almonds, 1 pound of shelled pecans, previously ground very fine, and 4 ounces of concentrated wild cherry syrup. If the mixture is too thick, dilute with syrup.

To serve, place a round ball of perfectly white vanilla ice cream on a suitable dish and pour over it some of the above dressing, then add a good dab of stiff whipped cream (flavored with pistachio and colored a pretty green), and a red cherry on the stem, the latter being placed in the centre on the top. Serve with snow or vanilla nabiscos.

PAWPAW

Take one-half pound of roasted almonds and one-half pound of pecans and pass them through a meat chopper until reduced to very fine pieces; mix well. Then take 4 pounds of sugar and 1 quart of water and make a syrup, stirring until the sugar is completely dissolved, strain through cheesecloth, and to the strained liquid add three ounces of best vanilla extract. Keep the syrup thus made in a dispensing bottle, well-corked, in a cool place. To serve take a 6-inch dish and place on it a No. 20-to-the-quart scoopful each of chocolate, vanilla and strawberry ice cream. Over the cream pour a ladleful of vanilla syrup made as above, and sprinkle on two teaspoonfuls of the mixed nuts. Place four fresh ripe strawberries around the base. Sells for 20 cents. (Theo. Louvis.)

RAISIN

Seeded raisins ...... 1½ pounds
Simple syrup 3   quarts
Wash raisins and boil, then add:
Lemon extract...... 8   drops
Caramel color ...... sufficient
Boil 10 minutes more, cool, and serve.

PRUNE SOUFFLE

Prunes .... ¾ pound
Simple syrup 1   gallon
Lemon rind 1
Chop and seed prunes and cut lemon rind in small cubes; add to syrup and boil 10 minutes, stirring well. Cool and serve.

PEANUT DOPE

Peanut butter, 4 ounces (finely ground peanuts can be used also). Salt, just a pinch; powdered gum acacia, ¼ ounce; water, 1 ounce; syrup, ½ gallon. Rub the peanut butter, salt and acacia together in a mortar, add all of water; beat up. Then add small lump of ice cream with syrup poured over. In this formula it may prove advantageous to increase the amount of peanut butter to as much as 12 ounces.

PISTACHIO DRESSING FOR SUNDAES

(P. A. C.)—We know of no standard formula for pistachio sauce or dressing made directly from pistachio nuts, although such a combination might be easily made. One method of using pistachio nuts in connection with sundaes is to sift the finely chopped nuts on a dressing made with whipped cream or one of the marshmallow dressings now so extensively employed.

Or, take one pound of pistachio nuts, shell and drop them into boiling water for a minute or until the skin can be rubbed off easily, which should be completed after they are dropped into cold water. Dry the blanched nuts on a towel, and pound them in a mortar with a few drops of rose water, a cupful of sugar, and a cupful of cream, to make a fine, smooth paste. This may be colored a pale green with spinach or other coloring. The paste thus made can be worked up as the basis of the dressing, using, if desired, one of the commercial marshmallow creams instead of the sweet cream previously suggested.

Another suggestion is to make a flavoring extract directly from pistachio nuts and use it to flavor any desired dressing you may have in mind. Here is a formula:

Crushed pistachio nuts 4 ounces
Bruised cinnamon ...60 grains
Bruised cloves ......60 grains
Lemon peel .... a few slices
Diluted alcohol .....16 fluid ounces

Macerate for seven days, agitating occasionally, and filter. As stated above, use a sufficient quantity of this extract to flavor the dressing; the quantity necessary will have to be determined by experiment. With these suggestions you should have no great difficulty in hitting upon a satisfactory dressing possessing the pistachio flavor.

STRAWBERRY

Boil together for 10 minutes ¾ cupful of sugar and ½ cupful of water. Rub through a vegetable press a pint of strawberries and when the syrup is cool add the strawberry pulp and a teaspoonful of vanilla. Serve over ice cream for a sundae.

CRUSHED STRAWBERRY

Select ripe strawberries, stemmed and washed, 1 quart; powdered sugar, 1½ pounds. Put in a glass bowl and stir well together. If the fruit is fully ripe, a heavy syrup will soon form on the top of which the berries will float. In ladling out, dip the ladle into the syrup and draw up through the fruit. Half an ounce to an ounce of this syrup as a "topping" to ice cream soda is sufficient.

HOT STRAWBERRY

Over a service of vanilla ice cream pour

a ladleful of hot crushed strawberries. Do not let the crushed fruit reach a boiling degree as the heat will tend to destroy the flavor.

STRAWBERRY SAUCE

This is used on sundaes and specials. Dissolve one tablespoonful of granulated gelatin in half a cup of cold water. Heat a pint of plain syrup hot and add to gelatin. Cool and combine with a quart of crushed sweetened strawberries. Set in cool place until the mixture is partly set. It is now right to serve and should be kept at ordinary temperature to retain its soft, jelly-like consistency.

RASPBERRY FOAM

Separate the yolks from the whites of eight eggs; beat the yolks very lightly, add 2 cupfuls of sugar, the grated rind of 1 lemon and the juice of half a lemon; put into a double boiler and boil until a thick mixture is produced; then add 6 ounces of concentrated black raspberry syrup and a little color. Beat up the whites of the eggs, add to the mixture and whip until very light. To serve, take a No. 12 disherful of ice cream in a sundae dish and over it pour a ladleful of the raspberry foam, and top off with whipped cream and a whole cherry.

LEMON FOAM

Take the yolks of 6 fresh eggs, the grated rind of 1 lemon, the juice of 2 lemons, and 1½ cupfuls of sugar. Mix thoroughly, place on a water bath and boil until the mixture thickens, stirring constantly, and allow to cool. In a separate dish beat the whites of the six eggs, mix with preceding and set in a dish on ice.

To serve · Put ice cream in the dish in the usual manner, spread over it a disherful of the "lemon foam," add some chopped nuts and top off with a cherry. (Leonard J Finkle)

ORANGE COCOANUT

Remove the skin from 12 large, juicy navel oranges, and chop the fruit fine in a chopping bowl, add 2 ounces of port wine and enough simple syrup to make half gallon. Beat up the whites of three eggs, add to the mixture, put all in a double boiler, add 2¼ pounds of granulated sugar and boil until of the consistency of heavy syrup. Remove the mixture from the fire, and when cool, beat in half pound of "feathered" cocoanut. To serve, place a cone of vanilla ice cream in an individual custard pot, pour over the cream a ladleful of the orange cocoanut, cover with whipped cream and decorate with a red and green cherry. Can be sold for 15 cents at a good profit (Harry T Frame)

CRUSHED PINEAPPLE

Select pineapple, fully ripe, 1 pound; powdered sugar, 1 pound. Pare the fruit and slice it crosswise ½ inch thick. Cut and slice it crosswise ¼ inch thick. Cut these in a glass bowl, add the sugar and stir well together. Use with ice cream soda.

PINEAPPLE PIPPIN

Grated pineapple ... 1½ pints
Granulated sugar ... 2 pounds
Whites of eggs...... 8

Cook pineapple and sugar and add whipped egg whites, stirring well for 10 minutes.

CHERRY SUEY

Crushed cherries
Crushed pineapple
Crushed strawberry
Chopped pecans, and
Chopped walnuts, of each.. 1 pint
Tame cherry syrup........ 2 pints
Price, 15 cents.

CHERRY-ALMOND

Roasted almonds, 1 pound; whole cherries, 8 ounces Grind or chop quite fine, then add simple syrup, 1 quart. Boil for 10 minutes, when cold add simple syrup, to make 1 gallon; almond extract, 5 drops; rose extract, 3 drops. Mix and stir thoroughly.

CHERRY TRILBY

Mix together crushed cherries, English walnuts, raisins, sliced oranges cut fine. Put the mixture in a fruit bowl as is done with other crushed fruits. To dispense, put 2 scoopfuls of ice cream in a salad dish, over it put the above mixed fruit, and top off with whipped cream and maraschino cherries. Price, 15 cents. (Robert Vonderheid.)

GRAPE PUREE

Pare about a dozen large sour apples and stew them in water until they become thick. Sweeten to taste and add a small quantity of nutmeg Then into a half-gallon fruit jar put 1 pint of grape juice and fill remainder of the jar with the apple sauce. Let the mixture stand for two days to allow the grape color to work through the sauce. Serve one ladleful of the puree on two small scoopfuls of vanilla ice cream. Sells for 10 cents. (E. Dean Matteson.)

GRAPE AND NUT

Boil two cups of sugar in one of water four minutes Cool and add half a cup of grape juice, one cup of chopped sultana raisins, one cup chopped walnut meats and one cup of whipped cream. Price, 15 cents.

GRAPE PUFF

One quart fresh cream, whites of 4 eggs, one glass of grape juice, two small cups powdered sugar Whip half the sugar with the cream, the balance with the eggs. Mix well. Add grape juice and pour over sweetened strawberries, pineapples, oranges or bananas. Serve ice cold.

APRICOT

Select large, fine apricots of a good color, wash them in fresh water and drain on a sieve, or better, on a napkin Arrange the fruit in the jar, so as to make it hold the largest number of pieces without crowding Fill the jars with white cold syrup, fasten the cover down, put in a water bath and boil for three minutes.

FRUIT FUDGE

Take equal parts of fresh bananas, peaches, walnuts and nabisco wafers and put them through the finest cut of a Universal food chopper. This, with a little grape juice added, makes a fine dressing for sundaes when served with whipped cream and a maraschino cherry on top. (Miss Winifred Lambert.)

TUTTI FRUTTI

Candied cherries, 1 pound; candied pineapple, 1 pound, granulated sugar, 1 pound; maraschino syrup, 1 pint. Chop the fruit fine, mix all together, add sufficient red coloring and let the mixture stand 24 hours; then thin with plain syrup. (P. A. Mc-Cole.)

FRENCH TUTTI FRUTTI

Into a pan put one box of French glaced fruit mixture and fill the pan with boiling water. Let the mixture stand for 10 minutes, drain the water off, and remove the pits from any of the fruit which may happen to contain them. Then chop the fruit, but not too fine (the fruit may be cut with a knife, if desired). Now add one pint of strawberry syrup and one and a half pints of simple syrup, and the mixture is ready to serve. To prepare the sundae, put two 16-to-the-quart disherfuls of vanilla ice cream on a fancy plate or side dish, and over them pour a sufficient quantity of the fruit dressing; sprinkle on some chopped burnt almonds, and decorate with a cherry. Sells for 25 cents. (Norman E Latta.)

FRUITTI NUTTO

Chop 1 pound of mixed nuts and add 10 ounces crushed strawberry and 10 ounces crushed pineapple sauce. Pour over plain ice cream.

SAMPLER SUNDAE

Take one-half dozen bananas and one grape fruit; cut into small pieces, then add half pint of crushed pineapple fruit and one quart of crushed strawberries. Mix well and flavor with one pint of simple syrup and half pint of bisque flavor To serve, place a No. 10-to-the-quart dipper-

ful of strawberry ice cream in a cake cup, cover with a ladleful of the fruit dressing, and top with a cherry. Sells for 15 cents. (Walter S. Bachman)

ROYAL FLUFF

White of 5 eggs, sugar, 1 pound; whipped cream, 1 quart, maraschino, 2 wineglassfuls. Into a pan, with a little water to dissolve it, put the sugar and bring it to the boiling point. Meanwhile, whip the white of eggs to a froth If the sugar is already boiling, take it off and cover with a damp cloth, or sprinkle a little sugar on it to prevent a crust forming and subsequent crystallization. The froth being stiff, pour it into the syrup gradually, stirring with a paddle the meanwhile and until it is cool. The cooling operation may be hastened by setting the vessel on ice. Sweeten two quarts of whipped cream with two pounds of sugar, stirring it to keep from falling to the bottom and add to the mixture previously made; then add the Maraschino. Price, 15 cents

EASTER

Add to 1 pint of marshmallow cream, 8 ounces each of vanilla syrup and chocolate syrup. Take ¼ pound of hazel nuts, bleach them in hot water, chop fine and add to the mixture. Then add 1 quart of fresh strawberries, previously prepared with sugar as is done in serving strawberry sundaes. Serve sufficient of the mixture over vanilla cream and top with violet whipped cream and a cherry.

The author states that in his experience this sundae is a good "leader" for making money; it catches the eye, and has a taste like that found in good bon bon candies. The whipped cream can be colored with a little concentrated violet syrup to give it the Easter color After Easter the mixture can be called "Bon Bon Sundae," using plain whipped cream instead of violet. "The sundae sells for 15 cents and the mixture costs only 27 cents a quart, or less than any fruit sundae on the market" (John Fox.)

BRYAN'S FAVORITE

Take a basket of crabapples, peel and core and then crush them to make about two quarts. Add five pounds of sugar and one quart of water and let it come to a boil. Then let the mixture cool and add one-half quart of grape juice To serve, place in a silver sundae cup two dipperfuls of vanilla ice cream, cover with the crabapple and grape juice mixture, and top with whipped cream

KATRINA

Scrape out a ripe cantaloupe and run the pulp through a colander. Add an equal amount of crushed pineapple, and one-fourth as much raspberry fruit as pineapple. Stir in one tablespoonful of lemon juice to each pint of the mixture and add nutmeg and sugar to taste. (F. F. Varney.)

NOUGAT FRAPPE

Nougat frappe dressing is prepared as follows. Vanilla marshmallow, 1 quart; chopped pecans, ½ pound; crushed cherries, ½ pint; simple syrup, ¾ quart. Heat slightly so as to mix thoroughly, and keep on ice. (C. Lawson Hughes.)

GIBSON GIRL

Peel, split and slice 2 bananas, and peel, halve, quarter and slice 2 oranges; cut into quarters whole cherries, about 6 ounces. Place these fruits thus prepared, with about 4 ounces of cherry juice, in a fruit or punch bowl and add sufficient syrup to cover. Stir and let the mixture stand for about six hours.

In a sundae dish place a ladleful of vanilla ice cream and over it 1 ounce of crushed pineapple. Over this pour a ladleful of the "Gibson Girl" mixture. "A very luscious sundae." Can be served for 10 cents. (Will Rollins.)

WALDORF-ASTORIA

Put a small dipperful of chocolate cream in a sundae dish and over the ice cream put a ladleful of crushed fruit syrup; over the syrup put a ladleful of whipped cream and top with broken pecan or hickory nut meats

The syrup is made by cutting up fine one orange, a small bunch of Malaga grapes, a few Maraschino cherries and a little crushed pineapple. Mix all together, add enough simple syrup to produce a mixture of about the same density as that of ordinary crushed fruit syrup, and enough of the juice from the Maraschino cherries to give the mixture the desired color, the syrup is then ready to serve. A fruit bowl filled with this mixture and placed on the service corner at the fountain, according to the author, "looks inviting and catches many an order for itself." The author also says that the name, "Waldorf Sundae" is suggested by the resemblance of the mixture to the well known "Waldorf Salad." It can be sold at a fair profit for 10 cents per dish. (Miss Lillian Woods.)

JACK FROST

Boil together for nearly an hour 1 pound of pineapple, 1 pound of cranberries and 2 pounds of sugar, using similar proportions if a larger quantity of the mixture is wanted. Then take a No. 10 dipperful of vanilla ice cream, place in a suitable dish, cover with the above fruit mixture, and top with shredded cocoanut and whipped

cream. Sells for 15 cents and costs about 6 cents to make. (E. Rowe.)

MT. VERNON

Granulated sugar....... 2 pounds
Dissolve in sufficient water and boil.

In another kettle beat whites of one dozen eggs and slowly add to cooked syrup. Stir vigorously and add 1½ pints of chopped Maraschino cherries and color delicate pink. Makes a capital Washington's Birthday special.

FRUITED ICE

Place a cone of lemon sherbet (No. 12 disher) in a glass sundae dish and over it pour a ladleful of the following prepared fruit: The pulp of one orange cut very fine, one cupful ripe strawberries crushed, one-half cupful of shredded pineapple, six Maraschino cherries, cut in small pieces, with a little of the juice; one banana cut in small pieces; sweeten to taste and stir until every particle of sugar is dissolved. Do not make too sweet. Pack the dish containing the prepared fruit in ice and keep very cold.

The author states that when unable to obtain strawberries she uses more orange and pineapple, and a little grape juice, "but there is nothing quite so delicious as the mixture with strawberries." (Mrs. L. L. Phillips.)

GARDEN SASS SUNDAE

Cook two pounds of cut and peeled rhubarb (garden "sass") with two pounds of sugar, without adding any extra water. Cut red ripe strawberries into small pieces, or use preserved strawberries slightly acid with fruit acid, and add two pounds to the cooked rhubarb. Then stir in half a pound of broken pecans, and half a pound of marshmallow. Dilute for service with heavy syrup. A fine grade of vanilla ice cream should be used for the cream portion of the sundae.

The author says this combination of two acid fruits is a new one, and the delightful flavor produced was a big surprise (C. L. Hadley.)

FRUITY

Over two quarts of ripe strawberries sprinkle two pounds of sugar, and allow the mixture to remain over night. Next day mash through a sieve, flavor with one ounce of vanilla extract, and add one pint of pure cream. Mix well and keep in a very cold place. To serve, place a 10-to-the-quart scoopful of vanilla ice cream in a sundae dish, and pour over it a ladleful of the above mixture; top off with a whole strawberry. The author states that the Fruity feature is "A good seller at 15 cents. (Theo. Louvis.)

HELEN OF TROY

Peel 6 oranges, cut up in blocks; 1 grated cocoanut, 12 ounces crushed pineapple. Mix well, serve over ice cream.

FROZEN PUDDING

Grind up in chopping machine one box raisins, two pints crushed pineapple fruit, two pints crushed Maraschino cherries Cut two whole oranges into cubes and add to mixture. Then add two ounces of rum flavor and mix thoroughly. Put into an ordinary double boiler and steam for about two hours. When cold add simple syrup sufficient to make amount required. Set away in hardening room or in salt brine for several hours. This mixture is served either plain or with any of several of the most called for flavors of ice cream. Served as a sundae dressing with whipped cream it should cost 15 cents. (Fireman's Pharmacy, Newark, N. J.)

SPRING PHANTASY

To each quart of new whipped cream add 3 ounces either of crystalized violet or rose leaves, coloring it if desired, but using dye sparingly as a very delicate shade is desired.

PALM BEACH

Into a porcelain container put 9 ounces of chopped pineapple, 9 ounces of chopped cherries, 9 ounces of crushed peaches, 9 ounces of crushed raspberries, 9 ounces of crushed or sliced oranges, 24 ounces of chopped assorted nuts, 8 ounces of grape juice, mix thoroughly and let stand for a few days Serve in the usual manner, pouring a small quantity over a dish of ice cream. Don't let stand too long, keep covered on ice. Price, 15 cents.

AMERICAN GIRL

Take 6 ounces of walnuts, 6 ounces of crushed pineapple, and 6 ounces of nice cherries, sliced in quarters; split and slice 4 large bananas and quarter and slice two Florida oranges; place all in a fruit jar and cover with pineapple syrup To dispense, place a ladleful of this mixture over a disherful of vanilla ice cream and serve on a suitable plate. The mixture of nuts and fruit should not be made in quantities too large for the day's service, as it is liable to spoil. Can be sold for 15 cents. (John A. Lassiter.)

BELLE ISLE

Mix 10 ounces of strawberry syrup, 10 ounces of vanilla syrup, 8 ounces of raspberry syrup, and 4 ounces of chocolate syrup. Pour a ladleful of this syrup over plain ice cream in a sundae glass.

MISSISSIPPI MIX

Mix crushed blackberries with grated black walnuts. Pour over ice cream and top off with whipped cream and one Maraschino cherry. Serve in sundae cup. Price, 15 cents.

CELESTIAL

Two pounds English walnuts, 2 pounds pecans chopped together with half pound of powdered sugar, add sufficient simple syrup and fruit syrup to flavor.

BASE BALL DOPE

Into a tall stem glass (6-ounce) pour half a ladleful of "base ball dope," add a scoopful (16-to-the-quart) of strawberry ice cream, another half ladleful of base ball dope, four thin slices of banana, and a few pecans; level off the top with whipped cream, and decorate with a green cherry. The "base ball dope" is made as follows: Cover 2 quarts of fresh strawberries with 1 pound of sugar and let the mixture stand for 3 or 4 hours, then mash and add 1 pint of simple syrup.

The author states that he uses all kinds and shapes of dishes—china, silver, glass, etc.—but he prefers "the tall stem glasses for sundaes, as these show up better and do not permit the sundae to spill over the sides as sometimes happens when oblong dishes are used Often I have noticed that a waiter going down the aisle with a tray of sundaes in tall stem glasses is stopped on his way back and asked what he just served, 'they looked so good we just wondered what they were'" He further states that he has a neatly printed menu, and every week he invents a new dish These delicacies are introduced to his patrons by means of a handwritten slip, bearing the name of the beverage, and the slips are fastened to the top of the regular menu with a clip. This attracts attention and sells many dishes, as it creates the impression the drink is new, and that is why many people always want it (Pendel Poledor)

LIBERTY BELL

Peel four large apples, grating three and chopping one, add 4 ounces of pineapple syrup and 1 pint of whipped cream, then mix, now take 5 bananas, slice into small pieces; also take 1 quart of fresh strawberries, crush, sugar well, and let stand for 2 hours to acquire a nice, sweet taste. Incorporate the three mixtures together. This makes a delicious dressing To serve, take a Colonial saucer and egg cup, one that comes narrow at bottom and tapers outward; then take a chocolate straw, cut in two and push one-half into a Maraschino cherry, and stand erect in the egg cup, into which put a well-filled No. 10-to-the-quart vanilla ice cream; flatten out the cream in the cup so that it will resemble the shape of a bell; pour the dressing as above made over the ice cream, then place the other half of the chocolate straw on the sundae to represent the crack in the bell. Top off with a cherry. (Peter Eichelman.)

WALDORF-ASTORIA

Mix a quart of crushed ripe strawberries with 1 pineapple, previously cut into cubes. Mix thoroughly with as much sugar as the fruit will absorb. Now add an equal quantity of ripe cherries or other fruit, and a quart of chopped pecan and pignolia nut meats. Add enough strawberry syrup to bring the mixture to the right consistency and use to pour over ice cream in the preparation of sundaes. Price, 15 cents.

BAR HARBOR

Peel and cut a pineapple into cubes and cover them with sugar. In another vessel crush a quart of ripe strawberries, add as much sugar as the juice will absorb, mix with the pineapple, and add any other suitable crushed fruits and some chopped walnut meats, with enough syrup to allow the mixture to be readily served. Place a quantity on ice cream and serve as any other sundae.

SWASTIKA

Slice 3 bananas, allowing the pieces to drop into a fruit bowl; add half a pint of crushed cherries, 2 ounces of shredded cocoanut and simple syrup q.s. Use one ladleful to each sundae. Sells for 15 cents. (W. R. Sampson)

ICE CREAM ORANGE SUNDAE

Prepare half a gallon of fruit preserves as follows · Mix one pint of crushed strawberries, one pint of crushed or grated pineapple, four crushed bananas, and sufficient orange, raspberry and strawberry syrup to make up the batch to two quarts. Place all in a shallow preserving kettle and cook to the consistency of preserves, adding several pieces of orange peel. Allow to cool, and serve two ladlefuls or 10 teaspoonfuls of this preserves over an ice-cream orange.

STRAWNUPINO

Chop 1 pound of mixed nuts and add 10 ounces of crushed strawberry and 10 ounces of crushed pineapple sauce. Pour over plain ice cream.

FRUIT BON BON

Whole cherries, 5 dozen; black raspberry fruit, 1 pint; pecan halves, 3 ounces; English walnuts, 3 ounces; sherry wine, 10 ounces; simple syrup, 1 pint. Grind the cherries, raspberries and walnuts together, add the simple syrup and sherry wine, and then stir in the pecans broken into pieces. Serve in a tall glass with nabisco wafers and a glass of water. Put into the glass a small portion of pineapple and orange ices, and ice cream, cover with the salad and top off with whipped cream and a whole cherry. Price, 15 cents. (Guy E. ClaVell.)

FRUIT SALAD

In a suitable footed-sundae dish place one twelve-to-the-quart disherful of vanilla ice cream; over this pour a ladleful of fruit salad; take two nice large oranges, peel and chop them into cubes; split two bananas into quarters lengthwise; slice one-half pint of cherries into quarters; one-half pint of shredded cocoanut; mix the fruit thus prepared with cherry syrup, sprinkle well with sugar and let stand an hour before serving. (Warren Thomas.)

ICE CREAM AND WATER ICES

What has been jocularly called "the solidification of the soda fountain business" is one of the most significant developments of recent years. The growth in the popularity of all sundaes and fancy desserts and more recently the addition of the luncheonette to many fountains have a most marked effect on the character of the materials employed at the fountain. A natural part of this movement has been a tremendous increase in the quantity of frozen products used at the fountains, and as a natural consequence the great increase in the number of fountains that are now making their own ice creams and water ices.

This tendency to serve ice creams of their own making has been fostered by the many improvements in the various types of freezers. Refinements in the ever-popular tub-and-ice style of freezer make these now easier to handle and have improved their freezing quality. The brine freezers, both of the perpendicular and horizontal type, have been markedly improved in recent years, and they have been made in smaller models than was at first thought practical.

These mechanical improvements have lowered the cost of ice cream making, and many fountains have found that it is possible for them to make a better cream at less cost and with very little additional trouble than it was possible for them to buy.

When a fountain is making its own cream, the pushing of various frozen specialties has often proved to be a very popular and profitable feature. Curiously, the sale of sundaes at the fountain is greater during the winter than in the hottest months of summer, and the sale of fancy ice creams to family trade during the social season has been highly developed by many fountain operators. In the torrid season, the sale of water ices, sherbets, and frozen punches can be most advantageously pushed. These all show a splendid profit, and the fountain that makes its own ice cream and does not add ices and sherbets to its menu is neglecting an opportunity.

As in every other department of the successful soda fountain a sure foundation of quality materials is the safest guarantee of success. The freshest of fresh fruits only should be used. When extracts are employed for flavoring these should be of the highest quality. Care should be taken to freeze the mix properly and to store and pack the frozen products skilfully. But the very foundation of good ice cream is good cream, and the ice cream maker should satisfy himself that his cream is right.

Testing Cream

A number of methods of testing cream have been devised, one of the simplest being described in Circular No. 42 of the Purdue University Experiment Station, the apparatus required being a number of sample tubes or jars, a balance or scales, cream-test bottles, an acid dipper, and a Babcock centrifuge Samples of fresh cream of normal richness, and which is not perceptibly separated, can be tested accurately without special preparation, other than mixing thoroughly by shaking or pouring before use. Thick and semisolid samples which are otherwise in good condition should be warmed to about 90° F., then poured gently and weighed at once. Cream samples in which the butter fat is completely separated and churned, or has formed a compact, tough and leathery layer, as is the case with old samples not stored at a low temperature, should be heated high enough to melt the butter fat, 110° F. or above, then shaken thoroughly and weighed out at once. It should be understood that samples in this condition are at best difficult to handle and tend strongly toward inaccurate results.

The cream must be weighed into the test bottle, not measured. This is necessary in order to secure the correct amount by weight. Cream varies in weight with its richness and its mechanical condition, and no one measure will hold the correct amount of cream of varying richness. The correct unit of weight to take is nine grams, which is weighed on a suitable balance or scales, in a standard 9-gram 50 per cent. cream test bottle, the stem of which is marked with divisions representing 0 5, 1, and 5 per cent. To the cream in the test bottle, add commercial sulphuric acid, sp gr. 1 82 to 1.83, until, when properly shaken and all the white curd has disappeared, the mixture has a coffee-brown color. A light brown color shows that more acid is needed. A black color immediately after shaking indicates too much acid. When adding the acid, the bottle should be held in an inclined position and should be revolved once. In this way the acid washes the neck free from particles of cream and curd. After the acid is added the bottle should be shaken carefully by giving it a rotary motion. Care should be taken not to spill any of the contents. In case of spilling the test should be rejected and made over. The bottle is now ready for the Babcock centrifuge in which it is whirled at the proper speed, 1000 revolutions per minute for a tester with a 12-inch diameter wheel and 800 revolutions per minute for a tester with an 18-inch diameter wheel. Fill to the bottom of the neck of the bottle with hot, soft water, whirl for two minutes, fill to about the 45 per cent. mark with hot, soft water, and whirl for one minute. The temperature of the water added should be not less than 140° F., and preferably near that of boiling water. Remove the bottle from the tester to a water bath, where it should remain at about 135 to 140° F. for 10 minutes. Just before reading the test and when taking the bottle from the water bath, add a few drops of glymol (white mineral oil), which removes the meniscus or curve on top of the fat column, leaving a straight line which is sharply defined, and readily seen. All that now remains to be done is to read the percent. of fat from the graduations on the outside of the tube corresponding to height of the column of fat within. With the average percentage of a representative sample known, the amount of butter fat in any number of gallons of cream may be readily ascertained by weighing the entire quantity, the factor found being the proportion in pounds of butter fat present.

This matter of the determination of the percentage of butter fat in cream is important to the maker of ice creams for most of the States have adopted certain legal standards with a minimum of butter fat allowed by law in ice creams of various types. The local boards of health, the State and National authorities are all active in the enforcement of these regulations, and it is well that those who are manufacturing ice creams should post themselves on the legal requirements:

STATE STANDARDS FOR ICE CREAM

There are several things to be remembered by ice-cream manufacturers and retailers who deal in manufactured cream· (1) Ice cream shipped to a State other than that in which it is made comes under Federal jurisdiction; (2) ice cream sold in the State in which it is made comes under the State and city jurisdiction—State laws and city ordinances or regulations of the local boards of health; (3) in States where no laws exist there are instances where rigid local regulations govern the manufacture and sale of this product. Hence, it behooves a manufacturer of ice cream to investigate thoroughly the regulations, local or State, under which his business will be conducted.

In Circular 19 of Standards (U. S.), the following definitions, or standards, are thus given:

1. *Ice cream is a frozen product made from cream and sugar, with or without a natural flavoring, and contains not less than 14 per cent. of milk (butter) fat.*

2. *Fruit ice cream is a frozen product made from cream, sugar and sound, clean, mature fruits, and contains not less than 12 per cent. of milk (butter) fat.*

3. *Nut ice cream is a frozen product made from cream, sugar and sound, non-rancid nuts, and contains not less than 12 per cent. of milk (butter) fat.*

These standards—14 per cent. for ice cream, and 12 per cent. each for both fruit and nut ice cream—have been indorsed by many of the States having ice-cream regulations. In other States—Maryland for example—a higher percentage of fat is required in nut ice cream than in plain ice cream; in still other States, milk and cream, condensed milk, and a pure vegetable "filler" are allowable under the law. The following table of legal requirements is made up from a digest of the recent legislation on this subject. Where no changes in standards have been reported, the standard heretofore published is stated:

State Butter Fat Regulations

Alabama—8, 6, 6 per cent. Local regulations authorized by State enactment.

Arizona—10, 8, 8 per cent.

Arkansas—No State standard.

California—10, 8, 8 per cent.

Colorado—10 per cent

Connecticut—8, 6, 6.

Delaware—No legal standard. Unauthorized ruling 14 per cent.

Florida—14, 12, 12.

Georgia—8 per cent.

Idaho—14, 12, 12.

Illinois—Statute authorizes regulation by State Food Standard Commission, which establishes 8 per cent, milk fat.

Indiana—Not less than 8 per cent. milk fat and 18 per cent milk solids.

Iowa—12, 10, 10.

Kansas—10 per cent

Kentucky—10, 8, 8.

Louisiana—10, 8, 8; 1 per cent. of harmless filler allowable.

Maine—14, 12, 12.

Maryland—10, 8, 8.

Massachusetts—7 per cent.

Michigan—10, 8, 8; not over 7 per cent gelatin.

Minnesota—12, 10, 10.

Mississippi—8 per cent.

Missouri—14. 12. 12

Montana—10, 9, 9.

Nebraska—14, 12, 12.

Nevada—14, 12, 12.

New Hampshire—14 per cent.

New Jersey—8, 6, 6.

New York—8 per cent.

North Carolina—8 per cent.

North Dakota—12 per cent.

Ohio—8 per cent.

Oklahoma—10, 8, 8.

Oregon—10, 8, 8.

Pennsylvania—8, 6, 6.

Rhode Island—8 per cent.

South Carolina—No State standard, local regulations in force.

South Dakota—14, 12, 12.

Tennessee—8, 6, 6.

Texas—8, 6, 6.

Utah—14, 12, 12.

Vermont—14, 12, 12.

Virginia— 8 per cent.

Washington—8 per cent.

West Virginia—8 per cent.; allowances made for reduction in the percentage of milk fat and milk solids not fat to the extent to which other ingredients have been added.

Wisconsin—12, 10, 10.

Wyoming—10 per cent.

FORMULAS FOR ICE CREAMS AND WATER ICES

VANILLA

Boil 1 pound sugar with 2 quarts milk, and add the mixture to 1 pound sugar, 10 egg yolks already prepared by whisking up together. Mix these all well together and boil until the mixture thickens a little. Remove from the fire and add 3 quarts cream, which thoroughly incorporate by whisking Add vanilla flavoring just before finishing. Strain and freeze in the usual way.

VANILLA

For 10 gallons of cream· Take 50 pounds (about 6 gallons) of aged 18 per cent cream (or 5½ gallons of cream and ½ gallon of condensed milk) ; about 8 pounds of sugar; 3 to 4 ounces of vanilla extract; and, if a binder seems called for, from 3 to 4 ounces of gelatin. The sugar should be thoroughly dissolved in the cream before freezing

For 1 gallon of cream· 2 quarts of 22 per cent cream; 11 ounces of sugar; 1½ tablespoonfuls of vanilla extract. (Vermont Agri. Expt. Stat.)

VANILLA (FRENCH)

Place 12 ounces of powdered sugar, 15 egg yolks, 1 quart of cream and 1 split vanilla bean in a pan and heat over a slow coal fire, or, still better, in a hot water bath, until the mixture thickens, then strain through a coarse sieve. Put it back in the pan, set the pan in ice, or ice water, and beat until it becomes quite thick and firm. Then put in freezer and freeze. Next beat up 1 quart of double cream, sweeten lightly with fine sugar, and gently but thoroughly mix into the batch. Re-ice the can and let stand.

FRENCH VANILLA

Take two quarts of good cream, and a large vanilla bean split in half, the yolks of 12 eggs and a pound of sugar. Put the cream on the fire in a double boiler, and then stir in slowly the eggs and the sugar, the vanilla bean having already been added. When this begins to thicken take from the fire and allow it to cool. Do not freeze until it has become cold. Before it becomes cold, after taking from the fire, strain so as to remove any pieces of the bean. This quantity when frozen will make about a gallon of cream. It will be good, too (Dwight Kempton.)

FRENCH VANILLA

Use 8 egg yolks to 1 quart of sweet cream, and 1 vanilla bean to every 2 quarts, and freezing in a French freezer, or at least after the French style. This cream is especially suitable for molding.

VANILLA (FRENCH TYPE)

Take 5 quarts of cream, 2 vanilla beans, (or use a good vanilla extract), split the beans, scrape out the seeds and put them into the cream and add 2 pounds and 4 ounces of sugar. Put on a brisk fire, stir constantly and bring to the boiling point; then slowly stir in 20 egg yolks, previously beaten with a little milk or cream, and at once remove from the fire, strain and cool off, and freeze.

In the above formula vanilla beans are preferable to an extract; the former gives the better flavor.

FRENCH ICE CREAM

This is nothing more than the cream boiled with an addition of a certain number of eggs or egg yolks. Opinions differ greatly as to which of the two mentioned is the proper method. But by using the whole egg (yolk and white together) for the production of ice cream the effect will be similar to that obtained by gelatin; it will make the cream lighter, gaining in quantity but not in quality; and when standing any length of time it is apt to transform it into small lumps of ice. Using the yolk only the cream will be of a smoother texture and more solid.

CHICAGO PICNIC

Condensed milk, 14 quarts; fresh milk, 10 quarts; granulated sugar, 8 pounds; gelatin, 8 ounces; vanilla, 4 ounces.

PHILADELPHIA

Cook 8 pounds of sugar in 2 gallons of cream. Bring it to a boil, when it should resemble skim milk; add and work in an additional 3 gallons of cream, 6 eggs and 2 ounces of vanilla. It is now ready for freezing. Must be very cold before freezing. A very delicious formula and used in some high grade stores.

COMMERCIAL

Formula No. 1

(Sells to retailer at $1.25 a gallon.)

Cream, 40%, 11 qts. @ .45	$4.95
Milk, grade B, 5 qts. @ 06½	.33
Cond milk, 4 qts @ .20	.80
Sugar, 9 lbs. @ 05	.45
Extract, 4 ozs. @ .10	.40
	$6.93

When expanded by freezing this quantity of ingredients produces 40 quarts of ice cream, containing 20 per cent. butter fat at a cost of 80 cents a gallon

Formula No. 2

(Sells to retailer at 90 cents a gallon.

Cream, 40%, 3 qts. @ .45	$1.35
Milk, grade B, 13 qts. @ .06½	85
Cond. milk, 4 qts. @ 20	80
Gelatin, 4 ozs. @ .24 per lb	.06
Extract, 4 ozs.	40
Sugar, 7½ lbs. @ .05	38
	$3 84

These ingredients expanded by freezing yield 40 quarts of ice cream containing 7½ per cent. butter fat at a cost of 38 cents a gallon.

Formula No. 3

Cond. milk, 10 gals.	$8.00
Milk, grade B, 10 gals.	2.60
Plain water, 60 gals	
Gelatin, 4 lbs @ 20	.80
Color	.01
Flavor	1 00
Sugar, 60 lbs. @ .05	3 00
	$15.41

These ingredients when expanded by freezing yield 120 gallons of ice cream at a cost of 13 cents a gallon.

The above formulas were quoted in the course of a case before the Iowa Law Court. No. 1 should make a high grade cream and No. 2 is in general use. The Editors of the Formulary do not recommend formula No. 3.

It was shown by the evidence presented that the cost to manufacture ice cream containing 20% butter fat is 45 cents a gallon; containing 7.7%, 29 cents; and that where condensed milk is used and the product contains 1.9% butter fat the cost is 15½ cents a gallon.

Commercial

Vanilla Ice Cream Without Cream or Milk

1 vanilla bean.
8 gills of syrup at 20 degrees.
18 egg yolks.

Cook and freeze, and then work in a meringue made of two egg whites and ¼ pound of sugar.

This formula is presented for what it is worth.

Reduced Cost Mix

Mix four pounds of sugar thoroughly with one ounce of powdered gum tragacanth No. 2, previously dissolved in a little hot water or milk. To this add five quarts of milk, five quarts of cream and one-half ounce vanilla extract. Dissolve thoroughly and freeze.

Milk Formula

A fairly good ice cream can be made from milk as follows: One gallon of milk, 18 whole eggs, or 10 whole eggs and 20 yolks of eggs, 2 pounds of sugar, flavor Place ½ a gallon of the milk and half of the sugar on a slow fire to boil Meanwhile mix the other half of the sugar with the eggs, stir the boilng milk into it, replace on the fire, and stir till the composition covers the blade of a palette knife, but do not let boil. Take off the fire and add the other milk at once, then strain, cool and freeze The whole mixture may also be set on the fire at once, and beat with the egg beater until it comes to the boiling point, then finish similar to the preceding. Great care should be taken in selecting the eggs.

Hokey Pokey

Make a custard composed of 3 eggs, 1 quart of milk, 2 tablespoonfuls of corn starch, 6 ounces of pulverized sugar and sufficient of any desirable extract to flavor it. Bring the milk to the boil, mix the corn starch, 6 ounces of pulverized sugar and eggs; beat these smoothly together with a little cold milk and add it to the boiling milk, stir all till the mixture begins to thicken, then add and stir in the flavor. Now immediately remove it from the fire, and when it becomes cool stir it together and pour it into your freezer and freeze till solid.

Hokey Pokey

Dissolve three ounces of corn starch in one quart of milk, also soak two ounces of gelatin in a little milk or water. Place three quarts of milk and one pound and twelve ounces of sugar in a tin or porcelain-lined pan, set on the fire until boiling, then pour it over the dissolved starch and gelatin, set on the fire again and bring to a good boil, stirring constantly with the egg beater, then add one can of condensed milk, strain, cool and freeze. Flavor at will.

Another formula calls for six quarts of milk, one pound and twelve ounces of sugar and half a pound of corn starch. Dissolve the starch and one ounce of gelatin in one quart of milk. Then mix all together and stir on the fire till it boils; strain, cool, freeze and flavor

Too much boiling will tend to curdle. In above formula it might be advisable to bring just to the boilng point.

Hokey Pokey

Into a bright and perfectly clean basin put 1 pound of fine sugar and 1 dozen eggs; mix these well together, then add and stir in 2 quarts of fresh cream or milk, 1 spoonful of salt and 1 tablespoonful of extract of vanilla; set the mixture on the fire and stir constantly till it thickens, but not curdles; strain into an earthen pan, cool, and stir into it 1 ounce of gelatin, dissolved in milk or water; now pour it into the freezer and work slowly during the whole process till it becomes well frozen; then remove the dasher and pack the cream firmly in brick molds and bury them in ice and salt until the cream is thoroughly frozen and hard; then turn them from the molds in the usual way and keep them in the ice cave or in a can imbedded in ice, or it may be cut with a knife, dipped in warm water, into suitable squares, wrapped in waxed paper and put in boxes and kept in the ice cave ready for sale

Chocolate

Melt and make a paste of 10 ounces of chocolate with hot water and keep it warm until wanted Cook 1 dozen eggs and 1½ pounds sugar in 2 quarts of cream. Add the chocolate and work it in while hot; cool and freeze in the usual way.

Chocolate

Make the foundation cream and whip 1 pint of cream to serve with it. Heat 2 bars of sweetened vanilla chocolate with 2 tablespoonfuls of water, or enough to melt it. When smooth add gradually a little of the hot cream or custard, and strain through a fine strainer or cloth into the remainder of the cream. If unsweetened chocolate be used, add 2 tablespoonfuls of sugar to it while melting.

Half of a teaspoonful of Ceylon cinnamon may be mixed with the chocolate, or half an inch of stick cinnamon may be boiled with the cream or milk; it gives a rich, spicy flavor. Or add 1 tablespoonful of caramel.

Chocolate

Two quarts of cream, 1 pound and 4 ounces of sugar, ½ a pound of fine sweet chocolate, or 5 ounces of chocolate liquor, 1 piece of whole cinnamon, 1 vanilla bean. Cook the cream with the cinnamon, add the sugar and vanilla, warm the chocolate and dilute it with part of the hot cream, mix with the rest of the cream, strain through fine muslin, let cool and freeze. The fountain man may consider it best to leave out the cinnamon; not everyone likes it.

CHOCOLATE

Put 5 pounds of bitter chocoalte in a pan; place the pan in hot water and let it remain until the chocolate is melted, put 4 pounds of sugar and ½ pound of glucose in a copper pan, adding enough water to dissolve the sugar, then cook to a syrup (35° on a syrup gauge), and while the syrup is hot pour it in a small stream into the melted chocolate, stirring the latter while adding the syrup Keep up this stirring until the chocolate becomes a smooth paste, then set it away in an earthen vessel for use. In flavoring put a pound of the paste into a pan and warm it till melted by putting the pan in hot water, then add a little plain cream to it, mixing well, and afterward adding the chocolate to the cream to be flavored.

CHOCOLATE

Sweet cream, 2 quarts, sweet milk, 3 quarts, powdered chocolate, 1 pound, table salt, 1 teaspoonful; eggs, whipped, 4, extract vanilla, 1 ounce, sugar, 5 pounds Add the powdered chocolate to 1 pint hot milk and make a smooth paste; then add to balance of ingredients, and let the mixture stand in freezer well iced (no salt) until ice cold. Then salt the ice and freeze. N. B.—Three ounces French gelatin may be substituted for the eggs.

CHOCOLATE

Two quarts of cream, 12 eggs, 2 to 2¼ pounds of sugar, 10 ounces of chocolate. Melt the chocolate, dilute it with a little hot water into a smooth paste and keep it warm. Cook the eggs, cream and sugar and work into the mixture while hot the chocolate; then cool and freeze.

CHOCOLATE

Three quarts of cream, 1½ pounds of sugar, 12 ounces of chocolate, 1 ounce vanilla sugar. Cook the cream, then add the sugar and vanilla; heat the chocolate and work it with 4 ounces of boiling water or milk to a smooth paste; add it to the hot cream, strain, cool and freeze. When serving, spread a spoonful of whipped cream on each dish.

AMERICAN CHOCOLATE

Twelve ounces of unsweetened chocolate (chocolate liquor), 3 pounds of powdered sugar, 5 quarts of sweet cream, a small piece of whole cinnamon. Melt the chocolate over a slow fire, gradually add a little sugar and cream, also the cinnamon, have the chocolate quite thin and fully dissolved, then stir it into the cream, add a good flavoring of vanilla, strain into a can and freeze in the usual manner.

CHOCOLATE (FRENCH TYPE)

Four quarts of cream, 10 ounces of chocolate, 2 pounds and 6 ounces of sugar, vanilla flavor, 12 egg yolks. Slowly melt the chocolate in the boiler, adding sugar and cream gradually, constantly stirring until it has reached the boiling point, then add the yolks in the same manner as for vanilla cream, strain and cool, then add vanilla flavor and freeze.

VASSAR

Sugar, 2 pounds, chocolate, 4 ounces; milk, ½ gallon; cream, ½ gallon; ground hickory nuts, 2 to 4 ounces, or as much as desired. Freeze as you would prepare ice cream.

FUDGE

Four ounces of grated chocolate and one pound of sugar melted together. To this add one quart of milk and the well-beaten yolks of one dozen eggs. Add one ounce of caramel coloring Put over fire and stir until mixture coats spoon. Cool. Add beaten whites of eggs and one pint of whipped cream Serve with fudge sauce.

This ice cream must not be kept long as it will get frosty.

FUDGE

Chocolate, 4 ounces, sugar, 2 pounds; milk, ½ gallon; cream, ½ gallon; ground hickory nuts, 2 to 4 ounces Bring the milk to boiling, add the sugar, stirring all the time, and set aside Grate the chocolate and work it with about 8 ounces of boiling water to a smooth paste; add to the previous solution along with the cream, strain through fine muslin, cool, stir in the powdered nuts, and freeze the same as any ice cream. Too much chocolate makes the cream dark and rough and destroys its fine flavor.

COFFEE

Steep ¼ cup of coarsely ground coffee in 1 pint of cream or milk 20 minutes. Remove it, let settle, and pour off carefully, then strain it and add it to the remainder of the cream or custard. This is sufficient for 1 quart of ice cream made according to either recipe.

COFFEE

Make ¼ cup of filtered coffee, or, if you have no filter coffee pot, put 2 heaping tablespoonfuls of fine ground coffee in a fine strainer placed in a bowl. Then pour through it one-third of a cup of boiling water. Pour the liquid through a second time, and if not clear strain it through a fine cloth. Add this clear liquid to the hot cream or custard, and make the ice cream in the usual manner.

This formula is adapted more to home than to fountain use.

COFFEE

Cook a quart of cream; add to it and stir well in 4 ounces coffee finely ground and roasted to a pale brown. Let it draw for

15 minutes, then set aside to settle in a warm place. Strain through a fine muslin Cook another quart of cream, add 1 pound sugar and the coffee, thoroughly stir and allow it to cool, then freeze.

COFFEE

Place 3 ounces of finest ground coffee into a coffee machine and filter, and pour about 5 cupfuls of boiling water on top of it. When all the liquid has passed through the filter and has cooled, pour it into a large bowl with 12 ounces of pulverized sugar, 8 yolks of egg and 2 whites, 1 ounce of powdered tragacanth and 1 quart of double cream.

COFFEE

Four quarts of cream, 1 pound 12 ounces of sugar, 8 egg yolks, 3 ounces of good ground coffee (or the equivalent of extract) Place sugar, half of the cream and coffee in the pan over a slow fire, keep stirring until it has reached the boiling point, then mix up egg yolks with the remainder of the cream and pour it in, and bring to the point of boiling. Strain through a fine sieve or cloth, then cool off and freeze.

There are a few very fine coffee extracts on the market and a better cream may be obtained by adding one of them, from 8 to 10 ounces, to a 5 gallon batch. Every lot of "homemade" coffee extract varies so much that the quality of the ice cream is liable to suffer thereby

COFFEE

One pint of strong coffee, two cups sugar, one pint milk, one quart cream, one tablespoonful arrow root, one-half teaspoon vanilla, two eggs well beaten, wet arrow root in a little milk and add to the coffee when boiling, stir to keep from burning, add milk and let boil two or three minutes; when cold, add the other things and freeze as you would ice cream. When nearly frozen add one pound English walnuts ground or chopped very fine. Makes about three and one-half quarts. (Henri Delasse.)

COFFEE

The mix for coffee ice cream is made in exactly the same proportions as for vanilla and maple. In fact it is very often a practice to add the coffee flavor to a vanilla ice cream, made as above specified, and the result may be depended upon to be satisfactory. The real flavor is in the coffee syrup. That must be good, and the following method has been found to produce eminently agreeable results:

Take 10 rounding tablespoonfuls of high grade coffee and place them in 1½ quarts of cold water. Bring this to a boil quickly and boil for 5 minutes vigorously. Strain through several thicknesses of cheesecloth. Then to the resulting liquid add 2½ quarts of sugar, which is dissolved and the whole

mass brought to a boil. This will produce about 2 quarts of coffee syrup, which is enough to flavor about 10 gallons of ice cream If a darker color is required it can be secured by adding 2 or 3 ounces of burnt sugar (caramel) to the batch.

This coffee syrup may be kept in jars almost indefinitely, and used as a flavoring or for a dressing for coffee sundaes, etc. (Vermont Agri. Exp. Stat.)

VIENNA COFFEE

Place 1 gallon of vanilla ice cream into a can imbedded in ice and salt, work it well with a spatula in order to get it smooth Then beat up the whites of 12 eggs with 12 ounces of fine sugar over a slow fire (like you would prepare a sponge cake), add to the ice cream and freeze all until nearly solid When the mixture has reached this condition, add ½ pint of good strong Mocha coffee flavoring and keep freezing a while longer Flavor with kirschwasser and serve

COFFEE SUPREME

Freshly roast eight ounces of a good quality coffee Grind and add two quarts of milk and 2 pounds and a half of sugar. Set on fire and steep very gently one hour, finally letting it come to a boil. Set aside to cool. Strain, and pour upon the thoroughly beaten yolks of 20 eggs. Cook until mixture coats spoon but not a moment longer. Cool and fold in beaten whites of eggs, also one quart of whipped cream. Freeze

CARAMEL

Put ½ cup granulated sugar in a saucepan over the fire, and stir till melted and dark brown. Add ½ a cup of boiling water and simmer 10 minutes Make either ice cream you prefer, using only half the sugar given in the recipe. Add enough of this caramel to give the desired flavor and color. Caramel may be added to vanilla or coffee ice cream. Whipped cream or marshmallow whip may be served with it, or stirred in when the caramel cream is partly frozen.

EXCELSIOR CARAMEL

Four quarts of 22 per cent. cream, and sufficient liquid caramel to give an agreeable flavor. This should be only slightly bitter. Into a double boiler put one dozen beaten egg yolks, one quart of cream, a little salt and two and one-half pounds of sugar. Cook until the mixture will coat a spoon thickly, then add to caramel cream. Freeze.

MAPLE

Three quarts of cream, 1½ pounds of genuine maple sugar. Cook the cream in a farina boiler, stirring frequently, until the water in the outer pan is boiling; then take it off the fire, add the maple sugar previously pounded into small pieces, and stir until the sugar is dissolved; let stand a few minutes, strain, cover with gauze, and let stand till cold; then freeze like any other ice cream. Should the cream be too white, add a little burnt sugar to give it a rich color.

VERMONT MAPLE

For 10 gallons of cream Take 6 gallons of 18-22 per cent cream—or the cream-condensed milk alternative given in the vanilla recipe—from 6 to 8 pounds of maple sugar, varying according to taste; and, if desired, 3 to 4 ounces of gelatin.

For 1 gallon: Two quarts 22 per cent cream, 9 to 11 ounces maple sugar, and enough common sugar to complete the sweetening.

Light-colored and delicately flavored maple sugar is not the best for ice cream making. The dark brown, strongly flavored variety—be sure it is not burnt—makes by far the best cream, and the quantity used must depend upon the sugar itself. As made by the Vermont sugar farmers the sugar content varies greatly, and when the proper flavor has been obtained in the ice cream mix ordinary sugar can be used to bring the sweetness up to the required point. (Vermont Agri Exp. Stat.)

ARCTIC TAFFY

Dissolve 6 pounds maple sugar in a hot water bath, allow to cool, and then strain into 5 gallons of cream. Add 4 pounds of brown sugar, a little caramel and freeze. Should the brown and maple sugar be dark, no additional coloring will be necessary Nuts may be added to improve this delicacy.

GINGER ICE CREAM

Two cups scalded milk; 1 cupful of sugar; 1 tablespoonful flour; 1 egg. A pinch of salt. Make this into a smooth custard, adding one tablespoonful of extract of ginger Cool. Add one quart of light cream and one-half cup of Canton ginger cut in small pieces. Freeze.

GINGERED CREAM

Scald two quarts of milk and four quarts of cream. Add five cups of sugar and four ounces of extract of ginger. Freeze and serve with a dressing made of equal parts of ginger and vanilla syrup containing bits of chopped preserved ginger.

GINGER

Two quarts of heavy cream, one pound of sugar, one lemon, half a pound preserved ginger, grated rind of two lemons. Scald half the cream, the sugar, and finely chopped ginger in a double boiler. Cool Add the rest of cream, lemon juice, and grated lemon rind. It might be well in this formula to add the lemon juice to the sugar first.

FRUIT

If preserved berries, raspberries or strawberries, are used they should be added to the mix after it is partially frozen, else the fruit and heavy syrup will sink to the bottom of the mix and remain there If fresh fruit is used it should be well chopped or crushed, and sugar added to it some time before it is added to the mix. It, too, is put into the cream after the latter has been partially frozen, but in this case it is in order that the acid in the fruit may not coagulate the cream, as might be the case if it was added when the cream was quite warm. (Vermont Agric. Exp. Stat.)

FRUIT

One pint of milk, 2 cups sugar, 2 eggs, 2 tablespoonfuls gelatin soaked in a little cold water, 1 quart cream, 4 bananas, ½ pound candied cherries and other fruit if desired. Let milk come to a boil, beat flour, sugar and eggs together and stir in boiling milk Cool 20 minutes, then add gelatin When cold, add cream; put in a freezer, freeze 10 minutes, add fruit, and finish freezing.

STRAWBERRY

Six quarts of cream, 3½ pounds of sugar, two boxes of sweetened, crushed strawberries. Strain and freeze at once, as berries have a tendency to curdle cream.

CRUSHED STRAWBERRY

Best cream, 3 pints; pulverized white sugar, 12 ounces; 2 whole eggs Mix all in a porcelain-lined vessel, place on fire and heat to the boiling point, stirring constantly Remove and strain through a hair sieve. Place in a freezer and freeze Now take 1 quart of ripe strawberries, select, hull, and put in a china bowl Add 6 ounces pulverized white sugar and crush all down to a pulp. Add this pulp to the frozen cream along with 2 tablespoonfuls of extract of vanilla and mix well. Give the freezer a few additional turns until the mixture hardens.

STRAWBERRY

2 quarts strawberries
2 quarts rich cream
3 pounds sugar
2 tablespoonfuls vanilla

Mash the berries thoroughly and mix with the sugar, stirring until the latter has been perfectly dissolved. Then add the cream and the vanilla, and freeze Some people add a few whole strawberries to make the dish look pretty when served, but this is not always effective as the whole berries become icy. Do not expect this cream to be bright in color; it will shade on the pink, and will be somewhat mottled. Three or four scrapes of nutmeg to a quart of berries will bring out the berry flavor as in no other way, and no one will detect the spice. Nutmeg will accentuate the flavor of strawberries, raspberries or blueberries. The above amounts when frozen will make about six quarts of cream. Freeze hard. Previous soaking overnight in clear syrup and then draining, will keep the fruit from freezing hard. (Dwight Kempton.)

STRAWBERRY

Whip two quarts of cream, sweeten with 12 ounces of powdered sugar and add 1½ pints of crushed sweetened strawberries which have been strained. Freeze.

STRAWBERRY COLD CREAM

Two quarts strawberries and one quart sugar mashed together and put through a strainer. Combine this with one quart of cream and one quart of whipped cream. Freeze. A bit of nutmeg added to the fruit might improve the flavor of this cream.

STRAWBERRY (FRESH)

Four quarts of cream, 2½ pounds of powdered sugar, enough ripe strawberries passed through a sieve to make 1 quart of juice, mix all together, add a little color if needed, although fresh berries need little coloring. Strain and freeze at once. The mixture should not be left standing, as the juice will tend to curdle the cream.

RASPBERRY

1 quart of rich cream
1 quart raspberries
1 pound sugar

Wash and pick over a quart of red ripe raspberries and crush them carefully, saving all the juice. Dissolve a pound of sugar in a quart of rich cream, and when thoroughly dissolved add the raspberry pulp and juice. Stir this mixture well so that the fruit may not settle at the bottom of the freezing chamber, and then freeze hard. While this is an exceedingly simple recipe it is delicious when prepared according to the directions.

As in the case of all fruit or nut creams, it is best in the above formula to partly set or freeze the cream, then add fruit or nuts (Dwight Kempton.)

GOOSEBERRY TART

Prepare three quarts of nice gooseberries by washing and rubbing blows from the ends. Stew these with two and one-half pounds of sugar and one and one-half pints of water. When thoroughly cooked, rub through a strainer. Add a few drops of green coloring, three pints of sweet cream sweetened to taste, or a custard mix may be used. Freeze.

MARASCHINO

Take the yellow rind of 2 lemons, put this in the boiler with 2 quarts of cream and 1 pound of sugar, place the mixture over a slow coal-fire, constantly stirring until it thickens, not allowing it to come to a boil; add 10 egg yolks in the usual manner, then strain and occasionally stir it until it is cold. When cold pour in freezer and freeze. Then beat up stiff 1 quart of good double cream and incorporate it, with ½ pint of maraschino, paddling it up very lightly; let stand about one hour before serving.

WILD CHERRY

Two teaspoonfuls extract wild cherry, 1 ounce almond extract, 1 pint red currant jam, 1 pint preserved cherries, 8 ounces cherry syrup, 1½ pounds sugar, 4 quarts cream.

Proceed as before, adding blended chopped fruit when mixture is partly frozen.

WHITE CHERRY

Put 2 cups of sugar and 1 cup of water in a saucepan over the fire Stir until the sugar is dissolved and let the syrup come to a boil. Drop in carefully 1 quart of California white wax cherries and simmer gently for 15 minutes, strain carefully, add a quart of cream to the syrup and freeze. When the freezer begins to turn hard, beat well, take out the dasher and stir in the fruit. Pack and let stand for two or three hours before serving. The ice cream is a good novelty feature

RED CURRANT

One quart red currant jam, 4 quarts cream, 2 pounds sugar, 4 ounces lemon syrup, 1 ounce lemon extract.

Proceed as before, adding the red currant jam which has been reduced to a smooth mass with the lemon syrup, just as ice cream commences to stiffen.

RED CURRANT

Put four pounds of ripe, red currants, two pounds of sugar, four cupfuls of water into a small kettle. Let the mixture come to a boil. Strain and add two quarts of cream and one pound of sugar. Freeze.

TOM TUCKER

Two quarts plum or greengage jam, 4 quarts cream, 1½ pounds sugar, 6 ounces lemon syrup.

As plum skins are rather tough frozen, blend jam and lemon syrup and press through a coarse colander or sieve. Proceed as before, adding fruit when cream is partly frozen. If purple plums are used, add a few drops of purple coloring; if greengage, green coloring; red plums, red coloring. This formula may be improved by sweetening to taste.

QUINCE

Use one pound of preserved quince pulp to a gallon of vanilla mix. Freeze. Serve with a dressing made of the quince juice and walnut meats. (Benj. L. Barry.)

GRAPE

Mix in the proportion of one quart of grape juice to one quart of cream, one pound of sugar and the juice of one lemon. Freeze. In this formula add the lemon juice to the pound of sugar as the first step. Mix the sugar well and then add the grape juice. Again mix and finally add the cream. (U. S. Dept. of Agric.)

GRAPE

To each quart of any good vanilla mix, add one cup of sweetened grape juice and one-fourth of a cup of lemon juice.

Dissolve 1 pound of sugar in your lemon juice before adding to mix. It will curdle if you don't.

APRICOT

Put one quart can of apricots, syrup and all, through a sieve, rejecting the skins. Add an equal quantity of hot water and a saltspoonful of salt. When boiling, stir into this eight heaping tablespoonfuls of cornstarch rubbed smooth with one quart of cold milk. Cook until smooth and free from lumps. Beat into this the juice of two lemons, one-fourth cup of butter, and one pound of sugar. Freeze.

APRICOT

Three quarts of 22 per cent. cream sweetened with two pounds granulated sugar. To this add one-pound can of apricots which have been put through a sieve. Color with a dash of red and flavor with an ounce of extract of almond. Freeze.

APRICOT

To each quart can of apricots forced through a coarse sieve add one quart of water and one pound of sugar. Scald one pint of cream and add one tablespoonful of cornstarch rubbed smooth with water. Pour hot mixture over four well beaten egg yolks and return to fire until cooked. Cool and fold in the stiffly beaten white. Combine with apricot mixture and freeze.

APRICOT

One quart apricot pulp, prepared by peeling about two dozen apricots; boil with ½ pint of water till dissolved; stir while on the fire and rub the pulp through a hair sieve; 1 quart double cream, 1 quart syrup, 32 degrees. Flavor with a few drops of essence of apricot or peach kernels.

APPLE

Peel, cut and core about two dozen apples and make them into a stiff marmalade; pass through a sieve with 1 quart of cream; sweeten to taste; add a little lemon juice; freeze.

BAKED APPLE

Bake a dozen sound tart apples Remove skins and cores. Mash and sift pulp Incorporate with this half a teaspoonful of extract of cinnamon, two ounces of rose water, two ounces of strained lemon juice and sugar enough to sweeten. The amount will depend upon the tartness of the apples used. Scald a quart and a half of cream

and add when cooled to apple mixture. Fold in one pint of whipped cream. Freeze.

PINEAPPLE

Boil in three cupfuls of water for 15 minutes one pint of sugar and a pint of shredded pineapple. Add to this a teaspoonful of gelatin, softened in cold water. Press the mixture through a cheesecloth, and when it is cold add the juice of two lemons. Freeze it to a "mush" consistency, then add a cupful of cream beaten solid. Fill the chilled pineapple shell, set it in a mold, and bury in salt and ice for half an hour before serving. (Robt. J. McBride.)

PINEAPPLE ICE CREAM

One quart grated pineapple added to three pints of heavy cream. Let stand one-half hour. Add 1½ cups of sugar and freeze.

HAWAIIAN

One quart shredded preserved pineapple, 1 pound minced preserved ginger, 4 ounces lemon syrup, 4 quarts cream, 2 pounds sugar.

Scald sugar, ginger, and half the cream. Combine when cold with one quart of plain cream, one quart of whipped cream and lemon syrup. Freeze.

HAWAIIAN

To one-quart can of grated Hawaiian pineapple add a cup of sugar over which has been squeezed the juice of one lemon. Add a pint of milk, a pint of scalded cream, and a pint of whipped cream. Freeze.

LEMON

2 quarts milk
2 quarts cream
3 eggs (whites)
3 lemons (juice)
Grated peel of one lemon.

This must be cooked. Bring to a boil one gallon of the milk combination in a double boiler. Beat the whites of three eggs very light, or so stiff they will stand alone. When the milk-cream comes to a boil take from the fire and stir in the white of egg, stirring slowly Squeeze three large lemons upon the sugar, removing all seeds and pulp from the juice Let stand an hour. Then when the milk-cream is cool and the lemon juice and sugar have become incorporated stir the latter into the milk-cream, grate in the rind of one lemon, sweeten to taste—depending largely upon the acidity of the lemons—and freeze at once Do not mix the lemons and milk until just before you are ready to start freezing as the milk is liable to curdle On this account lemon ice cream is going out as a commercial product, and, instead, home cooks are making lemon ice.

LEMON

Rub off the yellow outside rind of **4**

lemons, on hard lumps of sugar, 4 quarts of cream, 2 pounds of sugar, including the lump sugar flavored with the essential oil, 4 egg whites. Mix well together, put in a lined kettle and place on the fire, constantly stirring until the cream has reached the boilng point, but not allowing it to boil. Then take it off, immediately strain it through a sieve and cool. When cool, pour into freezer; when nearly frozen add the juice of the lemons. Observe that while the zest of the yellow rind is to be worked into the batch at the outset, yet the juice is not to be added until the cream is nearly frozen The reason is that if the lemon juice is added before the mixture is frozen it is apt to curdle the cream.

While this formula may be used in the soda department it should be observed that an unnecessary amount of labor is called for.

LEMON TART

To the strained juice of a dozen lemons add three pounds of sugar. Dilute four cans of condensed milk with three times the same quantity of water. Add this to the sugar and lemon juice slowly. Fold in the stiffly beaten whites of 12 eggs. Freeze.

ORANGE

1½ pints orange juice
1½ pounds sugar
1½ pints milk
1½ pints thin cream

Dissolve sugar in orange juice and gradually add milk and cream, also a little salt. Freeze.

ORANGE

Two quarts orange juice, 8 grated orange rinds, 4 cups sugar, 2 pints condensed milk, 1 pint water.

Combine orange juice, grated rind and sugar. Freeze rather hard, then add condensed milk and the pint of water which has been used to rinse out milk cans. Freeze again and serve. This will not stand, but is very nice to serve to a special party or during rush hours, when it will all be used up soon.

ORANGE

To 4 quarts of cream, 2 large oranges and 1 lemon are required, with an addition of 2 pounds of sugar. Secure the orange flavor by rubbing off the rind on lump sugar. In default of hard sugar you may grate off the yellow skin on a grater. Be careful not to rub off the white pith beneath the surface. Using sugar flavored with the essential oil will bring out the flavor in all its purity and strength, and this mixed in turn with the juice will produce a satisfactory confection, beverage or cream.

ORANGE (WITH CONDENSED MILK)

Heat one can of condensed milk and one pint of plain milk in double boiler. Beat six eggs thoroughly and add half a pound of sugar. Pour heated milk over eggs and sugar and return to fire. Cook until mixture coats spoon. Remove from fire, cool, and add one pint of concentrated orange syrup, the grated rinds of four oranges, another can of condensed milk made thin with half a pint of cold milk, one ounce of orange extract, and a little pure food yellow coloring matter. Freeze.

FROZEN ORANGES A LA NIPPON

Take 4 quarts of rich cream, 2 pounds of fine sugar, 8 eggs, ½ pound of rice boiled soft in a quart of milk, 4 ounces of curacoa, and a compote of 4 oranges Mix the sugar, eggs and cream; place them on the fire and stir with a whisk until the mixture is at the boiling point; then remove it from the fire and add and stir in the boiled rice and liquor, and freeze the composition. Then fill the mold and imbed it in ice and salt till needed for use When turned out on a dish garnish round the base with pieces of oranges of the compote, and pour the syrup over all.

PEACH

Two quarts of cream, 1 pound of sugar, enough good, ripe peaches mashed and passed through a sieve to make 1 pint of juice, mixed with a little syrup or fine sugar. This all stirred together and frozen at once. All fruits which contain acid, being of a tart nature, should not be left standing after being incorporated with the cream, therefore it is advisable to add the juice when the batch is nearly frozen. A little pink coloring is preferred by some ice cream makers, this, of course, is only a matter of taste.

PEACH

2 quarts ripe peaches
1 quart of rich cream
6 drops almond extract
2½ pounds sugar

Take two quarts of ripe peaches, pare them and mash them fine, being careful to lose none of the juice. Make them very sweet, as freezing has a tendency to offset the sugar, and fruit thus prepared if "just right" to eat will taste sour after coming from the freezer. Measure the crushed peaches and to each quart of the juice and pulp add a quart of rich cream. Add 6 drops almond extract to the cream Then put into the freezer and freeze carefully. If frozen too hard the fruit will be icy. This quantity will make something more than three quarts. (Dwight Kempton.)

PEACH ROYAL

Add six cups of sugar, in which have been incorporated 1½ cups strained lemon juice, to a pint of scalding cream. Cool, and add two quarts of milk. When mixture is partly frozen, add three pints of mashed peach pulp and finish freezing.

BANANA GLACE

To the pulp of one dozen bananas add one pint of water, one pint cream, and the strained juice of three oranges. Boil water and sugar 10 minutes, cool, and add bananas and orange juice. Put in freezer and add whipped cream when it begins to stiffen.

BANANA WHIP

Peel and crush a dozen bananas. Squeeze over bananas juice of ½ lemon. Rub through sieve and mix with pulp two cups of strained orange juice and three cups of sugar. Soak one ounce of granulated gelatin in a little cold water and dissolve in a cup of boiling water. Beat fruit pulp smooth, adding slowly one pint of milk and dissolved gelatin. Place in freezer and when mixture begins to stiffen add a quart of whipped cream and half an ounce of banana extract. Let stand three hours after it is frozen. Serve in tall stemmed glasses and garnish with a cherry.

TUTTI FRUTTI

Make an ice cream of 4 quarts of rich cream, 2 pounds of white sugar, 4 eggs, 1 fine vanilla bean, split and cut crosswise into small pieces; mix all well together in a bright and clean copper basin; place on the fire and bring the mixture just to the boiling point, stirring it constantly with a wire whisk; then immediately strain it through a hair sieve into an earthen or stoneware pan; when cool, pour it into the freezer and freeze; turning the crank slowly till it is frozen in and difficult to turn; then remove the dasher and add about a quart of preserved and slightly dried fruits, cherries, pineapples, strawberries, apricots, greengages, peaches, etc., all cut small and in equal portions to form the required quantities; add also, if at hand, 4 ounces of kirschwasser and the juice of 2 lemons, work all these thoroughly well into the cream by means of a long-handled spatula; then draw off the surplus water from the tub and repack it with fresh ice and salt; cover all with blankets or cloths and set aside for an hour or two to harden and ripen.

TUTTI-FRUTTI (WITH CONDENSED MILK)

Mix one pint can of condensed milk with two quarts milk. Make a custard of this by using eight egg yolks, one and one-half cups of sugar, and a tablespoonful vanilla flavoring; bring just to the boiling point. Add a pound of candied, mixed fruits chopped. When mixture begins to stiffen in freezer, fold in beaten whites of eggs.

NAVY PUDDING

1½ cups orange juice
¼ cup lemon juice
½ cup grape juice
Sweeten to taste.

Whip 1 pint of heavy cream with ½ cup of powdered sugar and 1 teaspoonful of vanilla and fold in ⅔ of a cup of walnut meats.

Add one tablespoonful of gelatin soaked in cold water and dissolved in one cup of boiling water to the fruit juice mixture. Add a little more sugar if necessary. Pour this fruit mixture into brick molds, about one-third filling. Fill with the whipped cream mixture. Pack in ice and salt.

MILLE FRUITS

Apricot juice	....	½ pint
Black cherry juice	..	½ pint
Greengage juice	....	½ pint
Lemon wine	....	½ pint
Crushed sugar	......	2 pounds

Dissolve the sugar with gentle heat in the juices and wine, set aside in the refrigerator or on ice to cool.

Sweet cream	....	8 pints
Crushed sugar	......	2 pounds

Cook these in a water-bath boiler until the water in the outer pan boils and the sugar is dissolved. Then put the syrup on ice to cool. When thoroughly cold, add the before-prepared and cooled juices and sugar, and pour the mixture into the freezer; freeze well, occasionally scraping the mixture from the sides of the freezer to insure thorough admixture. Be sure that your freezer and all utensils used in the manufacture of the ice cream are scrupulously clean.

HONEYMOON

Make a good vanilla mixture leaving out the vanilla flavoring. To each gallon add one ounce of lemon flavoring and one ounce of peppermint. Tint a delicate pink and freeze.

LALLAH ROOKH

Cut some French cherries, apricots and angelique and pour over it some Madeira and stand in hot place. Then make a mixture of French vanilla and freeze, leaving one cup of the liquid behind; when frozen hard enough, add the fruit and some broken ladyfingers and finely crushed macaroons. Then let it stand and when firm fill in molds, imbedding them in broken ice and salt for fully one hour. Next dissolve some gelatin in a little warm milk or water and add it to the remaining custard. When wanted for use, turn the pudding on the dish upon which it is to be served and sprinkle a little chopped fruit over it, then add some whipped cream with the previously prepared custard, flavored with Madeira.

VIOLET S. C.

Sweet cream	....	1 gallon
XXXX sugar	....	1¼ pounds

Strain through fine sieve into freezer and

add a little violet color and violet extract to taste.

Especially good for teas. (W. O. Rigby)

ORANGE PEKOE

This ice cream takes its name from the kind of tea used in the making Take 3 tablespoonfuls of orange Pekoe tea, stir it into a saucepan containing a pint of hot milk and allow it to stand for five minutes Then add a cupful and a half of sugar, the yolks of 4 eggs and cook the mixture in a double boiler until it thickens. Strain, incorporate a little salt, the grated rind of an orange and 2 cupfuls of thick cream, freeze.

NUT, FRUIT AND BISQUE ICE CREAMS

PISTACHIO

Scald a quart of milk with two quarts of cream. Add three cups sugar and a pint of whipped cream, an ounce and a half of pistachio extract and a little certified leaf green coloring. Freeze.

MARRON

Split and roast 2½ dozen chestnuts, then remove the skin and place them in a copper kettle with 2 pounds of granulated sugar and 1 pint of water, place the mixture on the fire and cook to the hard crack, or about 300 degrees. Then pour it on an oiled marble slab. When cold pound it in a mortar with enough sweet cream to form a soft paste. Put this on the fire with 5 pints of cream, constantly stirring until it has nearly reached the boiling point, then beat in 20 yolks, previously mixed with some cream or milk Strain, and when cold add a good flavoring of vanilla

Another method: Take the same amount of preserved marrons, rub them very fine with 1 quart of sweet cream and pass the mixture through a sieve; pour this in a pan and dilute with 1 pint of vanilla cream, and then freeze. Then whip up one quart of double cream, sweeten lightly and flavor with maraschino, mixing it thoroughly. Charge 15 cents.

ROAST ALMONDS

One pound almond meats, 2 ounces caramel, 2 ounces vanilla, 4 quarts cream, 2 pounds sugar.

Prepare the almond meats by blanching and roasting in olive oil to a light golden brown. Pound to a paste and blend with this the caramel and vanilla extract. Scald 2 quarts of cream with 2 pounds sugar. Add almond mixture and cool. Mix one quart of plain, cold cream with this and one quart of whipped cream. Freeze. Charge 15 cents per service.

ROAST ALMOND

Roast 1 pound of blanched almonds to a nice yellow. Then put 2 pounds of sugar in a copper kettle, set on the fire and stir slowly all the time until the sugar becomes liquid and of a golden color, then add the roasted almonds, give the mixture a few turns and pour it on the greased marble, and when cold pulverize it in a mortar; then place this in the boiler with 4 quarts of cream. Proceed in the usual manner, adding 8 egg yolks.

BURNT

Put over the fire ¾ pound raw almonds, previously blanched, and ¼ pound sugar until the sugar has taken on a delicious brown Turn the batch, put on a greased slab and let it cool, then pound in a mortar. Put it into 3 quarts cream, add 1½ pounds flour and some vanilla flavoring Cook as for other cream, then strain and freeze.

ALMOND-COCOANUT SPECIAL

Two quarts of heavy cream, one pint of milk, one pound sugar, two tablespoonfuls of vanilla, one tablespoonful of almond. Scald half the cream with the sugar melted in' it. Flavor when cool. Add the rest of the cream and milk, one-half pint of dried and rolled macaroons and half a pint of dried and rolled cocoanut cakes. Charge 15 cents. (Robt. Sellers)

HAZELNUT

Roast 5 ounces of hazelnuts to a light brown color, then remove the skins. This is best done by rubbing the roasted nuts in a towel, removing the skin, then put in a sieve and the skin is easily shaken off. Pound them in a stone mortar with some milk to a fine pulp. Next put 4 quarts of cream into the boiler over the fire, 12 egg yolks, beaten up with some of the cream, and added before it has reached the degree of boiling The hazelnuts should be added to the cream at the outset, thus increasing the flavor. Pass through a fine sieve, and when cold freeze in the usual manner.

PEANUT

21 pounds 18 per cent cream
4 pounds granulated cane sugar.
1 teaspoonful peanut butter, dissolved in one-half cup of boiling water.
Caramel color to give light brown color
Freeze as usual. To prepare this ice cream two-thirds cream and one-third milk may be used. (Roy C. Potts)

NUT FUDGE

Heat one gallon of milk to boiling point in a water bath with a pinch of salt and add four pounds of sugar. Take one-half pound of powdered cocoa or grated chocolate and make into a smooth paste with boiling water.

From the scalded milk take one quart and add to the cocoa paste and cook thoroughly or there will be a raw taste Add this to the rest of the milk and combine with this one gallon of cream and 12 ounces of hickory nut meats cut fine. Freeze.

COCA COCOANUT

Mix fresh shredded cocoanut with chocolate ice cream thoroughly, taking care not to use too much cocoanut as this makes the cream hard, then pack in brick moulds. (C. W. Webb, Ice Cream Trade Journal.)

CARAMEL NUT

Put one pound of granulated sugar in a saucepan and stir until it becomes a fine, light golden brown. When nicely browned, add a pint of boiling water and boil until a smooth syrup has formed. Scald one quart of milk and mix one pound of granulated sugar with three ounces of corn starch Mix smooth with cold milk and add to hot milk. Beat four whole eggs light and pour hot mixture over it, stirring at the same time. Cook until smooth Add one pint of cream and one can of evaporated milk thinned with half a pint of cold milk Combine half of the caramel syrup with this mix and one pint (dry measure) chopped nut meats.

CARAMEL FIG

Place two pounds of sugar in an aluminum dish and stir slowly as it melts. Allow it to scorch slightly until it becomes a rich brown. Remove from the fire and pour over this a pint and a half of boiling water To this liquid add three pints of scalded milk. With this mixture make a cooked custard using the beaten yolks of eight eggs, a pound of sugar, half a cup of flour, and a pinch of salt. Cool and strain into the freezer can. Add three pints of heavy cream and when partly frozen stir in two pounds of figs cooked until tender in hot water, then drained and chopped. Charge 15 cents.

MAPLE WALNUT

Two quarts of cream, one pint maple syrup, standard thickener, two teaspoonfuls vanilla, one tablespoonful caramel, one pint chopped walnut meats.

LEMON NUT

Add the strained juice of 3 lemons to 2 teacupfuls of sugar. Add gradually a partly frozen mixture of 1 pint cream and 1 quart of milk. Work in ½ cupful chopped walnuts and freeze at once.

GEORGIAN SPECIAL

Make a rich fruited strawberry ice cream. Use a center mold and as a center use a combination of shredded cocoanut and sliced peaches, which have been stirred to a proper consistency, to make a firm center. (C. W. Webb.)

FROZEN NUT MOUSSE

Scald two quarts of milk. Mix two pounds of sugar with four tablespoonfuls of flour, a pinch of salt, two ounces of vanilla

extract and six beaten eggs. When these ingredients are thoroughly incorporated, pour the hot milk upon them. Stir and return to a water-bath until mixture thickens. Cool; add two quarts of plain cream, two quarts of whipped cream, and one quart dry measure of mixed chopped nuts. Freeze. Charge 15 cents.

FRENCH ROYAL

One gallon 30 per cent cream, 3½ dozen eggs, using yolks only; 3½ pounds granulated sugar, 1½ ounces extract of vanilla; 2 pounds assorted fruit (candied), chopped fine; 1 pound marrons (chopped), 1 pound pecans (chopped); 1 pound filberts (chopped). Take 2 quarts of cream and mix with it the egg yolks and sugar; put the mixture into a kettle and slowly cook under constant stirring, being very careful not to boil or burn the same When the mixture is thoroughly cooked, remove from the stove and cool, add the rest of the ingredients named in the formula and put all into the machine and freeze.

To serve, take a six-inch plate and on it place a small lettuce leaf; now take a disherful (10-to-the-quart) of the above mixture and put it on the lettuce leaf, add a spoonful of whipped cream flavored with a little sugar and Maraschino liquor and top off with a green cherry Sells for 20c with a nice profit. It might be well in this formula to add the nuts when the mix is nearly frozen or to beat in after and let set. (F. F. Thompson.)

FIG WALNUT

3	pints milk
1	pound sugar
10	eggs
2	teaspoonfuls salt
1½	pounds chopped figs
1	quart cream
1	ounce vanilla
½	pound walnut meats

Use milk, sugar, salt and egg yolks to make a custard. Cool, add flavoring, beaten egg whites and the cream whipped stiff and chopped nut meats. Freeze.

DELMONICO

Pure cream .... 2 gallons
Good milk .... 6 quarts
Yolks of 10 eggs.
Sugar .... 4 pounds
A standard foam producer 2 ounces

(2)

Ground nuts .... 1 pound
Broken cherries .... 1 pound
Sherry wine .... 1 pint
Mix all together.

Rub up the sugar, foam and eggs with part of the cream and heat a few minutes; gradually add the milk and half of the cream, and, lastly, add 2 ounces of essence of pepsin and put on ice to congeal.

Whip the remainder of the cream and white of the eggs separately, and then mix the two, when the cream begins to freeze add the whipped cream and, when nearly frozen, add formula No. 2

X'MAS DELIGHT

Take 3 quarts milk, 1½ pounds sugar, yolks of 10 eggs, 1 quart thin cream, ½ teaspoonful of salt, ½ cupful of pineapple syrup, and 3 cupfuls of sweet chestnuts Make a custard of the first four ingredients, then add the thin cream, pineapple syrup, and boiled chestnuts forced through a strainer Now take two 2-quart brick icecream molds, and line each with the mixture, add one cupful of candied fruits, cut into small pieces; ½ cupful of Sultana raisins, ½ pound of Malaga grapes cut into halves, and about one dozen chestnuts, also cut into halves. Fill the remainder of the space in the molds with the custard mixture, cover the molds and pack in salt and ice for several hours When ready to serve, remove the cover carefully and take out the brick, which slice into one-inch slices. In dispensing, add to each slice of the mixture whipped cream, sweetened and flavored with Maraschino. Place each slice on a neat plate, and serve with wafers and a spray of holly or mistletoe, or a paper napkin indicative of the holiday season (Walter Luick.)

BISQUIT TORTONI

To make 2 quarts Beat 12 egg yolks with ½ pound of sugar over a hot fire until steam begins to rise; remove from the fire to ice and continue beating until the mixture becomes quite stiff, then stir in wineglassful of sherry and 3 ounces of bisque crumbs Pour into a 2-quart brick or melon mold thinly lined with frozen apricots. Pack in ice and salt for two hours Be careful to overfill the mold, as the mixture will shrink somewhat as it congeals. Price 75 cents per quart. To serve price at 20 cents.

BISQUE MACAROON

Twelve macaroons, 12 sunshine biscuits, 4 quarts cream, 2 pounds sugar, 2 ounces vanilla.
Roll macaroons and biscuits to fine crumbs. Scald 2 quarts cream and all the sugar. When cool add one quart plain cream and one quart whipped cream and vanilla. When mixture begins to stiffen in freezer add crumbs. Adding at this time they do not soak but remain distinctive in taste.

MACAROON

2 quarts cream
1 pint rolled dry macaroons
1½ pounds sugar
1 ounce vanilla
Scald half the cream and add macaroons

and sugar to hot cream. Cool. Mix rest of cream and flavoring. Freeze. Charge 15 cents

MACAROON NUT (WITH CONDENSED MILK)

Plain cream one gallon, whole condensed milk one-half gallon, mixed with one gallon plain milk and three pounds of sugar. Pistachio flavoring 1½ ounces, and one pint each of chopped nut meats and powdered macaroons. Sweeten to taste.

BISQUE OF PINEAPPLE

One can of pineapple, 1 pound of sugar, 1 quart of cream Chop the pineapple small and put it in a bright pan or kettle with the sugar and a few spoonfuls of juice or water to dissolve the sugar to syrup, let it simmer at the side of the range a short time. Whip the cream till it is half froth, then freeze it first by itself, because the pineapple added before freezing has a tendency to curdle it. Pound the pineapple and syrup through a colander, mix them with the partly frozen cream, and freeze again. The pineapple in syrup should be prepared beforehand to be cold
In making these bisques it is not best to pound the fruit perfectly fine, but the small pieces, about like grains of wheat, should be perceptible, and show that the creams are mixed with fruits and not merely flavored.

FRUITED BISQUE

Whipping cream, 3 quarts; powdered sugar, 6 ounces, best vanilla extract, 1½ ounces; one pineapple, sliced in cubes; three oranges, sliced in thin strips; pecan nuts, in halves, 2 pounds Mix the sugar, vanilla extract, and whipping cream until the mixture is very stiff. Place the fruit in a separate bowl, cover with sugar and stand on ice until the sugar is dissolved. Pour off the juice into a bottle to use as a sauce Mix the fruit and nuts in whipped cream, then place in quart brick ice cream packers and freeze until hard. To serve, put one-eighth of a brick on a round china dish and pour on a small quantity of sauce with three Maraschino cherries neatly arranged on top in triangular outline. Serve with three nabisco wafers and a glass of water. Charge 15 cents per service. (Alexander McDonald.)

MAPLE NUT

Take 18 ounces of maple sugar and break into small pieces, place in a water bath with four ounces of cream. When softened add slowly 18 yolks beaten light. Beat constantly until mixture begins to thicken. Remove from fire and cool. Add to this three pints of whipped cream, four ounces of macaroon crumbs and four ounces of chopped walnut meats. Freeze. Give small servings as this is very rich. Charge 15 cents per service.

ROYAL BISQUE

Use any good formula for vanilla ice cream but caramelize half the sugar before using. To each gallon of the mix use one and a half cups of chopped hickory nut meats and a dozen finely rolled macaroons.

MACAROON FRUIT

To each quart of any good vanilla mix, stir one dozen dried and rolled macaroons and 12 ounces of fruit, using four ounces each of preserved strawberries, chopped seeded raisins, and chopped canned peaches Use fresh fruit when possible. Charge 15 cents per service. (Robt. Sellers.)

BROWN BREAD

Make an ice cream composition of 1 quart of cream, 12 ounces of sugar and 5 or 6 eggs and cook and freeze as usual. Pound 2 ounces of genuine dried Boston brown bread into dust, sift and beat into the ice cream.

CHOCOLATE MALTED

One-half pound of malted milk mixed with one-half pound of granulated sugar, one ounce of powdered chocolate and one and a half quarts of water. Put over fire and bring to boiling point. To this mixture cooled add half an ounce of powdered dissolved gelatin, one ounce of essence vanilla and one pint of whipped cream. Freeze.

CHOCOLATE ALMOND BISQUE

Cut one-half pound of cake chocolate into pieces. Place in water bath with one pint of milk. Stir until smooth, adding one-half pound of sugar and one quart of cream. Stir until smooth and cool Mix this with three quarts of plain cream, one quart of whipped cream and one-half pound of roasted almonds chopped fine. Freeze.

MALTED PINEAPPLE

Mix two quarts of cream and three quarts of milk in which one pound of malted milk has been dissolved, 2½ pounds of sugar and one pint of shredded pineapple. Freeze slowly.

MARSHMALLOW MACAROON

With sharp, clean scissors snip two pounds of marshmallows into tiny pieces. Dry and roll two pounds of macaroons to a fine powder. Soak marshmallows and macaroons in two quarts of cream for one hour. Soak 10 level tablespoonfuls of granulated gelatin in eight ounces of cold milk until soft. To this add two quarts of scalding hot cream and one pound of sugar. Allow to cool. Combine with marshmallow and macaroon mixture and add two quarts of whipped cream. When the mixture is partly frozen, stir in two pounds of chopped and drained cherries.

MOUSSES

CHOCOLATE

Put the yolks of 16 well-beaten eggs into a water-bath container. Add one quart chocolate syrup and cook until mixture coats spoon heavily. Set container in ice water and beat until frothy and cold. Turn into freezer and fold in two quarts of whipped cream. Pack in ice and salt until frozen.

CHOCOLATE

Melt over the fire 4 ounces of good chocolate, with half a glassful of water; let boil up several times, then cool. Pour the chocolate in a bowl; add 12 ounces of pulverized sugar, 8 yolks and 2 whites of eggs, 1 ounce of tragacanth, previously dissolved in hot water or milk, and 1 quart of double cream Beat and finish as for vanilla.

COCOA MOUSSE

Mix ½ pound cocoa and 3 cups sugar. Cook with 2 cups boiling water till smooth. Add to 3½ quarts milk scalded with cinnamon bark; cook for 10 minutes Beat in 3 beaten eggs, mixed with cup sugar and a pint of whipped cream. Cool, flavor with vanilla extract and freeze. Serve in cups garnished with whipped cream (Janet McKenzie Hill in Ladies' Home Journal)

COFFEE

Soak four tablespoonfuls of granulated gelatin in cold water. When soft, dissolve in one pint of hot, strong, black coffee. Allow to cool and then stir in one quart of heavy cream and one quart of whipped cream. Add three cups of sugar and a pinch of salt. Freeze.

COFFEE NEAPOLITAN

Two quarts strong, clear coffee, 2 quarts cream, 8 eggs, 2 pounds sugar, 4 level tablespoonfuls corn starch or ice cream powder, 1 ounce vanilla.

Cook one quart cream in double boiler with well-beaten egg yolks. Into this beat the blended flour and sugar. Cook until mixture will coat spoon. To this add coffee, boiling hot, stiffly beaten egg whites and the other quart of whipped cream Freeze.

To make this delicacy extra fine use hot milk, or boil the fine ground coffee in milk, then strain several times.

FRENCH COFFEE MOUSSE

Put 2 ounces of freshly roasted coffee in a mortar, just enough to thoroughly crush the berries without reducing them to powder. Put the crushed berries into a pint of milk with 6 ounces of sugar, let boil, then leave the mixture until cold, strain it on the yolks of 6 eggs in a double kettle, and stir the mixture over a fire until the custard thickens Be sure that it does not curdle. When quite cold work into it 6 ounces of whipped cream. Freeze the mixture in an ice cream freezer, then fill a plain mold with it and replace in the freezer until time to serve. Recommended as a dainty dish for fashionable trade in hot weather.

MAPLE MOUSSE

Six eggs whipped, one-half teacupful maple syrup and one quart of whipped cream Mix thoroughly and slowly freeze. Chocolate and coffee mousses may be made in the same manner by substituting these syrups and using sufficient to give the desired flavor.

MAPLE MOUSSE

Stir six ounces of maple syrup into the beaten yolks of eight eggs and cook in a double boiler until the mixture thickens Remove from the fire, turn into a mixing bowl and beat until cold Then add a pint of cream, previously whipped stiff, folding the two together thoroughly but not beating them after they are mixed, turn into a mold and pack in ice and salt for a few hours, or until the mixture is sufficiently frozen.

VANILLA

Take 1 quart of "double" cream, place half of it on the fire with two vanilla beans, boil it up; let cool and strain. Place 12 ounces of pulverized sugar into a large bowl; beat up with 8 yolks and 2 whites of eggs; then stir in with the beater the cream with the vanilla, and afterwards the other half of the cream; also 1 ounce of powdered tragacanth. Place the mixture on ice, with very little salt, and stir with the beater; as soon as it commences to rise in the bowl fill or pile in glasses or silver goblets; set them immediately in the freezing box, and let stand for two hours The mousse is then ready to serve. The whole operation should be performed in a cold place. Charge 15 cents per service.

LEMON CREAM

Heat two pounds of sugar with two quarts of water until thoroughly dissolved. To the strained juice of one dozen large lemons add two more quarts of cold water When the mixture is partly frozen add two quarts of whipped cream flavored with vanilla and almond. Finish freezing.

CHERRY

2 tablespoonfuls granulated gelatin
½ cup cold water
1 pint cherry syrup
5 tablespoonfuls lemon juice
1 pound sugar
2 quarts cream

Soak gelatin in cold water. Heat cherry syrup hot and add gelatin, also sugar and lemon juice. Allow to cool until mixture begins to thicken. Fold in the cream which has been whipped. Pack in salt and ice and let stand four hours.

STRAWBERRY

Wash and mash 5 ounces of clean strawberries through a sieve, add 1 pint of double cream previously whipped stiff. Now add 4½ ounces of icing sugar to which has been previously added a tablespoonful of lemon juice, transfer the whole to a small freezer and freeze, occasionally scraping the mixture from the sides of the freezer and mixing with the part not frozen, but without working the cream

STRAWBERRY

Wash and hull two boxes of ripe strawberries Sprinkle them with one pound of sugar and allow to stand in cold place one hour. Mash and force through a fine sieve. Dissolve two ounces of powdered gelatin in eight ounces of boiling water and add strained juice of two lemons. Add to strawberry pulp. When it begins to thicken fold in two quarts of slightly sweetened whipped cream, and one ounce of strawberry extract Pack in ice and salt and allow to stand four hours

PLUM MOUSSE

Boil two pounds of sugar and eight ounces of water until it will spin a thread. Pour this hot syrup over the stiffly beaten whites of 16 eggs Beat until cold and add four quarts of whipped cream Fold into this two quarts of sifted slightly sweetened plum pulp. Pack in ice and salt until frozen.

PINEAPPLE (CRUSHED)

One quart milk, 10 egg yolks, pinch salt and three cupfuls of sugar cooked over water until the spoon is coated. Cool, add one quart whipped cream, four cups shredded pineapple, two cups of pineapple juice and two ounces of pineapple extract. Freeze.

MELON MOUSSE

Press the fruit and remove the seeds; slice the fruit and put into a preserving kettle. To one good-sized melon add a half-pound of sugar and cook until the fruit is soft. Add a quarter of an ounce of gelatin which has been soaking in a very little cold water, and rub the mixture through a sieve and flavor with a tablespoonful of wine When the mixture is cool beat it with a whip until it is light, then beat in a generous quart of whipped cream and place upon a glass dish and serve very cold.

RUBIO

1 pint cooked prune puree
1½ pints milk
4 ounces lemon juice
1½ pints heavy cream
salt
1 pound sugar

Soak prunes all night in cold water. Cook until soft, remove stones, and press pulp through a strainer. Add sugar, lemon juice, and a little salt. Whip cream and fold in. Freeze.

NEVADA NUT MOUSSE

Scald one quart of milk in a water bath. Thicken with four heaping tablespoonfuls of corn starch blended with one pound of dark-brown sugar and mixed with water to make a smooth paste   Turn the hot milk on this and return to fire. Stir until thoroughly cooked. Beat four egg yolks and turn part of hot mixture on this and return all to fire for 20 minutes. Strain into freezer can, and add one quart of whipped cream, half an ounce of vanilla and half a pound each of walnut and pecan nuts cut fine. Freeze.

BRAZILIAN FRUIT MOUSSE

3   pints milk
1½ pounds sugar
10 yolks of eggs
1   teaspoonful salt
1   quart cream
½   ounce almond extract
½   ounce vanilla
1   pint of chestnut puree
½   pint Maraschino
1   pint glace fruits

Make a custard of milk, sugar, egg yolks and salt   Cut fruits in tiny pieces the night before and soak in Maraschino, covered with a plate and weight to keep fruit under liquid. Add soaked fruits to custard, also chestnut puree, cream and flavoring Freeze   Serve with a heavy sprinkling of chopped Brazil nuts. Charge 15 cents.

ELK

Place 10 yolks of eggs into a farina boiler, add 2 vanilla beans, split in halves, set on very slow fire and beat the yolks until they form a thick body, remove the boiler from the fire and beat until cold. Now make Italian meringue of four whites of eggs and 9 ounces of sugar, add this to the beaten yolks, and when the composition is entirely cold, add 1 strong pint of whipped cream. When the composition is well mixed, add 8 ounces of preserved fruits cut into small dice and soaked in good Maraschino, and last 2 ounces of finely crushed macaroons

AMBROSIA

Well whip 1 quart of rich cream (40% butter fat), then gradually work into it, by whipping, 8 ounces of powdered sugar, sprinkling on the sugar with one hand and beating the mixture with the other   When thoroughly mixed, put it into a gallon ice cream can and tub, selecting a can with a notched lid; pack the can and turn as in freezing ice cream, cutting away the frozen cream adhering to the sides of the can with a spatula at intervals of every three min-

utes. Continue the operation until the whole mass is frozen, then add two bananas previously cut and crushed in an earthen bowl or crock, two oranges sliced in quarter-inch pieces, and 3 ounces of freshly grated cocoanut, mixing thoroughly. The mousse is now ready to serve and should be made fresh each day. Serve a No. 16-to-the-quart dipperful in a sundae glass and top with a little whipped cream and a cherry. Sells for 15 cents   (A. Philipp.)

FANCY FROZEN DESSERTS

BERRY BANANA PARFAIT

Make the custard for the cream at least two hours before freezing, so that it will be very cold when wanted. For this custard bring three cupfuls of milk to a boil, dissolve one and one-half cupfuls of sugar in it and turn immediately over the well-beaten yolks of three eggs. Cook the custard over hot water until it thickens, then strain; add six tablespoonfuls of orange-flower water and set aside to cool   When this is ready to freeze add to this custard one dozen bananas that have been pressed through a fine sieve or fruit press and one pint of double cream that has been whipped to a stiff froth. Chill this well in the freezer before adding the strained juice of three lemons   Finish freezing it and leave it two hours to ripen. Serve in tall glasses or sherbet cups with a covering of fresh berries and whipped cream on top of each portion. Charge 15 cents.

FROZEN EGG SHERRY PARFAIT

Rich cream, 2½ gallons, granulated sugar, 3½ pounds; good sherry wine, 1 quart; eggs, 2½ dozen, powdered nutmeg, 1 heaping teaspoonful. Beat the eggs to a froth, add the sugar, cream, nutmeg and wine; stir thoroughly, place in a freezer and run about eight minutes. In serving, place in a sundae dish, top with whipped cream and sprinkle over with a little nutmeg. This formula is especially recommended.

EMPEROR

Grate 2 pineapples, also the rind of 2 oranges and 2 lemons, add the juice of 4 oranges and 6 lemons, half of a nutmeg grated   Next make a boiling syrup of 3 pounds of sugar and 2 quarts of water and pour this over it; let stand until cool, then strain   Put this in the freezer and add 1 pint of strawberry juice and freeze, then mix in 2 well-beaten egg whites. Just before serving add the following liqueurs: half pint of Maraschino, 4 ounces of kirschwasser, 1 pint of champagne cider and a little curacoa.

FROZEN CHOCOLATE PIE

Four ounces of powdered chocolate, four ounces of sugar and four tablespoonfuls of hot water. Melt chocolate and sugar in water and add one quart of cream. Scald. Turn hot mixture over four eggs well beaten with one cup of flour, one pint of milk, one teaspoonful of salt and two cups of sugar. Beat thoroughly and return to fire and cook half an hour in double boiler, stirring frequently. Remove and cool. Add one pint of whipped cream. Freeze. Serve small rounded mound from a patent scoop in a puff paste tart shell. Top with marshmallow dressing.

FROSTED PEACH PUDDING

Scald one quart of milk in double boiler. Into this stir four level tablespoonfuls of corn starch which have been rubbed smooth with a cup of cold milk. Cook half an hour, stirring frequently. In a separate dish beat five eggs, three cups of sugar and a dash of salt. Turn hot mixture upon this and beat briskly. Return to double boiler and cook five minutes. Remove and cool. Add one tablespoonful of almond extract, one quart of peach pulp and one quart of whipped cream. Freeze. Serve in tall stemmed glasses. Charge 15 cents.

ICED BOMBA A LA MONTROSE

Peach water ice, 1 pint; hazelnut ice cream, 1 quart; comfits, 1 ounce; rose pastilles or drops, 1 ounce. Line the mold with the peach water ice to form the coating or shell, and use the hazelnut ice cream in which the comfits and rose drops have been mixed, to fill the center; the bomba when filled and closed, is to be imbedded and remain in ice and salt, until needed.

CAFE BOMBA

This is another style of bomba ice cream the formula of which is as follows: Put a quart of rich cream into a bright copper basin and thoroughly mix with it the yolks of 8 fresh eggs, ½ pint of the strongest black coffee, and a dessertspoonful of pure vanilla extract; place the basin on a slow fire, stirring constantly (do not let it boil). When it begins to thicken, take it immediately from the fire and add 12 ounces of powdered sugar; mix all well together; pour it into the freezing can, cover well with ice and salt; let it freeze for several hours without working it. If it is to be molded, pour it at once into the mold and bury the mold in the ice.

FROZEN ORIENTAL DESSERT

Pour two quarts of scalding cream over a pound of freshly roasted and ground coffee and allow to stand until thoroughly cold. Beat 12 eggs very light and mix 1½ pounds of sugar. Combine with coffee and cream mixture. Place in a container over hot water and stir constantly until the mixture coats the spoon. Strain several times while hot through cheese cloth, add two quarts of rich milk and fold in one quart of whipped cream and two ounces of vanilla. Freeze.

GLACE A LA BIJOU

Blanch ½ pound of sweet almonds and 1 ounce of bitter almonds, finely pound them in a stone mortar with 4 ounces of orange flower water, then add 1 quart of water and strain the mixture through a cloth. Put the strained liquid in a pan and add 14 egg yolks and 1 pint of syrup of 33 degrees on the syrup gauge, heat on a hot water bath until thickened, then remove and beat ten minutes longer. Next beat up a scant pint of double cream, add this with an Italian meringue mixture of 2 egg whites. Fill in bricks and pack in salted ice until frozen firm. Then turn out the bricks of cream and cut them in slices with a knife dipped in hot water, spreading a thin coating of cherry ice over the surface of each slice; now place the slices as finished in a fancy paper case, depositing them in the so-called ice cave, a can with many partitions or shelves imbedded in ice. This dessert may be made by using strawberry, raspberry, peach pulp or any other flavor than almond milk, the proportions being one pint of water and 1 pint of pulp to the above formula, but adding the corresponding flavor as coffee, vanilla, etc.

CAFE ROYAL

Mix well together 1 pint of thick cream, 2 ounces of powdered sugar, 1 teaspoonful of extract of vanilla, and one-third of a cup of very strong coffee. Chill thoroughly, then whip, setting the bowl in a pan of ice water. Take off the frost as it rises and lay on a sieve. When no more frost will rise, turn the drained whipped cream carefully into a mold. Cover tightly, binding the edges with a strip of muslin dipped in melted butter; bury in ice and salt as for freezing; let stand for two or three hours, wipe off the mold, and turn out on a serving dish.

PARISIAN PLOMBIERE

Four ounces of French cherries, 4 ounces candied lemon, orange peel, also citron and currants. Flavor them well with rum. Next prepare the following custard: Two quarts of raw cream, 8 yolks and 12 ounces of sugar; make it after the manner of French ice cream. When frozen, incorporate the fruit and let stand for one hour. Then fill into melon molds, sprinkle with picked and washed currants and pack in ice until wanted. Serve with rum sauce.

ORANGE SOUFFLE

Put 2 cups of granulated sugar and 1 cup of water in a saucepan over the fire. Stir until the sugar is dissolved, then let the mixture boil without stirring until the syrup spins a thread. Add 1 pint of orange

juice and the juice of 1 lemon. Scald 1
cup of cream, add the beaten yolks of 2
eggs, stir them into the scalded cream, take
from the fire, cool, and mix with the syrup
Stand away to cool and when thoroughly
chilled add the remaining cup of cream,
whipped. Flavor with half a teaspoonful
of extract of vanilla   Color delicately with
yellow color paste, then turn into the freezer and freeze as sherbet.

PEACH SOUFFLE

Two quarts cream, 1 quart peach pulp,
1 box gelatin, 1½ pounds sugar, yolks of
12 eggs.

Soak gelatin in cup cold water one hour.
Add pint of boiling peach juice, stir until
gelatin is dissolved. Add sugar and peach
pulp and the thoroughly beaten egg yolks.
Stand container in ice water until mixture
begins to thicken, then add the cream which
has been whipped   Be sure all ingredients
are thoroughly blended   Pack in ice and
salt and set aside to harden. Do not stir
when freezing. The souffle should not be
so very solid.

PINEAPPLE SOUFFLE

One quart crushed pineapple; 3 quarts
warm water, ½ sheet or 1 teaspoonful
gelatin; 3 whole eggs; 1½ ounces prepared
lemon; ½ ounce solution acid phosphate.
Sweeten to taste.

FROZEN FRUITS SOUFFLE

Take 3 ounces of granulated sugar and 6
raw egg yolks and whip slowly, warming
over boiling water while beating. When
an almost solid froth remove and chill the
bowl. Add carefully 1 pint of cream whipped to a solid froth and 1 cupful of mashed
and sweetened fresh fruit—strawberries,
raspberries, or grated pineapple. Turn
quickly into wetted mold, cover tightly,
bind around with a greased cloth or a strip
of muslin and bury in ice and salt for 3
hours.

FROZEN CUSTARD

Frozen custard is composed of cream,
sugar and whole eggs made after the manner of French cream, the necessary flavor
being added to produce the different kinds
of custard. This cream can be changed or
cheapened by using half cream and half
milk, or all milk with a corresponding
number of whole eggs   The eggs are beaten
up well with some milk or cream before being added to the hot batch on the fire;
poured in slowly and kept stirring until it
thickens, but not allowing the batch to boil.
Then remove from the fire and strain, occasionally stirring until it is cold, then freeze
after the manner of other creams.

FROZEN CUSTARD

To a quart of scalding hot milk add 3
eggs and 2 cups of sugar well beaten together; boil 3 or 4 minutes, add a little
salt. When cool, flavor, put into freezer
and freeze.

FROZEN SWISS CUSTARD

Break 3 dozen strictly fresh eggs in a
mixing bowl and beat thoroughly. Then
take 3½ pounds of sugar and 15 ounces of
a standard cocoa, mixing well until the
mixture has taken the form of sweetened
chocolate   Beat this with the eggs previously prepared, until a perfectly smooth
paste is obtained. Add 2 gallons of 20 per
cent cream and one gallon of condensed milk, and cook slowly in a steamer
or "double boiler" until hot (do not boil);
remove from the fire, strain well, and surround with ice or set in a cold place to
cool   When cold, freeze slowly until the
custard is hard enough to stand, and then
put it into a dish.

The author states that by carefully following the instructions given the operator
"will experience no difficulty in making a
light Swiss chocolate having the smoothest
texture that ice cream can assume, and one
that takes well with the trade which appre-
ciates something new as a few days' special   It leaves a very pleasant after-taste
and has been particularly successful with
the 'hard-to-please' Chicago public   The
price is 20 cents a dish, but it can be served
at a very good profit for 15 cents "
This formula is particularly recommended
(Chas. Greenberg)

FRENCH MAPLE CUSTARD

Two quarts of cream or rich milk, he
eggs, 1½ pounds maple sugar. Pound the
maple sugar first, then beat the yolks of
the eggs, add the maple sugar and beat
again, whisk the whites of eggs to a stiff
froth, stir them briskly into the yolks and
sugar and mix with the cream, cook the
whole in a farina boiler over a good fire,
stirring constantly until it does not run off
easily from a knife which has been dipped
into it   Be careful not to let it curdle.
Strain, cover and let cool; then freeze.

Most maple creams are made ⅔ rich
cream and ⅓ rich milk. Pure maple syrup
may be added to advantage in place of the
sugar. Unless great care is exercised in
melting the sugar it will grain in the cream.
Plenty of maple flavor is also used, artificial, of course.

CRANBERRY FRAPPE

Boil two quarts of cranberries in one
quart of water until thoroughly cooked.
Strain through a sieve, add the juice of
two lemons, one quart sugar and one pint
of scalded and cooled milk. Freeze

PINEAPPLE FRAPPE

Place in a large bowl 1 quart of good
cream, 12 ounces powdered sugar, 4 whole
eggs or 8 yolks, white of 2 eggs and 1
grated pineapple; also a spoonful of pulver-

ized gelatin dissolved in a little milk or one ounce of finely powdered gum tragacanth Stir well until the sugar is dissolved, then set the bowl on ice, well salted, and beat with an egg beater When the mixture starts to rise considerably, fill in glasses or silver goblets and place in the ice cave. They are ready to serve in about an hour and a half to two hours. Charge 15 cents.

FROZEN GRAPE PUNCH

Heat 4 pounds of ripe grapes in an earthenware jar that has been placed in a larger vessel of boiling water and simmer until the fruit is tender and the skins burst Then squeeze the grapes and return the juice to a granite saucepan, add to every cupful of the liquid three-quarters of a cupful of sugar, the strained juice of an orange, and half a cupful of lime syrup. Simmer slowly five minutes, and when quite cold, freeze to the consistency of mush. Now remove the cover, stir in half a pint of whipped cream flavored with three drops of mint flavoring, and continue freezing until hard and firm Serve in crystal sherbet cups ornamented with crystallized mint leaves.

MARBLEIZED ICE

Contains five flavors—vanilla, chocolate, strawberry, pistachio and orange, which are combined in the following proportions· Take 1 gallon of vanilla, 1 gallon of strawberry, 5 quarts of chocolate, 3 quarts of pistachio, and 3 pints of orange. Place them in a large mixing can, and then mix with a paddle until the creams have been separated and woven evenly through the mass Then place the cream in molds, packing carefully, and remove to the hardening room where it should be allowed to remain 45 minutes. If you have no hardening room pack in ice and salt as you would any brick cream. (Chas Morgensten.)

NEAPOLITAN ICE CREAM

This cream consists of four different flavors packed in layers into brick molds and cut into slices when served. The first layer being orange or lemon water ice, the next strawberry ice cream, then chocolate ice cream and last, vanilla ice cream. Most ice cream makers use 3 ice creams and do not use ices

SILVER LEAF PARFAIT

Boil two cupfuls of sugar and two cupfuls of water until the mixture spins a thread Pour this on to the beaten whites of six eggs Add one quart of cream whipped until stiff Flavor with lemon and vanilla Put into freezer (adding one cupful of shredded, candied citron when partly frozen)

PROMISE OF YOUTH

Rub one pound of lump sugar upon cleanly washed lemon rinds until well flavored with the lemon oil. Drop this sugar into one quart of fresh buttermilk and allow to dissolve To this add one pint of scalded and cooled cream and one pint of whipped cream When the mixture has begun to freeze add the strained juice of four lemons.

BAKED ICE CREAM

Place a thin sheet of sponge cake on a waxed paper, on a board, and then put on a brick of ice cream and frost it thickly over all the sides, topping off with powdered sugar frosting Set the board in a hot oven long enough to brown the frosting Sometimes a salamander is used for heating, and the frosting is put on with a pastry bag. Serve at once and charge 20 cents per service

MERINGUE GLACE

Make the meringue shells of any suitable size, have them dry and crisp. Fill the halves with any cream desired, placing two together, then put them into the ice cave or into an empty can imbedded in broken ice and salt Before serving, bind together the two halves with a bright colored ribbon.

BACHELOR'S GLACE

This delicate dish is something like a frozen Tom and Jerry, needing neither cream nor milk Make a boiling syrup, 1½ pounds of sugar with 1 pint of water. Next beat up 28 egg yolks with ½ pound powdered sugar and slowly stir in the syrup, put in freezer and freeze. Then add ¾ of a pint of kirschwasser, and lastly 6 beaten egg whites. Fill in paper cases of any size and place in ice cave. Price, 20 cents.

JUNKET

Sweet new milk, 18 quarts; rich cream, 6 quarts, sugar, 10 pounds, extract of vanilla (or other flavor), 6 ounces, junket cream tablets (Hansen's), 6. Dissolve the sugar in the mixed milk and cream, add the flavoring and color if desired If the mixture is cold, gently heat it to lukewarmness (from 80 to 100°F., no more). Dissolve the junket tablets in a cup of cold water and pour the solution into the mixture of lukewarm milk, and stir vigorously for a minute or so to thoroughly incorporate the junket solution. Allow the mixture to rest undisturbed until it forms a jelly-like mass (from 15 to 30 minutes) If the milk is somewhat acid this will not take more than 5 or 10 minutes. Watch the mixture, trying it with a spoon on the top, but do not stir the body of the material When thickened, transfer to a ten-gallon freezer and freeze quickly and without interruption. Do not allow the mixture to stand in a warm place after it has thickened, and do not disturb it until it is to be frozen.

A good formula of its kind but only a very low grade fountain would use it.

FROZEN TONIC

Into one quart of freshly made and strained hot beef tea stir one tablespoonful of gelatin previously dissolved in one-half cup of cold water. Mix one-fourth pound of malted milk to a smooth paste with one pint of water, and add one pint of shredded preserved pineapple. Combine mixtures and freeze

FROSTED EGG NOG

Beat the yolks of 10 eggs until light and add slowly two cups of sugar and the grated rind of one orange and the strained juice of four. Add two quarts of rich milk and the beaten whites of the eggs. Freeze. Price, 15 cents

FROZEN PUDDING A LA NAPOLEON

Blanch 1 pound of filbert kernels; pound them with ¾ pound of sugar and a few drops of water to a soft and fine pulp, put them into a basin, add 1 quart of single cream, stir it well together and pass it through a sieve or tammy into a puree; then freeze in the usual manner While the above is freezing, a pint of cherry ice must be made, as follows Take 2 pounds of ripe cherries, bruise them thoroughly in a mortar so as to break the stones, take them up in a sugar saucepan, add 12 ounces of sugar and boil the whole together over a brisk stove fire for about five minutes; rub this through a hair sieve into a bowl and freeze it, adding a little thin syrup if necessary, mix also in about ¼ pound of French cherries cut in halves Line the mold with this delicate-tinted ice, and garnish the center with the filbert ice cream, cover the mold and immerse in rough ice until dishing-up time. The pudding must be turned out, garnished around with wafer cauffres, filled with some of the filbert ice cream reserved for the purpose and served immediately.

FROZEN PUDDING A LA EDWIN DAVENPORT

Make a custard of 1 pint of cream, 8 yolks of eggs, half a pint of pineapple syrup, 8 ounces of sugar, 6 ounces of chestnut farina or rice flour and 1 ounce of vanilla sugar, 4 ounces of pineapple, cut small, 4 ounces of Sultana raisins, a gill of kirschwasser and a half pint of double cream whipped, mix the custard and liquor, freeze the composition, add the fruit and whipped cream and mold the ice
The molds for frozen puddings are generally made round or oval and smooth, without any design, in order to facilitate remolding

PLUM PUDDING

Plum pudding ice cream is a delicious frozen goody. It is made up of chocolate ice cream, nuts, raisins, currants and candied citron peel, in the proportion of eight ounces each of nut meats, raisins and currants and two ounces of shredded citron peel to a gallon of cream. Soak fruits and nuts in syrup, drain, and add to cream when near finish of freezing This formula makes a good Thanksgiving or Christmas feature.

FROZEN BANANA PUDDING

Peel and cut in slices 18 bananas, then mash them fine, dissolve 1½ pounds of sugar in 2 pints of water by heating, strain, and, when nearly cold, add the bananas and the freshly expressed juice of 2 oranges. Put in a freezer, turning slowly until frozen, then remove the dasher and stir in carefully 2 pints of whipped cream. Serve in glace tumblers

BLACKBERRY FROZEN PUDDING

Into two quarts of scalded milk stir three level tablespoonfuls of cornstarch rubbed smooth with a cup of cold milk. Cook half an hour in double boiler. stirring frequently. Remove from fire, add two cups of sugar and one quart of whipped cream. Put in freezer, and when mixture begins to stiffen add two quarts of crushed, sieved blackberries and one cupful of orange juice Finish freezing and pack for two hours

FROZEN PUDDING A LA MARSHALL

Make the same custard as for frozen plum pudding, using vanilla flavor instead of curacoa. When frozen add the following ingredients, previously prepared· One pound of stewed pineapples, 1 pound of white pears, 4 ounces of sultanas, steeped in 4 ounces of Maraschino, ½ pound of lady cake, cut into cubes and sprinkle with kirschwasser. First mix the fruit into the batch, then lightly beat in the lady cake with 1 pint of double whipped cream Next in order is to line the molds, using in this case raspberry ice; fill the interior with the fruited batch, finish in the usual manner, and serve with Maraschino sauce. To make this sauce follow the formula for rum sauce, using Maraschino for flavoring

FROZEN BANANA PUDDING

Slice four bananas and soak in Maraschino syrup. Take one pint of banana pulp, 12 ounces of sugar, 1 pint of water and the juice of 4 lemons, strain and add the well-beaten whites of two eggs, and freeze. When this is done, line a pudding mold with good vanilla ice cream, place in the bottom a layer of banana ice, then a layer of soaked banana slices and a few lady fingers, then another layer of banana ice, and so on, until the mold is filled. Pack in ice to harden and serve with Maraschino sauce.

FROZEN PUDDING

4 pints milk
1 pound sugar
1 teaspoonful salt
5 eggs
2 tablespoonfuls cornstarch or arrowroot
1 pint heavy cream
1½ pints candied fruits—pineapples, apricots, raisins, figs, etc.
½ cup brandy or ½ cup Maraschino cherry juice

Cut fruit very fine and soak one hour in chosen menstruum. Make a custard of milk, sugar, eggs, salt and cornstarch, or arrowroot. Add cream and freeze. Add fruit near end of freezing. Charge 15 cents.

FROZEN PLUM PUDDING

Cut up a quantity of preserved fruits, such as dates, candied citron, seedless raisins, sultanas and figs; put them in a stewpan with some rum for flavoring and steep for one hour. Then make a custard in the usual manner of 1 quart of cream, 8 yolks and 6 ounces of sugar, add enough burnt sugar color to give it a coffee color, and a good flavoring of curacoa and freeze. When frozen hard enough mix in the fruit and continue freezing a few minutes longer. Next imbed the melon molds in salted ice and line them with orange water ice, then fill in the fruited batch and again cover the top with orange water ice; then lightly secure the cover and pack the molds in ice and let remain for two hours. This pudding is served in slices with a rum sauce This formula is more adapted to the catering business than for fountain use.

FROZEN PUDDING A LA INDIAN

Take a convenient size large melon mold and line it, cover and all, with a fine marron cream, made of 1 quart of cream, 10 yolks of eggs, 10 ounces of sugar, 4 ounces of marron pulp, vanilla and a little caramel sugar for flavoring; line the mold a little over half an inch thick Have previously a fine strawberry ice of 1 quart of water, 1 pound of sugar, 1 basket of crushed strawberries, the juice of 2 lemons, the whites of 2 eggs; freeze good and solid, fill the interior of the melon mold and set in rough, salted ice for two hours to harden At serving time turn it out of its dish and serve with sweet cream sauce, highly flavored with marron syrup. Charge 20 cents

PATRICIAN PUDDING

Make a rich custard by using four quarts of milk, two pounds of sugar, one and one-fourth cups of flour (use an eight-ounce measuring cup), one-fourth pound of butter, and the yolks of 16 eggs. Blend sugar and flour together. Heat milk in water bath. Mix sugar and flour with another pint of cold milk and pour hot milk upon it stirring so as to prevent lumps. Return to fire and add the butter. When smooth and thoroughly cooked pour the mixture upon beaten egg yolks and return to fire. When cooked, cool thoroughly, then fold in the beaten whites of the eggs and one quart of whipped cream. Tint a rich yellow and place in freezer. When mixture begins to stiffen add two pounds finely cut seeded raisins, one pound each of pecan nuts and almond nuts chopped and one pound of chopped cherries. Finish freezing. Charge 15 cents.

FROZEN PUDDING A LA MILANAISE

Line a large-sized ice pudding mold with the following cream: One quart of cream, 12 yolks of eggs, 12 ounces of sugar and a little vanilla; freeze until nearly stiff; add 2 ounces of smooth almond paste and 4 ounces of finely roasted and powdered macaroon crumbs and flavor with brandy. Previously freeze a water ice of 1 quart of water, 1 pound of sugar, 4 ounces sweet milk, and 1 pound of sugar, 4 ounces almonds, pounded; in addition to half a pint of water in order to draw the milk pressed through a napkin; 2 whites of eggs and the juice of 2 lemons; freeze the mixture. color a very delicate green and when frozen add 2 ounces of chopped pistachio almonds, 2 ounces of finely cut angelica, 2 ounces of finely cut green French prunes, 2 ounces of red cherries, cut in halves; mix well and fill the interior of the above lined mold. Allow two hours to harden before turning it out for use and serve with Maraschino cream sauce.

FROZEN SPONGE PUDDING

Break up 10 ounces of ladyfingers, place in a kettle and add 3 pints of boiled cream or milk, 10 egg yolks and 10 ounces of sugar, heat the mixture for about ten minutes without coming to a boil, then remove and let cool. Then strain into the freezer, add 1 quart of raw cream and a flavoring of orange flower water and freeze. Next prepare the molds (melon molds are generally used for this pudding) in the following way: Pack them in crushed ice, well salted, then line the mold with French vanilla ice cream or pistachio ice cream and place in the mold in the order named a layer of lady-fingers, dipped in Maraschino, a layer of the frozen custard, a layer of different kinds of chopped preserved French fruit, then again a layer of custard, and so on until the mold is nearly full, spreading over the top the same cream as that used for the mold lining Then pack in ice and salt for at least one hour; serve with rum sauce. This consists of vanilla cream sufficiently beaten in order to get it smooth, with an addition of whipped double cream and a strong flavoring of rum.

ARABIAN FROZEN PUDDING

One-half cup ground tapioca, two table-spoonfuls gelatin, one and one-half cups of sugar, one pint of milk, one quart of cream, one tablespoonful vanilla, and one tablespoonful ginger extract

Cook tapioca in boiling water until perfectly transparent and it has absorbed all the water with which it was covered Add a pint of cream and the sugar to this and scald. Soak the gelatin in part of the cold milk and add to hot mixture. Cool. Add rest of milk, vanilla, ginger, dates. Fold in rest of cream whipped. Serve with a garnish of currant jelly.

ICES

LEMON

Four quarts of water, 10 lemons, 4½ pounds of sugar. Grate half the lemons, squeeze out, and put rind, juice, half the water and sugar into a pan, set it on the fire and stir until the sugar is dissolved and it becomes quite warm. Then remove and add the remaining 2 quarts of water and strain into the freezer. If it is not tart enough, add a solution of citric acid to suit the taste; then freeze in the usual manner. Some makers add a few egg whites before freezing or when half frozen; this is not recommended, as it makes the ice too light, and also to become rough after standing any length of time.

LEMON GRANITO

Make a rich lemonade, using plenty of sugar Put into a freezer, imbedded in broken ice and salt; twirl the freezer first to the right and then to the left, and as the syrupy liquid freezes on to the sides or the cylinder of the freezer detach it by scraping it down into the center with a spatula, keeping in mind that the mixture must be only half frozen so as to resemble snow-like water, and just sufficiently liquid to admit of being poured into glasses. The caterer will find this a pleasant addition to the entertainment programme of a woman's afternoon whist or euchre club.

ORANGE

Take the juice of 8 oranges; sugar 2½ pounds; fruit acid, 2 ounces; gelatin, 2 ounces; adding enough water to make the whole measure 6 quarts Freeze.

RASPBERRY

One pint raspberry wine (unfermented), 1½ pints sugar syrup, 12 pounds to the gallon; 1½ pints water; mix and freeze in the usual manner. The fountain man may deem it advisable to use the fresh fruit instead of the wine in the above formula.

RASPBERRY

This is made in the same manner as strawberry, using raspberry juice; it should be brighter in color.

RASPBERRY

Press juice and fruit through a fine sieve to make three quarts. Add 7 to 9 pints water to the 3 quarts of juice, etc. Add the juice of three lemons and two pounds of pulverized sugar together with one ounce of raspberry extract. More sugar may be added per taste. Freeze.

RED CURRANT AND RASPBERRY

One quart of water, 6 ounces of red currant juice, 4 ounces of raspberry juice, 1 small lemon, 1 pound of sugar. Make a syrup of the sugar and water, adding the juice of the lemon; when nearly cold add the fruit juices, previously mixed When cold, strain and freeze. Red currants are the best kind to use with raspberries, but black currants and raspberries will blend fairly well. If black currants are used the ice will be a little darker in color. If an all black currant ice is desired use 10 ounces of the juice and omit the raspberry. A little pink color may be added to the red currant ice.

STRAWBERRY

Strawberry juice, 1 pint; simple syrup, 1½ pints; water, 1½ pints, lemon juice, 1 tablespoonful; black raspberry juice, 2 tablespoonfuls; orange flower water, ½ teaspoonful. Mix and freeze.

STRAWBERRY

Press enough ripe strawberries through a fine sieve, leaving the pits behind, to make 1 pint of juice. To the juice add 3 pints of water, 2 pounds of sugar and the juice of 2 lemons (see that the sugar is fully dissolved), then strain through a fine sieve or cloth and freeze.

STRAWBERRY

Four quarts of ripe strawberries sweetened with four pounds of sugar; mash thoroughly. Mix with this four quarts of water and the strained juice of six lemons. Freeze and serve in tall sherbet glasses. This is a good formula for everyday fountain use

FROZEN STRAWBERRIES

Crush two boxes of berries and sweeten. Allow to stand over night, for if the berries do not absorb the syrup they will be hard. Make a syrup of five quarts of water and 10 pounds of sugar. Add fruit and the strained juice of 10 lemons. Color red and freeze.

PINEAPPLE

One quart of pineapple juice or grated pineapple, 1 quart of water, 12 whole eggs or 16 yolks, 1 pound 10 ounces of sugar. Beat eggs and sugar to a cream. Cook all of the ingredients in a farina boiler to a soft custard, strain and beat till cold.

Freeze like water ice, working the mixture vigorously in order to have the product as light and snowy as possible. It may be served in glasses or filled in molds and kept frozen in the ice cave until wanted. Serve with sweetened cream, flavored with pineapple.

PINEAPPLE PHOSPHATE

Pineapple juice, 1 pint; water, 1½ pints, plain syrup, 1½ pints; lemon juice, ½ lemon; solution citric acid, ½ ounce. Mix and freeze

POMEGRANATE

Two dozen blood oranges; water, 4 quarts; simple syrup, 4 quarts. Peel the oranges and remove the seeds before pressing out the juice. This is a fine confection, but the scarcity of blood oranges at certain seasons makes its manufacture difficult as a regular thing Freeze as an ice. The "pomegranate" makes an excellent springtime special.

PEACH

Slice 10 ripe peaches, but do not peel them; boil till soft in one-half pint of water, then rub through a fine hair sieve Mix the pulp with one pint of simple syrup, the strained juice of a lemon, and three or four drops of oil of almonds Color if desired with a little carmine or cochineal. Put the preparation in a freezer and turn until frozen, then fill a mold with it, put on the lid and pack in ice. When ready to serve turn out on a fancy dish.

PEACH BLUSH

Mash up 4 quarts of peaches and 16 oranges, extracting all the juice and straining. Flavor with a little citric acid and the bitter almond extract. Add 3 quarts of simple syrup, color a delicate pink, and freeze. This formula is recommended. (Wm. A. Dennis.)

PEACH FROST

Take 2 quarts peaches, peeled and sliced, sprinkle with 1 pound of sugar and let stand 2 hours. Mash fine; add 1 cup of cold water, and freeze the same as ice cream.

CRANBERRY

One quart cranberries cooked with one quart water, pound of sugar, and a pinch of soda. Put through a colander. Freeze Serve with meats. An additional quart of water may prove advantageous in this formula.

FROZEN CRANBERRIES

2   quarts cranberries
1   quart water
2   pounds sugar
½ pint lemon juice

Stew cranberries in water. Mash and force through sieve. Add rest of ingredients. Freeze.

FROZEN PEACHES

One basket ripe, sound peaches, skinned, the pits taken out and quartered and a syrup made of 5 quarts of water and 10 pounds of sugar, put the peaches into the boiling syrup and allow to stand over night to become soft and absorb some of the syrup, otherwise the peaches will be very hard when frozen. Strain and freeze the juice, when hard enough, lightly work in the peaches, being careful not to mash them, repack the can and let stand for an hour

FROSTED PEACHES

Two quarts of chopped peach, one quart of water, two and one-half pounds sugar, the juice of two lemons, and a pint of canned cherries, juice and all. Boil sugar and water, add chopped cherries and peaches. Bring to boiling point again. Combine with rest of ingredients and freeze. Garnish with sugared almonds.

CHERRY

To 3 quarts of base syrup add 2 pints of cherry juice, made by boiling the fresh fruit with sugar and water, and freeze. It will usually be found advisable in this case to add a little red coloring.

CHERRY

Dissolve 3 pounds of sugar in 1 quart cherry ice and add juice of a couple of lemons to flavor The mixture will take more water, probably half a gallon or a little less, according to the degree of strength required. Mix, strain and freeze in the usual way.

CHERRY CONSERVE

Two quarts cherry conserve, one quart water, one pint grape juice. Freeze.

GRAPE

Grape juice, one pint; juice of two lemons; juice of 2 oranges; water, 1 quart; granulated sugar, 1 pound. If the water and sugar are brought to a boil and then allowed to cool, the water ice will be found to have a smoother consistency when frozen. If boiling is resorted to an additional pint of water may be necessary. Freeze slowly.

GRAPE FRUIT ICE

The juice of 18 grape fruit is mixed with 3 pounds of sugar and 2 quarts of water, and 2 ounces of soaked gelatin added just before the freezing. It should be observed that grape fruit vary considerably in flavor

GRAPE

Mix three quarts of grape juice with 1 quart of orange juice and 2 pounds of sugar. Freeze, and, when partly frozen, the whites of two eggs may be beaten in the mix, though this is not necessary.

APRICOT

To 4 quarts of simple syrup add the

juice of 6 quarts of good apricots and of 6 lemons, and water to make 12 quarts. This can either be made clear by straining or the apricot pulp left in. This ice has a delicious flavor.

APRICOT

Three quarts ripe apricots, 3 quarts of water, 8 pounds of icing sugar, 1 ounce of citric acid solution. Press the apricots through a colander, and add the other ingredients.

BANANA

Make a syrup by boiling and cooling three quarts of water and three pounds of sugar for fifteen minutes. Strain the juice of six lemons and four oranges. Press pulp of eight bananas through a sieve and thoroughly incorporate. Freeze. Let stand for two hours to ripen.

FROZEN PUNCH

This combination may be made directly from the fruit or from bottled fruit juices of any reputable manufacturer. If the former method be followed, first mash through a sieve the fruit, one part of raspberry to three of currants, until a pint of juice is obtained. Mix this with one pound of sugar, adding the juice of half a lemon, or syrup, a sufficient quantity. Dissolve by aid of heat. If a deep tint is desired use red coloring. Strain through the sieve into a bowl, add 1 quart of water and pour into the freezer and freeze. To color after freezing, mix the coloring with a little of the composition and work in smoothly.

PUNCH FRAPPE

1	quart water
1½	pounds sugar
1	pint currant jelly
1	pint orange juice
½	pint lemon juice
4	bottles ginger ale
1	pint Maraschino cherry juice

Freeze, serve in tall, stemmed glasses. It may be desirable to add more sugar to this formula.

FRUIT

Take a half gallon of crushed cherries, 1 pint of crushed pineapple, 1 pint of crushed strawberries, 1 can of sliced pineapple (chopped), ½ dozen bananas, sliced, 1 pound of chopped nuts, ½ bottle of Maraschino cherries (sliced), 1 gallon of syrup, then add an ounce of solution of citric acid, and water enough to make 3 gallons. Freeze, pack and let stand. Then serve with a little whipped cream and a cherry on top.

In this formula it is well to soak the fruit in the syrup over night. Also, do not freeze too hard at first.

FROZEN FRUITS

Take a quantity of ripe strawberries, hull and pass them through cold water in order to wash or rinse out all sand or grit. Now squeeze and press them to a pulp through a coarse hair sieve into a porcelain or earthenware bowl or crock, adding to each quart of the pulp so obtained a half pound of fine sifted pulverized sugar, half a pint of water and the juice of an orange. Mix and freeze as directed for ice cream, and immediately transfer the frozen fruits to a porcelain-lined can or stoneware or earthenware jar well set in ice and salt. Fruits other than strawberries may be similarly prepared, but it is essential that the frozen mixture be kept frozen until served, if the fruits are to be well preserved.

FROZEN FRUITS

Mix ½ gallon of crushed cherries, 1 pint of crushed strawberries, 1 shredded pineapple, 6 sliced bananas, 3 finely sliced oranges, one-half bottle of Maraschino cherries, 1 gallon of base syrup, and water to make three gallons. The mixture should be packed in a freezer and frozen without stirring. It should be served topped with whipped cream and a cherry. This is a big winner at any fountain

COMMUNE BONUM

Boil together, for twenty minutes, one pint of sugar, one quart of water and one pint of chopped pineapple. Add to this mixture 4 ounces of lemon juice and 8 ounces of orange juice. When cold strain and freeze.

LINCOLN FRAPPE

4	cups water
2	cups sugar
¼	cup lemon juice
2	cups grape juice
1	cup orange juice
1	cup pineapple juice

Increase the amount of sugar if not considered sweet enough

TUTTI FRUTTI

Boil four cups of sugar with two quarts of water 20 minutes. Add one cup of strained lemon juice and a cup each of diced grape fruit, orange and pineapple pulp, a cup of chopped raisins and a cup of chopped walnut meats. Freeze.

KIRCHE PUNCH

For this make a regular orange water ice, adding 4 ounces of kirschwasser to every quart of ice and meringue in the same proportion as for Maraschino punch.

JAPANESE

4	cups water
2	cups sugar
2	cups strained orange juice
1	pint chopped cherries
¼	cup lemon juice

Grated rind of two oranges
Grated rind of two lemons
Flavor with pistachio and Maraschino

When partly frozen add one pint of chopped cherries. More sugar may be required in this formula—add per taste.

ICELAND ICE

Peach juice (fresh) .... 3 quarts
Orange juice .... 1 quart
Sugar .... 4 pounds
Simple syrup .... 1 quart
Water .... 1 quart
Strain through fine sieve and freeze.

SUWANEE WATERMELON

Express the juice from the red pulp of a watermelon through a fine hair sieve, and for every quart of juice add 4 ounces of sugar, the juice of one orange and four ounces of grape juice. Mix well and freeze in the same manner as for other ices. If desired, the color may be heightened by the addition of cochineal solution.

ZEPHYR

Place one quart of syrup of 18° strength into a saucepan, add the yellow rind of one citron and one orange, also half of a vanilla bean. Set on the fire and let come to the boiling point, then pour out into an earthen bowl and cover well for two hours. Strain through a fine sieve, add the juice of two lemons and freeze.

WHITE HOUSE

One pound of sugar dissolved in two quarts boiling water. Add the strained juice of six lemons, an ounce of extract of spearmint, and a little pure food green coloring to tint.

EDEN

1½ pounds sugar
1 quart water
2 quarts sweet cider
1 quart orange juice
½ pint lemon juice

Boil sugar and water half an hour. Cool, add fruit juices and freeze.

FROZEN COFFEE

Six ounces Mocha coffee, 10 ounces Java coffee, 3½ pounds sugar, sufficient water. Grind and mix the coffee, pack in a glass percolator, cover tightly, and pour on boiling water in 8-ounce quantities until 40 ounces of liquid have been obtained. Serve 1 ounce to sherbet glassful of shaved ice, with a spoon. In this formula it might be well to start with 2 quarts boiling water. Charge 5 cents for 8-ounce glass.

FROZEN COFFEE

Three quarts water, 1½ pounds sugar, ¾ pound fresh roasted coffee, 1 white of egg. Grind the coffee quite fine and put it into a gallon jar, first scalding the jar with boiling water.
Put 3 quarts of fresh water into a kettle, on a quick fire; at the first boil pour it on the coffee, stir well, cover and set in a warm place to draw. Stir occasionally for five minutes, let stand till well settled, pour off the clear coffee through fine muslin, add water to make 3 quarts, dissolve sugar in it, and cool. Put in the freezer, add the egg, and freeze to a soft mush, like wet snow. It is served in tall goblets. This is a very popular ice in France, and is called "Cafe frappe a la glace"; also "Cafe mousseux."

Frozen tea and many wines and cordials are prepared likewise.

TEA FRAPPE

Upon 6 teaspoonfuls of mixed tea pour 2 quarts of freshly boiling water; allow to stand for 10 minutes; strain off and sweeten to taste. When cold freeze.

PISTACHE

Simple syrup, 3½ pints; water, 3½ pints; cherry juice, 2 ounces; lemon juice, 2 ounces, orange flower water, ½ ounce; essence of bitter almonds, ½ dram. Color green. Mix and freeze.

MAPLE LEAF

Use either fresh currants and raspberries to obtain a quart of juice and pulp equal parts or use a tumbler of jam made of these fruits dissolved in three cups of boiling water and strained. Boil one quart of maple syrup 10 minutes. Combine sugar and fruit juice and add the juice of two lemons and two oranges and two quarts of water. Freeze.

MALTED MILK

Dissolve four tablespoonfuls of powdered gelatin in one cup of cold water. Add one cup of boiling water and use this liquid to stir four ounces of malted milk to a smooth paste. To this add one quart of pineapple and orange juice, strain and freeze.

SHERBETS

HINTS FOR SHERBET MAKING

Do not as a rule add your flavorings until the syrup has thoroughly cooled.

Two ounces of gelatin to 10 gallons of "batch" will prevent separation and will also insure the ices from being too hard.

When boiling syrup, particularly if it is to be heavy, a scant teaspoonful of cream of tartar to 5 pounds of sugar will prevent crystalization.

LEMON NUT

One quart water, one pint sugar and grated rinds of four lemons boiled 10 minutes and cooled. Add the juice of six lemons, half a cup of shredded candied lemon peel, half a cup chopped nut meats and the stiffly beaten whites of eight eggs. Freeze. Serve with a sprinkling of chopped nuts.

LEMON JELLY

Boil two quarts of water with four cups

of sugar for 15 minutes. Dissolve one ounce of granulated gelatin by soaking in a little cold water and adding a cup of boiling water. Combine hot syrup, gelatin and two and a half cups of strained lemon juice. Put in freezer, and when it begins to stiffen add beaten whites of four eggs. Finish freezing. Serve in sherbet cups decorated with ripe strawberries or cherries or strips of candied lemon peel.

PINEAPPLE

Two pineapples grated, 2 quarts of water, 2 pounds of sugar, beaten whites of 2 eggs. Freeze same as ice cream.

PINEAPPLE

Peel and crush 2 pineapples; then make a boiling syrup of 2½ pounds sugar and 2 quarts of water and pour it over the pineapples. Let stand until nearly cold, then add the juice of 5 lemons; strain, press the liquid from the pineapples, pour into freezer, add the whites of 4 eggs and freeze. Then work in a good ½ pint of Maraschino.

REAL PINEAPPLE SNOW

Take 1 ounce of granulated gelatin and dissolve it in a quart of boilng water. Put 3 quarts of simple syrup and 2 quarts of water into a large vessel and stir in the gelatin solution, the juice of six lemons, the beaten whites of 2 eggs, and 1 pint of rich cream. Put the mixture in a freezer and freeze until almost hard, then add 1 pint of crushed pineapple and 1 pint of pineapple stock and freeze until quite hard. This quantity makes 3 gallons. Serve in a sherbet glass with a spoon and top off with a Maraschino cherry. This formula is especially recommended. (P. W. McCabe.)

PINEAPPLE FROST

Three quarts of water and four pounds of sugar made into a thin syrup. Shred four ripe pineapples; add to hot syrup, also the strained juice of six lemons and three oranges. Set aside until cool. Prepare two ounces of granulated gelatin by soaking it in cold water and dissolving with one quart of boiling water. Mix with the previous mixture. When the whole is cool put into the freezer and freeze as usual.

PINEAPPLE

One tablespoonful gelatin soaked in 1 cup cold water 15 minutes. Dissolve with 1 cup of boiling water. Take ½ can grated pineapple and 1½ cups sugar, juice of 1 lemon. Add strained gelatin, put in freezer and pack with ice and salt and freeze.

CHERRY

Spring or distilled water, 5 gallons; Maraschino cherries (cherries cut in half), ½ gallon; Morello cherry syrup, 1 pint; granulated sugar, 7 pounds; whites of 2 eggs. Soak cherries in syrup. Mix all together; stir and freeze. Top off with 1 cherry when served. Use a little red color.

CHERRY SIREN

Dissolve two pounds of sugar in three quarts of cherry juice. Freeze until it begins to stiffen. Stir in the stiffly beaten whites of four eggs sweetened with six ounces of powdered sugar. Freeze and pack.

CURRANT

Three quarts water, 1 pint currant juice; 2 pounds of sugar; white of 1 egg. Cook the sugar and water to a clear syrup; skim and cool it, add the white of egg and the fruit juice and freeze. A small portion of raspberry juice much improves the flavor.

GRAPE

Two pounds of sugar, 2 lemons, 1 orange, 2 quarts of red Tokay grapes, 1 quart of water. Put grapes, sugar and water in a kettle and place over a slow fire; under constant stirring bring the mixture to a boil, then pass it through a sieve, leaving skin and pits behind. Squeeze the lemons and orange and add the juice. When cold, freeze in the usual manner. If this is to be served in glasses, beat up 1 egg whites quite stiff and mix it into the batch until smooth and foamy. A few drops of red color may be added, and 2 or 3 whole grapes placed on each portion.

GRAPE JUICE

Sweeten 1 quart grape juice to taste, add ½ pound of sugar to the juice of 6 oranges, let stand till sugar dissolves, mix together and freeze slowly. Beat the white of an egg, adding a tablespoonful powdered sugar and stir into the sherbet, repack and set aside for 2 hours. Serve in sherbet cups.

GRAPE

For eight persons mix one pint of grape juice, the juice of one lemon, and one heaping teaspoonful of gelatin dissolved in boiling water. Freeze quickly, and add the beaten white of one egg just before it is frozen. (U. S. Dept. of Agric.)

GRAPE AMBROSIA

Use whites of 18 eggs, beat to a froth and add sugar, 5 pounds; mix well and add sweet milk, 1 gallon; water, 2 gallons; Welch's grape juice, 2 quarts; grated pineapple, 2 cans; fruit acid, 2 ounces; essence of lemon, ¼ ounce. Mix all well in a freezer. Let stand, after being well packed, for an hour or so to become harder. Serve same as ice cream.

NECTAR SHERBET

Strawberry syrup	2 quarts
Raspberry syrup	2 quarts
Vanilla syrup	1 quart
Lemons (juice of)	18
Water	4 quarts
Whites of eggs	3

Strain and freeze. This sherbet might possibly be improved by eliminating either the strawberry or the raspberry syrup.

MINT

Grate the rind of six lemons and six oranges. Add two pounds of sugar and a dozen stalks of mint. Dissolve in two quarts of cold water. Bring to the boiling point and boil for 10 minutes. Tint a dark green with pure food color, remembering that it will be much lighter when frozen. Strain. Add one teaspoonful of essence of peppermint. Freeze.

MINT

Combine two cups of sugar, one cup of strained lemon juice and one tablespoonful of mint extract to two quarts of boiling water. Cool, tint with a leaf of green certified pure food color and freeze. Serve in tall glasses with a sprig of mint in each glass.

CREME DE MENTHE

1 pint hot water
1 quart cold water
2 ounces creme de menthe cordial
8 lemons
¼ pound loaf sugar
¾ pounds sugar

Wash and wipe lemons and rub cut loaf sugar lumps over them until they have absorbed oil. Pour strained lemon juice over granulated sugar and add hot water. Lastly add cold water and cordial. Charge 15 cents.

TUTTI FRUTTI

Take 1 pint of simple syrup, 1 pint of water, 4 ounces of kirschwasser, a teaspoonful of pure vanilla extract, the juice of 2 lemons and a pint of mixed fruit, cut into small pieces; mix the syrup, water, kirschwasser, vanilla and lemon juice, and freeze the mixture; then mix into it a meringue mass, made of the whites of 2 eggs and 2 ounces of powdered sugar, freeze again and then add the fruit; mix lightly but thoroughly well in; the ice may then be molded and buried in ice and salt till needed for use.

FRUITED

Mash one dozen bananas and combine with the strained juice of one dozen oranges and one dozen lemons, six pounds of sugar, the stiffly beaten whites of a dozen eggs, three quarts of water. Freeze as usual.

LAND OF PROMISE

Mix one pint grape juice, one pint of orange juice, one-half cup of lemon juice and one quart of water, sweeten rather heavily. Freeze until this begins to thicken, then add one quart of whipped cream previously mixed with one cup of strained honey. Freeze and pack.

FOUR-IN-HAND

Dissolve by heat three pounds of sugar in three pints of water. Into this slice five bananas, half a dozen oranges, two lemons and add a shredded pineapple. When the mixture begins to stiffen add the beaten whites of four eggs.

ARCTIC

Sweeten one quart of grape juice to taste, add the juice of 6 oranges and ½ pound of sugar, and stir until the sugar dissolves; add 4 ounces of fresh lemon syrup, mix all well together, and freeze slowly. Beat the white of an egg with a tablespoonful of sugar, and stir into the sherbet, then repack and set aside for two hours. Serve in sherbet cups.

FRIENDSHIP

Peel and rub through a sieve equal parts of peaches, plums and apricots to make six cups or three pints. Boil three pints of water and three pounds of sugar for 10 minutes and allow to cool. Add to fruit pulp and fold in stiffly beaten whites of one dozen eggs. Flavor with peach extract and add eight ounces of Maraschino syrup. Freeze.

CAFE FRAPPE

Water, 3 quarts; coffee extract, 6 ounces; sugar, 1½ pounds; whites of 3 eggs, beaten thoroughly; caramel to color. Mix and freeze to a mushy snow. Serve in glasses.

THE LUNCHEONETTE

"Luncheonette" means a light lunch, offered at any hour of the day or evening. The luncheonette was never intended to take the place of the hotel or restaurant, but to be a pleasing adjunct to the well-established and popular soda fountain. Eating and drinking have always gone together since the world began and each naturally suggests the other. The first soda fountains offered phosphates, plain sodas, and plain cream sodas. Later an ingenious mind combined ice cream and soda and so began the great movement toward food drinks and soda fountain combinations of a more solid 'character. The serving of wafers or small cakes with certain "Specials" was the next step.

In localities where students, transients, and shoppers were numerous the idea of a toothsome sandwich to accompany a glass of soda proved profitable. Shrewd dispensers recognized this as a straw which pointed toward a new order of things. The soda fountain was well-established and its patronage a matter of course, yet there were times when people were eager for something more substantial than the straight soda fountain menu gave. Why not offer a wider variety of easily-served, simple but excellent foods, and so increase the appeal by means of a luncheonette service, auxiliary to the soda fountain itself? The development had been so gradual that several men tried out the same idea simultaneously and found it good. So the luncheonette was born.

From time to time ambitious individuals have essayed to enlarge the luncheonette, till it over-shadowed the soda fountain itself and took on regular eating house features. Where a locality warrants a regular eating house, it should be run as such, but it ceases to be a luncheonette. An automobile and a railroad train are both good. Each has a province of its own, that the other cannot fill with commercial success. Supplies, equipment, and service are entirely different, and a different class of trade is catered to. The luncheonette, as considered in these pages, is dealt with wholly from the soda fountain standpoint.

A well-managed luncheonette should yield splendid profits, but it should not be allowed to outgrow certain limits. There are hours in the day when soda fountain business is not at its height, when business is slower than at other times. These are the hours when people are not satisfied with food beverages or ice cream combinations. They feel the need of something that will stand by them longer. Perhaps time does not permit or inclination warrant the purchase of an elaborate meal. A well-made bowl of soup, an individual service of chicken pie, a sandwich, and a strawberry dessert, or even less, will satisfy. Or, an after-theatre party on a winter night, will find real satisfaction in hot chocolate, dainty sandwiches, and a suitable sweetmeat. Thus, the sale of the hot chocolate at ten cents has been augmented to a sale of from twenty-five to fifty cents. Each department, soda fountain and luncheonette, has pulled for the other.

If the luncheonette is allowed to grow to such proportions that mingled food odors permeate the air, the clatter of dishes and silver resounds, and the hurrying of many waiters is evident, the business will be in cramped quarters. It will be like a big tree trying to thrive in a wooden tub of earth. Buying, preparation, and service will all be handicapped. Departmental proportions should be observed or business symmetry will be disturbed. Remember, the luncheonette is the ally and junior partner of the soda fountain itself.

In buying for the two departments, the advantage is great, for the same supplies are used in many instances. Wholesale prices on larger quantities effect a saving through special discounts, and the same or little additional space takes care of both. The time of employees is advantageously used on dull days and at dull times in keeping the entire service up to the mark. ·The additional equipment for the average luncheonette is not very extensive. The foods served may be prepared on the spot or not, as circumstances warrant. Sometimes the proprietor is able to reserve a space in the basement, on the floor above, or on the same floor for the preparation of the foods. Sometimes he contracts with some one outside to furnish what he requires, furnishing the formulas and specifying the amounts to be delivered each day. Or, he may prefer to have them prepared in his own kitchen at home. The space at his disposal will determine this.

Menus should vary with the season—stimulating, heat-forming foods in winter; cooling, tart ones in summer; appetite-jogging ones in spring; and savory, satisfying ones in autumn. It is better to serve a modest, well-balanced menu of excellently prepared articles, than to offer a long list of indifferent quality.

To make the luncheonette popular, the food offered must be genuinely good; the prices must be right; the attendants immaculate in appearance and courteous in manner; the service unimpeachable; and the menus well balanced. To make the luncheonette profitable, supplies must be bought to the best advantage; everything must be properly stored and carefully conserved; there must be no waste; sanitary conditions must be observed from start to finish; and the public constantly informed as to what you have to offer and why it is worthy of their attention. *You* may know, but that is not enough. They must be informed and convinced also. Naturally, they are absorbed in their own affairs. They are not mind readers. Advertise. It will pay.

SOUPS AND BOUILLONS

The dividing line is very slight btween the hot beef tea, the tomato, and the clam bouillon of the hot soda fountain and the soup and bouillons of the luncheonette. The chowder is a step farther away from the soda menu.

A bouillon, in soda fountain parlance, is a broth or extract, and is served in a regular hot soda mug, with a spoon, saltines, or thin crackers, or else in a special bouillon cup which is low and squat in shape with two handles, with a saucer to match. The luncheonette as is considered desirable will use this or a small decorative bowl on a plate to match.

Soups form such an important part of our food and are so deservedly popular, that every dispenser should know how to prepare them. Soups are divided as follows:

(1) The bouillon, made from lean meat, delicately seasoned, and clear in color.

(2) Brown stock soup, made from approximately two thirds lean meat and the

remainder bone and fat. One third of the meat is cut in small pieces and browned in the marrow fat.

(3) A white stock soup is made from chicken, veal, lamb, or combinations of these.

(4) Consomme' is made of two or more kinds of light or dark meat. It is highly seasoned, strained, and served clear.

These constitute the meat stock soups and are varied according to the meat, the seasoning, and the combinations used. In addition to these, we have soups made without stock.

(1) A cream soup is made of vegetables, or fish, with milk. It is smooth, is always highly seasoned and slightly thickened.

(2) A bisque is made of fish, or vegetables, or game. It also is highly seasoned, often contains small squares of the meat or fish for which it is named, and is slightly thickened.

(3) Puree's are usually made from vegetables. These are forced through a sieve, bound together with a little thickening, and highly seasoned. Milk or white stock may be used as part of the body.

All soups and bouillons should be served very hot in a hot dish. Cold soup is not appetizing. The stock kettle will receive all fragments of wholesome meat, bone, and vegetables, thus saving what would otherwise be wasted.

Soups in the making should never boil hard. Should they boil hard, especially in the beginning, the extract will be muddy and difficult, if not impossible, to clear. First of all, wipe the meat to be used with a clean cloth wrung out of clear, cold water. Cut in small pieces and separate the meat with a cleaver or meat saw. Meat, bone, and fat are all necessary for the proper preparation of a good stock. The bone, cartilage, tendons, and ligaments provide the gelatine which makes a soup or broth rich in consistency and nourishing, but this gelatinous material is tasteless. Part of the fat is absorbed, part rises to the top, and this latter is always removed after the stock is cooled.

If a rich, brown stock and a full taste is required, remove the marrow from the bones or take some butter, heat very hot, and brown one third of the cubes of meat all over in this fat. When done, turn them into the soup kettle, rinsing out the frying pan with some of the soup liquor so as to lose none of the coloring matter.

Soup made of cold, cooked meat will be tasteless unless some raw meat is added. In selecting meat, be sure it is firm and sweet. Shin bone, middle of the round of beef, lean beef from the round, the fore quarter of lamb, ox tail, knuckle of veal, and fowl all make good soup material. Meat should be covered with cold water and heated gradually in order to dissolve all the nutritive and flavoring elements.

To make the ordinary rich soup stock, allow one fourth pound of bone, three fourths of a pound of meat, and one pint of cold water. Allow to stand for an hour or more, that the rich juices may be drawn from the meat. After this the browned portion of the meat may be added. Bring slowly to the boiling point, then draw back, and simmer briskly for six or seven hours. The scum which rises to the top contains the coagulated meat juices. Unless a clear soup is desired, it should not be removed, as this scum is very nutritious and much of it will pass through the strainer.

To clear a soup easily, allow it to cool, remove the film of fat from the top, and then allow one egg white and shell to each quart, or quart and a pint of strained stock. Beat the egg white lightly, break the shell in pieces, and add to the stock. Put the kettle back on the hot part of the fire and stir constantly until it boils. Allow it to boil for two minutes and then let it simmer on the back of the stove for twenty minutes. Finally strain through two thicknesses of cheese cloth placed for convenience in the inside of the strainer. The stock will be a smooth, rich brown in color, without flecks of either meat or vegetables.

During the last hour of cooking vegetables and other seasoning matter for which the recipe calls, may be added. After the stock has been made, that is, after it has received sufficient cooking, it must be strained and then cooled so that the fat will harden. "Raw" soup is greasy because the fat has not been removed. The cake of fat which forms on top may be removed by running a knife around the edge, or it may be left until the stock is to be used, as it keeps out the air. Stock may be kept a week in summer and several weeks in winter in a cool place. The liquid beneath the cake of fat, will be found to be a rich jelly which can be melted and diluted to the proper consistency. Clear soup is not as nutritious as a vegetable soup or one containing thickening, but is rather more attractive in appearance.

Some of the accessories which go with soups are, croutons, crackers, browned crackers, cracker crisps, soup biscuits, or soup sticks. Soup biscuits or soup sticks may be purchased and heated to renew crispness. Croutons are little squares or strips of bread which are placed in a frying basket and plunged into hot fat just long enough to brown, but not long enough to become hard. After this they are drained and sprinkled with salt. They may be reheated in the oven just before serving. Sometimes these squares are dipped in melted butter and browned in the oven just before serving. These are delicious tidbits to serve with a bean or pea soup. Browned crackers are ordinary crackers buttered, sprinkled with salt, cayenne or paprika, and browned in the oven. Crisps may be either crackers, or circles, or strips of bread browned in a slow oven.

Proper utensils are a necessity in soup making. There should be a good, hard-wood meat board, sharp knives, a saw, paring knives, several puree strainers of different sized mesh, and a generous soup kettle with a tightly fitting lid. A meat cleaver and scales are also useful.

The following are characteristic recipes of the class already named:

BEEF BOUILLON

8	pounds lean beef	1 teaspoonful peppercorns
3	pounds marrow-bone	¾ cup sliced carrot
5	quarts cold water	¾ cup diced turnip
1½	tablespoonfuls salt	¾ cup diced celery

½ cup sliced onion

Trim the meat after it has been carefully wiped, and then cut into dice. Brown one third of these dice in marrow fat, and soak the remainder of the dice in the water for thirty minutes. Add the brown meat, fat, and bones to the meat and water in the kettle, carefully rinsing the frying pan with some of the water as suggested above. Bring to a boil, and then allow the soup to simmer on the back of the stove for five hours. Now add the seasoning and the vegetables, and cook for one and one half hours. Strain; cool; remove fat; clear.

CLAM BOUILLON No. 1

Be sure the clams are absolutely fresh; pick them over carefully, and throw away all which are not plainly alive. Then wash thoroughly in cold water and scrub the shells with a clean brush until they are absolutely clean. Put a peck of clams in a kettle with two quarts of cold water, and steam until the shells open wide. Strain the liquor, allow it to cool, and then clear as usual. The clam meats can be used in any manner desired.

CLAM BOUILLON No. 2

As many people are unable to obtain clams in the shell, the following recipe is given for bulk clams:

Take two quarts of solid clam meat. With a sharp knife cut off the tough black heads, and separate the soft parts from the remainder of the tough portion. Chop both fine but keep separate. To the tough portions—not the black tips—add two quarts of water, a tablespoonful of salt, two stalks of celery cut fine, and a dash of cayenne pepper. Simmer slowly for one hour. Then add the soft parts of the clams, previously chopped, and simmer another hour to extract all the juices. Bring to the boiling point and boil briskly for a few minutes. Then cover and place on the back part of the stove and allow it to stand for a while. Strain through clean cheese cloth doubled. Return the contents of the strainer to the kettle and add two quarts of white stock, two quarts of cold water, and the clam liquor strained previously from the clams. Bring to the boiling point again and then strain. It is now ready to serve.

BROWN STOCK SOUP WITH TOMATO

6 pounds shin of beef	1 turnip
6 quarts of cold water	12 whole cloves
1 tablespoonful salt	3 stalks celery
3 sliced onions	1 carrot
3 sprigs of parsley	1 tablespoonful sweet herbs
10 whole peppercorns	

Trim the meat from the bones and cut into small pieces. Crack the bones. Brown the onions and one third of the meat in the hot marrow fat. Soak the rest of the meat and the bones in the cold water an hour. Add spices and herbs and browned meat and vegetables. Simmer four hours. Add vegetables. Cook two hours longer. Strain, cool, remove the fat.

To each quart of this brown stock, add one quart of tomatoes, two bay leaves, four tablespoonfuls of butter, one fourth cup of flour, one third cup each of chopped onion, carrot, and raw ham. Cook the onion, carrot, and ham in the butter until brown. Add the flour stirred smooth in a cup of cold water. Stir until incorporated. Add the tomatoes, the bay leaves, and a sprig of parsley. Cover closely and cook one hour. Rub through a strainer, add the hot stock, season with salt and pepper to taste.

JULIENNE SOUP

1 quart brown stock	⅓ cup of carrots
1 small minced onion	⅓ cup of turnips
¼ cup green peas	¼ cup string beans

Cut the carrot and turnip in thin strips one inch long. Cook these and the onion in boiling salted water until tender. Add the peas and string beans. Heat thoroughly. Drain, add to the hot soup stock.

VEGETABLE SOUP

7	pounds lean round beef	6	peppercorns
4	pounds marrow-bone	1	tablespoonful salt
4	quarts cold water	½	cup lean, raw chopped ham
2	quarts tomatoes	3	tablespoonfuls butter
1	sprig parsley	1	bay leaf
½	cup chopped turnip	½	cup chopped parsnip
½	cup chopped cabbage	1	cup chopped onion
1	cup chopped carrot	1	cup chopped celery
1	cup chopped potatoes	2	tablespoonfuls sugar
2	tablespoonfuls butter		Pepper to taste

Fry part of the beef, all of the ham, and a tablespoonful of the onion in the heater. Soak the rest of the meat in the water an hour, add the tomato and the herbs. Cook slowly for five hours. Parboil the cabbage, parsnips, potatoes, and onions for five minutes. Drain, fry the carrots slightly in a little of the butter and add all the vegetables to the stock. Simmer very gently until tender. Add the seasoning. Serve without straining. A little sugar as indicated is a great addition to any mixed vegetable soup.

Ox-Tail Soup

2 ox-tails
1 tablespoonful Worcestershire sauce
3 quarts brown stock

1 cup each of carrot, onion, celery, turnip
2 tablespoonfuls of rice

Separate the ox-tails in short lengths. Wash, sprinkle with salt and pepper, and roll in flour. Fry slightly brown in a little of the hot fat. Remove the ox-tails and fry the onion in the same pan. Put the ox-tails and the fried onion into the soup kettle, and cover with two quarts of water. Add one tablespoonful of salt, one tablespoonful of mixed herbs, and two peppercorns. Cook gently four hours. Skim off any fat which may be present. Add the vegetables. Cook until tender. Add the three quarts of brown stock and the Worcestshire sauce. Season and serve hot.

Spaghetti Soup

To two quarts of brown stock (make as above and keep hot over simmering flame), add ½ cup spaghetti, cook until tender in boiling salted water. Season with salt and pepper to taste, as the spaghetti requires additional seasoning. The spaghetti should be cut into short lengths before it is added to the soup stock.

Three-In-One Soup

1 quart can tomatoes
2 quarts brown stock
1 tablespoonful minced onion
1 bay leaf

6 cloves
½ teaspoonful peppercorns
1 teaspoonful extract of celery
1 pint oysters

Mix all the ingredients but the oysters, and boil the mixture for half an hour. In the meantime remove the hard muscle and any stray bits of shell from the oysters. When the soup is done, strain it and then add the oysters and cook again until the beards curl up. Too long cooking makes oysters tough and leathery. Serve this soup with bread sticks.

Alaska Soup

2 quarts brown stock
½ cup rice
1 quart cooked, strained tomato
1 bay leaf
1 small onion sliced

12 peppercorns
½ teaspoonful celery salt
4 tablespoonfuls butter
4 tablespoonfuls flour

Simmer the rice in the stock until tender. While this is cooking, cook the tomato, the onion, and the bay leaf in another container for forty-five minutes. Turn into the stock kettle, and rub through a sieve when done. Bind with the cooked flour and butter. To make the flour binder, melt the butter until it bubbles and then stir in the flour until it is smooth. Add a little of the hot stock to the flour and butter mixture, stir constantly, and then add to the contents of the stock pot as directed.

It will be observed that the soups are less rich in gelatinous content than the bouillons.

White Stock Soup No. 1

6 pounds knuckle of veal
1½ pounds lean beef
6 quarts cold water
4 cloves

1 onion
3 stalks celery
1 carrot
1 bay leaf

Remove the veal from the bone, cut it and the beef in small pieces, crack the bone, cover with the cold water. Add the seasonings, heat gradually to the boiling point. Add the vegetables and simmer four or five hours. Strain through three thicknesses of cheese cloth and the stock should be quite clear.

White Stock Soup No. 2

3 pounds of fowl	1 tablespoonful beef extract
2 pounds knuckle of veal	1 tablespoonful salt
3½ quarts cold water	1 sliced onion
2 stalks celery	1 bay leaf
1 carrot	salt and pepper

Cut up the meat, cover with the cold water, add the vegetables and seasonings, and simmer until all meat is tender. Remove the meat and reserve for other use. Strain the stock, cool, and remove the fat.

Chicken Soup

2 quarts white stock No. 2.	2 tablespoonfuls lean raw ham.

1 cup hot boiled rice

Add one cup of hot water and the raw ham to the stock, simmer for three fourths of an hour covered. Strain, save the ham for future use, add the boiled rice. Season.

Oatmeal Soup

3 quarts white stock	3 tablespoonfuls butter
½ cup oatmeal	3 tablespoonfuls flour
3 cups of milk	Salt and pepper to taste

Cook the oatmeal in hot stock for an hour, and then rub through a fine sieve, and add scalded milk. Bind with butter and flour—as explained in the recipe for Alaska Soup, and season to taste.

Mulligatawney Soup

2 quarts white stock	¼ cup rice
1 pint tomato	½ cup butter
½ cup sliced onion	½ cup flour
½ cup diced carrot	1 teaspoonful curry powder
½ cup diced celery	1 bay leaf
2 cups raw diced chicken meat	1 sprig parsley
2 sliced tart apples	3 cloves
1 green pepper chopped	Salt and pepper

Brown the vegetables and the meat in the butter, and then add the flour, stock, seasoning, tomato, and rice. Cook for one hour. Take out the chicken meat, and put the liquid through a sieve. Then return the chicken meat to the soup and add seasoning.

Sago Soup

3 quarts white stock	Yolks of four eggs
¼ pound pearl sago	Salt and pepper
1 pint milk	Whipped cream

Soak the sago for an hour in water enough to cover. Then add one quart of the stock and simmer until the sago is clear. Add the rest of the stock and the milk. Beat the egg yolks until they are lemon colored, and pour the hot soup upon them, stirring all the time. Keep hot. When ready to serve add a teaspoonful of whipped cream to each portion.

Cream of Oysters

1 quart white stock	½ onion sliced
1 quart oysters	3 stalks celery
2 cups stale bread crumbs	1 pint hot milk
1 bay leaf	1 tablespoonful chopped parsley
3 tablespoonfuls flour	3 tablespoonfuls butter

Salt and pepper

Pick over the oysters and remove the tough muscle. Chop these muscles and add to the white stock with bread crumbs, oyster liquor, sliced onion, celery, bay leaf, and half the parsley. Cook slowly for one hour and then rub through a sieve. Heat to the boiling point again, and then bind or thicken with the butter and flour—as previously explained; add the oysters and seasoning. Stir in the rest of the chopped parsley, and serve at once. The oysters will cook in a few moments in the hot soup.

CREAM OF CLAM SOUP

This soup is made exactly like the preceding except that clams are used instead of oysters.

Any clear soup that contains different kinds of meat which have been boiled to rags or consommed, may rightly be called a consomme'.

CONSOMME'

3 pounds shin beef	¼ pound lean, raw ham
3 pounds knuckle of veal	1 tablespoonful salt
3 pounds of fowl	1 tablespoonful mixed sweet herbs
4 quarts cold water	8 peppercorns
4 cloves	1 quart mixed, chopped vegetables
3 sprigs parsley	Rind and juice of one lemon
1 teaspoonful celery salt	¼ teaspoonful pepper

Divide the meat into two portions. Put half of it together with the marrow and bones into the kettle with the water. While these are gently heating, fry the rest of the meat and the vegetables in beef drippings until brown. Add to the liquid in the kettle, also the herbs and spices. Simmer eight hours. If the herbs and spices are tied in a muslin, the meat may be used for some other purpose such as a meat loaf with gelatine. Strain, cool, remove the fat. Clarify with the egg as directed. This should be of a rich, dark amber color and perfectly transparent.

Cream soups are very nourishing and form an acceptable dish for lunch or the evening meal. They are rather hearty to be used with heavy meat dishes.

CELERY CREAM SOUP

4 cups celery	1 quart scalded milk
2 quarts cold water	3 teaspoonfuls salt
1 small onion	A dash of cayenne
6 tablespoonfuls butter	A dash of celery salt
4 tablespoonfuls flour	1 blade of mace

Cook chopped celery until tender. Cook mace and onion in milk half an hour and strain. Melt butter, add flour, and milk, and seasoning. Cook a few minutes and serve. Tough pieces of celery are used to good advantage in this way.

POTATO SOUP

10 hot boiled potatoes	4 tablespoonfuls flour
3 tablespoonfuls onion	3 pints milk
3 tablespoonfuls carrot	A little celery salt
5 tablespoonfuls butter	A dash of pepper

Cook minced onion and chopped carrot in butter five minutes but do not brown. Add flour, milk, and seasoning. Put in double boiler and cook half an hour. Add hot mashed potatoes and two tablespoonfuls of tomato catsup.

PEA SOUP

1 pint of dried split peas	1½ tablespoonfuls flour
3 quarts cold water	1 teaspoonful sugar
2 tablespoonfuls butter	Salt and pepper

Soak the peas over night, put on in the double boiler in the cold water. If you have a ham bone, this is a good place to use it. Watch that the peas do not catch to the bottom of the kettle. When thoroughly soft, rub through a fine strainer. Return to the kettle, add either milk and water, white stock, or two thirds white stock and one third cream to make of the desired consistency. It should be thinner than a puree. Cook the butter and flour together and add a little of the strained soup to this and stir until smooth. Turn this binding mixture into the kettle and cook ten minutes. Season and serve hot.

CORN SOUP

1 quart can of corn	1½ pints milk
½ pint of cream	Salt and pepper
1 tablespoonful sugar	1 tablespoonful flour
1 tablespoonful butter	

Heat the corn, the milk, and the cream together. Add to this one pint of hot water, the salt, pepper, and butter. Bind with the butter and flour. Serve very hot.

CREAM OF FISH SOUP

3 pounds of cod, salmon, or haddock	1 large onion
3 quarts milk	3 ounces butter
3 ounces flour	Salt and pepper

Cook the fish in boiling salted water until it flakes easily. Drain, remove the skin and bones, and flake in small portions. Cook the onion with one quart of the milk. Strain. Add the other two quarts of milk, the fish, and a tablespoonful of chopped, sweet pimento. Bind with the cooked butter and flour. Serve very hot.

A bisque may differ from a cream soup in having portions of the meat left in it. In the case of the tomato bisque, however, the product is smooth and rich.

TOMATO BISQUE

1 can tomatoes	2 teaspoonfuls salt
1 quart milk	1 teaspoonful chopped parsley
2 tablespoonfuls minced onion	½ teaspoonful soda
3 tablespoonfuls flour	Celery salt and cayenne
¼ cup butter	5 cloves
1 tablespoonful sugar	

Fry the onion in the melted butter five minutes. Add flour and seasoning, lastly the milk. Cook in double boiler half an hour. Cook tomatoes and put through a sieve. Dissolve soda in a little water. Add to the tomato. Combine milk and tomato mixture and serve very hot.

LOBSTER BISQUE

3 pounds lobster	3 tablespoonfuls cornstarch
3 pints milk	2 teaspoonfuls salt
2 tablespoonfuls butter	1 onion
1 quart water	Cayenne pepper

Remove the lobster carefully from the shell. Flake this into small pieces, cutting the tough portions. Save the bones from the inside of the body and put over the fire with the water and the sliced onion. Let simmer three fourths of an hour, adding as much water as boils away. Strain. Add this to the milk. When scalding hot pour upon the butter and cornstarch which have been cooked together. Beat until smooth. Boil fifteen minutes. Add the lobster meat and the green fat to the liquid together with the seasoning. Add two or three drops of pure food coral pink coloring. Lastly add one pint of hot white stock and a cup of finely rolled cracker crumbs. Serve very hot.

OYSTER BISQUE

2 quarts selected oysters	2 tablespoonfuls butter
3 quarts white stock	3 tablespoonfuls flour
1 quart milk	3 cups hot boiled rice
3 egg yolks	1 pint of canned green peas

Remove the tough muscles from the oysters. Chop the oysters fine. Bring the milk to the boiling point, thicken with the butter and flour. Pour this upon the beaten egg yolks, return to the fire. Add the cream and rice. Put through a strainer, season with salt, cayenne pepper, and a dust of nutmeg. Add the oysters and the hot stock. Let simmer five minutes. Add the peas. Serve.

Purees are somewhat thicker than bisques, that is, the body of the soup itself is heavier, otherwise they are very similar.

PUREE OF GREEN PEAS

1 can green peas	3 tablespoonfuls flour
1 pint cold water	4 cups scalded milk
3 level tablespoonfuls salt	1 tablespoonful chopped onion
3 tablespoonfuls butter	Cayenne pepper

Cook peas and onion in cold water half an hour. Press through a sieve and make a sauce of the butter, flour and milk. Put mixtures together and season. Serve hot.

PUREE OF SALMON

1 quart milk	1 can salmon
1 quart white stock	2 ounces butter
	4 ounces flour

Scald the milk, thicken with the cooked butter and flour. Remove the skin and bones from the salmon. Chop very fine, add to the white stock, combine with the thickened milk, season with salt, pepper, and a dash of cayenne.

A chowder is particularly toothsome and nourishing as nothing is strained out. The most popular chowders are clam, corn, lobster, and fish. There is a good deal of body to a chowder, especially one containing sliced potatoes.

FISH CHOWDER

5 pounds haddock	1 tablespoonful salt
6 potatoes	½ teaspoonful pepper
¼ pound salt pork	1 quart milk
1 medium-sized onion	6 butter crackers
	1 tablespoonful butter

Cut the pork into tiny dice and fry the thinly sliced onion in this. Pour fat through a strainer, rejecting the pork scraps and onion. Put fat into a kettle. Put the potatoes which have been pared and sliced on to boil in water enough to cover. Prepare the fish by removing all the flesh from bones and cutting in small pieces. Put bones and head on to cook in water before preparing the potatoes. When potatoes have cooked about ten minutes, drain water from bones and head into potato kettle. When potatoes are boiling again, add fish which has been freed from skin. When fish begins to flake and potatoes are done, add the tablespoonful of butter and hot milk. Split crackers and serve two halves on each bowl of chowder.

LOBSTER CHOWDER

2 pounds lobster	½ cup butter
2 quarts milk	1 teaspoonful salt
8 crackers	¼ teaspoonful white pepper
	A dash of cayenne

Roll crackers and mix with butter. Work the green fat into this, also the seasoning Pour hot milk over this and cook in a double boiler. Add lobster meat diced. Heat and serve.

CORN CHOWDER

1 can corn	4 cups scalded milk
4 cups potatoes	3 tablespoonfuls flour
1½ inch cube salt pork	1½ teaspoonfuls salt
1 onion	A pinch of pepper

Fry pork cut in small pieces and onion together. Cool five minutes. Strain fat into sauce pan, add potatoes and water enough to cover, cook until potatoes are tender. Add corn and seasoning and heat to the boiling point. Bind with two tablespoonfuls of butter and the flour and milk, cooked together. Bring all to the boiling point and cook a few minutes. Add a little more milk if too thick.

CLAM CHOWDER

2 quarts shucked clams	3 ounces of fat salt pork
2 quarts milk	2 sliced onions
1 quart thinly sliced potatoes	2 tablespoonfuls salt
5 ounces butter	A little pepper
4 ounces flour	Round Boston crackers

Clean the clams and with sharp scissors remove the straps from the bodies. Chop the straps fine. Cut the pork in dice and slice the onion. Fry the pork and the onion until a golden brown. Leave this in the bottom of the kettle. Now put in a layer of sliced potatoes, sprinkle with salt and pepper, and dredge with flour. Next a layer of the chopped clam. Repeat until all materials have been used except the clam bodies, the butter, and the milk. Cover well with water and cook until the potatoes are tender. Add the scalded milk, the soft part of the clams, and the butter. Cook a few minutes. Season to taste, break the crackers in two. Serve half of one on the top of each bowl of chowder.

RHODE ISLAND CLAM CHOWDER

This is made as above until clam bodies are added, then one pint of stewed tomatoes is added together with one half teaspoonful of soda. The tomato may be strained or not as preferred. More may be used if liked. Some use one quart of tomatoes to the above recipe.

SANDWICH MAKING

A good sandwich is a delight, a poor one a disappointment. The bread used should be of fine, spongy texture. A crumbly bread makes an unsightly sandwich because it is impossible to cut it thin. A special sandwich loaf which cuts into from thirty-six to forty slices is most satisfactory. This may be white bread, whole wheat, graham, or nut bread.

The ordinary sandwich is made by taking two thin slices of bread, between which a filling is placed. These fillings may be meat, vegetables, fruit, cheese, or mixtures. An open sandwich is one without a top. Canape's are bread cut about one fourth of an inch thick in circles, or strips, fried in deep fat, and then covered with highly seasoned mixtures. They are served either hot or cold.

A very sharp knife is necessary for sandwich making and a bread slicer is likewise a necessity. This may be guaged so that any thickness may be cut and all dishes will be perfectly uniform. Crusts may be removed or not as wished. Butter should be beaten to the consistency of whipped cream. It spreads very readily and goes at least three times as far as if used without this preparation. Sandwiches may be cut diagonally or straight across to shape rectangles.

Rolled and fancy sandwiches call for a special price to pay for the extra time in making them. Sandwiches may be kept moist by being wrapped in paraffine paper, or a part of them may be prepared and covered with a napkin wrung dry out of hot water. They should be stored in a cool place. Bread is at its best for sandwich making when it is about a day old.

Unless the filling is very rich, the sandwich slices, (or at least one of them,) are better spread thinly with butter. Slices of meat never make a dainty sandwich because the meat is so likely to be dragged from its covers as the consumer bites through it. A minced mixture or a paste is more desirable and economical. Many sandwiches fail because they are tasteless. Here are a few good ones.

LETTUCE SANDWICHES

Wash and dry crisp, tender lettuce. Spread bread thinly with mayonnaise. Arrange the lettuce leaf so that a tiny frill of green edges the bread.

MINCED HAM SANDWICHES

Chop cold boiled ham, using one half ounce of the fat to each six ounces of the lean meat. Moisten with boiled salad dressing and add a tablespoonful of chopped sweet gherkins to each seven ounces of the mixture. Spread between thin slices of buttered bread. Press well together.

SARDINE SANDWICHES

Mash one can of sardines to a paste, using all of the oil in the can; combine with this an equal quantity of the mashed yolks of hard boiled eggs. Chop the whites and combine with the mixture. Season with salt, pepper, and lemon juice. Make moist enough to spread evenly with melted butter.

LOBSTER SANDWICHES

Grate full cream cheese and moisten with whipped cream. Season with paprika. Spread between slices of white bread.

CHEESE SANDWICHES

Chop very fine an equal quantity of lobster meat, celery, and hard boiled eggs. Moisten with mayonnaise, and use as a sandwich filling.

DANDELION SANDWICHES

Cook young dandelion greens until tender; drain; season with pepper, salt, butter, and vinegar. To each cupful add a cold boiled egg chopped. Spread hot upon a rather thick slice of buttered bread. Garnish with slices of cold boiled egg, and serve without a covering.

MINTED SANDWICHES

Bruise tender leaves of mint and chop finely. Work one teaspoonful of this into one half pound of creamed butter. Add a dash of paprika and spread on thinly buttered, whole wheat bread.

APRICOT SANDWICHES

Butter thin slices of white bread and spread with apricot jam. Sprinkle with lemon juice. Close.

CURRANT JELLY SANDWICHES

Butter slices of whole wheat bread with creamed butter. Spread with currant jelly and sprinkle with chopped nut meats.

RAISIN SANDWICHES

Chop seeded raisins and nut meats in equal parts. Moisten with boiled dressing and serve between slices of whole wheat bread.

FRIED EGG SANDWICHES

Fry fresh eggs in crisco; season with salt and a dash of red pepper. Pierce the yolk with a knife when the egg is frying and allow it to spread to cover a buttered slice of bread. Place between slices of buttered bread while very hot.

EGG AND BEEF CANAPE'S

Toast squares of white bread and cover with the following hot mixture: Pull apart three ounces of dried beef; cover with one and one half cups of unstrained tomato; add one half cup of grated cheese, a few grains of cayenne, two ounces of butter. When mixture is hot add four whole eggs which have been slightly beaten. Stir to keep eggs from sticking, and until they are of rich, creamy consistency.

HOT SARDINE CANAPE'S

Heat eight sardines in a very hot pan, turning carefully so as not to break. Toast a slice of rather thick white bread and dip in a mixture of salt, pepper, one pint of milk, and one beaten egg. Fry toast in oil turned from sardine can. Place hot sardines on toast and garnish with two small sections of lemon.

JAM CANAPE'S

Prepare bread as in last rule only fry in lard, cooking oil, or butter, and spread with jam, or fig, or orange marmalade.

PEACH CANAPE'S

Cut thick slices of stale sponge cake and fry lightly in butter. Take two halves of a canned peach, place on hot sponge cake. Sprinkle with powdered sugar and a grating of cinnamon. Put a little peach juice in a frying pan with left over butter and thicken with a tablespoonful of cornstarch to consistency of thick cream. Add a couple of tablespoonfuls of lemon juice and some of grated rind. Pour a little of this above peaches. Serve hot.

ROYAL SANDWICHES

Make a rich biscuit dough by using one quart of flour, one half teaspoonful salt, two teaspoonfuls of baking powder, and two tablespoonfuls of butter. Sift the dry ingredients together and rub in the butter. Mix to a soft dough with milk or half milk and half water. Roll out one half inch thick or a little less. Cut in rounds. Spread one half of the rounds with softened butter and a thick layer of very finely chopped, well-seasoned, cold chicken or veal, and place another round on top. Press well together, brush the tops with milk and bake in a hot oven in a greased pan. Serve.

SNOWFLAKE SANDWICHES

Make a paste by combining one cup of grated cocoanut, one cup of chopped English walnuts, one fourth cup of powdered sugar, one tablespoonful of lemon juice, and enough thick cream to mix to a smooth paste. Spread between thinly buttered slices of white bread.

PINEAPPLE SANDWICHES

Drain grated pineapple of its juice, setting this aside for some other purpose. Mix the shredded pineapple with chopped blanched almonds and powdered sugar to make the right consistency. Spread between slices of whole wheat bread.

CHICKEN SANDWICHES

Chop cold, cooked chicken, either roast or boiled, until fine. Add an equal quantity of hard boiled eggs, season with salt and pepper to taste, and mix to a soft paste with boiled salad dressing. Spread between unbuttered slices of white bread.

CLUB SANDWICHES

Arange on a slice of buttered bread, crisp curls of fried bacon. Place on top slices of cold roast chicken and cover chicken with mayonnaise dressing with which has been mixed a few chopped olives and pimento. Put on a second slice of bread, and press well together.

HAMBURG SANDWICHES

Fry an onion in butter. Remove the onion and put into the spider one pound of hamburg steak. Toss lightly until fried rare, not crisp. Remove, add salt, pepper and bind with enough tomato catsup to make it spread easily. Serve hot.

Onion Sandwiches
Chop Spanish onions very fine. Moisten with lemon juice. Season with salt and butter and spread on a thinly buttered slice of bread.

Egg and Olive Sandwiches
Chop cold boiled eggs and stuffed olives, using two olives to an egg. Season with melted butter, salt and pepper.

Honey Sandwiches
Beat together six tablespoonfuls each of strained honey and creamed butter. Work in three tablespoonfuls of shredded cocoanut. Spread between thin slices of moist bread.

SOME SWEET SANDWICH FILLINGS

Cuban Sandwich
To eight ounces of grape fruit marmalade add one half ounce each of chopped candied ginger and candied cherries. Spread thinly.

Honolulu Beauty
Pineapple preserve, eight ounces; chopped cherries, one ounce; chopped walnuts, one ounce.

Algonquin Maid
Shaved maple sugar and chopped dates, equal parts.

Tutti Frutti Sandwich
One pound stoned and chopped dates, two ounces of shredded ginger, one pound ground roasted and salted peanuts, one pound of seeded and chopped raisins, one half pound strained honey and the juice of two lemons. Pack in a jar and keep in refrigerator. Use as needed.

English Luncheon
Neufchatel cheese blended with three Spanish sweet peppers chopped and a teaspoonful of tobasco sauce, the flesh of three grated tart apples, and one cup of chopped almond stuffed olives.

A FEW FISH SPREADS

Canned Fish
Such as salmon or sardines, may be pounded to a paste, seasoned with equal parts of mayonnaise and lemon juice, and mixed with chopped hard boiled eggs.

Cold Boiled Salt Cod
Cold boiled salt cod, one cup; flaked and blended with one tablespoonful of Worcestershire sauce, and one tablespoonful of minced onions, makes a tasty filling.

Cold Boiled Fresh Fish
Cold boiled fresh fish, seasoned with chopped pimento, stuffed olives, and moistened with mayonnaise, is liked by many.

Shrimp Sandwich
Mix chopped shrimp and cream mayonnaise. Chill and spread thinly.

LOBSTER IMPERATOR

One pint lobster meat, one pint crisp celery, one pint chopped hard boiled eggs. Moisten with mayonnaise.

SOME MEAT RECIPES

CHICKEN SALAD SANDWICHES

Make by taking equal parts of cold boiled chicken, celery and cucumber moistened with mayonnaise.

LAMB FILLING

Take lean lamb, cook until tender, remove all fat. Chop and season highly with onion, salt, and paprika. Moisten with red currant jelly.

GOOSEBERRY GOOSE

Roast goose until tender, remove meat, chop fat and lean, using all. Season highly and moisten with gooseberry jam.

ROAST PORK SANDWICH

Chop cold roast pork fine, combine with one third as much highly seasoned dressing and moisten with equal parts of freshly stewed green apples and red currant jelly.

CHEESE FORMULAS

AMERICAN CHEESE

Warm and mash half a pound of American cheese, blend with a palatable seasoning of tomato catsup, melted butter, and paprika.

SEASIDE SANDWICHES

Mix one cream cheese with a tablespoonful each of chopped green pepper and chopped blanched almonds. Color with green coloring and mix smooth with cream salad dressing.

EGG AND CHEESE

Mix cream cheese with equal quantities of chopped cold boiled egg and moisten with cream salad dressing.

THE MAKING OF SALADS

Salads have become a pleasing addition to any luncheonette because they offer a wide variety of toothsome combinations.

A salad properly consists of a few leaves of salad plant, such as lettuce, watercress, roumaine, chickery, cucumber, or other crisp vegetables together with the salad mixture. This may consist of meat, vegetables, fruits, nuts, or combinations of these. Salad plants should be served crisp and cold. Suitable salad dressings should be selected for the special style of salad to be served. Individual salads are easily prepared and attractive in appearance. The salad dressing should be kept on hand and the salad plants are ready for use if washed, wrapped in a cheese cloth, and laid upon the ice.

A FEW SALAD DRESSINGS

TRUE MAYONNAISE SALAD DRESSING

In a large bowl containing cracked ice bed another and smaller bowl. Into this break the yolks of two fresh eggs, add a pinch of salt and one of paprika, and half a teaspoonful or more of dry mustard. Mix these thoroughly and then add olive oil drop by drop—an oil dropper made for this purpose can be bought at any kitchen goods store. Use a silver spoon or fork for mixing and beat constantly. When a cupful of the oil has been used, the dressing should be thick enough to cut with a knife, and then the juice of half a lemon or more should be added and beaten in. Cover with paraffine paper and place on ice for use when necessary. If the mayonnaise should curdle while in the process of making, place on ice for an hour, and then proceed as before.

For fruit salads omit the mustard and the pepper and at the last fold in a little cream, whipped solid.

Chopped sweet herbs, pickles, olives, capers, horseradish, etc., are employed as flavoring ingredients. Veal or chicken aspic (a very stiff jelly) is also mixed with mayonnaise.

WHIPPED CREAM MAYONNAISE

Make a cooked dressing of four tablespoonfuls of lemon juice, two of tarragon vinegar, half a cup of water, one tablespoonful of grated horseradish, a teaspoonful of salt, one of mustard, one of sugar, a dash of cayenne, and a tablespoonful of cornstarch. Just before serving whip in a cupful of stiffly beaten whipped cream.

SOUR CREAM MAYONNAISE

Heat together one cup of water, one of vinegar, three tablespoonfuls of sugar, one teaspoonful of salt, and a quarter of a teaspoonful of white pepper. Rub two tablespoonfuls of butter to a cream with two tablespoonfuls of flour and a teaspoonful of mustard. Add to hot vinegar and cook. Combine with four well beaten eggs. Take from fire and add a cup of thick, sour cream. Keep in a cool place.

COOKED DRESSING

Beat the yolks of three eggs, add one teaspoonful of salt, one of dry mustard, a little white pepper, two tablespoonfuls of melted butter, one half cup of white vinegar, and one cup of cream. Mix well, put in a double boiler, and boil until thick enough to spread easily, or about the consistency of molasses. Put in a wide-mouthed bottle and keep tightly corked when not in use.

BOILED SALAD DRESSING

Beat three eggs and add as many tablespoonfuls of melted butter. Into a double boiler put a cup each of hot water and vinegar. When hot, stir in one teaspoonful of mustard, two of flour, and three of sugar blended smooth with olive oil. Add a teaspoonful of salt and a dash of cayenne. Pour the thickened mixture over the eggs and butter and return to the fire for three minutes.

CREAM SALAD DRESSING

Melt four tablespoonfuls of butter and add six of flour and two cups of cream. Mix together two teaspoonfuls each of salt, mustard and sugar, and a dash of pepper, and add one cup of vinegar, and when boiling mix with six beaten eggs, also one teaspoonful of onion juice. Strain and keep in a cool place.

IROQUOIS SALAD DRESSING

Mix together four tablespoonfuls of olive oil, two tablespoonfuls of tarragon vinegar, five tablespoonfuls of tomato catsup, a dash of paprika or pepper, and salt.

WALDORF SALAD DRESSING

Put six tablespoonfuls of olive oil into a bowl which has first been rubbed with a clove of garlic or a slice of onion. Add a dash of cayenne and the strained juice of four lemons. Beat until creamy.

FRENCH SALAD DRESSING

Put in a salad bowl the following ingredients, in the proportions given: Four tablespoonfuls of the best olive oil, half a saltspoonful of salt, half a saltspoonful of paprika, and stir until the salt is dissolved. Then add one tablespoonful of vinegar—cider, white wine, malt, tarragon, or any one of the flavored vinegars, as you please—and beat the oil and vinegar together until no separate globules of oil are visible. If your customers prefer less oil, use three tablespoonfuls of oil to one of vinegar. To get the best results, rub the inside of the bowl with garlic before mixing the dressing.

FRENCH DRESSING FOR FRUIT SALADS

This is prepared in the same manner as above, omitting the garlic and the vinegar, and substituting fruit juice, claret or white wine. Lemon or lime juice is often used Powdered cinnamon, nutmeg, ginger, or mace, or chopped candied fruits can be used for flavoring.

SALAD FILLINGS

CHICKEN SALAD

Cook plump chickens tender. Free from skin and bones and chop fine. Mix with equal quantities of chopped celery and two chopped hard boiled eggs, to each pint of chicken meat. Moisten with mayonnaise and serve on lettuce leaves.

VEAL SALAD

Combine a tin of veal loaf with twice the same quantity of cold boiled rice. Toss the mixture until thoroughly mixed with Iroquois Salad Dressing. Serve a portion on lettuce. Garnish with slices of cucumber.

TOMATO SALAD

Peel nice, round tomatoes and scoop out the centers. Mix with Neufchatel cheese, two pimentos, four olives, one small onion, and a little parsley chopped very fine, one half teaspoonful salt, and a dash of paprika together. Fill centers of tomatoes, place on lettuce leaf and on the side a spoonful of mayonnaise.

CUCUMBER SALAD

Peel and chill on ice medium sized cucumbers. Slice thinly and lay on lettuce leaves. Serve with French Salad Dressing.

POTATO SALAD

Mix together one quart of cold boiled potatoes cut in dice, one cup diced celery, one medium sized onion chopped fine, one cup sliced, crisp cucumbers, four chopped hard boiled eggs. Season all with salt and pepper and moisten with Boiled Salad Dressing. Serve on lettuce and garnish with a spray of parsley.

CELERY SALAD

To one pint of chopped, crisp celery stalks add one and one half pint of chopped tart apples, and one half pint of chopped walnut meats. Dress to a moist consistency with mayonnaise. Serve on lettuce.

CLUB SALAD

Cook curls of bacon to a delicate crisp. Trim cold cooked chicken in pencil-shaped pieces. Roll lettuce leaf tightly and slice to thin ribbons with a sharp knife. Slice cold boiled egg lengthwise. Arrange a loose bed of shredded lettuce, chicken, bacon, and eggs. Dress with Cream Salad Dressing.

SHRIMP SALAD

Equal parts of shrimps, diced celery, sliced cucumber, and hard boiled egg moistened with mayonnaise dressing. Serve on lettuce.

SALMON SALAD

One can of salmon, freed from bones and flaked; four diced cold potatoes; two cups of green peas, mix moist with Boiled Salad Dressing. Serve on lettuce and garnish with slices of cucumbers dipped in French Salad Dressing.

BEET SALAD

Dice in small sections equal quantities of cold boiled potatoes, beets and celery. Mash the yolks of three hard boiled eggs with three tablespoonfuls of olive oil, a little anchovy essence to flavor, and salt and pepper. Mix with the salad. Place a spoonful of this on lettuce, dress with mayonnaise, and garnish with rings of hard boiled whites of the eggs.

MEXICAN SALAD

On a couple of lettuce leaves, place a slice of pineapple, three sections of sweet orange, half a dozen seeded malaga grapes, and a couple of Maraschino cherries. Dress with equal parts of whipped cream and Cream Salad Dressing. Sprinkle with ground nut meats and top with a green cherry.

CRAB SALAD

Moisten flaked crab meat, either canned or fresh, and half the quantity of diced celery, with mayonnaise. Serve on a crisp lettuce leaf and garnish with shredded red and white cabbage. Decorate with a slice of stuffed olive and a hard boiled egg.

ONION SALAD

Chill a lettuce heart; remove the outer leaves and roots so that it will stand in a small salad bowl; sprinkle with one onion and two radishes chopped fine. Dress with mayonnaise and serve with two or three tender, young onions on the side, so trimmed as to leave about two inches of the grown top.

STRING BEAN SALAD

Cook crisp young butter beans in boiling salt water until tender Drain and cool on ice. Prepare each salad as follows: Place a small quantity of salmon on a lettuce leaf and arrange string beans about it log cabin fashion. Dress with mayonnaise, sprinkle with chopped parsley and garnish with a teaspoonful of capers.

LOBSTER SALAD

Mix together one can of lobster meat and diced celery. Moisten with Cream Salad

Dressing, adding salt and pepper to taste. Place a spoonful in a nest of lettuce and garnish with hard boiled eggs.

SARDINE SALAD

Mix equal quantities of sardines and chopped hard boiled eggs, also one half the quantity of cucumbers, together. Arrange in nests of lettuce. Over the whole pour a little Iroquois Salad Dressing. Garnish with parsley.

FRUIT SALAD

Dice three oranges and one half pint of pineapple, and slice three bananas. Add one half cup whole walnut meats and three tablespoonfuls of cocoanut. Moisten French Dressing for Fruit Salad. Serve on crisp lettuce and garnish with a cherry.

LAMB SALAD

Slice cold roast lamb very thin, and mix with a finely minced small onion, two stalks of diced, tender celery, and moisten with French Dressing.

ASPARAGUS SALAD

Lay four stalks of asparagus on a thin slice of potted veal. Dress with lemon juice and oil, and garnish with hard boiled egg and a spray of parsley.

CANTALOUPE SALAD

Serve half a melon to a person. Remove seeds, chill, and in the center place a spoonful of cherry frappe. Sprinkle with chopped walnuts and serve with two crisp wafers.

BOHEMIAN SALAD

Chop one pint of cold boiled ham, three hard boiled eggs, and two tablespoonfuls of Bermuda onion. Mix with Boiled Salad Dressing and serve on lettuce.

DELICATE SALAD

By means of sugar tongs dip fresh marshmallows into mayonnaise which has been tinted green with pure food coloring. Place five of these on a slice of ripe, chilled tomato. Garnish with three candied cherries and a piece of crystallized orange peel.

HOT CAKES

DOUGHNUTS

Perhaps no single variety of sweet cake has ever enjoyed the popularity of the doughnut or fried cake, due to its delicious toothsomeness when it is at its best, and also to its convenience in serving. A tough, tasteless doughnut is a distinct disappointment. With coffee, a glass of milk, or as an accompaniment to a piece of pie, the New Englander is not alone in his love for the doughnut. Doughnuts are high in nourishing value.

Successful preparation of doughnuts is no mystery. It is simply correct compounding of proper ingredients, a knowledge of deep frying, and proper storage after the cakes are made. In some parts of the country a distinction is raised between doughnuts and fried cakes, the former being the raised variety made with yeast, and the latter the regular baking powder or soda and sour milk raised cake. In other parts of the country these are designated as plain and raised fried cakes.

The utensils necessary are, a kettle with a rounding bottom and a generous frying surface, a molding board, rolling pin, and doughnut cutter. The kettle may be of iron, aluminum, or agateware.

The secret of fried foods is to have the fat hot enough to harden the albumen on the surface instantly. *This prevents the fat soaking in and sodden, heavy food.* If a thermometer test is used, 380 degrees Fahrenheit is the frying temperature. The fat gives off a thin, blue haze not to be described as smoke. There is a peculiar odor due to chemical change. As soon as the fat begins to look "riley," it should be clarified with raw quarters of peeled potatoes put into the barely melted fat, which is then allowed to cook until it bubbles and the potatoes brown. Then the liquid is strained through cheesecloth. The starchy, porous potatoes absorb the odors and gases and collect part of the sediment, the rest settling to the bottom.

Doughnut mixtures are of three varieties—those made with sweet milk, with sour milk, and with yeast. The old stand-by varieties are liked best of all. Store the doughnuts in a stone jar or glass bell-shaped ones if desired to display them on the counter.

Sour Milk Doughnuts
(A famous recipe)

2 eggs beaten light	1 cup loppered milk
1½ cups sugar	1 teaspoonful soda (dissolved in a ta-
3 tablespoonfuls melted butter	blespoonful of boiling water)
½ teaspoonful salt	½ teaspoonful cinnamon
½ teaspoonful nutmeg	About 1 quart of sifted flour.

Mix until smooth. Divide into three parts. Roll one third on a well-floured board to a thickness of one third of an inch. Cut out with a doughnut cutter and lay on a clean, floured paper. Take the second third of the dough and mix with this the trimmings of the first batch. Cut out and repeat process. *Have all cakes cut before you begin to fry, as this requires your sole attention.*

Have the fat the right temperature and keep it at that heat. Cold fat will make grease-soaked cakes. When the fat is too hot it does not permit of proper rising or of cooking the dough all through.

Drop in cakes. They should rise to the surface instantly because of expansion of gases. Let brown on under side. Turn. When a delicate golden brown remove. Drain the cakes on brown paper or by stringing on a stout wire suspended at either end.

All this sounds intricate, but in reality it is very simple and when once done it is possible to quickly repeat each step.

Cheaper Sour Milk Doughnuts
(To be eaten fresh.)

1 well-beaten egg	4 cups flour
1 cup thick sour milk	½ teaspoonful mixed cinnamon and nut-
1 cup sugar	meg
1 tablespoonful unmelted butter	1 teaspoonful salt
1¾ teaspoonfuls soda	1¾ teaspoonfuls cream tartar

Sift soda, cream tartar, salt, and flour together twice. Rub in the butter thoroughly. Add the sugar. Beat the egg and mix with the sour milk. Combine the mixtures thoroughly. Knead lightly, adding more flour if necessary. Roll out as directed above and fry.

Sweet Milk Doughnuts

3 beaten eggs	1 cup milk
1 cup sugar	1 teaspoonful salt
½ teaspoonful mixed nutmeg and cin-	4 teaspoonfuls baking powder
namon	Flour to mix to a soft dough.
2½ tablespoonfuls butter	

Cream the butter and sugar. Beat the egg light and mix with the milk. Add to the first mixture. Sift two cupfuls of flour with baking powder, spices, and salt. Lastly add sufficient flour to roll.

RAISED DOUGHNUTS

2 eggs	¼ cup lukewarm water
1 cup sugar	1 teaspoonful salt
1 cup milk	Spice to season
¼ yeast cake	Flour to mix.
⅓ cup butter and lard mixed	

Soak the yeast cake in the lukewarm water. Scald and cool the milk. Add the dissolved yeast cake and flour to make a smooth batter. Let rise all night. In the morning add melted butter and lard, sugar, well beaten eggs, seasoning, and flour to make a stiff dough. Let rise in a warm place. Add as little flour as will permit the mixture to be handled easily. Roll and cut out. Let rise on floured paper in a warm room, avoiding standing the mixture in a draught. Fry.

POTATO FRIED CAKES

½ cup hot mashed potatoes	1 teaspoonful cream tartar
2 tablespoonfuls melted butter	½ teaspoonful soda
1 egg	2 cups flour
½ cup sugar	½ cup sweet milk
Pinch of salt	¼ teaspoonful nutmeg

Mash the potatoes, and beat the butter with them, add the egg well beaten, the sugar, flour, cream tartar, soda, nutmeg, and milk. Roll out lightly, cut, and fry in smoking hot fat. Drain and sift fine sugar over them when served.

GRIDDLE CAKES

The universal liking of the public for hot cakes is crystallized in the well-known saying that anything popular "sells like hot cakes." If hot cakes sell well, why not make them a cold weather luncheonette feature? They have much to recommend them. They are inexpensive, and as they are usually made to order, the amount of waste material is minimized

The Hot Cake family has many branches, all of which possess individual characteristics, notwithstanding a strong family resemblance. Some of the best known of these are: (1) Griddle cakes, (2) Flat pancakes, (3) French pancakes, (4) Fried muffins, (5) Fritters, (6) Waffles, (7) Flannel cakes.

Griddle cakes are small, rather thin, batter cakes cooked on both sides on a hot griddle.

Pancakes are larger in size and rather thicker and are sometimes made in a frying pan, hence the name pancakes.

The *French pancake* is a name applied to a griddle or pancake which is sugared or spread with a sweet preserve and rolled.

Fried muffins is a regular muffin mixture dropped by the spoonful into deep fat

Fritters are irregular or cone-shaped cakes made of a mixture thinner than a muffin mixture and fried by being dropped in spoonfuls into deep, hot fat. Fritters may be plain or may contain fruit, vegetables, meat, or fish.

Waffles are cakes made of a mixture not unlike a griddle cake mixture (shortening is usually added to make them more crisp), and fried in a double corrugated iron griddle. Both sides are heated, the mixture is poured in and the other side closed down upon it. In no part of the country does waffle-making reach its best among the rank and file of the people at large, as in our own Sunny South. A dish of waffles at their best is worth a trip to Dixie.

Flannel cakes are much like griddle cakes, but are of a texture more like bread or cake, as they contain eggs, the yolks and whites of which have been beaten separately. Sometimes instead of eggs yeast is used for the leavening factor.

Hot batter cakes are usually served with maple or cane syrup, a plain sugar syrup, one flavored with fruit juice, with butter and powdered sugar—white, coffee, or maple—or with country sausages. The gravy of the latter is particularly liked by many with griddle cakes and furnishes the fat necessary to balance the starches.

Hot cakes must be served piping hot and freshly fried. As soon as they stand they steam and lose their crispness. Cold days make hot cakes sell rapidly. In most home families griddle or pancakes or waffles are served only for breakfast or lunch, but in public eating places, such as restaurants, tea rooms, and luncheonettes, they are met at all times of the day and are in great demand. The fritter is used as a side dish with a heavier dinner and also as a dessert. The flannel cake being a twin sister to the griddle cake, fills the same menu office.

Griddle and pancakes include the following among many others: White flour, whole wheat, graham, cornmeal, buckwheat, bread, rice, cream rye, oatmeal, potato, fruit, huckleberry, etc., hominy, German, pease, squash, etc. Waffles and flannel cakes are usually just what they seem and do not change their mood at the will of the cook. Fritters, on the other hand, are exceedingly fickle as to contents. We have apple, banana, orange, peach, pear, corn, cumquat, mixed fruit, cauliflower, celery, parsnip, salsify, tomato, oyster, clam, etc.

Fritter sauces also afford variety. Chocolate, caramel, wine, orange, lemon, maple, honey, cream, jelly, or in fact any delicate pudding sauce. Of course the *kind of the fritter and the kind of the sauce* must be suitably co-ordinated. A chocolate or orange sauce will be relished with a banana, pear, or orange fritter, while a nicely seasoned white, unsweetened cream dressing will go nicely with clam or oyster fritters.

New griddle or waffle irons do not give as good results as those which have been used, but a few usings will temper the griddle surface and render it smooth when heated Cold or cool frying surfaces make tough cakes. If sour cream or rich milk is used, fewer eggs may be employed or they may be omitted altogether.

The objection to buckwheat cakes is often that they are so made as frequently to cause a rash on the skin of the eater. Overcome this by using only enough buckwheat to flavor, using graham or bread crumbs for the rest of the thickening.

Brown sugar—a tablespoonful to a pint of liquid—will make cakes brown to the desirable golden tint. Turn griddle cakes when they are cooked dry about edges and the center is set and bubbly.

Use soda with sour milk and baking powder with sweet milk. The amount of soda is governed by the acidity of the milk but the usual proportion is a rounded (not a heaped-up) teaspoonful of soda to a pint of sour milk. Vary this to meet condition of very sour or mildly sour milk.

Heat dish hot upon which cakes are served. To do good work, the griddle must be equally heated all over. A skillful cook does not need to make a stifling smudge. Watch the next man you see frying cakes in a show window and see how deftly and neatly he manages the whole operation. By the way, that same man probably sells cords of griddle cakes to people who would never think of them did they not see them being made. Such is the power of suggestion!

WHEAT GRIDDLE CAKES

1 quart white flour	1 quart sour milk
1 teaspoonful salt	2 level tablespoonfuls brown sugar
2 rounding teaspoonfuls soda	3 eggs.

Mix in order named. Beat thoroughly. If it is desired to omit the eggs, use very rich sour milk, or part sour cream, or lacking these, use a teaspoonful of melted butter in lieu of each egg omitted. The great secret, however, of omitting the eggs is to regulate the thickening just right.

HEALTH WHEAT CAKES

3 cups wheat flour	1 tablespoonful brown sugar
4 teaspoonfuls baking powder	2 eggs
2 teaspoonfuls salt	4 tablespoonfuls melted butter
1 pint sweet milk	

Mix in order named, adding egg yolks well beaten and lastly folding in stiffly beaten whites.

RICE SOUR MILK CAKES

1 quart of soft boiled rice	4 eggs
1 teaspoonful salt	1 tablespoonful white sugar
1 teaspoonful soda	1 pint flour
1 pint sour milk	

Mix rice, salt, milk, well-beaten eggs, soda dissolved in a little lukewarm water and flour. Fry as usual.

FRUIT PANCAKES

1 quart flour	1 quart rich sour milk
1 pint mixed currants and chopped raisins	3 eggs
2 teaspoonfuls salt	2 teaspoonfuls soda

Mix salt and flour, dissolve soda in water, and add to sour milk, combine with milk, add fruit and eggs. Beat thoroughly. Bake in small cakes. Serve with lemon syrup.

SWEET MILK PANCAKES

1 pint dry bread crumbs	(soak yeast cake in water until dissolved)
1 pint scalded milk (poured over crumbs until soft)	2 teaspoonfuls salt
1 yeast cake	1 quart buckwheat flour.
1 pint lukewarm water	

Mix and beat well. Let stand over night. In the morning the batter will have risen. Add two tablespoonfuls of brown sugar and half a teaspoonful of soda dissolved in a little warm water. If the batter is not of exactly the right consistency to dry well, add a little more milk or water, if needed, or a dust of flour if it is too thin.

FLANNEL CAKES

1 quart sweet milk	8 teaspoonfuls baking powder
4 eggs	5½ cups of flour.
1 teaspoonful salt	

Sift together salt, flour, and baking powder. Add beaten yolks to milk and mix with dry ingredients. Fold in stiffly beaten whites. Fry.

INDIAN FLANNEL CAKES

3 cups Indian meal	1 yeast cake
3 cups flour	1½ pints scalded milk
2 teaspoonfuls salt	½ cup melted butter.
3 tablespoonfuls brown sugar	

Scald meal and milk, add butter. Dissolve yeast cake in half a cup of lukewarm water. Add to mixture. Beat in flour, salt, and sugar. Let rise over night. In the morning fry as usual.

FRITTER BATTER

2 eggs
1 cup water
1 level teaspoonful salt

2 tablespoonfuls olive oil
1 pint flour.

Beat egg yolks well, add water, salt, oil, and flour. Lastly, fold in beaten whites. If to be used for fruit fritters, add a tablespoonful of sugar to batter, if for meat or shell fish one tablespoonful vinegar.

FRUIT FRITTERS

Prepare the fruit by separating into small pieces. Sprinkle lightly with powdered sugar and lemon juice. Add one cupful of sliced fruit to each pint of batter as given above.

DIXIE WAFFLES

1 quart flour
4 teaspoonfuls baking powder
2⅔ cups milk
1 teaspoonful salt

1 tablespoonful salt
4 tablespoonfuls melted butter
5 eggs.

Mix flour, baking powder, and salt. Add beaten yolks of eggs, milk, and melted butter. Lastly, fold in whites of eggs. Fry in a well-greased waffle iron.

SOUR MILK GRIDDLE CAKES

2 teaspoonfuls soda
1 teaspoonful salt
1 quart flour

3 well-beaten eggs
1 quart sour milk
1 tablespoonful sugar

Crush soda and sift with the flour, salt, and sugar. Add the milk, then the egg yolks beaten thoroughly. Add the stiffly-beaten whites. The mixture should be thin enough to pour upon the griddle. The sugar makes the cakes brown delicately. If the sour milk or buttermilk is very rich, the number of eggs may be lessened or omitted altogether, but the batter has to be a little thicker with flour.

SWEET MILK GRIDDLE CAKES

3 cups white or entire wheat flour
2 level teaspoonfuls salt
1 pint sweet milk

2 eggs
4 tablespoonfuls melted butter

Mix and sift the flour, baking powder, and salt. Add the well beaten yolks and melted butter. Fold in the stiffly beaten whites. Fry as usual.

BREADCRUMB GRIDDLE CAKES

1 quart stale bread crumbs
1 quart scalded milk
4 eggs
1 teaspoonful salt

2 cups flour
2 tablespoonfuls butter
4 level teaspoonfuls baking powder

Pour the hot milk over the dry bread crumbs and add the melted butter and let stand a couple of hours or until crumbs are thoroughly softened. It is sometimes convenient to do this at night and let the mixture stand until morning. Mix, and sift the flour, baking powder, and salt, and add to crumb mixture. It may sometimes be necessary to add a little cold milk to thin the batter if the crumbs have been rather closely packed in measuring.

BUCKWHEAT GRIDDLE CAKES
(These are made with yeast.)

1 quart buckwheat flour
1 cup white flour
2 teaspoonfuls salt
½ cup molasses

1 yeast cake
½ cup lukewarm water
4 cups warm water
2 teaspoonfuls soda.

Mix the buckwheat flour, the white flour, and the salt. Add the yeast cake dissolved in the lukewarm water and the molasses. Beat thoroughly. Add the rest of the warm water. Let stand over night. In the morning beat in the soda dissolved in a very little warm water, beat up again, and fry.

RICE GRIDDLE CAKES

1	pint warm boiled rice	1½	tablespoonfuls sugar
1	pint scalded milk	2	tablespoonfuls melted butter
3	cups flour	1	pint cold milk
4	eggs	4	tablespoonfuls baking powder
1	teaspoonful salt		

Pour the scalded milk over the rice and let cool. Add the flour, baking powder, salt, and sugar, which have been sifted together, then the melted butter, the well-beaten eggs, and lastly the cold milk. Beat thoroughly and fry. Eggs need not be separated for this. Boiled Hominy may be used in the place of rice in the same recipe for Hominy Griddle Cakes.

SHORTCAKES

The shortcake is essentially a luncheonette stand-by. When well-made and attractive in appearance nothing quite takes the place of it. In some places a one-egg cake batter well sweetened is used for the shortcake body, but this is not a true shortcake, the kind that "mother used to make." Shortcakes are very easy to make and quickly prepared. The following recipes may be increased as many times as wished.

TRIED AND TRUE SHORTCAKE

Sift together one pint of flour, two level teaspoonfuls of baking powder, and one teaspoonful of salt. Break one egg into a measuring cup and beat thoroughly, add enough milk to fill the cup. Combine the two mixtures and mix well. Bake in two thin layers.

OLD FASHIONED SHORTCAKE DOUGH

To each pint of flour add one half teaspoonful of baking powder, one tablespoonful of melted butter, and half a teaspoonful of salt, together with milk enough to make into a dough the consistency of biscuit dough Roll in two thin cakes, spread the lower one with butter and put the upper one on top of it. Bake in a hot oven. The cake will split where it has been buttered and will be lighter than if cut.

NEW MARKET SHORTCAKE BATTER

To each quart of flour take two and one half teaspoonfuls of baking powder, two tablespoonfuls of melted butter, one egg, two tablespoonfuls of sugar, and two cups of milk. Add one half teaspoonful salt. Spread in a buttered pan and bake.

SHORTCAKE FILLINGS

CRUSHED STRAWBERRIES

Wash, crush, and sweeten ripe, fresh strawberries. Fill the shortcake. Cover the top with whipped cream, and garnish with whole berries.

STRAWBERRY AND PINEAPPLE FILLING

Take equal parts of chopped, sweetened berries and diced, sweetened pineapple Mix. Set aside for an hour. Fill shortcake layers with the mixture, serving the juice in a small individual pitcher. Cover the top with powdered sugar, whipped cream, or fruit if preferred.

Tutti Frutti Filling

Mix equal parts of crushed berries, diced pineapple, and sliced peaches. Use as a filling.

Peach Shortcake

Use the Tried and True Shortcake previously given. Remove from the tins and butter. Use sufficient thinly sliced, sweetened peaches to serve as a filling and put a thick layer of same on top. Serve with whipped cream and powdered sugar.

MACARONI, RAREBITS AND SOUFFLES

It is the exceptional person who does not enjoy a well-cooked dish of macaroni. Many European and Oriental nations give macaroni an important place upon their national menu. This is true of the Italians with their different forms of macaroni, spaghetti, vermicelli, tallerini, whole wheat macaroni, egg macaroni, etc., etc.; the Japanese with their buckwheat and bean makaronis; the Koreans with their variations of the same delicacy; the Chinese with their bean, rice, tree-pith, and sea-weed makaronis. Then, there is Turkish makaroni not intended to be cooked in water, but rather to be braised in oil or cooked in steam.

The American people are ready to adopt anything good in the way of food products wherever they may find it, and with true native ingenuity, not only make it for themselves, but are most likely to improve upon the original idea.

Macaroni is no exception to the rule. Our native "Made in America" product is equal to any of the imported and in many cases superior. Some varieties we do not produce because of lack of market demand. In the foreign quarters of large cities the different kinds of macaroni may be had. Many of these are sold from large-sized open wooden boxes. The surrounding conditions are rarely as sanitary as we are accustomed to demand. Package macaroni sealed in suitable cartons appeals much more to the average buyer, and while some of the imported product (especially the French) comes in this form, the price is necessarily high in comparison with our own product.

Plain Boiled Macaroni

Break tube macaroni into inch strips. To each pint of broken pieces add one tablespoonful of salt, and three quarts of boiling water. Cook until tender. Drain in a strainer. Pour a couple of quarts of cold water through the macaroni and let stand a couple of minutes. Pouring cold water through in this manner prevents the pieces sticking together.

Put one pint of thin cream, a piece of butter the size of a couple walnuts, a little more salt, a dash of paprika over the fire to heat. Add the macaroni, re-heat and serve.

Baked Macaroni

Put alternate layers of macaroni boiled in salted water, and white sauce in a buttered baking dish. Cover with buttered crumbs and bake until brown. Prepare the white sauce as follows:

To each two ounces of butter take two ounces of flour, one pint of scalded milk, salt, and pepper to taste. Melt the butter in a saucepan, add the flour, and seasoning. Blend thoroughly. Pour on the milk, adding a little at a time and beating swiftly. Cook until the mixture is smooth and shiny.

BAKED MACARONI WITH CHEESE

Alternate layers of boiled macaroni with grated cheese and white sauce. Cover with buttered crumbs and bake.

MACARONI AND CHEESE WITH TOMATO SAUCE

Prepare as above using tomato sauce in place of the white sauce. The tomato sauce is prepared as follows:

Take one pint of brown stock and heat with a quart can of tomatoes and two slices of onion. Season with a tablespoonful of sugar, a teaspoonful of salt, pepper, and a bay leaf. Let simmer half an hour. Rub through a strainer. Cook five ounces of butter and five ounces of flour together, gradually adding the tomato liquid.

MACARONI WITH HAM

To each pint of cooked macaroni allow two thirds of a cup of grated cheese and two thirds of a cup of chopped cold boiled ham. Arrange in layers, the macaroni, cheese, ham, and white sauce. Have a layer of cheese on top, set in the oven until nicely crisped, decorate with parsley and serve. This is nice in individual dishes.

ALABAMA MACARONI

Fill a buttered baking dish with cooked macaroni. Heat sufficient milk to cover the contents of the dish. Gradually add to this peanut butter in the proportion of seven level tablespoonfuls to a quart of milk and one half tablespoonful of cornstarch Season with two teaspoonfuls of salt. Finish the dish with buttered crumbs. Brown in the oven.

NEW ENGLAND MACARONI

Cook macaroni in boiling salted water. Prepare thinly sliced dried beef in the proportion of one half pound to each pint of uncooked macaroni pieces. Cover the meat with hot water and let stand twenty minutes. Place a layer of macaroni in a buttered dish, a layer of dried beef, cover with white sauce. Repeat until the dish is full. Cover with buttered crumbs and bake until brown.

MACARONI RAREBIT

Put a layer of cooked macaroni in a buttered baking dish, sprinkle with grated cheese, and cover thinly with a white sauce to which mustard has been added in the proportion of a scant tablespoonful of mustard to two and one half cups of white sauce. Repeat the layers until the dish is full, finish with buttered bread crumbs, and bake.

ITALIAN SPAGHETTI

Do not break the spaghetti. Dip in hot water and it may be easily coiled. Cook in boiling salted water, dash cold water over it, and drain. Put in individual dishes, cover with the following sauce:

Fry six slices of onion brown in olive oil. Add one quart can of tomatoes, salt and pepper to taste. Simmer gently for one hour. Force the tomato mixture through a strainer and pour over the dish of spaghetti. Serve.

AMERICAN SPAGHETTI

Prepare as above, using bacon fat in place of the olive oil.

EGG MACARONI

Chop two hard boiled eggs finely to each quart of cooked macaroni. Chop the latter coarsely. Mix and moisten with a dressing made of equal parts of white sauce and milk. Heat these together and the resulting sauce will be very thin. Stir into this a teaspoonful of made mustard to each pint of sauce. Pour over the egg and macaroni. Cover with buttered crumbs. Bake.

RAREBITS

WELSH RAREBIT

One pound of cream cheese cut in small pieces, one pint of milk, two ounces butter, one level tablespoonful cornstarch, one egg, one half teaspoonful salt, one half teaspoonful mustard, a little cayenne, slices of toasted bread.

Break or grate the cheese, put it and the milk in a double boiler. Mix the cornstarch, salt, pepper, and mustard thoroughly. Beat the egg well and add to the dry mixture. Incorporate as thoroughly as possible. Add the butter to the scalding milk and cheese, which by this time should be melted. Pour over the egg mixture and beat thoroughly. Return to the double boiler and cook until the mixture is thickened and coats a spoon. Pour over the toasted slices.

TOMATO RAREBIT

Four ounces butter, four ounces flour, one pint milk, one pint stewed, strained tomatoes, one fourth teaspoonful soda, one pint grated cheese, three slightly beaten eggs, one half teaspoonful salt, one half teaspoonful mustard, a little paprika.

Melt butter, cook the flour with this, gradually add the milk and beat until smooth. Mix soda with the tomato and add to the mixture. Lastly, add the slightly beaten eggs, the grated cheese, and the seasoning. Serve on toast.

CHICKEN RAREBIT

One pint minced, cold cooked chicken, four ounces butter, three fourths of a pound of cream cheese, one and one half pints milk, one half teaspoonful salt, a few grains cayenne, three eggs, one heaping tablespoonful cornstarch.

Melt the butter, add the cornstarch, cook together. Slowly add the milk, the melted cheese, and the seasoning. Fold in the slightly beaten eggs and the chicken. Serve on toast.

OYSTER RAREBIT

Prepare as above, using as much less milk as you have oyster liquor

NEWPORT RAREBIT

Melt two ounces of butter, add one pint of milk, a teaspoonful of salt, and a dash of cayenne. When hot, stir in eight slightly beaten eggs. Cook like scrambled eggs. Have one small cream cheese worked smooth with a couple of tablespoonfuls of cream. Stir in at the last moment. Serve on toasted bread.

ITALIAN RAREBIT

Two ounces of melted butter, four tablespoonfuls of green pepper, two tablespoonfuls of chopped onion, one cup of stewed tomato pulp, one pound of mild cheese, salt, cayenne pepper, three tablespoonfuls of made mustard, and two eggs.

Cook the butter with the pepper and onion, tossing constantly until a golden brown. Add the tomatoes, using very little of the liquid part. Cook ten minutes slowly. Melt the cheese and add to the mixture. Season with the salt, cayenne, and mustard. Lastly, add the slightly beaten eggs, stir just enough so portions of cooked egg will be discernible. Serve on squares of bread toasted on one side.

Bean Rarebit

This is a good way to use up a few cold baked beans. Melt two ounces of butter in a saucepan, add one cup of milk, a teaspoonful of salt, and a little paprika. Put a pint of cold baked beans in a dish and mash thoroughly with one cup of cold milk. Put through a strainer. Add to the hot milk, also one half teaspoonful of grated onion and one half pound of grated cheese. Cook until smooth. Add a tablespoonful of tabasco sauce. Serve upon quarters of crisp toast.

Australian Rarebit

Melt two ounces of butter, add one cup of milk, a pinch of soda, teaspoonful of salt, a pound of thinly sliced cream cheese, and one quart of canned tomatoes. Cook until the cheese is all melted. Add six slightly beaten eggs and one tablespoonful of made mustard. Serve on buttered toast.

SOUFFLES

Souffles are dishes which may be baked or frozen (see chapter on Ice Cream). They depend for their lightness mainly upon eggs.

AL and Chicken Souffle

Make one pint of rich white sauce as follows:

Melt two ounces of butter in a saucepan, add two ounces of flour, and cook until bubbly, then add one pint of milk, stirring constantly, and cook until thick and smooth.

Season this with a teaspoonful of onion juice and a teaspoonful of minced parsley, also a level teaspoonful of salt and a little cayenne. Fold into this one pint of minced, cold cooked chicken and veal. Add the beaten yolks of three eggs. Cook until the mixture coats a spoon. Set away until cool. When cool fold in the stiffly beaten whites of the eggs to which a pinch of salt has been added. Bake in a buttered dish in a moderate oven twenty-five minutes. Serve at once with mushroom catsup.

The same rule may be used for Lamb or Oyster Souffle.

Cheese Souffle

To each pint of rich white sauce add one cup of hot boiled rice, one cup of grated cheese, and the well-beaten yolks of two eggs. When cool fold in the stiffly beaten whites of the two eggs. Bake in a buttered dish for twenty-five minutes.

Salmon Souffle

To each pint of rich white sauce allow one can of salmon, one cup of bread crumbs, three teaspoonfuls of lemon juice, the yolks of two eggs, and the whites of two eggs. Cook the bread crumbs a few moments in the white sauce, add the flaked salmon which has been freed from skin and bones, the lightly beaten egg yolks, salt and pepper to taste. Set aside until cool, fold in the whites of the eggs beaten stiff and the lemon juice. Bake in a moderate oven until well set and firm—about twenty-five minutes. Serve with tomato catsup.

Onion Souffle

Cook sliced onions in boiling salted water. Drain. To each pint of pulp allow one half pint of rich white sauce and one half pint of water in which the onions have been boiled. Season with a tablespoonful of butter and thicken with a tablespoonful of flour stirred smooth in a little cold milk. Bring to the boiling point, add the onion pulp, the beaten yolks of three eggs. Let cook a few minutes. Fold in the beaten whites. Bake in a buttered dish for twenty-five minutes.

CORN SOUFFLE

To each pint of canned corn add one pint of rich white sauce, salt and pepper to taste. Heat the sauce, add the corn and the beaten yolks of three eggs. When partly cool, fold in the stiffly beaten whites and bake twenty-five or thirty minutes.

FRUITS AND PASTRY

The serving of fruits at the luncheonette should be marked by simplicity and style. The main thing is to have sound fruits, delicately chilled, and properly prepared.

Berries should be gently washed before the hulls are removed or much of the rich juice will be lost. Oranges may be sliced or diced, being first freed from the white portion inside the rind. Grape fruit can be removed from the shell or the core taken out and the sections loosened, with a sharp knife which comes for this purpose.

Baked apples with cream or plain, stewed prunes, apricots, or peaches, or the uncooked ripe fruit are relished in season. Pears are best served in a salad. Apples may be used in salad or served raw or baked. Pineapples should be diced or shredded after the eyes and peeling have been removed. Grapes should be washed and served on the stem or seeded and served in salads. The white grapes are adapted to the latter use.

In the serving of fruits some ingenuity is permissible. Honey, maple syrup, and fig jam are all relished with grape fruit. Powdered sugar, a sprinkling of cocoanut and a candied cherry add attractiveness to sliced oranges. Bananas lose their insipidity when a teaspoonful of lemon juice is added to each serving with the sugar. This should be done at serving time. Bananas and cream are not so treated.

Most fruits are relished served plainly with sugar. The keynote is excellence rather than elaborateness.

PASTRIES

The luncheonette pastry will include plain paste and puff paste. Out of these all suitable delicacies in this line can be made. The main thing in making good pastry is to have good shortening material, pastry flour, and ice water.

PLAIN PASTRY

For one large pie allow one and one half cups of flour, one half teaspoonful of salt, a generous one third cup of lard, and ice water. Mix salt, flour, and lard together with the tips of the fingers. Moisten to a dough with the water. Toss on a floured board. Pat into a cake and roll out, handling as little as possible. Dot with little pieces of cold butter and sprinkle with flour, fold over, and roll up like a jelly roll. Divide in two parts. Now roll out, using one for the upper crust and one for the lower crust By brushing the upper crust with milk before it is baked a nice brown color will be insured For a custard or cream pie prick the lower crust full of air holes and press out all of the air beneath. Now pat the crust in place to close the holes

TENDER RECIPE

Make exactly as above only add a generous saltspoonful of baking powder to the flour and salt allowed for each pie.

Either of the above recipes is suitable for an open pie with a soft filling or a two crust pie.

PUFF PASTE

Take one pound of best pastry flour, one pound of butter, and a little ice water. Have everything used about the paste *ice cold,* even the flour should be chilled. Divide the butter into three parts and wash the salt out until you have three little oblong cakes. Drop into a bowl of ice water. Remove one pat, dry it on a linen napkin and rub into the flour, adding just as little ice water as possible to make a paste. Knead the mass into a ball and roll into an oblong shape. Dry another pat of butter, roll out one fourth inch thick, and lay on the paste, dredge lightly with flour and fold over. Roll up snugly and it will look like a jelly roll. Gently roll with a chilled rolling pin. Repeat the process with the rest of the butter. After all the butter has been added, fold and roll five or six times, as the more air is enclosed the lighter the paste will be. The rolling must be done gently. When it begins to get warm, fold in a napkin and set on a clean, white blotting paper on the ice. Roll and cut out and put in oven very cold. Oven should be hot. Turn frequently.

APPLE PIE

Line a pie plate with a rich pastry crust. Fill the plate with peeled, sliced apples. Mix together one half cup of sugar and one fourth teaspoonful nutmeg Sprinkle this mixture over the apples, dot with little pieces of butter, add one teaspoonful of lemon juice (if apples are old ones), and put on the upper crust, pressing the two crusts well together. Prick the top quite full of holes, brush with a little milk, and bake in a hot oven, cooling it as the apples commence to be tender. When they are well cooked and the crust nicely browned, remove from the oven and cool.

DELICIOUS LEMON PIE

Prepare shells of rich pastry. For each pie allow the grated rind and the juice of one lemon, one cup of flour, one tablespoonful butter, one well-beaten egg, a little salt, a rounding tablespoonful of cornstarch, and a cup of milk.

Heat the milk in a double boiler, mix the cornstarch smooth in a little cold water, adding it to the sugar, salt, and the beaten egg. Put the butter in with the hot milk and when melted, pour the milk over the egg mixture. Return to the double boiler and cook for five minutes or until thick. Remove from the fire, add the lemon very slowly. Beat steadily for several minutes. Pour into the pastry shell, cover with a meringue made of the beaten whites, and brown in the oven a moment.

CUSTARD PIE

Line a pie plate with pastry crust. For each pie allow three beaten eggs, one half cup sugar, a teaspoonful vanilla, one half teaspoonful salt, and one pint of milk. Mix salt and sugar, vanilla and beaten eggs, slowly adding the milk Stir until sugar is thoroughly dissolved. Pour into crust, sprinkle with a little nutmeg or cinnamon, and bake in a moderate oven. When a knife comes out of the custard clean, it is done.

BERRY PIE

Line a tin with rich pie crust. Wash and pick over enough berries to fill it Add sugar to taste (about one cup to a quart of fruit). Place on the top crust, prick with air holes, and bake in a moderate oven, cooling at the last so the juice will not cook out. If the berries are very juicy, add a tablespoonful of flour to the sugar and mix well together.

CREAM PIE

Heat in a double boiler one pint of milk. When hot add a mixture made of the following ingredients: Two beaten egg yolks, a pinch of salt, three fourths of a cup of sugar, a teaspoonful of vanilla, and two level tablespoonfuls of cornstarch. Cook until thickened. Remove from the fire, pour into the ready baked shell of rich pastry, and cover with a meringue made by beating the whites of the two eggs until stiff and adding two tablespoonfuls of granulated sugar. Set in the oven to brown slightly.

CHOCOLATE PIE

Make same as the above filling, adding two squares of chocolate which have been melted and added just after the egg and sugar mixture, and cook. Fill shell in the same way and cover with the meringue and brown in the oven.

BLUEBERRY PIE

Line a tin with rich pie crust as usual. Prepare two and one half cups of blueberries by washing and picking over. Mix together two level tablespoonfuls of flour and one half cup sugar, also a pinch of salt. Sprinkle this mixture over the blueberries in the tin and add a teaspoonful of lemon juice. Cover with the second crust, prick with air holes, and bake in a moderate oven.

RHUBARB PIE

Fill a rich pie crust with rhubarb cut in short lengths. Over this sprinkle one and one half cups of sugar which has been previously mixed with two level tablespoonfuls of flour and a pinch of salt. Dot with bits of butter and season with cinnamon. Bake between two crusts.

RHUBARB MERINGUE PIE

To each cupful of finely chopped rhubarb, allow one cup of sugar, three tablespoonfuls of flour, the yolks of two eggs, a cup of cold water, a pinch of salt, and butter the size of a small hen's egg. Fill a rich crust and bake. Beat the whites of the eggs, add two tablespoonfuls of powdered sugar, cover the pie, and return to the oven until a golden brown.

RAISIN PIE

Make individual pies in tart pans. Fill with the following: Heat one quart of milk in the double boiler; add the yolks of six eggs, two cups of sugar which have been mixed with two heaping tablespoonfuls of flour. When the filling begins to thicken add a piece of butter the size of an egg and one half teaspoonful salt. Stir into this mixture four cups of seeded, chopped raisins and one tablespoonful of vanilla. Pour into the individual shells Whip the whites of the eggs to a stiff froth, adding a tablespoonful of powdered sugar to each egg. Spread on pies and return to the oven until a delicate golden brown.

MINCE PIES

Cook together the following ingredients: One cup of chopped cold cooked meat, one cup cold boiled rice, four cups of chopped raw apples, two teaspoonfuls each of salt, allspice, and cinnamon, two cups of brown sugar, one cup raisins, one cup currants, two cups of cider, juice of one lemon, and one glass of apple jelly. Cook until well seasoned through. Cool.

Fill rich pastry shells and bake in a moderate oven between two crusts.

PUMPKIN PIE

For each pie allow one cup strained pumpkin pulp, one half cup brown sugar, two tablespoonfuls molasses, one teaspoonful cinnamon, one half teaspoonful ginger and salt, one egg, and one cup of rich milk. If necessary a little more milk may be added.

Mix in the order given. Fill a rich pastry shell and bake for at least one and one half hours in a moderate oven.

SQUASH PIE

Select sound Hubbard squash. Cook in boiling salted water until done. Remove the pulp from the shell and mash perfectly smooth. To one quart of mashed, sifted squash, add one and one fourth pounds of sugar, one level tablespoonful of cinnamon, one half teaspoonful of nutmeg, one level tablespoonful of salt, two beaten eggs, two tablespoonfuls of rolled cracker crumbs, one tablespoonful of vanilla extract, two tablespoonfuls of melted butter, and one quart of milk. Fill deep pie shells with this mixture and bake in a slow oven for an hour. The pie should be a delicious, golden brown.

THREE CRUST LEMON PIE

Grate the outside of two small lemons. Express the juice and make a filling of this, one egg, one cup sugar, one tablespoonful flour, and one half cup cold water. Cover the pie tin with a rich crust; put in half of the lemon filling, and cover with a thin crust perforated with a number of thimble holes; put in the rest of the lemon filling and the top crust. Bake and cool.

CAKES, COOKIES AND PUDDINGS

In order to make a good cake the materials must be first class, the process of mixing exact, and the baking attended to with care and judgment.

Broadly speaking, cakes are divided into three classes—sponge cakes, or those made without butter; butter cakes, or those requiring shortening to make them tender, and fruit cakes, which have rich fruit as one of the main ingredients.

Sponge cakes depend for their lightness upon the air in the beaten egg whites. Sometimes soda and cream tartar or baking powder are used to replace part of the eggs, thus cheapening the cake. Pastry flour is to be preferred for cake-making to bread flour. Should bread flour be used, allow from one to two tablespoonfuls less for each cup. All flours are not alike in thickening properties. For this reason a small trial cake is sometimes a good means of testing the amount of thickening to be used. Only good butter and thoroughly fresh eggs should be used. Fine granulated sugar makes a finer grained cake than that of coarse granulation.

A thick loaf cake requires a slower oven than a thin cake. Cakes containing molasses burn quickly and require a moderate oven. Any butter cake recipe may be varied by the addition of fruits, nuts, spices, or flavoring matter. When cake tins are lined with buttered paper, as is sometimes done for loaf cake, there is less danger of burning. Unsalted butter or fresh lard is better to grease the tin with than any form of fat containing salt. Soda, cream tartar, or baking powder are usually mixed with the flour. Spices may be mixed with either the flour or the sugar Creaming butter and sugar means to work them together until they are the consistency of cream. An earthen bowl and a wooden spoon are preferred by many cake makers, although one of the patent cake mixers now on the market makes excellent cake with a minimum of trouble. The directions are that all the ingredients are to be put into the mixer at once unless otherwise specially directed.

The baking of cake is important. Divide the time into quarters. During the first quarter the cake rises; during the second it browns slightly and evenly; in the third quarter it gradually takes on a golden brown hue   In the last period of the baking time the cake should shrink a little from the pan and it may show tiny cracks. There are various ways of testing cake. A clean tooth pick or a sanitary straw which comes for this purpose may be gently inserted into the middle of the cake. If it comes out clean, it is done; if doughy, let it remain in a little longer. An experienced cook will hold a cake to her ear. If it sings softly she returns it to the oven. When it is silent, she knows that the baking has ended

When fruits are used in a cake they should be divided into small pieces, floured and added to the cake the last thing. Cake should be removed from the pan as soon after baking as possible.

ONE EGG CAKE

1 egg	Butter half the size of an egg
1 cup sugar	1 teaspoonful cream tartar
½ cup sweet milk	1 teaspoonful soda, or
1½ cups flour	2 teaspoonfuls baking powder

Cream butter and sugar, add the beaten egg, milk and flour, which has been sifted with the baking powder, or soda and cream tartar. Mix well and add any kind of flavoring desired. This may be used as a loaf or a layer cake.

PLAIN BUTTER CAKE

Two eggs well beaten, one cup sugar, one tablespoonful butter; blend thoroughly together. Add one half cup milk, one and two thirds cup of flour in which has been sifted two teaspoonfuls of baking powder, and one teaspoonful of vanilla. Beat well. This may be used as a layer cake, making two large layers, or three small ones, or as cup cakes (by adding a trifle more flour), or as a loaf cake. It is also nice when orange flavoring is used in place of the vanilla. It may be frosted with white frosting or chocolate.

CHOCOLATE LOAF CAKE

Melt together one tablespoonful of butter and two squares of chocolate. The yolk of one egg beaten until light, one cup sugar added gradually, one half cup sweet milk, one and one fourth cups of flour in which has been sifted one teaspoonful of soda, and another half cup of milk. Add melted chocolate and butter, one teaspoonful of vanilla, and beat until thick. Bake forty minutes in a moderate oven and top with White Mountain Frosting.

WHITE MOUNTAIN FROSTING

Boil one cup of sugar and one half cup cold water until it "hairs" without stirring. Remove from the fire and have the white of an egg beaten stiff. Add hot syrup slowly to egg, beating all the time, and one half teaspoonful of vanilla. After syrup is added, beat with spoon until cool and thick and put on cake when it is cool.

LEMON SPONGE CAKE

Separate four eggs. Beat the yolks until thick and lemon colored. Add one cup of granulated sugar very slowly. Then one half teaspoonful salt, the grated rind and juice of one lemon. Beat all twenty minutes. Add stiffly beaten whites and fold in very carefully one cup of sifted flour. Bake in very slow oven for forty minutes. Cut in squares and frost with confectioners' sugar.

ALMOND CAKE

Five tablespoonfuls butter, one cup sugar, one half cup milk, one and three fourths cups flour, two and one half teaspoonfuls baking powder (even), whites of three eggs, one cup blanched and chopped almonds, one half teaspoonful almond flavoring.

Cream butter, add sugar gradually, also milk and flour into which baking powder has been sifted. Fold in beaten whites last Bake in moderate oven.

NOTE—A cup of grated or shredded cocoanut may be substituted for the almonds, or one half cup of chopped citron peel. This cake should be frosted and cut in squares. Garnish each square in the center with a small dot of candied red cherry.

POUND CAKE

One pound butter worked until creamy, one pound fine granulated sugar thoroughly beaten into the butter. Add ten egg yolks, one at a time, beat thoroughly, and one cup Maraschino cherry syrup. One teaspoonful each of vanilla, almond, and lemon flavoring, a few gratings of nutmeg, and one pound and one ounce of pastry flour. Fold in the flour and lastly the egg whites beaten stiffly. Bake in slow oven one hour.

DEVIL'S FOOD CAKE

One and one half cups of butter, four cups of sugar, eight eggs, one pint of milk, sixteen tablespoonfuls grated chocolate, two teaspoonfuls cinnamon, one half teaspoonful ground cloves, one half teaspoonful salt, eight teaspoonfuls baking powder, four and one half cups flour. Cream the butter and sugar, add the melted chocolate, well-beaten egg yolks, spices, and milk. Beat in flour and lastly fold in egg whites. Bake in good sized pan. Finish with Marshmallow Frosting.

FEATHER LAYER CAKE

For each cake, cream one half cup butter, and gradually add a cup of sugar. Add three well-beaten egg yolks, one and three fourths cups of flour into which has been sifted three level teaspoonfuls of baking powder, and one half cup of milk. Use a little milk and a little flour alternately until all is used. When the batter is thoroughly beaten fold in two stiffly beaten whites. Flavor with orange and bake in three layers. Put together with Date Filling made as follows: One cup chopped dates, one half cup whipped cream, one beaten egg white, two tablespoonfuls lemon juice, one half cup powdered sugar. Spread between layers.

MOCHA CAKE

Use any good layer cake and the following filling: Beat two eggs thoroughly. together with two cups of fine granulated sugar. Mix one fourth of a cup of flour smooth with one half cup cream. Put one half cup cream, one half cup butter, and one half cup strong coffee on to boil. When heated, pour first over the egg mixture, then stir in the flour and cream mixture Return to fire and cook in a double boiler until nicely thickened. Stir constantly. Flavor with a teaspoonful of vanilla and one half cup of walnut meats

SOFT GINGER BREAD

One half cup pure beef drippings, cream to a smooth paste with one cup sugar. Add one cup New Orleans molasses, one half teaspoonful salt, one level teaspoonful ginger, one teaspoonful soda, one cup milk, and three cups flour. Bake in gem pans. This can also be used for individual hot puddings and served with a lemon sauce.

RELIABLE CAKE

The following cake is excellent to serve with ice cream. It is fine grained and moist.

One half cup water, three eggs, one and one fourth cups of sifted pastry flour, one half cup cocoa, one half teaspoonful cinnamon, three teaspoonfuls baking powder, one cup sugar, one half cup butter.

Sift flour and baking powder, sugar, cocoa, and cinnamon together twice. Beat eggs, add water and melted butter, and combine the mixtures. Beat thoroughly. Bake in a loaf or layers. If layers are made, combine with a simple white icing.

VIRGINIA CHOCOLATE CAKE

2 eggs	½ cup milk
1½ cups sugar	1½ cups flour
½ cup butter	1 teaspoonful vanilla
2 teaspoonfuls baking powder	

Grate a little more than two squares of chocolate fine. Add five tablespoonfuls of sugar taken from the one and one half cups, and set on the back of the stove until it cooks smooth. Then add three tablespoonfuls of boiling water. Beat butter and the rest of the sugar to a cream, add cooked chocolate, two beaten eggs, milk, flour and two teaspoonfuls of baking powder sifted together, and a teaspoonful of vanilla.

SOFT MOLASSES CAKE

Put three tablespoonfuls shortening, three tablespoonfuls of cold water into a cup and fill the cup with molasses. Allow one egg for each cup, one cup of flour, one teaspoonful of soda, and a little ginger and salt.

NUT CAKE

2 cups sugar	⅔ cup sweet milk
½ cup butter	3 cups flour
3 eggs	1 heaping teaspoonful baking powder
1 teaspoonful nutmeg	1 cup nut meats

Cream the butter and sugar together, add the beaten eggs, the milk, and the flour, baking powder, and nutmeg sifted together. Mix well and flavor with one teaspoonful of vanilla. Add the nut meats cut in small pieces and rolled in flour. Bake in a loaf.

ROCHESTER JELLY CAKE (OR PREMIER WASHINGTON PIE)

1½ cups sugar	2 heaping cups of flour
2 eggs	1 heaping teaspoonful cream tartar
½ cup butter	½ teaspoonful soda
¾ cup milk	

Mix in the usual order. Put two thirds of the batter in two layer cake tins. To the rest, add spice, black molasses, raisins, and a little more flour. Use this for the middle layer. Frost the top and use apple jelly for the middle fillings.

SPONGE CAKE

2 eggs	½ cup boiling water
1 cup sugar	2 teaspoonfuls baking powder
1 cup flour	Flavoring.

Separate the eggs and beat the whites stiff, then beat in half of the sugar. Beat the yolks until thick and then beat in the rest of the sugar. Add to the first mixture. Sift flour and baking powder and add to the mixture. Then stir in boiling water and flavoring

ANGEL FOOD CAKE

Whites of 10 large or 11 small eggs 1 teaspoonful cream tartar
1½ cups granulated sugar   1 teaspoonful vanilla
1 cup flour

Beat the whites of the eggs, add the sugar, which has been sifted three times, the flour sifted with the cream tartar three times. Add the vanilla. Do not grease tin and bake in one with a central chamber. Bake with rising heat until nearly done. This should take an hour or a little less.

EXPOSITION SPONGE CAKE

5	eggs	1	cup pastry flour
1	cup sugar	1	teaspoonful baking powder
1	tablespoonful cold water	1½	teaspoonfuls vanilla

Separate the eggs and beat the yolks until thick and lemon colored. Add the sugar gradually, beating all the time, then the cold water. Beat the whites stiff and fold into the first mixture. Lastly add the sifted flour and baking powder, then the vanilla. Bake one half hour in a slow oven.

UNION CAKE

¾	cup sugar		Whites of 2 eggs
½	cup sweet milk	1¼	cups flour
½	cup butter	1	teaspoonful baking powder

Cream butter and sugar, add the milk, then the flour and baking powder sifted together. Lastly fold in the stiffly beaten egg whites. This makes a white cake of two layers. For the dark part take the following.

½	cup sugar	1¼	cups flour
	Yolks of 2 eggs	1	teaspoonful soda
¼	cup butter	½	teaspoonful cloves
¼	cup sweet milk	½	teaspoonful nutmeg
½	teaspoonful cinnamon		Raisins
¼	cup molasses		

Cream butter and sugar, add the well-beaten yolks of the eggs, the milk, molasses, soda dissolved in a little of the milk, and the flour and spices sifted together. Mix well. Chop the raisins and flour well Add to the batter. Bake in two layers. Put together, using first a light and then a dark layer, with White Mountain Frosting.

MacDONALD CAKE

1	cup butter	½	cup milk
1½	cups sugar	½	cup cornstarch
4	eggs	1½	cups pastry flour
1	teaspoonful vanilla	3	teaspoonfuls baking powder

Cream butter and sugar, add the well-beaten yolks of the eggs, the milk, and the flour, cornstarch, and baking powder sifted together, then the vanilla. Lastly, fold in the stiffly beaten whites of the four eggs. Bake in two shallow pans in a moderate oven.

OLD TIME FRUIT CAKE

1	pound butter, or	¾	pound seeded chopped raisins
½	pound each of butter and Crisco	¾	pound currants
	mixed	½	pound sliced citron
½	pound brown sugar	8	ounces molasses
4	eggs	½	pint milk
1	quart flour	1	teaspoonful soda
1	tablespoonful cinnamon	1	teaspoonful allspice
1	teaspoonful mace	½	teaspoonful ground cloves
1	teaspoonful lemon extract	1	teaspoonful vanilla
1	teaspoonful almond extract	1	tablespoonful salt

Cream the butter and sugar, beat the whole eggs thoroughly, add to the sugar and butter. Sift the flour, salt, and spices together, prepare the fruit and mix it thoroughly. Flour the fruit until well coated. Dissolve the soda in a little milk, add the molasses, beat until foamy, add the rest of the milk, turn into the butter, sugar, and egg mixture. Fold in the flour, and lastly add the fruit, adding the extracts gradually.

The mixture should be quite stiff. As there is a difference in the thickening properties of flour, a dust more of flour may be necessary.

Oil deep, narrow tins, line with clean, white paper which also has been oiled. Bake in a moderate oven from one and one fourth to one and one half hours. Fruit cake may be iced or not, as desired. Only such portion of it should be iced as will be used up in a short time, as the icing turns yellow if it stands on fruit cake. Keep these cakes in deep stone jars. Cut as needed.

ECONOMY FRUIT CAKE

2	ounces butter	1	teaspoonful allspice
6	ounces clarified shortening	½	teaspoonful cloves
7	eggs	½	pound seeded raisins
½	pound powdered sugar	1½	pounds currants
½	pound brown sugar	½	teaspoonful mace
1	quart milk	2	pounds flour
1	teaspoonful salt	¾	ounce baking powder
1	tablespoonful cinnamon		

Sift together the flour, baking powder, salt, mace, cinnamon, allspice, and cloves. Mix the fruit together and flour until well coated. Cream the butter, shortening and sugar. Add the beaten eggs When thoroughly incorporated add the milk. Beat in the flour mixture and lastly fold in the fruit.

Bake in a prepared tin in a cool oven. If baked in one large loaf, it will take two and one half hours. If in smaller loaves, a correspondingly less time. There is as much in the baking of a good fruit cake as in the mixing.

SUGAR COOKIES

2	eggs	1	teaspoonful vanilla
2	cups brown sugar	3	cups flour (about)
1	cup lard	1	level teaspoonful soda
½	cup butter	1	heaping teaspoonful cream tartar
1	large cup sweet milk		

Cream the butter, lard, and sugar together. Add the well beaten eggs, the milk, vanilla, and lastly the flour, cream tartar, and soda sifted together. Flour a moulding board well. Mix in as little flour as possible to roll out. Sprinkle the top with granulated sugar before cutting out. Cut with a scalloped cutter and bake as quickly as possible in quite a hot oven. If desired a raisin may be thrust into the top of each one just before placing in the oven, or they may be sprinkled with chopped nut meats or shredded cocoanut

---

CREAM COOKIES

2 cups buttermilk, or	1 egg
1 cup sour cream, and	2 cups sugar
1 cup sour milk	1 heaping teaspoonful soda
1 cup shortening	1 teaspoonful vanilla
Pinch of salt	Flour to roll

Cream the shortening and sugar, add the beaten egg, the buttermilk or cream and sour milk, salt, and soda dissolved in the milk, and lastly the sifted flour. Roll out and bake in a hot oven.

MOLASSES COOKIES

1 egg	3 teaspoonfuls soda
2 cups molasses	1 heaping teaspoonful ginger
1 cup melted lard	1 . heaping teaspoonful cinnamon
⅔ cup boiling water	

Dissolve the soda in the hot water and mix the ingredients into a soft dough with pastry flour. Let stand over night. Use as little flour as possible to make a dough that can be rolled. If the ingredients are very cold, less flour will be needed. Roll very thin and bake quickly. Especially nice to serve with afternoon tea or coffee.

GINGER COOKIES

1 egg	2 teaspoonfuls soda
½ cup sugar	1 teaspoonful ginger
1 cup molasses	Little salt
½ cup lard (scant)	3 cups flour (about)
½ cup boiling water	

Cream lard and sugar, add the beaten egg, molasses, boiling water with soda dissolved in it, flour sifted with ginger and salt. Roll out and bake as usual.

OATMEAL FRUIT COOKIES

1 cup sugar	1 cup chopped raisins
½ cup butter	1 teaspoonful soda
1 cup dry oatmeal	1 scant cup sour milk
1 cup shredded cocoanut	Flour
2 cups flour	

Mix in the usual order, and either drop in tablespoonfuls on a buttered pan or add enough flour to roll.

GRAHAM COOKIES

1 egg	2 cups graham flour
1 cup brown sugar	1 cup raisins
1 cup sour milk	1 teaspoonful cinnamon
2 ounces melted butter	Flour to drop from spoon.

Mix in the usual order, adding as little flour as possible to make thick enough so the cookies will keep their shape when dropped from a spoon on to a well greased pan. Bake quickly.

SOUR MILK COOKIES

1½ cups sugar	1 teaspoonful soda
½ cup butter	Flour to roll
1 cup sour milk	Flavor with vanilla.

Mix the butter and sugar. Dissolve the soda in a tablespoonful of warm water and add to the sour milk. Combine with butter and sugar. Add the seasoning and flour enough to roll out into a sheet one half inch thick. Do not have oven too hot.

SWEET MILK COOKIES

1 cup sugar	⅓ cup sweet milk
1 cup shortening (butter and lard mixed)	½ teaspoonful vanilla
	½ teaspoonful lemon
1 heaping teaspoonful baking powder	1 cup English walnuts (chopped)
Pinch salt	

Mix sugar and shortening, add the milk, flavoring, and salt. Sift the baking powder and flour together, add to the first mixture. Roll out and bake quickly.

CHOCOLATE COOKIES

½ cup butter
1 cup sugar
1 teaspoonful vanilla
1 egg
½ cup sweet milk

½ cup grated chocolate
½ cup hot water
Pinch of salt
teaspoonful soda
Flour to roll

Mix the butter and sugar and add the seasoning. Dissolve the chocolate in the hot water, add the salt, and combine with the butter and sugar mixture. Beat the egg thoroughly and stir in. Dissolve the soda in the milk, add to mixture, and lastly stir in the flour.

COCOANUT COOKIES

½ cup butter
1 cup sugar
2 eggs
½ cup fine cocoanut

½ cup sweet milk
1 teaspoonful lemon flavoring
2 cups flour
2 level teaspoonfuls baking powder.

Mix the butter and sugar, add the well-beaten eggs, cocoanut, milk, flavoring, and lastly the baking powder sifted with the flour. If desired to roll a little more flour may be added, but these are nice dropped from a spoon on a buttered pan. Do not crowd as they will spread. After they are baked ice with a white icing and sprinkle with cocoanut.

DATE COOKIES

1 pound dates (stoned and chopped)
1 cup sugar
2 eggs
¼ pound walnut meats
1 teaspoonful cinnamon

1 teaspoonful cloves
1 teaspoonful soda
½ cup chopped citron peel
4 tablespoonfuls hot water
½ cup flour.

Mix in the usual order, flour the fruit well before adding to the mixture. Bake.

SPICE COOKIES

¼ cup sugar
1 tablespoonful milk
3 tablespoonfuls shortening (butter and lard mixed)
Pinch of salt
1 tablespoonful vanilla

½ cup molasses
2 cups flour
½ teaspoonful soda
½ teaspoonful cinnamon
½ teaspoonful cloves
½ teaspoonful nutmeg

Bring the molasses to the boiling point, add the sugar, shortening, and milk. Mix and sift all dry ingredients and combine with the liquid. Divide the mixture in three parts. Take each third separately, roll on a well-floured board, and cut out. Gather the trimmings and combine with the second third, and so on.

JELLY COOKIES

1 cup butter
2 cups sugar
2 eggs
1 teaspoonful soda

1 cup sour milk
½ teaspoonful salt
Flour

Mix butter, sugar and eggs. Add the soda mixed with the milk, salt and flour. Chill. This will make a soft dough. Roll on a well-floured board very thin. In the center of half of the circular pieces put a little currant jelly. With a small, sharp cutter or a large thimble make two openings in the other circles. Place these on top of the circles containing the jelly and press well together. Bake in a hot oven.

SEED COOKIES

2 eggs	3 cups flour
1 cup sugar	3 teaspoonfuls baking powder
1 cup sweet cream	1 teaspoonful salt
1½ tablespoonfuls caraway seeds	Flavor with pistachio

Cream eggs and sugar, add cream, caraway seeds, flour, and baking powder sifted together, salt, and seasoning. Roll and bake in a moderate oven.

SCOTCH COOKIES

½ cup butter and lard mixed	1¾ cups rolled oats
1 cup sugar	½ cup raisins
1 egg	½ cup chopped nut meats
Pinch of salt	½ teaspoonful soda
1½ cups flour	1 teaspoonful cinnamon
⅔ cup sweet milk	

Mix the shortening and sugar, add the egg, milk, rolled oats, nuts and fruit. Drop by the spoonful on a buttered tin, leaving plenty of room for them to spread. Bake in a rather slow oven.

PLAIN MOLASSES COOKIES

1 cup sugar	1 heaping teaspoonful soda
1 cup black molasses	½ teaspoonful cinnamon
⅔ cup shortening	½ teaspoonful allspice
Flour	½ teaspoonful cloves

Mix in the usual order, roll, and bake.

NEW ENGLAND JUMBLES

1½ cups sugar	1 teaspoonful soda
2 eggs	2 teaspoonfuls cream tartar
½ cup butter	Flavor with vanilla
½ cup milk	

Mix soft, turn upon a floured board, roll out half an inch thick, cut, and sprinkle with cocoanut and chopped nut meats.

PEANUT COOKIES

3 cups brown sugar	½ cup milk
1¼ cups butter and lard mixed	1 teaspoonful soda
2 eggs	2 quarts unshelled peanuts
1 teaspoonful salt	Flour to roll

Cream the butter and sugar, add the eggs, and the soda dissolved in the milk. Shell the peanuts and free from the inner skin. Chop and add one half of them to the batter. Add about three pints of flour, a little more or less as needed to roll nicely to the usual thickness. Use the rest of the peanuts to sprinkle thickly on top. Cut in squares and bake.

HERMITS

1 cup butter	2 heaping teaspoonfuls baking powder
2 cups sugar	1 cup seeded, chopped raisins
3 tablespoonfuls milk	Flour to roll
4 eggs	

Roll thicker than for cookies. Bake in a moderate oven.

POOR MAN'S RICE PUDDING

2 quarts milk	1 cup sugar
⅔ cup rice	Grated rind of one lemon
1 teaspoonful salt	Dust of nutmeg

Wash the rice carefully, mix ingredients, pour into a buttered pudding pan, bake in a very slow oven, stirring several times during the first one and one half hours to prevent the rice lumping. After that bake from one and one half to two hours. The pudding may be covered during the last portion of the baking if it is likely to get too brown on top. If raisins are liked in this pudding, stir in one cupful of seeded raisins when the pudding is stirred the last time. If they are put in before they will make the pudding brown.

CUSTARD RICE PUDDING

Boil one cupful of rice in boiling salted water for thirty minutes, stirring gently so as not to break the rice, and yet to prevent its sticking. Drain. Put the partially cooked rice into a double boiler with one quart of milk. Cook twenty minutes. Beat three eggs until light with one cupful of sugar. Add to the rice and milk mixture. Add one tablespoonful of butter, stirring gently until the custard is set. Cook until the pudding coats the spoon. Set away until partly cooled, add one half teaspoonful each of vanilla and lemon. Raisins may be added if liked with custard and cooked at the same time.

TAPIOCA CREAM

Take one half cup of pearl tapioca soaked all night in cold water or three table-spoonfuls of minute tapioca. Cook the tapioca in a double boiler until it is trans-parent with one quart of milk. Beat the yolks of four eggs, one cup of sugar, and one half teaspoonful of salt together. Pour the hot mixture slowly on the egg mixture. Return to the double boiler and cook until the mixture is nicely thickened. Beat the whites stiffly and fold this in. Cook a moment longer, remove from the fire, partly cool, flavor with two teaspoonfuls of vanilla.

PUDDING ROYAL

1	pint cake crumbs	1 teaspoonful soda
1/4	cup molasses	1 cup seeded, chopped raisins
1	cup sweet milk	1/4 cup tiny strips candied citron peel
1	egg	3 tablespoonfuls flour

Mix well and steam two hours. Serve with any favorite sauce or with whipped cream.

BLACK PUDDING

1	cup molasses	1 1/2 cups flour
1/2	cup water	Little salt
1	egg	1 teaspoonful soda

Mix, and steam one hour. Serve with the following sauce:

1	cup sugar	1/2 cup melted butter
2	or 3 eggs	Flavor with vanilla

Mix well beaten eggs with sugar, add melted butter and beat thoroughly, and flavoring. Cook.

DATE PUDDING

1	cup dates	2/3 cup sugar
	Juice of one half lemon	Whites of 2 eggs
1/2	pint cream (whipped)	

Squeeze the lemon juice over the dates which have been stoned and cut finely. Whip the cream, add the sugar, then the dates. Serve very cold.

GRAHAM PUDDING

½ cup sugar
½ cup molasses
1 cup sweet milk
2 cups graham flour

1 teaspoonful soda
1 teaspoonful cinnamon
   A little salt, nutmeg, cloves, and if
   desired, fruit.

Steam for two hours. Serve hot with any butter sauce or sour gravy.

GRAHAM FRUIT PUDDING

½ cup molasses
½ cup melted butter
1 cup sour milk
1 egg
1 teaspoonful soda

½ cup raisins
1 teaspoonful cloves
1 teaspoonful nutmeg
2 cups (level) graham flour

Steam two and one half hours. Serve with Foam Sauce.

FOAM SAUCE

1 cup sugar
½ cup butter
1 tablespoonful flour

1 egg
1 cup boiling water

Mix together sugar, butter, flour and the yolk of the egg. Pour on this the boiling water and cook well. Stir in beaten white of the egg and whip until light. Cook a few moments longer. Whip thoroughly after taking from the fire. Whip again before serving.

CRUMB PUDDING

1 pint cake crumbs
¼ cup molasses
1 cup sweet milk
1 egg

1 teaspoonful soda
1 cup seeded raisins
2 cups flour

Mix well, steam two hours, and serve with whipped cream.

SUET PUDDING

1 cup suet
1 cup sour milk or buttermilk
1 large teaspoonful soda
   Flour to thicken

½ cup sugar
½ cup molasses
   Spices as desired
1 cup raisins

This should be quite thick. Steam and serve with a lemon sauce.

EVELYN BREAD PUDDING

2 quarts of milk
2½ cups sugar
1 quart bread crumbs

3 eggs
1 level teaspoonful salt
2 teaspoonfuls vanilla

Caramelize one cup of the sugar and add to the milk, which has been placed in the double boiler and is now scalding. When dissolved add the bread crumbs and let soak thirty minutes. Beat the eggs lightly, add the rest of the sugar, the salt, and the vanilla. Combine the two mixtures, stir well, pour into a buttered baking dish and bake about an hour in a moderate oven. Serve with any sauce desired, or with whipped cream.

GINGER BREAD WITH LEMON SAUCE

½ cup shortening
½ cup sugar
½ cup sour milk
½ cup molasses
1 teaspoonful ginger

1 teaspoonful soda
1 teaspoonful salt
1⅓ cups flour
1 egg

Mix in the order given. Bake in a shallow cake tin. Serve very hot with the following sauce:

Lemon Sauce

1 cup sugar	1 egg
¼ cup butter A little nutmeg	¾ cup boiling water
1 lemon (all of juice and half grated rind)	

Cream butter and sugar, add egg, lemon and nutmeg. Beat well. **Add water,** cook in double boiler till slightly thickened.

Cottage Pudding

1 quart flour	1½ cups sugar
4 teaspoonfuls baking powder	7 tablespoonfuls melted butter
1 teaspoonful salt	1 pint milk.
2 eggs	

Sift the salt, baking powder, and flour together. Beat the eggs, add the milk, sugar, and lastly the melted butter. Combine and bake. Cut in squares and serve with Lemon Sauce.

Apple Pudding

Pare, core and slice a dozen medium sized apples. Put a few slices into buttered individual dishes. Sprinkle sugar and spices over the apples and dot with a little butter. Make a batter as follows:

½ cup butter	4½ cups flour
2 eggs	4 teaspoonfuls baking powder
1 pint milk	1 teaspoonful salt

Mix butter with the sifted flour, baking powder, and salt. Add the beaten eggs to the milk and combine with the flour. Pour over the apples. Bake and serve with Vanilla Sauce.

Corn Pudding

2 quarts sweet corn	5 ounces sugar
1 quart milk	3 ounces butter
6 eggs	Salt and pepper to taste

Place the corn in a casserole. Beat the eggs and add milk, butter, and **seasoning.** Add this to the corn. Bake in a slow oven two hours.

Fig Pudding

1 pint chopped figs	3 cups graham flour
1 pint milk	3 teaspoonfuls soda
1 pint molasses	Little hot water

Mix flour with soda dissolved in the hot water, milk, molasses, then **the fruit.** Mix well and steam for three hours.

Fig and Nut Pudding

1 pint suet	2 teaspoonfuls soda
1 pint molasses	1 teaspoonful grated nutmeg
1 pint milk	1 teaspoonful salt
1 pound chopped English walnut meats	1 pound chopped figs.
5 cups flour	

Mix suet, milk, molasses, flour sifted with soda, nutmeg, and salt, and lastly the nut meats and figs. Steam three hours. Serve with a hot sauce.

Apple Tapioca

Cook one cup of pearl tapioca which has been soaked over night in cold water with one quart of milk until transparent. Add two and one half cups of brown sugar and a good sized piece of butter. Stir until sugar is dissolved and the butter melted. Have a baking dish filled with whole apples which have been pared and cored. Pour the tapioca mixture over the apples and bake until the apples are done.

APPLE SNOW

Peel and grate four good sized sour apples, sprinkling with about two cups of powdered sugar as you grate them. Beat the whites of four eggs stiff. Add the grated apple to this and beat until very light. Place this in a large dish and over the top pour a nice boiled custard. Serve very cold.

BLANC MANGE

To each quart of milk use, four level tablespoonfuls of cornstarch, two eggs, one cup of sugar. Place the milk in the double boiler and when hot add the sugar and cornstarch moistened with the beaten eggs. Cook until thickened, flavor to taste, and place in buttered individual molds. Serve with plain cream, whipped cream, or a good cold sauce.

INDIAN TAPIOCA

To each quart of scalded milk add two thirds of a cup of pearl tapioca which has been soaked over night and one half cup of corn meal. When tapioca is transparent add one cup of molasses, a little salt, and a good sized piece of butter. Add one and one half cups of milk, stirring constantly. Remove from the double boiler at once, and place in a buttered baking dish and bake about an hour. Serve very cold.

ENGLISH PLUM PUDDING

1 cup molasses	1 teaspoonful cassia
1 teaspoonful baking powder	Pinch salt
3 eggs	1 heaping dessert plate of mixed raisins,
½ (large) cup suet	currants, and citron
1 cup milk	1½ cups flour (about)
1 teaspoonful cloves	

Steam three hours. Serve with the following sauce: Two dessertspoonfuls of flour mixed with a very little water, the yolks of two eggs, butter the size of an egg, one half cup of sugar, one cup of boiling water, and one cup of grape juice. Bring to the boiling point. Add a dash of nutmeg.

BLUEBERRY PUDDING

Mix together in the order given the following: One cup sugar, a piece of butter the size of an egg, one teaspoonful cinnamon, one egg, one scant cup of milk, one teaspoonful soda, two teaspoonfuls cream tartar sifted with two cups of flour. Lastly, add two cups of blueberries after they have been floured. Bake in a rather hot oven. Serve with the Lemon Sauce.

FILLINGS, SAUCES AND CUSTARDS

A complaint against public eating places is the sameness in the flavor and appearance of many foods offered. This arises from two causes. The first is lack of interest in preparing sufficient variety of dishes, and the second reason is that articles prepared by the same person and in close proximity to each other are apt to partake of the same flavors.

One great help in affording luncheonette variety is different sauces, relishes, fillings, and frostings. The same cake may be given an entirely different appearance and taste by using an orange filling or a mocha filling. A scant quantity of turkey or chicken will take on quite a festive appearance when served with cranberry jelly or Bechamel Sauce. Fish rather tasteless in itself, will be appetizing in the extreme if served with egg sauce, a spray of parsley, and a cut of lemon.

The wise luncheonette caterer will keep sauces and fillings with which he can speedily change the dress of the familiar dish. Economy is duly considered by this means also as frequently a small quantity of material insufficient for other purposes may be converted into a delicious dressing of some sort.

The following are simple and reliable:

CARAMEL FILLING

3 cups scalded milk	2 eggs
1 cup sugar	1 teaspoonful vanilla
	2/3 cup flour

Caramelize one half of the sugar in a clean pan; add the scalded milk to this and allow to stand until thoroughly dissolved. Mix the rest of the sugar and the flour and pour the hot milk upon it. Cook twenty minutes; then add the beaten egg yolks and flavoring.

This may be used between layers of cake or Washington Pie or in individual pastry tarts. For the latter cover with a meringue.

ORANGE FILLING

1 pound sugar	3 cups milk
½ cup cornstarch	Pinch of salt
2 tablespoonfuls butter	2 tablespoonfuls lemon juice
4 eggs	Juice and rind of two oranges

Mix cornstarch, sugar, and eggs; add milk and butter, and cook in a double boiler thirty minutes. Add fruit juice and grated rind.

This filling may be used for soft pies or tarts with a meringue top or for a cake filling. If a further variety is wished add one cup of orange pulp freed from seeds and skin to the dressing and use for cake or Washington Pie filling.

WELLSLEY FILLING

1 pound sugar	4 ounces butter
1 pint rich milk	1 teaspoonful vanilla
	4 squares chocolate

Melt the chocolate and butter, add milk and sugar. Cook until a soft mass is formed. Beat until creamy. Spread on cake.

VARIETY FILLING

1 pint heavy cream	1 dozen marshmallows
1 cup powdered sugar	2 ounces candied cherries
1 teaspoonful granulated gelatine	1 ounce macaroons
2 tablespoonfuls cold water	½ teaspoonful vanilla
2 tablespoonfuls hot water	1 teaspoonful lemon extract

Whip the cream, add the sugar, then the gelatine dissolved first in cold and then in the hot water. Cut marshmallows and cherries in small portions, dry and roll the macaroons. Add to the sweetened cream and flavor.

FRUIT FILLING

1 cup raisins	2 tablespoonfuls lemon juice
1 cup nut meats	Little salt
1 egg white	½ cup powdered sugar

Chop raisins and nuts. Beat the egg white stiff, add the sugar gradually, then the lemon juice, nuts, and raisins.

MAPLE FILLING

1 cup maple syrup	A little salt
½ cup whipped cream	1 egg white

Boil the syrup until it spins a thread, pour on the stiffly beaten white of the egg, whipping at the same time. Add whipped cream and salt.

COFFEE FILLING

1 pint milk	1 pound powdered sugar
2 ounces butter	4 ounces cornstarch
4 egg yolks	1 cup strong, black coffee

Mix egg yolks, sugar, and cornstarch with the milk and butter. Cook twenty minutes and when thick and smooth add the coffee.

DATE OR FIG FILLING

ᴄ cups chopped figs or dates	2 tablespoonfuls lemon juice
½ cup sugar	1 tablespoonful butter
1/3 cup boiling water	A little salt

Mix sugar, butter, salt, and water together, add lemon juice and figs or dates. Cook in a double boiler until of the right consistency to spread.

COCOANUT FILLING

1 egg	1 cup grated coocanut
1 cup whipped cream	Grated rind and juice of 1 orange
	½ cup sugar

ead on cake and sprinkle with fresh cocoanut.

PLAIN COCOANUT FILLING

1 cup milk	2 tablespoonfuls cornstarch
1 tablespoonful butter	1 cup grated cocoanut
2 egg yolks	Juice and rind of one lemon
	1 cup sugar

Mix sugar, egg yolks, and cornstarch with milk and butter. Cook twenty minutes, stirring to keep it smooth. Add lemon and cocoanut.

Frostings are the outer finish of cake or fancy pastry although they are sometimes used as a binding material between layers.

The following offer a fair variety:

MOCHA FROSTING

1/3 cup butter	1 tablespoonful cocoa
1½ cups powdered sugar	Strong, black coffee

Cream butter, add sugar previously mixed with cocoa, and blend thoroughly. Add the coffee drop by drop until the right consistency to spread is reached.

PLAIN BOILED ICING

1 cup granulated sugar	1/3 cup cold water
White of 1 egg	Pinch cream tartar

Boil the sugar and water until it spins a thread. Add the cream tartar to the well-beaten white of the egg, and pour hot syrup in a fine stream upon it, beating well meanwhile. Beat until frosting is thick and smooth, flavor and spread at once, if necessary dipping the spreading knife in hot water.

UNCOOKED ICING

White of one egg   1   cup powdered sugar
1   teaspoonful lemon or orange juice

Put egg white and fruit juice in a bowl and stir sugar in slowly. Beat thoroughly.

MAPLE FROSTING

½ pound maple sugar   Whites of 2 eggs
3   tablespoonfuls water

Boil the sugar and water until it spins a thread. Pour in an even stream on the beaten whites of the eggs. Beat until smooth.

MARSHMALLOW FROSTING

2   tablespoonfuls milk   ¼ pound marshmallows
6   tablespoonfuls sugar   2   tablespoonfuls boiling water

Heat the milk and sugar over the fire until well dissolved. Put the marshmallows and water into the double boiler. Cook until smooth. Stir in the boiling milk and sugar. Beat until practically cold.

CHOCOLATE FROSTING

Make as for boiled icing, stirring in at the last moment one and one half squares of melted and cooled chocolate.

ORANGE FROSTING

2   cups sugar   ¼ cup strained orange juice
¾ cup water   ¼ cup candied, shredded orange peel
Whites of 3 eggs

Boil sugar, water, and orange juice until syrup will spin a hair. Pour gradually on egg white. Beat until smooth and add orange peel.

SAUCES

Meat and fish sauces are a great help in making a little go a long way in a satisfactory manner. The familiar White Sauce easily comes first. Its goodness depends upon its smoothness and flavoring.

WHITE SAUCE

1   ounce butter   1   cup milk
1   ounce flour   Salt and pepper to taste

Melt the butter in a sauce pan. Stir the flour into this when it is hot. Stir until smooth. Add little by little one cup of milk, the salt and pepper, cook until thick and smooth.

Very useful in making creamed dishes, patties, ramekins, etc.

BECHAMEL SAUCE

Made according to directions for White Sauce only the liquid is half cream and half chicken or veal stock.

EGG SAUCE

To each cup of White Sauce is added two chopped hard boiled eggs, one tablespoonful chopped parsley, and one teaspoonful of lemon juice. Parsley is added after sauce is taken from fire.

BROWN SAUCE

2 tablespoonfuls minced onion	1 pint white stock
2 tablespoonfuls butter	Salt and pepper
2 tablespoonfuls flour	

Fry the minced onion in the butter five minutes. When brown, but not burned, stir in the dry flour. Stir until brown. Add the hot stock a little at a time and stir until perfectly smooth. Add salt and pepper to taste. Strain. If color is not right, add a few drops of caramel.

ALLAMANDE SAUCE

3 tablespoonfuls flour	1 cup chicken stock
3 tablespoonfuls butter	½ cup cream
Yolks of two eggs	Salt and pepper

Melt butter, add flour. When well cooked pour on stock and cream. Bring to the boiling point, add the beaten egg yolks and one teaspoonful of chopped parsley, salt, and pepper.

If desired, one half cup of mushrooms may be added.

TOMATO SAUCE

1 can tomatoes	½ teaspoonful pepper
2 onions	4 cloves
1 teaspoonful salt	

Simmer the tomatoes with the sliced onions, salt, pepper, and cloves. Rub through a sieve. Cook together two tablespoonfuls each of butter and flour, add the strained tomato gradually. Cook slowly ten minutes.

CURRANT SAUCE

To each two cups of White Sauce add one third cup of melted currant jelly, one tablespoonful of lemon juice, and a few drops of tabasco sauce.

HOLLANDAISE SAUCE

½ cup butter	Salt and pepper to taste
Yolks of two eggs	½ cup hot water
1 tablespoonful lemon juice	

Cream the butter and add the egg yolks. Incorporate lemon juice, salt, and pepper with this, lastly stirring in the hot water. Cook in a double boiler until the consistency of custard. Serve at once.

SAUCE TARTARE

To each cup of plain Mayonnaise Dressing, add one tablespoonful of chopped capers, olives, parsley, and sweet cucumber pickles. Serve with fried or broiled fish.

Custards are an easily prepared, delicate dish. They are all nourishment and if properly cooked are relished by nearly every one. Over cooking will cause a custard to whey. A baked custard should be removed from the oven as soon as a knife blade thrust into the middle will come out clean. A boiled custard is done when it will coat the spoon. Four eggs to a quart of milk is the rule. If a richer custard is desired, more eggs may be used. Too much sugar makes a porous custard. The right proportions of ingredients and correct cooking will insure a velvety, delicious mixture.

BAKED CUSTARD

1 quart milk	½ cup sugar
4 eggs	¼ teaspoonful salt
1 teaspoonful vanilla	A dust of cinnamon or nutmeg

Beat thoroughly the eggs, sugar, and salt. Upon this pour the scalding milk slowly. Beat until thoroughly incorporated. Butter individual molds and pour an equal quantity into each, using the ground spice for a little sprinkling on top of each. Set the custard cups in a pan of hot water. Use sufficient hot water that it does not reach the boiling point while the custard is baking. If it shows signs of getting too hot a little cold can be added. Slow baking is essential for a good custard and the water merely serves the purpose of equalizing the temperature. As soon as the knife comes out clean, remove the custard from the oven.

This same recipe may be used for a steamed custard, the individual molds being cooked over boiling steam. The benefit of baking is that each custard has a rich brown top.

BOILED CUSTARD

1 quart milk	½ cup sugar
Yolks of four eggs	½ teaspoonful salt
1 tablespoonful cornstarch	1 teaspoonful vanilla

Beat the eggs thoroughly, scald the milk. Stir the cornstarch, sugar and salt together. Pour the scalding milk upon the eggs and incorporate thoroughly. Turn enough of this mixture upon the flour and sugar to mix it smooth, then add the rest of the egg and milk mixture. Do not add the seasoning until the custard is partly cool.

This makes a nice custard sauce if not cooked too thick, or the boiled custard may be poured upon diced fruit or small portions of stale cake, and a meringue of egg whites put on top.

COFFEE CUSTARD

1 quart milk	½ cup sugar
4 eggs	½ teaspoonful salt
4 tablespoonfuls ground coffee	½ teaspoonful vanilla

Scald the milk with the coffee and strain, or else use one tablespoonful of coffee extract to each quart of milk. Beat the eggs, sugar and salt. Add the scalding milk containing the coffee to this. Turn into buttered molds. Bake until firm in a pan of hot water.

CARAMEL CUSTARD

1 quart milk	1 teaspoonful salt
5 eggs	1 teaspoonful vanilla
	1 cup sugar

Put the sugar into a clean pan and stir steadily until it melts and becomes a golden brown color. When properly cooked, add the milk gradually, stirring so that it may not foam and go over the stove. Allow a few minutes for the sugar to melt in the milk. In the meantime, beat the eggs, salt and flavoring, and turn the hot milk mixture over this. Bake as directed before.

SPANISH CREAM

½ box plain gelatine	6 tablespoonfuls sugar
½ cup cold water	Yolks of five eggs
1½ cups boiling water	Whites of five eggs
½ teaspoonful salt	1 quart milk
1 teaspoonful vanilla	1 teaspoonful lemon

Soak the gelatine in the cold water for half an hour. Dissolve it by means of the boiling water. In the meantime while this is completely dissolving, make a custard of the well-beaten yolks of the eggs mixed with the sugar and salt. The scalding milk will be poured upon this and the whole cooked in the double boiler until the mixture thickens.

Now add the gelatine water which has been strained through cheese cloth. Lastly fold in the stiffly beaten whites of the eggs. Mix well, and pour into individual molds which have been rinsed in cold water.

ORANGE JELLY

1	box gelatine		Juice of 2 lemons
1	cup cold water	1	pound sugar
1	quart boiling water	1	pint orange juice

Soak the gelatine in the cold water until soft. Add the boiling water, the lemon juice, the sugar, and the orange juice. Stir and strain. Turn into individual molds and set in a cool place. Serve with soft boiled custard or whipped cream.

BANANA CUSTARD

Arrange alternate layers of stale cubes of cake and sliced bananas. Pour a rich boiled custard over this. Finish with a meringue of beaten egg whites, set in the oven until slightly brown.

PEACH CUSTARD

Make as above, only using sections of peaches in place of bananas.

ORANGE CUSTARD

Sections of orange are used for this with a couple of lady fingers or macaroons and the boiled custard poured about this.

CHOCOLATE CUSTARD

For chocolate custard make a regular baked or boiled custard mixture and add half a square of melted chocolate for each quart of milk used.

COCOANUT CUSTARD

To a regular custard mixture add one cup of grated cocoanut or one cup of cocoanut cake crumbs to each quart of milk.

ORANGE CHARLOTTE

1½	tablespoonfuls gelatine	2	cups orange juice
1	cup cold water	3	cups whipped cream
1	cup boiling water		Grated rind of two oranges
	1½ cups sugar		

Soak the gelatine in the cold water and dissolve in the boiling water, add the sugar, orange rind and juice. Set away to cool. When partly cold, whip the cream and add to the first mixture. Put into individual molds and let harden. Serve with plain or whipped cream.

CHARLOTTE RUSSE

To each pint of heavy cream add one teaspoonful of vanilla, one half cup of fine granulated sugar. Mix cream, sugar, and seasoning, chill until very cold, whip to a stiff froth. Line a dish or a charlotte russe cup with lady fingers, fill with the whipped cream, finish with a maraschino cherry. Serve very cold.

MEATS, SCALLOPS AND STUFFINGS

The luncheonette does not call for an extensive variety of meats cooked in fancy ways, yet there are certain meats which adapt themselves particularly well to the luncheonette service. The preparation of these is important that the very best results may be obtained and every scrap of meat used to advantage.

Roast beef, roast pork, roast veal and roast lamb are all excellent if nicely cooked and sliced cold. These should be rubbed thoroughly with a mixture of flour, salt, and pepper, and put into a hot oven. After the meat has been seared over in order to retain the juice, the heat may be reduced somewhat. Put one-half cup of water and three tablespoonfuls of beef drippings in the bottom of the pan and put the cover of the roasting pan in place so that the condensation of steam will perform the service of automatic basting.

If liked rare, beef should be baked ten minutes to the pound and if liked well done, from eighteen to twenty minutes to the pound. This may be served hot ir slices or in hot roast beef sandwiches, or cold.

A leg or loin of lamb may be similarly roasted or the bone removed, stuffed with dressing, rolled, and baked. Lamb calls for long, slow cooking.

```
Leg of mutton or lamb to the pound......14 minutes
Stuffed shoulder of lamb.................18 minutes
Plain loin of veal.......................15 to 18 minutes
Loin of veal stuffed.....................20 minutes
Loin shoulder of pork....................20 to 30 minutes
Boiled corned beef to the pound..........25 to 30 minutes
Ham to the pound.........................15 to 20 minutes
Roast chicken to the pound (average).....20 to 22 minutes
Roast turkey to the pound................18 minutes
Roast goose to the pound.................20 minutes
Tame duck (of average size) to the pound..60 to 80 minutes
Wild duck to the pound...................40 to 60 minutes
Venison to the pound.....................15 minutes
Fish in a solid chunk to the pound.......15 minutes
Thin fish to the pound...................10 minutes
A small fish.............................25 to 30 minutes
```

BOILED HAM

Select a fine ham of medium weight. Soak over night in sufficient cold water to cover. This will dissolve some of the superfluous salt near the surface and the ham will absorb some of the water. In the morning trim off some of the hard skin near the bone at the small end. Put the ham in a large kettle, cover once more with cold water, heat to the boiling point, then draw to the back of the range so that the heat will be below this point, but the meat will continue to grow tender. If a fireless cooker is used, exceptionally fine results are obtained. Cook the ham about twenty minutes to the pound, or until thoroughly tender. Cool in the ham liquid. Remove and put in a cool place. Slice as needed.

BAKED HAM

Prepare as above. Allow the ham to partially cool in the ham liquor. Remove and place in a baking dish. With a sharp knife take off the outside skin. Sprinkle with a mixture of one-fourth sugar and three-fourths fine cracker crumbs. Stick with cloves. Bake in a slow oven until brown and crispy on the outside. Cool and slice thinly.

BROILED BOILED HAM

Grease a wire broiler with bacon fat. Broil thin slices of boiled ham over glowing coals until well heated through. Serve on a hot plate with a spoonful of currant jelly.

HAM TIMBALES

Four tablespoonfuls of butter mixed with one half cup of stale bread crumbs and one and one-fourth cups of sweet milk. Into this beat four eggs, a pinch of salt, pepper to season, and one tablespoonful of chopped parsley. Add one pint of chopped ham.

One pint of white stock, one half of a sliced onion, half a bay leaf, a sprig of parsley, one chopped green pepper, a tablespoonful of salt, and a little pepper. Simmer an hour or so, strain. Add one cup of milk. Melt three tablespoonfuls of flour. Slowly add the hot stock and milk. Season to taste.

CASSEROLE OF HAM

Grease a casserole and dot the bottom of the dish with a tablespoonful of butter cut into small flakes. Take one fourth glass of currant jelly and dot the bottom of the dish with this. Next put in a layer of chopped ham, using both fat and lean meat. Sprinkle with cracker crumbs, dot once more with butter and jelly. Finish with buttered cracker crumbs. Bake until brown.

HAM AND CAULIFLOWER TIMBALES

Cook one head of cauliflower in boiling salted water until tender. Chop coarsely. Prepare a white sauce by rubbing two level tablespoonfuls of flour into two tablespoonfuls of bubbling hot melted butter. Slowly add to this one pint of milk, salt and pepper to taste. Beat until smooth. Add the cauliflower, four well-beaten eggs, and one cupful of chopped cold boiled ham. Turn into buttered timbale molds, sprinkle with buttered crumbs, and bake.

HAM OMELETTE

Make a plain omelette as follows: Beat eggs separately. Put the whites in a cool place when stiff. To each beaten egg yolk, add one tablespoonful of milk, one small rolled cracker, and one fourth teaspoonful of melted butter. Salt and pepper to taste. Fold in the beaten whites. Heat the omelette pan and butter the bottom and sides. Turn in the omelette mixture. Cook evenly. Occasionally let the omelette mixture through to the bottom of the pan with a sharp knife. When well puffed and firm enough to be pressed by the finger, set upon the top grate of the oven a few moments to "set." Before folding, sprinkle with finely chopped ham, fold, and serve at once on a hot platter.

DEVILED HAM

Take slices of raw ham, cut one-fourth inch thick, place in a greased broiler and broil for three minutes on each side. Remove from the broiler and roll each piece in the following dressing· Melt one ounce of butter. Mix with one-half teaspoonful of ground mustard rubbed smooth with two tablespoonfuls of vinegar. Add to this one egg yolk, one-half teaspoonful salt, and a little cayenne pepper, also one tablespoonful of Worcestershire sauce. Dip in cracker crumbs, return to the broiler, broil a minute on each side. Serve on a hot dish, garnish with parsley.

BRAISED HAM

Soak half a ham in cold water over night. Drain and place in a large container. Add two slices of carrot, one slice of onion, a little garlic and parsley, a couple tablespoonfuls of tarragon vinegar, one-half teaspoonful of curry powder, and one quart of cider. Set aside until the next morning in a cool place. Put the pot in the oven and bake two and one-half hours, basting it with the liquid. Remove the ham to a hot dish. Serve with a sauce made from the liquid in the pan, seasoned with one-half ounce of butter and thickened with one and one-half ounces of flour.

SAUTED HAM

Take very thin slices of ham. Fry in butter three minutes on each side. Serve with a nicely fried fresh egg.

VEAL AND HAM PIE

Cut two pounds of veal and three-fourths of a pound of ham into thin slices. Roll each piece of meat in the following mixture: One cup of flour seasoned with salt, red pepper, poultry seasoning and grated lemon rind. Sprinkle with a tablespoonful of chopped parsley, add a cup of white stock, cover with puff paste, and bake in the oven for one and one-half hours. Serve hot. These can be baked in individual dishes if desired.

CHICKEN PIES

Cut the chickens or fowls into pieces of suitable size for serving. Cook in boiling water with one sliced onion, a sprig of parsley, and one-half of a bay leaf, until tender. When partly done, season with salt and pepper. Simmer a little longer. If there is too much fat, remove part of it and thicken the stock with a heaping tablespoonful of flour rubbed smooth in a little cold water, to each pint of the liquid.

Into individual dishes which have been well buttered, place a couple pieces of the meat and cover with gravy. Have ready a rich biscuit dough which has been prepared as follows, and roll to a thickness of three-fourths of an inch. Make incisions in the crust to allow the steam to escape, and bake.

To each quart of flour, take four heaping teaspoonfuls of baking powder, one teaspoonful of salt, and sift together. Into this quantity of flour rub two tablespoonfuls of lard, two tablespoonfuls of butter, and wet with one and one-half cups of equal parts of milk and water. Bake until the crust is done and a golden brown.

SPANISH STEAK

2 pounds round steak	½ cup diced fried bacon
2 ounces butter	3 pints rich brown stock
1 minced onion	4 ounces flour
1 small can mushrooms	1 tablespoonful meat extract
2 diced carrots	1 tablespoonful Kitchen Bouquet
2 diced potatoes	

Fry the meat cut in neat squares in the melted butter lightly together with the minced onion. Make a sauce of the brown stock, the flour, and the meat extract. Put the beef in the dish and turn over it the crisp bacon scraps, the mushrooms, the diced carrots and potatoes, and the Kitchen Bouquet. Salt and pepper lightly. Pour the brown sauce over this and bake four hours.

VEAL PIE

2 pounds veal	4 hard boiled eggs
½ pound ham	2 tablespoonfuls chopped parsley
2 ounces flour	1 tablespoonful sweet herbs
1 pint stock	Biscuit dough—very short

Slice the veal and ham in thin slices and roll in flour seasoned with salt, pepper and paprika, also the sweet herbs. Alternate layers of meat and slices of hard boiled eggs. Cover with chopped parsley and turn over the pint of stock. Put crust over all and bake an hour and a half.

CHICKEN EN CASSEROLE

1 five-pound fowl	8 mushrooms
½ pound sliced bacon	1½ pints white stock
1 onion	1 ounce cornstarch
1 pint tomatoes	Salt and pepper

5 stalks celery

Singe the fowl and clean it and cut up into pieces of suitable size to serve. Line casserole with bits of bacon and lay chicken in place. Turn over this the tomato, mushrooms and chopped onions. Make a well-seasoned dressing of white stock and cornstarch. Add diced celery and turn into dish. Bake four hours.

SHEPHERD'S PIE

Chop sufficient cold roast mutton to make one quart. Add enough gravy to moisten. In a buttered baking dish put layers alternately of mashed potato well seasoned with butter, salt and hot milk and meat. Have potato on top. Bake until nicely brown and done.

SOME USES FOR POTTED AND POTTED MEATS

DEVILED TONGUE CROQUETTES

Open a can of a good brand of deviled tongue and pour over this one cupful of hot meat stock. Mash fine and add three times this bulk of hot mashed and seasoned potatoes. Add an egg yolk and shape in rolls. Dip in egg white diluted with a tablespoonful of ice water and roll in cracker crumbs. Fry in hot fat. Serve with a white sauce.

HAM PEPPERS

One can of pressed ham minced fine, one cup of stale bread crumbs, half a cup of cold boiled eggs chopped, and one cup of hot mashed potato. Moisten with meat extract and bake in halves of sweet pepper shells which have been freed from seeds and soaked in cold salt water.

DEVILED TURKEY MOLDS

One cup of deviled or potted turkey highly seasoned, one-half cup of buttered crumbs, thoroughly mixed. Gradually add two well-beaten eggs and a cup and a half of milk. Turn into buttered molds and set in a pan of hot water. Bake until a knife will come out clean from the center. Serve with a white sauce in which a cup of green peas have been heated.

Ham or a mixture of ham and turkey are very tasty cooked this way.

POTTED HAM WITH MACARONI

Cook macaroni in boiling salted water until tender and then drain. Cover with a rich white sauce and put in layers in a baking dish or in individuals. Top each layer with a mixture of potted ham and cracker crumbs. Bake. Garnish each serving with parsley. Serve hot.

CHICKEN AND CELERY A LA CHINESE

Dice one can of chicken and an equal quantity of celery. Let simmer one-half hour in enough rich white sauce to moisten thoroughly.   Season with paprika and celery salt.   Serve in a border of hot boiled rice and garnish with two curls of bacon, a spray of parsley, and a lengthwise section of hard boiled egg.

LOBSTER CURRY

Take one pound can of lobster meat and dice fine.   Put a quarter of a cup of butter in a hot skillet and in this cook one small sliced onion, two tablespoonfuls of flour, and a teaspoonful of curry powder.   Add a dash of paprika and a pint of either meat stock or milk.   Strain to remove the onion and add lobster meat.   Cook ten minutes and serve over one spoonful of rice and one of hot mashed potato.

A dish which is prepared by using alternate layers of meat, fish, or vegetables together with seasoned bread crumbs and the whole moistened with milk or stock is called a "scallop."

SCALLOPED POTATOES

Peel and slice thinly nice sound potatoes.   Butter a baking dish and in the bottom place a layer of fine buttered cracker crumbs.   Next place in a layer of the potatoes and season well with salt, pepper and butter.   Add another layer of bread crumbs, another of potatoes, and so on until the dish is filled.   Have the crumbs on top.   Fill the dish with milk and bake until the potatoes are well done.   If desired, a light sprinkling of flour may be used in place of the bread crumbs.

SCALLOPED OYSTERS

Remove the tough portion from each oyster, also any particles of shell.   Butter a baking dish as usual and place in a layer of crumbs, oysters and seasoning.   When the dish is full, cover the whole with milk, and bake until nicely brown and the oysters are done.

SCALLOPED TOMATOES

Butter a baking dish and place in a layer of seasoned bread or cracker crumbs, a layer of tomatoes juice and all, and so on until the dish is filled, seasoning each layer with salt, pepper, butter, and if desired a very little sugar.   Bake until set and firm.

SCALLOPED SALMON

Prepare a baking dish in the usual manner, using first a layer of crumbs, then a layer of salmon which has been freed from any bones, and seasoning until the dish is full, having the crumbs on top.   Fill the dish with milk and bake until nicely browned and set.

SCALLOPED ONIONS

Prepare as for scalloped potatoes, using sliced onions in place of the potatoes. Bake as usual.

Almost any kind of meat or vegetables may be prepared in a similar manner.

STUFFINGS

Many kinds of stuffing are used for fowls and roast meats, but the simple ones will please better than the unknown ones.   Stuffings offer an excellent way of using up dry bread.

BREAD STUFFING

Use bread not less than twenty-four hours old. Cut two five-cent loaves into thick slices and dip a moment into cold water. Drain and chop fine. Mince one good sized onion and chop into bread. Season with a tablespoonful of salt, half a teaspoonful of pepper, and two tablespoonfuls of poultry seasoning. To this amount use half a cup of melted butter. Taste and decide whether more seasoning is required. Bind together with the yolk of an egg. The bird should be full and the opening sewed up.

POTATO STUFFING

4 cups hot mashed potatoes	1 minced onion
1 cup salt pork cubes	2 tablespoonfuls poultry seasoning
Salt	Pepper

Mix and use either one pint of sausage meat or two cans of deviled ham. Cook pork and onion until golden, adding remaining ingredients.

OYSTER STUFFING

4 cups cracker crumbs	1 cup butter
4 cups bread crumbs	1 cup chopped celery
1 minced onion	2 tablespoonfuls poultry seasoning
1 quart of oysters	1 cup boiling water

Parboil oysters and mix with dressing made of rest of ingredients.

CHESTNUT STUFFING

Make as for oyster stuffing, using boiled and chopped chestnuts instead of oysters. Some prefer to mash the chestnuts after they are chopped. For the extra moistening needed, use hot water.

VEGETARIAN ROAST

Two cups grated cheese, two cups bread crumbs, one-fourth cup minced onion, one-fourth cup butter, two cups chopped walnut meats, two lemons, one and one-half cups hot water, one teaspoonful salt, a dash of paprika, and one tablespoonful chopped parsley. Add bread crumbs, salt, cheese, paprika, nut meats, and the juice of one lemon. Bake in individual ramekins half an hour. Decorate with parsley and thin slices of lemon and thin slices of hard boiled egg.

HOT COFFEE

FINISHED HOT COFFEE

Pack ½ pound of pulverized coffee in a percolator. Percolate with 2 quarts of boiling water, letting it run through twice. Add to the infusion thus obtained 2 quarts of milk, keep hot in an urn, and draw as a finished drink To serve, fill the cup with finished coffee, add a lump of sugar, and top with whipped cream. Charge 10 cents per cup.

HOT COFFEE

This coffee must be made daily, or as much oftener as required: Use a separate urn and a fine quality of ground coffee Put ½ pound of the ground coffee in a bolting cloth bag, place the bag on the diaphragm of the urn and pour over it 1 gallon of boiling water In five minutes draw off ½ gallon of the infusion and pour it back over the coffee; repeat this once or twice. After fifteen minutes remove the bag containing the coffee grounds and keep the infusion hot. In serving use ½ ounce of cream and fill up the cup with the hot coffee. Serve with loaf cut sugar. Extracts cannot be used for this coffee.

The above formula is especially recommended for fountain use.

HOT COFFEE

One pound of finely ground Mocha and Java coffee, 44 ounces of sugar, 2 drams of vanilla extract, and sufficient boiling water Pack the coffee in a percolator and pour boiling water upon it until 2 pints of liquid are obtained. In the latter dissolve the sugar and add the extract. This makes, when served with cream, a most pleasant cup of coffee.

HOT COFFEE

Another good coffee is made of 4 cubes of loaf sugar, (a wellknown pulverized coffee may be used in this formula to advantage), dessertspoonful of extract Mocha coffee, 1 dessertspoonful prepared milk, a cupful hot water, 1 tablespoonful whipped cream.

HOT COFFEE

Hot coffee may be also served by using extract and sugar, mixing them as required For extract of coffee use either of these two formulas: Ten ounces Mocha coffee, 10 ounces Java coffee, sufficient glycerin and water. Mix the two coffees and grind to fine powder. Then moisten with a mixture of 1 volume of glycerin and 3 of water, pack in a percolator and percolate slowly until 16 ounces of percolate are obtained. More complete extraction will be obtained by pouring the menstruum in a hot condition on the ground coffee. If on the residue be poured the same menstruum, until about 20 ounces of percolate are obtained, the latter may be used to make a subsequent preparation of the same kind, thus insuring a stronger extract. Only a glass percolator and the very finest coffee should be used. Some coffee extracts are only one-half as strong as this one and made with diluted alcohol as a menstruum.

Five ounces moderately fine Java coffee, 5 ounces moderately fine Mocha coffee, enough hot water to make 30 ounces, and 1 ounce of the best French brandy. Moisten the coffee with the water, pack into a percolator, pour on the remainder of the coffee and add the brandy In serving, take about 1 ounce of either of these extracts for an 8-ounce mug, add sufficient sugar and about 1 ounce of cream, fill with hot water, top with whipped cream, and serve with spoon and sweet crackers. Hot coffee served by using the extract may be called "hot coffee boshea."

HOT COFFEE

Another way is to take coffee of any good kind in any desired mixture. About 32 ounces is the usual amount. Take 4 ounces of sugar and enough water to make 64 ounces. Moisten the coffee thoroughly, let stand in a covered vessel until softened, pack in a percolator, cover the coffee with a heavy filter paper turned up at the edge, and upon the whole pour boiling hot water. Allow the percolate to flow into a funnel or percolator containing the sugar, and continue adding the boiling water until 4 pints of syrup are obtained, taking care that all the sugar is dissolved. If the process is conducted in the manner prescribed, the odor of coffee will scarcely be observed in the room. Serve like the preceding.

HOT COFFEE

Sixteen ounces of coffee, freshly roasted and ground, may be mixed with 48 ounces of sugar, 2 ounces of brandy, and sufficient boiling water. Moisten the coffee with some hot water mixed with the brandy, pack in a percolator, pour on boiling water until 32 ounces of percolate are obtained, and in this dissolve the sugar by agitation. About the best mixture of coffee to be used is one part of Java with two of Mocha. Serve like the preceding.

HOT COFFEE

Take 5 ounces of the best Java and Mocha coffees mixed and powdered moderately fine, 4 ounces of glycerin, 2½ pounds of sugar, and sufficient water. Mix the glycerin with 28 ounces of water, moisten the coffee with this mixture, let stand ½ hour, pack firmly in a percolator, not tin; pour on the remainder of the liquid, previously heated to boiling, and when this liquid has disappeared from the surface of the coffee, add boiling hot water until 40 ounces of percolate are obtained; to the latter add the sugar and dissolve by agitation. Serve by drawing 2 ounces to an 8-ounce mug, add 1 ounce of cream, fill with hot water, top with whipped cream, and serve with spoon and sweet crackers.

MALTED COFFEE

Prepare a syrup of 8 ounces malted milk, 16 ounces sugar, 2½ ounces coffee extract, 24 ounces water Dissolve the malted milk in the water, not too hot. Strain, add the coffee extract and color with caramel.

(THE END)

INDEX

THE DISPENSER'S FORMULARY

THE DISPENSER'S FORMULARY